THE PAPERS OF

WOODROW WILSON

VOLUME 19

1909-1910

SPONSORED BY THE WOODROW WILSON
FOUNDATION
AND PRINCETON UNIVERSITY

THE PAPERS OF
WOODROW WILSON

ARTHUR S. LINK, *EDITOR*
DAVID W. HIRST AND JOHN E. LITTLE
ASSOCIATE EDITORS
JOHN M. MULDER, *ASSISTANT EDITOR*
SYLVIA ELVIN FONTIJN, *CONTRIBUTING EDITOR*
M. HALSEY THOMAS, *CONSULTING EDITOR*

Volume 19 · 1909-1910

PRINCETON, NEW JERSEY
PRINCETON UNIVERSITY PRESS
1975

L.C. Card 66-10880
I.S.B.N. 0-691-04633-6

Printed in the United States of America
by Princeton University Press
Princeton, New Jersey

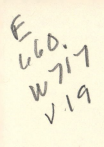

INTRODUCTION

THE documents in this volume, covering the period from January 20, 1909, to January 11, 1910, reveal momentous developments in Wilson's thought and in the history of Princeton University. They also cast much light on Wilson the university administrator and budding politician, as well as on his personal relationships.

The preparation and delivery of a Lincoln centennial address in Chicago prompts Wilson to ponder, systematically for the first time, what the Civil War President's life and career meant to contemporary America. To Wilson the conclusion is clear: the strength and hope of America lies in the common people, not in those born to wealth and special privilege. This address and subsequent articles and speeches printed in this volume reveal Wilson's rapid movement toward a radical social democratic philosophy.

Wilson applies his egalitarian social ideals most specifically in 1909 to the situation prevailing in American universities and colleges, and he did not spare Princeton in his assessment. Many institutions of higher learning, he says, have become strongholds of wealth and snobbery. Lincoln would not have been as "serviceable" had he gone to a private eastern university in 1909. Private schools and colleges that cater only to the wealthy are in fact "country clubs" and do not deserve to survive. Convinced that the rebirth of democracy in academic communities could come only through radical social reorganization, based squarely upon the principle of non-exclusiveness, Wilson through articles and frequent addresses continues his crusade for his quadrangle plan not only among Princetonians, but in the nation at large. Moreover, only through such reorganization of undergraduate life can intellectual pursuits gain their proper place as the main business of the university. As it was, he says, the side shows of athletics and extracurricular activities are swallowing up the main tent. In the same articles and addresses, Wilson reveals his philosophy of liberal education in its maturest form.

A dispute between Wilson and the Dean of the Faculty concerning the proper distribution of the staff of the scientific and non-scientific departments, in addition to a growing annual deficit, prompts the Finance Committee of the Princeton Board of Trustees to ask whether reductions in personnel in the non-scientific departments could be made. In response, Wilson requests the chairmen of these departments to undertake a comprehensive five-year review of the preceptorial system. Their detailed reports, printed herein, shed remarkable light on the curriculum, course loads, and teaching methods at Princeton in 1909-10. They also reveal certain defects in the preceptorial system which have not heretofore been exposed or discussed.

Of particular interest and significance are the documents in this volume relating to a much-publicized and controverted case involving the disciplining of ten freshmen. Wilson plays the crucial role in the final disposition of the case, and his letters about it express forcefully his academic ideals.

Meanwhile, the greatest crisis in Wilson's career to date begins in the spring of 1909 and develops during the following months. William Cooper Procter, a Cincinnati soap manufacturer, at the instigation of Andrew F. West, Dean of the Graduate School, offers $500,000 (to be matched by other contributors) for the construction of a graduate college and endowment of professorships and fellowships. Another provision was that a site well removed from the campus be used for the new graduate establishment. The trustees accept Procter's offer, subject to the settlement of a legal difficulty, on October 21, 1909. Wilson had always strongly believed that the graduate college should be in the heart of the campus, in order that it might constitute, as he put it, the energizing force in the life of the university. By this time it was obvious that West intended to build an elaborate and luxurious establishment and, as Wilson thought, to cater to rich students. The letters in this volume from the Wilson collections and from the private papers of the leading participants in the controversy reveal how sharply the lines are already drawn by late 1909 between Wilson and West. In a letter to Moses Taylor Pyne, chief supporter of the Procter-West plan, Wilson says that control of academic policy has been taken from his hands by the acceptance of the Procter offer, and announces his intention to resign unless the trustees agree to build a graduate college on the campus. He also clearly implies that West could have no further hand in the conduct of the Graduate School and the graduate college.

As the documents in this volume also divulge, Wilson's political fever rises in direct response to the heat of this controversy. Still spurning open alliance with the rising progressive movement, he continues to oppose direct primaries, the initiative and referendum, the commission form of city government, and other favorite progressive political instrumentalities and to condemn direct governmental regulation of business, railroads, and public service corporations. Instead, in several addresses, notably in St. Louis and Philadelphia, he launches his own movement for political regeneration through the short ballot and helps to organize and serves as president of the Short Ballot Organization to further the cause. In addition he issues a blast in the *North American Review* against the Payne-Aldrich Tariff Act, inaugurates the New Jersey gubernatorial campaign of 1910 in an address to the Democratic Club of Plainfield, and outlines the "Democratic opportunity" in the monthly published by the chairman of the Democratic National Committee.

Finally, in numerous lengthy, intimate letters to Mary Allen Hulbert Peck, published in full herein for the first time, Wilson reveals his innermost thoughts and reactions to persons and passing events.

Thus this volume provides the background of the violent eruption of the graduate college controversy in the first half of 1910 and of Wilson's decision of July 15 to accept the Democratic nomination for Governor of New Jersey.

Readers are again reminded that *The Papers of Woodrow Wilson* is a continuing series; that persons, events, and institutions that figure prominently in earlier volumes are not re-identified in subsequent ones; and that the Index to each volume gives cross references to fullest earlier identifications. We reiterate that we print texts *verbatim et literatim*, and that we make silent corrections only of obvious errors in typed copies.

Dr. John M. Mulder, Research Associate, Princeton University, and Assistant Editor, resigned on June 30, 1974, to accept a position in American church history at Princeton Theological Seminary. Dr. Mulder came with us three years ago as a graduate assistant in research and worked part time in this capacity while he was completing his doctoral program in the History Department at Princeton, including an excellent dissertation on Wilson's religious and intellectual development to 1910. We value him not only as a fine scholar but also as a friend and will miss him greatly, and wish for him a long and distinguished career at our sister institution.

With this volume we welcome to our staff as Assistant Editor, Edith James Blendon, Ph.D. We look forward to a long and happy association with her. We are grateful to Lewis Bateman of Princeton University Press for editorial help and to Marjorie Sirlouis for deciphering Wilson's shorthand. We also thank an old friend, Lewis L. Gould of the University of Texas, for discovering the letters printed as addenda in this volume, and Ms. Daurene V. Aubrey of the Bermuda Library for her frequent assistance.

THE EDITORS

Princeton, New Jersey
July 22, 1974

CONTENTS

ILLUSTRATIONS

Following page 386

TEXT ILLUSTRATIONS

ABBREVIATIONS

ALI	autograph letter initialed
ALS	autograph letter signed
CC T MS	carbon copy of typed manuscript
CCL	carbon copy of letter
hw	handwriting, handwritten
HwL	handwritten letter
HwLS	handwritten letter signed
LS	letter signed
MS	manuscript
T	typed
T MS	typed manuscript
T MS S	typed manuscript signed
TCL	typed copy of letter
TCLS	typed copy of letter signed
TCR	typed copy of report
TL	typed letter
TLS	typed letter signed
TRS	typed report signed
WW	Woodrow Wilson
WWhw	Woodrow Wilson handwriting, handwritten
WWhw MS	Woodrow Wilson handwritten manuscript
WWsh	Woodrow Wilson shorthand
WWsh MS	Woodrow Wilson shorthand manuscript
WWT	Woodrow Wilson typed
WWT MS	Woodrow Wilson typed manuscript
WWTCL	Woodrow Wilson typed copy of letter
WWTCLS	Woodrow Wilson typed copy of letter signed
WWTLS	Woodrow Wilson typed letter signed

ABBREVIATIONS FOR COLLECTIONS AND LIBRARIES

Following the National Union Catalog
of the Library of Congress

CtY	Yale University, New Haven
DLC	Library of Congress
LU	Louisiana State University, Baton Rouge
MH	Harvard University, Cambridge
MH-Ar	Harvard University Archives
MWC	Clark University, Worcester
MiU-H	University of Michigan, Ann Arbor–Michigan Historical Collection
NHi	New-York Historical Society, New York
NN	New York Public Library
NNC	Columbia University, New York
NcD	Duke University, Durham
NjHi	New Jersey Historical Society, Newark
NjP	Princeton University, Princeton
PLF	Franklin and Marshall College, Lancaster

RSB Coll., DLC	Ray Stannard Baker Collection of Wilsoniana, Library of Congress
UA, NjP	University Archives, Princeton University
ViHi	Virginia Historical Society, Richmond
WC, NjP	Woodrow Wilson Collection, Princeton University
WHi	State Historical Society of Wisconsin, Madison
WP, DLC	Woodrow Wilson Papers, Library of Congress
WU	University of Wisconsin, Madison
WWP, UA, NjP	Woodrow Wilson Papers, University Archives, Princeton University

SYMBOLS

[Jan. 23, 1909]	publication date of a published writing; also date of document when date is not part of text
[[Feb. 12, 1909]]	delivery date of a speech if publication date differs
[*July 6, 1909*]	composition date when publication date differs
⟨College⟩	matter deleted from document and restored by editors

THE PAPERS OF

WOODROW WILSON

VOLUME 19

1909-1910

THE PAPERS OF

WOODROW WILSON

From Charles Williston McAlpin

My dear Dr. Wilson: [Princeton, N. J.] January 20, 1909.

Allow me to remind you of the Committee to be appointed under Mr. Garrett's Resolution.[1] Mr. Garrett agrees with you that the Committee should consist of himself and Messrs. Imbrie and Thompson.

I call your attention also to the Minute on the Resignation of Mr. Morgan, which you were requested to prepare;[2] and to the notification you were requested to give to the Graduate Presidents of the Upper Class Clubs of the action taken by the Board at the October meeting.[3]

Yours very sincerely, [C. W. McAlpin] Secretary.

CCL (McAlpin File, UA, NjP).

1 At the meeting of the Board of Trustees on January 14, 1909, Robert Garrett proposed and the board adopted a resolution providing "that the President be authorized to appoint a committee of three to consider the need for the student body of Princeton of a comprehensive plan of physical training, and if in their judgment a suitable plan can be devised and can be put into effect, to report their findings in detail to the Board of Trustees at the meeting in April." Wilson subsequently appointed Garrett, H. B. Thompson, and A. C. Imbrie as the committee. Minutes of the Trustees of Princeton University, Jan. 14, 1909.

As it turned out, the committee did not present its report until January 13, 1910. It recommended creation of a Department of Physical Education, to be staffed by a professor and one or more associate professors or instructors. These men were to have "the control and direction of all matters connected with physical training,—including competitive athletics,—subject to the ultimate control of the Faculty and Board of Trustees." The board accepted the committee's recommendations. *Ibid.*, Jan. 13, 1910. A Department of Hygiene and Physical Education, with Joseph Edward Raycroft, M.D., as head, was inaugurated in September 1911 and at once began a program to involve all undergraduates in some form of athletics. See the *Princeton Alumni Weekly*, XII (Oct. 4, 1911), 20.

2 This minute is printed as an Enclosure with WW to C. W. McAlpin, Jan. 23, 1909.

3 The Board of Trustees at its meeting on October 15, 1908, had adopted the recommendation of its Committee on Conference with the Alumni "That the upper class clubs should unite in appointing a duly authorized graduate committee to deal with themselves and with the University authorities in all matters affecting club life and club relations to the University." See the extract from the Minutes of the Board of Trustees printed at Oct. 15, 1908, Vol. 18.

At the meeting of the trustees on January 14, 1909, Wilson stated that he "proposed personally" to notify the clubs of this resolution but had forgotten to do so; and he therefore requested McAlpin to make a note to remind him of the matter. See H. B. Thompson to J. S. Morgan, Jan. 18, 1909, *ibid.* Wilson finally sent letters to the graduate presidents in late January 1909. See WW to F. Murphy, Jr., Jan. 26, 1909.

Charles Williston McAlpin to Robert Garrett

Princeton, New Jersey
My dear Mr. Garrett: January 20, 1909.

In answer to your letter of the 18th inst., I would say that I had a talk with President Wilson on Friday last about the composition of the Committee to be named under your Resolution. The President feels very strongly that Mr. Thompson is the only Trustee, in addition to Imbrie, suitable for appointment. I am to bring the matter to his attention upon his return from the South,[1] when he will undoubtedly appoint the Committee you suggest.

Yours very sincerely, C W McAlpin Secretary.

TLS (Selected Papers of R. Garrett, NjP).

[1] Wilson had gone to Chapel Hill, N. C., to speak on Robert E. Lee at a special convocation at the University of North Carolina. His address is printed at Jan. 19, 1909, Vol. 18.

From George Cullen Battle[1]

Dear Sir, Chapel Hill, N. C. Jan. 20, 1909.

When you had finished your address here, I did not presume to push forward, crowding those more worthy than I am, in order that I might tell you how thoroughly I enjoyed it but the desire to do so was equal to that of any who did go forward.

It was not the desire to gain notoriety by shaking hands with a *great* man and congratulating him upon having delivered an eloquent address but rather the humble desire to thank a *noble* preacher for having delivered a powerful sermon.

It had never before fallen to my lot to hear so eloquent and so polished an address, one in which every word was so peculiarly fitted to its place and yet had I been called upon, when you finished, to quote a single phrase from it, I doubt very much if I could have done so.

Such phrases truly deserve to be remembered for their force and beauty but they have no practical value to the hearer after they have conveyed the thoughts to him.

It was your thoughts which remained in my memory after you had finished speaking.

They were a great stimulus to do better things and I count myself a wiser and I hope better man for having received them.

I shall try to follow your advice and, with my eyes to the front, forge ahead doing my humble part in the work which is before us all but nevertheless I shall repeatedly look back upon the past and recall ple[a]sant memories to mind and among the plesantest will be the fact that it was my great fortune to be in Chapel Hill and hear your address.

Yours truly, George C. Battle (Student)

ALS (WP, DLC).

[1] A medical student at the University of North Carolina, 1908-10, he received the M.D. degree from the University of Maryland in 1912.

From Frank Miles Day and Brother[1]

Dear Dr. Wilson: Philada. January 20th, 1909.

In conference with Mr. Henry B. Thompson yesterday upon the plans of the Sage Dormitory, it became evident that it would be desirable to have the wording of the Fitzrandolph inscription[2] at as early a time as might be convenient. Mr. Thompson asked us to write to you for the inscription in order that the size and character of the tablet might be determined for inclusion in the working drawings of the building.

Very truly yours, Frank Miles Day & Brother.

TLS (WWP, UA, NjP).

[1] Architects of 925 Chestnut St., Philadelphia, who were drawing the plans for and supervising the construction of what was to become Holder Hall.

[2] It is printed as an Enclosure with WW to F. M. Day and Brother, Jan. 26, 1909.

To Charles Williston McAlpin

My dear Mr. McAlpin: Princeton, N. J. January 21st, 1909.

In reply to your letter of January 20th, kindly reminding me of the items assigned to me by the various actions of the Board at its last meeting, let me say that I will appoint as the committee under Mr. Garrett's resolution Mr. Robert Garrett, Mr. Henry B. Thompson and Mr. Andrew C. Imbrie. I would be very much obliged if you inform these gentlemen of the appointment.

I will try to send you a minute on the resignation of Mr. Morgan tomorrow. I have just come back from a trip to the South and do not like to attempt to prepare it offhand.

Always cordially and faithfully yours,

Woodrow Wilson

TLS (McAlpin File, UA, NjP).

From Melancthon Williams Jacobus

Hartford, Conn.,
My dear President Wilson: January 21st, 1909.

I thank you very much for your kind letter,[1] informing me of the meetings of the Committee on Curriculum and of the Board of Trustees.

I do sincerely congratulate you upon being relieved of this burden of detailed administration, especially in view of the most competent hands in which you have been able to place it.[2] Surely this will give you a new feeling of freedom for the splendid public work, in the interests of Princeton, which you are carrying on.

Have you seen the article in the "Independent" of two weeks ago, on Harvard University?[3] From the good word it has to say of Princeton's preceptorial system, I look for an appreciative article when our time comes to be written up.[4] Surely it is evidence that Princeton has met the present need in University education in this country as no other institution has met it, and should be of the greatest encouragement to us all to persevere in the carrying out of the logical results of that system.

The list of honorary degrees which you present is most attractive, and I am sure it will give an intellectual character to our coming Commencement at the alumni banquet, which we have missed hitherto.

In going over the minutes of the October meeting, I see there are several matters which, perhaps, should have been placed upon the Docket of the January meeting of our Committee. I enclose them herewith, on a separate sheet,[5] and would ask you to consider the matter of reporting on them at the April meeting.

I notice, in the "Princetonian's" account of the Trustee meeting,[6] that Mr. Junius S. Morgan, Associate Librarian, resigned and his resignation was accepted. Is there any reason for the resignation which has to do with Mr. Morgan's opposition to the Quad plan? I am sorry indeed that the University should lose his enthusiastic interest in the Library; but I am wondering whether he has become convinced that things are moving, if slowly, yet inevitably, in the direction of the carrying out of some scheme of Residential Quad. If such is the case, perhaps his resignation has been wise.

I enclose herewith my record of Dr. McPherson's suggestion regarding the entrance requirements in languages for the C.E. course,[7] as I took it down at the meeting of the Board when it was made.

With kind regards and renewed thanks for your thoughtfulness in informing me as you have done, I am

Yours very sincerely, Melancthon W. Jacobus

TLS (WP, DLC).

[1] WW to M. W. Jacobus, Jan. 15, 1909, Vol. 18.

[2] That is, the creation by the trustees at their meeting on January 14, 1909, of the new Deanship of the Departments of Science and the appointment of Henry B. Fine as the first incumbent.

[3] Edwin E. Slosson, "Harvard University," *The Independent*, LXVI (Jan. 7, 1909), 23-40. This was the first of a series of articles by Slosson for the *Independent* on "Great American Universities." The series was later published under that title as a book by Macmillan in 1910.

[4] Edwin E. Slosson, "Princeton University," *The Independent*, LXVI (March 4, 1909), 458-77. This was the third article in the series, following one on Yale University.

[5] It is missing.

[6] "Result of Trustees Meeting," *Daily Princetonian*, Jan. 15, 1909.

[7] See M. W. Jacobus to WW, Jan. 5, 1909, n. 1, Vol. 18.

To Charles Williston McAlpin, with Enclosure

My dear McAlpin: Princeton, N. J. January 23rd, 1909.

I take the liberty of enclosing the minute with regard to Mr. Junius S. Morgan's resignation. It has given me pleasure to write it, and I hope it is so framed as to convey to him an expression of our real feeling in the matter.

Always faithfully yours, Woodrow Wilson

TLS (UA, NjP).

E N C L O S U R E

A Tribute

[Jan. 23, 1909]

In accepting the resignation of Mr. Morgan the Board wishes to express its very warm appreciation of the unusual services he has rendered the University as Associate Librarian and in many other ways, and its very great regret that he feels obliged to give up the duties of the office and his official association with the administration of the University. His knowledge of library affairs, his intelligent devotion to the interests of the library, great and small, his appreciation of all its relations to the work of the University, his admirable taste and invariable good judgment have rendered him a singularly valuable officer and delightful colleague. The Board yields to his desire to be released from his present duties with the utmost reluctance and wishes to thank him for the many and varied services which he has rendered Princeton University.

T MS (UA, NjP).

To Melancthon Williams Jacobus

My dear Dr. Jacobus: [Princeton, N. J.] January 23rd, 1909.

I am very much obliged to you for your kind letter of the 21st and beg to assure you that the matters you have noted will be taken up by the proper committees of the faculty.

So far as I can make out, Mr. Morgan's resignation as Associate Librarian did not have any special connection with his feeling with regard to our quad controversy or the movement of opinion in the matter. He has withdrawn from active participation in the business of the firm of Cuyler, Morgan & Co., from the vestry of the Episcopal Church here, and from other positions, with the feeling, I think, that he has scattered his energy and attention over too many matters and has given his real energy to none of them. So far as I can make out, he wants to draw off for a little and make up his mind what one thing he wishes to do, feeling that he has perhaps frittered away his life instead of using it. He seemed to leave with the most cordial feeling towards all of us.

Thank you also for the minute of Dr. McPherson's suggestion regarding entrance requirements in languages for the C.E. course. We had, by joint recollection, recovered it, and I shall bring it before an early meeting of the Committee on the Course of Study.

You say nothing in your letter about your health. I sincerely trust that no news is good news and that you are continuing to gain in strength.

Always cordially and faithfully yours,

[Woodrow Wilson]

CCL (RSB Coll., DLC).

From Andrew Fleming West, with Enclosure

My dear Wilson, Princeton January 24 1909

On the next sheet of this letter I have written two short *prose* mottoes or legends for you to consider. I have kept in mind your suggestion that some personal suggestion regarding Nathaniel

Fitz Randolph is desirable. Also that the space allows probably not more than half a dozen words.

Ever yours Andrew F. West

ALS (WP, DLC).

ENCLOSURE

I

IN AGRO IACET NOSTRO IMMO SUO

Within our field he lies; nay, in his own.

II

NON SIBI TANTUMMODO DIVES

Not rich for himself alone.

N. B. Perhaps I can make one or two more in a day or so.

A F. W.

Hw MS (WP, DLC).

Notes for an Address

Monday Night Club.[1] 25 Jan'y, 1909.

THE RECENT CAMPAIGN AND THE PRESENT STATE OF PARTIES

Contrasted men
Contrasted proposals } rather than contrasted principles

Mr. Taft in the South: the South without *convictions* opposed to the acceptance of his overtures.[2]

Mr. Bryan a preacher whose proposals were accepted by millions because his sermons were indisputable.

Statesmanship should be a guide to the national life

No one can guide who does not know the country

The country = our present social and economic order.

1) Inquiry, analysis.
2) Some system (i.e. some *principle*) of regulation.
3) Some non-economic standard and ideal.

Is it likely that we shall discover new principles, as, e.g., that gov't. power is now safe, efficient, and dependable?

A. Negative control
B. Individual responsibility, private and public.
C. Simplification of all processes. (I.e. publicity)

Machinery the enemy alike of efficiency and of liberty (i.e. democracy)

The American passion for organization opposed to political and administrative success.[3]

24 Jan'y, 1909[4]

WWhw MS (WP, DLC).

1 About this organization, see n. 2 to the notes for a talk printed at Nov. 13, 1905, Vol. 16.

2 In 1908, William Howard Taft had become the first Republican presidential candidate to campaign in the South, making a tour in October through Kentucky, Tennessee, North Carolina, and Virginia. Partly because of this effort, but principally because of a conservative reaction against Bryan's candidacy, the Republican vote increased significantly in all the southern states. Indeed, Taft came close to carrying North Carolina and Tennessee.

In numerous speeches both during and after the campaign, Taft took a basically pro-southern position on the question of race relations in the South. In particular, in a brief but widely quoted address to the North Carolina Society of New York on December 7, 1908, Taft asserted that election laws which excluded "an ignorant electorate, black or white" were acceptable so long as they were not technically in violation of the Fifteenth Amendment; that the federal government should not attempt to enforce "social equality" of the races; that the best hope for the Negro lay in vocational education; and, finally, that "the best friend that the southern Negro can have is the Southern white man." He also said that the increasing industrialization and prosperity of the South, together with Republican acquiescence in the southern position on race relations, would lead to a gradual breakdown of the "solid South." Wilson's comments were probably inspired by this speech. See William Howard Taft, *The South and the National Government* (n. p., n. d.). See also C. Vann Woodward, *Origins of the New South, 1877-1913* (Baton Rouge, La., 1951), pp. 467-68, and George B. Tindall, *The Disruption of the Solid South* (Athens, Ga., 1972), p. 19.

3 No local newspaper printed a report of this address.

4 Wilson's composition date.

To Cyrus Hall McCormick

My dear Cyrus: [Princeton, N. J.] January 25th, 1909.

Thank you for your letter of January 22nd[1] and also for the copies of the letters you wrote Pyne and Fine regarding Professors Capps and Abbott.[2]

I think that on the whole it would be most prudent for me to decline to speak at the banquet of the Industrial Club. It will give me great pleasure to attend it, and it would be a very rare pleasure indeed if I might attend it without a speech on my mind and at liberty to feel the full enjoyment of the occasion. I know that the gentlemen in charge of the banquet will appreciate the feeling I have that one address is all that I should undertake on a single visit,[3] and that they will accord me the pleasure of this exemption.

As for the matter of Professor Capps, he has actually been called to Harvard and it is by no means certain that he will decline.[4] This is not at all because we have not made his life here sufficiently pleasant and attractive, for he has become, I think, very much attached to Princeton and to us, but only because he feels very much discouraged about the prospects of graduate work here. Indeed, we are convinced that a radical reorganization on that side will be necessary, if we are to keep Capps or Abbott or Conklin or any of the new men we have added to our faculty and in whom our hopes of distinction for the University so much center. I wish very much that you were going to be in the East some time in the near future, in order that these matters might be fully discussed before our fears in the matter of Capps' going can be realized.

I return the memorandum which your letter enclosed.

Always faithfully and affectionately yours,

[Woodrow Wilson]

CCL (WWP, UA, NjP).

1 It is missing.

2 C. H. McCormick to M. T. Pyne, Jan. 23, 1909, and C. H. McCormick to H. B. Fine, Jan. 23, 1909, both CCL (WP, DLC). They were enclosed in F. A. Steuert to WW, Jan. 23, 1909, TLS (WP, DLC). In both letters, McCormick warned that Harvard University was making strenuous efforts to persuade Edward Capps and Frank Frost Abbott to accept professorships and urged that Pyne and Fine make every effort "to make the social life and atmosphere of these two eminent men, with their families, agreeable and attractive at Princeton." "I think you would be perfectly justified," he wrote to Fine, "in doing what you could to awaken the interest in these two men among those who have homes at Princeton and are in a position to invite them to the hospitality of their homes."

3 Wilson was scheduled to give an address on Lincoln in Chicago on February 12, 1909. His address is printed at that date.

4 Capps declined the Harvard offer.

To Abbott Lawrence Lowell

My dear Mr. Lowell: Princeton, N. J. January 25th, 1909.

I have kept your letter of January 13th[1] longer than I should have kept it, but only because I wished, if possible, to accept the very kind invitation which it conveyed to me to deliver the Phi Beta Kappa oration at Harvard next June.

I take it for granted that your Commencement exercises come this year, as usual, a little after our own, and, if that is true, I think that it would be possible for me to come, and I can assure you that I would consider it an honor and pleasure to do so.[2] Our Commencement date this year is June 15th.

Allow me to thank you very sincerely for your letter and also for your letter[3] acknowledging the receipt of my very sincere congrataultions [congratulations] to you and to Harvard on the recent action of the Fellows and Overseers.[4]

With warmest regard,

Cordially and sincerely yours, Woodrow Wilson

TLS (A. L. Lowell Papers, MH-Ar).
1 It is missing.
2 Wilson's oration is printed at July 1, 1909.
3 A. L. Lowell to WW, Jan. 15, 1909, Vol. 18.
4 Lowell had replied to a telegram from Wilson of January 14, 1909, congratulating Lowell upon his election to the presidency of Harvard University.

To Cleveland Hoadley Dodge

My dear Cleve., Princeton, N. J. 26 January, 1909.

I was so much distressed by the turn the discussion took yesterday at the meeting of the Finance Committee[1] that an important piece of business about which I wanted to speak to speak [*sic*] to you went entirely out of my head.

Conklin, our crack biologist, and Dahlgren, who in his way is going to bring us reputation also, are in need of money for their necessary supplies, Conklin of five hundred dollars and Dahlgren of almost as much more. When I spoke to Pyne about it he suggested that I ask you whether there is any accumulated interest on the fund you have been generous enough to provide for the endowment of the work to be done in Guyot Hall which would be available now for the purchases these men must make. We brought Conklin here under express assurances with regard to our willingness to support his work; but if there is any money to be had from that fund it will spare the already staggering general budget.

With warmest affection,

Faithfully Yours, Woodrow Wilson

WWTLS (WC, NjP).
1 The discussion revolved around the question of whether the non-scientific departments were overstaffed with preceptors. For the resolution which emerged from this discussion, see H. G. Duffield to M. W. Jacobus, Jan. 26, 1909, printed as an Enclosure with M. W. Jacobus to WW, Feb. 3, 1909.

To Andrew Fleming West

My dear Professor West: Princeton, N. J. January 26th, 1909.

Thank you most sincerely for your kindness in sending me the Latin mottos. The first one, "In agro jacit nostro immo suo" seems to me particularly beautiful and suitable, and I shall take the liberty of sending it to the architect. It is very happily done, as always when you do these things.

Always faithfully yours, Woodrow Wilson

TLS (UA, NjP).

To Franklin Murphy, Jr.[1]

My dear Mr. Murphy: Princeton, N. J. January 26th, 1909.

Through a misunderstanding as to who was to send out the notification, there has been a delay, which I regret, in sending out the following notice:

At its October meeting, the Board of Trustees of Princeton University adopted the following resolution: Resolved, that the Upperclass Clubs should unite in appointing a duly authorized graduate committee to deal with themselves and with the University authorities in all matters affecting club life and club relations to the University.

The object of the Board in taking this action was to request the Upperclass Clubs to establish a committee which should be regarded as representing all of them and which should be ready to advise with the Faculty of the University or the Trustees or with the officers of the University whenever it seemed desirable to communicate with the governing bodies of the clubs. This action was taken with a view to avoiding the inconvenience of consulting the several governing bodies of the different clubs separately whenever such communications seemed necessary, and to facilitate all official intercourse between the authorities of the University and the clubs as members of the University community.

Allow me to beg that you will lay this communication before the Board of Governors of the Tiger Inn Club.

With much regard,

Sincerely yours, [Woodrow Wilson][2]

CCL (WWP, UA, NjP).

1 President of the Board of Governors of Tiger Inn Club and Vice-President of the Murphy Varnish Co., Newark, N. J.

2 Wilson sent the same letter to the graduate presidents of all the eating clubs.

To Frank Miles Day and Brother, with Enclosure

My dear Sirs: Princeton, N. J. January 26th, 1909.

I have delayed a few days in replying to your letter of January 20th about the wording for the Fitz-Randolph inscription, in order to give it careful consideration. I now enclose on another sheet what seems to me a suitable inscription.

Sincerely yours, Woodrow Wilson

TLS (WC, NjP).

E N C L O S U R E

An Inscription

January 26th, 1909.

Near this spot
lie the remains of
Nathaniel Fitz Randolph
The generous giver of the land
upon which the original buildings
of the University
were erected

IN AGRO IACET NOSTRO IMMO SUO[1]

CC T MS (WWP, UA, NjP).

[1] This inscription appears on a tablet in the archway on the east side of Holder Hall.

From Cleveland Hoadley Dodge

My dear Mr. President: New York January 27, 1909.

In reply to your good letter of yesterday, you will remember that when Guyot Hall was first talked of, I agreed to give $200,000 as an endowment fund to maintain the building; but I do not think there was any understanding as to whether the income of that fund should be used for necessary laboratory supplies or simply the heating and lighting of the building. The understanding was that I should pay interest on the sum named, beginning with the 1st of January, 1908, and I have therefore already paid $10,000 interest, and there will be nearly as much more paid in before the building is in active use. I do not know definitely what the Treasurer has done with this interest which I have paid in, but I very much fear that it has been used for the necessary expenses of the University, for which purpose you very well know that it was much needed.

Now, however, that money is actually needed for the legitimate wants of the Departments which will use the building, it certainly does not seem that the applications of Prof. Conklin and Dahlgren are out of the way, and I should be in favor of giving them the sums you name. Of course, however, you must recognize that I really have nothing whatever to say about it, as my money has been turned over to the University and I suppose the Finance Committee ought to determine to what use this special fund should be put. Of course, if the whole income of the $200,000 is used for specimens in the Museum and supplies in the laboratory,—which is the case with the endowment of Palmer Hall,—the University will have to add a large amount to next year's budget for the mere heating, lighting and maintenance of Guyot Hall, as has been the case with Palmer Hall.

I think we ought to give the Professors what they need in this instance and if the Finance Committee does not approve it, I will be glad to make it up myself, although I do not want to establish any bad precedents.

I wish that a dear friend of ours[1] would go away for six months and get his nerves in a little better condition and drop all thought of a certain vexed question.[2] I absolutely refuse to discuss it with anybody now, and if Momo would only adopt the same policy and let this confounded agitation die out, it would be the best for everybody. It worries him frightfully and so many people speak to him that he does not seem to be able to get it out of his head. We had a good talk with Imbrey [Imbrie] and [Harold Griffith] Murray yesterday afternoon about the plans for the graduate Council,[3] and I feel confident that Murray is doing the best he can when he sees the alumni to stop all talk and agitation about the "Quad" system.

With best wishes, hoping that you will not let yourself be worried by the revamping of this miserable business,

Yours very sincerely, C. H. Dodge

TLS (WP, DLC).

1 Moses Taylor Pyne.

2 That is, the quadrangle plan.

3 Plans for reorganizing the Committee of Fifty, about which see J. L. Cadwalader to WW, March 5, 1909; WW to J. L. Cadwalader, March 6, 1909; and the "Plan for the Organization of the Graduate Council of Princeton University," printed at March 29, 1909.

To Cleveland Hoadley Dodge

My dear Cleve: Princeton, N. J. January 28th, 1909.

Thank you most heartily for your kind letter of yesterday. The matter of the endowment of the new laboratory has given me a good deal of thought and concern. It is evident to me that so far as the budget of the University is concerned, it is almost a matter of indifference whether the endowment be applied to the physical maintenance of the building and to heating and lighting, etc., or be applied to the support of teaching in it. I mean to the purchase of the necessary supplies and specimens. If it is applied to the physical maintenance of the building, it will simply mean that the University will have to pay out at least as much more for the supplies and specimens necessary to the teaching. Inasmuch as it is possible to skimp on that side and is not possible to skimp on the side of lighting and heating and the actual maintenance of the building, and inasmuch as the skimping on the teaching side is the very thing above all others that should be avoided, particularly since these Departments have heretofore been sadly starved, my own judgment would be that it would be wisest to definitely apply the endowment as it has been applied in the case of the [Palmer] Physical Laboratory. I know that the men of the teaching staff in Biology and Geology have expected that the same arrangement would be made for them that has been made for the physicists, and I know that their uneasiness and disappointment would be very great if they were to feel that they were to be dependent upon a shifting budget for their absolute necessaries of life. This is a matter of considerable concern with me, because with the coming of Professor Conklin we are entering upon a new era of teaching in Biology under one of the most eminent men in the country, and have undertaken new obligations, both implicit and explicit, with regard to him and the facilitation of his teaching.

It was characteristic of your generous way of doing things to pay the endowment in without any prescription or restriction as to its use, but I am sure that the Trustees would feel that you still had the right to designate the purposes for which it should be used.

While you are considering that subject, I will write to Pyne about the present question and am sure that he, as Chairman of the Finance Committee, will authorize the application of the part of the income now needed by Conklin and Dahlgren as I have suggested, especially now that I can tell him that that use of it meets with your approval.

I am very grateful for the rest of your letter. I often find myself in very great perplexity as to what is my own proper personal course of action, and words of reassurance are inestimably valuable to me.

Always affectionately yours, Woodrow Wilson

TLS (WC, NjP).

To Moses Taylor Pyne

My dear Momo: [Princeton, N. J.] January 28th, 1909.

I consulted Dodge with regard to the matter I spoke to you of, namely Professor Conklin's and Professor Dahlgren's need for certain moderate sums, Professor Conklin $500 and Professor Dahlgren a little less, for the maintenance of their work in Biology.

Cleve tells me that the interest ($10,000) which has been running on his endowment fund since the first of January, 1908, he has so far paid into the Treasurer of the University without any direction as to how it should be expended. From what Mr. Duffield tells me, I think that it has come in as if part of what we were deriving from the Committee of Fifty and has been applied to the general expenses of the University.

Dodge entirely agrees that Conklin and Dahlgren should have their money—indeed, that is an absolute necessity—and he espresses [expresses] himself as approving your suggestion that a portion of the interest which he pays in during the present calendar year should be devoted to that use. If you will be kind enough to let me have your authorization as Chairman of the Finance Committee, I can arrange the matter with the Treasurer of the University.

Always faithfully yours, [Woodrow Wilson]

CCL (WWP, UA, NjP).

From George Bryan Logan[1]

Dear Sir, Pittsburg. Jany 29/09

It has been my intention to send my son to Princeton next Fall, but I have been recently led to doubt the wisdom of so doing & am writing you for information.

Persistant & definite rumors have reached me, that the instructor in Bible,[2] teaches & advocates the teachings of destructive criticism, & the most liberal views regarding the person of Christ, the Trinity & the Atonement. I do not care to subject the immature mind of my son to this kind of teaching. He must of course meet these things later in life, but I want him to have solid ground for anchorage, before the storms reach him. Please let me hear from you on this subject & oblige

Yours truly Geo B. Logan

ALS (WP, DLC).

1 President of the Logan-Gregg Hardware Co., Pittsburgh.

2 Lucius Hopkins Miller, Assistant Professor of Biblical Instruction.

To Frank Arthur Vanderlip

Personal

My dear Mr. Vanderlip: Princeton, N. J. February 1st, 1909.

I wonder if you remember a conversation I had with you last winter about interesting Mr. Carnegie in giving the money that would enable us to put into operation at Princeton a system of undergraduate life which would bring our college spirit, perhaps, back to something like its old democracy of motive and action and supply us with an atmosphere in which serious work would be possible and even natural?[1] I wonder whether what I then urged remained in your mind and whether you have had an opportunity to judge whether I made any impression on Mr. Carnegie himself?

The importance of the whole subject has grown, even beyond my expectation. The whole college world is awaking to it slowly but very definitely, turning vaguely towards the very solution I have thought out for Princeton. If I could carry the change out here, it would be of universal and revolutionary influence. But I cannot without money; and some one man must give me the money. My whole administration of the University waits for that particular consummation, is embarrassed, very seriously embarrassed, because there is a sense of revolution in the air and a slow turning of conviction in my direction, and yet no definite movement but only a sort of disturbed and arrested life. It has come to the point where I must move forward or else turn in an utterly different direction, to the complete marring of all I had conceived and planned. The college world that has of late begun to look to us for leadership will be disappointed, and a great opportunity lost. The thought is very hard for me to bear. I must get the money.

It is three and a half millions. I do not know from whom I could get it, if not from Mr. Carnegie; and I believe that if you have faith in my plans, Mr. Carnegie would yield to your representations and Dr. Pritchett's, as he would respond to no others. I understand Dr. Pritchett to be thoroughly of my mind in the matter; but I do not know whether I interested you or not.

Would you have the leisure and opportunity to have another talk with me on the subject this week? I am going to be in New York on Friday and on Saturday, but could come any other day that might better suit your convenience. If you would be free on Friday or Saturday, I could fix an hour, if you would give me more than one to choose from, because I am liable to a call on one or other of those days for an important committee meeting, which I will know about certainly within twenty-four hours.

Things have come to the turning point with me, for reasons which I can explain to you. If I cannot do this thing I have spoken of, I must turn to something else than mere college administration, forced, not by my colleagues, but by my mind and convictions and the impossibility of continuing at an undertaking I do not believe in and could change, if Mr. Carnegie or some other man of large free means believed in me enough to trust me with the money and the enterprise.

With warm regard,

Faithfully yours, Woodrow Wilson

TLS (F. A. Vanderlip Papers, NNC).

[1] He of course meant the quadrangle plan.

From George Howe III

Dear Uncle Woodrow, Chapel Hill, N. C. Feb 1, 1909.

At last the stenographer's copy of your speech[1] has come. It is in very bad shape in some places, but for the most part I think you can straighten it out. The bill amounted to $12.05, and I learn that the $100 handed you was supposed to cover it. You can make the check payable either to me or W. T. Patterson, Bursar.[2]

We are still hearing your praises on all sides. You won every one. And you can have no idea how deeply happy Maisie[3] and I were to have you. We are both well, and planning just now to go to New Orleans to the meeting of the Classical Association.[4] I followed your advice & accepted the vicepresidency.

Unbounded love from Maisie & myself to you & all the dear family. Affectionately, George Howe

ALS (WP, DLC).

[1] That is, of his address on Robert E. Lee.

[2] Wylie Thomas Patterson, Bursar of the University of North Carolina.

[3] His wife, Margaret Smyth Flinn Howe.

[4] The Classical Association of the Middle West and South.

From Charles Alexander Richmond[1]

My dear Dr. Wilson, Albany New York 1st Feby 1909.

I want to thank you for your kind note. My election was unanimous, really, not formally, so they say. I shall therefore take up my new work with good heart. The best ideals of Princeton shall be mine.

It is natural of course that I should look to you to make the address at my Inaugural. The date would be, tentatively, the seventh or eighth of June the week before the Princeton Commencement and early in the week.

Could you come at that time? I want my Princeton friends about me at that time and I should like to feel that you are back of me in this promising, but untried field.

It would greatly please us all, if you could come.[2]

Faithfully Yours Charles Alex. Richmond.

ALS (WP, DLC).

[1] Princeton 1883; Princeton Theological Seminary, 1888; most recently pastor of the Madison Avenue Presbyterian Church of Albany. He was elected President of Union College and Chancellor of Union University on January 26, 1909.

[2] Wilson did attend and speak at Richmond's inauguration. His address is printed at June 7, 1909.

From Charles Francis Adams

PRIVATE AND PERSONAL

My dear Mr. President: Boston February 2, 1909.

I have received a printed notice from the Secretary of the Princeton University, containing an invitation to attend the next Annual Commencement on Tuesday, June 15, in order then to receive an honorary degree.

Needless to say, I highly appreciate this compliment on the part of Princeton University, and by it feel greatly honored. Meanwhile, before accepting, would you kindly intimate to me the circumstances, etc. of this occasion? How many honorary degrees are likely to be conferred, and upon whom; and is this merely an ordinary Commencement of the University, or is it to commemorate some special occasion? You will probably appreciate the motive of these enquiries on my part. While I appreciate to the fullest extent an honorary degree from so ancient and prominent a seat of learning as Princeton University, I at the same time would like to be somewhat advised as to the circumstances which may accompany the conferring of the degree. Believe me, etc, Charles F. Adams

TLS (WP, DLC).

To Henry Green Duffield

My dear Mr. Duffield: [Princeton, N. J.] February 3rd, 1909.

The enclosed letter concerns the matter about which I had a short conversation with you on the railway train coming back from the last meeting of the Finance Committee. I have seen Mr. Dodge and Mr. Pyne, and therefore feel authorized to authorize you to honor the drafts of Professor E. G. Conklin for supplies for his laboratory during the present academic year, to the extent of $500, and the drafts of Professor Dahlgren to the extent of $475, these moneys to be entered against what Mr. Cleveland H. Dodge pays in as interest on his gift of $200,000 to the University for the endowment of Guyot Hall. I have no doubt that a line dropped by you to Mr. Dodge would enable you to distinguish these credits from the others which you receive from him. Very sincerely yours, [Woodrow Wilson]

CCL (WWP, UA, NjP).

From Melancthon Williams Jacobus, with Enclosure

Hartford, Conn.,

My dear President Wilson: February 3rd, 1909.

Thank you very much for your kind letter of the 23d ultimo, the information contained in which I have greatly appreciated.

I received from Henry Duffield, Secretary of the Committee on Finance, copy of the resolution presented to and carried by that Committee at a recent meeting held in the city of New York.

I enclose herewith a copy of this resolution, and ask you whether in your judgment it will be necessary to call a special meeting of the Committee on Curriculum to give it consideration before the April meeting of the Board of Trustees. If you feel this is implied in the request of the Finance Committee, and will give me some idea of the time when it would be most convenient for you to have such an extra meeting called, I will see that the call is made out.

There is one other inquiry I wanted to lay before you. I take for granted that the January meeting of the Board is the last meeting at which nominations for honorary degrees, to be granted at the coming Commencement, are possible. If, however, I should be mistaken in this and it is possible to make them as late as the April meeting, I should like very much indeed to present for the honorary degree of Doctor of Divinity the name of Rev. Robert Forman Horton, M.A., D.D., minister of the Lyndhurst Road Church, Hampstead, London, educated at New College, Oxford, where he held the place of a distinguished scholar and secured the Fellowship connected with that College—in fact, where he was a Lecturer on History until 1883.

He was the Lyman Beecher Lecturer on Preaching at Yale University in 1893, was Chairman of the London Congregational Union (an office corresponding to the Moderator of the Presbyterian Assembly here) in 1898, and Chairman of the Congregational Union of England and Wales in 1903. His publications have been numerous and of wide-spread influence.

He is to be in this country the latter part of May and the early part of June, and Princeton could not do itself better honor than recognizing his international reputation and influence as scholar and minister.[1]

I understand that George Adam Smith, the well-known historical scholar,[2] is at present or is soon to be in this country. Such a degree to him, or even a Doctor of Laws, will be recognized as most fitting and would doubtless be more popular than a degree of Doctor of Divinity to Dr. Horton. But I am not sure that his stay in this country is to extend into the summer.[3]

In either case, if it is too late to present the degrees, nothing further need be said; though, as you know, I am anxious to have Princeton honored with as goodly a number of splendid men for her honors this Commencement as it is possible for us to secure.

With kindest regards,

Yours very sincerely, Melancthon W. Jacobus

TLS (WP, DLC).

1 He did not receive an honorary degree from Princeton.

2 The Rev. Dr. George Adam Smith, Professor of Old Testament Language, Literature, and Theology at the Free Church College, Glasgow, since 1892. A specialist in Old Testament studies and the historical geography of the Holy Land, he became Principal of Aberdeen University in late 1909.

3 He did not receive an honorary degree.

ENCLOSURE

Henry Green Duffield to Melancthon Williams Jacobus

Dear Sir: Princeton, N. J., Jan. 26, '09.

At a meeting of the Committee on Finance held in New York City on the 25th inst., the following resolution was unanimously passed. The Secretary of the Committee was directed to forward a copy to you.

"WHEREAS, the relative number of students in the various Departments varies from time to time, while the present assignment of instructors has been practically unchanged for years;

"RESOLVED, that the Committee on Curriculum be requested to report to this Committee regarding the effectiveness of the teaching force of the University, whether in its judgment the distribution of the appropriations given by the University for instruction is made in a manner calculated to produce the best results, and whether any retrenchment might be made in any Department without interfering with the necessary and desirable work of that Department."

Very respectfully,

(Signed) H. G. Duffield, Secretary.

TCL (WP, DLC).

To Charles Francis Adams

My dear Mr. Adams: Princeton, N. J. February 4th, 1909.

Allow me to acknowledge the receipt of your letter of February 2nd. We hope most sincerely that we may look forward to the pleasure of having you with us at our next Commencement. The occasion is of no unusual sort. It is merely our annual Commencement, but we have tried for a great many years to make our list of honorary degrees a very distinguished one. This year, besides yourself, Earl Grey, the Governor-General of Canada, Mr. Abbott Lawrence Lowell, and Dr. Frank Hartley, the distinguished surgeon of New York City, now probably the leading surgeon there, have been invited to receive the degree of Doctor of Laws, and it is not likely that the list will be added to. If any name is added, it will, I think, be the name of the present Chinese ambassador to the United States,[1] though that is improbable.[2] Mr. John W. Alexander, the artist, and the Rev. Samuel Crothers[3] have been invited to receive the degree of Doctor of Letters; President W. H. S. Demarest of Rutgers College the degree of Doctor of Divinity; and Mr. Gutzon Borglum, the sculptor, the honorary degree of Master of Arts.

A luncheon follows the exercises at which the degrees are conferred, and it would be our hope that at that luncheon we might have the pleasure of hearing a few remarks from you. No one would speak on that occasion except those who had received honorary degrees and myself as President of the University, except of course the toastmaster of the occasion.

It was a disappointment to me not to find you at the last dinner of the Round Table Club.[4]

With much regard,

Sincerely yours, Woodrow Wilson

TLS (photostat in RSB Coll., DLC).

[1] Wu T'ing-fang, Chinese Minister to the United States, 1897-1901 and 1907-1909.

[2] He did not receive an honorary degree from Princeton.

[3] For re-identification of Crothers, see n. 1 to the essay printed at Aug. 3, 1909.
[4] About this organization, see WW to C. H. Marshall, Dec. 26, 1902, n. 3, Vol. 14.

To George Bryan Logan

My dear Sir: Princeton, N. J. February 4th, 1909.

Allow me to acknowledge the receipt of your letter of January 29th and to express my appreciation of its candid inquiry. It gives me pleasure to return as candid a reply.

The only course in Biblical literature offered by the University is an elective for Seniors. I quite appreciate your point that a boy coming to college is apt at the outset to have too immature a mind to be plunged into any critical inquiry concerning the contents and meaning of the Bible. The course we offer in [is] open only to Seniors, whom we find very much more mature than Freshmen and who, before taking this course, have pursued studies calculated to raise many questions about life, religion, and the Bible, which it seems entirely to their advantage to discuss with them very frankly. You will understand, however, that no one is obliged to take the course. The class consists generally of some twelve or fourteen men who have specially selected that study.

While we believe in the necessity of studying the Bible by critical methods, if it is to be a part of a university course, I can assure you that you are wrongly informed if you suppose that the methods or the effects of the instruction given in the course are destructive. The consistent aim of the instructor is to emphasize the positive conclusions to be reached by a sane, constructive, historical method, and to enable the students to see the real depth and beauty and power of the books both of the Old and New Testament. You may rest assured, also, that the person of Christ as the cardinal and essential Christian fact, the real Saviour of mankind, is dwelt upon with all the emphasis of profound conviction.

A strong proof of the positive emphasis of the course and its very strong religious influence is found in the fact that it has influenced men in an unusual degree to join the church and take up religious work as their calling in life. This fact alone would seem to allay fear and disarm criticism.[1]

I am fully alive to the difficulty and the dangers of a course of university instruction in the Bible. It cannot, if it is to have the character of other university instruction, be anything else than a study of the Bible as a great body of literature. It cannot be, in the ordinary sense of the word, a course of religious instruction. It inevitably becomes so, however, because of the extraordinary character of the books studied, their place in the whole history and development of the church and of civilization, and their inevitably divine character as a revelation of God to man. While the method of the course, therefore, is not the method of religious instruction, I have abundant testimony from my young friends among the undergraduates that its effect is deeply and noticeably religious.[2]

With much respect,

Sincerely yours, [Woodrow Wilson]

CCL (WP, DLC).

[1] To this point Wilson was paraphrasing a draft of a reply written by Lucius Hopkins Miller. The draft is a typed MS in WP, DLC.

[2] This letter must have allayed Logan's doubts. George Bryan Logan, Jr., entered Princeton in 1909 and was graduated with the Class of 1915.

From Arthur Crosby Ludington[1]

Dear Mr. Wilson: [New York] February 4th, 1909.

Thanks ever so much for your letter in regard to direct primaries. I fully agree with you that the most important reform of all to be worked for is the reduction of the number of elective offices, and I think you will be interested to hear that most of the members of the C. U. Committee on Legislation[2] are so alive to the necessity of this change that they will probably favor a provision to this effect in the constitutional revision of 1914.[3] Governor Hughes also suggests in his message that if the voters will not show a proper interest in choosing candidates under the direct primary, and find the Massachusetts ballot with the present number of names too much for them, the solution will be to lessen the number of offices to be voted for.[4] He believes —and Professor Merriam expresses the same opinion in his recent book on "Direct Primaries"[5]—that direct nominations, the Massachusetts ballot, and the "shortened ballot" should go hand in hand.

We have had some bad experiences with conventions in New York State of recent years, especially in the Democratic party, and I think the up-state voters will welcome any measure which gives fair promise of "downing the bosses." I must say I sympathize with this point of view, and look on the direct primary, not as a step toward pure democracy, but as a means of checking and controlling the action of party leaders. They will make selections as before,—indeed the Governor's bill[6] will provide for this specifically—but such selections will be subject to the approval of the enrolled members of the party, who, if they disapprove, will be able to submit a rival candidate for nomination. The average participation elsewhere in direct primaries runs from 50 to 95%, averaging about 75%, whereas under the convention system in New York it runs from a fraction of 1% to 10%. But I shall hope to have a chance some day to discuss the subject with you.

I am very sorry to hear that your daughter has scarlet fever, but am glad to know that the case is such a light one. I wish you would give her my best wishes for a speedy recovery. I shall certainly not forget Mrs. Wilson's and your invitation to spend a week end with you, and shall look forward to doing so without fail if you are able to have me. With kindest regards to you all, believe me ever sincerely yours Arthur Ludington

ALS (WP, DLC).

1 A gentleman of independent means who had served as Instructor in Jurisprudence and Politics at Princeton, 1905-1907, and was now devoting his full time to political reform work in New York City and State.

2 The Citizens Union was founded in 1897 as an independent political party in the newly consolidated city of Greater New York. That year it nominated a slate of candidates headed by Seth Low; though unsuccessful then, it played a key role four years later when Low was elected mayor on a fusion ticket. In subsequent years the organization gradually metamorphosed from a party into a civic group especially concerned with problems of city government. From 1905 onward, the Union's Committee on Legislation scrutinized proposed legislation of the New York city government and that of the New York state government affecting the city. Ludington was at this time a member of the Committee on Legislation.

3 Ludington seems a bit confused here. The New York Constitution of 1894 required that the question of calling a constitutional convention be submitted to the voters of the state at the general election of 1916 and every twenty years thereafter. Under the procedure established by the constitution, the proposed convention, if approved, could not have been held before 1918. However, the state legislature could initiate a convention at any time it saw fit. As it turned out, on the advice of Governor Martin H. Glynn, the question of a convention was submitted to the voters on April 14, 1914, and a constitutional convention met on April 6, 1915. The resulting amendments to the constitution of 1894 were defeated by the voters, and the old constitution remained in effect until 1938. The Editors have been unable to find any evidence that the possibility of an earlier submission of the question to the voters was under serious discussion in 1909.

4 Annual Message to the Legislature, Jan. 6, 1909, printed in State of New York, *Public Papers of Charles E. Hughes, Governor,* 1909 (Albany, N. Y., 1910), pp. 21-52. Ludington was paraphrasing a passage on p. 41.

5 Charles Edward Merriam, Associate Professor of Political Science at the University of Chicago. The book referred to is *Primary Elections: A Study of the History and Tendencies of Primary Election Legislation* (Chicago, 1908).

6 In his Annual Message (cited in n. 4 above), Governor Hughes had called for a system of direct primary nominations for all elective offices, except presidential electors, to be made by the enrolled voters of the respective parties. Whereas he had formerly suggested that such a system be optional, he now urged that it be binding on all parties.

The bill actually presented to the New York legislature on March 14, 1909 (known as the Hinman-Green bill), was a complicated compromise measure worked out by many hands. Under its provisions, a system of party committees—a state committee, congressional district committees, judicial district committees, county committees, etc.—would select candidates who would then run in the primaries, either unopposed or against other candidates whose names might be placed on the ballot by petition. The members of the various party committees were also to be chosen by the eligible voters at the primary elections. Obviously, in practice such a primary system would have given much power to the established party managers. However, as it turned out, the politicians of New York State were unwilling to accept even this watered-down direct primary bill, and it was soundly defeated by the legislature in both 1909 and 1910. See Robert F. Wesser, *Charles Evans Hughes: Politics and Reform in New York, 1905-1910* (Ithaca, N. Y., 1967), pp. 252-301.

From Edward Wright Sheldon, with Enclosure

My dear Woodrow: New York. February 4, 1909.

Pyne has talked with me regarding the proposed change in the management of the Graduate School and has shown me a draft amendment of Chapter VIII of the University By-laws, embodying this change. At his request, I have re-cast this by-law, and enclose it herewith for your consideration in advance of the meeting of the Graduate School Committee which is to be held at two o'clock tomorrow. If you see serious objection to any part of this new chapter will you kindly let me know before the meeting?

Yours sincerely, Edward W. Sheldon.

TLS (WWP, UA, NjP).

ENCLOSURE

A Draft of a Proposed By-Law of the Trustees of Princeton University by Moses Taylor Pyne and Edward Wright Sheldon

[Feb. 4, 1909]

CHAPTER VIII.

Of the Dean and the Faculty Committee of the Graduate School.

1. The Dean of the Graduate School shall be ⟨the chief executive officer of the School,⟩ a member *ex officio* of the Trustees' Committee on the Graduate School, and Chairman of the hereinafter mentioned Committee of the University Faculty on ⟨such⟩ School. He shall make a written report for that Committee to the Trustees' Committee before the January and Commencement meetings of the Board.

2. The administration of the Graduate School shall be in the hands of a Committee of the University Faculty, to be known as the Faculty Graduate School Committee. ⟨This Committee shall be appointed by the Board on the recommendation of the Com-

mittee on the Graduate School, and shall continue in office during the pleasure of the Board.⟩

3. They shall have supervision of graduate courses and instruction, of the admission of students to the Graduate School, of the studies of members of the Graduate School, of the work leading to higher degrees and the examination therefor, and of recommendations to the University Faculty of appointments to fellowships and graduate scholarships.

4. They shall also have supervision over fellows, graduate scholars and other graduate students, and in general over all matters affecting the administration of the Graduate School.

5. They shall conduct and administer the affairs of the Residential Graduate ⟨College⟩ Hall, and the Master of that ⟨College⟩ Hall shall be associated with the Committee as a voting member in the administration of the ⟨College⟩ Hall.

CC T MS (WWP, UA, NjP).

A Draft of a Proposed By-Law of the Trustees of Princeton University

[c. Feb. 4, 1909]

CHAPTER VIII.

Of the Administration of the Graduate School.

1. The administration of the Graduate School and of the residential Graduate College shall, under the President of the University, be in the hands of a Committee of the University Faculty, of which the Dean of the Graduate School shall be chairman. The Committee shall be called the Faculty Committee on the Graduate School.

2. It shall have s[u]pervision of graduate courses and instruction, of the admission of students to the Graduate School, of the studies of members of the Graduate School, of the work leading to higher degrees and the examinations for the same, and of all recommendations to the University Faculty of appointments to Fellowships and Graduate Scholarships.

3. It shall also have supervision over Fellows, Graduate Scholars, and other graduate students, and, in general, over all matters affecting the administration of the Graduate School.

4. It shall conduct and administer the affairs of the Graduate College, the Master of the College being associated with the Committee as a voting member in the consideration of the administration of the College.

5. The Dean of the Graduate School shall submit to the University Faculty, or to the President, or to the Trustees, or both, as the case may be, for their sanction, such measures as the Committee may recommend. To this end he shall be a member, *ex officio*, of the Committee of the Board of Trustees on the Graduate School, and shall make a written report for the Faculty Committee on the Graduate School to the Trustees' Committee on the Graduate School before the January and Commencement meetings of the Board.[1]

WWT MS (WWP, UA, NjP).

[1] There is an earlier WWT draft of this by-law in WWP, UA, NjP. The by-law as finally approved appears in the extract from the Minutes of the Board of Trustees printed at April 8, 1909.

From Henry Green Duffield

Dear Sir: Princeton, N. J., Feb. 4, '09.

I am in receipt of yours of the 3rd inst. enclosing letter of Mr. Pyne authorizing appropriations to be made from the income of the pledge of Mr. Dodge, concerning which we were speaking on the train the other evening. This matter has been straightened out and there is considerably more than sufficient income to make the appropriations asked for, viz:

$500. for Prof. Conklin,
475. " " Dahlgren.

I am also in receipt of a letter from Mr. Pyne in this mail in regard to these appropriations. I will arrange with Professors Conklin and Dahlgren in regard to the orders for payment.

Very respectfully, H G Duffield Treasurer.

TLS (WP, DLC).

To Frank Arthur Vanderlip

My dear Mr. Vanderlip, [New York, Feb. 5, 1909]

I am coming into town again on Monday, the 8th, and will take the liberty of calling at the City Bank, as you so kindly said I might. Your kind words of encouragement over the telephone the other day heartened me more than I can say. They happened to come at a moment when I was engaged upon a matter particularly perplexing and difficult (I may have *sounded* over the telephone as preoccupied as I was) and were like water to a dry land.

I will consult your convenience as to the hour of my call by telephone after I reach town.

With warm regard

Sincerely Yours, Woodrow Wilson

ALS (F. A. Vanderlip Papers, NNC).

A News Report of an Address in New York to Williams College Alumni

[Feb. 6, 1909]

NEW IDEAS FOR COLLEGE LIFE.

President Harry A. Garfield, recently installed head of Williams College, and President Woodrow Wilson of Princeton announced at the sixtieth annual dinner of Williams College, held at Delmonico's last night, several policies calculated to make a stir in college life.

President Garfield told the 250 Williams alumni at the tables that he intended to eat his meals among the students of the college in the new dining hall which is being completed in the new dormitory in the Berkshire Quadrangle. He added that he was going to make as many members of the Williams Faculty as he could dine there also.

"We won't dine at a high table apart, either," he added, while the diners cheered. "We'll dine at the same table as the students."

President Wilson, who followed President Garfield, said that he agreed with President Garfield, but that the latter hadn't, in his opinion, said enough.

"Our problem is not merely to help the students to adjust themselves to world life," he said. "Our problem is to make them as unlike their fathers as we can. Their fathers are specialized persons. The problem of the college faculty is to generalize the younger generation all over again.

"Take Abraham Lincoln, for example. He couldn't have been born in the present City of New York. He would have fought New York. Any one who thinks New York to-day doesn't think American. This city doesn't make generalized Americans, and that is just the kind of Americans that the American universities must make. Our colleges are not doing this to-day.

"Colleges must not be mere country clubs in which to breed up a leisure class. I don't blame the leisure classes for doing wrong. If I belonged to a leisure class I would try to see how near I could come to getting into jail. College must make students of its young men. I don't give a shell of corn what they study. But they mustn't be idle."

Both President Garfield's and President Wilson's remarks were frequently interrupted by applause and cheers.

Printed in the *New York Times*, Feb. 6, 1909; one editorial heading omitted.

To Melancthon Williams Jacobus

My dear Dr. Jacobus: [Princeton, N. J.] February 9th, 1909.

It was tantalizing to get so brief a chance to speak with you last Friday. There were so many things I wanted to talk to you about, and a letter is so inferior and unsatisfactory a means of discussing things.

I sincerely hope that it did not too much fatigue you to attend that very important meeting on Friday,[1] and I hope with all my heart that the good results we expect from the changes then effected[2] may be realized. Certainly we now have made it possible to do the work of the Graduate School in the right way.

I did not understand that it was the desire of the Finance Committee that we should specially push forward the inquiry which they requested, into any possible retrenchment in the teaching expenses of the several Departments. I think that it will quite meet their wishes if we report before the next meeting of the Board. In the meantime, I am asking the Heads of the several Departments for full particulars as to the time devoted to teaching in their several Departments, in order to get something like a comparative view of the demands made upon the teaching staff in the different branches.

In answer to the question contained in your letter of February 3rd with regard to honorary degrees, the Committee is scheduled to report both at the January and April meetings. It is, therefore, quite feasible to add Dr. Horton's name to our list at the next meeting of the Board, if you should wish to bring it before the Committee for that purpose. It has also been proposed to us that we add the name of the Chinese ambassador, but I feel a good deal of hesitation about that. We gave a degree to the Japanese minister[3] last Commencement, and to confer it upon the Chinese minister so soon afterwards would seem merely like going through the oriental list.

Pray let me know as soon as convenient how you are and

that the special exertion you underwent in coming to our aid did you no harm.

With warmest regard,

Always faithfully yours, [Woodrow Wilson]

CCL (RSB Coll., DLC).

[1] That is, the meeting of the trustees' Committee on the Graduate School in New York on February 5, 1909.

[2] The revision of the by-law on the administration of the Graduate School.

[3] Kogoro Takahira, Japanese Minister to the United States, 1900-1906, and Ambassador to the United States, 1908-1909.

From Frederick Paul King[1]

My dear Dr. Wilson: New York, February 9, 1909.

As Secretary of the Board of Governors of Tiger Inn, I am instructed to communicate to you the following resolution passed at a meeting of the Board held yesterday to consider your recent letter to Mr. Murphy, President of the Board, referring to a resolution of the Board of Trustees, passed at the October meeting.

> "RESOLVED: that the President of this Board be appointed as the representative of The Tiger Inn, in any conference with representatives of other Clubs, or representatives of the Faculty, or Board of Trustees of Princeton University, on matters affecting Club life, or Club relations to the University, provided, however, that nothing herein contained shall be construed as making any action which shall be taken by any such conference, binding upon The Tiger Inn, unless such action shall be confirmed by the further action of this Board."

I beg to remain

Very respectfully, Frederick P. King.

TLS (WWP, UA, NjP).

[1] Princeton 1900, lawyer of New York.

From Charles Francis Adams

My dear Mr. President: Boston February 10, 1909

What you tell me of the circumstances connected with the offer to me of an honorary degree is wholly satisfactory. As a Harvard man, I feel especially complimented at being invited to accept a degree at just this time, in company with Mr. Lowell, who will then have freshly entered upon his new duties. Nevertheless, I apprehend that President Lowell may himself be quite occupied at about that date, and it seems questionable at least whether it will be in his power to attend your Commencement exercises.[1] Perhaps, however, in this case, personal attendance would not be called for.

So far as I am concerned, it will afford me much satisfaction to be at Princeton on the date named, in response to the invitation I have already acknowledged; and there to accept the degree which the University will then do me the honor to confer upon me.

I have been much disappointed this year at my inability to attend the dinners of our Round Table Club. I always look forward to them as the most satisfactory dinners I attend in the course of the year. I meet there more men worth meeting and hear better talk.

Nevertheless, up to this time, the dates of the dinners and my engagements have refused to conform. I hope it will prove otherwise during the remainder of the winter.

I remain, etc, Charles F. Adams

TLS (WP, DLC).

[1] Lowell did attend and received the honorary degree of LL.D.

An Address in Chicago on Lincoln

[[Feb. 12, 1909]]

ABRAHAM LINCOLN: A MAN OF THE PEOPLE

My earliest recollection is of standing at my father's gateway in Augusta, Georgia, when I was four years old, and hearing some one pass and say that Mr. Lincoln was elected and there was to be war. Catching the intense tones of his excited voice, I remember running in to ask my father what it meant. What it meant, you need not be told. What it meant, we shall not here to-day dwell upon. We shall rather turn away from those scenes of struggle and of unhappy fraternal strife, and recall what has happened since to restore our balance, to remind us of the permanent issues of history, to make us single-hearted in our love of America, and united in our purpose for her advancement. We are met here to-day to recall the character and achievements of a man who did not stand for strife, but for peace, and whose glory it was to win the affection alike of those whom he led and of those whom he opposed, as indeed a man and a king among those who mean the right.

It is not necessary that I should rehearse for you the life of Abraham Lincoln. It has been written in every school book. It has been rehearsed in every family. It were to impeach your intelligence if I were to tell you the story of his life. I would rather attempt to expound for you the meaning of his life, the significance of his singular and unique career.

It is a very long century that separates us from the year of his birth. The nineteenth century was crowded with many significant events,–it seems to us in America as if it were more crowded with significant events for us than for any other nation of the world,–and that far year 1809 stands very near its opening, when men were only beginning to understand what was in store for them. It was a significant century, not only in the field of politics but in the field of thought. Do you realize that modern science is not older than the middle of the last century? Modern science came into the world to revolutionize our thinking and our material enterprises just about the time that Mr. Lincoln was uttering those remarkable debates with Mr. Douglas. The struggle which determined the life of the Union came just at the time when a new issue was joined in the field of thought, and men began to reconstruct their conceptions of the universe and of their relation to nature, and even of their relation to God. There is, I believe, no more significant century in the history of man than the nineteenth century, and its whole sweep is behind us.

That year 1809 produced, as you know, a whole group of men who were to give distinction to its annals in many fields of thought and of endeavor. To mention only some of the great men who were born in 1809: the poet Tennyson was born in that year, our own poet Edgar Allan Poe, the great Sherman, the great Mendelssohn, Chopin, Charles Darwin, William E. Gladstone, and Abraham Lincoln.[1] Merely read that list and you are aware of the singular variety of gifts and purposes represented. Tennyson was, to my thinking, something more than a poet. We are apt to be so beguiled by the music of his verse as to suppose that its charm and power lie in its music; but there is something about the poet which makes him the best interpreter, not only of life, but of national purpose, and there is to be found in Tennyson a great body of interpretation which utters the very voice of Anglo-Saxon liberty. That fine line in which he speaks of how English liberty has "broadened down from precedent to precedent" embodies the noble slowness, the very process and the very certainty, of the forces which made men politically free in the great century in which he wrote. He was a master who saw into the heart of affairs, as well as a great musician who seemed to give them the symphony of sound.

[1] Actually, Chopin was born in 1810 and William Tecumseh Sherman in 1820.

And then there was our own Poe, that exquisite workman in the human language, that exquisite artisan in all the nice effects of speech, the man who dreamed all the odd dreams of the human imagination, and who quickened us with all the singular stories that the mind can invent, and did it all with the nicety and certainty of touch of the consummate artist.

And then there were Chopin and Mendelssohn, whose music constantly rings in our ears and lifts our spirits to new sources of delight. And there was Charles Darwin, with an insight into nature next to Newton's own; and Gladstone, who knew how to rule men by those subtle forces of oratory which shape the history of the world and determine the relations of nations to each other.

And then our Lincoln. When you read that name you are at once aware of something that distinguishes it from all the rest. There was in each of those other men some special gift, but not in Lincoln. You cannot pick Lincoln out for any special characteristic. He did not have any one of those peculiar gifts that the other men on this list possessed. He does not seem to belong in a list at all; he seems to stand unique and singular and complete in himself. The name makes the same impression upon the ear that the name of Shakespeare makes, because it is as if he contained a world within himself. And that is the thing which marks the singular stature and nature of this great—and, we would fain believe, typical—American. Because when you try to describe the character of Lincoln you seem to be trying to describe a great process of nature. Lincoln seems to have been of general human use and not of particular and limited human use. There was no point at which life touched him that he did not speak back to it instantly its meaning. There was no affair that touched him to which he did not give back life, as if he had communicated a spark of fire to kindle it. The man seemed to have, slumbering in him, powers which he did not exert of his own choice, but which woke the moment they were challenged, and for which no challenge was too great or comprehensive.

You know how slow, how almost sluggish the development of the man was. You know how those who consorted with him in his youth noted the very thing of which I speak. They would have told you that Abraham Lincoln was good for nothing in particular; and the singular fact is he *was* good for nothing in particular—he was good for everything in general. He did not narrow and concentrate his power, because it was meant to be diffused as the sun itself. And so he went through his youth like a man who has nothing to do, like a man whose mind is never halted at any point where it becomes serious, to seize upon the particular endeavor or occupation for which it is intended. He went from one sort of partial success to another sort of partial success, or, as his contemporaries would have said, from failure to failure, until—not until he found himself, but until, so to say, affairs found him, and the crisis of a country seemed suddenly to match the universal gift of his nature; until a great nature was summed up, not in any particular business or activity, but in the affairs of a whole country. It was characteristic of the man.

Have you ever looked at some of those singular statues of the great French sculptor Rodin—those pieces of marble in which only some part of a figure is revealed and the rest is left in the hidden lines of the marble itself; where there emerges the arm and the bust and the eager face, it may be, of a man, but his body disappears in the general bulk of the stone, and the lines fall off vaguely? I have often been made to think, in looking at those statues, of Abraham Lincoln. There was a little disclosed in him, but not all. You feel that he was so far from being exhausted by the demands of his life that more remained unrevealed than was disclosed to our view. The lines run off into infinity and lead the imagination into every great conjecture. We wonder what the man might have done, what he might have been, and we feel that there was more promise in him when he died than when he was born; that the force was so far from being exhausted that it had only begun to display itself in its splendor and perfection. No man can think of the life of Lincoln without feeling that the man was cut off almost at his beginning.

And so it is with every genius of this kind, not singular but universal, because there were uses to which it was not challenged. You feel that there is no telling what it might have done in days to come, when there would have been new demands made upon its strength and upon its versatility. He is like some great reservoir of living water which you can freely quaff but can never exhaust. There is something absolutely endless about the lines of such a life.

And you will see that that very fact renders it difficult indeed to point out the characteristics of a man like Lincoln. How shall you describe general human nature brought to its finest development?—for such was this man. We say that he was honest; men used to call him "Honest Abe." But honesty is not a quality. Honesty is the manifestation of character. Lincoln was honest because there was nothing small or petty about him, and only smallness and pettiness in a nature can produce dishonesty. Such honesty is a quality of largeness. It is that openness of nature which will not condescend to subterfuge, which is too big to conceal itself. Little men run to cover and deceive you. Big men cannot and will not run to cover, and do not deceive you. Of course, Lincoln was honest. But that was not a peculiar characteristic of him; that is a general description of him. He was not small or mean, and his honesty was not produced by any calculation, but was the genial expression of the great nature that was behind it.

Then we also say of Lincoln that he saw things with his own eyes. And it is very interesting that we can pick out individual men to say that of them. The opposite of the proposition is, that most men see things with other men's eyes. And that is the pity of the whole business of the world. Most men do not see things with their own eyes. If they did they would not be so inconspicuous as they consent to be. What most persons do is to live up to formulas and opinions and believe them, and never give themselves the trouble to ask whether they are true or not; so that there is a great deal of truth in saying that the trouble is, that men believe so many things that are not so, because they have taken them at second hand; they have accepted them in the form they were given to them. They have not reëxamined them. They have not seen the world with their own eyes. But Lincoln saw it with his own eyes. And he not only saw the surface of it, but saw beneath the surface of it; for the characteristic of the seeing eye is that it is a discerning eye, seeing also that which is not caught by the surface; it penetrates to the heart of the subjects it looks upon. Not only did this man look upon life with a discerning eye. If you read of his youth and of his early manhood, it would seem that these were his only and sufficient pleasures. Lincoln seemed to covet nothing from his business except that it would give him leisure enough to do this very thing—to look at other people; to talk about them; to sit by the stove in the evening and discuss politics with them; to talk about all the things that were going on, to make shrewd, penetrating comments upon them, to speak his penetrating jests.

I had a friend once who said he seriously thought that the business of life was conversation. There is a good deal of Mr. Lincoln's early life which would indicate that he was of the same opinion. He believed that, at any rate, the most attractive business of life was conversation; and conversation, with Lincoln, was an important part of the business of life, because it was conversation which uncovered the meanings of things and illuminated the hidden places where nobody but Lincoln had ever thought of looking.

You remember the very interesting story told about Mr. Lincoln in his early practice as a lawyer. Some business firm at a distance wrote to him and asked him to look into the credit of a certain man who had asked to have credit extended to him by the firm. Mr. Lincoln went around to see the man at his place of business, and reported to this effect: that he had found the man in an office which contained one table and two chairs, "But," he added, "there is a hole in the corner that would bear looking into." That anecdote, slight as it is, is typical of Mr. Lincoln. He sometimes found the character of the man lurking in a hole; and when his speech touched that character it was illuminated; you could not frame otherwise a better characterization. That seemed to be the business of the man's life; to look at things and to comment upon them; and his comment upon them was just as fearless and just as direct as it was shrewd and penetrating.

I know some men can see anything they choose to see, but they won't say anything; who are dried up at the source by that enemy of mankind which we call Caution. God save a free country from cautious men,—men, I mean, cautious for themselves,—for cautious men are men who will not speak the truth if the speaking of it threatens to damage them. Caution is the confidential agent of selfishness.

This man had no caution. He was absolutely direct and fearless. You will say that he had very little worldly goods to lose. He did not allow himself to be encumbered by riches, therefore he could say what he pleased. You know that men who are encumbered by riches are apt to be more silent than others. They have given hostages to fortune, and for them it is very necessary to maintain the *status quo*. Now, Mr. Lincoln was not embarrassed in this way. A change of circumstances would suit him just as well as the permanency of existing circumstances. But I am confident that if Mr. Lincoln had had the gift of making money, he nevertheless would not have restrained his gift for saying things; that he nevertheless would have ignored the trammels and despised caution and said what he thought. But one interesting thing about Mr. Lincoln is that no matter how shrewd or penetrating his comment, he never seemed to allow a matter to grip him. He seemed so directly in contact with it that he could define things other men could not define; and yet he was detached. He did not look upon it as if he were part of it. And he was constantly salting all the delightful things that he said, with the salt of wit and humor.

I would not trust a saturnine man, but I would trust a wit;

because a wit is a man who can detach himself, and not get so buried in the matter he is dealing with as to lose that sure and free movement which a man can have only when he is detached. If a man can comment upon his own misfortunes with a touch of humor, you know that his misfortunes are not going to subdue or kill him. You should try to instill into every distressed friend the inclination to hold himself off at arm's length, and should assure him that, after all, there have been worse cases on record. Mr. Lincoln was not under the impression that his own misfortunes were unique, and he was not under the impression that the misfortunes of his fellow-men were unique or unalterable. Therefore he was detached; therefore he was a wit; therefore he told you a story to show that he was not so intense upon a matter that he could not recognize the funny side of it.

Not only that, but Lincoln was a singularly studious man –not studious in the ordinary conventional sense. To be studious in the ordinary, conventional sense, if I may judge by my observation at a university, is to do the things you have to do and not understand them particularly. But to be studious, in the sense in which Mr. Lincoln was studious, is to follow eagerly and fearlessly the curiosity of a mind which will not be satisfied unless it understands. That is a deep studiousness; that is the thing which lays bare the map of life and enables men to understand the circumstances in which they live, as nothing else can do.

And what commends Mr. Lincoln's studiousness to me is that the result of it was he did not have any theories at all. Life is a very complex thing. No theory that I ever heard propounded will match its varied pattern; and the men who are dangerous are the men who are not content with understanding, but go on to propound theories, things which will make a new pattern for society and a new model for the universe. Those are the men who are not to be trusted. Because, although you steer by the North Star, when you have lost the bearings of your compass, you nevertheless must steer in a pathway on the sea,–you are not bound for the North Star. The man who insists upon his theory insists that there is a way to the North Star, and I know, and every one knows, that there is not–at least none yet discovered. Lincoln was one of those delightful students who do not seek to tie you up in the meshes of any theory.

Such was Mr. Lincoln,–not a singular man; a very normal man, but normal in gigantic proportions,–the whole character of him is on as great a scale–and yet so delightfully informal in the way it was put together—as was the great frame in which he lived. That great, loose-jointed, angular frame that Mr. Lincoln inhabited was a very fine symbol of the big, loose-jointed, genial, angular nature that was inside; angular, not in the sense of having sharp corners upon which men might wound themselves, but angular as nature is angular. Nature is not symmetrical like the Renaissance architecture. Nature is an architect who does not, in the least, mind putting a very different thing on one side from what it has put on the other. Your average architect wants to balance his windows; to have consistency and balance in the parts. But nature is not interested in that. Nature does what it pleases, and so did the nature of Lincoln. It did what it pleased, and was no more conventionalized and symmetrical than the body of the man himself.

Mr. Lincoln belonged to a type which is fast disappearing, the type of the frontiersman. And he belonged to a process which has almost disappeared from this country. Mr. Lincoln seemed slow in his development, but when you think of the really short span of his life and the distance he traversed in the process of maturing, you will see that it can not be said to have been a slow process. Mr. Lincoln was bred in that part of the country—*this* part, though we can hardly conceive it now—where States were made as fast as men. Lincoln was made along with the States that were growing as fast as men were. States were born and came to their maturity, in that day, within the legal limit of twenty-one years, and the very pressure of that rapid change, the very imperious necessity of that quick process of maturing, was what made and moulded men with a speed and in a sort which have never since been matched. Here were the processes of civilization and of the building up of polities crowded into a single generation; and where such processes are crowded, men grow. Men could be picked out in the crude, and, if put in that crucible, could be refined out in a single generation into pure metal. That was the process which made Mr. Lincoln. We could not do it that way again, because that period has passed forever with us.

Mr. Lincoln could not have been born at any other time and he could not have been made in any other way. I took the liberty of saying in New York the other day that it was inconceivable that Mr. Lincoln could have been born in New York. I did not intend thereby any disparagement of New York, but simply to point the moral that he could not have been born in a finished community. He had to be produced in a community that was on the make, in the making. New York is on the make, but it is not in the making.

Mr. Lincoln, in other words, was produced by processes which no longer exist anywhere in America, and therefore we are solemnized by this question: Can we have other Lincolns? We cannot do without them. This country is going to have crisis after crisis. God send they may not be bloody crises, but they will be intense and acute. No body politic so abounding in life and so puzzled by problems as ours is can avoid moving from crisis to crisis. We must have the leadership of sane, genial men of universal use like Lincoln, to save us from mistakes and give us the necessary leadership in such days of struggle and of difficulty. And yet, such men will hereafter have to be produced among us by processes which are not characteristically American, but which belong to the whole world.

There was something essentially native, American, about Lincoln; and there will, no doubt, be something American about every man produced by the processes of America; but no such distinguished process as the process, unique and separate, of that early age can be repeated for us.

It seems to me serviceable, therefore, to ask ourselves what it is that we must reproduce in order not to lose the breed, the splendid breed, of men of this calibre. Mr. Lincoln we describe as "a man of the people," and he was a man of the people, essentially. But what do we mean by a "man of the people"? We mean a man, of course, who has his rootage deep in the experiences and the consciousness of the ordinary mass of his fellow-men; but we do not mean a man whose rootage is holding him at their level. We mean a man who, drawing his sap from such sources, has, nevertheless, risen above the level of the rest of mankind and has got an outlook over their heads, seeing horizons which they are too submerged to see; a man who finds and draws his inspiration from the common plane, but nevertheless has lifted himself to a new place of outlook and of insight; who has come out from the people and is their leader, not because he speaks from their ranks, but because he speaks for them and for their interests.

Browning has said:

"A nation is but the attempt of many
To rise to the completer life of one;
And they who live as models for the mass
Are singly of more value than they all."[2]

[2] Robert Browning, *Luria, A Tragedy*, Act V, Lines 299-302.

Lincoln was of the mass, but he was so lifted and big that all men could look upon him, until he became the "model for the mass" and was "singly of more value than they all."

It was in that sense that Lincoln was "a man of the people." His sources were where all the pure springs are, but his streams flowed down into other country and fertilized other plains, where men had become sophisticated with the life of an older age.

A great nation is not led by a man who simply repeats the talk of the street-corners or the opinions of the newspapers. A nation is led by a man who hears more than those things; or who, rather, hearing those things, understands them better, unites them, puts them into a common meaning; speaks, not the rumors of the street, but a new principle for a new age; a man in whose ears the voices of the nation do not sound like the accidental and discordant notes that come from the voice of a mob, but concurrent and concordant like the united voices of a chorus, whose many meanings, spoken by melodious tongues, unite in his understanding in a single meaning and reveal to him a single vision, so that he can speak what no man else knows, the common meaning of the common voice. Such is the man who leads a great, free, democratic nation.

We must always be led by "men of the people," and therefore it behooves us to know them when we see them. How shall we distinguish them? Judged by this man, interpreted by this life, what is a "man of the people"? How shall we know him when he emerges to our view?

Well, in the first place, it seems to me that a man of the people is a man who sees affairs as the people see them, and not as a man of particular classes or the professions sees them. You cannot afford to take the advice of a man who has been too long submerged in a particular profession,—not because you cannot trust him to be honest and candid, but because he has been too long immersed and submerged, and through the inevitable pressure and circumstances of his life has come to look upon the nation from a particular point of view. The man of the people is a man who looks far and wide upon the nation, and is not limited by a professional point of view. That may be a hard doctrine; it may exclude some gentlemen ambitious to lead; but I am not trying to exclude them by any arbitrary dictum of my own; I am trying to interpret so much as I understand of human history, and if human history has excluded them, you cannot blame me. Human history has excluded them, as far as I understand it, and that is the end of the matter. I am not excluding them. In communities like ours, governed by general opinion and not led by classes, not dictated to by special interests, they are of necessity excluded. You will see that it follows that a man of the people is not subdued by any stuff of life that he has happened to work in; that he is free to move in any direction his spirit prompts. Are you not glad that Mr. Lincoln did not succeed too deeply in any particular calling; that he was sufficiently detached to be lifted to a place of leadership and to be used by the whole country? Are you not glad that he had not narrowed his view and understanding to any particular interest, —did not think in the terms of interest but in the terms of life? Are you not glad that he had a myriad of contacts with the growing and vehement life of this country, and that, because of that multiple contact, he was, more than any one else of his generation, the spokesman of the general opinion of this country?

Why was it that Mr. Lincoln was wiser than the professional politicians? Because the professional politicians had burrowed into particular burrows and Mr. Lincoln walked on the surface and saw his fellow-men.

Why could Mr. Lincoln smile at lawyers and turn away from ministers? Because he had not had his contact with life as a lawyer has, and he had not lectured his fellow-men as a minister has. He was detached from every point of view and therefore superior,—at any rate in a position to becoming superior,—to every point of view. You must have a man of this detachable sort.

Moreover, you must not have a man, if he is to be a man of the people, who is standardized and conventionalized. Look to it that your communities, your great cities, do not impose too arbitrary standards upon the men whom you wish to use. Do not reduce men to standards. Let them be free. Do not compel them by conventions. Let them wear any clothes they please and look like anything they choose; let them do anything that a decent and an honest man may do without criticism; do not laugh at them because they do not look like you, or talk like you, or think like you. They are freer for that circumstance, because, as an English writer[3] has said: "You may talk of the tyranny of Nero and Tiberius, but the real tyranny is the tyranny of your next-door neighbor. There is no tyranny like the tyranny of being obliged to be like him,"—of being considered a very singular person if you are not; of having men shrug their shoulders and say, "Singular young man, sir, singular young man; very gifted, but not to be trusted." Not to be trusted because unlike your own

[3] Walter Bagehot.

trustworthy self! You must take your leaders in every time of difficulty from among absolutely free men who are not standardized and conventionalized, who are at liberty to do what they think right and say what they think true; that is the only kind of leadership you can afford to have.

And then, last and greatest characteristic of all, a man of the people is a man who has felt that unspoken, that intense, that almost terrifying struggle of humanity, that struggle whose object is, not to get forms of government, not to realize particular formulas or make for any definite goal, but simply to live and be free. He has participated in that struggle; he has felt the blood stream against the tissue; he has known anxiety; he has felt that life contained for him nothing but effort, effort from the rising of the sun to the going down of it. He has, therefore, felt beat in him, if he had any heart, a universal sympathy for those who struggle, a universal understanding of the unutterable things that were in their hearts and the unbearable burdens that were upon their backs. A man who has that vision, of how—

"Now touching good, now backward hurled,
Toils the indomitable world"—[4]

a man like Lincoln—understands. His was part of the toil; he had part and lot in the struggle; he knew the uncertainty of the goal mankind had but just touched and from which they had been hurled back; knew that the price of life is blood, and that no man who goes jauntily and complacently through the world will ever touch the springs of human action. Such a man with such a consciousness, such a universal human sympathy, such a universal comprehension of what life means, is your man of the people, and no one else can be.

What shall we do? It always seems to me a poor tribute to a great man who has been great in action, to spend the hours of his praise by merely remembering what he was; and there is no more futile eulogy than attempted imitation. It is impossible to imitate Lincoln, without being Lincoln; and then it would not be an imitation. It is impossible to reproduce the characters, as it is impossible to reproduce the circumstances, of a past age. That ought to be a truism; that ought to be evident. We live, and we have no other choice, in this age, and the tasks of this age are the only tasks to which we are asked to address ourselves. We are not asked to apply our belated wisdom to the problems and perplexities of an age that is gone. We must

[4] The Editors have been unable to identify this quotation.

have timely remedies, suitable for the existing moment. If that be true, the only way in which we can worthily celebrate a great man is by showing to-day that we have not lost the tradition of force which made former ages great, that we can reproduce them continuously in a kind of our own. You elevate the character of a man like Lincoln for his fellow-men to gaze upon, not as if it were an unattainable height, but as one of those conspicuous objects which men erect to mark the long lines of a survey, so that when they top the next hill they shall see that mark standing there where they have passed, not as something to daunt them, but as a high point by which they can lengthen and complete their measurements and make sure of their ultimate goal and achievement. That is the reason we erect the figures of men like this to be admired and looked upon, not as if we were men who walk backward and deplore the loss of such figures and of such ages, but as men who keep such heights in mind and walk forward, knowing that the goal of the age is to scale new heights and to do things of which their work was a mere foundation, so that we shall live, like every other living thing, by renewal. We shall not live by recollection, we shall not live by trying to recall the strength of the old tissue, but by producing new tissue. The process of life is a process of growth, and the process of growth is a process of renewal; and it is only in this wise that we shall face the tasks of the future.

The tasks of the future call for men like Lincoln more audibly, more imperatively, than did the tasks of the time when civil war was brewing and the very existence of the Nation was in the scale of destiny. For the things that perplex us at this moment are the things which mark, I will not say a warfare, but a division among classes; and when a nation begins to be divided into rival and contestant interests by the score, the time is much more dangerous than when it is divided into only two perfectly distinguishable interests which you can discriminate and deal with. If there are only two sides I can easily make up my mind which side to take, but if there are a score of sides then I must say to some man who is not immersed, not submerged, not caught in this struggle, "Where shall I go? What do you see? What is the movement of the mass? Where are we going? Where do you propose you should go?" It is then I need a man of the people, detached from this struggle yet cognizant of it all, sympathetic with it all, saturated with it all, to whom I can say, "How do you sum it up, what are the signs of the day, what does the morning say, what are the tasks that we must set our hands to?" We should pray, not only that we should be led by such men, but also that they should be men of the particular sweetness that Lincoln possessed.

The most dangerous thing you can have in an age like this is a man who is intense and hot. We have heat enough; what we want is light. Anybody can stir up emotions, but who is master of men enough to take the saddle and guide those awakened emotions? Anybody can cry a nation awake to the necessities of reform, but who shall frame the reform but a man who is cool, who takes his time, who will draw you aside for a jest, who will say: "Yes, but not to-day, to-morrow; let us see the other man and see what he has to say; let us hear everybody, let us know what we are to do. In the meantime I have a capital story for your private ear. Let me take the strain off, let me unbend the steel. Don't let us settle this thing by fire but let us settle it by those cool, incandescent lights which show its real nature and color."

The most valuable thing about Mr. Lincoln was that in the midst of the strain of war, in the midst of the crash of arms, he could sit quietly in his room and enjoy a book that led his thoughts off from everything American, could wander in fields of dreams, while every other man was hot with the immediate contest. Always set your faith in a man who can withdraw himself, because only the man who can withdraw himself can see the stage; only the man who can withdraw himself can see affairs as they are.

And so the lesson of this day is faith in the common product of the nation; the lesson of this day is the future as well as the past leadership of men, wise men, who have come from the people. We should not be Americans deserving to call ourselves the fellow-countrymen of Lincoln if we did not feel the compulsion that his example lays upon us—the compulsion, not to heed him merely but to look to our own duty, to live every day as if that were the day upon which America was to be reborn and remade; to attack every task as if we had something here that was new and virginal and original, out of which we could make the very stuff of life, by integrity, faith in our fellow-men, wherever it is deserved, absolute ignorance of any obstacle that is insuperable, patience, indomitable courage, insight, universal sympathy,—with that programme opening our hearts to every candid suggestion, listening to all the voices of the nation, trying to bring in a new day of vision and of achievement.[5]

Printed in Nathan William MacChesney (ed.), *Abraham Lincoln: The Tribute of a Century, 1809-1909* (Chicago, 1910), pp. 14-30.

[5] There is a WWT detailed outline, dated Feb. 12, 1909, along with a typed abstract of this address in WP, DLC. A copy of the abstract is also in WC, NjP.

A News Report of an Address to the Princeton Club of Chicago

[Feb. 14, 1909]

Woodrow Wilson Wants Colleges to
Make "Generalized Americans."

"Would a man like Lincoln have been more or less serviceable to the country if he had gone through a modern university?"

In answering this question Woodrow Wilson, president of Princeton University, last night denounced the trend toward specialized intellectual training. He declared that it is only by insistence upon a varied course of study that the universities can produce the Lincoln type of man, the broad, many-sided man, who is able to turn his hand to any emergency.

President Wilson was the principal speaker at a banquet of the Princeton Club of Chicago at the University Club. John Maynard Harlan,[1] president of the club, was toastmaster.

"If we hold Lincoln up as a model it is our duty to contribute as much as we can to making such men," said Mr. Wilson. "It is our duty to ask how much are universities qualified to produce that type of man.

"In a great many parts of the country men are saying that universities are producing a specialized class of individuals. I always undertake to defend that charge, for they ought above all to produce generalized Americans."

The distinguished educator strikingly illustrated his viewpoint by asserting that the young generation should be made as much unlike their fathers as possible.

"It ought to be the object of the university to make young men as much unlike their fathers as possible," he said. ["]By the time a man is old enough to have a son in college he has become so specialized in his particular business that he has ceased to be a generalized American. We can't afford to reproduce after that kind.

"It is indispensable that we shall regeneralize each generation as it comes along. We should make young men so generalized that they, like Lincoln, shall be able to turn in any direction and be serviceable in anything.

"You can't specialize a man and at the same time leave him as serviceable for general usefulness. If the universities are producing a specialized class they are not enriching the general energies of the country.

"If I knew that a man had a career cut out for him I would

make him study for another career in order that he could understand the career he was entering."

President Wilson gave athletics credit for having a part to perform in the development of a man, but remarked that one "can't be distinguished in society as an animal."

"I believe that no well grounded development can take place without a great deal of unintellectual training," he said. "I believe therefore that a university ought to be a place where play finds more men to enter into it with a zest than any other place in the world.

"But all this I believe ought to be merely for the sake of what we do with our brains.

"You can't be distinguished in society as an animal. It makes no difference how handsome you are nor how ugly you are. The mind was born king and will always remain king."[2]

Printed in the *Chicago Record-Herald*, Feb. 14, 1909; some editorial headings omitted.

[1] Princeton 1884, lawyer of Chicago; son of Associate Justice John Marshall Harlan (1833-1911) and father of Associate Justice John Marshall Harlan (1899-1971).

[2] There is a WWhw outline of this talk, dated Feb. 13, 1909, in WP, DLC.

To Harriet Hammond McCormick[1]

My dear Mrs. McCormick, Princeton, 16 Feb'y, 1909.

The locomotive of my train grew asthmatic in the night and could not make steam; but, though we were three hours late, I reached Philadelphia in time to catch the last Princeton train and got home about half past eight instead of half past five,—very tired, but very content, and full of truly delightful recollections of my little visit to you. You always make me delightfully welcome and treat me as I best like to be treated. Mrs. Wilson joins me in warmest regards to you all.

Gratefully Yours, Woodrow Wilson

ALS (WP, DLC).

[1] Mrs. Cyrus Hall McCormick.

To Moses Taylor Pyne

My dear Momo: [Princeton, N. J.] February 16th, 1909.

I have just received a notice from West that you have called a meeting of the Trustees' Committee on the Graduate School for Friday afternoon, to consider the plans for the Thompson College. I am very sorry, but I shall be speaking in Baltimore that evening[1] and could not make connections with my appointment there, if I came to New York. I am to be Mr. Garrett's guest, and I know that he also will be kept away from the meeting. I think it very necessary that we should go slowly in the matter of the consideration of the plans for Thompson College. If we are not to get into immediate trouble under our prospective new arrangements, it will be necessary that the members of the committee of the Faculty which is to be appointed should have an opportunity and time enough to form their judgment regarding the plans. I hope very much, therefore, that nothing definitive will be done until this suggestion is carried out. I should regard it as very unfortunate to come to any conclusions yet.

Always cordially and faithfully yours,

[Woodrow Wilson]

CCL (WWP, UA, NjP).

1 To the Presbyterian Union of Baltimore. His address is printed at Feb. 19, 1909.

To Daniel Moreau Barringer

My dear Moreau: Princeton, N. J. February 16th, 1909.

Thank you very heartily for your kind letter of the 14th.[1] Unhappily, I can seldom go where I want to go, and can go only where I must. It would give me real pleasure–more than pleasure, genuine delight–if I could accept your invitation, but the truth of the matter is that I am squeezing the Hampton Institute meeting[2] into a very narrow place on my calendar. I shall be obliged to hurry back early the next morning, to meet an engagement in Princeton, and I cannot go down until the afternoon of the day on which the meeting occurs.

This is a genuine disappointment to me. It seems to me half an age since I saw you, and I am tempted to cut everything and go, but I cannot, in conscience, and must be a steady-wheel horse.

I hope it is only a pleasure postponed and that I will at least have a glimpse of you at the meeting.

With cordial regards to Mrs. Barringer,[3]

Always affectionately yours, Woodrow Wilson

TLS (D. M. Barringer Papers, NjP).

1 It is missing.

2 Wilson's notes for this address in Philadelphia are printed at Feb. 26, 1909.

3 Margaret Bennett Barringer.

From Edward Parker Davis[1]

My dear Wilson: Philadelphia. February 16, 1909.

Acting upon your request the majority of the Faculty of the Jefferson College, teaching in the Freshman Year, have compared the Schedules of Princeton and Jefferson and find that without altering your Curriculum, it will be possible for Princeton Students to study medicine at Jefferson at considerable advantage.

We find that work done in Princeton corresponds and is practically identical with work done in the Freshman Year at Jefferson in the following Departments:

Embryology including the study of Vertebrates, The Comparative Anatomy of Vertebrates, General Biology, Comparative Osteology, Advanced Histology and Neurology, General Inorganic Chemistry. Physics could, of course, best be done at Princeton.

In the following Departments Princeton does not give instruction in her Senior Year and this could best be done at Jefferson:

Bacteriology, Human Anatomy, Materia Medica, Pharmacy, Medical Biology which is practically Physiology, Parasitology, Toxicology.

The advantage to the Princeton Student coming to Jefferson would be that he had done in Princeton so much work of the Freshman Medical Year, that he would be enabled to do advanced work in two Departments which are the foundation of modern medicine, namely, Human Anatomy and Pathology and Bacteriology. Additional work in these Departments would fit him pre-eminently for the later study of Surgery and Internal Medicine.

We were glad to find that the Schedules dove-tail to such an extent as to offer especial advantages to Princeton Students entering upon our medical course.

We at Jefferson are actuated in this by the desire to improve the educational standard of medicine. The benefits of a working agreement between these Schools[2] would be mutual, for Princeton would derive the benefit of association with an established technical school, whose students in their acquaintance and association would bring increased numbers and interest to Princeton.

We shall be glad to confer with you further and to receive the expression of your views on this subject, in any way convenient to you.

With kind regards and best wishes,

Very truly yours, Edward P. Davis.

TLS (WP, DLC).

1 Wilson's classmate, Professor of Obstetrics at the Jefferson Medical College.

2 That is, an affiliation between the two institutions making Jefferson the medical school of Princeton University. For further discussion of this proposal, see C. H. McCormick to WW, March 2, 1909; WW to C. H. McCormick, March 3, 1909; and WW to C. C. Cuyler, April 13, 1909.

From William Henry Roberts[1]

My dear Sir: Philadelphia, Pa. Feb. 17, 1909.

I forward to you herewith your Commission duly signed as a delegate from the Presbyterian Church in the U.S.A. to the Ninth Council of the Alliance of the Reformed Churches throughout the World holding the Presbyterian System.

The Council will meet in the Fifth Avenue Presbyterian Church, New York City, beginning June 15th, 1909, and will remain in session until June 25th.

Kindly acknowledge receipt of the Commission.[2]

With best wishes, Yours cordially, Wm. H. Roberts

TLS (WP, DLC). Enc.: commission dated Feb. 16, 1909.

1 Stated Clerk of the Presbyterian Church in the U.S.A.

2 Wilson attended at least one session of the council.

To Edwin Grant Conklin

Princeton, N. J.

My dear Professor Conklin: February 18th, 1909.

The Curriculum Committee of the Board of Trustees wishes to report at the next meeting of the Board somewhat systematically with regard to the question of the distribution of teaching work among the Departments.

I would be very much obliged to you, therefore, if you would be kind enough to prepare for me, or have prepared, a careful statement of the number of teachers in your Department and of the amount of teaching work reckoned in hours, whether classroom or laboratory hours, done by each member of the staff. Your early attention to this would very greatly oblige,

Yours very sincerely, Woodrow Wilson[1]

TLS (E. G. Conklin Papers, NjP).

1 Wilson sent similar letters to all departmental heads.

From Henry Smith Pritchett

Personal

My dear Dr. Wilson, New York Feb'y 18, 1909

Since our conversation I have had a conference of some length with our friend,[1] the details of which, I can better give you in talk than on paper. If you happen in N. Y. some day soon perhaps you can spare the time to chat about it. The result was not, I am sorry to say, very encouraging.

Monday next is a good day for me.

Yours faithfully, Henry S. Pritchett

ALS (WP, DLC).

[1] That is, Andrew Carnegie, who Wilson hoped would provide the money for the quadrangle plan.

From Moses Taylor Pyne

My dear Woodrow: New York February 18th, 1909.

I am very sorry that you will be unable to be at the meeting of the Trustees' Committee on the Graduate School on Friday afternoon to consider the plans for the Thomson College. I called the meeting because we have had the plans in our possession now for two months and it seems to me that some definite general policy ought to be agreed upon. Of course, this is simply for the preliminary consideration of the plans and not for their final approval, but it seems to me that the Graduate School Committee should get together and take some notice of these plans, which will have to be considered at a joint meeting of the two Committees[1] hereafter.

Yours very sincerely, M Taylor Pyne

TLS (WP, DLC).

[1] The other committee was the trustees' Committee on Grounds and Buildings.

An Address to the Presbyterian Union of Baltimore[1]

[Feb. 19, 1909]

Mr. President and gentlemen, it is indeed a sincere compliment when you invite a man to speak to you a second time.[2] I do not know how many of you have undergone the experience before, but I myself remember with the greatest pleasure the occasion to which Mr. Garrett has referred, when I had the privilege of addressing this company before. I feel particularly safe in speaking, after being introduced by one of the trustees of Princeton University, and I am very much gratified that he can give so satisfactory an account of his impressions of me. Certainly I can return the compliment, for I feel that we have been greatly strengthened at Princeton by the loyalty, not only, but by the sobriety of counsel and the sane view of things which Mr. Garrett has brought to our council. (Applause.)

I feel that, as I get older, I become less and less fit to make after dinner speeches, for after dinner speeches ought to be made by gentlemen who are very light-hearted indeed, who stand upon a very easy poise, and can lightly turn in any direction. I feel that I do not become cooler as I grow older, but hotter. I find that there is a certain ardor that rises in the blood and increases from year to year as one's experience broadens and one's contact becomes more intimate and direct with the important things that have to be handled every day, even by those of us who handle very little of the broad circumstances of the age in which we live. And in the experience that I have had in recent years in attending public banquets it has been very noticeable how much changed has become the note of after dinner speaking. American bodies of men nowadays seem to have a certain hunger for the discussion of the broader and more serious kinds of questions. There was a time within my easy recollection when a company of American gentlemen after dinner were impatient if they got anything but entertainment; they are now distinctly impatient if all that they get is entertainment. The truth is that we are aware that the circumstances of our national life are thickening about us; that the light-hearted day in which we can take it for granted that things would take care of themselves has gone by; that nothing will take care of itself, not even in happy America, and that Americans, like men bred in hotter ages and under more difficult circumstances, must be men whose thoughts thread the intricacy of many puzzling circumstances and undertake to attack even the most complex problems, with that direct courage and that readiness to apply moral judgments which we would like to have the world believe to have been always characteristic of America.

It happens that my thoughts have been turning in recent days, as the thoughts of mose [most] men in this country have been, to the study of the extraordinary career of Abraham Lincoln. I myself was called upon to do a very interesting thing. First of all, to go into the South and pronounce a eulogy upon the memory of the incomparable Lee; and then to go into a northern state and pronounce a eulogy upon the equally incomparable Lincoln, and the delightful circumstance in my mind was that there seemed to be no conceivable incompatibility between the two tasks now, in this generation; that in the same place you could get the same acquiescence, if it had been the same place, for the eulogy of both men.

But there are some things about the career of Lincoln not present in the career of Lee which set me very seriously to meditating upon the responsibilities and the character of my own particular task in life. It has been the chance of my life that I have been elevated to the head of a university, and I have been asking myself during the last few days whether Lincoln would have been rendered more serviceable to the country or less serviceable to the country by having received a modern university education. If we are in the least sincere in our admiration of Lincoln, if we are not merely using phrases and talking to please the ear of the ordinary citizenship of this country, we who are college men must examine ourselves and see whether we wish our universities to produce men like Lincoln or wish them to produce men unlike Lincoln, and to ask ourselves, if we wish to produce men like Lincoln in quality, in general character, whether we are using the means suitable to that end—a very interesting, and, I must say, as it has gone through my thinking, a very searching question.

Undoubtedly the impression in this country is that we are not using methods suitable for the production of men like Lincoln. You get the impressions in this country, if you travel about as I do, very frankly; men do not conceal them from you. I do not find anybody hesitating to tell me what he thinks of American universities, and the opinion which I hear most commonly expressed is that the universities of this country are producing a class of persons distinguishable from the general body of the nation; that they are making a specialized body of Americans, separated by very recognizable lines of distinction from that generalized body, from the mass of which men like Lincoln arise.

The interesting thing about Lincoln is that you cannot pick him out for any special gift or quality. He seems to have been a sort of universal instrument for whatever he was called upon to do, and the powers slumbered in him until they were challenged; but wherever they were challenged, they responded in splendid and abundant fashion. He was, as it were, a generalized American, ready to turn in any direction, to any task, and bred with a shrewdness, an appreciation of the general circumstances of his day and people, which rendered him almost as fit for one task as for another. A singularity of his whole career is that he seems to have been just as full of promise when he died as when he was a lad, and that the chief feeling we have about him is that he was unexhaustive and inexhaustible; not a man trained and fit for some particular thing which we called upon him to do, but so universally gifted that we might have called upon him to do other things and he might have done them as well. Surely, here is the picture of the serviceable citizen.

I was addressing a party of college alumni the other night, and I told them that it had occurred to me that the particular task of the American college in our generation was to make boys just as unlike their fathers as we possibly could, not because their fathers were not admirable persons, but because every man in America, nearly, old enough to be the father of a college undergraduate, has specialized and centered himself in some particular task, and is like the man who said when he was an undergraduate he thought of humanity, when he grew a little older he thought of the steel industry, and when he grew still a little older his thought was centered upon his bank account. Now, the whole tendency of American life is, first, to center your attention upon an occupation, and then to center your interests upon the profits of that occupation, and by the time you are old enough to have a son in college you have so submerged yourself in a particular interest that you have lost the horizons of the country.

What we must do with your sons, therefore, is to plunge them once more into that reviving bath of the general atmosphere of the country at large, regeneralize them as Americans, and make them serviceable for the general opportunities of a great and varied country, and for the general services of a great and varied country. (Applause.) Our object in each generation, in other words, if we understand it properly, is to reimpregnate the new generation with the general consciousness of the country, as distinguished from the general consciousness of any class in the country. Do you not see how difficult that is? Do you not see how imperative it is? If we are merely going to reproduce after our several kinds, we are going to reproduce and intensify the points of view of particular separated interests, and if we do that, every finger of prophecy in our affairs will be directed towards a warfare of classes. That is the problem, of producing Lincolns, of planting the young trees in the rich and general soil of the country.

How are we going to do that? It seems to me that, in the first place, you cannot do that unless the point of view and the purpose of the teacher is unprofessional. If the teacher has as his object to draw the special attention of his pupil to a particular and narrow line of inquiry, and so capture his interest as to withdraw it from other lines of inquiry unlike his own, then his whole object is professional, and in proportion as he succeeds he will do the very thing that, according to my present view, he should avoid. He will be narrowing, specializing, standardizing the mind that is under his control. He will be sophisticating it with the point of view of a particular profession or a particular inquiry.

Every professional man is deeply sophisticated with the associations of his own calling. The lawyer looks at all life from his point of view, bred so by reason of his constant practice. The physician looks at life from the point of view of the care of the human body and the general hygienic conditions which produce either that which is normal or that which is morbid. The merchant looks at questions of peace and of war, of public policy and of private interest, from the point of view of the trade in which his mind is submerged, and in the terms of which he constantly thinks. And so the scholar, if his interests be in the development of a particular line of inquiry, becomes at once sophisticated with that line of inquiry. The logician will accept nothing but logical proof. The student of the literature of imagination will be impressed by nothing except the imagery in which ideas body themselves forth. And the man who tries to stamp upon his pupil that particular bias is doing the very thing which, in the undergraduate period of his instruction, it is imperative in a free country that he avoid doing. We should try above all things to let every lad under our instruction see that what we are teaching him is only part of the general story of human life, of human observation, of human impulse, of human experience, and that each item we lay before him is one sentence in one chapter of a great work that covers all the experiences of mankind. We are trying to orient him in the world; we are trying to show him where men have gone, where they have struggled, what they have gained, what they have lost, what they have hoped for, and in proportion as we do that we are uniting that young mind with the general body of humanity, and are rendering him fit for the sort of service which a man like Lincoln could and did render.

Then it involves also an unprofessional point of view on the part of the student. This is the ground for my conviction that the very thing that a boy ought not to have in mind at the outset of his undergraduate course is the profession which he intends ultimately to pursue. You know that at Harvard University they have a system of advisors. Every undergraduate who enters Harvard is assigned to some member of the faculty who is to act as his advisor in the choice of his electives, and I asked a very distinguished member of the Harvard faculty how the system was working, and he said "Very badly." I said, "Do you mean that the fellows do not get advice?" "No," he said, "I mean they are getting bad advice." "In what respect?" I said. "Why, in this respect," he replied, "they are almost without exception advised to choose those studies which lead directly to the profession they have in view." "Oh," I said, "I think that is bad advice, but I did not know you did." "Yes," he said, "I think that is very bad. I think they ought to be advised to take the studies which lie as remote as possible from the things they ultimately immerse themselves in." I said "Amen." That, and that only, is a liberal education.

In proportion as you make it the standard of choice that the lad is going to enter such and such a profession, you professionalize him at the very outset of his general studies, and in proportion as you professionalize him you narrow the range of his interests and throw him just that much out of sympathy with America, for America is made up of all of us, and not of any of us, and the particular thing which individual men of success in this country are most apt not to know is this country itself. The particular limitation of the minds of educated men in this country is their provincialism. This country is one of provincial minds, and so long as the country is one of provincial minds, there will be contests of interests so sharp as to endanger the peace and render improbable a wise general policy. You must have an unprofessional point of view if you are going to make a soil for the general use of America. In our colleges we must have an unprofessional point of view on the part of the teacher and an unprofessional point of view on the part of the pupil. So that Mr. Lincoln is carrying us a good ways, and I take it for granted that we cannot dispense with Mr. Lincoln.

Moreover, there is another and equally important thing you must have if there is to be any operative virtue in these things I have been speaking of. These are mere negations. The absence of a professional point of view is a mere negation. We must have a life in our universities which is fundamentally democratic in its make-up, and which includes in its democracy the men who teach as well as the men who are taught. The peculiarity of our American colleges just now is that they consist of two air-tight compartments—one compartment is occupied by the faculty, the other compartment by the students. The walls are not sound-proof, and there is communication (laughter); but there is not atmospheric communication, and the whole association in the one chamber is different from the association in the other. The peculiarity of our American universities at this moment is that the sideshows have swallowed up the circus. (Applause and laughter.) The life of our American universities, I mean the independent life, organized by the undergraduates themselves, the life that has nothing to do with study, is so various, so interesting, essentially so innocent, so free from fundamental vices, that it has come to absorb the whole interest and attention and energy of the men who attend the universities, and the attention which we get is merely the residuum, left over after them [they] have satisfied themselves in their own light (laughter), and there is a considerable degree of solemn truth in the statement that the reason that undergraduates consent to prepare themselves for and pass examination is that they may be allowed the privilege of staying in that place and enjoying that delightful life. (Laughter.) Study is a formal means of qualifying for an experience which has nothing to do with study. (Laughter.)

The democratic element lacking in that life is that it consists only of a youthful body of persons: a democracy consists of elderly persons, as well as young persons, and a democracy is given its whole saturation, in respect of the experience of the race, by its elderly portion, and not by its young portion. I am told by psychologists that I know who I am today because I remember who I was yesterday, and that if I forgot who I was yesterday I could not for the life of me tell you who I am today. If you depended on your youngsters to say what the country is and shall do, you could not for the life of you tell what the country was yesterday. It would have lost its identity. You must fall back upon the lobe of recollection in order to maintain your identity and continuity. Not only so, but it is only persons who have passed a certain period of life who really know what fun it is to use the mind, in addition to using the body. Youngsters use the mind on compulsion; their elders use it because it is a luxury to use it, if they happen to have one. (Laughter.) And the interesting circumstance in your experience, so far as teachers are concerned, is this—take my own experience as an example, I never remember to have been thanked by any pupil of mine for anything he ever got from me in the class room. I lecture to my classes to the best of my ability. I am sure I put into my lectures, try to put into them, everything that I am and everything that I know, but it does not get transmitted. I have several times had the delightful experience of being thanked by men younger than myself for something they got from me outside the class room. When, by reason of the fact that we came into personal association, we laid our minds alongside each other's as comrades and shared counsel upon some common point, and the additional mind advantage, the little more experience, a little more balance of judgment on the part of the older man, were able to contribute to the steadying of the lad, or he guided him in some point of determination, often opened some subject to him that he had never seen opened before as a matter of special and vital interest to him—he carried that for the rest of his life. In other words, in so far as I had been introduced into his companionship and being I had been his real teacher, and not because I had stood behind a desk and lectured to him out of what I supposed to be the fullness of my mind.

Unless, therefore, you can organize your colleges so that the faculties and the students are undistinguishable from the point of view of the community that exists among them, you will not have the proper process of education set up at all. The older I get the more I am convinced that the real education takes place between the last class exercise on one day and the first on the next. It takes place in the process which occurrs [occurs] in the mind of the pupil after the formal instruction is over. If any of it has stuck, if any of it enters into the circulation of his blood, then the infection has taken, but generally the infection is utterly thrown off. (Laughter.) A Yale friend of mine cheered me, in a moment of depression, by saying that after twenty-five years of teaching he had come to the conclusion that the human mind had infinite resources for resisting the introduction of knowledge. (Laughter.)

Now, the interesting point is that when a man is professedly trying to teach you, you naturally regard him as odiously didactic and resist him. I do not blame you; I do myself. Whenever anybody stands up and proceeds to instruct me, then I become critical and resist. If I can sit down by him and match my ideas with his, and find the true candor of his mind, that he is not didactic, that he is not dogmatic, that he is another human being searching, as I am searching, for things that are true and that will satisfy all the questionings of the mind and all the anxieties of the spirit, then his personality begins to work on me like a leaven, and the whole power of learning, if it be in the man, is communicated to me. You must make a life out of learning, or else you will not penetrate life by learning. The two things will be distinct, the one formal, the other real; the one an attempt, the other a reality.

So that these unprofessional comrades, these men not bent upon anything except diffusing the common consciousness of the intellectual portion of the race, must live as members of the same community, or else their living together is of no avail whatever. The way Lincoln trained himself in that mastery which afterwards gave him the leadership of the nation was by sitting in country stores and standing on street corners and matching his mind with everybody who would match it with him, and seeking those phrases, those exact terms of demonstration, those illuminating processes of speech, which would enable his mind to conquer the other man's mind. That was his process of self-education; he educated himself on other men. Nobody ever educated himself on a book; nobody ever educated himself on anything but living spirit. If you can recall the living man who wrote the book out of the pages as you read it, then you have caught the spirit. But the book will not give you learning; the book will not give you power. It is the communication, the transmission, the enlargement, the great, universal partnership of the human mind, that is the object of education and the means of enlightenment.

Another question that we have to ask ourselves in this searching inquiry is this: The Nation cannot live on what it has been; it can live only on what it is to be, and the whole process of life, if I understand anything about it, is a process of renewal; not a process of keeping the old tissue, for it cannot be kept, but a process of constantly, not replenishing, but replacing it with new tissue, and where does the new tissue of a nation come from? Does it come from above? Not at all. It comes from below. All the renewal of a nation comes out of the general mass of its people. Nations have no choice, in respect of power and capacity, but to be democratic. Do you know how the Middle Ages survived their aristocratic order? By means of the Roman Catholic Church. The administrative ability of the Middle Ages was supplied from the Roman Catholic Church, and the Roman Catholic Church was an organization fundamentally and essentially democratic. There was no peasant who might not become the chancellor of an empire or a pope of all Christendom, and because that has been an open channel through which all the common energies of those countries could rise to the top for their renewal, they were kept alive in an age pretending to be aristocratic, but drew all its sources from a democracy. Now, the function of a university is the function which, in that respect, was performed by the Roman Catholic Church during the Middle Ages. The function of a university is to afford open, unclogged channels for the rising of the obscure powers of a nation into observation and supremacy. The moment you impede this process of the rising sap, you kill the whole tree. When I see men pretending to be cultivated who speak with condescension of the masses of the people, I know that they are dying at the top; they have cut their tap roots; they do not know where their sources of strength come from, and presently some man born in a log cabin, some man born of some despised portion of the race, will rise and dominate them, as Lincoln dominated all the cultivated men of his time.

These indomitable powers, which will not be abashed, will not be held back, will rise whether you open the university channels to them or not, and if you do not open the university channels to them, they will be impoverished and sterilized, so that you must remember that you must look for the feeding of your universities down in that dusky soil from which all the fruitage comes, and not up to see the sap run to you from the gaudy flowers that move in the noticeable circles of great cities. (Applause.) It is a very obvious lesson, when you think of it, but a very much neglected lesson. What do we regard our universities as nowadays? As places, for the most part, for those who are privileged by unusually fortunate circumstances to afford to give their sons this additional advantage. If that were true–happily it is not wholly true–if that were true the universities would all be going to seed and I, for my part, would want to climb down out of the branches, for I do not know which way the tree is going to fall. If the educators of this country could once look at the undergraduate organization of our universities at this moment, they would see that at last they were awake and they knew what the task of the day was, to open those channels, to clear them of all the artificial social obstructions, to simplify the process, to coordinate the life, to make this thing a product of the general strength of America, and not in any respect a resort for privileged classes in America. (Applause.)

It is no self-denial on the part of those who are trying to conduct universities to take this point of view. On the contrary, the most interesting men I know are the men who have never attended universities, but who have shown their extraordinary, indomitable strength by succeeding in spite of that fact, and who therefore have known what it means to have their intellectual achievements cost them the sweat of their brow. That is the reason they are interesting. These gentlemen who are coddled and nursed and coaxed into an education have suffered the same consequences that other persons physically reared in that fashion have suffered, they have grown up without any fiber, they are mush. (Laughter.) I am interested sometimes in noticing how many of the men of our educated classes interested in some of the most important undertakings of our day, the moment they get out of the field of their business become sentimentalists and try to settle great questions in this country as if they could be settled with a sentiment. Men who have not had the indulgence of too many books do not try to settle things by sentiment, and if you have not forced your way through this soil, which is the common source of our strength, and have not come out into the upper strata of life riddled with all these life-producing juices of the soil, you do not know what business is; you do not know how costly sentiment is; you do not know how inefficacious mere sentiment is in settling the real, fundamental difficulties of life. If you want to hear a real debate go down and hear men debate who are in hot contact with the facts, and you will hear debate such as no college teams have ever dreamed of.

It goes without saying that I am not depreciating our universities, for they are not what many men say that they are and what they seem to be, but if we do not constantly remind ourselves of the circumstances I have been dwelling upon, they will become so. The interesting circumstance that makes men of us all is that everything in this world has a tendency to run down. If we could only once fix things right and then go about other business, and pay no further heed to them, there would be no other business worthy our steel, worthy our metal. But you have to turn back next morning to see that the thing has not run down. You have to watch it, you have to invigorate it, you have to mend it from day to day, as well as from generation to generation, if you do not wish it to deteriorate, and you must never forget for one moment or the kernel and heart of the whole moralizing process is changed. Some of my fellow Princetonians will say that in this part of my discourse I have mounted a favorite hobby. I have only to say that if it were a hobby I would not have thought it worth while to mount it. It is not a hobby; it is a vehicle of thought, so big that if you do not get on top of it it will turn out to be a Juggernaut and crush you. But this is the process of national life, and there is no hobby in recalling the vast, organic, cosmic, creative processes of the world, and these processes have their triumph, their expression, their vindication, in the life of universities as in the life of nations, and we cannot neglect them.

It is not within our choice to choose any other way of life than this way of which I have spoken. So that it is true that the business of the university is to put under each generation that has arisen a new generation drawn back to some original model, and not permitted to be like the generation that has arisen; held back in close, warm, renewing contact with those unspecialized, unsophisticated processes which are the youth-producing, youth-renewing, the life-containing processes of all the world. We want men drawn, in this liberal fashion, from the richness of the general world, communicated to the thoughts of our boys as they come on into that life which they cannot calculate, the vicissitudes of which they cannot see, the aspect of which constantly changes, the future problems of which will tax new powers and produce unforeseen situations, and our universities must see to it that we get this generalized stuff out of which we can manufacture a new generation unlike the past generation because set in new circumstances and addressing itself to new tasks. That, gentlemen, is the argument for a liberal education, and no other education is liberal, either in spirit or in fact. (Great applause.)

T transcript (WP, DLC).

[1] An organization of Presbyterian laymen which met monthly for fellowship, discussion, and lectures.

[2] For the earlier occasion, see the news report printed at Dec. 5, 1902, Vol. 14.

A News Report

[Feb. 19, 1909]

OLD NORTH'S LIONS TO GO.

Two Royal Bengal Tigers in Bronze
To Be Put in Their Place by Class of 1879.

The bronze lions on the steps of Nassau Hall will soon be removed, and two bronze tigers substituted in their places. The Class of 1879, which presented the University with these lions on its graduation, recently decided that tigers would be more appropriate and suitable, and the final contract with Mr. A[lexander]. P[himister]. Proctor of New York, who was chosen as sculptor, was signed on February 9.

Mr. Proctor is a sculptor of no small fame in this country, having designed the Lincoln Statue in Chicago, and being one of the best animal sculptors in America. In this connection Mr. Proctor has done considerable work, and among his productions might be mentioned the elephant heads in the White House and the animal studies on the buildings of the New York Zoölogical Garden in the Bronx. Small working models of the tigers which he is designing for Old North may be seen at his studio in McDougall Alley, which is just off of Waverly Place, near Sixth Avenue, New York City.

The tigers, when finished and set in place, will be of heroic size, nine feet long and four and a half feet in height, or nearly twice the size of the present lions. The contract calls for their completion and being put in place not later than April 15, 1910, a little over a year from the present time. The present figures, however, will have to be removed in the near future, in order to facilitate the work on the proposed tigers, but the Class Committee, consisting of Robert Bridges, Cornelius C. Cuyler, John Farr, A. Woodruff Halsey, William B. Isham, Jr., Cyrus H. McCormick and William R. Wilder, expect to have plaster casts made in full size and placed in position before the annual Yale-Princeton baseball game. The cost of the tigers will be ten thousand dollars, the half of which has already been pledged by the members of the Class of 1879. Needless to say, the Board of Trustees of the University has given consent to the project.

Printed in the *Daily Princetonian*, Feb. 19, 1909.

From John Watson Foster[1]

My dear Dr. Wilson, Washington, D. C. Feb. 20th 1909

I have your letter of the 18th, and in reply to your inquiries would state that it is expected to have two leading addresses at the Witherspoon statue dedication.[2] Ambassador Bryce has made a conditional promise to make one of the addresses, and if so he will speak on the Scotch contribution to America, and in this connection discuss Witherspoon's political services.

We should like you to review in about twenty five minutes, his work as President of Princeton College and his services to the church, but would not expect you to confine yourself closely to that topic, as you will naturally be tempted to refer to his work in the Continental Congress.[3]

We hope we may induce President Taft to attend and say a few words.[4] Mr. Macfarland, as President of the City Government,[5] will make a short talk, and I shall make a brief sketch of the Memorial Association's work. The exercises will begin probably at 3.30 P.M. and the addrésses will be delivered in the Church of the Covenant, immediately adjoining the statue.

At five o'clock Mrs. Foster[6] & I should like to give a reception at our residence in honor of you and Mrs. Wilson, to which we would invite the resident Alumni of Princeton and their wives, and the visitors to the dedication.

As soon as the program is definitely arranged, we will send you a copy. Very truly, John W. Foster.

HwLS (WP, DLC).

[1] United States Secretary of State, 1892-93; lawyer of Washington; scholar of diplomacy and international law; and President of the Witherspoon Memorial Association, which was erecting a statue of John Witherspoon near the Presbyterian Church of the Covenant at Connecticut Avenue and N Street, N.W., in Washington.

[2] That is, on May 20, 1909. The two main speakers were Ambassador James Bryce and Wilson.
[3] Wilson's address at the dedication of the Witherspoon statue is printed at May 20, 1909.
[4] The President was represented by Vice-President James Schoolcraft Sherman, who spoke briefly.
[5] Henry Brown Floyd MacFarland, President of the Board of Commissioners of the District of Columbia.
[6] Mary Parke McFerson Foster.

From Edith Rockefeller McCormick[1]

My dear Mr. Wilson: [Chicago] February 20th, 1909.

I was most interested in what you said about the problems and difficulties at Princeton, but we never overstep the rule, now of a number of years' standing, to present no appeals to my Father.

I would be glad to write to my brother[2] or to Mr. Gates,[3] if this would be of help to you.

We enjoyed so much your visit, and I hope that we may have the pleasure of meeting before so very long again.

Sincerely, Edith Rockefeller McCormick

ALS (WP, DLC).
[1] Mrs. Harold Fowler McCormick, sister-in-law of Cyrus H. McCormick.
[2] John D. Rockefeller, Jr.
[3] The Rev. Frederick Taylor Gates, business associate of and adviser on philanthropic matters to John D. Rockefeller.

From Charles Ernest Scott[1]

Dear Sir: Tsingtau Shantung Province North China. 2-22-1909.

It is quite improbable that you remember me; but during three delightful years at Princeton Seminary I did graduate work at the University and "drank in" every one of your courses possible. I have long wanted to pay my modest but very sincere tribute to your great helpfulness to me, both in your public speech & in your attitude generally towards life; but haven't dared to intrude upon your busy hours, so full of important things. However, as a humble but ever-loyal Princetonian, I have at last plucked up my courage, from an obscure corner on the far rim of the planet, to tell you the goodness of the Lord in permitting me ever to be under your influence and example.

Your words & principles were no small factor in helping me to decide to go, for my life work, to the hardest field I could fill; for the Lord is surely pleased to have us, for love to His Son, man the neediest places, unsurfeited with workers. . . .

I always think of you with especial pleasure on Washington's birthday, not merely because it is Princeton's jollification time, nor because I have often conned your "George Washington" & loaned it to isolated missionaries all over N. China; but especially because of a delightful evening spent in your study, when you invited my dear friend, John Fairman Preston[2] (already one of the able & vigorous missionary leaders in the spiritual awakening of Korea) and me to discuss Washington with you; rather, it was, to listen with greatest delight to your account of the Old Dominion, its plantation life, social condition, etc "befoh de Wah." It was a great night in my life, & twelve o'clock came all too soon. . . .

With prayers for God's abundant blessing upon your life & work, Gratefully Yours Charles Ernest Scott.

P.S. If you should ever be able to favor me with a note, I should be glad to know what books you have published.

ALS (WP, DLC).

[1] Secretary of the American Presbyterian Mission in Shantung, China; student at Princeton Theological Seminary, 1899-1900, 1901-1903.

[2] Princeton Theological Seminary, 1899-1902; Presbyterian missionary, at this time stationed in Kwangju, Korea.

From Thomas Maxwell Henry[1]

My dear Wilson: Washington, D. C., Feb. 22, 1909

It is not among the burning issues, but I would meekly protest to you, in your double capacity of President of Princeton and probably most prominent '79er, against a substitution of tigers for lions by our usually infallible Class Committee. Tho' not a Buffon[2] or anything of that sort—nor a buffoon either—I have a distinct impression, instilled perhaps in the nursery, that the tiger is a man-eating brute of cruel and ferocious instincts unrelieved by the gentlemanly appearance which his leonine relative wears, or has been represented as wearing in heraldic and other blazonry, time out of mind. The tiger donated for the gymnasium by my Pittsburg friend, Mr. E[dward]. A[ugustus]. Woods, was not liable to the same objection as the two proposed for the steps of North, inasmuch as the locus in quo is everything in such matters: and a concession to the athletic spirit of recent years was more appropriately made by placing this demi-god of our football rooters in the temple of football training than in that of Lady Minerva. Perhaps I have been too much out of the current to view college matters in all respects as most of our contemporaries view them, and doub[t]less I am wrong in making this particular criticism, or in ever criticising anything approved and sanctioned; but of this you are a better judge than I, and, if you regard my protest as untimely or otherwise objectionable, dispose of it as you think wisest–I will submit. This, like other dissenting opinions, is not made with the hope of accomplishing or preventing anything, but is perhaps doubly pardonable where one is asked to contribute to a barbarism "without representation," so to speak. I am for a reproduction of lions.

Very sincerely yours, T. M. Henry

TLS (WP, DLC).

1 Wilson's classmate, lawyer of Washington.

2 Georges Louis Leclerc, Comte de Buffon (1707-88), French naturalist.

To Thomas Maxwell Henry

My dear Henry: Princeton, N. J. February 23rd, 1909.

I think that there is a great deal of force in your interesting letter of yesterday, and I know that what you say about the substitution of tigers for the lions has been a very general thought among our classmates. At the same time, I have felt that a radical change of circumstances has rendered this substitution timely and suitable. The fact is that for the past ten or fifteen years the most frequent question that those of us who were here on the ground have had to answer, alike from undergraduates and colleagues of the faculty and strangers, has been: "Why lions? Why not tigers? What association has the lion with the history or traditions of the place?", and it has always been necessary to explain that at the time we put the lions there the college association with the tiger had not been established. This makes the class sound rather antediluvian, in the opinions at any rate of the passing generation of Princeton men, and when the Class Committee suggested the substitution of tigers for lions, I felt bound to say that I thought it would be the right thing to do.

I quite agree with you that the tiger is not an emblem of qualities desirable in human society, but on the other hand it is to be said that there is no more common symbol in carving of all kinds than the lion, and that it is very much more possible for a sculptor to give us something vital and distinguished in the shape of a tiger than in the shape of a lion, which would at best have a touch of the common-place and the expected about it.

The sculptor whom the Class Committee has chosen is himself of that judgment and is a man of very unusual gifts, is indeed the greatest of our animal sculptors. He has made sketches for the tigers which promise something very fine indeed.

I thank you for your letter and for this opportunity to explain what I understand to be the grounds of the action by the Class Committee. I think the first general impression was that which you expressed.

Always cordially and sincerely yours,

Woodrow Wilson

TLS (UA, NjP).

From Henry Burling Thompson

Greenville P. O. Delaware

Dear President Wilson: February twenty-fourth, 1909.

Before submitting the completed plans and specifications of the Sage Dormitory to the Committee on Grounds and Buildings, it would be wise to hold a meeting of the Sub-Committee, which Committee consists of Pyne, yourself and myself. I would suggest some afternoon, either the 9th, 10th or 11th of March. If any one of these dates suit you will you kindly let me know at your earliest convenience, so that I can arrange with Messrs. Day and Pyne for the meeting.

I am most pleased with the development of the plans, and am inclined to believe this is going to be one of our best buildings,—both from the point of view of use and good architecture.

Yours very sincerely, Henry B Thompson

TLS (WP, DLC).

To Frank Miles Day

My dear Mr. Day: Princeton, N. J. February 26th, 1909.

Thank you for your letter of February 25th. I am just now trying to arrange a day for a conference with you and Mr. Thompson and Mr. Pyne, the sub-committee, and am looking forward with a great deal of interest to discussing the details of the plans.

Thank you very much for your thoughtful kindness in planning to send me photographs of the drawings.

With much regard,

Sincerely yours, Woodrow Wilson

TLS (WC, NjP).

Notes for an Address[1]

Academy of Music Phila.,
For Hampton Institute 26 Feb'y, 1909

Problem of providing a place and training for the negro in America much more complicated now than formerly, because of economic changes and *other races*,—a more complicated problem in *adjustment*.

The freedom of the negro?

Liberty is *adjustment*. The negro has been thrown out of adjustment. Reconstruction a colossal example of *mal*-adjustment.

Here are *means* of adjustment, social and economic at hand,— *in education*.

Education *is* adjustment
a) by enlightenment
b) by training,—familiar skill

Private aid: the opportunity, the privilege, the duty } Of wealth and influence

WWhw MS (WP, DLC).

[1] The only report of this meeting, at which Booker T. Washington also spoke, in the Philadelphia newspapers appeared in the *North American*, Feb. 27, 1909. It devoted most of its coverage to Washington's speech and said about Wilson only that he spoke.

From Edwin Grant Conklin

Princeton, New Jersey
My dear President Wilson, February 26, 1909.

In answer to your request of Feb. 18 for a careful statement of the number of teachers in this department and of the amount of teaching work reckoned in hours, whether classroom or laboratory hours, done by each member of the staff, I beg to submit the following report:

The persons engaged in giving instruction in the Department of Biology, with the number of hour's work actually given by each during the current academic year, as well as the number of hours of graduate instruction, which they have offered through the catalogue, but have not been called upon to give this year, are the following:

Scott, W. B., 2 hrs. lecture, Senior Course #44
3 " Graduate Course #109, offered but not given this year.

(Time about equally divided between class-room & lab.)

Rankin, W. M., 6 hrs. lecture and laboratory, Junior Courses #33 and #34.
6 " " " Graduate Courses #103 and 107, offered, but only 2 hrs. actually taken this year.

McClure, C. F. W., 6 hrs. lecture and laboratory, Senior Courses #41 and 42.
6 " " " " Graduate Courses #105, 106, offered but not taken this year.

Conklin, E. G., 6 hrs. lecture and laboratory, Junior Courses #31 and 32.
6 " " " " Graduate Course #102
6 " (about) Supervision of Graduate Research work.

Dahlgren, U., 6 hrs. lecture and laboratory, Senior Courses #43 and 46.
6 " " " " Graduate Course #101.

Farr, M. S., 6 hrs. lecture and laboratory, Senior Course #45.
2 " preceptorial work Senior Course #44.
6 " lecture and laboratory, Graduate Course #110, offered but not taken this year.

Sylvester, C. F., 6 hrs. laboratory assistance, Senior Courses #41 and 42.

Crampton, G. C., 6 " " " Junior Courses 31 and 32.

In addition to the above all members of the staff except Professors Scott and Farr have regularly given at least one hour per week to the graduate Seminary in Biology.

Very truly yours, E. G. Conklin[1]

TLS (WWP, UA, NjP).

[1] For other replies to Wilson's request of February 18, 1909, see, e.g., W. F. Magie to WW, Feb. 24, 1909, TLS (WWP, UA, NjP); W. M. Daniels to WW, March 1, 1909, TLS (WWP, UA, NjP); H. B. Fine, typed memorandum dated March 3, 1909 (WWP, UA, NjP); and T. W. Hunt to WW, March 4, 1909, ALS (WWP, UA, NjP). There will be much subsequent correspondence about Wilson's report on the preceptorial system to the Committee on the Curriculum. He finally prepared a report on the non-scientific departments (it is printed at May 13, 1910, Vol. 20), but apparently did not submit it to the committee.

From Lucius Hopkins Miller

Princeton, New Jersey
My dear President Wilson, Feb. 26. 1909.

Mr. Duff[1] has just asked me to explain to you concerning a special work we are planning for the week beginning March 7th under the leadership of Mr. E. C. Mercer.[2] We did not think it necessary to trouble you about it, or to request permission as we did last year, because practically all that is to be done will be done quietly with small groups of men—there is to be no series of large meetings as there was last year.

Mr. Mercer has been here before but not for any period of days. His success at Yale, Williams & other colleges of our type has been marked. We debated having him last year but decided we would wait until his work elsewhere guaranteed the wisdom of asking him to come. He aims especially at gambling, drinking & immorality & I am confident that his visit will result in much good. You may count on our handling the matter with care. As you know men like Duff & Pfeiffer[3] know how the run of men feel about such "special efforts" & are naturally conservative—perhaps too much so.

With your permission we should like to plan a Conference here on May 6th whose end will be to open the eyes of the inhabitants of Mercer County to the opportunities for cooperation on the part of religious organizations in the County for the bettering of the welfare of the County Community. We have been laying much emphasis this year on securing *definite* religious & philanthropic work for groups of our Students & have been fairly successful. We think there is a large field for service in the County which will appeal to faculty & students alike, & result in the Philadelphian Society becoming a medium through which the best that we have to give may be passed over into the surrounding community & incidentally our men will be trained up in the first principles of Christian Citizenship. The bearing of all this upon the training up of Christian Laymen & of good men for the Ministry as well as upon the Moral Life of the University is evident. We wish to invite representatives from towns & villages & from Trenton, as well as Princeton People & the University Community—probably men only.

Subject to your approval, we have secured Dr. Josiah Strong to give three addresses, the first at 11:00 a.m. on "How may the Good Elements in Mercer County cooperate effectively & Concretely for the County's Welfare."
2:00 p.m. "The Religious Significance of Social Service"

8:00 p.m. "Concrete Ways of Service open to the Faculty & Students of Princeton University in Promoting the Welfare of Mercer County."

These are merely tentative phrasings of the topics. The Addresses will be about 45 minutes in length, to be followed by open discussion if desired.

Realizing that the outsiders will bulk largely in morning & afternoon & will probably go home before Evening, we have planned the Program accordingly—the morning session being planned to meet the needs of the Visitors especially. The Aim of the Scheme is purely Inspirational—Inspiration through Information. We do not wish to suggest any new organization. We think such a Conference is particularly within the Province of the Religious Organization of a University & feel that we have been lacking in our sense of Community Responsibility.

Could you preside at these Sessions, introducing Dr. Strong and conducting the discussions, we would deem it an especial favor for that would insure the success of the undertaking both in the matter of attendance & in efficiency.[4]

If you so desire, I will come over to see you and explain the situation more in detail. In conclusion I may say that this move is merely the natural result of some very successful, though limited, work carried on this year for the first time. I am convinced that we have found *a* solution of one of the great problems of our Religious Life here in Princeton.

Very truly yours, Lucius Hopkins Miller.

ALS (WP, DLC).

[1] George Morgan Duff '07, graduate student at Princeton and Secretary of the Philadelphian Society, 1907-1909. About this organization, see n. 1 to the news item printed at Nov. 1, 1890, Vol. 7.

[2] Edward C. Mercer, evangelist and former mission worker in New York.

[3] Timothy Newell Pfeiffer '08. He was still in residence, completing the work for his A.B., which was awarded him in June 1909 as of the Class of 1908.

[4] The conference took place as scheduled on May 6, 1909, following exactly the program outlined above by Miller. Wilson presided when Josiah Strong gave his three addresses. *Daily Princetonian*, May 6 and 7, 1909.

From Platt Kent[1]

Dear Sir: Princeton, N. J. February 27, 1909.

I have been asked to inform you that in accordance with the request contained in your letter of January 26, 1909, Mr John A Stewart III[2] has been selected as representative of the Board of Governors of the Princeton Charter Club on the proposed graduate committee to advise with the university authorities.

His address is, care of Brown Brothers and Company, 59 Wall St. New York City.

Very sincerely yours Platt Kent
Secretary, Board of Governors[3]

ALS (WWP, UA, NjP).

1 A member of the Senior Class at Princeton and Secretary of the Board of Governors of the Princeton Charter Club.

2 Princeton 1905, a clerk in the New York banking firm of Brown Brothers and Co.

3 For other replies to Wilson's letter, see J. H. Walker to WW, Jan. 30, 1909, ALS (WP, DLC); C. G. Meinken to WW, Feb. 25, 1909, TLS (WWP, UA, NjP); F. W. Stelle to WW, March 17, 1909, ALS (WWP, UA, NjP); O. H. McPherson to WW, April 2, 1909, ALS (WWP, UA, NjP); and W. O. Morse to WW, May 18, 1909, TLS (WWP, UA, NjP).

From Winthrop More Daniels

My dear Wilson: Princeton, N. J. March 2, '09.

Whittlesey, Arner, and Willard[1] have all been informed that they will not be retained on the teaching staff. Arner and Willard have been told that they will not be continued after June next, and Whittlesey was told that he might have, if necessary, until June 1910 to make a final exit.

I told Arner that there was no complaint made as to his teaching, but that I thought you felt his basic concepts in Politics were not firmly grounded, and that his logical processes were lacking in precision. I told Willard that you regarded his methods as lacking in scholarly poise, balance, and proportion. Whittlesey was told that you did not regard him in the line of promotion for a Preceptorship, and that he ought to prepare more thoroughly, if he intends to take to teaching as his final profession. I told them all to see you and confirm themselves as to the reasoss [reasons] you held for their non-continuance here. So you are probably in for some interviews with them. I confess in my talks with them to have felt like the English judge who in sentencing a man to hanging for counterfeiting the coin of the Realm, added: "And may you in the next world find that mercy which a regard for a sound currency must forbid you to expect in this." If "sound learning" be substituted for "currency," the analogy is complete.

Faithfully yours, W. M. Daniels

TLS (WWP, UA, NjP).

1 Walter Lincoln Whittlesey, George Byron Louis Arner, and Ralph Claude Willard, all Instructors in History, Politics, and Economics.

From Cyrus Hall McCormick

Dear Woodrow: Seaboard Florida Limited March 2. 1909.

I was in Princeton last evening on my way with Mrs. McCormick south by the physicians advice to find a better climate where she can recover from the severe cold which she has taken and cannot throw off.

I was sorry to find that you were absent and so I send this letter to make some suggestions I would have made verbally.

1. Please take up the Jefferson question[1] seriously with a view to *some* report to the Trustees at the April meeting. This involves preliminary work and there is not a day to lose. (a) I should think you would like the opinion of some of the Faculty on the subject (b) Get some of the Trustees to go and look over the Jefferson plant. I spoke to Pyne & Dodge about it and they were both deeply interested in the matter. They will go and make a report if you ask them to, I am sure. If the Trustees should act favorably on the question in April we could consummate things by June and make the announcement for the coming year. If we are to turn down the plan surely Jefferson ought to know without delay.

2. There is a mix-up on the question of assigning the vacant rooms in '79 Hall but I am taking this up with Duffield, Cuyler & Pyne to prepare a resolution for the Trustees to act upon at the April meeting, laying down the rules of occupancy and not leaving it as it now is to a matter of personal preference and private "pull" for a boy to get in.[2] I do not know whether you care to go into this question but if you do I can send you more details. I want to help C. C. C. to get rid of an embar[r]assing position he is put in when he tries to distribute this patronage! Dodge & Pyne both agree with me that the present system is very bad. Duffield says it is *very* bad & makes hard feeling among the boys.

3. Have you had an opportunity to write out the notes of that Chicago address to the Alumni? If not would you rather give it up than still keep it on your docket? *We* are just as anxious for it as ever but we don't want to add a feather weight to what you already have in hand.

4. The question of "Industrial teaching" is being considered at Harvard[3] and elsewhere, and sometime I would like to talk this over with you to see if the idea has any merit for Princeton.

5. I received notice of a meeting of Graduate School Committee but I cd not attend. Before the Committee makes its report as to the plans for the buildings will you give those who

were necessarily absent from the meeting a chance to be heard by letter or verbally? Cordially yours C. H. McC.

My address is Jekyl Island Club
Brunswick Ga.

ALI (WP, DLC).

[1] That is, the affiliation of the Jefferson Medical College with Princeton University.

[2] See WW to C. H. McCormick, March 3, 1909, ns. 3 and 4.

[3] McCormick probably referred here either to the ferment at Harvard about the abolition of the old Lawrence Scientific School and its replacement by a Graduate School of Applied Science between 1906 and 1910 or to the establishment of a Graduate School of Business Administration in March 1908.

From John Ralph Hardin[1]

Dear Mr. President: Newark, N. J. March 2, 1909.

The Princeton Club of Newark very badly needs stirring up, and it is the present thought of the officers, provided they can secure your attendance, to have a dinner of the Club some time this spring.

Can you give us a date, either in April or May? We will be glad to have you name your own time, and if we can be assured of your presence we are confident we can have a large and enthusiastic body of the alumni to meet you. Please do not turn us down.[2]

Kindly let me hear from you, and oblige,

Yours very truly, John R. Hardin

TLS (WP, DLC).

[1] Princeton 1880, lawyer of Newark and President of the Princeton Club of Newark.

[2] Wilson accepted. A news report of his address to the Newark alumni is printed at May 6, 1909.

To Cyrus Hall McCormick

My dear Cyrus: Princeton, N. J. March 3rd, 1909.

I am sincerely sorry to hear that Mrs. McCormick has had so much trouble throwing off her cold and hope that the change to Jekyl Island will work an immediate and delightful cure. I am glad that incidentally you are getting a taste of a vacation.

I am very sorry I was not in Princeton when you came through. A talk on the important matters mentioned in your letter would be so much more satisfactory than speaking of them in this way.

First. With regard to the Jefferson College matter, it is imperatively necessary that we should go slowly. It would not be wise to act upon the matter this academic year at all. I say this because, though I am convinced of the excellence of the Jefferson faculty and of the Jefferson equipment, the Jefferson is now one of the few colleges which are upon a purely proprietary basis (in effect) and which, without endowment, could hardly be brought up to the standards with regard to entrance to which all the other first class medical colleges of the country are coming. The Carnegie Foundation for the Advancement of Teaching, to whose Executive Committee I belong, is just now engaged in a very careful consideration of the whole matter of medical education in this country and of the relations, real and nominal, between medical schools and universities.[1] I have been in conference with President Pritchett of the Foundation, who is conducting this inquiry very thoroughly and intelligently, and I feel that it is imperative, if we would act with prudence and wisdom, that we should await an opportunity to study this report and know exactly what we wish the relationship between the University and the Jefferson to be, before we act at all. Haste would be highly imprudent. I will, nevertheless, of course discuss the matter with my colleagues here and take all the preliminary steps towards information and the formation of opinion which may be possible on our part.[2]

Second. I am very glad indeed that you are taking up the matter of the assignment of rooms in Seventy-Nine Hall. Without having gone into the matter myself in any detail, I have long felt that the present system[3] is very unwise and very distressing to those who have to administer it. I hope that you will count on me to cooperate in any way that is necessary in putting the thing upon a systematic basis and taking it out of the category of patronage.[4]

Third. As for my address to the Chicago alumni, I made practically the same address to the Presbyterian Union in Baltimore the other evening and had a competent stenographer present to take it down. I have not yet had time to examine his notes, but I think it very likely that I can base upon them what will be substantially a report of what I said in Chicago. I sincerely hope so.[5]

Fourth. The suggestions for "industrial teaching" at Harvard do not seem to me consistent with our system and purposes, but I will of course be very glad to go into the merits of anything that might be suggested for Princeton in this line.

Fifth. As to the plans for the Graduate College, I was very sorry that Pyne called the Graduate School Committee together on such short notice. It turned out that only three or four members of the committee could be present. I was necessarily absent, and I do not see that the meeting served any particular purpose. Undoubtedly, the other members of the committee must have an opportunity to form and express an opinion before final action is taken. You will remember that the Board referred the matter to the Committee on the Graduate School and the Committee on Grounds and Buildings jointly. It will not be concluded before that joint action is taken. In the meantime, I am going to submit the plans to the criticism of the members of the faculty who are to constitute the new Faculty Committee on the Graduate School. I think this quite indispensable and shall ask them to submit their opinion in some definite way to the Committee of the Board.

Please give my warmest regards to Mrs. McCormick, and believe me,

Always faithfully and cordially yours,

Woodrow Wilson

TLS (WP, DLC).

1 Wilson referred to the examination of American medical schools begun in December 1909 by Abraham Flexner under the auspices of the Carnegie Foundation. Flexner's report, *Medical Education in the United States and Canada . . .*, was published by the foundation about the middle of 1910 and caused a public furor. The report evaluated all the medical schools of the country individually and by name and revealed that a large proportion of them, even many connected with reputable colleges and universities, were simply diploma mills, with few or no standards or requirements for admission or graduation. As a direct result of the report, many of the schools closed, and those remaining greatly tightened their standards. Interestingly, the Jefferson Medical College received a relatively good rating in Flexner's report.

2 The trustees never formally considered the affiliation of the Jefferson Medical College with Princeton University during Wilson's presidency.

3 The allotment of rooms in Seventy-Nine Hall was under the control of the Class of 1879, with preference going to sons of class members. In practice, Cornelius Cuyler Cuyler had taken charge of the allotment of rooms. See WW to D. M. Barringer, April 3, 1909.

4 The trustees took no action at the April 1909 meeting, or, for that matter, during the remainder of Wilson's administration, concerning the assignment of rooms in Seventy-Nine Hall.

5 Wilson did not revise the stenographic report of his address to the Presbyterian Union of Baltimore for publication.

To Winthrop More Daniels

My dear Daniels: Princeton, N. J. March 3rd, 1909.

Thank you very much for your letters of March first[1] and second, containing the teaching statistics about the Department, and reporting on what you said to Whittlesey, Arner, and Willard. I have already had an interview with Arner and am about to appoint one with Willard. I will, of course, be very glad to see Whittlesey too, if he desires it.

I know how painful a matter this is, and I hate to ask anyone to share the burden with me, but it seems to me that unless the initial steps at any rate are taken by the Heads of Departments, the departmental organization will lack something of its reality.

Always cordially and faithfully yours,

Woodrow Wilson

TLS (Wilson-Daniels Corr., CtY).

[1] W. M. Daniels to WW, March 1, 1909, TLS (WWP, UA, NjP).

From John Fairfield Dryden

My dear Dr. Wilson: [Newark, N. J.] March 3, 1909.

I beg to inform you that, pursuant to the authority given to the President at the organization of the Cleveland Monument Association, I have filled up the Board of Trustees and filed the certificate of incorporation, a copy of which will be mailed to you by the Secretary.

At the meeting at which the Association was organized, it was resolved to put up a monument, to cost about $100,000, and President Woodrow Wilson and Mr Moses Taylor Pyne were appointed a Committee, with the President, to select a site and to procure plans and specifications for such a monument. The Committee expects to be able to report in ample time for the consideration and determination of the Trustees.

Meantime, the Executive Committee has thought it desirable to proceed at once to raise the necessary funds, and to that end has had subscription blanks prepared, three copies of which I enclose you herewith.[1] I am sending three of these to each Trustee, asking him to take such means for bringing the same to the attention of Mr. Cleveland's friends, and the public generally, in his locality, as may seem to him to be most appropriate. The Executive Committee thinks that popular subscriptions, to some extent at least, ought to be invited, but that before this is done it would be better to get in the larger amounts from among Mr. Cleveland's known friends who are in a position to give liberally. We are pursuing that course here, and have already obtained some One-Thousand-Dollar subscriptions, and are hoping to get some of even larger amount. I should be very glad indeed of anything that you could do in the way of obtaining subscriptions, and I suggest that you prepare a list of persons in your locality who would be likely to contribute, and then either submit the subscription list to them yourself or get some proper person to do it. Or if this, for any reason, is not convenient, send it to me and I will arrange to have them seen or communicated with from here.

I have, of course, no desire to burden you with any work which may not be entirely convenient, but I am hoping that each Trustee can do something in his own locality in this matter, and I have no doubt that every one will be pleased to do what he can.

Kindly let me hear from you at your convenience, and much oblige Yours truly, John F. Dryden

TLS (WP, DLC).

[1] These enclosures are missing.

From David Benton Jones

My dear Doctor, Cairo [Egypt] March 4, 1909

Judging from my brother's account of your visit to Chicago I am very heavily the loser for being away from home. His rating of the Princeton dinner talk was such as to place it quite by itself. As his disposition is supposed not to be as "ardent" as mine it only shows what I have missed. The term in quotation is the quality Mr. [John Aikman] Stewart objected to in my case and was satisfied when told my brother was less so than I. I am sure the mills are grinding and if so how little it matters whether this one or that one is elected.[1] It delights me to hear, as in this case, the sledge hammer blows you are delivering, all the more effective, because they concern fundamental principles and for the time ignore the formal facts of the case.

I am very sorry the chief disturber is not to be entirely eliminated,[2] but even that will come in time, as his absurdity becomes more evident.

I am sending you this note simply to relieve my own feelings in regard to Princeton and what you are doing for it and the larger problem. It makes me ill in spirit to feel what Princeton is in danger of missing by declining to follow in the path[3] you are making so plain, and which, to walk in, would bring it more distinction & influence than it can reach in any other way. Ultimately it will have to "tag on," when now it can lead if only it would.

I hope you are not overtaxing your endurance & that you are more & more establishing your health as I fear the laggards will require a lot of time to catch up or to catch on. The chief difficulty now is a real failure to understand.

Please remember me most kindly to Mrs Wilson.

Very Sincerely David B. Jones.

ALS (WP, DLC).

[1] His brother, Thomas Davies Jones, had been elected a Life Trustee by the Board of Trustees on October 15, 1908. D. B. Jones had retired at the end of his term as an Alumni Trustee in June 1908.

[2] That is, that Dean West had not been removed entirely as a result of the recently proposed reorganization of the administrative structure of the Graduate School.

[3] The adoption of the quadrangle plan.

To Frank Miles Day and Brother

My dear Sirs: Princeton, N. J. March 5th, 1909.

Allow me to acknowledge with appreciation the receipt of the photograph of the water color drawing of Mrs. Sage's portion of the Freshman Dormitory. It seems to me in every way admirable, and I feel very glad at the prospect of adding so handsome and useful a building to the University.

I shall see Mr. Thompson on Saturday and confer with him as to the best means of pushing our plans for the erection of the building forward.

Very sincerely yours, Woodrow Wilson

TLS (WC, NjP).

From John Lambert Cadwalader

My dear Mr. President: New York, 5 March, 1909.

Since the last meeting of the Board, when an Alumni Council was approved, the Committee of Fifty have been working on the scheme in order to meet your views and the views of the trustees as evidenced by the proceedings of the last trustees' meeting.[1]

While it was left to the Committee to work out the details, I wish to keep you informed and therefore enclose to you a copy of the form of organization now suggested by the Committee of Fifty,[2] who will become the Alumni Council and who gradually will retire and be succeeded, as appears by the certificate.

The points which were criticised by you, as well as by the Committee, have, it seems to me, been satisfactorily disposed of. At the request of the Committee, and not on the motion of the Committee of Fifty, there has been eliminated from the scheme—properly and wisely, I think—the idea of approving the composition of this body by the trustees. In my judgment, it ought to be an alumni body, pure and simple.

They have also modified paragraph 3, at the top of page 3, on publicity, by making the Committee cooperate with the Secretary of the University. Paragraph 4 they have changed by making the

Committee cooperate with the University authorities, and subject to them.

I think the Committee of Fifty have no possible desire to secure any undue authority, and I also think that the Alumni Council will be a much more effective body, and, in fact, that it will prove, if properly directed—as I think it will be—a real power and very important adjunct of the University. . . .

Whether you agree in this or not, I shall be glad to have your views as soon as possible as to this particular form of organization, which really goes to put the Committee of Fifty on some logical and business basis.

Believe me, with great respect,

Faithfully yours, John L. Cadwalader

TLS (WP, DLC).

1 There are many documents in Volume 18 relating to the reorganization of the Committee of Fifty. See especially the report printed at Oct. 15, 1908, and WW to J. L. Cadwalader, Dec. 17, 1908.

2 Wilson returned it. The plan of organization is printed at March 29, 1909.

To John Lambert Cadwalader

My dear Mr. Cadwalader: [Princeton, N. J.] March 6th, 1909.

Thank you for your letter of yesterday. I have read the Plan of Organization of the Graduate Council very carefully and think that it is no longer open to any exception whatever. I am very much obliged to you for sending it to me promptly. I take it for granted that you will want the copy you sent me. I therefore return it.

With much regard,

Faithfully yours, [Woodrow Wilson]

CCL (WWP, UA, NjP).

An Address to the Civic League of St. Louis

[[March 9, 1909]]

CIVIC PROBLEMS

Mr. President, Ladies and Gentlemen:

I think that as I grow older, I grow less and less qualified to make after dinner speeches; for I grow more and more serious. I have certain friends whom I look upon with hopeless envy; they are so poised, they are so cool; their judgment is always so removed from the heated processes which seem to go on inside myself. For, as I grow older, instead of growing cooler, I grow hotter, and I think that of all the unfavorable seasons for heatable persons, the season through which we have just passed has been the worst. We have had for the past seven years a gentleman at the head of the Government whose purpose seemed to be to keep us all at white heat, and for a person so susceptible to that condition as myself, it has been a very serious series of years. Because there are various sorts of warmth. There is the warmth by which you are attracted, and there is the warmth by which you are repelled—and I am not sure which warmth excites you the most, though I am sure which makes you genial and which makes you disagreeable.

We have gone through a season, as I just now playfully said, of heat, of excitement. When we do not wish to speak disparagingly, but wish to speak hopefully, we say that it has been a season of awakening, of moral and civic awakening; and we take heart from the circumstance that we are now at last aware of the difficult problems we have to solve; aware of the abuses which have sprung up in this country, and of the necessity that we are under to correct those abuses by any process which will be effectual.

I hope that we realize, however, that we have gone through merely a process of awakening. I hope we realize that we have in fact accomplished almost nothing. It is one thing to be cried wide awake by the rumors of trouble, and it is a very different thing indeed to correct the trouble which our now wide-open eyes perceive. It seems to me, therefore, that we have now come to the most interesting, because the most difficult, period of our recent national life. We must now stop preaching sermons and come down to those applications which will actually correct the abuses of our national life, without any more fuss, and without any more rhetoric. For a nation of the American disposition, that is a very unpromising prospect,—not to be expected to talk but to be expected to work in the stubborn stuffs of human nature and to correct those things which all of us know reside potentially in ourselves.

You know it was one of the whimsical remarks of Mr. Carlyle, Thomas Carlyle I mean, that the problem of politics was how, out of a multitude of knaves, to make an honest people. Even if you were to admit that every nation is made up of a multitude of knaves, I do not think that the problem is entirely hopeless, even in Mr. Carlyle's terms. I picture it to myself in this way: Suppose that you were one of a multitude made up, as we often see multitudes made up now, a multitude seated around a great amphitheatre in the midst of which is an open space upon which a great game was to be played,—let us say a football game,—and suppose that two men not in football suits, not expected to do the rough and tumble work of the game, were to emerge upon the open space, and there in your presence were presently to come to blows. You would instantly condemn them, and the interesting part of it is that probably one of them said an intolerable thing to the other, and that if you or I (I am now referring to the gentlemen in the room) had been in the same position, the same result would have followed. The remark would have been resented by a blow, the blow would have been returned, and we should have done a thing which, done in that place, would have been more intolerable as an exhibition of manners than if done anywhere else. The point is that the men in that audience who condemned the action would probably have acted in the same way; but not being concerned, and therefore being in their right minds, they condemn the thing. Similarly, the hope of every nation with regard to each transaction is that most persons are with regard to that matter, disinterested; most persons are in possession of their calm judgment, and can pass judgment upon it though they may not be superior to the persons concerned. That is the way in which out of a multitude of knaves you can make an honest people. There are enough of them not to receive the heat of the temptation, or the heat of the passion. They stand off and judge those who are in danger of forgetting themselves.

That, therefore, is the task that is before us, not merely to resist temptation ourselves, but to judge and deal with those who yield to temptation. In an age full of temptation, full of concealments, full of coverts, the real trouble about the modern corporation is not that it is a body of conscienceless men, for generally it is not, but that it is so large a body of men that any one of them can run to cover; and that just because, in the language of an old law writer, corporations have neither bodies to be kicked or souls to be damned they are very difficult things to deal with. The only way you can deal with them is by singling out the individuals who have been guilty of the wrong things.

When we come to the civic problems that are before us, we are, as Americans, faced first of all by this singular difficulty, that all our governments, our national governments, our state governments, our city governments, were made in the Eighteenth Century. It does not make any difference whether the actual date of a particular state constitution is later, or not, it gets its theory and form from the Eighteenth Century. The Eighteenth Century was dominated by a particular theory, which was the theory of the universe that we get from Sir Isaac Newton; and every one of these modern governments was made upon Sir Isaac Newton's theory of the universe. It is a mechanical contrivance, the parts of which were balanced off against each other.

Have you never read the theory of the several parts of the Constitution of the United States? Have you never been told how admirable a circumstance it is that the House is balanced against the Senate, that the House and Senate are balanced against the President, that the President and Congress together are balanced against the courts, and the courts against them? You would suppose that in constructing a government we were seeking an equipoise, that we were seeking undisturbed and separate orbits for its several parts; that we dreamed of nothing like co-operation, nothing like union or a single will; that we supposed a contrivance containing as many wills as possible was the best contrivance upon which to model a government. We have been living under an impossible thing,—a Newtonian system of government. A government is not a mechanism, it is an organism; because it consists of us who are organisms. A government must act by some combined force which is the will of one person, or the will of many persons united; and what we are witnessing now and what we have witnessed under the last two presidents has been the transformation of our constitution from a Newtonian contrivance, into a Darwinian organism.

I was traveling in the train not long ago with a Senator of the United States who had not long been Senator, had not settled down to the disappointments of his life, and he said to me in an almost peevish tone, "I wish the Constitution had not given the President the right to send messages to Congress." And I said, "Why, what harm does it do you?" I said, "Suppose it had not given the President the right to send messages to Congress, you cannot imagine it forbidding him to make speeches to the people of the United States." "Now, the difficulty about these messages," I said, "is not that they are sent to you, but that they are published throughout the country, and if the country happens to agree with the message and not with you, I admit it is extremely awkward, and I admit also that you are at a very considerable disadvantage, because all the country hears the message of the President, and only a very small part of the country cares to hear your reply. There is not another national office in this country except the office of President of the United States. Whatever he says is printed everywhere. Now, it unfortunately happens there is not one gentleman in the United States Senate whose remarks are printed everywhere in the United States, and, therefore, there is no man in the Senate whose voice can compete with the voice of the President. If the country agrees with the President, therefore, the President has you on the run. It is not that it is a message to you, it is an address to the country, and you cannot conceive of a constitution in which the President would be forbidden to address the country."

This leadership of one leading person is the Darwinian process. It is the process by which the various organs of a government are being made either to assent or to dissent to some leading series of proposals. There is no government anywhere which can be successfully conducted amidst difficult circumstances on any other plan; and therefore, we might as well get accustomed to it now as later, for we shall be obliged to grow accustomed to it some time.

Suppose you constructed any other organism on the Newtonian principle. Suppose my lungs were set off against my liver. I should not care to be an organism at all under the circumstances. Unless there is instant harmony, unless there is constant co-operation among the organs of my body, I would rather be dissolved than not; and there must reign over this organism the domination of a single will. If there were a couple of wills in my head, there would be some disaster in my personal career, as there are disasters in personal careers when there are a couple of wills in the household because you cannot steer by two north stars, you must steer by one.

Our present political process, therefore, is a process of reduction from a mechanical to an organic theory, and it is just as inevitable as the law of nature. Government is a living thing, and not a mechanical contrivance. And yet you will notice that we build not only our state government upon that plan, but conduct our city government upon the same plan. We talk about the 'legislative' part of the city government, and the 'executive' part, and the 'judicial' part, and we separate them so carefully that one would suppose there was something immoral in their communicating with one another.

There is a great moral significance in respect of the situation of our Federal Government in the mere length of Pennsylvania Avenue. The White House is set as far as it can conveniently be set away from the Houses of Congress; and the theory of that is that it isn't exactly moral for the President to come to understandings with the Houses. Well, if it is not moral, then we must move them nearer nevertheless and have a successful immoral government, because that is the only way in which it can be conducted. And we must particularly get rid of this idea that the several parts of government must be shy of each other when it comes down to the intimate administrative business which is characteristic of a modern city.

You know we have heard a great deal recently about the government of the country by the people of the country, and I must say that it seems to me we have been talking a great deal of nonsense. A government can be democratic only in the sense that it is a government restrained, controlled by public opinion. It can never be a government conducted by public opinion. What I mean to say is this: That popular initiative is an inconceivable thing. Not only is popular initiative an inconceivable thing, but the initiative of a body of persons no more numerous than this audience is an inconceivable thing. Suppose this company seated here wanted to do something. Can anybody in the room now guess what all the rest of you want to do about anything? The first thing that you would have to do would be to appoint a committee and preferably a small committee. That committee would retire and bring in certain resolutions. Now are those resolutions brought in upon your initiative? No; a committee went out upon your initiative, but the resolutions do not come in on your initiative; they come in on the initiative of, I should shrewdly guess, not even of that committee, but of some single member of it;—for I have belonged to a good many committees and have never known the initiative of more than one member to be effective. When you began to debate these resolutions, you would be debating the resolutions of a single individual. Your judgment of the resolutions may be a common judgment after there has been sufficient debate to bring you to a common opinion, but there has been no common initiative. There has been the initiative of a single person, or a very small group of persons, and there never can be anything else.

I remember saying this in the presence of a gentleman who had been prominent during one of the spasmodic reforms of the city government of New York, a good many years ago, and he said, "Do you mean to say that the people did not take the initiative in the recent reform in New York City?"

I said, "What did the people do in the recent reforms in New York City?"

"Why," he said, "a committee of one hundred was appointed after the Lexow investigation,[1] and reported upon the abuses which had been discovered."

"Yes," I said, "I know; but what did the people do?"

[1] An investigation into police corruption in New York City in 1893-94 by a special committee of the New York State Senate headed by Clarence Lexow. The revelations of this investigation led to the election of the reform Mayor William Lafayette Strong in 1894 and the temporary eclipse of Tammany Hall.

He said, "Why, the people perceived the necessity of reform."

I said, "Was that initiative? You uncovered unsavory things, and they smelled a smell. Is it taking the initiative to smell a smell? All noses can perceive the same odor, but I don't see any initiative in that."

And yet the illustration illustrates. There can be no common movement which does not centre upon the proposal of a small number of persons. You never knew of any instance in which that was not true. Let us never dream, therefore, that any body of people can govern upon their own initiative; they can do nothing of the kind. They can ask somebody to govern them, they can criticise that person when he has attempted the task, but they cannot govern, they cannot originate measures, they cannot originate even amendments to measures. All of that must be done by a small number of persons.

And, if you want the real free judgment of opinion which is genuinely democratic, how are you going to get it? There is only one channel; the channel of knowledge. The only way in which to have a common knowledge is to have a common information with regard to what is going on: to have that information absolutely candid; to have it abundantly full, so that there will be no debate as to the facts after the people know the circumstances, and then let opinion form as it will. But that is a process of judgment, it is a process of restraint; it is a process of ascertaining whether the people think the persons with power have exercised that power in a public spirited way, or have not, and that is all that democratic government can ever accomplish. Every time anybody in this country thinks that the people are not taking part enough in the government, he suggests the necessity of something else the people ought to be asked to do in addition to what they are doing now, or rather in addition to what they are trying to do now,—which is only a process of confusion.

I met a young member of the New Jersey legislature a few months ago, and fell into conversation with him in regard to a commission the desirability of which the legislature was debating; and I said,

"How, are the members of the Commission to be given their places? By appointment?"

"No," he said, "we thought that it should be left to the people."

"Oh," I said, "what do you mean? That they ought to be elected?"

"Yes."

"Well," I said, "you were elected, were you not?"

"Yes."

"Were you elected by the people?"

He colored a little bit and said, "Professor, I see you know something about politics."

"Well," I said, "its my business to know something about politics. I would be ashamed if I did not. Let us get down to business," I said, "I can name the gentleman who elected you; his name is known to everybody in this State; he lives in .... County, it is not necessary that I should mention him. You were elected by him, not by the people of your district."

"Well," he said, "you can put it that way if you choose."

I said, "Isn't that true? I am not choosing to put it that way; I wish it were not; but isn't that true?"

"Well," he said, "Yes; just between us, it is."

I said, "It is interesting to know why that is true. You were elected on a ticket that contained, I will say at a guess, one hundred and twenty-five names. Now there is no community in this country that can select for itself one hundred and twenty-five persons to be voted for. It is too elaborate a job; it cannot be done in that way. It can select three or four persons, but outside that number I doubt if it can select any."

You have given the people of this country so many persons to select for office that they have not time to select them, and have to leave it to professionals, that is to say, the professional politicians; which, reduced to its simplest term, is the boss of the district. When you vote the Republican or Democratic ticket you either vote for the names selected by one machine or the names selected by the other machine. This is not to lay any aspersion upon those who receive the nominations. I for one do not subscribe to the opinion that the bosses under our government deserve our scorn and contempt, for we have organized a system of government which makes them just as necessary as the President of the United States. They are the natural, inevitable fruit of the tree, and if we do not like them we have got to plant another tree. The boss is just as legitimate as any member of any legislature, because by giving the people a task which they cannot perform, you have taken it away from them, and have made it necessary that those who can perform it should perform it.

You say that your legislatures do not represent you,—and sometimes, I dare say, they do not, though I think they are generally just as good as you deserve,—and, therefore, you say, let us directly vote upon the measures which they vote upon. Do you not see that this is simply adding another piece of machinery, which, after you cease to be interested in it, is going to be used by the same set of persons for the same objects? If you do not see it, you will see it after you have tried it awhile.

The direct primary was introduced in a city which I could name, greatly against the opposition of the local bosses, and it had not been operating two years before the bosses said,

"Why, good gracious, we don't see how we got along without this!"

That does not proceed from the professor's chair; that is what the bosses said. I leave it to you to explain it; I am not here to explain it—that was the feeling of the bosses. They did not see how they had got along without it.

Elaborate your government; place every officer upon his own dear little statute; make it necessary for him to be voted for, and you will not have a democratic government.

Just so certainly as you segregate all these little offices and put every man upon his own statutory pedestal and have a miscellaneous organ of government too miscellaneous for a busy people either to put together or to watch, public aversion will have no effect on it; and public opinion finding itself ineffectual, will get discouraged, as it does in this country, by finding its assaults like assaults against battlements of air, where they find no one to resist them, where they capture no positions, where they accomplish nothing. You have a grand housecleaning, you have a grand overturning, and the next morning you find the government going on just as it did before you had the overturning.

What is the moral? This is the moral, which I have presented very often to college classes; and this is the first time I ever presented it to a body of my fellow citizens, outside college halls; because when you think how many fellow citizens I have, the task is discouraging. The remedy is contained in one word, *Simplification*. Simplify your processes, and you will begin to control; complicate them, and you will get farther and farther away from their control.

Simplification! Simplification! Simplification! is the task that awaits us: to reduce the number of persons voted for to the absolute workable minimum,—knowing whom you have selected; knowing whom you have trusted, and having so few persons to watch that you can watch them. That is the way we are going to get popular control back in this country, and that is the only way we are going to get political control back. Put in other elected officers to watch those that you have already elected, and you will merely remove your control one step further away.

Let me take an example. There are a great many persons in

this country who are beginning to perceive this in regard to city government, but we are in danger, I think, of going a little too far and a little too fast. Government is a very complicated thing, ladies and gentlemen. If you supposed that one man can wisely be made responsible for the affairs of a great city, you are very much mistaken. Those affairs are too various and complicated. If you suppose that a very small body of men, five or six, can fairly be made responsible for so complicated a body of business, I think you are mistaken. But, leaving that aside for the moment, I want to call your attention to this significant fact, that the best governed cities in the world are on the other side of the water. I am now comparing our government with those of cities of nations in a like class with ourselves of political development and civilization; and, confining myself to that field of comparison, it is true to say that the best governed cities are on that side of the water, and most of the worst governed cities are on this side of the water,—and that the American people have a political genius superior to that of any other people in the world!

It cannot be an accident that the government of Berlin and the government of Glasgow are substantially alike in principle and organization. It cannot be an accident that excellent and truly successful city governments have substantially the same organization, no matter where you find them. And the significant feature of their organization is this,—that no voter, roughly speaking, in any one of those cities, ever has an opportunity to vote for more than one or two persons in that government.

Take the government of an English or Scottish city, for example. They have a city council elected, not at large, but by wards, exactly as we elect them, and each voter has an opportunity to vote for one person, the representative of his ward. These various representatives in council assembled, elect a mayor. The citizen is not troubled with that, for the mayor is merely the chairman of the council, with the powers of a justice of the peace added. The council divides itself into committees on the various branches of the city government, and all the appointments of the city government emanate from these committees. Every action that is taken in council is printed the next morning in the papers, with all the names of those who voted Aye and all the names of those who voted No, so that from session to session every voter in the city can see how his representative voted on every question. There is no possibility of shifting a personal, individual responsibility.

You remember one of the most famous cartoons drawn by Thomas Nast in the old days of the Tweed Ring of New York.

He represented the various members of that ring as standing in a circle. Each man had his thumb towards his neighbor, and each man said, " 'twarn't me," and the " 'twarn't me" went all the way around the circle. Now, we have devised a " 'twarn't me" system of government, to escape from which we must substitute a system of government in which it will be impossible for any man to shift the responsibility; where we will know exactly what he did, when he did it; and be able to check any statement he may make by our knowledge, as if we had been present.

If you had, in any one ward, to select only one person, do you suppose you would need a political machine to make out your ticket? If you had to elect only one person in any one ward, do you suppose it would take much trouble to know who that person was, and what his character was?

In the little borough of Princeton, where I live, I vote a ticket of some thirty names, I suppose. I never counted them, but there must be quite that number. Now, I am a slightly busy person, and I never have known anything about half the men I was voting for on the tickets that I voted. I attend diligently, so far as I have light, to my political duties in the borough of Princeton,—and yet I have no personal knowledge of one-half of the persons I am voting for. I couldn't tell you even what business they are engaged in,—and to say in such circumstances that I am taking part in the government of the borough of Princeton is an absurdity. I am not taking a part in it at all. I am going through the motions that I am expected to go through by the persons who think that attending primaries and voting at the polls is performing your whole political duty. It is doing a respectable thing that I am not ashamed of, but it is not performing any political duty that is of any consequence. I don't count for any more in the government of the borough of Princeton than the veriest loafer and drunkard in the borough, and I do not know very much more about the men I am voting for than he does. He is busy about one thing, and I am busy about others. We are preoccupied, and cannot attend to the government of the town.

That is what I mean by talking of simplification. But I am afraid that we are carrying simplification too far. For example, take the Des Moines and the Galveston plans of city government.[2] If you reduce the number of persons who are to have the

[2] Wilson referred here to the two most widely known and copied versions of the commission form of city government. Galveston was the first city in the United States to adopt the commission form, doing so in 1901 following a disastrous hurricane and tidal wave the previous year. Under the Galveston plan, a board of five commissioners was chosen by the voters of the city at large. These commissioners exercised the full legislative and administrative power of the

full responsibility for conducting the affairs of the municipality to four or five, I doubt if four or five men can thoroughly enough inform themselves with regard to the various things that it is necessary to do through the instrumentality of a modern city government. For you must remember how much we are multiplying our city government's tasks and how impossible it is for a small number of persons really to inform themselves thoroughly with regard to them. I doubt also whether it is wise to have these persons elected on a general vote,—that is to say, to have all your candidates at large, not for particular portions or sections of the city; because, in some of our cities there are sections in which there is nothing that can properly be called public spirit which can by combination outvote those sections of the city which can fairly be called public spirited and intelligent. You involve yourselves again in the dangers of a long ticket made up by bargain and conference. By polling the vote as a whole you sometimes secure the domination of the least desired portion of it. It is one of the most significant and discreditable facts of our balloting that the persons we least like to see vote are the ones that always vote, and those we most desire to have vote are the persons who most often refrain from voting. Most of the handsome lessons that I have heard read from lecture platforms about municipal government, have, I have afterwards gathered, been delivered by persons who did not vote at the last municipal election where they lived. It is a very easy question to approach from the outside, but it is a very embarrassing one to approach from the inside.

There are many things to be debated with regard to the detail of distribution, or detail of number; but there is one thing that is not debatable, and that is the necessity for utter simplification. My prediction is that just so soon as you give every voter only one man to vote for, so soon will difficulties in respect to government by the people disappear,—and that not until then will they disappear. Give voters five men to vote for, and it is five times

---

city and appointed all subordinate city officials. One of the commissioners was designated as mayor and had general supervision of city business as a whole, but no veto over legislation, while each of the other commissioners was the head of one of the four major departments of the city government. The Des Moines plan, adopted in 1907 and put into operation in 1908, was similar in form to that of Galveston but in addition included provisions for the popular initiative of legislation, the referendum to the voters of ordinances passed by the commission, the popular recall of members of the commission, nonpartisan primaries and elections of the commissioners, and a separate civil service commission. For an historical and comparative study of all city commission governments created up to the middle of 1911, see Ernest S. Bradford, *Commission Government in American Cities* (New York, 1911).

less likely that they will do it intelligently and independently than if you give them one man to vote for.

I was trying the other day to count up how many persons a qualified voter in Great Britain can vote for, for any office, and I believe I am correct when I say that there are only two, a member of Parliament, and a member of the County Council, or City Council, as the case may be. Now, if there were only two persons I ever voted for, I should know more about politics than I do now, and I should never meet a political boss anywhere. There would not be enough for him to do; his business would disappear. I can attend to choosing two persons, but when it comes to choosing twenty-five, I must have experienced assistance.

There is another matter that concerns this whole thing very nearly. Are you going to have representative government, or are you not going to have representative government? With this newly favored method of 'recall' exemplified in the Des Moines plan, and the newly popular devices of initiative and referendum, which will work at all only while they are novel and the interest in their use fresh,–and I am afraid that will not be very long,–it will make mere agents of those whom you trust with your city government, and not representatives. I, for my part, would be willing to be a representative of the people, but I would not be willing to be an agent. I will tell you why I would not be willing to be an agent; that kind of principalship on the part of the people is not based upon an inside knowledge of business. Do you suppose anybody would consent to be a director of an important business corporation if the stockholders could insist upon voting upon any questions that they chose to demand to vote upon, or if the stockholders could withdraw the director at any time they chose to withdraw him? Certainly not, and for this reason: if I am a member of a board of directors, I know a great deal more about the business than anybody outside of that board can know. I have never gone into a committee, I have never gone into an assembly where something was to be debated, from which I did not come out realizing two things: first, that I knew a great deal more about the business than when I went in; and, second, that my own judgment had been materially modified by what the other men had said. There is no sound piece of business that is not based upon the debate of men, all of whom are concerned; and you cannot carry that debate outside the body. Why? Well, for one thing, because the body generally consists of persons representing various political opinions. The newspapers read outside by any one person represent only one political opinion. The voters,–I say this with regard to intelligent voters, as well as the others,–seldom hear more than one side, and the men in the body necessarily hear both sides, and all sides.

If you insist upon having agents, you will have agents. If you want to have representatives, you can get representatives; and representatives will give you better government than agents can possibly give you, as they will try to conduct the business as their own judgment dictates after conference. Moreover, they have time in which to try the thing out and determine whether it is wise or unwise. One of the things of which I grow weary as I grow older is theory, and sentimental theory above all other sorts. When I hear gentlemen say that you must allow the people to have a voice in affairs, I am not in the least interested. I am only interested to hear an answer to this question: How are you going to put your government in the hands of the people? Concrete methods are the only things worth debating.

We are here to discuss ways and means of getting the government in the hands of the people to which it belongs. You know that at present government in the United States is not in the hands of the people. You can go in one direction or the other. You can multiply machinery or simplify it. You have been creating machinery for the past century, and you have been getting farther and farther away from the people. Is it not worth trying to see if human nature is not the same in the United States as it is in Germany and Scotland? Is it not worth trying to see whether successful popular government is not as good and as practicable in the United States as it is in any foreign country?

I am for the real rights and not the rhetorical rights of the people. I am for those things which are really and practically in the interest of self-government; and I say that the interests of self government are served by nothing except by reducing the number of elective officers to the absolute minimum of efficiency.

And there is another thing that is imperative in my mind. It is publicity at every step, so that we shall know what these officials are doing. One of the things that seems most wasteful is the number of governmental reports sent out that nobody reads. We have just had a monetary commission traveling all over Europe discovering things that we could have found in books that could have been furnished by the faculty of any university.[3] I

[3] The Aldrich-Vreeland Act of 1908, designed to provide a supply of emergency currency for the United States, also established a National Monetary Commission to study the continuing problem of the nation's banking and currency systems. Headed by Senator Nelson Wilmarth Aldrich of Rhode Island and made up of members of both houses of Congress, the commission conducted sporadic investigations from 1908 to 1912, sponsored the writing of monographs on many phases of the banking problem, and presented its final report and recommendations to Congress in 1912. Wilson here referred specifically to a trip to the

don't mean to object to their taking the trip, and I don't mind their getting their minds broadened by contact with public men in other parts of the world, but what I do object to is that they should publish the results of their findings in many ponderous volumes. Nobody, not even the members of Congress, will ever read their report, and nobody but the commission itself will ever be the wiser for their trip.

I attended a meeting of the National Bankers' Association last autumn,[4] and they were preparing to have all sorts of interesting reports made. I plead with them not to do this in similar fashion. I said, "Be kind enough to have somebody at least digest the reports and set forth the results in a way that an ordinary man can understand." I have never met a banker yet who could explain banking to me in terms that I could understand. I asked what trading on a margin was, and I don't know yet. I suppose if I were to try it once, I would know. I never had the money or the intelligence to understand it without trying it. If information were made intelligible and accessible, then in the course of time people would become really informed. I know hundreds of persons who, if they were allowed to do so, could reduce this lot of information to brief readable pamphlets which everybody could understand. That is the way in which to get information in the hands, and not only into the hands, but also into the heads of the people.

You know that every time a difficult question arises in this country, we have to have what we call a campaign of education, and the education has to be given in the briefest, simplest language. The man who is valuable at such a time is the man who knows how to reach people of every sort and kind, and the most unserviceable persons are the persons who really know the most, but have peculiarities, and want to tell you about it continually. The essential part is an outline of the main details.

There is another matter, and that is the salary paid our public officials. We pay them such absurdly small salaries that it is not worth a capable man's while to leave his business and accept office. On such terms you cannot get the kind of government you want.

There is another disappointment for which you must prepare yourselves. I was saying to a body of college men the other day

---

financial centers of Europe made by Aldrich and several members of and advisers to the commission in late 1908, during which extensive interviews were conducted with many banking officials.

[4] When he spoke to the American Bankers' Association on September 30, 1908. The text of his address is printed at that date in Vol. 18.

that, as I understood it, the task of the college teacher is to make the young gentleman sent them as unlike their fathers as possible; for by the time a man is old enough to have a son in college he has become established and absorbed in a particular business, and his sympathies are largely confined to that business. The object of a college is to regeneralize each generation. We should put our youngsters at as many different points of view as possible, and let them know what other men are doing who are out of the circle of their ordinary acquaintance. We have this interesting reason for this. Every successful business man, while he may not be guilty of accepting money for anything, has already been bribed. Society as it stands has allowed him to have some of its prizes. Therefore, he stands bound to keep society as it stands. The circumstances of his success would be altered by change and his success might disappear. Never allow successful men in the same kind of business to combine in any large affair. Always try to mix interests, because if you do not, you will have a body of gentlemen who are obliged beforehand to reach a particular conclusion.

I am simply stating what every man knows to be a fact; for whenever I have stated this to an audience, the men have looked very solemn. There is a famous story told of old Mr. Pettigru of South Carolina, that having lost a certain case on one occasion, his client called him out of the Court and called him all sorts of names, a liar, a thief, and so on; but Mr. Pettigru did not pay the least attention to him until he called him a Federalist. Then he knocked him down. Someone said to him,

"Why did you knock him down for that; it was the least offensive thing he said?"

"Yes," he replied, "but that was the only true thing he said,"

I noticed a great many solemn faces just now. Every man knows it in his own conscience. He does not want society to be changed so as to disturb him. But society needs change. There isn't any arrangement which you can leave alone. Everything you do needs watching in order to keep it up. Everything you arrange will run down if you do not keep it wound up. The tendency of everything is to deteriorate. Therefore it is constant change that is going to keep things alive.

You cannot expect everybody to be a happy person, but you should desire them to be conscientious persons. Constantly knowing his tendency to run down, every man winces under the efforts of the public to wind him up. All of this renewal and correction is an extremely expensive process, expensive in motive power, expensive in time, expensive in the true conceptions, which, if we undertake to make the government even tolerably good, we must possess. Civic reform is not a matter of enthusiasm for the people; it is a very practical matter of giving the government to the people. It is a matter of concrete and difficult business to be arranged on business principles.

We have come to days full of perplexities. Like older countries, we must now do away with ornate ideas in government which cannot be realized, and devote ourselves to the practical problems which are constantly arising. I believe we are on the eve of one of the most practical eras in the history of American politics. I believe this great awakening which we have experienced in the past eight or ten years is an awakening which will lead us all to a hopeful success. I think that nothing is more inspiring than the hope which makes practicable business, nothing more futile than the hope which is carried on the wings of mere ecstacy. Let us come soberly down now to the direct issue, whether we shall or shall not bind ourselves to make this in true practical fashion a government of the people.[5]

Printed in *Civic Problems: Address delivered March 9, 1909, at the Annual Meeting of the Civic League of St. Louis by Woodrow Wilson . . .* (St. Louis, n. d.).

[5] There is a WWhw outline of this address, dated March 7, 1909, in WP, DLC.

A News Item About a Speech to the Virginia Society of St. Louis

[March 11, 1909]

FINES LEAD TOWARD SOCIALISM

President of Princeton Criticises
Corporation Law.

A national socialism will be the outcome of that treatment which fines corporations guilty of law breaking but does [not] punish the individual who really is responsible, declared Dr. Woodrow Wilson, President of Princeton University, in an address to the Virginia Society of St. Louis Wednesday evening [March 10] at the University Club.

Henry T. Kent, president of the Virginia Society, introduced Dr. Wilson and the other speakers, Dr. A. Ross Hill, president of the University of Missouri, and the Rev. Dr. Samuel J. Niccolls, pastor of the Second Presbyterian Church.

Printed in the *St. Louis Post-Dispatch*, March 11, 1909.

A News Report of an Address in Philadelphia to the University Extension Society

[March 13, 1909]

UNIVERSITY'S PART IN POLITICAL LIFE

Woodrow Wilson, president of Princeton University, speaking before the University Extension Society in Witherspoon Hall yesterday on public life in this country and the part the university should play in it, said that he thought the country would be better governed if audiences would leave when the speakers to whom they were listening failed to be specific. He was referring to political speakers. He had heard many speeches himself; a large number of them had been composed of generalities belonging to all men equally.

Then he proceeded to some specifications of his own, as follows:

The relation of those who occupy public office to the people is very remote. The access of the people to the rulers of the country is only atmospheric. We are in an age when we are allowing ourselves to be fooled.

The nation was born unhappily with relation to the philosophy which prevailed at our birth. The Newtonian philosophy, which would reduce all things to one principle, prevailed. Life has always been so complex as to defy such reduction and is particularly so in the United States today.

We are not a democratic country. We should not abuse the political boss. We have made him necessary by our form of government, and he will continue until the machinery of elections is made simpler than it is today.

The part of the university in this condition should be to keep alive through its attitude toward the undergraduates being trained for life generally and not for specialized employment, the university ideal. Through them the subjective, scientific habit of mind should be grafted upon the more complex, objective habits of thought of the political life of the country. No man should be excused for lack of knowledge of public questions. Out of keen, intelligent observation, combining scientific thought with knowledge of life as it is outside the university's quiet halls, should emerge a situation in which it should become so uncomfortable to be untrue to a public trust that the practice would cease to be fashionable.

Doctor Wilson hoped to see the day when both the House of Representatives and the Senate would talk about things instead of accomplishing their work through the subterranean channels of their committees. The public might then be permitted to assist at the "general assize" of a subject. The country would then be able to weigh the men who come out into the open. It would reject those who remained in the background.

"A Senator complained rather peevishly to me some time ago," said Doctor Wilson, "of the injustice which had been done Congress when the President had been given the right to address it with messages. I replied that I thought it was fortunate that it had been so. The President's messages are given to the newspapers and through them he speaks to the people. Few members of Congress speak in such a manner that their words are read so widely.

"It is [not] an ideal situation in which Speaker [Joseph Gurney] Cannon suspects everything the President does and the President rejects everything Mr. Cannon does, while the Supreme Court stands between them. I think it desirable to have a President who can express himself forcibly. The President understands the foreign relations of the country as few others do. He is in a position to possess such knowledge of its domestic condition as few may possess."

Doctor Wilson believed that we had emerged from the era of "regulation." We had been making experiments and the men who know most had not been advising us. Lawyers had been "standing pat" with the corporations by which they had been employed, saying that they would take advantage of every opportunity the law afforded to withstand the tendency. It had become the duty of every corporation lawyer to advise the corporation by which he was employed to correct the abuses which had caused the criticism of them.

Time was when public life had been easy. It had ceased to be easy. America had become a world power. It must cease to be provincial if it would grow, keep abreast of the times.

"The purpose of a university should be to make a son as unlike his father as possible," he said. "By the time a man has grown old enough to have a son in college he has specialized. The university should generalize in its treatment of its undergraduates, should struggle to put them in touch with every force of life. Every man of established success is dangerous to society. His tendency is to keep society as it is. His success has been founded upon it. You will not find many reformers among the successful men. A man told me once that he left college interested in humanity. At 40 he was interested only in an industry to which he had applied himself. At 60 he was interested only in his bank account. Any social change affects that bank account. Society cannot progress without change."

The relation of the university to life was the relation of the conception to the act, he said; the relation of the vision to that slow, toiling process by which an end was accomplished. University extension societies should extend the influence of the university to the general public.[1]

Printed in the Philadelphia *Public Ledger*, March 13, 1909; some editorial headings omitted.

[1] There is an undated WWhw outline of this address entitled, "Academic Ideals and Public Service," in WP, DLC.

To Walter Mead Rankin[1]

My dear Mr. Rankin, Princeton, N. J. 16 March, 1909

Mrs. Wilson is confined to her room with a serious cold, but I had promised myself the pleasure of calling this afternoon on your father,[2] as you so kindly suggested, until a few minutes ago when the imperative necessity of making another engagement for this afternoon presented itself. I am *very* sorry. Please present my warmest regards to your father, with assurances of my high respect and admiration, and say to him that I hope many more years will be added to his honoured life.

With much regard

Sincerely Yours, Woodrow Wilson

ALS (photostat in WP, DLC).

[1] Professor of Biology at Princeton.

[2] William Rankin, who reached his centennial on March 16.

From Cleveland Hoadley Dodge

Dear Woodrow [New York] March 16th 1909

I have had a very interesting day & a successful one as far as I could go. Mr. C[arnegie]. had a cold & couldn't play golf under orders of Dr. [Jasper Jewett] Garmany ('79) but Mr. [Richard Watson] Gilder was of the party & played a round with me & then took a kindly nap leaving me with the laird for half an hour & I had on the whole a satisfactory talk with him about Princeton & your plans for social reorganization. It was so long ago—considering the number of other matters that have filled his mind—since you saw him[1] that I had to refresh his mind a little regarding your plans but he showed considerable interest & remembered very well his objections regarding the feelings of the Trustees & alumni. I feel sure that what I said *thoroly* convinced him that all who had the best interests of Princeton at heart would welcome your scheme if it could be carried out on the lines you propose—so that obstacle is out of the way, & I think the time is ripe for a new & vigorous approach by Pritchett & Vanderlip.

He is full of his Anglo American alliance plans but nothing came out in the conversation which indicated that he was thinking of any new scheme involving money,

I am a little afraid of Murray Butler. He A.C. asked what he N.M thought of it & had a vague idea that Butler did not approve of your quad scheme. Butler is South now & it might be well for you to lose as little time as possible. I am already late for dinner up town & can't write more but before you see P. or V. it might be well for me to see you & tell you a little more of our conversation

I think the affair is hopeful if Pritchett really means business

I trust that I have done my share & if I have made any impression it should not be allowed to cool.

Bayard Henry & his wife[2] spend Thursday night with us but I should love to have you come here tomorrow or Wednesday to dine & sleep or if you want I can see you any time or place morning or evening up or down town

Don't be too sanguine but let the good work go on.

Yrs affly & sympathetically C H Dodge

ALS (WP, DLC).

[1] When Wilson visited Carnegie at Skibo Castle in Scotland, August 12-15, 1908.

[2] Jane Irwin Robeson Henry.

A News Report about Wilson's Speeches in St. Louis

[March 17, 1909]

President Wilson in Saint Louis

During his visit to St. Louis last week, President Wilson '79 made three addresses, one before the Civic League, one at Washington University, and the third before the Virginia Society.

The address before the Civic League was heard by over five hundred men and women, in attendance on the annual banquet of the League, at the Hotel Jefferson, March 9th. . . .

On the following morning, March 10, President Wilson visited Washington University, where he addressed the students and members of the faculty, setting forth his conception of the purposes of a college education and his ideas of what student life in a university should be. He spoke for about twenty minutes, and was frequently interrupted by enthusiastic applause.

That evening Dr. Wilson was the guest at the annual dinner of the Virginia Society of St. Louis. At this meeting he spoke particularly of the unbroken political traditions of the South, because of the derivation of its white population from the original settlers.

Printed in the *Princeton Alumni Weekly*, IX (March 17, 1909), 359-60.

After-Dinner Remarks in New York to the Friendly Sons of St. Patrick[1]

[[March 17, 1909]]

MR. PRESIDENT,[2] YOUR GRACE,[3] SONS OF ST. PATRICK, WHO PROVE YOURSELVES *MOST* FRIENDLY:

I hesitate to follow Chauncey Depew, because I am a Democrat, and I particularly hate to follow him so late at night. There is no telling where he might lead. [*Laughter*]

I have found melting away in me as I sat here to-night the slight feeling of irritation against the Irishmen of New York which I felt mounting in my bosom this afternoon as I spent an hour and a half trying to cross Fifth Avenue. I had to go into the next county to cross it, and I then realized more than I ever had before how difficult it is to circumvent an Irishman. [*Applause*] I have had misgivings about the Irish race of late. Not many years ago, upon the 17th of March, certain members of the senior class in Princeton University, not finding the day suitable for addiction to their books, put their heads together to find out what would be the most amusing way to spend the day, and concluded that they would organize a St. Patrick's Day parade. The juniors, finding that this left them a little in the cold, determined to organize an Orangeman's parade, and then there was a preconcerted and most interesting meeting between the processions. [*Laughter*] Somebody took this seriously and wrote it up for the newspapers, and I got a fierce letter from an Irish gentleman

1 At the one hundred and twenty-fifth anniversary dinner of the Society of the Friendly Sons of St. Patrick in the City of New York, held at Delmonico's Restaurant. The other speakers were William Temple Emmet, president of the society and lawyer of New York; Most Rev. John Joseph Glennon, Archbishop of St. Louis; Chauncey Mitchell Depew, United States Senator from New York; Edward Richard O'Malley, Attorney General of the State of New York; and Thomas Francis Grady, state senator of New York.

2 William Temple Emmet.

3 There were two archbishops of the Roman Catholic Church in attendance at the dinner: Archbishop Glennon of St. Louis, mentioned in note 1 above, and Most Rev. John Murphy Farley, Archbishop of New York.

saying that it was outrageous that a great university should permit the Irish race thus to be insulted. I replied to him that there was only one cause of misgiving in my mind from his letter, and that was the fear that the Irish were losing their sense of humor. [*Laughter*] I did not suppose that any Irish fellow-countryman of mine could so mistake the spirit of college students.

I myself am happy to believe that there runs in my veins a very considerable strain of Irish blood. I can't prove it from documents, but I have internal evidence. [*Laughter*] There is something delightful in me that every now and then takes the strain off my Scotch conscience and affords me periods of most enjoyable irresponsibility [*Laughter*] when I do not care whether school keeps or not, or whether anybody gets educated or not. [*Laughter*] Certain I am that the gentleman who was my beloved father and the gentlemen who were his six brothers could not have come from the North of Ireland with their temperament if they were pure Scotch-Irish. They did not resemble the other Scotch-Irish that I have known except in their belligerency.

It is the belligerency of the Scotch-Irish character that is rendering me more and more unsuitable, as I grow older, to be an after-dinner speaker. You have to have a very light heart to be an after-dinner speaker, and a very easy conscience. [*Laughter*] You have to be able to say something and yet say it as if it were nothing at all; and I find myself, as I grow older, instead of growing cooler, growing hotter, taking the world more and more seriously, feeling more and more as if it were my particular function to straighten it out. As a man finds that mood grow upon him, he becomes very unsuitable for the light touch of after-dinner speaking.

And yet I suppose there is a very valuable asset in the belligerency of the Scotch-Irish character and that it does lend an element of freedom to speaking, whether it be after dinner or at any other time; for the Scotch-Irishman does not care a peppercorn whether you agree with him or not; having you there and trusting to your manners, he expects to keep you there until he has had his say.

And there is a great deal that excites belligerency in our day. It isn't a matter of race. I have never objected to the race, to the blood, of other men. I have objected to their opinions. [*Laughter*] All that I require of a man is, not that he should be of the same blood as myself, but that he should hold the same sound and sensible views. [*Laughter*] If he holds the same sound and sensible views I am perfectly willing to regard the documents as authentic which show him to be an American citizen.

It is true, as your President has said this evening, that the prejudice, which never went very deep, I take it, in this country, against Irishmen has long since passed away. If it were not for the Irish we should be very short of governing material [*Laughter*] and we should be very short of those persons who are willing to do the work whether it is necessary or not. [*Laughter*] I reminded myself last summer of the position of an Irishman I heard about. I started out on a bicycle tour from Glasgow, in Scotland, on a day which, I learned the next day from the newspapers, was the hottest day there had been in Scotland for thirty years. I worked all day long, in Mark Twain's phrase, "sweating like an ice-pitcher," wondering why in the world I was working so hard when I didn't have to, and recalling the story of the Irishman who was working without his hat in the broiling sun in the streets and to whom the boss of the gang said, "Pat, don't you know it will ruin your brains if you work on a day like this without your hat?" and Pat said, "Be jabbers, do you think I would be working a day like this if I had any brains?" [*Laughter*] I thought the story very pertinent to my own performance. I doubted very much if I would have been working a day like that if I had any brains.

But there is something in the Scotch and in the Irish that is in me which tempts me to work on off days when it is not necessary to work. It was not at all necessary, for example, that I should come here and do the work which you have imposed upon me to-night. But I take it that you must have had some rational reason for desiring me to be here. I suppose that it was not out of idle curiosity to see a specimen of that large class of gentlemen, growing larger every year, who are expected to go about and make public speeches and have nominally something to do with the administration of universities. [*Laughter*] The class of college presidents is a class of gentlemen expected to disseminate opinions which they are not required to put into practice and which therefore are for the general entertainment if not for the leadership of their fellow-citizens. But I take it that you did not send for me because of that curiosity, because you have seen many college presidents—they are not hard to find—and they generally come in response to an invitation. The only explanation I could think of was that you had learned that I was one of those persons who are eminently uneasy if they are obliged to bottle up their views and not allowed occasionally to explode them.

And I have some views to expound to you to-night. I have been reflecting upon the whole question upon which Senator Depew touched, the blending of races in this country, and I have come to the conclusion that it is not necessary in a country like ours that you should blend in blood. The real blending in this country is an intellectual and a social blending. It is the process of living in the presence of each other's opinions that makes us all Americans. [*Applause*] It isn't that we intermarry. That is the more pleasing aspect of it. It is that very much more extended view of affairs which brings us into the presence of each other's opinions. And in proportion as the atmosphere of America is a conducting medium, just in that proportion are races blended. There is nothing else, so far as I can make out, that determines the blend. The reason that we wish all of our fellow-citizens to speak the English language is that we wish a medium for the communication of common views, and that we do not wish any man, no matter what his family connections and ramifications, to be shut off from that general impulse of common motive and of common principle which constitutes the unity of America. [*Applause*]

What disturbs me, gentlemen, with regard to the processes of this country, is not that races do not blend fast enough, is not that the processes of blood are not the normal processes which make a composite nation, but that there is not a quick and spontaneous enough process of the mingling of interests in this country. I wish to see, not the intermarriage of bloods—that will take care of itself—but the intermarriage of interests. What I am afraid of in a company of men even like this, dwelling in one city and associated in many common enterprises, is that each man will think upon his own interest and will not give a sufficient number of hours in the month to thinking about the common interest of the country. [*Applause*] When I see public policies meet upon the basis of mere give and take, I know that public policies will not be compounded of the general interest. Unless every man has not only the perception to see the common interest but the instinct to serve it he has not yet become a true citizen of America. [*Applause*]

We are in danger in this country of there being no sufficient intermingling of interests because there are not enough national processes. Did you never reflect upon the circumstance that we have no national newspaper? It falls to me to do a good deal of traveling in this country and to read a great many newspapers, and they are all alike in this respect, that their view is bounded by their locality and that every newspaper in this country, the metropolitan newspapers not excepted, is a provincial newspaper. [*Applause*] The difference between the newspaper of a great city and the newspaper of a country district is that the newspaper of a great city is more provincial than the newspaper of a country district, for the reason that in the city there is more local news than in the country, and the country newspaper, in order to fill its columns, prints more of the Associated Press despatches. The Associated Press is a national instrumentality. The local press is not a national instrumentality. I do not say this to the discredit of our great newspapers. It is a circumstance of our life and is the reflection of the larger circumstance that there are no common national interests which it is necessary that every newspaper should exploit in order to satisfy its readers.

There is only one national voice in this country, and that is the voice of the President of the United States. A Senator of the United States complained to me, in a tone that I thought was actually peevish, a couple of years ago, that the Constitution had given the President the right to send messages to Congress. [*Laughter*] I said: "Senator, I don't think that is your real difficulty. The trouble is not that the Constitution gives the President the right to send messages to Congress. The trouble is that the Constitution could not prevent the President from publishing his messages to the country. It would not do you any harm if the messages were merely sent to you. They are sent to everybody else, and if the country happens to agree with the President it doesn't stop to hear what you have to say." [*Applause*]

That is the real circumstance in this country. The President's views are printed everywhere by every paper, and there isn't a man in Congress in either house whose views are printed everywhere by every paper. The consequence is that the voice of the President is the only national voice in our affairs, because it is the only universally audible voice in our affairs. The President can sow his opinions broadcast. No man else can sow except in his own private field. If you want national processes, therefore, elect Presidents who will have national thoughts and national principles, and then you will see slowly taking head under the inevitable leadership of such men those impulses, those thoughts, those convictions, those determinations which are slowly to link us together in a common understanding and a common sympathy.

For, after all, gentlemen, nations are not conducted upon reasoned opinion; they are conducted upon the common impulses of the heart. I have heard it said that this is an age in which mind is monarch. I take it for granted that if that is true mind is one of those modern monarchs that reign and do not govern. The rule of this generation is in a great House of Representatives made up of the passions, and the best we can do is to see to it that the handsome passions are in the majority.

For, after all, for what is it that we are assembled here tonight? It is to express a passion, that noble and handsome passion which recollects as its chief glory the sacrifices men have made, the lives they have spent, not for themselves, but for a cause. The only thing that quickens our blood is to think of the things that have nothing to do with our business, to think of those things that spring from the heart, those things that make a man forget that he is a private individual, forget the clinging hands of his wife and his children, and turn away from the pride of his home to go out and fight the battle of the people. Those are the things that make gatherings like this enjoyable. We are not gathered here to celebrate the victories of the mind, but we are here to celebrate the victories of the heart. [*Applause*] And the thing that will link all America together is the quickening of universal understanding and universal sympathy.

The great difficulty in America, if I may say so, is her prepossession in favor of things which, though fundamentally true, she continues to express in terms which do not fit the situation. America is constantly trying to express herself in old policies with the idea that she is getting back to old principles. Her real interest is to express the old principles in new policies [*Applause*], to find a new and modern translation for the things that she has time out of mind believed in; and in order to do that she must realize above all other things that she has ceased to be a closed and domestic nation. We have now to think in the terms of the world and not in the terms of America. [*Applause*] We have come out upon a stage of international responsibility from which we cannot retire. That responsibility is not the responsibility of showing the world the way to material success, because the world knows the way to material success without our suggestion. Germany knows some of the ways of material success, for example, a great deal better than we do. Germany does not need to be drawn into the tutelage of America to learn how to make money, but every nation of the world needs to be drawn into the tutelage of America to learn how to spend money for the liberty of mankind [*Applause*]; and in proportion as we discover the means for translating our material force into moral force shall we recover the traditions and the glories of American history.

America was born by an impulse of intellectual and spiritual freedom, and America has lost her aristocracy in the company of nations if she forgets how to translate her power into the terms of intellectual and spiritual liberty. [*Applause*] Of whatever blood we spring, from whatever original sympathy we take our derivation, when we come together as Americans we have to ask ourselves this searching question: What sort of men ought we to be if America is to be a country in which subsequent generations will remember us in the way in which we are remembering great self-sacrificing Irishmen to-night? We are not remembering these gentlemen because they were successful, for politically speaking they were not, they were defeated—and yet there was a triumph in their defeat which makes them great in our eyes. [*Applause*] Men went down to their graves in sorrow to be resurrected in the hearts of their fellow-countrymen on evenings like this. [*Applause*] Would you wish upon some future day to be remembered as a great merchant, to be remembered as a great lawyer, to be remembered as a great manufacturer, to be remembered as a great engineer? Do you suppose that anybody will ever celebrate your birthday on any such account? It is very satisfactory when you are living to be successful in these material callings, but when you are dead you will wish it different. [*Applause*] When you are dead you will wish a certain aroma of sweeter flavor than that to permeate the air of your birthday. You will wish men to look back to you as a man whose eyes were lifted to the horizon, who led great companies of his fellow-men in their struggle up the steep and difficult ways which lead to the elevation and exaltation of nations. The dreams that we have heard of to-night were not dreams of personal success; they were dreams of the apotheosis of principle; they were the dreams of men who were willing themselves to be forgotten provided the great ideals which they had sought to embody in their lives might inform the minds and invigorate the generations that followed them.

There is no patent of nobility in a free country except this patent of spiritual and intellectual distinction which makes a man who is great a member of no generation, but one of that select company of immortals the roll of whose names is the book of our hope. [*Great applause*][4]

Printed in *The 125th Anniversary Dinner of the Society of the Friendly Sons of St. Patrick in the City of New York, Held at Delmonico's, March 17, 1909* (n. p., n. d.), pp. 28-33.

[4] There is a WWhw outline of these remarks, dated March 17, 1909, in WP, DLC.

From Robert Marion La Follette[1]

Dear Doctor Wilson: [Washington] March 17, 1909.

I read in one of the papers of Saturday, March 13th an extract from an address which you delivered the 12th inst. before the Philadelphia branch of the University Extension Society. From the extract published, I feel certain that the address was one of the most timely which has been delivered in recent years upon the tendency of our government.

If you have a copy of the address in its entirety and could spare it to me, I would appreciate its receipt.[2]

With kind regards, I am,

Very truly yours, [Robert M. La Follette]

CCL (R. M. La Follette Papers, WHi).

[1] Governor of Wisconsin, 1901-1905; United States senator from the same state since 1905.

[2] Wilson's reply is missing in the La Follette Papers in the Wisconsin Historical Society and the Library of Congress.

From Arthur Judson Brown[1]

My dear Dr. Wilson: New York, N. Y., March 17, 1909.

We are sure that you are interested in the extraordinary intellectual movement that is taking place in China, and that you appreciate with us the opportunity and duty which it affords. A Committee of eminent men has been appointed in Great Britain including such men as Sir Robert Hart, the Archbishop of Canterbury, the Bishop of London, and the Lord Mayor of London and others. The Committee on Reference and Counsel, representing the Boards and Societies of Foreign Missions of all the Protestant communions of the United States and Canada, has been authorized to appoint a similar Committee for America. I enclose a copy of our report, entitled "Educational Opportunity in China,"[2] which will give detailed information as to our plans.

You will note that our Committee is to select twelve laymen to serve with us in this matter. We earnestly desire that you should be one of these men. The others whom we have selected thus far are President Arthur T. Hadley of Yale University, the Hon. Seth Low, LL.D., of New York, the Hon. John W. Foster, LL.D., formerly Secretary of State, Washington, D. C., the Hon. Charles E. Hughes, Governor of New York, Mr. John R. Mott, M.A., Secretary World's Student Christian Federation, Mr. Robert E. Speer, Secretary Presbyterian Board of Foreign Missions,[3] Mr. Cleveland H. Dodge, of New York, the Hon. W. Murray Crane, United States Senator from Massachusetts, President Edgar [Edwin] A. Alderman, LL.D., of the University of Virginia and George Wharton Pepper, of Philadelphia.

Governor Hughes writes: "In view of the extreme importance of this matter I feel that I cannot decline to comply with your request. Highly appreciating the honor of your invitation, and with best wishes for the success of the work, I am, Very sincerely yours,"

President Hadley answers: "It will give me great pleasure to accept a place on this Committee. I appreciate the magnitude and importance of the work, and like exceedingly the names of the other members who are being invited to serve."

It will be a great pleasure to be assured that you can co-operate with us in this great movement.[4] While the work of the Committee will be exceedingly important, it is not expected to require much time of its individual members, as detailed work will of course have to be done by a secretary to be appointed.

Sincerely yours, Arthur J Brown

TLS (WP, DLC).

[1] Secretary of the Board of Foreign Missions of the Presbyterian Church in the U.S.A. since 1895; however, he was writing in his capacity as Chairman of the Committee on Reference and Counsel Representing the Boards of Foreign Missions of the United States and Canada, which he identifies in the first paragraph of his letter.

[2] *Educational Opportunity in China From Report of Committee on Reference and Counsel to Conference of Foreign Mission Boards . . .* (n. p., 1909).

[3] Brown, Speer, and Abram Woodruff Halsey all held the title of Secretary of the Board of Foreign Missions of the Presbyterian Church in the U.S.A.

[4] Wilson's reply is missing; however, as W. H. Grant to WW, Dec. 2, 1909, reveals, he agreed to serve.

An Interview

[March 19, 1909]

SEES NO HOPE OF NATIONAL JOURNAL

Dr. Woodrow Wilson, Explaining First Statement, Says Such a Newspaper Is Impossible Here.

When asked yesterday whether he believed a national newspaper possible in this country Dr. Woodrow Wilson, president of Princeton University, who declared in his speech on Wednesday night that no such publication was printed anywhere in the United States, said:

"I believe that conditions make the newspapers what they are. The conditions in this country are such that a national newspaper is an impossibility. If an editor started out to publish a national newspaper in New York or anywhere else owing to the existing conditions I don't believe that he could carry out his purpose. Even with unlimited means and trying to get out an ideal publication with a national scope the task, in my opinion, could not be successfully accomplished. I would not know how to tell him to go about it. But I have never been a newspaper man myself."

"Do you think it would be possible to eliminate local news to get a national paper?" he was asked.

"No, I don't, especially in New York. The only place where it would be at all reasonable or feasible to try the scheme would be in some large capital like Washington, maybe, and I hardly think that it would be possible there. It is impossible to get national news and the local news, too, in a paper in this country, because it is so big.

"By a national newspaper I mean one that publishes all the news of interest from all over the country. The local events in New York are of so much interest that the Associated Press despatches from elsewhere are crowded out. I read the country newspapers for national news, because their columns cover a much wider range, having less local matter to print.

"As for foreign news, the papers in this country print practically none, with the possible exception of the HERALD. It is the only American paper that pays any attention to foreign news at all. I have to get the London Times to read the foreign news, and then it is a week or so old."

"Do you believe that a national newspaper exists anywhere?" Dr. Wilson was asked.

"Yes, I believe the London Times is a national newspaper. But then, you see, England is a snug little country and very small as compared with our great area. London is the one great centre of English life as well as the capital of the country. It is fairly simple to make a London paper national.

"But in this country we have so many centres that there is no one great capital of all American interests. As I said, the President of the United States is the only national figure. It might be possible to get up such a newspaper in Washington, but then it would largely be devoted to politics and national only in that sense. New York would overshadow it as a news centre, and then we would get back to the local bugaboo. No, I don't believe that the scheme is now possible in this country."

Printed in the *New York Herald,* March 19, 1909; some editorial headings omitted.

A News Report of a Speech in New York at Temple Rodeph Sholom

[March 19, 1909]

DR. WILSON URGES NATIONAL STABILITY

"The Only Permanent Thing We Have Is Changed [Change]," Says Princeton's President.

Before the Culture Society of the Temple Rodeph Sholom, at Lexington avenue and Sixty-third street, Dr. Woodrow Wilson, president of Princeton University, delivered an address on "Americanism" last night.

"Now that we have become a grown up member of the family of nations," he said, "the foreign Powers are asking us, and we are asking ourselves the question, 'What are we going to do?' Are the foreign peoples yet coming here in such numbers that we are not yet ready to speak of American stock and characteristics?

"Until 1890 we always had frontiers in this country, and then we got the Philippines as a place to put out a lot of our frisky young colts to grass. The only permanent thing we have is change. No artistic or lasting work can be accomplished on this unstable basis.

"We have never finished our governments. Certainly our city governments are not finished. I sometimes think that they are done for, but they are certainly not finished. We have to admit that the best governed cities are on the other side of the water.

"There has never been a typical American who would not be at home on the frontier. Americans must see to it that the things we have gained are not lost by whimsical experiments. We must choose men to lead us who are saturated with experience and who do not change their opinions every day."

Printed in the *New York Herald*, March 19, 1909.

A News Report of an Address to the Princeton Club of Philadelphia

[March 20, 1909]

CLASS LINE UN-AMERICAN, SAYS PRINCETON PRESIDENT

In a stirring address before the Princeton Club of Philadelphia, which held its forty-first annual dinner at the Bellevue-Stratford last night, Woodrow Wilson, president of Princeton University, declared that the college or university which encouraged social stratification and made a bid for the exclusive patronage of the rich, is de-Americanizing the nation, and is not contributing any part to the real development of the country.

He deplored the fact that there are some universities which make a specialty of "social courses," and expressed the hope that Princeton would continue to stand ever ready to help the obscure youth and bring to light the undiscovered men, upon whom, he asserted, rested the future welfare of the nation.

"Could Abraham Lincoln have been of more or less service to this country had he attended one of our modern universities?" asked Dr. Wilson. "It is a question I hesitate to answer."

Referring to the growth of classes and the tendency of law-makers throughout the country to serve the large money interests, Dr. Wilson cited the method adopted by the ways and means committee of Congress to adjust the tariff. He said that they called before them the big steel men and asked them what the tariff should be on steel, and then called the wool men and asked them what the duty should be on wool, and then tried to pull the wool over the eyes of the American people by giving them a tariff that had in view the protection of the great interests.[1]

Printed in the Philadelphia *North American*, March 20, 1909; one editorial heading omitted.

[1] There is a WWhw outline of this address, dated March 19, 1909, in WP, DLC.

From Melancthon Williams Jacobus

Hartford, Conn.,

My dear President Wilson: March 20th, 1909

It has been with great interest that I have heard indirectly from some of the Princeton students here and through the families of others who are still undergraduates, that the practical abandonment of the Inter-club Treaty has brought about, this spring, a condition of affairs that even to the most enthusiastic Club men is utterly humiliating and intolerable.[1]

It is, of course, a situation which we could easily have shown them would necessarily issue and for which all temporary expedients that can be devised will never be a remedy. I am interested that matters should have developed so quickly, and I can not but believe that the thing for us to do in the situation is to keep absolutely silent not only in the way of criticism but especially in the way of offering advice or suggesting remedy.

We might perhaps come to them now and say, "I told you so," but it would intensify what seems to me to be the utterly wrong ideas which their prejudices in the matter have given them, namely that this whole question of Residential Quads is simply a partisan matter in which the party of the Club is offset against the party of the Quads. As long as the men hold this utterly wrong idea, the irritation of the question will be always to the front, and they will be less ready to see things in their right relations.

I have always found that when I approached the Club men and told them that, while I had nothing to say at present and realized and recognized that there was much in the proposition which radically concerned their financial and social interests, nevertheless when they came to see this matter in its right light they would find that when the Quad System, either in the shape in which it was originally propounded or in some modified shape, was finally adopted, it would place Princeton at the unquestioned head of the whole University educational life of the country, and I have not hesitated to add that when they saw this they would be just as enthusiastic as those were whom they now look upon as their partisan foes. *We* were quite willing to be patient and let them come to see this in their own way, but that they would so see it was absolutely inevitable, and when that day came it would be the greatest thing that ever happened to Princeton's life.

I confess that it is a great temptation just now to rub it in on the Club men, but I feel that we must restrain ourselves and as quietly as possible let the men so see the intolerableness of the situation that they will, rather than we, be the proposers of a taking up again of the question of the Quads.

Of course, what I am saying is my own individual opinion and it may be entirely contrary to your views. I do hope, consequently, if you have another view, that you will not hesitate to let me know what it is. You may be sure that I will do everything I can to further what you think to be the interests of the cause at the present moment.

I should like also to ask what you feel is the paramount issue in the present debate regarding the character of the Graduate School buildings and the organization of the Graduate Department, as conditioned by the new home into which they are to go?

I must confess that I am utterly discouraged at the luxurious views which Dean West seems to have, regarding the Graduate students' living. If these are carried out, it will result in simply making the Graduate School a great big upper class Club.

You will remember that I said some time ago I thought we had an opportunity to develop the Residential Quad idea in this Graduate College in a way in which it would be non-irritating and at the same time most effective as an object lesson to the undergraduates. In view of this suggestion, have you anything concrete to propose in the present debate?

I am very sorry that the joint meeting of the Graduate School and Grounds and Buildings Committees is to be called for Saturday, April 2nd, a day upon which it will be impossible for me to be absent from Hartford. But I should like to convey through you or through Mr. Pyne my views on this matter, if you feel there is any definite point at which they can be made effective.

With kindest regards and best wishes,

Yours very sincerely, Melancthon W. Jacobus

TLS (WP, DLC).

[1] For the Inter-Club Treaty regulating the election of sophomores to the upperclass eating clubs, see G. C. Fraser to H. B. Fine, March 18, 1907, n. 1, Vol. 17. Several editorials in the *Daily Princetonian* during March 1909, though vague on the exact details, make it clear that the old abuses of electioneering and bargaining for admission to the clubs, which the successive versions of the treaty had been designed to curb, had broken out once more. An editorial on March 8, 1909, indicated that several clubs had withdrawn from the treaty and flatly asserted that "practically all the signatory clubs" had broken the treaty "intentionally and purposely"; hence, it concluded, the treaty had been abolished for all practical purposes. Intensive negotiations among undergraduate representatives of the clubs went on during March 1909, but apparently the only agreement that could be reached was that notifications of election would not be sent to sophomores until March 22 and that all acceptances had to be in hand by March 25 (*Daily Princetonian*, March 17, 1909). This agreement was apparently honored by all parties; at any rate, there was no further comment on the subject in the *Daily Princetonian* for the rest of the academic year.

From James Hopwood Jeans

Princeton, New Jersey
March 20 1909.

Dear President Wilson,

I write, with extreme regret, to ask you to accept my resignation from my Professorship, to date from June.

I cannot here mention all the causes which have led me to wish to sever my connexion with Princeton, but among the principal are—

The climate, which has an unfavourable influence on my health and on the productiveness of my brain, and

The failure of the Graduate Department to develop in the way in which we had hoped it would, and the utter absence (as it seems to me) of hope for it in the future.

I feel that I am accomplishing nothing satisfactory here, either in the way of my own research, or of graduate teaching, and so feel forced to move. At the same time, I can assure you that I leave with many regrets, and shall always feel a warm appreciation for the cordial way in which I have been received during my time here.

I hope that, by giving you this early notice, I shall have reduced the trouble of filling my place to a minimum.

Yours sincerely, J. H. Jeans.

ALS (WWP, UA, NjP).

To Melancthon Williams Jacobus

My dear Dr. Jacobus: Princeton, N. J. March 23rd, 1909.

Thank you very much for your kind letter of the 20th. I take the liberty of returning the copy, knowing that you would like to keep your files complete.

I entirely agree with you as to the wisdom of keeping absolutely quiet about the present club turmoils and difficulties and letting the thing work itself out without either assistance or criticism on our part. That seems to me both the kind course and the wise course, and you may be sure that I shall use all my influence to prevent the faculty from taking any assisting hand, even if they should show a disposition to do so, which I think most unlikely.

I got Professor West to call together the gentlemen who are to constitute the new Graduate School Committee of the Faculty, and they spent some three hours together, going over the plans which Mr. Cram has submitted for the Graduate College. I understand, though I was not able to be present at the meeting (indeed, I did not desire to be), that it was the unanimous opinion of the gentlemen of that committee that the plans are in every way too costly and elaborate. I think that what we should insist upon is that the plans be sent back to the architects for a thorough re-consideration upon several points; that we should ask, in the first place, that if possible the whole scale of the building be reduced and its appointments rendered more simple by the elimination of many things, such as very numerous baths and very large studies and an unnecessary number of public rooms, which are now the chief features of the plan. My own suggestion would be that the new faculty committee should be asked to draw up a definite memorandum of the changes they would suggest and that that memorandum should be given to Mr. Cram with the suggestion that he act upon it, after consulting with the Chairman of the Graduate School Committee of the

Board, the Chairman of the Grounds and Buildings Committee, and the President of the University. This, it seems to me, would be in accord with the new proceedure [procedure] we have adopted, inasmuch as Professor West is a member of the new Faculty Committee and its Chairman and would have his part in the preparation of the memorandum. I feel it very important that these several elements should be included in the preparation of the decision, because it involves many financial and general administrative questions, as well as those more intimately associated with the life and administration of the Graduate College itself. But the main point is a radical re-consideration of proportions and details.

I hope that your health is established once more and that we are to have the pleasure of seeing you at the meeting of the Board. I take it for granted that you will select, as usual, the evening before the meeting of the Board for the meeting of the Committee on the Curriculum. I will hold my office at the disposal of the committee for that evening until I learn your pleasure. I wish I were going to see you at the joint committee meeting on April 2nd.

Always cordially and sincerely yours,

[Woodrow Wilson]

CCL (RSB Coll., DLC).

To Robert Bridges

My dear Bobby: Princeton, N. J. March 23rd, 1909.

I have not heard from Pittsburgh or Chicago yet,[1] but will of course let you know the minute I do hear. Meantime, I enclose the little bunch of nomination blanks that you suggested.

In haste, and with warm gratitude,

Faithfully yours, Woodrow Wilson

TLS (WC, NjP).

[1] As to whether Wilson's friends in these cities would nominate a candidate for Alumni Trustee to succeed John Lambert Cadwalader, who had declined to be a candidate for re-election.

From Joseph Bernard Shea

Confidential

Dear Mr. President: Pittsburgh, Pa. March 23rd, 1909.

I am laid up at home with a bad cold which after having me in its grip for some three weeks has now insisted upon being recognized. Your letter has been sent out to me and as time presses I will see that this answer goes east tonight.

I know of no agreement either expressed or implied whereby Pittsburgh and Chicago were to support [Wilson] Farrand this year. I think I had something to do with his withdrawal last year and so should know.[1] Of course there may have been individual promises given but I do not even know of one such case. I saw the original nomination circular last year and protested strongly at its tenor. Three Chicago [alumni] nominated McIlva[i]ne and I had some correspondence with Bob Annin[2] in which I told him that the place belonged to the West and that if McIlvane was defeated it would harm Princeton west of the Allegheny's. Other things were said and finally Farrand most gracefully pulled out. I wrote to Farrand at that time telling him how much I appreciated his action & reminding him that he was a young man and could wait. That to the best of my recollection is as far as I went. This spring Annin has urged me and others to have Pittsburgh nominate Farrand. We talked it over out here & decided that it was not proper for us to do so. The place belonged to the East & the East should choose the man. Anyway if any association outside of New York should do it Chicago was the one. So we have kept out. But I consider the situation most deplorable and do hope that this still hunt will not succeed. I can not vote for Farrand and many Pgh. men feel as I do.[3] I sent in a nomination blank for Parker Handy[4] as he seemed to me one who might be elected. If it were only possible to get two or three names on the official ballot all would be well. I feel that as an alumnus you have just as much right in this contest as any one—as a man you have infinitely more. I know Parker wants it. So does Alex Gulick.[5] Both would have a very strong following in New York. How about Tracy Harris.[6] I suppose *he* would not oppose Farrand. A very little fire would start a big blaze in this matter & if the alumni knew of F's last year's platform he could never win. One thing is sure. Pittsburgh will never support an anti-administration candidate Yours most sincerely J B Shea

P.S. After reading this letter I find it is not as warm as I could wish it but it must go as it is. I only wish I could talk to you about it and could help as I should be happy to do.

ALS (WP, DLC).

[1] As Shea indicates below, in the election of an Alumni Trustee in 1908 Farrand had withdrawn in favor of William Brown McIlvaine of Chicago, Princeton 1885. See M. W. Jacobus to WW, Jan. 10, 1908, n. 2, Vol. 17.

[2] Robert Edwards Annin, Princeton 1880, at this time in the stock brokerage business in New York.

[3] Farrand was generally known as an anti-administration man, especially on the quadrangle plan.

[4] Parker Douglas Handy, Princeton 1879, President of Handy & Harmon, dealers in precious metals in New York.

[5] Alexander Reading Gulick, Princeton 1889, lawyer of New York.

[6] Tracy Hyde Harris, Princeton 1886, lawyer of New York.

To Robert Bridges

My dear Bobby: Princeton, N. J. March 23rd, 1909.

Here is Mr. Shea's reply to my inquiry about Pittsburgh. It makes very interesting reading in the circumstances, and I think that it shows that it is highly desirable that some other men should be put in nomination. If Pitney[1] seems too near the same constituency that Mr. Farrand belongs to, I think that Shea's suggestion of Parker Handy is excellent. I am hoping for an early letter from Cyrus. If none comes with the next forty-eight hours, I will write again to you.

In haste, Affectionately yours, Woodrow Wilson

TLS (WC, NjP).

[1] John Oliver Halsted Pitney, Princeton 1881, lawyer of Newark, N. J., and resident of Morristown, N. J.

From Robert Bridges

Dear Tommy: New York, March 25th 1909

I have just had word from Munn[1] on the telephone that he has talked with Cauldwell, '81.[2] He thinks we had better hold off until he has a conversation to-night with John Pitney. Cauldwell seems to think that Pitney will not be inclined to run and that the Farrand nomination has got too far along in New Jersey. At any rate, he expects to let us know Pitney's own opinion to-morrow morning. In the meanwhile I shall withhold the blanks, as it would be unfortunate to have a flash in the pan.

Very truly yours Robert Bridges

P.S. Pitney is just getting over typhoid. We certainly do not want to get into a contest without good backing. I may see Bob McCarter[3] tonight at the U. C.[4]

TLS (WP, DLC).

[1] Charles Allen Munn, Princeton 1881, publisher and co-editor of *Scientific American.*

[2] Thomas William Cauldwell, Princeton 1881, lawyer of New York and Morristown, N. J. and at this time Mayor of Morristown.

[3] Robert Harris McCarter, Princeton 1879, lawyer of Newark, N. J.; Attorney General of New Jersey, 1903-1908.

[4] That is, the University Club.

Cyrus Hall McCormick to Robert Bridges

Chicago Ill March 26 [1909]

Telegram received dreadfully disappointed about Pitney what man shall we propose parties here mostly unfavorable to Farrand if no New Jersey or New York man available why not Philadelphia man Cyrus H McCormick

T telegram (WC, NjP).

To Andrew Clerk Imbrie

My dear Mr. Imbrie: Princeton, N. J. March 26th, 1909.

Now that I have an unusual number of days at home, I have been looking over some of the papers lying on my desk which had been laid aside for more careful consideration, and I find among them Dr. Samuel Cochran's letter to you,[1] enclosing the letter from the Imperial Chinese Legation in Washington upon the subject of attracting Chinese students to Princeton.[2]

I have had a number of talks with Lucius Miller upon this matter and have returned to it once and again in conversations with others who were in a way to give me the necessary information. I have had several plans in mind which might prove suitable to bring about what Dr. Cochran suggests and have first and last given the matter a good deal of thought. The net result of all the thinking is this:

In the first place, as the letter from the Chinese Legation states, most of the Chinese students come in search of engineering and professional courses, which we cannot give them. In the second place, they will be best suited by universities whose course of study offers them a miscellany from which to choose and ties them down to no necessary combination of studies for a degree. In the third place, I fear, and I am sure that you will agree with me that the fear is well grounded, that our present social organization at Princeton would be sure to result in making any Chinese students who might come here feel like outsiders, not received into the real life of the University but set apart for some reason of race or caste which would render them most uncomfortable. There is no door that I can see by which they could really enter our university life at all, and to have them come and form a group apart would certainly be most undesirable.

For these reasons I have come very reluctantly to the conclusion that there is nothing that we can wisely do to press our claims for recognition in the distribution of the numerous Chinese students who are about to be brought to this country in the expenditure of the indemnity money by the Chinese government. I should like very much, when you have leisure, to know if these conclusions seem to you sound.

With warm regard,

Sincerely yours, [Woodrow Wilson]

CCL (WWP, UA, NjP).

[1] Samuel Cochran, M.D., Princeton 1893, Presbyterian medical missionary in China.

[2] That is, students whose expenses were to be paid by the Chinese government out of funds returned to China by the United States Government from the so-called Boxer Indemnity. About this matter, see WW to L. H. Miller, Jan. 15, 1909, n. 1, Vol. 18.

From Melancthon Williams Jacobus

Hartford, Conn.,

My dear President Wilson: March 26th 1909

I have just received notice of a special meeting of the Graduate School Committee on Friday Apl. 2nd, preceding the joint meeting at Princeton the next day.

I do not know what it is planned to do with the findings of the Faculty Graduate Committee; but if they could be got before this special meeting of the Graduate Committee on Friday and be adopted by them, it would contribute not a little towards simplifying the discussion at the joint meeting on Saturday; for it is obvious that if the plans are too costly, other plans must be prepared which will come within the means at our disposal.

If the College is to serve the purposes of the Graduate School you are wholly right in insisting that the Faculty Graduate Committee should express its ideas as to what sort of a building it should be. This is done with laboratories; it ought to be done with such specific buildings as this College is intended to be, and with the Faculty Committee should be consulted also the President of the University, as well as the Chairmen of the two Committees particularly interested in the undertaking. The main thing is however that the opinion of the Faculty Graduate Committee should be brought to bear upon the Trustee Graduate Committee as expressing an expert estimate of the situation, which must not be ignored.

From what Mr Pyne has written me I have reason to fear that he thinks the Trustee Graduate Committee should themselves reconstruct the present plans, holding them essentially as they are & consequently building only a portion of them at the present time, since this is all our money allows us to do. He is reinforced in this opinion by certain statements regarding soon to be expected large gifts to the Graduate School made to the Committee, which, if realized, will enable us to complete the building on its present scale.

I have never quite believed in this policy & now that the Faculty Graduate Committee has spoken I am wholly of the view that the present plans should be laid aside and a new scheme presented by the architect which will enable us to build the College complete with the money of the bequest.

I am writing to Ed Sheldon & will express to him my views. I hope however you will consider yourself commissioned to cast my vote for the above measure if it is needed.

I greatly fear that either at this special meeting of the Graduate Committee, or at the following joint meeting of the two Committees, the question of the site of the Graduate College will be brought again to discussion. I think Bayard Henry has stirred up Cleve Dodge and trouble is brewing. I have talked with Harry Thompson & I have written Pyne & they both hold to my view, that this is a closed incident. After long discussion a site has been determined upon,[1] submitted to the Board, and adopted by them. The site is not only excellent in itself, but represents a compromise of views which cannot be disturbed without serious results. I trust no foolish action will come before the Board. Should the site be again thrown into debate, the Executors of the bequest would have good cause for action.

I trust that you were gratified with the review of Princeton in the *Independent* of March 4th.[2] It is to my mind one of the most significant utterances in modern educational things, and places Princeton gloriously in the lead—certainly of the two (Harvard & Yale) already discussed—and the basis of its commendation is your preceptorial policy which I believe belongs to the great *democratic* movement in modern American education and American university life.

Pardon this manuscript letter; but I am in bed again with rheumatism & find it hard to *write right*. It is nothing serious: I will be out again in a day or so.

Yours very cordially Melancthon W. Jacobus

ALS (WP, DLC).

[1] On the grounds between Prospect and Seventy-Nine Hall. There is much discussion of this matter in Vol. 18.

[2] Edwin E. Slosson, "Princeton University," *The Independent*, LXVI (March 4, 1909), 458-77.

From Robert Bridges

Dear Tommy: New York, March 26th, 1909.

Cauldwell has heard from John Pitney, who has been very ill but is now recovering. Pitney says that under no circumstances would he run against Farrand who is a personal friend of his. The '81 men, therefore, could not make a fight for him. It therefore seems advisable not to nominate him, particularly so if the names appearing should be principally men of our Class. I am sorry that the whole matter was not taken up sooner because I am convinced that at this late date it will be almost impossible to secure the right man to accomplish what we want. Halsey,[1] Munn and I were ready to secure the necessary signers, but of course we shall not go ahead with it as Pitney undoubtedly would withdraw.

If you are in New York please let me know, or come in to see me.

With best wishes

Faithfully yours Robert Bridges

TLS (WP, DLC).

[1] Abram Woodruff Halsey, Princeton 1879, Secretary of the Board of Foreign Missions of the Presbyterian Church in the U.S.A.

Cyrus Hall McCormick to Robert Bridges

Chicago Ill Mch 26 1909.

McI[l]vaine recommends John W Barr Junior president fidelity Trust Co Louisville Ky for alumni trustee barr was spoken of for secretary of treasury he is a very representative southern alumnus think will be very desirable to have trustee from South consider this & telegraph your opinion we can get ten or fifteen nominations for anyone agreed upon

Cyrus H McCormick

Hw telegram (WC, NjP).

To Robert Bridges

My dear Bobby: Princeton, N. J. March 27th, 1909.

I must say that I feel, as you do, that the situation is so complicated that it really is not possible for us to do anything wisely and intelligently before the first of April. I am deeply chagrinned to have been so tricked and taken in, but there is nothing to do but to submit to this added mortification, so far as any active steps are concerned.

McIlwaine's suggestion of Barr of Kentucky seems to me an admirable one. I have no doubt, for my part, that if he were nominated, a sufficient support could be worked up for him in Chicago and Pittsburgh, among other places, to make his election very likely, and I regret extremely to think that this is now impracticable. Clearly we have acted too late, and I suppose that is all we can say to Cyrus.

I need not tell you how warmly I appreciate your interest and activity. It was like you to act so promptly and so generously.

Always affectionately yours, Woodrow Wilson

TLS (WC, NjP).

To Melancthon Williams Jacobus

My dear Dr. Jacobus: [Princeton, N. J.] March 27th, 1909.

I am greatly distressed to hear that you are in bed again with rheumatism and hope with all my heart that your prophecy of being out in a day or two will be fulfilled.

A good many things in your letter disturb me. The suggestion you make about action by the new Graduate School Committee of the Faculty jumps with my own judgment, and I shall act upon it, if possible. The only trouble is that this group of gentlemen is not yet a committee of the faculty. It is possible that they will not be willing to make a formal recommendation until the new bylaw of the Board is adopted and they are given formal authority. I will at once consult with them, however, (though unfortunately West is away, having gone South to cure a cold) and see how far and in what way they will be willing to act.

It is very singular that if new and large gifts to the Graduate School are expected, I should have heard nothing whatever of them. All of this movement of groups in entire independence of each other makes me very uneasy and really renders proper government of the University impossible.[1]

What your letter contains will be of great value to me when the committee meets. I shall then know what information to draw out and what course to pursue myself. Things must certainly be handled now very definitely and without more backing and filling.

With warm regard and sympathy for your suffering,

Cordially and faithfully yours, [Woodrow Wilson]

CCL (RSB Coll., DLC).

[1] Wilson apparently was not kept long in the dark. Dean West, according to his own account, told the trustees' Committee on the Graduate School at its meeting on April 2, 1909, that a gift of $500,000 for the Graduate School and Graduate College by William Cooper Procter, Princeton 1883 (his degree was conferred in 1903), President of Procter & Gamble Co., soap manufacturers of Cincinnati, was in the offing, provided that the trustees raised an equal sum and selected some other site than Prospect for the Graduate College. Andrew F. West, "A Narrative of the Graduate College of Princeton University . . ." mimeographed MS (UA, NjP), pp. 45-46.

To Daniel Moreau Barringer

My dear Moreau: Princeton, N. J. March 27th, 1909.

I had to consult the Treasurer before answering your letter of March 25th.[1] He keeps track of the boarding places and knows more about them than anyone else in Princeton. He recommends very strongly No. 39 Van Deventer Avenue, Mrs. [M. A.] Stiger's house, which is marked with a cross on the enclosed list. He thinks that the other three marked are also excellent places, but that Mrs. Stiger's is much the best. She always secures an excellent class of boarders and seems to know how to look after the boys, as much as it is necessary or desirable to look after them. Very likely if Mr. Law[2] were to come up this spring some time, he could make a provisional engagement with Mrs. Stiger.

All the freshmen eat, under the new rules of the University adopted some three or four years ago, at what we call the Freshman Commons. They are not really commons, that is to say the men do not all eat together in one great room, but eat in groups in a series of rooms, arranging themselves very much as they please. We found under the old system that they were being unconscionably cheated by the boarding-house keepers, and the new arrangement has given universal satisfaction.

I am very much interested in what you tell me of young Edward Law and hope most sincerely that he will get in without difficulty.

It was very delightful to hear from you. We missed you very much at the Princeton dinner the other night in Philadelphia. I was looking forward to that evening with the hope that you would be there. Please give my warmest regards to Mrs. Barringer and believe me,

Faithfully and affectionately yours, Woodrow Wilson

TLS (D. M. Barringer Papers, NjP).

[1] It is missing.

[2] Edward Law of St. David's, Pa., who entered Princeton in the autumn of 1909.

To Moses Taylor Pyne

My dear Momo: [Princeton, N. J.] March 29th, 1909.

Here is the tentative draft of a report on the site and monument that I promised to send you. If you approve of it, I will write to Senator Dryden asking for a meeting of our committee, or send him a copy of this report as I am sending it to you, as you think best. My own feeling is that a meeting would be better, if we can get it, where we can talk the matter over and be sure of Senator Dryden's real acquiescence and approval.

Always faithfully yours, [Woodrow Wilson]

CCL (WWP, UA, NjP).

A Draft of a Report to John Fairfield Dryden

[c. March 29, 1909]

Monument and Site

Your committee appointed to consider the important matter of suitable form and appropriate site for a memorial to Mr. Cleveland to be erected in the town of Princeton beg leave to report as follows:

It has seemed to your committee unwise to recommend the erection of a monument in the ordinary meaning of that word. None of the forms usually given to monuments seems to them suitable or desirable in this case. They entirely agree with what they have understood to be the generally expressed opinion of the members of this Board, that it is not likely that any bronze or marble statue could be designed which would be artistically acceptable. They deem it most unlikely that any monument could be designed which was meant by the artist to be symbolical of what Mr. Cleveland has stood for in the political annals of the country which the Board of Trustees of the Foundation would be willing to adopt: a simple shaft, or a massive body of stone bearing inscriptions upon bronze tablets, or a structure resembling a mausoleum such as has often been adopted for memorials of this kind, seems to them more suitable for a place of burial than for such a site as this Board would wish this particular memorial to have.

Moreover it would be as difficult to find an appropriate site for a monument of the ordinary kind in Princeton as it would be to find an appropriate form for the monument itself. Princeton is a very small place. It has no public squares and no large open places. The single central and appropriate place for a monument has already been set apart for a monument commemorative of the battle of Princeton.[1] Even if there were to be money enough available for the purchase of an appropriate site in town where land is extremely expensive, your committee would be at a loss to point out any piece of land now obtainable at any price which would be suitable in location and approach for a monument.

In the circumstances, therefore, your committee recommend that the monument to be erected be given the form of a memorial tower built on the grounds of Princeton University in connection with the most conspicuous and architecturally-important group of buildings on those grounds, the group a portion of which is about to be erected on Nassau street at the corner where the street leading up from the railway station [University Place] merges upon the busiest corner of town, its very heart and center.

Two members of your committee are connected with the administration of Princeton University. So far as they are concerned, therefore, this recommendation is made with a great deal of diffidence and hesitation, because it may seem a recommendation prompted by their interest in the architectural beautification of the university rather than by their zeal to do well what you have appointed them to do, namely to serve the interests of this association by making the best possible recommendation with regard to a monument memorial to Mr. Cleveland. They urge the adoption of this recommendation, however, none the less earnestly and confidently on that account. They believe that it will bear examination and criticism on its own merits.

Such a memorial tower would be of no monetary value to the university whatever. Its form would preclude its use for any demeaning purpose or for lodging rooms or for any other use to which the university has been accustomed to put any of its buildings. It would lend itself admirably, however, to such intrinsic use as, for example, a museum or place of exhibiting prints, documents, books, or other objects illustrative of the time and services of Mr. Cleveland,—to a memorial room, in short, which could be made a center of no small interest to visitors. A memorial arch, flanking the tower, could contain a bronze tablet with a suitable inscription and could be so placed in relation to the group of buildings as to become a much frequented passageway alike for citizens of the place and for visitors to the university town. Nowhere else and in no other way that we can suggest could so beautiful and impressive an architectural monument be erected in this delightful university town.

Mr. Cleveland's closing years were spent in Princeton. He became closely identified with the place not only in the minds of his fellow-countrymen, but also with the administration of the university, in which he became deeply interested, to its great benefit. It is a practical form of national sanction to give to memorials of great public men the form of a beautiful tower erected in connection with some institution removed from the noisy field of affairs to which they have devoted their thought and attention at times when public business did not absorb them. Many of the most beautiful at Oxford and Cambridge had such an origin. They are in no sense utilitarian. They were erected in memory of some great public man or some great class dignitary, who was at once a statesman and patron of learning; and they more than any other form of monument have arrested the attention and the world's admiration to those who leave great names and great works behind.

It is the conviction of your committee that a monument of this kind could be given unusual dignity and beauty and would enjoy an unusual distinction. They have reason to believe, moreover, that it would meet with the approval of those most deeply interested in the proper commemoration of this great career.

Respectfully submitted,[2]

Transcript of WWsh MS (WP, DLC).

[1] The battle monument was to stand at the juncture of Stockton Street and Bayard Lane.

[2] There is an undated WWhw outline of this report in WP, DLC.

A Plan for the Organization of the Graduate Council of Princeton University

March 29th, 1909.

I. MEMBERSHIP.

(1) The Graduate Council shall be composed of one representative from each of the thirty-five classes last graduated, and fifteen members at large. The present Committee of Fifty shall constitute the first Graduate Council.

(2) The Secretary of each class on graduation shall become *ex-officio* a member of the Graduate Council to serve 5 years.

(3) At or before 1 P.M. on Tuesday of Commencement week, the Secretary or other authorized representative of each of the classes then having been graduated 5, 10, 15, 20, 25 and 30 years shall certify in writing to the Secretary of the Graduate Council the choice of his class for representative upon the Graduate Council to serve 5 years.

(4) At the stated meeting of the Graduate Council in October of each year 3 members at large shall be elected by ballot to serve 5 years.

(5) *Vacancies.* Vacancies, whether by death, resignation, failure of a class to certify to the election of a representative or otherwise, shall be filled by ballot at any stated meeting of the Graduate Council. A member who shall be absent from two consecutive meetings shall thereupon cease to be a member, unless upon his application he shall be excused by the Council.

II. OFFICERS.

The officers shall be a Chairman and a Secretary, who shall be elected by the Council at the stated meeting in October of each year. The Secretary of the Council shall also act as Secretary of each of the Committees.

III. PLAN OF ORGANIZATION.

There shall be six committees appointed by the Chairman at the October meeting in each year to serve for one year and until their successors shall be appointed. Vacancies in Committees may be filled at any time by appointment of the Chairman. Every member of the Graduate Council shall be expected to serve on a committee.

(1) *A Committee on Finance.* It shall be the duty of this committee to co-operate with the authorities of the University as to the raising of money, and to lay before the several classes or alumni organizations desiring to contribute to the University, the several purposes for which funds are needed, and to report to the Graduate Council for transmission to the Board of Trustees, information as to what specific purposes the said organizations desire their contributions to be devoted, and in what manner credit shall be given therefor; and to perform such other duties as may be delegated to them from time to time, by the authorities of the University or the Graduate Council.

(2) *A Committee on Class Records and Organization.* It shall be the duty of this committee to encourage efficient class organization and to co-operate with the Secretary of the Alumni in the preparation of the alumni directories.

(3) *A Committee on Publicity.* It shall be the duty of this committee to co-operate with the Secretary of the University in communicating to the public such information regarding University affairs as may be of general interest.

(4) *A Committee on Preparatory Schools.* It shall be the duty of this committee, in co-operation with the University authorities

and undergraduate organizations, to secure information with regard to the sources from which the University is drawing its students.

(5) *A Committee on Alumni Associations.* It shall be the duty of this committee to secure information regarding the character of work undertaken by the Alumni associations and to increase and to improve the same for the best interests of the University.

(6) *A Committee on Undergraduate Activities.* It shall be the duty of this committee to obtain information regarding the athletic, literary, musical and other interests of the undergraduates, and from time to time to make suggestions concerning the conduct of such of the same as affect the alumni or bring the University before the general public.

(7) *Executive Committee.* There shall be an Executive Committee composed of the officers of the Graduate Council and the chairmen of the several committees, which shall have all the powers of the Council when the Council is not in session. At each stated meeting of the Graduate Council, the Executive Committee shall make a report upon the work of the several Committees; and as soon thereafter as may be convenient shall prepare and publish a statement for the information of the alumni.

(8) *Meetings.* There shall be two stated meetings of the Council in each year; one in October and one in April; which shall be held in Princeton. A special meeting may be called at any time by the Chairman or by a majority of the Executive Committee; but notice of such special meeting must be mailed to each member at least two weeks in advance.

(9) The Council may appoint such other Committees as may from time to time be advisable and may adopt by-laws or rules and regulations for the more ready transaction of its business.

MEMORANDUM TO ACCOMPANY PLAN OF ORGANIZATION OF THE GRADUATE COUNCIL.

As soon as the present Committee of Fifty shall be reorganized as the Graduate Council, lots shall be drawn to determine the expirations of the terms of the 15 members-at-large—the terms of three members to expire in October of each of the years 1909, 1910, 1911, 1912 and 1913.

At Commencement in June, 1909, the representatives of the classes prior to and including the class of '74 shall retire. The Secretary of the class of 1909 shall become, *ex-officio* a member of the Graduate Council. The classes of '79, '84, '89, '94, '99 and 1904 shall elect representatives to serve 5 years in place of their present representatives in the Committee of Fifty.

Printed document (WWP, UA, NjP).

From Joseph Bernard Shea

Dear Mr. President: Pittsburgh. March 30th 1909

Yours of March 27th reached me last evening. I am indeed glad that you feel as you do towards me and I trust that that condition will be permanent. I think you know how heartily I am in favor of the reforms you are urging though we may not now agree as to the methods by which they are to be accomplished. I think we have at least a fighting ground secured for the Alumni Trustee contest. At least 12 nomination blanks will go from here for John W. Barr Jr. of Louisville: Chicago has promised ten to fifteen more and I have taken steps which I think will get him some from Philadelphia and New York. So: there will be at least two names on the ballot. After that the contest can either be carried on or not but at least we have the chance to fight. Yours most sincerely J B Shea

I am happy to say that I seem at last to have the best of my cold.

ALS (WP, DLC).

Two Letters from Moses Taylor Pyne

My dear Woodrow: New York March 30th, 1909.

I have read the report and approve it thoroughly. I should suggest that at the top of the second page you make it a little more clear that the Memorial tower to be erected on the grounds of Princeton University is expected also to front on Nassau Street, so that it will be clear that it will not be in the interior of the Campus, but that it will be seen publicly as well.[1]

I think it might be well to arrange, if possible, an interview with Senator Dryden either in Princeton next Saturday or Monday some time, or at his office. If the latter, we should bring the drawings and pictures of the proposed improvement, but if he could be induced to come to Princeton, it would be better as then he could see for himself.

Saturday would be the only day this week on which I could

be present, and yet it would be an awkward day to have him, for the reason that the Committee on Grounds and Buildings will have so much work to do that it will take up the greater part of the morning and most of the afternoon, so that we could not pay him proper attention. I shall be in Princeton on Monday but I have a Township Committee Meeting at 2.30 and a Board of Education meeting at a quarter to four, so that I can not see much of him that afternoon. You might arrange it for the following Wednesday or Thursday afternoon but, in any event, if you and he can get together it will not be necessary for me to be present, and you know your own engagements and what day will be convenient.

Yours very sincerely, M Taylor Pyne

[1] As subsequent documents in this volume and in Volume 20 will disclose, Dryden and the Cleveland Monument Association accepted the idea of a memorial tower to be located on the Princeton campus. However, the site proposed by Wilson and Pyne was abandoned, and the tower was eventually built as an integral part of the Graduate College on the Springdale golf links.

My dear Woodrow: New York March 30th, 1909.

On showing your report to Mr. [Archibald Douglas] Russell he suggests that it would be advisable to get Mrs. Cleveland's consent to the matter. I told you that I practically had it last January, but I think, before closing the matter, I had better see her and try to obtain her formal consent, as it would have a great deal of influence on the whole Board. This I think I can do probably better than you can.

Yours very sincerely, M Taylor Pyne

TLS (WP, DLC).

From Edward Capps[1]

My dear President Wilson: Princeton, March 30, 1909

In response to your request I am sending you a statement concerning the proposed building for the Graduate College.

The graduate student of the better sort, as I know him, is a young man very much in earnest in the pursuit of his professional training. He is like the student of law or medicine. He has largely abandoned the outside interests of his undergraduate days and is eager to devote himself unreservedly to the serious business of study. He is now generally thrown more or less wholly upon his own resources; very likely he earns by teaching or summer work a portion at least of his income; and he is less disposed than before to call upon his father for financial assistance. As compared with the undergraduate, as his resources are slighter so his wants are fewer. He prefers to order his life simply, with a view to the maximum of intellectual efficiency combined with the minimum of expense for purely physical comforts. He will unhesitatingly prefer to undergo what a few years before, as an undergraduate, he would have considered hardships, if by so doing he may be able to buy more books or otherwise advance his scholarly interests.

The life which the graduate student chooses to lead is wholesome and good, the same sort of life, we must remember, as that for which he is preparing himself,—eventually a professorship on a modest salary after eight or ten years of apprenticeship. In laying our plans for the development of a superior graduate school here at Princeton, I think we should do well constantly to bear in mind the needs of the class which we wish to attract to us, and to devote our resources consistently to the provision of advantages which will determine the choice of the best men. They demand, in the first place, the best possible facilities for advanced study in the way of instruction, books, and equipment, and, in the second place, the possibility of securing, either in the town or on the campus, simple but comfortable quarters at moderate expense. The proportion of graduate students who can afford expensive rooms and board is so small as to be negligible; in this respect there is a noticeable difference between graduate students and students of law or medicine.

The plans of the Graduate College seem to me to have been drawn on the basis of a radically different conception, both as to what the graduate student desires and as to what it is desirable to offer him. For a counterpart of the quarters provided for in these plans one would have to go to the most expensive of the private dormitories at Harvard, erected as investments and patronized by wealthy undergraduates, and even in these I do not believe that the suites are so large or expensively built, and nothing like so much space is given to halls, corridors, commons rooms, servants' rooms, and the like. Even if we cared to furnish such quarters to our graduate students at the prices which they could afford to pay—and this would be in effect the setting aside of an endowment to meet in part their ordinary living expenses —I fear that we should only be preparing the students for lives of discontent in the future. We are not likely to draw students to Princeton by the quarters we provide for them, in any event. Therefore, whatever saving we can reasonably effect in the construction of this dormitory and whatever increase we can secure in the income to be derived from it, the greater our progress will be in building up a graduate school at Princeton that will rank with the best in the country.

I am accordingly in favor of a radical modification of the present plans. There should be a good many suites of three rooms for the use of two students, the less desirable to rent for about $75 per student, heat and light included, others at say $100, and a few single rooms (bedroom and study) at perhaps $125. For the sake of greater economy in construction and a greater degree of privacy for the occupants of the building I should favor the grouping of the rooms in separate entries, as is done in the undergraduate dormitories. The building should house, I should think, at least 100 students. We ought to have more than this number in residence within a very short time. It will of course contain, besides, a dining room and library, which should be open to the whole body of graduate students whether they are residents of this hall or not. Provision should be made, further, for simple furnishings for the bed rooms and studies.

Yours sincerely, Edward Capps

TLS (WWP, UA, NjP).

[1] Wilson soon appointed Capps, Henry Burchard Fine, Winthrop More Daniels, Edwin Grant Conklin, and John Grier Hibben to the newly-constituted Faculty Committee on the Graduate School. He had notified them of their impending appointment and solicited their views on the plans for the Graduate College.

From Edwin Grant Conklin

Princeton, New Jersey

My dear President Wilson, March 30, 1909.

I understand that you desire an expression of my opinion of the plans of the proposed Graduate College in so far as they bear upon the needs of the graduate work of the University; I therefore beg to submit the following statement:

1. I assume that it is desirable that the building shall be the center of the graduate life of the University and that it shall be occupied by as large a number as possible of our graduate students, and further that the principal aim of such men while here is to become productive scholars.

2. To this end the building should provide comfortable, but not luxurious, rooms for men of small financial resources as well as for those of average means. My own experience justifies the view that graduate students are usually dependent upon their own resources; I could show you at the present time letters from at least a dozen good men, several of them instructors or

investigators elsewhere, who say that they desire to come to Princeton for graduate work in Zoology, but that they cannot do so unless living expenses here are low, or financial aid can be had from the University. The cost of living in the Graduate College must be kept as low as possible in order to provide for such men. Furthermore I believe that the real aims of graduate work can be best promoted by plain and simple living. The present plans seem to me to provide for too small a number of men, and if the building is to be self supporting I fear that the cost per man is likely to be too great to be of much service to our graduate students.

3. For these reasons it seems to me desirable that a larger number of smaller and cheaper rooms should be provided in the Graduate College, that there be more double suites, and perhaps fewer bath rooms, and that in general the building be so planned as to minister to the needs of a large number of students rather than to the luxuries of a few.

Very respectfully yours, E. G. Conklin

TLS (WWP, UA, NjP).

To Edwin Grant Conklin

Princeton, N. J.

My dear Professor Conklin: March 31st, 1909.

Allow me to thank you for your letter of yesterday which reached me this morning. I am very much obliged for it and will take pleasure in submitting it to the Committee of the Board.

With much regard,

Faithfully yours, Woodrow Wilson

TLS (E. G. Conklin Papers, NjP).

From Winthrop More Daniels

My dear President Wilson: Princeton, N. J. Mch. 31, 1909.

In reply to your request for my individual opinion upon the plans submitted by Mr. Cram for the Graduate College, I beg to say:

FIRST: that the plan submitted, in my judgment, involves unnecessary expense. The funds available for the structure I understand to be not greatly in excess of $300,000.00. The building as planned is to accommodate 60 students. This means an average expenditure of $5000.00 per student. Of course it is true that the terms of the bequest require the inclusion of a dining hall of some kind, and this feature somewhat increases the per capita expenditure as previously estimated. At the same time the cost of recent structures such as Little Hall, into which I have inquired, makes the proposed cost of the Graduate College seem by comparison to be excessive. In particular I would cite as affording opportunity to reduce the cost per capita the following: the present uniform provision of separate studies for every student. In the case of students engaged in such studies as Physics and Biology the laboratory is, of necessity, the workshop; and the separate provision of separate studies in every case is wasteful. Second, the size of many of the studies—some of them 20 feet in length—savors of unnecessary expenditure. Third, in some cases, the suites are planned to run along one side only of a corridor, there being no rooms on the opposite side. Walls are thus built at unnecessary expense when they might as well serve for suites on both sides of a central corridor. Fourth, a fireplace in every study is unnecessary. Fifth, the provision of bath and toilet-rooms admits of retrenchment. TO SUM UP, FOR THE SAME COST A BUILDING COMPARABLE ARCHITECTURALLY WITH OUR BEST RECENT DORMITORIES OUGHT TO BE BUILT TO ACCOMMODATE 100 MEN INSTEAD OF 60.

SECOND: the idea which seems to underlie the architect's plans misconceives the whole nature of the kind of graduate school and graduate student we are likely to have. The typical graduate student is a man of very limited means, to a very much greater extent than is true of our undergraduates taken generally. He is commonly a mature man to whom the idea of group or family-life does not necessarily appeal. The idea seemingly underlying the architect's plans is of a relatively small number of well-to-do graduate students, docile enough to submit to restrictions upon their freedom which would not infrequently seem irksome to the undergraduates. It appears clear to me that what is desirable is to afford the maximum opportunity to mature men to accomplish the maximum amount of advanced work. Any plans for a dining-hall and for magisterial supervision that are mandatory under the terms of the bequest must, of course, be observed; but where such arrangements are not mandatory, but optional, they should be strictly subordinated to the one main controlling principle of applying the money available so as to give the greatest opportunity to advance the cause of graduate work and research.

I am, Very sincerely yours, W. M. Daniels

TLS (WWP, UA, NjP).

Recommendations by Henry Burchard Fine

[c. March 31, 1909]

DEPARTMENTS OF MATHEMATICS AND PHYSICS:

Professor J. H. Jeans and Preceptor C. E. Stromquist have resigned from the teaching staff of the University. Their salaries have been $5,000 and $1,300 respectively. In view of the situation thus created it is recommended that the following appointments and adjustments of salary be made.

1. After careful consideration of all available men qualified to give the instruction in Applied Mathematics which Professor Jeans has been giving, we have concluded that no better man for our purposes can be found than E. P. Adams, now one of the Assistant Professors in the Department of Physics. Moreover, as it happened, at the very time we were considering the matter, Mr. Adams received from the University of Illinois practical assurances of a call, if he would promise to accept it, to the chair of Mathematical Physics in that University, with a salary of at least $3,000, so that it became necessary, in order to hold him, to assure him that he would be recommended for promotion here. It is recommended that he be appointed a Professor of Physics with a salary of $3,000.[1] The title Professor of Physics is suggested rather than that of Professor of Applied Mathematics, held by Professor Jeans, because of the strong desire of Mr. Adams and his colleagues that he continue to be a member of the Department of Physics.

2. It is recommended that the salary of Professor A. Trowbridge, now $2,500, be increased to $3,000. Mr. Trowbridge is one of our ablest lecturers and has charge of the course in Physics required of academic Sophomores. His scientific reputation is high. When he came to Princeton he gave up a larger salary than that offered him here, and in the course of the present year he has refused a call at a salary of $3,000. It seems unfair to ask him any longer to do the important work he is doing in the Department on the salary he is now receiving.

3. In undertaking his new duties, Professor Adams will require a release from the preceptorial work in Sophomore Physics which he is now doing. Moreover there will be need next year of additional help in the course of instruction in Freshman Laboratory Physics. It is therefore recommended that B. J. Spence, who has held the Experimental Science Fellowship this year, be appointed Instructor in Physics on a salary of $1,000.

[1] This and all subsequent recommendations were approved and put into effect.

4. It is recommended that Mr. L. P. Eisenhart be appointed a Professor of Mathematics. His mathematical and pedagogical ability, and the very exceptional service he has rendered and is rendering the University not only in connection with the Department of Mathematics, but in administrative work entitle him to this promotion. It is especially desirable that he should receive it now in view of his recent appointment to be Vice-Chairman of the Committee on Examinations and Standing.

5. It is recommended that the salaries of Mr. J. G. Hun and Mr. C. R. MacInnes be increased from $1,300 to $1,500, and that Mr. E. Swift be promoted to a preceptorship and his salary increased from $1,200 to $1,500. These men are among the most valuable teachers in the Department of Mathematics. Mr. Swift last year refused a call to Yale which, had he accepted it, would have given him next year a salary of the amount proposed and a still larger salary the year following, and Mr. MacInnes last fall refused a call to McGill University at a salary of $1,800.

6. While the advanced courses which Mr. Jeans has been giving will be conducted by Mr. Adams, the Honors Course in Analytical Mechanics will fall to Mr. Eisenhart. Moreover, the great increase in the amount of graduate instruction which must be given by the Department of Mathematics next year (when three of our graduates come up for the degree) will necessarily occupy a good deal of the time of certain members of the staff; the teaching done by Stromquist must be provided for; and the Freshman class is likely to be larger than this year. To meet this situation it will be necessary to add two men to our depleted staff. The teaching might be done by two instructors. But it is difficult to secure any but inexperienced teachers in mathematics at $1,000. And it is highly important to make good so far as is possible the loss in prestige suffered by the Department by the departure of Mr. Jeans. It is therefore recommended that Mr. M. Wedderburn of the University of Edinburg be appointed Preceptor in Mathematics at a salary of $2,000 if he will accept the post;[2] and that an instructor be appointed at a salary of $1,000.[3] Mr. Wedderburn is one of the ablest of the younger mathematicians of Scotland and has a fine reputation as a teacher. He is well known in America and is used to American conditions, having spent two years at the University of Chicago.

[2] Joseph Henry Maclagan Wedderburn did accept and came to Princeton in September 1909.

[3] Actually, a preceptor, George David Birkhoff, was appointed at a salary of $2,000.

SUMMARY

Salaries of Jeans and Stromquist		$6,300.00
Increase in Adams' salary	$1,000.	
Increase in Trowbridge's salary	500.	
Salary of Spence	1,000.	
Increase in Hun's salary	200.	
Increase in MacInnes' salary	200.	
Increase in Swift's salary	300.	
Salary of Wedderburn	2,000.	
Salary of Mathematical Instructor	1,000.	6,200.00

DEPARTMENT OF GEODESY:

The efficiency of instruction in the Department of Geodesy has for some time been suffering from the lack of a sufficient number of assistants to instruct the students in the use of instruments and in the conduct of surveys. It is therefore recommended that an additional assistant be appointed next year and that the force of assistants consist of G. G. Cornwell $900, H. W. Ralph $600. and a third man, as yet unknown,[4] at a salary of from $800. to $1,000. as may be found necessary to secure him. The two assistants this year have received $1,600.

DEPARTMENT OF ASTRONOMY:

Professor [R. S.] Dugan is to be married this summer and must therefore give up the rooms he is now occupying in the Observatory of Instruction on Prospect Avenue. It is recommended that his salary be increased by $200. from $2,000 to $2,200, in other words, that the same allowance be made him toward house rent that was made his colleague Professor [H. N.] Russell. It is hoped that the budget of the Department of Astronomy will be the same next year as this, namely $5,400. This year $2,200 was appropriated to Russell's salary, $2,000 to Dugan's and $1,200 to a fund for repairs and recording, with the understanding that any unexpended balance of this $1,200 was to be applied to a fund for the purchase of a transit instrument. Next year the proper distribution would be $2,200 to Dugan's salary, $2,200 to Russell's and $1,000 to the fund for repairs and recording.

Respectfully submitted, Henry B. Fine

T MS S (WWP, UA, NjP).

[4] As it turned out, Henry William Ralph did not teach in 1909-10, and the Instructors in Geodesy for that year were George Gilbert Cornwell, Milton Argyle Campbell, and Edward Davis Townsend.

From Henry Burchard Fine, with Enclosure

Dear Tommy: [Princeton, N. J.] April 1, 1909.

I enclose a note from Cyrus McCormick received about a week ago in which he declares his willingness to provide a course of lectures for us next session on Trusts by Professor Gore[1] if we think well of his doing so. You of course are the one to decide. McCormick will be here next week at the meeting of the Board and you can then give him your answer. What probably suggested the scheme to McCormick is the fact that Professor Gore recently delivered such a course of lectures at Yale.

Sincerely yours, H. B. Fine

[1] James Howard Gore, Professor of Mathematics at George Washington University, 1883-1909. Gore had written numerous textbooks in such varied fields as mathematics, geodesy, geography, and the German language, as well as monographs in history and political science.

E N C L O S U R E

Cyrus Hall McCormick to Henry Burchard Fine

My dear Fine: Chicago 24 March, 1909.

I thank you for your note of the twenty-first, and am so glad that you and Mrs. Fine had an opportunity of meeting Professor Gore. He writes me most enthusiastically of his visit, and hopes he was of some benefit to the students.[1] He says that he would be glad to give a course of lectures next session on "Trusts, or Industrial Combinations," and he feels that much good could be accomplished by arousing an interest in this subject with the students, inducing them to take sane views on this great economic question.

If you or President Wilson think that this would be of interest to Princeton, I should be glad to provide the Honorarium and the expenses for Professor Gore for this purpose,—the lectures to be delivered whenever you and Professor Gore may determine that it is mutually convenient.[2]

I am,

Very sincerely yours, Cyrus H. McCormick

TLS (WP, DLC).

[1] Gore had been in Princeton to coach the members of the Princeton debate team on the negative side of the question, "Resolved, that all corporations engaged in interstate commerce should be compelled to take out a federal charter."

[2] There will be subsequent correspondence and notes about this matter. However, Gore did give six lectures on "The Corporation Problem" on March 18 and 19 and April 1, 2, 8, and 9, 1910, and McCormick paid the honoraria.

The reports in the *Daily Princetonian* of Gore's lectures make it clear that he was an ardent apologist for great industrial corporations, and he might well have been a paid propagandist.

From Henry Burchard Fine

Dear Sir: [Princeton, N. J.] April 1. 1909

In response to your request for an expression of my opinion as to the proposed plans of the Graduate College, I beg to submit the following:

To provide quarters for but 60 men at a cost of over $300,000, or at nearly twice the rate per man spent in erecting the best of our dormitories for undergraduates, would in my opinion be a very extravagant and unjustifiable use of money. The proposed building is far too luxurious in its appointments and use of space, and provides quarters for too few men. Accom[m]odations which are luxurious enough for our well to do undergraduates should suffice for graduate students who as a class are and always have been men of small means and simple tastes. It will not dignify the position of the graduate student in the community to surround him with luxuries for which he cannot pay, nor will the enjoyment of such luxuries benefit him.

There is a double reason for making the capacity of the building to quarter students much greater than in these plans. Graduate students on the average cannot afford to pay more than $100 for room rent, heat and light included. At this rate 60 students would pay but $6000, a sum not sufficient to maintain the proposed building. The difference must be paid out of the college funds. I can imagine no greater folly than for an institution of learning to devote any part of its revenues to the maintenance of luxurious living quarters for its students.

The other and equally important consideration is this: There is every reason to expect that within a period of two or three years we shall have at least 100 graduate students devoting all their time to higher studies at the University. Three or four of our Departments have taken pains during the past few weeks to bring the opportunities for graduate work at Princeton to the notice of our colleagues in other colleges and universities. We have been as much surprised as gratified by the results. For the fellowships in the Dept. of Classics there are 16 applicants, and Professor Capps tells me that from them it will be possible to select as fine a group of graduate students of the classics as he has ever seen. Professor Conklin speaks with like enthusiasm of the candidates for fellowships in the Dept. of Biology, of whom there are 10. For the fellowships in Physics also there are 10 candidates, and for those in Mathematics 17, of the same high quality as in the Departments already mentioned–one of the candidates in mathematics being a young professor in a Southern college who has already won distinction for himself by his mathematical writings.

I do not mean to imply that the candidates to whom we cannot award fellowships will enter Princeton next fall, though it is to be hoped that some of them will. They are for the most part unable to come without some financial aid. But in the fact that this large number of able advanced students desire to come, many of them being willing to give up University instructorships which they are now holding, or to refuse offers of fellowships elsewhere, to secure for themselves the opportunity to prosecute their studies here, we have one of the most gratifying indications possible of the position Princeton is beginning to hold among American universities. It is on this that my expectation of a rapid increase in the number of our graduate students rests. And may I say incidentally that the process would be greatly promoted at the start by the appropriation of a few hundred dollars each year to fellowship purposes. By a little assistance to the Depts. of Biology, Physics, and Mathematics of the kind already assured the Classics, the present numbers of graduate students not hailing from the Seminary might be doubled next fall.

With such a number of graduate students in prospect in the near future it is of the first importance that we provide quarters for them now that we have the opportunity of doing so. The sum of money at our disposal should be sufficient to erect a building that will accomodate 100 of them as comfortably as the undergraduates are housed in our best dormitories. It should be our effort to secure such a building. Nothing could be more unfortunate than that almost at the beginning of the new life of our Graduate School it should become necessary to separate its students into two classes, the one class admitted to the enjoyment of the life of the Graduate College, the other left to shift for itself in the town. Such a situation would almost certainly lead to a class distinction in the Graduate School like that between Club and non-Club men among the undergraduates. The Graduate College should be the center of the life of the entire Graduate School, not the home of a privileged class of graduate students.

I prefer not to make specific suggestions as to the plans of the building, except tentatively, until I have had a better opportunity to study the question. But it requires no serious study to see that as compared with the proposed building one constructed like our undergraduate dormitories on the entry plan would be far more economical in the use of space. It is on this plan that the English Colleges are constructed. I see no sufficient reason for departing from it.

Mr. Cram's plans provide for each student an apartment in which the study is larger than those connected with double rooms in our undergraduate dormitories. Many of the graduate students will prefer to room in pairs and should be allowed to do so if they wish. I therefore advise that a considerable number of the apartments consist of two bedrooms and a study not larger than those connected with undergraduate double rooms, and the rest of a study of smaller size and a single bedroom.

Finally I advise that all the toilet arrangements and baths (shower baths seem to me sufficient) be placed in the basement as in '79 Hall.

By arrangements of this kind a building of the size planned by Mr. Cram could, I think, be made to accomodate 100 students, or nearly that number, and that without encroaching upon the space which ought to be reserved for other purposes than students' rooms.

Clearly it was contemplated by Mrs. Swan[n] that the Thompson College should not only maintain itself, but yield a considerable revenue—sufficient to pay the stipends of a large number of Fellows even after rooms had been assigned these Fellows rent free. The gross income from the building will be but $10000 even if by economy of space it be made to accomodate 100 men, or far less than the sum in the mind of the donor. It seems to me that her wishes constitute a very important reason for not by needless extravagance making the income some $4000 less, thus not only putting all provision for the Fellowships to which she attached so much importance out of the question, but even making the maintenance of the College in part a burden on the University treasury. Sincerely Yours, H. B. Fine

ALS (WWP, UA, NjP).

From John Grier Hibben

My dear President Wilson, Princeton April 1/09

In response to your request, I would submit the following statement for the consideration of the Trustees Committee on the Graduate School:

In examining the architect's plans of the Graduate College, it seems to me the cost of construction can be substantially lessened, without detracting in the least from the dignity and beauty of the proposed building. More particularly I would suggest that (1) the number of bath rooms can be cut down considerably; (2) the size of the study in the several suites can be reduced; (3) there need not be so great an elaboration and extension of corridor space.

I think a thorough reconsideration of the treatment of the interior of the building is desireable.

Faithfully yours John Grier Hibben

ALS (WWP, UA, NjP).

Harold Griffith Murray to Cleveland Hoadley Dodge

Sir: New York, April 1, 1909.

The following is a report of the Committee of Fifty of Princeton University to date, covering the period from my last report made to you June 1, 1908.

The total income of the Committee of Fifty for the last fiscal year ending July 31, 1908, was $145,956.

The pledges in the Endowment form of subscription amounted, on July 31, 1908, to $643,125. Of this $323,300 was paid in; the balance $319,825 was drawing interest at 5% according to the terms of the pledge.

For the present fiscal year, ending July 1, 1909, the pledges under the Term form and interest on unpaid pledges under the Endowment form amount to $98,360, $50,613 of which has been paid into the treasury of the University. It is uncertain, of course, how much of the sums pledged we shall be able to collect, but I estimate that not more than 1-1/2% is uncollectible.

Total pledges in endowment form $643,125 of which $348,300 has been paid in.

In addition to the sums above mentioned, there are ten of the Alumni who have made Princeton a beneficiary under their wills. It would, of course, be unwise to include any of the amounts that I have seen mentioned in these wills in any financial statement, owing to the uncertainty of life and the possibility of changes in the wills or depreciation in the values of the estates. Also I have secured since August 1st in written or tentative pledges for endowment in the form of dormitories approximating a quarter of a million.

DORMITORIES

The plan for erecting an Alumni Dormitory on the campus, to which various classes desiring class memorials will contribute to entries, have [has] been mentioned in several of my annual reports. I am glad to say that, as matters now stand, we may, without doubt, count on the following classes, each to contribute an entry:

'81; a tower by the class of '84, '02, '03, '04, '06, '07 and '08, as well as two entries from the principal of the old Alumni fund.[1]

THE PRESS BUREAU

During the past year the Bulletin of the Committee of Fifty has been published three times a year in the Alumni weekly, and sent to practically all of the Alumni not subscribers. I believe that the result of this has been beneficial, judging from what I have been told by the Alumni on my trips around the country. The Press Bureau has been sending out regularly weekly articles relative to Princeton until the 1st of February, when I discontinued the Bureau for the time being owing to my prolonged absence in the West. As far as I am able to ascertain we have been benefitted by these articles.

THE ALUMNI

At this time the following classes are contributing to special class funds:

'73, '77, '81, '88, '90, '94, '96, '98, '99, '00, '01, '02, '03, '04, '05, '06, '07, '08.

The Alumni in these classes, with few exceptions, are immune from my solicitation under the arrangement by which the Committee of Fifty is making its canvass; the number left open to approach is therefore reduced over one-half.

Believing that the present organization of the Committee of Fifty was not as efficient as it might be made, I presented to you a plan for re-organization about a year ago, and you appointed a Committee on Plan and Scope to draw up a new plan of organization. The Committee on Plan and Scope submitted a plan to the Committee of Fifty at their meeting held October 13, 1908,[2] which was adopted by them and forwarded to the Board of Trustees for their consideration and action.

[1] About the Alumni Fund, see M. T. Pyne to WW, July 23, 1904, n. 2, Vol. 15.
[2] It is printed at Oct. 15, 1908, in Vol. 18.

Since October 1, 1908, I have made a thorough canvass of the following cities:

Baltimore		
Camden	Minneapolis	Salt Lake
Chicago	New York	St. Louis
Cincinnati	Omaha	St. Paul
Denver	Pasadena	Scranton
Detroit	Philadelphia	Washington
Greensburg [Pa.]	Pittsburg	Williamsport
Los Angeles	Reading	Wilkesbarre

Many of these cities had been visited before, and it was not expected that a very material increase would be made in the number of contributions.

In the new centers which I visited in the far West I was impressed with the loyalty and enthusiasm manifested everywhere by the Alumni, and I think it is worth particular mention that, in Denver and Los Angeles, while I did not secure a subscription from every man, owing to financial inability[,] I received only one absolute negative. When one takes into consideration the great distance these centers are from Princeton, and the inability of the majority of the men to visit Alma Mater, except at rare intervals, in not a few cases extending over many years, it appears to be a very remarkable exhibition of loyalty and interest. It seems entirely probable that, in the near future, the Western trip may result, in one dormitori [dormitory], an entry to a dormitory, some $12,000 to Endowment and $3,000 annually toward current expenses.

I believe the work of this Committee is cumulative; that the Alumni to-day are more interested in Princeton than at any time in her history; that from among the younger men that have graduated recently, we may expect the same interest and support that has been given in the past by the older Alumni. Their enthusiasm and constantly increasing number, give me every right to feel that, in the near future, Princeton may depend upon her Alumni for adequate financial support. At the present time, however, so many classes are tied up on memorial funds that it is impossible to expect very much of an increase for the next few years in our annual collections, but I think we should also remember that the contributions and pledges of the Alumni each year since the Committee of Fifty have been organized, have been over $200,000. outside of any big individual gift, a sum sufficient to take care of the deficit, if it could be devoted wholly to that purpose.

Respectfully, H. G. Murray Secretary.

TLS (Trustees' Papers, UA, NjP).

A News Report

[April 2, 1909]

SPLENDID ADDRESS.

President Wilson Pleads for Social Independence Before Philadelphian Society.

A stirring address was delivered by President Wilson before the midweek meeting of the Philadelphian Soicety [Society] in Murray Hall last evening. He took as the basis of his talk, St. John I, 17: "For the Law was given by Moses, but Grace and Truth came by Jesus Christ." This law of rectitude was necessary when nations were young, but when the world came to maturity, the law was no longer imperative. At this time Jesus Christ brought grace and truth to the world. By grace is signified all the felicities of the mind and of nature, all that tears away the crust of mere custom and awakens us to the consciousness of our manhood. Truth means every verity, candor, sincerity and courage of heart. Our hearts understand the truth only when the conscience speaks.

Many a man is released from former allegiances while in a University, because there he begins to think for himself. And this release of the faculties is education's greatest function. But the processes of life in Princeton at the present time tend to standardization, to subordinate us, as individuals, to the organization. The entering man is forced, at the penalty of ruining his college career, to conform to the standards of thoughts of others and to imitate them. In this manner the processes of education are nullified. Independence of opinion is taken away. Education, however, should break up the tyranny of the social process. President Wilson said his words were a challenge that we become our own masters, a petition that we dismiss our silly fear of each other, and a request that we become real men. There are processes in Princeton that smother real opinion. As long as these prevail, Princeton, ostensibly a Christian university, is neither university nor Christian.

In closing he said that he looked for some splendid day when there should be a declaration of independence, when every one should feel that he was responsible for his opinions not to mankind but to God.

Printed in the *Daily Princetonian*, April 2, 1909.

To Daniel Moreau Barringer

My dear Moreau: Princeton, N. J. April 3rd, 1909.

[E. P.] Davis is mistaken.[1] I have never had anything to do with the administration of Seventy-Nine Hall. It has always been in Cuyler's hands. He has felt the difficulty of it very greatly, I have reason to believe. It has really become a very serious matter of patronage. Undergraduate opinion is very much disturbed by the way in which Seventy-Nine Hall is excepted from the ordinary rules with regard to the opportunities of students to obtain rooms, and I know that several members of the class are very anxious to have the matter put upon a more regular footing.[2] I am sure that you can find out all there is to be learned on the subject by writing to Cuyler. I must frankly say that I fear it will not be possible for members of the class to get youngsters in on the ground that they are sons of friends, because there would be no possible way of setting a limit to that, and the whole use of the building would in that way become a matter of patronage. I know that you will appreciate how serious a difficulty this would impose upon the University authorities and how important it is that we should not put the building in a class by itself which would "queer" it in general undergraduate opinion.

It was a great pleasure to hear from you again.

Always faithfully and affectionately yours,

Woodrow Wilson

TLS (D. M. Barringer Papers, NjP).

[1] Barringer's letter to which this was a reply is missing.

[2] See WW to C. H. McCormick, March 3, 1909, ns. 3 and 4.

A News Report of an Address in Princeton at the Witherspoon Street Presbyterian Church

[April 3, 1909]

Lecture by President Wilson

A representative audience assembled in Witherspoon Street Presbyterian Church on Wednesday evening to hear President

Woodrow Wilson deliver a lecture before the Men's Association of the church on the subject "What Ought a Man to Do?" President Wilson emphasized the fact that the so-called "negro problem" is a problem not of color, but capacity; not a racial, but an economic problem. The negro's problem rather than the negro problem. To industrious and progressive people of color this is pleasing and desirable, as is evidenced by schools such as Tuskegee and many smaller institutions conducted along similar lines. We sincerely thank President Wilson and acknowledge with gratitude the generous assistance given by many friends in all parts of the country and particularly in Princeton. The work of the Men's Association of the Witherspoon Street Presbyterian Church is made possible by the coöperation of the Institutional Work Committee of the Brotherhood of the First Presbyterian Church. This committee arranged for a series of lectures which were delivered during the winter and closed with the lecture delivered by President Wilson. On behalf of the Men's Association I desire to thank the committee, and particularly Prof. Winans and Prof. Foster, by whom the series was conducted.

George Shippen Stark.[1]
Witherspoon St. Presbyterian Church.

Printed in the *Princeton Press*, April 3, 1909.

[1] Pastor of the Witherspoon Street Presbyterian Church of Princeton, 1905-19.

To Robert Bridges

My dear Bobby: Princeton, N. J. April 5th, 1909.

If you had an opportunity to buy an established newspaper in the South, say at Baltimore, and desired to find a man to act as editor and control its policy, who could give the paper a character which would make it deserve national attention and be calculated to widen its interest in all national matters and attract the attention of thoughful people everywhere, in brief a man of patriotic purpose, thoughtfulness, and sufficient scholarship and energy, whom would you choose? I am asking this question in the interest of someone else whose name and plans I cannot give but whom I should like very much to assist in this important choice. I know that your acquaintance with men in the editorial fraternity is wide enough to give you a pretty general view of the field. Always affectionately yours, Woodrow Wilson

TLS (WC, NjP).

To Henry Smith Pritchett

[Princeton, N. J.]

My dear President Pritchett: April 6th, 1909.

I am extremely sorry that I cannot attend the meeting of the Executive Committee on Thursday. The Board of Trustees of the University meets that day here, as I wrote you.

Quite aside from my feeling that it is a real dereliction to be absent in any case, there is a special case concerning which I wished particularly to ask your opinion and the opinion of the committee. I mean the case of Professor Shepherd, of Baltimore,[1] about whom of course you have had many papers, no doubt.

I happen to know a great deal at first hand about Professor Shepherd, and it has seemed to me worth our while to give the case very special consideration. While Professor Shepherd retired from official connection with any college before the date of Mr. Carnegie's gift and therefore could not be considered in the ordinary way, it is literally true, as his papers state, that he has devoted himself exclusively to teaching until a very recent date and that his lectures and his work in general have been of a very unusually high quality, winning recognition in the most authoritative quarters. His role among Southern educators during the time of his greatest activity was a very noticeable and very useful one. It covered the period immediately following the War, when there was practically nothing more than a bare living to be got out of teaching, and throughout that period he devoted himself to the promulgation of the highest ideals and played no small part in reviving literary study in particular throughout Georgia and the Carolinas. A man of unusual parts and character, his seems to me certainly an exceptional case, and I hope that I shall have an early opportunity of hearing what you and the other members of the committee think about it, upon a statement of the whole case.[2]

Always cordially and faithfully yours,

[Woodrow Wilson]

CCL (WWP, UA, NjP).

[1] Henry Elliot Shepherd. Born in Fayetteville, N. C., on January 17, 1844, he attended the University of Virginia, 1860-1861. Entering the Confederate Army in 1861, he was severely wounded at Gettysburg on July 3, 1863. After the war he taught school for a time at Louisburg, N. C., and was Professor of English and History at Baltimore City College, 1868-75. He became Superintendent of Instruction of Baltimore in 1875 and remained in this post until 1882, when he became President of the College of Charleston. He returned to Baltimore in 1897 and devoted the rest of his life to lecturing and writing. The author and editor of many books and articles on English and American literature and American history, he died on May 29, 1929.

[2] Shepherd did not receive a Carnegie pension.

From Cleveland Hoadley Dodge

My dear Mr. President: New York April 6, 1909.

I spoke to you early in the winter regarding my desire to have Princeton University confer a degree upon Mr. John R. Mott, and we both thought at that time it might be better to defer the matter until, possibly, the dedication of the new statue at Princeton.[1] I find, however, that it will be some three or four years before that will be ready, and in talking the matter over with Mr. McCormick I found that he sympathized fully with my desire and was exceedingly urgent that there should be no delay, as he feared some other university would get ahead of us and have the honor of giving a degree to Mr. Mott, which really belongs to Princeton owing to his leadership in the great students' movement which started at Princeton.[2]

I would, therefore, like to suggest that your committee consider this matter now. There is one consideration which would make the conferring of the degree peculiarly appropriate at the present time. Mr. Mott will complete, in June, a series of visits to the great European universities which is unparalleled in the history of university life. Commencing with English universities, he spent a week each at Oxford and Cambridge, where he made a remarkable impression upon the students and dons; and from there he went to the leading universities in the Scandinavian countries, and has just finished, in March, a series of lectures at the four great Russian universities, and during this month and next expects to visit universities in Austria Hungary, Italy, Germany and Spain. These lectures have all been upon the invitation of the students of the several universities, and the accounts which I have received from the places which he has already visited indicate that he has produced a profound impression wherever he has been.

I do not know anyone in the United States to whom the degree of Doctor of Laws could be more fitly given than to Mr. Mott. He has for twenty-five years led the great student movement in this country, which has been the most potent factor in the development of the spiritual and moral life in the American colleges and universities, and from which has grown a corresponding movement in Europe and all over the world. It is needless for me to recount the wonderful growth of this movement in heathen countries, where some two hundred of the very picked men from American universities are now working amongst the students in the colleges and universities of these countries. All of this work has been a direct growth of Mr. Mott's genius.

He is the Secretary of the World's Student Christian Federation and will preside at the great triennial meeting of the Federation at Oxford at the end of June, and it would add much to his prestige and influence to have received from Princeton an important degree. He is a man of great intellectual attainments, a graduate of Cornell University, and has already received from Yale the degree of Master of Arts.

Recommending this matter to your thoughtful consideration,[3] believe me,

Very respectfully yours, Cleveland H. Dodge

There is hardly a college in the world from Tokio East to California & from Pekin South to New Zealand including all continents—So Africa & So America which Mott has left unvisited & all over the civilized world he is known admired & loved by college men. He thinks in continents

TLS (WWP, UA, NjP).

[1] The statue, later known as "The Christian Student," was being executed by Daniel Chester French to commemorate the founding of the intercollegiate movement of the Y.M.C.A. in Princeton in 1877 (see n. 2 below). Completed and dedicated in 1913, it stood for many years between Murray-Dodge Hall and Pyne Library. It is now located at Chesterwood, the home and studio of Daniel Chester French, in Stockbridge, Mass.

[2] About this matter, see the news report printed at Dec. 8, 1902, Vol. 14.

[3] The trustees voted to confer an LL.D. on Mott in 1910, but he was unable to receive the degree until the following year. See J. R. Mott to WW, Jan. 21, 1910; WW to C. W. McAlpin, Jan. 25, 1910; and J. R. Mott to WW, Jan. 27, 1910, all in Vol. 20.

From Henry Burling Thompson

Greenville P. O. Delaware

My Dear President Wilson: April sixth, 1909.

Saturday, May 1st, will suit us exactly, and I have ordered notices sent out for the Delaware dinner for that night.[1]

I am delighted to know that you can come, and I want you and Mrs. Wilson to arrange to spend Sunday, May 2d, with us. I hope to have Cleve Dodge and his wife at the same time.

I shall see you to-morrow night at the Curriculum Committee meeting. Yours very sincerely, Henry B Thompson

TLS (WP, DLC).

[1] That is, the meeting of the Delaware alumni in Wilmington. The only newspaper report of this address, in the Wilmington, Del., *Every Evening*, May 3, 1909, was a brief account noting only that Wilson was one of the speakers. There is a WWhw outline of his address, entitled "The Ideals and Objects of the University," with the composition dates of April 22 and 30, 1909, in WP, DLC.

A Resolution

8 April, 1909

RESOLVED that Mr. Andrew C. Imbrie, of this Board, be constituted Financial Secretary of the Board, and that he be authorized to cooperate with the President of the University in the oversight of all its business interests, to attend all meetings of the Committee on Finance, the Committee on Grounds and Buildings, and the Committee on Library and Apparatus, and to perform such duties as those Committees or their Chairmen may direct, to the end that the various business departments of the University may be as much as possible coordinated and that system and economy may be furthered in their administration.

RESOLVED, that the matter of the salary to be attached to this office be referred to the Committee on Finance, with power, to be reported to this Board at its next meeting[1]

T and WWhw MS (Trustees' Papers, UA, NjP).

[1] The trustees adopted this resolution at their meeting on April 8, 1909. There is nothing about Imbrie's salary in the Minutes of the Board of Trustees for 1909-10.

From the Minutes of the Board of Trustees of Princeton University

[April 8, 1909]

The Trustees of Princeton University met in stated session in the Trustees' Room in the Chancellor Green Library, Princeton, New Jersey, at eleven o'clock on Thursday morning April 8, 1909.

The President of the University in the chair. . . .

Mr. Pyne, of the Committee on the Graduate School, reported as follows:

Princeton University, April 8, 1909.

TO THE TRUSTEES OF PRINCETON UNIVERSITY.

Gentlemen:

Your Committee on the Graduate School respectfully presents the following recommendations for adoption:

First–That the Theodore Cuyler Prize in Economics be made the Theodore Cuyler Graduate Scholarship without allotment to any particular department.

Second–That the present Chapter VIII of the By-Laws of the Board of Trustees be replaced by the following new Chapter VIII:

CHAPTER VIII.

OF THE DEAN AND THE FACULTY COMMITTEE OF THE GRADUATE SCHOOL.

1. The Dean of the Graduate School shall be a member *ex officio* of the Trustees' Committee on the Graduate School, and Chairman of the hereinafter mentioned Committee of the University Faculty on such School. He shall make a written report for that Committee to the Trustees' Committee before the January and Commencement meetings of the Board.
2. The administration of the Graduate School shall be in the hands of a Committee of the University Faculty, to be known as the Faculty Graduate School Committee.
3. They shall have supervision of graduate courses and instruction, of the admission of students to the Graduate School, of the studies of members of the Graduate School, of the work leading to higher degrees and the examination therefor, and of recommendations to the University Faculty of appointments to fellowships and graduate scholarships
4. They shall also have supervision over fellows, graduate scholars and other graduate students, and in general over all matters affecting the administration of the Graduate School.
5. They shall conduct and administer the affairs of the Residential Graduate Hall, and the Master of that Hall shall be associated with the Committee as a voting member in the administration of the Hall.

(Signed) M. Taylor Pyne, Chairman, *pro tem.*

RECOMMENDATIONS OF COMMITTEE ON GRADUATE SCHOOL ADOPTED

The report of the Committee on the Graduate School was accepted and the recommendations of the Committee adopted.

"Minutes of the Trustees of Princeton University, April 1908-June 1913," bound minute book (UA, NjP).

From Robert Bridges

Dear Tommy: New York, April 8th, 1909.

In reply to your letter of April 5th—I have thought considerably about the matter, and the best suggestion that occurs to me is the name of Francis E[llington]. Leupp, who is now Indian Commissioner. He was, as you know, for more than twenty years connected with the *Evening Post*—for a great part of the time as

Washington correspondent. He knows everybody in public life, and has had training in almost all the departments of journalism. Whether he would be tempted by a journalistic offer at this time, I do not know, but I am certain as to his ideals and as to his equipment. He is not a young man, but he is vigorous and capable.

I talked with Dr. Albert Shaw confidentially about the matter and he immediately suggested Fabian Franklin, who was for some years the Editor of *The Baltimore News* until it passed into the hands of Frank Munsey. Shaw said that you would know all about him and that he believed that Franklin was an ideal man for the place. He had, I believe, the entire respect of the best people in Baltimore and was given a remarkable dinner when he resigned. Shaw said, however, that you were fully informed in regard to him and his history. If I think of any other suggestions I shall let you know.

I hope that you talked over fully with McCormick and Cuyler the question of an Alumni Trustee? We had a Class Committee dinner last night and Cyrus believes that the Chicago, Louisville, and Pittsburg associations will support Barr with practical unanimity. Cuyler also thinks that a great deal can be done here in New York. I notice by the *Alumni Weekly* that the Jersey Associations have organized a Confederation with Farrand as President.[1] I have little doubt that the immediate object of this was to promote his candidacy.

Faithfully yours Robert Bridges

TLS (WP, DLC).

[1] The Princeton Alumni Federation of New Jersey had been organized recently by delegates of the alumni associations of Newark, Montclair, Plainfield, the Oranges, and Hudson County. Wilson Farrand was chosen president at the organizational meeting. See the *Princeton Alumni Weekly*, IX (April 7, 1909), 409-10.

From Arthur Crosby Ludington

Dear Mr. Wilson: [New York] April 11th, 1909.

The other night at the City Club a little group of us met to take the first step toward forming an organization to promote the plan of cutting down the number of elective offices. Those present were Mr. Henry C. Wright, the former director of the active municipal work of the City Club, and before that the executive secretary of the reform organization in Cincinnati, Professor [Charles Austin] Beard of the Political Science Department of Columbia, Robert [Studebaker] Binkerd, the secretary of the

Citizens' Union, Richard Childs, the author of the pamphlet which I left with you, and his partner in the advertising business, a man named Ericson,[1] Henry Sanford, a young lawyer, and myself. Mr. Clinton Rogers Woodruff,[2] and a Mr. Brown,[3] an associate editor of Collier's weekly, expected to be there, but were both prevented at the last minute.

After some discussion of the general question of reducing the number of elective offices, we discussed the best method of organizing for an active propaganda. We decided to prepare a brief prospectus in the form of a folder, setting forth as simply as possible the significance of a "short ballot" and the principal reasons which lead us to advocate it. This folder we plan to send out to a selected list of perhaps a hundred or a hundred and fifty men in various parts of the country, with the idea of forming from among them a preliminary organization, or "correspondence committee," for the collection of information and the further distribution of our prospectus.

Before preparing this prospectus, however, or taking any active steps, we decided that we should consult with a few older and more experienced men, for two reasons; first, in order to secure their advice as to the best method of launching such a movement, and their criticism of our tentative plans; second, that we might secure their backing and, if they were willing, the right to use their names as advocates of this proposed reform. Our idea was to call on them for practically no active work—we are planning to take care of that part ourselves!—but to ask from them advice from time to time, and general moral support. Your name was almost the first mentioned in this connection and the most unanimously agreed upon. The others are President Butler whom Professor Beard thought that he could surely induce to come to our assistance, President Finley of the City College, whom Beard will also approach, Norman Hapgood of Collier's Weekly, Albert Shaw, and Lawrence Abbott of the Outlook. Coming down from the direct primaries hearing at Albany the other night I had dinner with Mr. Hapgood and laid the matter before him, and he said he would be glad to come to a conference. Could you find time to come to such a conference at the City Club at some date on which all these gentlemen could be brought to-

[1] Alfred William Erickson, President of the A. W. Erickson Advertising Agency of New York.

[2] Lawyer of Philadelphia; Secretary of the National Municipal League.

[3] There was no "Mr. Brown" on the editorial staff of *Collier's, The National Weekly* at this time. Ludington was possibly referring to Roscoe Conkling Ensign Brown, Managing Editor of the *New York Tribune*. He was a member of the City Club and involved in various civic and good government organizations.

gether? I had hoped to come to Princeton to-morrow night with Binkerd for his address before the Municipal Club, and to see and talk with you then, but he postponed his trip,[4] so I am taking the much less satisfactory method of laying the plan before you by letter. Merely as a tentative proposal we agreed upon Thursday afternoon, the 22nd, at four o'clock, as a good hour for this conference. In case you are able and willing to attend such a conference, would this hour be convenient for you?[5] If not, is there any other day on which you could be here?

Attending this conference would not commit you to anything unless you wished it. I know it is a good deal to ask of anyone who is as busy as you are—yet on the other hand I know that you are strongly in favor of the object for which we mean to work, and I feel pretty confident that the right sort of an organization to promote this object will sooner or later secure very widespread support. It would be better if older and better-known men could take our places as the originators of an active movement, but at least we can make a start, and we are ready to put in some hard work. Beard strikes me as a first-rate man. He has had a couple of graduate students collecting material on this subject for several months, and is a member of the programme committee for the next conference of the American Political Science Association, so that he can perhaps arrange to have the subject presented there. Childs is inexperienced, but very enthusiastic and ready to work, and his father[6] will give us financial assistance. Mr. Clinton Rogers Woodruff will include this movement—or rather its object—as a topic at the next conference of the National Municipal League.

Childs has had very cordial and approving letters from a number of men including Bryce, President Eliot, and [Frank Johnson] Goodnow of Columbia, and the two latter will probably be willing to help. I should think, too, that Mr. [Henry Jones] Ford would approve of our plan, and I shall write to him, or talk with him about it.

If the plan for a conference such as I have outlined does not strike you as wise, can you perhaps suggest an alternative. It may be too late to call it off, but we could follow it up with some different plan if it seemed best.

[4] Someone was confused about the date of Binkerd's address. "Tomorrow night," April 12, fell during the spring vacation at Princeton. Binkerd did not speak at Princeton during the remainder of the spring term. About the Municipal Club, see WW to H. W. Turner, Oct. 19, 1908, n. 2, Vol. 18.

[5] As R. S. Childs to WW, July 10, 1909, discloses, Wilson did attend this meeting.

[6] William Hamlin Childs, President of the Barrett Manufacturing Co. (makers of coal tar products) of New York.

Hoping that you will approve of our undertaking, and will feel able to give us your assistance, believe me

ever faithfully yours Arthur Ludington.

ALS (WP, DLC).

To Cyrus Hall McCormick

My dear Cyrus: Princeton, N. J. April 12th, 1909.

My thoughts were so preoccupied with other matters lying very near to my heart in connection with the internal administration of the University when you were here, that I realized after you had gone how little interest I had shown in the very important matter of the Alumni Trustee election. I hope that you realize how warmly I appreciate and admire the efforts you are making to get Barr elected. I believe that it will be very difficult to elect him unless you can get considerable support in New York City and in Philadelphia, where I dare say the majority of our alumni voters are. I am the more appreciative, therefore, of the influences you have set going there in behalf of Barr. I think the whole thing can be done in a way which will not seem to the friends of the other candidate to make it a personal fight, as indeed it is not, but it seems to me a matter of critical importance. I think that you will find Mr. Shea of Pittsburgh very much interested, and he has so large a group of friends in New York that I venture to suggest that it is possible that through him something further might be done there in behalf of this candidacy. I feel that I myself must of necessity keep in the background, but it is delightful that you should have taken hold of the matter so vigorously and patriotically.

Always cordially and affectionately yours,

Woodrow Wilson

TLS (WP, DLC).

To Robert Bridges

My dear Bobby: Princeton, N. J. April 12th, 1909.

Thank you very much for your letter of April 8th and for your suggestion of Fabian Franklin. I know Dr. Franklin very well and think the suggestion an admirable one so far as his intellectual equipment is concerned. He lacks a little the planning and executive powers which would be needed in developing the enterprise I spoke of, but I am sure that the frields [friends] who consulted me will be very much interested in the suggestion you have made.

I had only a brief talk with Cyrus about the matter of the alumni trustee election, but enough, I hope, to get a correct idea of what he is doing to feel very much cheered by it. I think Cyrus feels as strongly as I do the necessity of quietly effecting our purpose in this matter, and I do not see why, if managed correctly, it may not be done in a way which will rob it of all appearance of personal opposition. I warmly appreciate, for my part, the interest that you and the other men are taking in it. It seems to me of first rate importance that a large number of votes should be quietly secured in New York and Philadelphia, since I suppose that after all that is where the majority of alumni votes are to be found.

Always faithfully and affectionately yours,

Woodrow Wilson

TLS (WC, NjP).

To Robert Randolph Henderson

My dear Bob: Princeton, N. J. April 12th, 1909.

I take real pleasure in enclosing the letter you ask for about George,[1] and I sincerely hope that it will be of service to him in securing the appointment as Rhodes Scholar.[2] I am very much interested indeed to hear that he is applying.

I was very much distressed the other day to learn that you had not been well. I hope, my dear fellow, that it is only a temporary setback and that you are on the high road to be perfectly strong again. It would distress us all very much if you were not strong by the time our next reunion comes around. The reunion would not be complete without you. Do take care of yourself and be sure to be here.

Always affectionately yours, Woodrow Wilson

TLS (WC, NjP).

1 George Henderson '09, son of Robert R. Henderson.

2 George Henderson did not win a Rhodes Scholarship.

From Melancthon Williams Jacobus

My dear President Wilson: Hartford, Conn. April 12/09

In a note just received from Harry Thompson I am distressed to learn of the discussion which prevailed at the meeting of the Curriculum Committee.

I regret all the more that my illness prevented my being present, if for no other reason at least because I might have had the satisfaction of standing up for the Preceptorial System, which I understand was the subject of debate[1]

I should be glad indeed to have a word from you regarding such situation as may have developed. If there is anything I can do by written or spoken word; or if you care to see me in New York, please let me do what I can to be of service to Princeton

I have received the minutes of the Committee meeting from Mr Imbrie for which I have to thank you.

Sincerely yours Melancthon W Jacobus

ALS (WP, DLC).

[1] As M. W. Jacobus to WW, April 19, 1909, and M. W. Jacobus to H. B. Thompson, April 20, 1909, disclose, there had been an acrimonious debate about the preceptorial system, with Dean Fine arguing that the scientific departments were understaffed as compared with the non-scientific departments.

To Mary Allen Hulbert Peck

Dearest Friend, Princeton, 13 April, '09.

I know that it must seem to you that I have been giving you advice which took too little heed of the sacrifice you were to make and the all but intolerable burdens you were to bear[1] and was merely a bit of worldly wisdom, and your letter of comment upon it, received this morning,[2] filled my eyes with tears,—not because you misjudged me (the letter itself shows you do not, really) but because your anguish and hopelessness are written in such pathetic terms through every sentence and I have been offering you no comfort but only wise advice which must of necessity seem wholly hateful to you. You know what my sympathy is. It could not be deeper or truer. I sometimes think that I understand you better than you understand yourself. Not one word of your bitter dispraise of yourself makes the slightest impression upon me. This is a time of deepest humiliation and unspeakable suffering for you. You are not capable of judging your own nature or your own motives in such circumstances. In the very midst of your disparagement of yourself there gleams unconsciously out the real self which thinks just and unselfish thoughts. I dare not, in such circumstances, use my heart in counselling you: I *must* use my head, and try to supply, if I may, some of the elements of counsel which for the time you cannot yourself supply. I must risk seeming cold in order to be of any real service at all. And I am not urging any irrevocable decision. I am only urging that you give yourself time to discover a workable modus vivendi, after you have for a little while been in a position to know all the possibilities you have to deal with.[3] Things may look one way in Bermuda, another when you see them at close range in America. I do not mean that they will look better; I mean only that they will disclose themselves more entirely and calculably.

But enough of advice: I only chill your heart with it, and suggest nothing that does not form quite as clearly in your own mind. Forgive me for having wounded you with apparently cold counsel. When the suffering is over and you have rested you will know that it was not cold, whatever else it may have been.

I am greatly distressed to learn that the handles did not come. I took them with my own hands to the express office two days before the steamer sailed and sent them off (from Philadelphia) addressed, as you had told me to address them, to "Miss Holmes, S. S. Bermudian, Pier 47 North River[.]" Your name was not on them, because you had asked me to leave it off, because of the customs. I supposed Miss Holmes to be one of the stewardesses.[4] This was more than two weeks ago. I will try to have the package traced. I am *very* much annoyed and disappointed. I was congratulating myself that I had been able to get them in plenty of time for your use. Did you inquire of Miss Holmes, or did you forget the directions you had given me? It makes me uneasy about the caning. I wonder if that will reach you. I addressed it, you remember, to the chief steward of the Bermudian, not knowing whether I was right or not in supposing that Miss Holmes was a stewardess and a permanent passenger. If I had been sure of that, I would have addressed it also to her, as I did the other package.

It gives me a delightful glimpse of you to hear about your poor friends and their troubles. In those glimpses I know that I see the real woman you are, and the sweet life that would have been yours if peace and love had set you free to follow your own instincts. It is as interesting and delightful as it is pathetic to have you thus unconsciously refute all your own judgments about yourself. You never can prove your case. You can only heighten the contrast between what you think you are and what you really are to the friends who are privileged to see you truly, a very noble woman distracted by suffering and yet displaying her lovely gifts in spite of herself whenever her active spirit turns to other things.

I have been chiefly resting since I last wrote. I was utterly worn out by the end of last week, and stayed all day Sunday in bed, sleeping, sleeping, sleeping without stint or end, and it has refreshed me a good deal. A week with the trustees of the University wears my spirits out more than it fatigues my body, and after it is over I sadly need sleep and silence. I am not naturally sanguine with regard to anything affecting myself. I simply fight stubbornly and circumspectly on. But fighting tells all the more severely on a man who fights without a knack for hoping confidently. I am simply a Scots-Irishman who will not be conquered. I am also, with utter steadfastness,

Your devoted friend, Woodrow Wilson

You have not told me yet what I am to do about engaging a room for your son.[5]

WWTLS (WP, DLC).

1 The difficulties in her relationship with her husband, Thomas Dowse Peck.

2 It is missing.

3 Wilson was apparently suggesting a trial separation instead of a divorce.

4 She was Mrs. Peck's friend in Bermuda who was teaching her how to refinish her antiques and cane her old chairs.

5 Allen Schoolcraft Hulbert, who planned to move to New York and look for a job in business.

To Cornelius Cuyler Cuyler

My dear C. C.: Princeton, N. J. April 13th, 1909.

Barringer and E. P. Davis and Cyrus McCormick have all talked with me on the matter of the affiliation between Jefferson College and Princeton, and I have visited the college and hospital and gone through them very carefully with several members of the Jefferson faculty, E. P., of course, included. Moreover, a committee of that faculty has been here in Princeton to lunch with me and talk the matter over. I am very much interested, but there are many reasons why we should move with a great deal of caution in this matter and be sure what we are doing before we take any steps at all. There is one thing that I feel it imperative to wait for. The Carnegie Foundation for the Advancement of Teaching has undertaken a very thorough-going examination of the whole question of medical education in the country, including of course the relations between medical schools and universities, the standards required and actually maintained in the medical schools, the opportunities for physicians, and the relation between demand and supply in that field of education. I have talked with Dr. Pritchett about this report from time to time, and he has given me many data which make me feel that we should be acting very blindly and unwisely, were we not to wait for the result of this investigation and be sure just where we would be placing Princeton in the general development of professional education in the country by such an affiliation, and by this affiliation in particular.

Jefferson College does not now maintain the standards to which the medical colleges of the country in general are being lifted and to which it will soon be necessary that they all should come, and I do not see how it is possible for it to maintain them unless it secure large endowments and relieve itself of the necessity of depending upon its students' fees. It has an admirable faculty, so far as I am able to judge, but is hampered by the fact that its fees must support it and that it is really in this essential character a proprietary institution. You can see, therefore, how affiliation with it might subject the University to very great additional financial burdens. The University could not afford to maintain a medical school whose standards did not conform to the best. Neither could it afford to affiliate in any merely nominal way with an institution over whose administration and personnel it would have no actual control. We must be very sure that the thing could be managed and that the University would gain more than it risked by the connection.

I say these things without wishing to prejudice the final conclusion and without meaning in any degree to disparage the school, which is doing the best work that can be done in the circumstances which condition it. I am only trying to show you that I have gone into the matter pretty thoroughly and have thought it over from end to end and have come to this conclusion for the present, that we must wait for the materials for a very thorough study and must refrain from committing ourselves for the present in any way or degree.

I have stated these conclusions to Cyrus, who seemed to think them entirely wise and justifiable.[1]

Always cordially and faithfully yours,

[Woodrow Wilson]

CCL (WWP, UA, NjP).

[1] There is no evidence of any further correspondence or discussion about this matter.

From John Sanburn Phillips[1]

My dear President Wilson: New York April 15th, 1909.

I am sending you, herewith, proofs of an article, which we are soon to publish, by William Allen White, on the Schools.[2]

I am sending advance proofs, for I would like very much to have any comment that you might feel like making about the article. I hope I am not presuming in assuming that you will be interested in it.[3]

Very sincerely yours, John S Phillips

TLS (WP, DLC).

[1] Editor of *The American Magazine* and President of the Phillips Publishing Co., publisher of *The American Magazine.*

[2] William Allen White, "The Schools–The Main Spring of Democracy," *The American Magazine*, LXVIII (August 1909), 376-83.

[3] No comment by Wilson was published in *The American Magazine.*

Notes for an Address in Detroit[1]

University Club 16 April, 1909

Political Reform

Recent ardour for reform (of all kinds)
Dissatisfaction with legislative, administrative, and judicial instrumentalities

Consequent desire for *political* reform
E. g. Municipal }
State }
These two *moving in opposite directions* (*concentration–dispersion*), except in respect of initiative and referendum (i. e. *ad interim*, occasional, as contrasted with periodic, control, non-representative in character)

The *argument for Representation*
Debate
Leadership

Real representation:
Simplification, simplification, simplification
Limit of simplification: Comprehension of all parts of the business=*Efficiency.*

Opinion must be formed, and must take hold.

A period of reconsideration and reconstruction at hand, which should be
(1) Systematic
(2) Formed, not on theory, but *on experience*, as in 1787.

Note: 'All just gov't derived from the people,' but we have so elaborated the process of election that gov't. is *not* derived from the people

WWhw MS (WP, DLC).

[1] The Editors have been unable to find a newspaper report of this address.

From Robert Garrett

My dear Mr. Wilson: Baltimore, April 16th, 1909.

I have been thinking a little bit about the matter of securing a fund with which to meet the salary of Littmann if he should be called back to Princeton.[1] I dislike extremely, as we all do, to go constantly to the men who have furnished so much money for all kinds of purposes in Princeton, and I therefore have determined to make up a tentative list of men, most of them among the younger alumni, who might be asked for comparatively small sums, say $250 or $500 each; possibly it would be well in some cases even to ask for only $100. All these subscriptions should, I presume, be payable each year for a period of three or five years. Not knowing very well the financial resources of many men it is hard to get up a satisfactory list, but these are the men who have occurred to me, or who have been suggested by others.

Alexander Van Rensselaer '71	Harold F. McCormick '95
Howard A. Colby '95	A. J. A. Alexander '97
E. D. Balken '97	Howard C. Brokaw '97
Frank G. Curtis '97	Richard E. Dwight '97
A. H. Hagemeyer '97	A. W. Jamison '97
H. B. Jamison, '97	Ario Pardee '97
F. Sturgis, Jr. '97	William B. Trainer '97
Robert C. Wilkins '97	Percy H. Williams '97
C. B. Derr '97	Ralph Derr '97
G. J. Geer, Jr. '97	George K. Crozer, Jr. '98
Archibald S. Alexander '02	Childs Frick '05
Edward K. Ream '05	

Will you not kindly give me your opinion of these men and let me have any suggestions you may care to make with regard to the points that should be mentioned in a letter to them about Littmann?

With kind regards,

Sincerely yours, Robert Garrett.

TLS (WP, DLC).

[1] Richard Ludwig Enno Littmann, former Lecturer on Semitic Philology and Librarian of the Oriental Department of Princeton University Library and Professor of Semitic Philology at the University of Strassburg since 1906.

To Robert Garrett

My dear Mr. Garrett: Princeton, N. J. April 19th, 1909.

I would have replied sooner to your letter of April 16th, had I not been absent from home. I was speaking, the day it was written, in Detroit.

Ardently as I desire to have Professor Littmann come back and make use of our collection here and develop our neglected Semitic studies, I find myself increasingly alarmed by the growing proportion of the work of the University which is carried by subscription. So far as the plan you suggest is concerned, I think it a wise one, and I believe the list you have made up a list of men from whom the money could be obtained, but I wish very much that before you go any further with the matter you would make a point of having a talk with Mr. Dodge, to see what his own feeling, as Chairman of the Committee of Fifty, is with regard to the whole question of adding further subscriptions to our already enormous list.

It is in this way, of course, that we take the government of the University out of our hands and put it in the hands of those who are supplying the money, and of late I have felt this pressure and embarrassment very keenly. Will you not be coming this way some time soon, and can we not have a conversation about the matter? I was so preoccupied with many things at the time the Board met that I spoke upon impulse, and I would like to have a talk with you which would look in several directions and make sure of the ground we are on.

Always cordially and faithfully yours,

Woodrow Wilson

TLS (Selected Corr. of R. Garrett, NjP).

To Albertina Pyne Russell[1]

My dear Mrs. Russell, Princeton, 19 April, 1909.

My delay in replying to your note written just before Easter[2] has been due to my absence from home.

I will write to Major Higginson with pleasure, as you suggest.[3] I shall be a little at a loss, I foresee, as to how I may put the matter to him, but I will do it as well as I can. From the way in which he *offered* the concert to us last year I got the distinct impression that, at any rate in his mind, he was offering us a gift from himself. I supposed that he *expected* the concert to cost him something personally. Therein lies my embarrassment.

But I dare say I shall find a way to put it which will disclose the facts and not wear the appearance of asking a favour of Major Higginson. At any [rate] I will be pleased to try, rather than not get a concert by the Boston Symphony for lack of trying.

With warmest regard,

Sincerely Yours, Woodrow Wilson

ALS (WC, NjP).

[1] Mrs. Archibald Douglas Russell.

[2] It is missing.

[3] See WW to H. L. Higginson, May 19, 1909, in which Wilson wrote to inquire whether Major Higginson would send the Boston Symphony Orchestra to Princeton in 1909 as he had done the year before.

From Melancthon Williams Jacobus

My dear President Wilson: Hartford, Conn., April 19th, 1909.

I thank you most heartily for writing me so fully regarding the unfortunate debate over the Preceptorial System at the last meeting of the Curriculum Committee.[1]

Some time ago Dean Fine said to me that he felt money could be saved to the University by reconsidering the distribution of the preceptors, and I was quite willing to agree with him then, as I am now with the Finance Committee, that if there is any way in which the budget of the University can be helped it is certainly our obligation to do all we can to find the way, and I am quite willing, on general principles, to believe that we may be able to accomplish something. On the other hand, I wish to assure you that I am absolutely and utterly in agreement with you as to the essential purpose of the Preceptorial System and the resultant necessity under which we are of essentially differentiating between the Reading Departments and the Laboratory Departments. Nothing could be better said than what you have said as to the object of the Preceptorial System in getting teacher and pupil into conference on subjects which come into vital contact with life. This is to me the democracy of education, and it does have an importance in the Reading Departments that it can never have in the Laboratory Departments. I do not believe any more than you do that Dean Fine's test between the Departments is in principle correct. It does not see the deeper thing which you point out and which the Committee must never lose sight of.

I do not know that my presence at the meeting of the Committee would have helped the situation at all, for it is evident that the matter must be talked out fully before we can come to united conclusions. In the meantime, however, will it not be possible for us to, in some way, prepare for the meeting we must have before Commencement? Would you propose any conferences in New York where we might get down to a full discussion on this matter and clear the way for the next Committee meeting?

I wish sincerely that you would be willing to come up to Hartford for a day or two of real rest and talk the matter over with me in our home. Mrs. Jacobus[2] unites with me in this suggestion, and I do hope that you will consider it carefully. We will have lots of room for you, and you can be just as quiet as you wish, and we can talk the matter over in any way you would like. You could also have a chance of a talk with Dr. Mackenzie,[3] but I would promise not to give you any more publicity than would be compatible with the idea of a rest.

With kindest regards,

Yours very sincerely, Melancthon W. Jacobus

TLS (WP, DLC).

[1] Wilson's letter is missing.

[2] Clara Cooley Jacobus.

[3] The Rev. Dr. William Douglas Mackenzie, President of Hartford Theological Seminary.

Melancthon Williams Jacobus to Henry Burling Thompson

My dear Harry: Hartford, Conn., April 20th, 1909

. . . I confess to being utterly discouraged regarding the wrangle in the Curriculum Committee meeting, over the Preceptorial System. I know perfectly well what Dean Fine's criticism is, that there has not perhaps been the right kind of judgment exercised, from the expense point of view, in the securing and distributing of the preceptors, and I am quite willing to believe that a more judicious oversight, from this financial point of view, might help the budget of the University and not disturb the real effectiveness of the system. But his debate with Wilson, at least as I gather it from a long letter received from the President the other day, seemed to lack in its understanding of the essential differences which must lie between the Preceptorial work in the Reading Departments and those in the Laboratory Departments. The test which Dean Fine suggested that, in order to determine whether there was the most economical distribution of preceptors, one should consider the number of students in these two Departments and the amount of money spent on them in the University budget, together with the results obtained in turning out good men I cannot believe any more than does President Wilson is the proper way to look at it.

I am perfectly convinced that one of the real objects in the

Preceptorial System is what I am accustomed to call the democracy of education, in other words the close association of teacher and pupil in conference on those subjects which have contact with life, and which are intended to do a vast deal more than merely convey the necessary items of instruction for examination. Now this must obtain more in the Reading Departments than it does in the Laboratory Departments, and I think it ought to be taken into consideration in all this criticism on the distribution of preceptors.

You will understand, of course, that I quite stand by the request which the Finance Committee has made to us that we should seek every means in our power to reduce the expense of the preceptors, and it may be that even on this basis of the essential difference between the Reading and the Laboratory Departments the assignment to the Reading Departments is still too large; but we should not allow ourselves to lose sight of the fact that the distribution can never be put on the same level in both Departments.

I am very glad that the answer to the Finance Committee's inquiry has been postponed. I only wish that we could have a talk with Fine before the next meeting.

Would you be willing to come over to New York if I could get him to come down there, and we could spend an afternoon in discussing the matter? If we could have [Thomas D.] Jones with us, it might be even better. Perhaps this is not convenient to you, but I thought you might be coming up to Farmington some day soon, in which case I would like to have you either do this or stop and spend the night with me in Hartford. In fact, you know you have promised, when you came next to Farmington, that you would make my house your headquarters. This you must do anyway. Please let me hear from you as soon as possible. I am anxious also to have a talk with Wilson, and am writing him today with a view to arranging some time convenient to us both.

Yours very sincerely, Melancthon W Jacobus

TLS (H. B. Thompson Papers, NjP).

From George Brinton McClellan

My dear Mr. President: New York Apl. 21, 1909.

I should like to again express to you my appreciation of what you said last night.[1] I can only assure you that I most sincerely value your good opinion and your friendship.

I am, with best wishes and kind regards,

Yours ever, Geo B McClellan

TLS (WP, DLC).

[1] At a dinner at the Waldorf-Astoria in New York, given by Princeton alumni to honor Mayor McClellan. A news report of Wilson's address is printed at April 28, 1909.

To John Lambert Cadwalader

My dear Mr. Cadwalader: Princeton, N. J. April 21st, 1909.

After the Mayor spoke last night, I did not withdraw from the dinner, as I hope you understand, but went up and joined Mrs. McClellan[1] in her box and sat with her while Mr. Hedges[2] and Mr. Edmund Wilson[3] spoke. I tried to find you after the diners had dispersed, but was unable to do so, and write now to say how much I enjoyed sitting by you, how much I appreciated your introduction of me, and how appropriate a thing I thought it that you should represent the University on such an occasion. I do not know anyone whom I would rather sit under or acknowledge as a representative of what we stand for.

Always, with warm regard,

Faithfully yours, Woodrow Wilson

TLS (CtY).

[1] Georgianna Heckscher McClellan.

[2] Job Elmer Hedges, Princeton 1884, lawyer of New York.

[3] Edmund Wilson, Princeton 1885, Attorney General of New Jersey, 1908-14, father of Edmund Wilson, Princeton 1916, writer and critic.

From Robert Garrett

My dear President Wilson: Baltimore, April 21st, 1909.

Thank you for your letter of the 19th inst. I am in entire sympathy with your view of this question of carrying on so much of the work on insecure foundations, and giving over some degree of control to those who are supplying the money.

I hope to be in Princeton before very long, and shall endeavor to find you so that we may have a further talk about Littmann.

Sincerely yours, Robert Garrett.

TLS (WP, DLC).

From William Wirt Phillips

My dear Doctor Wilson: New York, April 22, '09

I have received your letters of April 12th and 21st in reference to an inter-club conference, and appreciate very much the kind spirit in which you have met us. I have communicated with all the clubs, asking them to give me the names of their representatives authorized to act for them in future conferences, as I am not sure that all the men who met with us were the ones so authorized. As soon as I have this list complete I will send it to you for comparison with yours.

I am very much pleased with the Committee which the Faculty have appointed to consider this subject, as I know from personal acquaintance how efficient they will be.

I can but assure you again that our Committee is more than desirous of doing whatever lies in their power to improve club conditions in Princeton.

With kindest regards,

Very sincerely, William W. Phillips

TLS (WP, DLC).

From Adrian Riker[1]

My dear Doctor: Newark N. J. April 23, 1909.

I am delighted to hear that you have been able to accept an invitation to address the Princeton Club of this city on May 5th.[2]

I hope that you will be able to spend the night with me at my house. If you will let me know the train by which you expect to arrive in Newark, I will meet you at the station and will be at your entire disposal from that time on until you leave Newark.

Yours very truly, Adrian Riker

TLS (WP, DLC).

[1] Wilson's classmate, a lawyer in Newark, N. J.

[2] A news report of this address is printed at May 6, 1909.

A News Item

[April 24, 1909]

HONOR FOR EDUCATOR.

PATERSON, April 24.—A complimentary dinner was tendered last night to Dr. A. J. Reinhart[1] to mark his completion of twenty-five years of service in the local High School. Woodrow Wilson, president of Princeton University, and William H. Demarest, president of Rutgers College; Judge Francis Scott,[2] Mayor McBride[3] and a large body of educators were present.

Rev. Anthony H. Stein, rector of our Lady of Lourdes Church, made the invocation. The address made by President Wilson was on the topic, "The Schoolmaster," while President Demarest spoke upon "The High School and the Colleges."

Printed in the *Newark Evening News*, April 24, 1909.

[1] J. Albert Reinhart, Principal of the Paterson High School.

[2] Judge of the Passaic County Court.

[3] Andrew F. McBride.

From Robert Randolph Henderson

My dear Woodrow, Cumberland, Md. April 24th, 1909.

Your warm letter to me and the splendid letter that you wrote about George both touched me very deeply, and Mrs. Henderson[1] as well. It gave me the pleasantest afternoon I have had since I have been sick. I have not acknowledged it sooner because almost immediately upon receiving it, I was taken with the grippe which has had me down ever since until now when I am about ready to get around a little again in a wheeled chair. It is very certain that I cannot be at the reunion. The Doctor has pronounced my case tuberculosis and while he seems not to take a hopeless view of it, I recognize the fact that my age and constitution are somewhat against me. He thinks the infection came from being confined in the bad air of our ill-ventilated Court House, as I have no family history that would presage any trouble, nor had I any preliminary symptoms. I am living out of doors, or will be in a day or two, on our back porch. I shall miss the reunion more than I can say. Princeton is the place I love best of any in the world, next to my home, and my class mates are the friends to whom my warmest affections go out.

With most cordial remembrances for all your family from whom I have received such constant kindness and hospitality, I am, affectionately yours,

Robert R. Henderson

HwLS (WP, DLC).

[1] Louisa Patterson Henderson.

To Andrew Fleming West

My dear Professor West: Princeton, N. J. April 26th, 1909.

I have notified the Clerk of the Faculty of the appointment of the following members of the Faculty to constitute the Committee on the Graduate School: Dean Fine, Professor Daniels, Professor Hibben, Professor Capps, and Professor Conklin. I know how eager Mr. Cram is to get forward with the plans, and I would suggest that you call these gentlemen together for organization as early as possible and determine the best way to facilitate conference with Cram, to the pressing forward of the business in hand.

Very truly yours, Woodrow Wilson,
President of the University.

TLS (UA, NjP).

A News Report

[April 27, 1909]

MINISTERIAL CLUB MEETING.[1]

President Wilson Addressed the Club Yesterday Afternoon. Officers for Next Year Elected.

The last meeting of the Ministerial Club for this year, held yesterday afternoon in Murray Hall, was addressed by President Wilson, who spoke on "The Claims and Character of the Christian Ministry." Dr. Wilson opened his address by pointing out the fact that it was becoming very difficult for churches to find the right kind of men for the ministry.

That the Church is losing hold is a subject for much contemporaneous literature. A symptom of this is the immediate popularity which any religious fad enjoys. And yet these fads are only a means of satisfying a hunger for spiritual things which is very marked at the present date. The only explanation of the fact that the churches do not satisfy this spiritual craving is the loss of the Christian ministry's old power. It should be a challenge to all Christian men of the best intellects that they should join so honored an organization that stands in need of being revived. College men who can go into the pulpit and can assist in the interpretation of modern knowledge in a religious light, have an unparalleled chance for doing good.

The claims of the ministry are imperative. They are crushing to the man who is weak in his convictions, but they bring out all the strength in the strong man. The minister should not only exercise his individual helpfulness in the family life of his parishioners, but he should also be the intellectual guide to show men the certain path of truth. In the ministry there is something worth while which appeals to the best men and the best minds, and this is its claim.

Unlike the men in other professions, who are only expected to do something, the minister is expected to do something and also to *be* something. The minister must add to his knowledge a peculiar attitude toward life. He should appreciate that his capacity is that of an ambassador from God, and should so act that the dignity of his sovereign may be recognized. He should carry about with him an atmosphere, of his own, which is the result of his profound conviction in the tenets of his belief.

Such a man is successful, for it is always the sincere, the convinced man who appeals to his fellow-men. And men who intend to enter the ministry should think of this, and ask themselves whether or not they fully believe the Christian faith, and whether they are willing to subordinate their conduct to this belief. No man worthy of the name should go into the ministry, regarding it as a means to make a living or as a way to get a certain kind of social standing.

The character of the ministry demands that men who enter it should be unmistakably chosen for this mission. Their spiritual and intellectual make-up should compel them to such a course. Thus the reason for going into the ministry is not a philosophical one, but the imperative "you must," coming from within the soul.

After President Wilson's address a meeting of the club was held, at which the following officers were elected for the coming year: President, Jesse Hermann 1910, of Stirling, N. J.; Vice-President, David John Terry 1910, of Philadelphia, Pa.; Secretary and Treasurer, Ernest Paxton Janvier 1911, of Philadelphia, Pa.

Printed in the *Daily Princetonian*, April 27, 1909.

1 The Ministerial Club was organized on January 9, 1908. As the name implies, it was composed of students who intended to enter the Christian ministry.

To Mary Allen Hulbert Peck

[Princeton, N. J.] 28 April, 1909

There was no steamer sailing to-day. I can therefore add a few lines to say that I found your letter of the 24th[1] awaiting me here when I got back from Philadelphia, with its delightful news that you had 'recovered' from the grippe (I am trying to accept the word as literally as possible) and the very reassuring announcement that you would not try to rush the packing but would wait for the steamer on the sixth or even on the thirteenth. I will send a line to your son, to meet him when the steamer comes in, to say that I will be in N. Y. on Monday on an errand wh. should leave me a partially free afternoon and to ask him where I may see him then to consult as to what assistance I can render him in the matter of finding a suitable room, or in any other matter. I will also try to find some one of whom I can make inquiries about the standing of Dick Brothers.[2] I can readily find out all about them from some of the men I know on Wall St. Do you not know the members of the firm? How does Allen happen to go to them?

By the time this letter reaches you your son will have sailed—out into the world, to make his own way, his moorings cut and your relations once for all changed! I know what it will cost you, —your 'boy' gone,—a man substituted to whom you can play mother only in your heart, by yearning solicitude, tender counsel, a word now and again when the dear chance of seeing him comes,—all the sweet intimacy and dependence gone,—your baby gone out of your arms, and in great part out of your ken; and my heart is heavy for you. I know how desolate you will feel—how the sense of loneliness will thicken like something that chokes your faculties, weakens your sense of reality—of identity even—and makes all your life seem strange and disconnected from memory. I never had a son, but I *was* a son and had a mother whom I devotedly loved and in whom I saw all these things when I was separated from her for life. She lived long enough to be very proud of her son's success, and he loved her always as he had loved her when he was a lad, but he had gone from the household, his call was not in her ear, the days went by without him. I am sorry, so sorry, and wish I knew the right words of comfort with which to wing my words of deep, affectionate sympathy. Perhaps you will go to live with him—and the years bring you the love of new friends of whom I am proud to be one. Woodrow Wilson

ALS (WC, NjP).

[1] It is missing.

[2] A banking firm located at 30 Broad St., New York.

A News Report of an After-Dinner Address in New York

[April 28, 1909]

The Dinner in Honor of Mayor McClellan

Nearly five hundred Princeton alumni foregathered at the Waldorf-Astoria in New York on the evening of April 20th, to show their appreciation of the public services of the Hon. George B. McClellan '86, Mayor of New York City. . . .

Parker D. Handy '79, President of the Princeton Club of New York, began the speech-making by presenting Mr. Cadwalader as toastmaster. . . .

When Toastmaster Cadwalader introduced President Wilson

there was much cheering. Dr. Wilson began by saying that since the product of a university is the men it makes, he was glad of an opportunity to speak of a particular product of Princeton—Mayor McClellan.

"The Mayor of New York," he continued, "has won his distinction in a way which I am sorry to say has come to be regarded as peculiar in American life. He has made his way slowly. There has been no self-advertisement, but in the midst of many difficulties he has mastered them, even while in the toils of an irrational city charter, without key or principle. It is a fine thing to note that the integrity of a city officer can win out in spite of the trammels laid upon him by the law itself. Now he has won his way to the place of trust and affection that he enjoys, by the characteristic of manhood—a big word that includes self-respect, integrity and courage."

President Wilson went on to say that knowledge in men is much rarer than honest desire, but that the Mayor had not only lived up to his lights but "they have shone bright and have illuminated." He spoke of the Mayor's name for scholarship, saying that this was a fine thing in a day when "many university men at least conceal their knowledge of letters." A cheer from the back of the room followed and President Wilson remarked: "I trust that was a cry of hope."

President Wilson discussed the relation of the university to public affairs. He pointed out that the days when men went to college solely to prepare for the learned professions had passed and that now the majority of college men entered the business world. This, he said, together with the fact that hardly a generation has passed since science secured a sure foothold in our universities, accounted for the changes that have taken place. To-day, he said, the great need was for change.

"Society always renews itself from the bottom. This renewal must come from the young men pressing up like sap in the trees—the sap hasn't always reached their heads, but when it does a wholesome intoxication follows which is dangerous to restrain."

President Wilson pointed out further that the university must not produce a few types, but must be democratic above all things. It must be a place where all new forces are drawn and welcomed in a spirit that will challenge them to express themselves and give them free leave to exercise the fermentation that is sure to result when these are introduced into the old order of things.

President Wilson closed with the statement that Mayor McClellan was such a man as the modern university sought to produce and that the diners were met not only to celebrate the success of a man, but to redevote themselves to a principle of patriotism.[1]

Printed in the *Princeton Alumni Weekly*, IX (April 28, 1909), 454-55.

[1] There is a WWhw outline of this address, dated April 20, 1909, in WP, DLC.

To Cleveland Hoadley Dodge

My dear Cleve: Princeton, N. J. April 30th, 1909.

I have been a long time returning these letters, but it was a long time before I had a leisure moment in which to read them with attention. I have read them with the greatest interest and quite agree with you that Mott is an extraordinary man, marked out for an influence and a career which is in many ways quite unprecedented.

Always affectionately yours, Woodrow Wilson

TLS (WC, NjP).

To Edwin Silas Wells Kerr[1]

My dear Mr. Kerr: Princeton, N. J. April 30th, 1909.

I am quite tied up for the present, but if Monday evening, May 10th, would suit the convenience of the men at Dial Lodge,[2] I would be very pleased to dine with them on that evening and shall look forward to it as a pleasure. If you will kindly let me know whether that date is perfectly convenient and at what hour you would expect me, I would be very much obliged.

Cordially yours, Woodrow Wilson

TLS (received from H. W. Bragdon).

[1] A member of the Class of 1909.

[2] An eating club founded in 1907 by members of the Class of 1909 who had failed of election to the older clubs. According to the anonymous historian of Dial Lodge, both Woodrow Wilson and Mrs. Wilson took special interest in the new organization, and it was in deference to Wilson's dislike of the word "club" that the group called itself a "lodge." For several years the lodge was located in the building on Prospect Avenue formerly occupied by the Tiger Inn Club. In 1912 Dial Lodge was incorporated as a club and in 1917 moved into a permanent clubhouse built to its own specifications on Prospect Avenue. See *The 50th Anniversary of Dial Lodge* (n. p., n. d.).

From Charles Ernest Scott

Dear Sir: Tsingtau North China. 4-30-09.

As I have been out preaching in the dirty streets of these mud-villages, explaining the "Jesus doctrine" to these unspeakably poor & degraded people—not because they are intrinsically lovable, but because their souls are precious for the great [price] paid to redeem them—your article in March 1909 "Assembly Herald" on "Being Something in the Ministry,"[1] came to me like a breath of pure air. It has energized my will. Thank you.

May I show my appreciation by sending some kodaks for comparison & contrast—a camera commentary on Confucianism & Christianity? Perhaps you can use them for His cause

Sincerely & Gratefully Yours Charles Ernest Scott

ALS (WP, DLC).

[1] A paragraph entitled "On Being Something in the Ministry" appeared in the Philadelphia *Assembly Herald*, xv (March 1909), 131. The paragraph was an exact quotation of the penultimate paragraph of Wilson's address, "The Minister and the Community," printed at March 30, 1906, Vol. 16.

A News Report of a Speech at the Annual Banquet of the *Daily Princetonian*

[May 1, 1909]

THE DAILY PRINCETONIAN ENTERTAINS.

The eleventh annual banquet of The Daily Princetonian was held last evening at the Princeton Inn. The dinner was the largest ever given by the Princetonian, one hundred and fifty covers being laid. . . .

President Wilson in response to the toast, "University Ideals," said:

"The delightful relaxations, friendships and sports which constitute a legitimate part of college life, should be relaxations only, and not occupations. There is a peculiar danger to which we are exposed as college men and as young men. It will not do to conceive college life from the view-point of boys. We should stop being boys when we leave the preparatory school. Let us be men and look upon the things around us with the eyes of men who have put away childish things and are desirous of seeing the world as it is. The characteristic process of a university is a maturing process, is the process which lifts us out of mere youthfulness into that thoughtful period of life when we look upon the world as a place where we shall have to move as those who understand.

"I have heard men with sons in college say that they had not put them in college with any particular desire that they should study or learn anything, but that they should there experience a certain life, and should subject themselves to the processes of a school of friendship and of manners. These men were proposing deliberately to subject their sons to an interval between one process and another. These gentlemen are proposing that there should be a pause in the process of life, in the processes of maturing.

"More thoughtful men complain of their sons' experiences in college; that whereas in certain schools of preparation they were made to work and that after the college period they will be again made to work in their professions or in business, they have lost in the meantime the momentum which they gained when they were younger, and go inexperienced to the places where they should know how to work.

"It seems to me a dangerous heresy to think of college as a place of interval between the ardent processes of life. On the contrary I believe that a university is, of all places a place where there should be a conception of unchosen discipline and particularly in a democratic country. The men who are the real enemies of the country are not the men who deliberately purpose evil but the men who are so situated that they are cut off in understanding and in sympathy from the body of their fellow-citizens. One of the things which makes us unserviceable citizens is that there are certain classes of men with whom we have never been able to associate, and whom we have, therefore, been unable to understand. I believe that the process of a university should be a process of unchosen contacts where a man is put in contact with modern thought and life and particularly with the life of his own country. Discipline does not consist in experiencing the things you prefer. Discipline consists in experiencing the things the world presents to you, whether you like them or not.

["]This University is not going to be made by its Faculty or its Trustees. It is going to be made, and given its color and character by its sons, and if this nourishing mother can send her sons out with this idea of a university, then Princeton will reign in the field of education, for she will then be the distinctive American university, where no caste or privilege is recognized, but where America herself is reproduced in small.

"I look forward to the annual Princetonian banquet as an evening on which we can renew our pledges, upon which we can again conceive the intellectual responsibility which is laid upon us, so that we can again join hands and say 'We are sworn to this cause and our mother shall not find us recreant.' "[1]

Printed in the *Daily Princetonian*, May 1, 1909; one editorial heading omitted.

[1] There is a WWhw outline of this speech, dated April 30, 1909, in WP, DLC.

From Ernest Ludlow Bogart

My dear President Wilson: Princeton, N. J., May 1, 1909.

Professor Daniels on Saturday communicated to me the results of his interview with you, and suggested that I submit his memorandum to you in order to be certain that he represented his understanding with precision. Accordingly I reproduce herewith his letter, which I should be glad to have confirmed. I may say that upon receipt of it I telegraphed Professor Kinley, of the University of Illinois,[1] declining his offer, as my reply had already been delayed. Professor Daniel's memorandum is as follows:

"In consideration of your offer from the University of Illinois, which offer you agree to decline, the President on his part engages: (1) to add to the staff of instruction in our Department at the earliest time he may be able to obtain funds for that purpose, the first addition in the University to be made in our Department; (2) to advance you so soon as such addition is made to the staff of instruction, to the position of Professor in the University with such functions and duties as attach to such rank; (3) to advance your pay when you are a Professor to a figure commensurate with the work of the position, such advance of pay to be made as soon as the resources of the University permit. On the other hand you agree, in case you accept the suggested arrangement, to continue the work you are now engaged in, and in the rank of Preceptor which you now hold. It is also understood that in case you assent to and accept this arrangement, you are at liberty to assume, with the President's assent thereto, (which assent on his part is assumed to constitute a part of this agreement) that you will be continued as Preceptor until you are advanced to a Professorship in accordance with the foregoing arrangement."

I cannot close this letter without expressing my appreciation of your kindness, and my plesaure [pleasure] at the thought of remaining in Princeton.

Yours very sincerely, Ernest L. Bogart

TLS (WP, DLC).

[1] David Kinley, Professor of Economics and Dean of the Graduate School, University of Illinois.

From Henry Smith Pritchett

Personal

My dear President Wilson, New York May 1, 1909.

I have tried unsuccessfully for a week to send you a line relative to the matter discussed in our last conversation.

I endeavored the best I could to make an opportunity for Mr. Vanderlip & myself to make a special plea with Mr. Carnegie in this matter. During the last month however a number of matters were under discussion with him of such importance to the Foundation and other interests that I did not feel it wise to try to inject any other thing until they were settled which was only accomplished in the last day or two before Mr. Carnegie sailed. Meantime such passing references as were made to it satisfied me of the hopelessness of getting any measure of success. For all these reasons I was obliged to let the time go by without any actual trial of the thing. For this I have much regret but it seemed impossible to avoid.

Yours sincerely, Henry S. Pritchett

ALS (WP, DLC).

From Francis William Dinsmore[1]

My dear President Wilson, Trenton, N. J. May second [1909].

Allow me to express to you my appreciation of the speech you made at the Princetonian banquet. Although not the first time I have heard you express the same thought it seemed to me that you put it before the men on Friday evening in a particularly effective manner.

I know that it is your purpose to inspire Princeton to the fullest understanding of what you mean when you say that a University should be first of all and always a place for intellectual development. Expositions of the ideal such as you present whenever called upon cannot help but carry conviction to those who love Princeton and who can already see the first fruits of the working out of the ideal.

Your time is too fully occupied for me to ask you to take more of it in reading longer lines.

Kindly accept the sincere appreciation of one more Princetonian for the great work you are doing.

Respectfully, Francis W. Dinsmore.

ALS (WP, DLC).

1 Princeton 1904, at this time employed by the Imperial Porcelain Works of Trenton, New Jersey. Dinsmore had been editor-in-chief of the *Daily Princetonian* during his senior year in college.

From Walter Hulme Sawyer[1]

My dear Dr. Wilson: Hillsdale, Mich., May 3, 1909.

The committee appointed by the Board of Regents to recommend to it a successor to Dr. [James Burrill] Angell, has had suggested to it, among many others, the name of Dr. John [Huston] Finley, Pres. of the University of N. Y. as being eminently fitted for this duty. Will you be kind enough to give me your opinion of his qualifications? If you will do this I shall be grateful. While I have felt that an offer from Michigan might not attract him, because of his happy relationships at New York, yet, as his name has been urged, we are desirous of getting all the information we can to help us in our final determination and recommendation.

With kindest regards, I am,

Yours sincerely, Walter H. Sawyer

TLS (WP, DLC).

[1] Physician of Hillsdale, Mich., and a member of the Board of Regents of the University of Michigan.

To Henry Smith Pritchett

My dear President Pritchett: Princeton, N. J. May 4th, 1909.

Thank you for your letter of May 1st. I must admit that it has brought me keen disappointment, but I am of course confident that you exercised the best and wisest judgment in the matter of speaking to Mr. Carnegie. Without money, my tasks here look to me almost impossible, and I have recently been tempted in my weakness to wish that they would call me to the University of Michigan or somewhere else where with a change of venue I might approach the problem of university life from a fresh quarter. There are other men with money, of course, but I do not know how to get at them.

The Executive Committee of the Association of American Universities met, as you know, in the offices of the Foundation yesterday, and I was disappointed that I did not get a glimpse of you. I left my warmest messages of regard for you with Mr. Bowman.[1] I was sorry to hear from him that you had not been well and that you were in Atlanta. I hope that you are entirely strong and fit again.

With warm appreciation of the way in which you have kept my interests in mind,

Cordially and faithfully yours, Woodrow Wilson

TLS (H. S. Pritchett Papers, DLC).

[1] John Gabbert Bowman, Secretary of the Carnegie Foundation for the Advancement of Teaching, 1907-11.

To Ernest Ludlow Bogart

My dear Mr. Bogart: [Princeton, N. J.] May 5th, 1909.

I sincerely hope there has not been a misunderstanding. I am sure that when Professor Daniels used the word "professor" in the second clause of the understanding which he conveyed to you from me he used it in the sense in which I used it when I spoke with him. What I said to him was, first, that it was my purpose to add to the staff of instruction in the Department of History and Politics at the earliest time at which I might be able to obtain funds for that purpose, and that the first addition to the University would be made in our Department. Second, that upon the appointment of such an additional preceptor in our Department I would recommend to the Board of Trustees that you be given a position similar to that which has already been assigned to Mr. Meeker. That is to say, that you would be transferred from the strictly preceptorial work to a position which entitles the occupant to give lectures and to conduct a course, with the corresponding difference in the title of your rank. And, third, that I would secure an advance in your salary either at that time or as soon thereafter as the resources of the University permitted. Of course, it went by implication with all of this that you were to be continued in your present position until these changes became possible.

You will see that this is simply what Professor Daniels said to you, with the exception that the implication of his wording would seem to be that you would be advanced at once, should such an opportunity arise, to the rank of full professor. Standing, as I do, at the center of all Departments of the University, I feel that that promise would be very rash, because it would invade so many precedents and create so many collateral difficulties in other Departments, if the opportunity we have in mind should occur soon. If it should be somewhat delayed, then it might be possible to advance you to the full professorship.

You will understand that in my view a professorship differs from a preceptorship only in the way I have indicated, namely that the professor, whether of full rank or of the rank of assistant professor, is put in charge of a course and gives lectures besides doing preceptorial work, whereas the preceptor does only preceptorial work so far as the undergraduates are concerned. I am very anxious that no contrasts of rank should be thought of, though it is true that a larger salary in almost every instance goes with the title of assistant professor and professor.

I am sure that these are the terms which Professor Daniels understood me to name and that they are the terms which he meant to convey to you in his letter. I trust that the use of the word "professor" without qualification has not led to any misunderstanding.

With much regard,

Sincerely yours, [Woodrow Wilson]

CCL (WWP, UA, NjP).

To Walter Hulme Sawyer

My dear Mr. Sawyer: Princeton, N. J. May 5th, 1909.

Allow me to acknowledge the receipt of your letter of May 3rd and to express my gratification that you should value my judgment in the very important matter of the choice of a successor to Dr. Angell. I know how difficult and responsible the task is and would be very much gratified to feel that I was lending any assistance of any kind.

I know Dr. John Finley, President of the College of the City of New York, very well and entertain a very warm admiration for him. So far as engaging character is concerned and great power to please and, therefore, to lead, and unusual social gifts, making him everywhere a much desired guest and speaker, he is an ideal man for such a post as you now have to fill. But my association with him has led me to the judgment that he has no great constructive power. He does not seem to me a man who can make large plans or carry them out with consistency, and he lacks, I should judge, the aggressiveness and clearheadedness necessary to lead public opinion and carry his policy forward in the debate of committees and legislative bodies. His administrative ability, in other words, is better suited for the conduct of a completed institution, I should think, than for one that has constantly to be adjusted to the growth of circumstances and the changes of the time.

I have given you my frank judgment in this matter because I feel in duty bound to do so. One ought not to offer counsel in a matter of so great consequence to the university world without giving it with the utmost frankness and explicitness. I feel sure that you will know how to make use of this letter without prejudice to Mr. Finley, for whom I have the warmest affection.

I hope you know how deep an interest the whole university world takes in the choice you are about to make and how unanimous the feeling is that the presidency of the University of Michigan is one of the first posts of influence in the country.

Sincerely yours, Woodrow Wilson

TLS (W. H. Sawyer Papers, MiU-H).

From Henry Smith Pritchett

PERSONAL AND CONFIDENTIAL

My dear President Wilson: New York May 5, 1909.

Your note of May 4 really touches me quite deeply. I know exactly how your problem stands to you and the discouragement that you must feel. I felt thoroughly discouraged myself after my efforts with Mr. Carnegie. It is really so difficult to get before him any conception of the difference between the problem you are dealing with and the problem of some ambitious high school that wants to call itself a college that I feel hopeless over the matter. However, I have had some rather encouraging talks with the General Education people, and I still feel sure that the only way to get Mr. Carnegie's help is through their action, and you may count on me for anything I can do in this matter.

Let me say a word concerning another matter, which I am sorry I have not had the chance to talk with you about. The Michigan authorities have consulted me a good deal concerning the new president. This is one of the great opportunities for a man who believes in a genuine democracy. The institution is a great one, suffering a little bit from the fact that President Angell, with all his fine qualities, has held on about ten years longer than he ought to. I have taken the liberty to urge the Michigan people to go in and try to secure you for the presidency, saying to them that I hadn't the slightest idea whether you would accept or not, but that if they wanted a president who could do what needed to be done at Michigan, they ought not to stop short of the best man, and the way to get the best man was to go after him. Whether you should finally conclude to take this place or not, I hope very much they will offer it to you and hope you will not say no without giving me a chance to talk with you.[1]

Faithfully yours, Henry S. Pritchett

TLS (WP, DLC).

[1] Documents in the W. H. Sawyer Papers, MiU-H, indicate that Wilson was considered informally as a candidate for the presidency of the University of Michigan by at least some members of the Board of Regents of that institution, including Walter Hulme Sawyer himself. However, the Editors have found no documentary evidence that Wilson was actually offered the

position, although he may have been approached informally by some intermediary from the Board of Regents. As it turned out, Harry Burns Hutchins, at this time Dean of the Department of Law, was elected Acting President in August 1909 and President in June 1910.

A News Report of an Address to the Newark Alumni

[May 6, 1909]

DR. WILSON FOR BROADER STUDY

Tells Princeton Club Evils of Predatory Wealth
Arise from Educational Defects.

In stirring speech and happy-hearted song and yell, "Old Nassau" was praised and vociferously cheered at Achtel-Stetter's last night. It was at the dinner of the Princeton Club, with President Woodrow Wilson and Governor [John Franklin] Fort as the guests of honor, that the merits of the "Tiger" were backed against the world, and not until well on toward 1 o'clock this morning was there any let up in the festivities and the last "Siss, boom, ah" was sounded.

"Problems of College Life" was the subject Dr. Wilson elected to discourse on, but he had not gone far before he branched into a discussion of vocational schools, declared for general educational institutions where the college youth would be disciplined and directed in the course he must pursue without being allowed to satisfy his own tastes, and finally he reached a thought that turned the talk toward politics and the country's citizenship.

It was along this line the university head stirred the gathering. His references to the "predatory interests," the real criminals and enemies of the government, the selfishly ambitious seekers for political preference, and Americans who love their country for their country's gain were repeatedly applauded. . . .

At the outset Dr. Wilson told of the changes in college life, asserting that these days a majority of the young men who go to the universities expect to follow a business life afterward. It is becoming fashionable, he said, for youth of means to go to educational institutions merely for something, but it is becoming greatly confusing as to what this "something" is. Princeton and one or two other universities, the president said, belong to a separate class which maintains an ideal and which insists on a general education for its students. As opposed to these institutions he referred to vocational universities as establishments which do not profess to impart a general education, but which seem to think their chief duty to supply the commonwealth with graduates who hold a diploma, no matter what its worth.

Continuing, Dr. Wilson said there was a certain danger in a

college which represents the latter ideal, and it is debatable whether it is proper in this busy world to have institutions where men go to seek nothing in particular. There are competitive ideals of education, and every college man to-day must make up his mind on entering a university just what ideal he wishes to pursue. Men of large means, said Dr. Wilson, are not men anxious to pursue an ideal other than their own self-indulgence, and he regretted to say there were certain phases of education which greatly add to these tendencies. Throughout life, he said, there seems to be growing more and more a section of American manhood which refuses to rise above the level of occupation, and the speaker asserted that he did not believe the duty of a college ended in the imparting of useful information alone, as useful information solely will not make useful citizens.

College educations [education], Dr. Wilson said, instead of being narrow and semi-vocational in its intent, should be broad and liberal in its training and should fit its graduates not alone for the business world, but for a true citizenship that will work for the nation's good and prosperity. Men cannot attain this education, however, in a leisurely and self-indulgent spirit. A student cannot go through college in the spirit of a boy and become a man.

"This brings me to a point I wish to touch on briefly," went on Dr. Wilson, "and this is the country's good. The chief enemies of government to-day are the men who are using their wealth for predatory purpose. These men are criminals, ingenious criminals, however, who sooner or later will be brought to the bar presided over, I hope, by these eminent jurists sitting with me, who will understand their criminality and will give them what they deserve. The criminals of this age, though, are not more numerous than the criminals of the age past. They are merely more ingenious, more clever. We have no more criminals. We simply have better ones, more able ones. We have criminals who are more covert, and sooner or later we will smoke them out.

"These criminals are men who in their supreme consciousness seek their own private interest under the belief they are doing their country a great favor. They believe they are serving their country rightly, enhancing its power, increasing its ambitions. These are the men who are the real enemies of the nation; men who are opposing its general interests and don't know it. These are the men, or some of them, who go to Washington, thinking that in favoring themselves and patronizing their government the country is being uplifted. These are the men who do not know the general condition of affairs throughout the land. Absolutely untutored they are, unschooled in that field of statesmanship which makes self-indulgence impossible and which puts country above self, nation above ambition.

"The country is not served by indulging your private tastes. It is best served by taking what is coming to you and not in picking out what you want to come to you. There is much of this private taste in our land. There is a great deal of this private taste in this part of the country, but I say to you that if you cannot generalize yourself as an American you had far better seek life under another colony where you can seek indulgence of your private interests."

The educator then put forth his remedy of a broader and more general education at the colleges. There is too much information imparted at the schools to-day, he said, that has for its sole intent to make business, to confine the recipient to a knowledge that will be of but personal interest to him in later life. There should be more time spent in educating college men to a true patriotic spirit, and more attention should be given to the needs of the country and to those traits of manhood which will make toward good citizenship.

The time is coming, Dr. Wilson declared, when the country will need just such men. It is making itself more evident each day. He explained, he did not expect a day of revolution, no matter how discontented interests may be, as the nation is too self-possessed. The special duty that should be considered by the man of to-day is for him to divest himself of special class, and be a universal democrat, whether spelled with a small or big "D."

"We are on the eve of an interesting period in the politics of the country," said the president in closing. "The existing political interests are going presently to suffer a great reform. An age is about to dawn as difficult to us as when the Constitution of the country was framed, and when we face it we shall need the men and the experience to meet it."[1]

Printed in the *Newark Evening News*, May 6, 1909; some editorial headings omitted.

[1] For this address, Wilson used the outline referred to in H. B. Thompson to WW, April 6, 1909, n. 1.

To Henry Smith Pritchett

PERSONAL AND CONFIDENTIAL.

My dear President Pritchett, Princeton, N. J. 8 May, 1909.

Your letter of the fifth of May is very generous and I am very grateful to you for it.

My suggestion about the University of Michigan was, as I am sure you understood, not seriously made. There are many important tasks waiting to be done here which are not impossible, and I should feel a good deal like a man running away were I to turn my back upon them now. I hold my ideals so very seriously that I am perhaps too easily discouraged by apparently insurmountable obstacles, and I have to guard against my temperament.

At the same time, I appreciate the entire truth of all that you say about the opportunity at Ann Arbor. It is a very great field and an opportunity to challenge the very best that is in one. It gratifies me very deeply that you should feel about me and about my fitness for the great task as you do; and you may be sure that, if the Regents were to offer me the presidency, I would look the question through from end to end before declining, seeking your counsel very earnestly in the matter. I rather hope that I shall not be tempted!

With warmest regard,

Faithfully Yours, Woodrow Wilson

WWTLS (H. S. Pritchett Papers, DLC).

William Cooper Procter to Andrew Fleming West

My dear Professor West: [Cincinnati] May 8, 1909.

I have read with much interest the book prepared by you outlining the scheme of The Proposed Graduate College of Princeton University.[1] Believing in its great value to Princeton, provided the scheme is carried out on these lines, I take pleasure in making the following proposition for acceptance by the Board of Trustees.

I will give the sum of Five Hundred Thousand Dollars to be expended for such objects, in furtherance of the plans, as I may designate, provided an equal sum is secured for the Graduate College in gifts or responsible pledges by May 1st., 1910. I do this on the understanding that my subscription is to be paid in ten equal quarterly installments beginning July 15th, 1910, and that the money for the other subscriptions or gifts shall be paid into the Treasury of the University not later than October 15th, 1912.

I have visited and examined the proposed site at Prospect, and beg to say, that in my opinion, it is not suitable for such a College. I feel, therefore, obliged to say that this offer is made upon the further understanding that some other site be chosen, which shall be satisfactory to me.

Yours very truly, Wm. Cooper Procter.

TCL (WWP, UA, NjP).

[1] [Andrew F. West] *The Proposed Graduate College of Princeton University* (Princeton, N. J., 1903).

To Robert Bridges

My dear Bobby: Princeton, N. J. May 10th, 1909.

I write for both Mrs. Wilson and myself to say that we eagerly hope that you will be our guest during Commencement and the Reunion of Seventy-Nine. I am inviting the rest of the gang,[1] and we should be very much disappointed if we could not get them together again under our roof. Poor Bob Henderson cannot come, but we are strongly hoping that all the rest can.

Always affectionately yours, Woodrow Wilson

TLS (WC, NjP).

[1] That is, the Witherspoon Gang, members of the Class of 1879 who had roomed in Witherspoon Hall.

To Winthrop More Daniels

My dear Daniels: Princeton, N. J. May 10th, 1909.

Here is Bogart's decision. I am sorry to say that he is going. I had another interview with him in which he asked assurances so specific that it seemed to me quite out of the question to give them.

His going frees us to do, or at any rate to attempt, the things which you suggested the other day in our conversation. I hope it will enable us to get Crane[1] and some other equally good man. I shall hope that we may soon hear from Conyers Reed.[2]

Always faithfully yours, Woodrow Wilson

TLS (Wilson-Daniels Corr., CtY).

[1] Probably Robert Treat Crane, who had received the Ph.D. in political science from The Johns Hopkins University in 1907. At this time he was United States Deputy Consul-General at Montreal, was soon (on May 31, 1909) to be appointed Consul at Guadeloupe, and remained in the consular service until 1913. He later went on to a notable career as Professor of Political Science at the University of Michigan and Executive Director of the Social Science Research Council.

[2] Read, who had received the Ph.D. in history from Harvard in 1908, was at this time engaged in historical research. He was an Instructor in History, Politics, and Economics at Princeton in 1909-10 but then went on to the University of Chicago.

From George Brinton McClellan Harvey

Dear Mr. Wilson [New York] May 10 [1909].

The country is red-hot over the tariff atrocity.[1] Why not sound a bugle blast in the N. A. Review—and take the lead?[2]

I am sailing Wed. the 19th and am dining with Balfour[3] and Sir Gilbert Parker[4] on the 26th. I think Parker is coming over in October and he will probably ask me if I have spoken to you of the possibility of his making a lecture on "Imperialism."[5] Have you thought about it?

Sincerely yours George Harvey

ALS (WP, DLC).

1 Harvey referred to what was to become the Payne-Aldrich Tariff Act of 1909. President Taft had called a special session of Congress to begin on March 15, 1909, to consider tariff revision. Representative Sereno E. Payne of New York, chairman of the Ways and Means Committee, introduced a bill which provided for substantial downward revision of the existing rates. The bill moved rapidly through the House of Representatives, although many amendments were added lowering the rates still further, and was passed by a substantial majority on April 9, 1909. On April 12, 1909, Senator Nelson W. Aldrich of Rhode Island, chairman of the Finance Committee, introduced a bill in the Senate which made over eight hundred amendments to the Payne bill, most of which revised its rates upward. The Aldrich bill set off a storm of newspaper criticism across the country. On April 22, 1909, Senators Robert M. La Follette of Wisconsin and Jonathan P. Dolliver of Iowa made the first of a series of scathing attacks on the bill by insurgent Republican senators in debate on the Senate floor. Despite the opposition of the progressive Republican senators, the Aldrich bill was passed by the Senate on July 8, 1909, and the Senate-House conference committee thereafter accepted most of its provisions. President Taft signed the final version of the bill into law on August 5, 1909. For a thorough discussion of the passage of the Payne-Aldrich Act, see George E. Mowry, *Theodore Roosevelt and the Progressive Movement* (Madison, Wisc., 1947), pp. 44-65.

2 Wilson responded with "The Tariff Make-Believe," printed at Sept. 5, 1909.

3 Arthur James Balfour, former Conservative Prime Minister, at this time M.P. for the City of London.

4 Sir Horatio Gilbert George Parker, writer of historical novels and M.P. for Gravesend, 1900-1918.

5 Parker did not deliver this lecture at Princeton.

To Mary Allen Hulbert Peck

My dearest Friend, Princeton, 12 May, 1909.

Welcome back! It is delightful that you should again be within actual reach of your friends and that they can at least think the chances of seeing you now and again increased a hundred fold! You come back with a stout heart, and I do not believe for a moment that you will not win out, and make a life for yourself in the new circumstances which you can live with dignity and without too much anxiety. I wish that I could report at once that the lad[1] is pleasantly placed in a boarding house that he will probably like, but, alas! the rascal put off room hunting because

Mrs. Bacon[2] invited him to remain with her until the fifteenth, and only starts out to-day to take the business seriously in hand. I would have gone in on Monday to finish the selection, as I had promised, had he not written me that he had postponed the search. It now looks as if he would hardly be ready for the final choice before you yourself arrive.

I am very much interested in what you tell me of the Knox party.[3] It would be delightful to welcome them here. Unfortunately Ellen is to be away both on Saturday, the day of your arrival, and on Monday. She asks me to beg that they will come down and spend Tuesday with us, the eighteenth. If Saturday and Monday are the only days they are to be free to come, however, Margaret and Nellie will be here: they can take their mother's place as hostesses, and I should be very happy to have Sir James and Lady Knox and their daughters come down on either day, if it will suit their pleasure and convenience. Ellen would be disappointed at not having the opportunity to meet them, but they must not miss seeing Princeton. How delightful it would be if You and Mr. Peck could come also! Do you expect to have to hurry on to Pittsfield the very day you land? If you can come do not let Mrs. Allen[4] drop out of the party. We have so long wanted to see her here. The morning trains to Princeton (Pennsylvania Railroad)

Leave West 23rd. St. Ferry	Arrive in Princeton
9.25	11.03
10.55	12.57
11.55	1.45

Slow trains, all of them, but the best we have! The second one is especially tedious. If they should come on Monday, there is an earlier train which leaves at 8.25 and reaches Princeton at 10.16. In arriving time it is the most desirable of the day. It would be our preference because it would give us a full day with our guests and they would not feel hurried.

Princeton is just now more beautiful than at any other *moment* of the year. The Spring hues are here in their first freshness, the trees are but just coming to their full leaf: on some of them there is yet only a tender veil of green, for our season has been very backward. I have not been sorry to have the languour of Spring postponed: it makes hard, concentrated work very trying, and this is my season of hardest work. There are nine difficult addresses ahead of me, in addition to the closing work of the term, always the most miscellaneous and pressing. If it were not pressing, you may be sure I would make a point of being in

New York on the fifteenth. I simply cannot be. I have an early forenoon appointment on that day which I must keep or hold important work on college buildings up to the loss not only of time but of money. I am perfectly well, and fortunately too busy to *feel* tired. I shall take a perfect loaf this summer at Lyme!

I hope with all my heart that you have not utterly worn yourself out by the packing and all the hurried last things that must have made your last days in Bermuda a bit overwhelming, and that your summer is to be planned with a view to genuine rest! It will, I should suppose, in view of our mild winter, be on the whole a mild summer also, so that we shall not wilt at any rate. We shall remain in Princeton until the tenth of July (the day on which Jessie and Nellie sail, with friends, for Europe, to be gone until the very end of November) and shall then go up to Lyme to throw in our lot with the artists there, Ellen, Margaret, and I.[5] I have no work in view for the summer, except, perhaps, an article on the tariff for the North American Review (!) to keep me out of mischief. While Ellen paints and Margaret practices her music I shall play golf (if my left eye will serve me),[6] go wherever the motor cars will permit me to go on my bicycle, and indulge my quite unlimited capacity for sleep. Doesn't that sound like vegitating,–a programme for a man of active mind? It's the best I can think of. It will be full of many thoughts of you, and, I hope, of news from you. Please give my warmest regards to Mrs. Allen and believe me always and in all things

Your devoted friend, Woodrow Wilson

WWTLS (WP, DLC).

1 That is, her son, Allen Schoolcraft Hulbert, now in New York City.

2 It is impossible to identify this Mrs. Bacon among the numerous Bacon families listed in the New York City directories and social registers for this period.

3 Sir James Knox of Kilbirnie, Ayrshire, and his wife, Anne Eliza McCosh Knox. The Knoxes had two daughters. The first cannot be identified, but the younger was Janet Knox (Mrs. Charles Massy) Mathew. Lady Knox was the daughter of a James McCosh of Merksworth, Dalry, Ayrshire. She may well have been related to President James McCosh, who was also born in Ayrshire.

4 Anjenett Holcomb (Mrs. Charles Sterling) Allen.

5 At the home of Florence Griswold, about which see WW to EAW, June 26, 1908, n. 9, Vol. 18.

6 That is, if his left eye, which had been partially blinded by the stroke of 1906, would permit. About this illness, see WW to J. D. Greene, May 30, 1906, Vol. 16.

Notes for an Address to the Graduate Students of Princeton University

MERWICK, Wednesday evening, 12 May, 1909.

Political Reform.

Spreading discontent with existing political institutions, and universal discussion of reforms.

City government

State government.

Vogue of Socialism, though as a sentiment rather than as a programme.

Accompanying tendency towards centralization,—preference for the federal government,—showing an interesting instinct to turn to the most conspicuous and definite agency

Special objects of movement:

To get rid of the "boss"

To realize direct, or at any rate genuine, government by the people.

Aggregate initiative } Alike impracticable
Checks and balances }

The simplified representative process and concentrated responsibility.

Their natural and their exaggerated application.[1]

WWT MS (WP, DLC).

[1] No local newspaper printed a report of this talk.

Moses Taylor Pyne to William Cooper Procter

My dear Mr. Procter: [Princeton, N. J.] May 12th, 1909.

At a meeting of the Trustees' Committee on the Graduate School held today, your very generous letter was presented and received with the greatest appreciation. We are anxious to make it possible to meet the conditions mentioned in your letter, and, to that end, the Committee passed a resolution,[1] copy of which I enclose.

In order to give the Committee time to report to the Board, it is very desirable that a conference with you be held before the Commencement season, as the final meeting of the Board for the year will take place on Monday morning, June 14th, and we are anxious to have the whole matter settled at that meeting.

The President and the Dean will be away the first part of the week preceding Commencement, but if you could in any way arrange to meet us either in Princeton or New York on Saturday, June 5th, we would then have the opportunity to consider all the details of the matter. Inasmuch as the question of site is involved, we should prefer to have the conference in Princeton, so that the various sites may have the fullest consideration.

Dean West tells us that you are to be in Princeton on Saturday, June 12th, to attend the Yale game. While we should be delighted to see you at this time, it would be impossible, I fear, for the sub-committee to be able to report to the Trustees' Committee in time for them to prepare a report for the Board meeting on Monday morning.

If any other date would be more convenient for you, we should appreciate it very much if you would kindly let us know as soon as possible.

In conclusion, my dear sir, I beg to assure you of the most sincere and hearty thanks of the Committee for your very generous and munificent offer.

Yours very sincerely, M. Taylor Pyne, Chairman.

TCL (M. T. Pyne Coll., NjP).

[1] The resolution read as follows:

"At a special meeting of the Committee of the Board of Trustees of Princeton University on the Graduate School, it was

"RESOLVED: That this Committee has heard read with great satisfaction the letter of Mr. William Cooper Procter, as affording a prospect of the early completion of the scheme for a Graduate School on a permanent and dignified basis;

"FURTHER RESOLVED: That a Committee consisting of the President, the Dean of the Graduate School and the Chairman of the Trustees' Committee, with Mr. Cadwalader and Mr. Sheldon, seek an early occasion for a conference with Mr. Procter to discuss and consider certain of the details, prior to the meeting of the Board of Trustees to be held on the 14th day of June." T MS (WWP, UA, NjP).

From Robert Bridges

Dear Tommy: New York, May 13th, 1909.

Thank you very much for the kind invitation from Mrs. Wilson and yourself to stay with you during the Reunion at Commencement time. It gives me great pleasure to accept.

I am sorry that Henderson feels that he cannot come, but I still have some hope that perhaps he may improve.

I have had several letters from Cyrus about the Trustee matter and told him that from my conversation with various people in a position to know, I do not believe that there is any chance for Barr. My sole interest in the matter is that you shall not appear to be put in a wrong position, and it is my firm belief that under the circumstances the best way out is for Barr to withdraw.[1] The other side are undoubtedly making strong use of the fact that the opposition comes from inside the Board of Trustees.

With best wishes always

Faithfully yours [Robert Bridges]

CCL (WC, NjP).

[1] In fact, Barr had already declined his nomination as a candidate for Alumni Trustee in a letter to Charles W. McAlpin of May 8, 1909, stating that, in view of Wilson Farrand's withdrawal from the contest in 1908, Farrand was now entitled to the position. Barr's letter is printed in the *Princeton Alumni Weekly*, IX (May 19, 1909), 502.

From John Watson Barr, Jr.

Dear Doctor Wilson: Louisville. Ky., May 13, 1909.

We are delighted with the prospect of having you in Louisville on Saturday, May 22nd.[1] If you could arrange to arrive in Louisville on Friday forenoon, the principal of the Louisville High School would be much pleased to have you address the students at the High School; in fact, he has extended to you an invitation to that effect.[2]

A few hours before the regular business of the Princeton Alumni Association might be pleasantly and profitably spent by you in meeting persons who are interested in educational matters, and especially in University work. If you can so arrange, we will be delighted to have you, and it will be a pleased [pleasure] to me to be your escort for that day.

Sincerely yours, Jno W Barr Jr

TLS (WP, DLC).

[1] Wilson was to address the Western Association of Princeton Clubs on that date. A news report of his speech is printed at May 23, 1909.

[2] As the news report printed at May 22, 1909, discloses, Wilson did not speak at the Louisville High School because he did not arrive in Louisville until the evening of May 21.

To Cyrus Hall McCormick

My dear Cyrus: Princeton, N. J. May 15th, 1909.

Inasmuch as you were not able to attend the recent meeting of the Trustees' Committee on the Graduate School, I send you the enclosed papers as a memorandum of what we were called together to consider, and the action taken. The letter from Mr. Procter speaks for itself, and it is of course deeply gratifying, if we can manage to meet his terms. The conference spoken of in the resolution adopted we hope may take place about the fifth of June, and I think there is a hopeful prospect of coming to some satisfactory conclusion which we can report to the full committee at a convenient time before the Board meets. It may be that copies of Mr. Procter's letter have already been sent you, but for fear there should have been some oversight I am taking the liberty of making sure.

Always cordially and faithfully yours,

Woodrow Wilson

TLS (WP, DLC).

Henry Burling Thompson to Melancthon Williams Jacobus

[Greenville P. O., Del.]

Dear Jacobus: May Seventeenth, 1909.

It gave me much pleasure to have had the opportunity of seeing you in your own home, last Thursday night, although it was a source of regret to me that I was unable to see your wife. . . .

I spent Saturday morning in Princeton, and had the opportunity of a talk with Fine,–meeting him by chance on the campus. Fine is a difficult man to talk to, due to the fact that he does not differentiate between obstinacy and firmness. However, I believe my talk, on the whole, has helped the situation. I told him very briefly that, at the last Committee meeting, the question under discussion was not the important question, but a more important situation developed at that meeting, which was this: Due to his attitude in the discussion, he was rapidly putting himself in the position of asking our Committee to decide a question by a vote, which would either turn him down or turn the President down, and the instant affairs drifted this way, it made a condition which was impossible. He stated that he did not agree with me, and that he was glad he said just what he did; that we could not expect to muzzle him at meetings if he chose to differ from the President. My answer was that nobody expected to muzzle him, but it would be wise, in so far as possible, for him and the President to settle their differences out of Court, and not ask the Committee to act as judges.

Notwithstanding what Fine said to me, I know he saw the point I was trying to make, although unwilling to acknowledge it. He did back down on his statement with regard to the necessary number of preceptors for academic studies as opposed to the lesser number for the scientific side. He is positive that reforms can be made in the preceptorial system. I told him that I would not question this statement; it was worthy of investigation.

Now, he is willing to leave it this way, and it seems to me a good solution of the problem: That a Committee of three, consisting of the President, the Dean and yourself, (as Chairman), should take this matter up, and, if necessary, take the year for a calm, dispassionate discussion of the whole subject, and then make a report back to our Committee. This would not question, in any way, Wilson's report, which applies to present conditions. The contracts for terms of service are virtually made for the next year or two, so the present conditions cannot be disturbed, but it would be entirely reasonable to take up the whole question for the future; and I think, if such a resolution was offered, without any discussion, it should be acceptable to the President.

I spent the better part of two hours with the President on Saturday,–principally, on Grounds and Buildings matters. I told him of my visit to you; and took occasion to tell him that I felt certain conditions existed which were forcing a number of students who had formerly gone into the B.S., into the Lit.B. courses, –the result of which is over-crowding in certain departments and a diminution in the Scientific departments, which is deplorable. He admitted the necessity of looking into conditions.

Please let me know if you think the appointment of the above Committee, with duties as outlined, is feasible.

Very sincerely yours, [Henry B Thompson]

TLS (Thompson Letterpress Books, NjP).

From Melancthon Williams Jacobus

My dear President Wilson: Hartford, Conn., May 18th, 1909.

I thank you for the courtesy of your communication of the 15th instant,[1] with its enclosure of Mr. Proctor's letter and the resolutions adopted by the Graduate School Committee at its last meeting.

I cannot help but wonder somewhat how Mr. Proctor came to his prejudice against the present site selected for the School, for I cannot readily see how anyone could see the location for himself without being greatly attracted to it. It looks as though he must have been shown it by those who are interested in another site, and the arguments against the present location have been furnished him at the time.

I sincerely trust and I have every confidence that the Committee appointed to interview Mr. Proctor will succeed in showing him the difficulties that gather around every other location save this, and that he will be moved from his present mind to do us the generous thing he has offered to do, without this condition.

I am sorry that you could not accept the invitation I sent you in my last letter, replying to your full and most satisfactory statement of what happened at the Curriculum Committee meeting. It would have been a great pleasure to have you at our house where you could take a rest and talk these matters over at your leisure.

But you will not forget that you are to be my guest next week when you come to the Anniversary exercises of the Seminary.[2] Can you not make up in some way for your not coming two weeks ago by coming a bit earlier this time? On Saturday of this week Mr. Bridgman of Norfolk,[3] President of our Board of Trustees, is placing at the disposal of the Faculty and Trustees, together with any of the invited guests who may be here at that time, a parlor car in which we are to take the little journey from Hartford up to his palatial residence in Norfolk, leaving here at 11:00 in the morning, being entertained by him at lunch, and returning at 4:00 in the afternoon. Cannot you come Friday night, or early enough Saturday morning, to go with us on this delightful expedition? We will be so glad to have you. Then this will give you Sunday, Monday and Tuesday for a quiet time and such enjoyment of the surrounding country as our automobile can give you, and I can assure you Hartford and its environs look beautifully just now.

With kindest regards,

Yours very sincerely, Melancthon W. Jacobus

TLS (WP, DLC).

1 It is missing.

2 When Wilson was to speak at the seventy-fifth anniversary of the Hartford Theological Seminary on May 26, 1909. His address is printed at that date.

3 Henry H. Bridgman, New York publisher, whose estate, Fox Hill, was at Norfolk, Conn.

From Cyrus Hall McCormick

My dear Woodrow: Chicago 18 May, 1909.

I am greatly interested in the letter from Mr. Procter, copy of which you have enclosed to me and which I had not seen before. I think the first step should be to show Mr. Procter the legal difficulties in the way of going off to a different site for the Graduate School. Personally, I have never been very strongly impressed with the site which is now under consideration next to '79 Hall, but I have supposed it was the best one available for us under all the circumstances. I do not remember what was the second choice when this one was selected, but I am under the impression that it was the little elevation of ground down by the canal and I wonder if that location legally would be impossible.

Do not trouble to write me about this further, but take the matter up only in the Committee.

I am, Very sincerely yours, Cyrus H. McCormick.

TLS (WP, DLC).

Moses Taylor Pyne to Ralph Adams Cram

My dear Mr. Cram: [Princeton, N. J.] May 18th, 1909.

I have your letter of the 17th inst. regarding the Graduate College and fear, however, that while we wish, if possible, to secure this money, it is a very doubtful quantity. In the first place, he offers us $500,000, and seems inclined to force us to put it on the Merwick property. In that case, we should lose the Swann money, so that what he practically offers us is $180,000 provided we raise $500,000 more which, in itself, is not a good proposition. We have made an appointment with him to meet us in a couple of weeks and go over the whole matter, and we shall be ready, I think, to make a final decision on the 14th when the Board meets. I regret this delay extremely, the more so as it does not seem at all sure that this $500,000 will amount to anything, as the conditions are so onerous. . . .

Yours very sincerely, M. Taylor Pyne.

TCL (M. T. Pyne Coll., NjP).

To Henry Lee Higginson

[Princeton, N. J.]

My dear Major Higginson: May 19th, 1909.

I hope you will not think it presumption on my part if I write to ask whether the visit of the Boston Symphony Orchestra to Princeton last season proved so satisfactory to you and to the performers as to seem worth repeating in the same way. The leader of the orchestra[1] expressed himself at that time as so highly pleased with the visit that I think he felt that it would be very pleasant to repeat it, and certainly no musical event of the year was so greatly enjoyed here as was that. We are a little community, but a community of music lovers, and would be very grateful if the visit could be repeated.

I make this suggestion with a great deal of diffidence because I am not sure that the visit last year did not involve some expense on your part. If it did, I do not feel that I ought to ask for its repetition, but if the orchestra could come to us in the same way that it did last year without involving you in inconvenience or expense, we should deem it a great privilege to hear it again. I dare say that we could arrange for almost any date that would suit the convenience of the orchestra itself.

With warmest regard,

Cordially and sincerely yours, [Woodrow Wilson]

CCL (WWP, UA, NjP).

[1] Max Fiedler, conductor of the Boston Symphony Orchestra.

To Moses Taylor Pyne

My dear Momo: [Princeton, N. J.] May 19th, 1909.

I am to deliver the Commencement Address at St. Paul's School on June 3rd.[1] I am taking it for granted that there is a night train by which I can get away from there, and I will make a point of being in New York on Friday morning, June 4th, as near 11 o'clock as train schedules will permit. If I am not there on time, pray do not delay the meeting for me, since it is probably the only time we can get hold of Mr. Procter.

Always faithfully yours, [Woodrow Wilson]

CCL (WWP, UA, NjP).

[1] A news report of this address is printed at June 3, 1909.

To Melancthon Williams Jacobus

My dear Dr. Jacobus: [Princeton, N. J.] May 19th, 1909.

I hasten to acknowledge your letter of yesterday just as I am about to take a train. I am going down to Washington to be present at the unveiling of the statue of John Witherspoon there tomorrow, and from there tomorrow night I must start for Louisville, Kentucky, where the Western Association of Princeton Clubs is to hold its meeting on Saturday. This makes it impossible for me to get back home earlier than Monday evening at the soonest. I must linger at home a little while and clear my desk of the most pressing business and then I will come on to you on Tuesday evening, if I may. I will let you know later by what train to expect me.

It is a great disappointment to me that I have to hurry and

skimp in this way, but this meeting in Louisville has caught me in a tight place, and I do not feel that I can be absent from it. It would be delightful if I could fall in with the generous suggestions of your kind letter.

I shall be obliged to postpone the discussion of the Graduate College business until I see you.

In haste,
With warmest regard,
Faithfully yours, [Woodrow Wilson]

CCL (RSB Coll., DLC).

A Commemorative Address in Washington on John Witherspoon[1]

[[May 20, 1909]]

Mr. Foster, ladies and gentlemen: It is my interesting task this afternoon to try to recall for you the man whose memory we celebrate. Fortunately it is not difficult to recall John Witherspoon. He made so strong and definite an impression upon his own generation that there are abundant records which display to us his qualities, his person, and his achievements.

The story of his life, viewing it in the bulk, is a very simple one. He was forty-six when he came to America in 1768, and he had by that time become the leader of the orthodox party in the Church of Scotland. I dare say that the leaders of the other party, which was known as the Moderate Party, were not unwilling to see him depart for America, because he had made their lives very uneasy, not only by worsting them in argument, but also by penetrating their armor with a touch of wit which went to the quick very much more than the solid point of his argument. No party, particularly no ecclesiastical party, can afford to be made ridiculous, and Dr. Witherspoon had the gift of making those who opposed him ridiculous, not with the broad laughter of a more southern race, but with the quiet, significant, dismaying smile which precedes the chuckle of the Scotchman. I say that they were probably not unwilling to see him depart for America, and America was most willing to receive this redoubtable champion of an orthodox people, because he had established in Scotland a fame as a writer and a preacher which bespoke in him something more than the mere minister of the Gospel, bespoke in him the qualities of the statesman, of the man

[1] About this affair, see J. W. Foster to WW, Feb. 20, 1909.

whose gift it is to lead, no matter what the sphere of leadership may be which he attempts.

When he came to America he reorganized the course of study and revivified the whole administration of the College of New Jersey at Princeton; but he did more, as had been expected. It was only eight years before the signing of the Declaration of Independence. Affairs were gathering for a very significant period of history. He was almost immediately sent to the Legislature of New Jersey, the Colonial Assembly, and he was presently sent to the Convention which framed the first constitution of the State. Just before the signing of the Declaration of Independence he was made a Delegate to the Continental Congress, and added his voice to those counsels which brought about the promulgation of that great epoch-making document.

Then, more important still, he, more assiduously than any other member, continued to lend his counsel to the proceedings of the Continental Congress throughout the Revolutionary War; and no man in it represented so consistently as he did the wise counsel which was necessary to sustain that difficult and sometimes discouraging contest. He, more than any other man in the Continental Congress, urged the maintenance of such measures as Washington felt to be indispensable for the support of his armies and the success of the cause. It was as if Washington himself spoke in council for the things which Washington in the field needed, when John Witherspoon stood upon his feet in the Continental Congress.

Then he returned to Princeton to pick up the scattered threads of the organization of that demoralized institution, which had gone to pieces like so many other things during the Revolution; and the closing work of his life was the habilitation of the college to which he had devoted so much of his thought and energy.

That, in the main outline, is the story of his life; but we are not interested in the historical and biographical detail so much as in the effort to recover a distinct image of the man and to make a reasonable assessment of the powers that were in him and the qualities which distinguished him.

One of the most interesting things about Dr. Witherspoon was that he had no sooner landed on this side of the water than he made the interesting discovery that he was an American. He was one of those sturdy Scotchmen who do not take things upon report; and one of the first things that he did was to journey up and down the length of the coast, all the way from Massachusetts to Virginia, meeting every man of consequence, seeking counsel not so much as information, seeking to test the quality of the men who were influential in that day not only in the field of education, but also in the field of public affairs. And then when he more deliberately undertook the work at Princeton he consciously stood at the center of things that were going on in America, and felt that he was able to determine what sort of an institution must lend itself to the public necessities of that age.

Scotchmen are not averse to advertising, and Dr. Witherspoon very early set himself diligently to advertising throughout the Colonies the purposes he had, and at the heart of his advertising stood this declaration of purpose—that he intended at Princeton to fit young men for the service of their country. He proposed that they should not only follow the ordinary course in the liberal arts, but that they should be encouraged, if they were diligent in their purpose, to return to the college after the ordinary course and take up more particularly a study of public affairs, of the philosophy of politics which should underlie the successful operation of public affairs.

There is an interesting passage in one of Dr. Witherspoon's lectures to his classes, in which he asks this question: "What is the advantage of civil liberty?" "I suppose," he replies, "that it chiefly consists in its tendency to put in motion all the human powers. Therefore it promotes industry, and in this sense happiness; it produces every latent quality and improves the human mind. Civil liberty is the nurse of riches, literature, and heroism."

Certainly in him it was the nurse of literature and of heroism, and this man, touched with the indomitable freedom of the Scottish people, found when he came to America that here was an air which blew that spark into a flame, which made that flame a thing which illuminated every purpose that men undertook.

He rejoiced in the wild character of the forest roads; the song of the birds in the trees seemed to him to be significant of an ample air, and to interpret this primeval place in which picked men had set up their habitations and were feeling a new and noble discontent and a new and threatening aspiration.

He did not need to be schooled in the legal case for the colonies. I dare say, as an ecclesiastical lawyer he knew that the legal case for the colonies was a very weak case indeed. The true case for the colonies was that they had grown up such men, and had made for them such communities, as rendered the domination of a foreign government no longer tolerable. Therefore he felt his pulse from the first in this free air to be the pulse of America. He needed no novitiate.

Scotchmen are easily transplanted, for the reason that Scotchmen have a strong acquisitive energy; they do not so much identify themselves with the communities in which they live as take possession of them. (Laughter.) You have never known a Scotchman, I venture to say, who did not show, in spite of what you call the stiffness of his fiber, a singular adaptability. He at once becomes a part of the community and not only that, but an enterprising part of the community, and makes the community his own by making it like himself.

This was the spirit, I dare say, that was in Witherspoon. To describe a man like this is just as difficult as to describe General Washington, and for the same reason. There is, I venture to say, a quality which is more difficult to describe than any other, the quality of greatness, an ineffable, indefinable quality, indefinable because of the singular symmetry and completeness and universality which lies back of it in the nature of the person who possesses it. The great men of critical periods are men marked by great versatility, and yet not by a very marked degree of originality. Walter Bagehot has a very interesting phrase in which he describes a constitutional statesman. He says he is a man of ordinary opinions and extraordinary abilities; not original, but extraordinarily strong in the movement of his powers; and not only strong, but also giving you the impression that his powers are not to be discriminated as the one is weak and another strong, because they are all strong, a uniform strength in the several powers, so that they only wait to be challenged to respond to the challenge.

And then, too, there is in such men a sense of mass and solidity, as of a body that moves all together, that has not an eccentric and variable course, but moves with the steadiness of mass and of weight, which gives the impression of irresistibility.

Those, I suppose, are the things we have in mind when we speak of that undefinable thing which we call greatness. Washington would be describable in terms of that sort; Lincoln may be described in terms of that sort. You cannot pick out in Lincoln or in Washington any dominating gift, any singular and peculiar trait. The interesting thing about a man like Lincoln, for example, is that he was not fit for anything in particular, but for everything in general. Every power that is given to a fully equipped man slumbered in him and waited only the challenge of circumstance to spring into full action. So that the interesting circumstance of Lincoln's life is that, not having a drilled and schooled youth like Washington and Witherspoon, he was disclosed only by degrees, discovered in sections, made evident to the Nation in his complete greatness only when the large scale of his career was unfolded. You would not belittle such men by picking out qualities; you say there was a symmetry, a completeness, a mass, a solidity, a discernment and power in this man that proclaimed him great; so that at every point where he was touched with fire he kindled. You know that some men are not combustible; though they seem dry they will not burn. (Laughter.) These man were combustible throughout. There was not a dead, irresponsive piece in them. Therefore, wherever you touched them with sufficient warmth you got the flame of action.

Do you wonder that this man Witherspoon, who had touched Scottish life at so many points and kindled at every point, burst into flame when he felt the electrified air of America; that he seemed suddenly to epitomize in himself the impulses that America felt growing in her like growing pains, and instantly recognized the significance of the situation into which he had almost unawares stepped? And the interesting thing about the man when he actually entered upon his career was this: He put into everything that he touched the spirit of scholarship and the spirit of affairs.

It is true, as the British Ambassador has said, that it is a distinguishing characteristic of the Scottish mind that it is intensely logical, exact in its processes, precise. There is something in the Scottish mind that reminds you of the German mind—its preference for the abstract and metaphysical. But there is a very radical difference between the Scottish and the German mind. The German mind is satisfied with its metaphysics, but the Scottish mind has an awkward habit of translating its abstract principles into action. If you get a perfectly logical man like John C. Calhoun, if you get a man who has reasoned out the destiny of man and the purpose of God, like Witherspoon, and then allow him to play a part in affairs and to interpret in action what he conceives to be the truth, you will find that you have come into contact with something that seems like a living incarnated principle, and which therefore seems irresistible.

By the spirit of scholarship I mean the spirit which looks into the facts and then gives them their true interpretation. That I take to be the spirit of scholarship. The scholar insists upon knowing what the facts are, as Witherspoon did the moment he set foot in America, and then sets his trained mind to work to interpret the significance of the facts.

The spirit of affairs I take to be that practical sense of what is possible, that knows how principles which truly interpret facts can themselves be made to generate new facts in the field of action; that knowledge of men, that knowledge of human nature, that willingness to confine the mind and the plan to what is possible, which shows conviction the way of action—that is the spirit of affairs.

Another interesting circumstance that you will find here is that those who eulogize Witherspoon speak of him as a great orator, and he was a great orator; but not of the sort that this phrase usually suggests. He was not a rhetorical speaker; he was not a man who spoke with much warmth. He spoke with singular self-restraint, and what overcame you was not the exquisite phrase, but the indisputable truth of what he said. We think sometimes, ladies and gentlemen, that the men who create revolutions are the emotional orators. No emotional orator has ever created a revolution, much less has any emotional orator ever led a revolution. The man who led, who formed the revolution of 1688 in England was John Pym; and what sort of a speaker was John Pym? A short, heavy, sedate, indomitable man, who spoke business all the time, who knew what he was talking about, and was not to be perturbed by any contradiction; a man in whom you felt you touched a conviction of what was true and what was possible which could be withstood by no emotional objection. You remember the quiet speech of the town clerk in one of the chapters of the Acts, when that great assembly in Ephesus, like a lot of excited children, exclaimed for the space of two hours, "Great is Diana of the Ephesians"; how the town clerk said, "You will be called in question for this day's business." And you remember what had happened? The men who had caused this outcry, the men who had preached the Gospel, had announced an indisputable fact which, though the assembly should cry its throat out, had once and for all put Diana of the Ephesians out of business. Those humble preachers could afford to ignore the cries of the mob and the excitement of those who incited the mob, and simply repeat that there had been a transaction upon Calvary which changed the history of the world.

There is no excitement in the oratory which creates and leads revolutions. I suppose that most of you have heard of William L. Yancey, one of the chief orators of the Southern cause, when the war between the States was coming on, and I suppose you think that Yancey excited his audiences by rhetoric. He did not. He was one of the plainest speakers that this country has ever heard. He excited them by that thing which is compact of fire, namely, absolute, irresistible logic. He showed them their situation and the inferences from their situation and their choice; and he challenged them to make the choice and they made it. Not an appeal, not an emotional passage; simply the facts and the reasoning springing out of the facts—and that was the man who kindled a revolution.

Similarly, John Witherspoon was not an orator. By oratory you think of the emotional phrases and the visions of poets; but an orator is one who has seen the vision of what is going to happen and is able to lead up to it by those lines of lucid light which are the lines of unanswerable statement.

And so when Witherspoon came to reorganize his college he touched it with the spirit of affairs. He found it sleeping over its books. He made them devote themselves more to the natural sciences and to the mathematical studies. He himself undertook to lecture all around that great field which the Scotchmen of that day called the field of Moral Philosophy; and in moral philosophy he included the philosophy of government. He had no sooner reached the college than every youngster that rose to speak spoke upon some public theme. The presbytery to which he belonged in New Jersey [New Brunswick Presbytery] forbade its representatives to speak of politics in the pulpit; but there is a grave suspicion at Princeton that Mr. Witherspoon wrote many of the speeches of the undergraduates. (Laughter.) They contained with singular exactness an image of his own thought, like a mirror held up to the teacher, so that every public occasion at Princeton heard some young voice raised in exposition of the principles of liberty. Then at last he got his presbytery to rescind its rule, and there began to be spoken from his own pulpit those things which were so helpful in changing the history of the world.

He taught eagerly and gave a touch of what is modern and liberal and of active force to the studies of the youngsters who crowded about him. When you think of the men whom he taught you will see how various his product was. Here was a man who had an outlook in all directions, and his two typical pupils were James Madison and Lighthorse Harry Lee—the man whose thought was efficient in council, and the man whose action was efficient in the field—the two sides of the man given admirable expression in two lads who came from his teaching, the young man who guided the deliberations of the Constitutional Convention, and the dashing youngster who reminded men of Harry Hotspur himself in the field of battle. These were his characteristic pupils.

And then when we turn to affairs, he insisted, to the great embarrassment of many other persons in the Continental Congress, upon always basing what he had to say upon the actual facts not only, but upon the foundation of common sense. There were some of the strongest minds in that body, minds like the mind of John Adams and the mind of Benjamin Franklin, that were touched with some of the absurd and dangerous heresies of the time. There were moments when John Witherspoon was almost in a minority of one, in insisting that if you were going to fight a war you must have armies; that if you were going to have armies you must pay them with money, real money, not imitation money; and that if you were going to pay them with real money you must have an organization of States in which you did not beg the States to give you money, but could levy taxes and get it. He insisted upon actual levies, hard cash, and a solid union of the States. And these were the foundations of the American Union and of the American Nation.

He was a moderate man. He never flashed out into exaggeration. He had a great deal of the reserve of the canny Scotch. For example, in the Convention which he had just joined when it was framing the Declaration of Independence, he insisted that the list of mercenaries, of which complaint was made in that document, should not include the Scotch. Many bodies of mercenaries were complained of, and among the rest the Scotch; but he insisted that that be stricken out. I dare say that he did not himself care to be included in so objectionable a generalization. And throughout he was watchful not only to see that the Scotch were not libelled, but that the truth was nowhere libelled; that those moderate phrases of statement should be used upon which you could stand, and stand to the end, not having to explain away exaggerations, but insisting that a thing had been stated which could be proved and so always have a defensible case.

You see thus the image of the man–indomitable, a natural leader, a very formidable debater, tireless, never defeated, of that admirable cast of schooling which never knows when it is defeated but acts after nominal defeat exactly as it acted after triumphal success; never to be surprised, never to be overlooked, never to be expected to be absent, always in his seat, always ready to be upon his feet, always in the way if you wanted to do anything unwise or foolish–that is the sort of Scotchman who is at once troublesome and indispensable.

It is not difficult, then, to recall this sturdy and admirable man, a man serviceable in everything that he turned to, a man in some things a preacher, in other things a teacher, in still others a man of affairs, but always the same man–preaching what he taught, insisting in legislative councils and out of them, upon what he preached and taught; always self-consistent, self-respecting, indomitable, master of himself and of his fellows—such was John Witherspoon, whom it would belittle to call the greatest President of Princeton, one of the greatest citizens of the United States! And one of those men who typify in himself those steadfast qualities of thought and of purpose which will lead this nation stage by stage to the realization of its sober and manifest destiny.[2]

Printed in *The Witherspoon Memorial: Sketch of the Association and Unveiling of the Statue* (n. p., n. d.), pp. 18-29.

[2] There is a WWT outline of this address entitled "John Witherspoon" and dated May 18, 1909, in WP, DLC.

From Henry Lee Higginson

Manchester by the Sea [Mass.]

Dear Doctor Wilson, May 21st, 1909.

Your note is kind in its invitation to play for you.

My road-manager has died & so the Manager, Mr. [Charles A.] Ellis, must pass on your concert.

All the concerts cost me something i.e. the year leaves a deficit—always has, always will—& was expected to do so. That was in the scheme when made by me in '81—& it has not failed. The deficit has run from perhaps $10,000 to $50,000 odd—& has averaged $25,000 to $30,000. I rarely look at it—any more than the bread-bill, because it is a necessary & legitimate expenditure—& as I am not a rich man, I work for it—with pleasure, just as you work for your University—a much finer object—but is not one rule of the citizen "We each do what we can?" I say this to you as a man who sees things in a true light—& who puts work at its true value. The citizen owns his country, & sees to it that it is decent, habitable & wholesome, eh?

Our orchestra ought to go to the Universities, but then a limit to my purse & to the time & strength of my men restricts our wishes. I'll report later & ask your indulgence for my words.[1]

We have parted with our President this week, & have welcomed our new President.[2] *You* can judge what a delightful club, committee or knot of men—our Harvard Corporation of seven—we are—(is this vain?). Twice a month or oftener we meet & consult four hours with our President & indulge in free talk & action. Yours is a great profession. With kind regards I am yours H. L. Higginson

ALS (WP, DLC).

[1] The Boston Symphony Orchestra did not return to Princeton during Wilson's presidency.

[2] Charles William Eliot had just retired as President of Harvard and had been succeeded by Abbott Lawrence Lowell. Eliot had requested that his resignation take effect as of May 19, 1909, the fortieth anniversary of his assumption of the presidency.

A News Report About Wilson's Arrival in Louisville

[May 22, 1909]

PRINCETON CLUBS OF WESTERN ASSOCIATION MEET HERE TO-DAY.

Elaborate Entertainment Is Arranged For Visitors.
Going to Churchill Downs In Afternoon.

PRESIDENT WILSON IS HERE.

. . . About twenty of the members of the alumni arrived last night, including President Woodrow Wilson, of the university, and Joseph B. Shea, of Pittsburgh, Pa., president of the association of clubs. . . . Scott Bullitt and Pratt Dale[1] met President Wilson at the depot last night and escorted him to The Seelbach. President Wilson was down in the lobby shortly after arriving, shaking hands with the local alumni and those who arrived last night. All greeted each other with the usual college warmness and some time was spent in talking over old college days.

President Wilson said that he had been in Louisville once before, but that he knows many persons from this city. He makes it his business to attend the meetings of the association, unless detained at home by illness. He will leave Louisville to-morrow night for his home in Princeton. He came to Louisville from Washington, D. C., where he had gone on business. He was in fine spirits last night and said that he was really enjoying his visit. Said he:

"We continue to draw our quota of students from this section of the country and especially from Kentucky. Two professors in Princeton college hail from Kentucky. George [Madison] Priest, of Henderson, Ky., has been an instructor in the college for a number of years. He is instructor in Germany [German] and is well liked by the faculty and student body. By the way, he is wearing a Vandyke beard now and looks the part of the European instructor. Our university is in excellent condition now and its future is brighter than ever before in its history."

Printed in the Louisville *Courier-Journal*, May 22, 1909.

[1] Alexander Scott Bullitt, Princeton 1898, and William Pratt Dale, Princeton 1899.

A News Report of a Meeting of the Western Association of Princeton Clubs

[May 23, 1909]

COLORS OF TIGER

Everywhere In Evidence In Louisville Yesterday.

PRESIDENT WILSON'S SPEECH.

The "Black and the Orange," famous colors of old Princeton University, were in evidence on all sides in Louisville yesterday in honor of the annual meeting of the Western Association of Princeton Clubs. . . .

The members of the alumni attending the meeting, together with President Wilson, went on a special car to the Country Club. They first assembled in the red room of The Seelbach. As soon as they reached the Country Club, which was after the noon hour, luncheon was partaken of and the election of officers took place. St. Louis won the next meeting without opposition. After the business was attended to the delegates dispersed, and some went one place and some another. Automobiles and cars were furnished. Many of the delegates went direct to Churchill Downs, where the afternoon was spent.

The banquet last night at The Seelbach was a real treat in more ways than one. Fully 100 of the sons of Princeton were about the banquet board with John W. Barr, Jr., of Louisville, presiding, and Woodrow Wilson, president of the university, on his right. . . .

The feature of the banquet was the speech of President Woodrow Wilson on "Princeton," the keynote of which was what will be the future of the higher educational institutions of the United States, in view of the conditions that now exist socially, morally and from a business point of view. . . .

In the beginning of his address President Wilson said that he felt as he grew older perhaps less and less suited to after-dinner speaking. Said he:

"I do not know whether increasing responsibilities are sobering me or whether it is the processes of increasing years. I will say now that colleges like Princeton are now on trial. The question is how suited are they for modern life? Princeton is a great university among the institutions of education of this country. As I said, colleges in America are undergoing a severe test. You can't look around unless you see what is going on. It is not unlikely that our secondary schools will advance their standards of learning in the future. It will be the lot of the universities to undertake vocation[al] instruction. We will likely become as the great universities of Germany. There will not be any intermediary institutions.

"I must say that the vast majority of the State universities are working on vocational lines. The State university is typical of an American university. Still, though, the high universities must be free from the dictation of the taxpayers. The State universities must do what is popular, for the reason the taxpayers pay the bills. I believe that unless something is done colleges will only exist as leisure resorts of wealthy persons. I tell you that the next ten or twelve years will settle the fate of the kind of colleges that will continue to exist. We will know whether they will stand as they now are or be radically changed."

The speaker said that in former times it was the professionally inclined persons who sought college educations mostly, but now the vast majority of persons going to college expect to go into business. He declared that as the colleges now are, very little about modern business methods can be learned. It was clearly discerned from the speaker's address that he was more for intellectual learning than for athletics. He was against the idea of college life being four years of recreation as between the hard years of real learning at school and the hard years of earning a livelihood to follow. He advocated the college life being one of work and duty just as well.

The speaker dwelt at length on the comradeship and social intercourse among the students at college. He said that the colleges must become more democratic in their ideals. He said men become public enemies when they became segregated in their interests and ideas. Said he:

"The trouble in Congress to-day in the attempt to revise the tariff is that the members are individually blinded by self interests. Each has an interest to protect and each is working for the good of the United States as a whole. You can't make a reasonable tariff revision by items. It can only be done by system. All interests must be united."

The speaker discussed the democratic principles from a broad viewpoint. The trouble to-day is that many men think that the college has been lifted out of sympathy with the vast majority of men. He said if college education classified men by tastes it is not worth the while of a democratic country. Said he:

"There are two institu[t]ions that fully meet democratic expectations of America. These are the military and naval educational institutions. Men are taught in these to make themselves common instruments for the good of the country. I do not know any men more in touch with these principles in the United States than the soldiers and sailors."

The speaker said that the college had no monopoly in making good fellows. He declared that learning should be the chief aim of any college.[1]

Printed in the Louisville *Courier-Journal*, May 23, 1909; some editorial headings omitted.

[1] For this address, Wilson used the outline referred to in H. B. Thompson to WW, April 6, 1909, n. 1.

To Mary Allen Hulbert Peck

My dearest Friend, N. Y., 25 May, '09

Only last night did I get the news for which *all* my thoughts had been waiting ever since the little note in which you let me know that you had landed.[1] I did not know when or where or how to write until I did learn something definite. While I waited I had to go to Washington and thence to Louisville, Ky., and try to make speeches (how weary I grow of them!) by force of will, in spite of my pre-occupation with what might be happening for your happiness or unhappiness! I was in Princeton when I telephoned you this morning; now I am on my way to Hartford, to fulfil an engagement of long standing there,—and am forced to leave the Grand Central Station just a few minutes before you reach it! Isn't that typical of the way life teases and tantalizes us? If I could only be here to-morrow! To-morrow is your birthday. How I should love to put a *little* cheer and consolation into it by seeing you and letting you know how deeply, how utterly I sympathize, how entirely I trust you and believe in you, and how confidently I yet hope that your happiness will eventually come, with your freedom, out of all this tangle of utter distress! May that not be my birthday message to you? Did you get the little birthday memento I sent to meet you when you came in on the *Bermudian*,—a brooch? I sent it by express, in plenty of time. You spoke of my letters, but not of the little package. If I had known I was to see you (with what impatience I look forward to it!) so near the 26th I would have brought the little ornament to you in person. I will *try* to get away from Hartford to-morrow night. If I do, I shall reach N. Y. too late to see you, but will call you up early on Thursday,—say about 8.30 or 9. If I *cannot* get away then, I will take the earliest possible train on Thursday morning and should get in about 10.30 or 11.

It was deeply delightful to hear your voice over the telephone and I was more grateful than I can say to learn that you were well. I am well, but very tired, and deeply excited with impatience to hear everything that concerns you. May God bless you and keep you!

Your devoted friend, Woodrow Wilson

ALS (WP, DLC).

[1] The "little note" and letter are missing.

To Charles Andrew Talcott

My dear Charley: Princeton, N. J. May 25th, 1909.

Do try and break away from the young gentleman in Seventy-Nine Hall with whom you have promised to share quarters. It will be so hard to get hold of you if you are not at Prospect, and we shall be so much disappointed. Whether you break away or not, we shall claim as much of your time as possible, and I am looking forward with the greatest pleasure to seeing you again.

Always cordially and faithfully yours,

Woodrow Wilson

TLS (WC, NjP).

An Anniversary Address at the Hartford Theological Seminary[1]

[[May 26, 1909]]

THE PRESENT TASK OF THE MINISTRY.

Ladies and Gentlemen: I feel that there is a touch of temerity in an outsider's coming to estimate the task of the ministry, and yet I suppose that every profession is best estimated from the outside. There is a degree of self-consciousness on the part of those who practice it which prevents their proper estimation of their own service. There is among every conscientious party of men, perhaps, also, an exaggerated sense of short-coming and of failure, and therefore those who stand outside of the profession see it more in the mass, can estimate more the net results, overlooking the little discouragements and the details which are seen so clearly by those who are inside the daily life. I had thought that the theme which has just been announced would

[1] Wilson's address was part of the ceremonies in celebration of the seventy-fifth anniversary of the founding of the Hartford Theological Seminary held from May 23 to May 26, 1909. Wilson spoke at the commencement on the morning of May 26, 1909.

be an appropriate theme for an occasion like this, because it is natural that a great institution, upon every anniversary of its beginning, should make some sort of estimate of what it is that it has done, not only, but of what it intends to do, what its spirit is, and what its purpose must continue to be.

I suppose that the graduating class today must feel that they are in some sense the mature fruitage of this institution and that it is particularly incumbent upon them to know what they would be about, to know what they would represent, to know what they would try to undertake and attempt in this day, this interesting generation of ours.

I do not envy the young minister who sets out upon his task in the present age, because I know of no more difficult, no more delicate, no more tremendous undertaking than his. It is an undertaking to daunt any man who depended upon his own strength to accomplish it. Unless a man goes, in this age, on this errand with the conscious support of the spirit of God, I do not see how he can have the audacity to go out at all. We live in an age when a particular thing cries out to be done which the minister must do, and there is no one else who can do it. A very interesting situation has arisen, intellectually, in our own day. There was a time, not many years ago, marked by an entirely different intellectual atmosphere. There was a time, which we can all remember, when men of science were content, were actually content, with a certain materialistic interpretation of the universe. Their antagonistic position with regard to spiritual matters was not a defiant position. It was a position of self-assurance and of self-content. They did not look into such matters, because they were convinced that it was vain to look into them, that there was nothing that would come of their examination of the secret motives, of the secret springs of action among men, of the secret source of life in the world itself. But that time has gone by. Even men of science now feel that the explanation which they give of the universe is so partial an explanation, so incomplete an explanation, that for the benefit of their own thought—quite aside from the benefit of their own souls—it is necessary that something should be added to it. They know that there is a spiritual segment in the complete circle of knowledge which they cannot supply and which must be supplied if the whole circle is not to show its imperfection and incompleteness.

In connection with the administration of universities in our day there is an exceedingly interesting situation in the field of science. It used to be possible to draw sharp lines of division between the several fields of science. But it is no longer possible to do that. The science of physics can no longer establish a scientific frontier as against the science of mathematics. The science of physics, on the other side, cannot determine with definiteness where its jurisdiction ends and the jurisdiction of chemistry begins. Chemistry, on its further borders, cannot clearly discriminate between its field and the field of organic biology. Biology knows that it shades off into that great historical biology that lies in the field of paleontology, recorded in the buried records of what the earth's surface contains. And all of these sciences are aware that, linked as they thus are together, they must have some common principle and explanation; that we cannot stop at any frontier because there is no frontier; that the domain of knowledge, like the globe itself, is round and there is no stopping place; that what we have to do is to complete, at whatever cost, the map of knowledge, to press onward into the field where lie the unknown things both of physical knowledge and of spiritual knowledge.

In other words, we are in the presence of the absolute necessity of a spiritual coördination of the masses of knowledge which we have piled up and which we have partially explained, and the whole world waits for that vast task of intellectual mediation to be performed. Who shall mediate between our spirits and our knowledge? Who shall show our souls the tracks of life? Who shall be our guides, to tell us how we shall thread this intricate plan of the universe and connect ourselves with the purpose for which it is made?

I do not know who is to tell us if not the minister. I do not know in whom these various bits of knowledge should center and bear fruit if not in him. The world offers this leadership, this intellectual mediation, to the minister of the gospel. It is his if he be man enough to attempt it; man enough in his knowledge, man enough in the audacity and confidence of his spirit, man enough in the connections he has made with the eternal and everlasting forces which he knows to reside in the human spirit.

I believe that we have erroneously conceived the field of the Christian Church in our age. If my observation does not mislead me, the Christian Church nowadays is tempted to think of itself as chiefly a philanthropic institution, chiefly an institution which shall supply the spiritual impulse which is necessary for carrying on those great enterprises which relieve the distress, distress of body and distress of mind, which so disturbs the world and so excites our pity, among those men particularly who have not had the advantages of fortune or of economic opportunity. And yet I believe that this is only a very small part of the business of the Church. The business of the Church is not to pity men. The business of the Church is not to rescue them from their suffering by the mere means of material relief, or even by the means of spiritual reassurance. The Church cannot afford to pity men, because it knows that men, if they would but take it, have the richest and completest inheritance that it is possible to conceive, and that, rather than being deserving of pity, they are to be challenged to assert in themselves those things which will make them independent of pity. No man who has recovered the integrity of his soul is any longer the object of pity, and it is to enable him to recover that lost integrity that the Christian Church is organized. To my thinking, the Christian Church stands at the center not only of philanthropy but at the center of education, at the center of science, at the center of philosophy, at the center of politics; in short, at the center of sentient and thinking life. And the business of the Christian Church, of the Christian minister, is to show the spiritual relations of men to the great world processes, whether they be physical or spiritual. It is nothing less than to show the plan of life and men's relation to the plan of life.

I wonder if any of you fully realize how hungry men's minds are for a complete and satisfactory explanation of life? I heard a very pathetic story told the other day about a poor woman, a simple, uneducated woman, in one of our cities, who had by some accident, got hold of one of Darwin's books—I don't know whether it was the Origin of Species or not—and who had found, even to her unlettered mind, a great revelation in the book, a revelation of the processes of physical life and of the plan of physical existence. She told a friend that it had taken out of her—in her expression—"all the kick there was in her." She said: "I don't find anything in the preaching that I hear. It listens good, but it is so soft. It doesn't seem to give me anything to chaw on. It doesn't enable me to understand what happens to me every day any better than I understood it before. It doesn't even put bread in my mouth or in my children's mouths. But I read that book and I saw that there was something doing. I saw that there was something going on of which I was a little part, and it has taken all the kick out of me."

I believe that her experience is typical of the modern intellectual situation. We are infinitely restless because we are not aware of the plan. Just as soon as we are aware of the plan and see that there is "something doing," something definite, something to which we are related, even if by mere inexorable necessity, we at least know that it is futile to "kick," that it is inevitable that the processes of the gods should be ground out, and that, therefore, the whole operation of life is something to which we may properly relate ourselves if we choose, but must relate ourselves in some fashion whether we will or not. How arid, how naked, how unsatisfying a thing, merely to know that it is an inexorable process to which we must submit! How necessary for our salvation that our dislocated souls should be relocated in the plan! And who shall relocate them, who shall save us by enabling us to find ourselves, if not the minister of the gospel?

Shall he stand up in his place of teaching and talk as if there were antagonism between science and religion? If he does, he is taking religion out of the modern mind, for religion cannot remain there if it is antagonistic with science. Religion is the explanation of science and of life, that lost segment of the circle of which I was speaking just now. Think of the knowledge, therefore, with which the minister must equip himself! Not at the outset, for that is impossible, but as he grows in power and in his own understanding of the plan of the world. Think what it is that he must do for men!

In the first place, it seems to me that he must interpret the plan, not only in terms which will satisfy men of science and the deeper students of theology, but also in terms and from a point of view that will aid the man in the street who can see only a little part of the plan. The minister must seek out for him such part of the plan as can be made visible to his obstructed eye, and lead him on from this little door where he enters the plan to that larger comprehension to which every door which enters the plan at all must ultimately lead. He must show men that there is a plan and he must show that plan to them ultimately in its completeness.

In that way he must discover for men their spirits. I sometimes think that men in our age are either losing their spirits or thinking that they have lost them. It is a very confusing age for a man of conscience. In the modern organization of economic society, for example, no man is a complete whole, every man is a fraction. No man is an integer. His conscience has to reckon out for itself what part the fraction plays in the whole and what possibility of independent action there is for the fraction. The undetachable fraction lies imbedded in the mass and cannot be entirely discriminated from it, and men have allowed their consciences to run down because the mechanism in them seemed to be affected by great magnets outside, which made it impossible for them to work independently. All their little individual compasses were disturbed by great masses—chiefly of gold,—in their neighborhood, and they have asked themselves how they could disengage their consciences and become independent instrumentalities in the sight of God. The task is so tremendous and so perplexing that many men have adjourned the effort and have decided that all they can do is to drift with the general movement of the mass. They are craving to have someone rediscover their spirits for them.

Not many men in my hearing profess scruples in respect of their business and occupation; not many men indulge their consciences, and they are a little ashamed of evidences of indulging their consciences. Ask the majority of men why they go to church and, if you get the same answer that I get, you will get an answer something like this: that it is decent to go to church; that it is expected of them to go to church; moreover, that they have lived in that community, men and boys, a great many years, and their fathers and mothers went to the same churches before them; they like to maintain the moral traditions and the vague spiritual connections which go with the habit of attending church. Don't believe a word of it. It is a pure sham. Every man who is not absolutely dried up is kept alive by an inexhaustible well of sentiment. It is the fashion of our age to cover the well over with concrete so that you cannot even see or guess the gleam of the waters, but they are there, creeping up in the soil and maintaining all that produces living fruit.

What the minister has to do is to blast away these concrete covers and say to men "Here are the only sustaining waters of life, here is the rediscovery of your spirits." In that wise they must reveal God to men, reveal God to them in their own spirits, reveal God to them in thought and in action, reëstablish the spiritual kingdom among us, by proclaiming in season and out of season that there is no explanation for anything that is not first or last a spiritual explanation, and that man cannot live by bread alone, cannot live by scientific thought alone; that he is not only starving but that he knows that he is starving, and that digestion of this dry stuff that he takes into his mouth is not possible unless it be conveyed by the living water of the spirit.

I take that to be a very great and a very difficult task—a challenge to the best things that are in any man. I congratulate you, young gentlemen, that this is your high and difficult function in life. I beg you not to apologize for the Scripture to any man. I beg you not to explain it away in the presence of any audience, but to proclaim its sovereignty among men, the absolute necessity of the world to know these things if it would know itself. For it is a very significant matter, in my mind, that the gospel came into the world to save the world as well as to save individual souls. There is one sense in which I have never had very much interest in the task of saving individual souls by merely advising them to run to cover. It has never seemed to me that the isolation of the human soul, its preservation from contamination such as the Middle Ages attempted, or any modern substitute for that, was graced with any dignity at all. If men cannot lift their fellow-men in the process of saving themselves, I do not see that it is very important that they should save themselves, because they reduce Christianity by that means to the essence of selfishness, and anything that is touched with selfishness is very far removed from the spirit of Christianity. Christianity came into the world to save the world as well as to save individual men, and individual men can afford in conscience to be saved only as part of the process by which the world itself is regenerated. Do not go about, then, with the idea that you are picking out here and there a lost thing, but go about with the consciousness that you are setting afoot a process which will lift the whole level of the world and of modern life.

Until you believe that, there is absolutely no use in your going into a pulpit, you will have to have musical entertainments in order to get an audience; and then I hope you will be distinctly aware that it is the music and not you that brought the people. But if you have something to say to these people that fills you as with a living fire, it will not be necessary to have any music or any cooking classes or any bowling alleys or any gymnastics in order to bring men to the source of the things for which they most long. If you feel this, you can preach in such seething syllables as to make them feel it; and unless you preach in that wise I advise you to go into some more honest occupation. This work in the modern world is assigned to you by invitation, and if you decline the invitation then you have shown that there was some mistake in the address on the envelope. It was not intended for you. It was intended for you only if when it meets your eye your spirit leaps to the challenge and accepts it, as those do who accept the obvious lesson of every impulse that is in them, the very dictate of their conscience.

And so, standing outside the ministry, longing to see it come to the relief of those of us who undertake the imperfect processes of education, longing to see the modern world given the privilege of witnessing a day when the human spirit shall come unto its own again, I congratulate you, I welcome you, and above all, I would challenge you to do this high thing in such wise as shall mark the Seventy-fifth Anniversary of this seminary as nothing else could mark it—by taking your part, at any rate, in giving to the world the vision of God which it was intended to exhibit.[2]

Printed in the *Hartford Seminary Record*, XIX (July 1909), 226-33.
[2] There is a WWT outline of this address, dated June [May] 26, 1909, in WP, DLC.

From John Grier Hibben

My dear Woodrow, Princeton May 27/09

I had a talk with Mr. Eliott[1] today about my resigning from the Discipline Committee. I told him that I wished to be relieved of the duties of this Committee, & also that I felt that he should have a free hand at the very beginnings of his administration. Both for his sake and my own, this course is a wise one, I am sure. Mr. Elliott understands my position, & our conversation was most satisfactory to me. Will you kindly allow me therefore to terminate my service on the Discipline Committee at the close of this Academic year.[2]

Ever faithfully yours John Grier Hibben

ALS (WP, DLC).
[1] That is, Edward Graham Elliott, Dean-designate of the College.
[2] Wilson did permit Hibben to resign from the Discipline Committee.

From Henry Ferguson[1]

My dear President Wilson Concord, N. H. May 27th [1909]

We are looking forward to your visit at the school next week and hope that you can spare us as much time as possible

The boat races are on the first, and the anniversary itself[2] is on the third.

We shall be glad to welcome you whenever you can come, and if you will let us know by what train we may expect you, will meet you at the station.

With very kind regards

I am Yours very sincerely Henry Ferguson.

ALS (WP, DLC).
[1] Rector of St. Paul's School in Concord, N. H.
[2] The fifty-third anniversary of the founding of St. Paul's School.

To Charles Francis Adams

My dear Mr. Adams: Princeton, N. J. May 29th, 1909.

We are looking forward with a great deal of pleasure and satisfaction to having you here at Commencement, and I am writing, both for myself and on behalf of Mr. Henry W. Green of our Board of Trustees, who is Chairman of our Commencement Committee, to ask if you will not give us the pleasure of hearing a few words from you after lunch on Commencement Day, Tuesday, the 15th of June. The Alumni Lunch is given in the University Gymnasium at one o'clock on Tuesday, after the formal exercises of the day, and is concluded before the afternoon reception at Prospect.

With warmest regard,

Cordially and sincerely yours, Woodrow Wilson

TLS (photostat in RSB Coll., DLC).

From Edgar Starr Barney[1]

My dear Pres. Wilson, New York May 30, 1909.

The Union College Men are looking forward with pleasure at meeting you next Monday at the inauguration of President Richmond.

I am arranging for the Union men in New York to go up to-gether on Monday June 7th, 10.30 a.m. train from the Grand Central Station, and due to arrive in Schenectady at 2.14 in time for the exercises at 4 o'clock.

May I ask if you are going up on that train and if I may reserve a Pullman chair in our car for you?

Sincerely yours, Edgar S. Barney (Trustee)

ALS (WP, DLC).

1 Principal of the Hebrew Technical Institute of New York and a trustee of Union College.

From Charles Alexander Richmond

My dear Dr. Wilson Schenectady, New York 30th May 1909

We want you to stop with us when you come to Schenectady next week Monday.

Let us know when to expect you.

You will be very welcome as you know

Cordially yours Charles Alex Richmond

ALS (WP, DLC).

To Mary Allen Hulbert Peck

Dearest Friend, Princeton, 31 May, 1909.

I had been away from home on so many errands and for so many days that when I got back from Hartford and New York I was quite overwhelmed with the arrears of work that had piled up against me. I have just begun to see daylight through it, after three days of burrowing, and am blinking and rubbing my eyes at sight of the day.

It was a deep pleasure to see you in New York. You seemed to me to be looking very tired indeed and I am impatient to learn that you have begun to rest and to *feel* rested. But you have simply wonderful vivacity,—I mean physical vivacity, as well as every other kind. The word seems to me to imply so many more elements of life than any other,—so much more than elasticity or vitality. It is the quality of *youth*, and it is so characteristic, so delightfully characteristic, of you. You will have it to the end. Death, when he comes, will come to you like a stranger, an interloper. You will not know him. May his coming be put off till many, many years of peace and happiness have given you a taste of life whose sweetness can never leave you. Selfishness would make me wish, also, that it might not come till all who love you and depend upon you are gone! So long as you live you will be a source of life and happiness to them.

I am in the throes of writing my baccalaureate address,—"We are unprofitable servants: we have done that which was our duty to do,"[1] and the idea is searching me pretty thoroughly,—that mere duty does not profit, but only that which we volunteer over and above. I write my sermons to myself. I at least know what *I* need to hear! There may be others like me whom it will touch to the quick. I think that some part of the secret of the happiness that friendship brings lies hidden in the things I have been trying to say in my little layman's sermon. Friendship is all largess. Nothing is given from a sense of duty. It all lies in the delightful region of voluntary service. The affection which supports it is wholly spontaneous,—and only the spontaneous is delightful. The road you *must* walk grows very dreary: it is the paths you pick out of your own choice that you follow with zest, in search of delights. The perfect moment comes when duty and inclination, obligation and choice, join hands and forget that there is any difference between them. Isn't that deliciously didactic? I am afraid the teacher in me often draws a smile from you! Why is it that when one is in the midst of the tasks of a very practical world, deciding actual questions of administration and action every hour, it is so natural, on the slightest occasion, to turn aside and utter a gentle homily? I suppose the mind is really at every turn registering a sort of comment on the movement and action of its life,—and we all love to moralize!

I am very tired, using up every hour all the energy there is in me, and yet persistently well and seemingly very strong. The heat suitable to Commencement is beginning to descend on us. I hope it will sweat all the bad humours out of me and make me docile to my tasks. Madge Axson is back from her six months by the Pacific, and would, I am sure, send you her love if she knew I was writing to you. She is very well and as sweet and inscrutable as ever. Your devoted friend Woodrow Wilson

ALS (WP, DLC).

[1] It is printed at June 13, 1909.

To Isaac Chauncey Wyman[1]

My dear Mr. Wyman: Princeton, N. J. June 1st, 1909.

I had the pleasure, the other day, of receiving a call from Mr. and Mrs. Raymond,[2] who were kind enough to convey to me your messages of regard and of good will for the University and also to speak of your kind interest in your Alma Mater.

I ventured to send to you through them my very warm expressions of regard and appreciation, and give myself the pleasure of adding this line of direct and personal greeting. I do not know of anything that more heartens us in the administration of the University than the support and affectionate regard of those of our older alumni who have gone out into the world and made a place for themselves, thereby honoring their Alma Mater, and who as years draw on find themselves still full of a feeling of thoughtful loyalty towards the college.

I sincerely hope that I may have the opportunity upon some early occasion to pay my respects to you in person at Salem, should my engagements draw me in that direction.

With much respect,

Sincerely yours, Woodrow Wilson

TLS (UA, NjP).

[1] Princeton 1848, of Salem, Mass., who had made a fortune in real estate.

[2] John Marshall Raymond of Salem, Mass., Wyman's lawyer and friend, and his wife, Jennie Abbott Ward Raymond.

An Announcement

[June 2, 1909]

A very graceful compliment is to be paid to the President of the University by the present graduating class, who will give a dinner in his honor at the Princeton Inn on the evening of June 10th, just before the Commencement season begins. The event is "in recognition and appreciation of President Woodrow Wilson's services to the University and to the Senior Class," in accordance with a motion adopted at a recent meeting of the seniors. This will be the first time, we believe, that a graduating class his [has] given such a dinner to the President of the University.

Printed in the *Princeton Alumni Weekly*, IX (June 2, 1909), 533.

A News Report of an Anniversary Address

[June 3, 1909]

ST. PAUL'S ANNIVERSARY.

"Old Boys" see their famous school today under best conditions.

A SPLENDID GATHERING.

A day nearly ideal in temperature and with a bright June sun marked the 53rd anniversary of St. Paul's school. The "old boys" returned in great numbers for the annual ceremonies, in many cases accompanied by wives and children; and in instances not a few greeted their own sons, now students at Concord's favorite school.

It was a typical anniversary day, with all the traditional services and functions and with the reunions which always make memorable an occasion of this kind. . . .

In the new upper school, after the chapel exercises, a lunch of salads, croquettes and ices was served. Following this, Rev. Dr. Ferguson introduced President Woodrow Wilson of Princeton as a college president who believes in an education which educates.

President Wilson said that the figures above the door represented the span of his own life. He had not produced as much as St. Paul's school, he said, but he had had just as much trouble. He was pleased, he said, to speak to the fathers and mothers, as well as the students, for fathers and mothers frequently have less conception than their children of what an education really is. We have forgotten what our schools are for. He asked if the fathers and mothers thought that what their sons are doing at St. Paul's has any vital connection with what they are to do later. He believed in a broad education and said that the object of a college is to make young gentlemen as unlike their fathers as possible. The man whose son goes to college has become immersed in his own affairs and his eyes are below the horizon. He forgets the country in minding his own business. A generalized American is preferable to a specialized American. "I believe in athletics," said President Wilson. "I believe in all those things which relax energy, that the faculties may be at their best when the energies are not relaxed. But only so far do I believe in these diversions. When the lad leaves school, he ceases to be an athlete. It is of no consequence whether he can play hockey or not. The modern world is an exacting one and the things it exacts are mostly intellectual. Machinery has largely exempted us from manual labor. To the president of a corporation, the corporation is a thing of the imagination. He never sees it. You cannot see a government. The whole thing is a projected brain. The modern world will demand from your son a quick comprehension of things he can never see; and if he has merely played baseball, played football or rowed in a crew, he must begin to go to school again.

"The modern world is governed by intellectual power. The only man who is a master in the modern world is the man who is master of things he never saw. The modern world is a world of the mind.

"A danger surrounding our modern education is the danger of wealth. I am sorry for the lad who is going to inherit money, for it is no longer distinguished to be rich. The lad who is to inherit money is foredoomed to obscurity. You can't distinguish yourself by pleasure; you can't amuse yourself by adventure. I fear that the kind of men who are to share in shaping the future are not largely exemplified in schools and colleges. So far as the colleges go, the sideshows have swallowed up the circus, and we don't know what is going on in the main tent and I don't know that I want to continue as ringmaster under those conditions. There are more honest occupations than teaching if you can't teach.

"I don't want you to think that I contemplate going out of the business. I shall not, until I have made as many of my fellow countrymen as uncomfortable as possible.

"When once we have the gracious assistance of fathers and mothers, we shall educate their sons. Given that assistance, in a single generation we shall change the entire character of American education, and it has to be changed. Schools like this one and universities like Princeton must pass out of existence unless they adapt themselves to modern life.

"All the education that takes place in a school or college takes place in the student's mind outside the classroom. We have gone ridiculously far in our college and school life, but we have generated an opposite tendency."[1]

Printed in the Concord, N. H., *Evening Monitor*, June 3, 1909; one editorial heading omitted.

[1] There is a WWT outline of this address, June 3, 1909, in WP, DLC.

From Melancthon Williams Jacobus

Pittsfield, Mass.

My dear President Wilson: Thursday June 3/09

My doctor has ordered me away for a month's rest and I am at present thus far into the Berkshires which were thought to be the best thing in the way of an immediate, near by resort.

This change in my plans throws me out again of the meeting of the Board, and I cannot well tell you how disappointing and discouraging it makes my service in the Board during this last year, that I can look back to but one meeting which I was privileged to attend.

However, I seem to have no alternative but to obey commands, and I am writing you at once to inform you of the situation & to ask you as President of the University to issue the call for the Curriculum Committee at such time as is most convenient to yourself.

Added to my disappointments is my failure to have had a conference with Fine regarding the matters of which we had a moment's conversation during your visit to Hartford last week.

I sincerely hope nothing will be brought before the Committee in connection with this matter which is not the outcome of full agreement between yourself & Fine. I stand with Thompson in opposition to the use of the Committee for referee work and will vote from first to last to support the President of the University in his judgment as against the contentions of his subordinate officers.

May I ask to have Mr. Imbrie do me again the favor of forwarding for filing a copy of the minutes of the Committee meeting, as well as a copy of the report to the Board.

I enclose herewith a communication from Prof. Magie which should come before the Committee[1]

With renewed regrets at my inability to attend the Annual

Meeting of the Board and the sincere hope & prayer that all matters will issue to the best interests of the University

I am yours very cordially Melancthon W Jacobus

PS Your corrected address[2] has been received & placed in proper hands for publication. Thank you for your letter. MWJ.

ALS (WP, DLC).

[1] The minutes of the Committee on the Curriculum held on June 12, 1909, do not reveal what Magie's communication was about.

[2] That is, "The Present Task of the Ministry," printed at May 26, 1909.

To Mary Allen Hulbert Peck

Dearest Friend, N. Y., 4 June, 1909

I am *in transitu*, as usual. I invaded New Hampshire night before last, and spoke yesterday at St. Paul's school, on a sort of nondescript occasion,—a luncheon, which seems to be the chief event of their Finals. How I did wish that Pittsfield were on the route from N. Y. to Concord! It was Boston instead, not half so interesting a place,—to me! Today (I arrived at half after six this morning, and feel already, at nine, as if the day were half spent) I am due at two conferences here—one of a committee of our Board,[1] the other of the Executive Committee of the Carnegie Foundation. I hope to be at home to-night, only to start out again on Sunday evening for a visit to Schenectady on Monday, to assist at the inauguration of a new President of Union College,—a Princeton man to whom I must carry the blessing of his *alma mater*. Are you coming down to visit Mrs. Roebling?[2] When I was on my way up to Concord on Wednesday I met her at the ferry and we had some fifteen or twenty minutes together,—very enjoyable minutes for me, for she is truly delightful. She told me that you were back from Bermuda, and that she had meant to see you in New York the other day,—that you had been down for a day or two and she had talked to you over the telephone,—but that a po[u]ring rain had prevented! She said, too, that her friends, the Rivers,[3] at the Webster, had seen you and had told her that you were not looking at all well. I thought you looked well, but worn out and depressed. I wish I could hear from some disinterested witness that you were looking rested and bright again now. I had not heard from you since your return to Pittsfield when I left home on Wednesday. I am feeling pretty well 'played out' myself,—but every engagement puts me just that much nearer vacation—which is now less than two weeks off—and I have plenty of strength to hold out. I am *only* tired—and that kills nobody. It is just such another day as that on which Mrs. Roebling could not come in to see you. I shall come to think of it as the normal New York day. It was threatening on Wednesday when I saw Mrs. R. and she had come off with the Colonel's[4] umbrella—"the one thing in the house she had been absolutely forbidden to touch." She did not know whether she would dare go back home,—was thinking of telegraphing, "Have eloped with the umbrella. Good-bye." The last I saw of her she was waving her hand to me out of a taxicab as she flew past the slow four-wheeler I had taken.

There is no news—and nothing has happened to me that was in the least entertaining since I saw Mrs. R. I saw the Garfield's[5] at Concord and Mrs. G. asked after you. She asked if something had not happened in the Peck family,—very kindly, but I thought it strange she should ask.

God bless you.

In haste, Your devoted friend Woodrow Wilson

ALS (WP, DLC).

1 The Committee on the Graduate School, which was in New York to meet with William Cooper Procter.

2 Cornelia Witsell Farrow (Mrs. Washington Augustus) Roebling, of Trenton. She had married Roebling on April 21, 1908, the second marriage for both.

3 One of the several Rivers families of Charleston, S. C.; however, it is impossible to determine which one it was. Mrs. Roebling was from Charleston. The Webster was a hotel in New York.

4 Washington Augustus Roebling, who had been a colonel in the Union Army.

5 Harry Augustus Garfield and Belle Hartford Mason Garfield.

From Lawrence Crane Woods

My dear Dr. Wilson: Pittsburg, Pa. June 5, 1909.

Under separate cover I am sending you a copy of yesterday's Pittsburg Post. In my judgment the marked article (Associated Press Dispatch) upon the first page can do you and the cause no good, and may do great harm.[1] I regret it, therefore, exceedingly. The opposition will welcome an early issue. Every day that we can be patient our forces are being strengthened. At the close of the university year, when one's physical limitations are most sorely taxed, it seems to me peculiarly important that great care should be taken as to what is said or done.

Pray forgive me for writing to you as frankly as I do. If I were not heart and soul with you in the campaign, anything which struck me as a tactical error would not trouble me.

Very sincerely yours, Lawrence C. Woods

TLS (WP, DLC); P.S. omitted.

1 The Associated Press dispatch purported to give the highlights of Wilson's

speech at St. Paul's School on June 3, 1909, and consisted primarily of alleged direct quotations from Wilson's speech. One controversial quotation was the opening sentence of the article: "Schools like this one and universities like Princeton must pass out of existence unless they adapt themselves to modern life." Another was a paragraph which read: "A danger surrounding our modern education is the danger of overwealth. I am sorry for the lad who is going to inherit money. I fear that the kind of men who are to share in shaping the future are not largely exemplified in schools and colleges."

An Address at the Inauguration of Charles Alexander Richmond as President of Union College

[[June 7, 1909]]

Princeton has not the responsibility of being the oldest of American universities, and I feel that it is an especial privilege for me to stand here to-day, not to bear any formal congratulations from a vague body of university men, but to bear the special, affectionate greeting of Princeton men to the Princeton man who is assuming the presidency of this aged and distinguished seat of learning. We are a very compact family, we Princeton men. We are proud to believe that we inherit a common spirit, and I believe that you will not think that I am taking away from the dignity of the occasion when I say that I prefer to think of the gentleman who is assuming the presidency of Union at this present moment, as the very much beloved Charlie Richmond of '83.

We have known Dr. Richmond for a long time, and we know absolutely nothing to his disadvantage. It is our pessimistic idea about the world we live in that only the men who push themselves, that have a shrewd eye for the main chance, are the men who are preferred in the fortunes of society. The contrary is the case. Many a man in American life who has no thought of promoting his own fortune has, by the mere circumstance of letting the gold in him gleam, caught the idea more effectively than the man who has flaunted his powers by his advancement in the face of the world. And this modest gentleman has been unable to conceal his worth, and America now sees him elevated to an additional post of trust, which shows that men not intimately associated with him have seen, in a difficult point of selection, that this was the man who would supply Union with the leadership which she needed at this turn in her life. We can guarantee to you that the man we knew at Princeton, and have loved ever since he graduated, was always the sort of man whom we have recognized.

And so it is with a sort of personal and affectionate greeting that I welcome Dr. Richmond into the questionable privileges of the fraternity of college president. It is a very happy life, sir, for those who love strife; it is a very interesting life for those who like to tell their fellow men what they really think of them. It is especial[l]y a life of an extraordinary number of demands upon one's energy, one's time and one's brains. Inside the college, a college president has to co-ordinate and guide the processes of his own institution, and that is by no means a simple or easy task. College faculties are sometimes touched with as much sensitiveness and personal jealousy as church choirs, and it is a very delicate task to moderate and modulate and personally conduct the processes of accommodation which must be sought and found in the administration of a college.

And then there is another thing which a college president must do. He must constantly remind his college that it is its business not to serve as a clearing house for all modern ideas in education. Most modern ideas are so exceedingly modern that nobody knows whether they are sound or not. They are very much in the same condition that the so-called science of child-psychology is,—nobody but the child knows whether it is sound or not, and he can't tell it.

It is characteristic of our school systems that they should lack system, and of our school methods that they are so miscellaneous as not to be methodic. We are not only trying everything, but we are trying everything at once. We might if we tried things in sequence discover which were workable and which were not, but when we try them all at once, it is impossible to discriminate between them. The college is under the temptation to follow the lead of the school and try to teach everything at once, establishing no sequences, assessing no values, giving no advice, throwing everything into the pot and hoping that the result will be a savory mixture.

It is the business of the modern college president to lead his college out of chaos into order; and that is not an easy thing in this modern time. He has to deny himself the pleasure of teaching some things. It is a pleasure to teach things that nobody else understands. It is a very difficult matter to teach things that everybody else understands. I have often thought of the extraordinary position of Plato, who for a whole life time had Aristotle for a pupil. I am happy to think that our pupils last only four years. The important part of the inside work of a college president is to drive his team and to see to it that the energies of the college are not dispersed along a thousand ineffectual lines, that they are co-ordinated and directed toward definite purposes and that those purposes are never apologized for to anybody, but are spoken of with authority. For if the college does not know its job, certainly the community does not. If it did, the part should be reversed.

The college president is now expected to speak everywhere upon every subject. There is a certain freedom that goes with it, because it is never easier to speak than upon subjects that you do not understand. It gives absolute scope to the mind. There is no restraining or limiting information. Your conscience is not checked by the feeling that you may be making inaccurate statements. There is a delightful sense of adventure, for you are going into new territory without chart, without direction, and without method, and speaking upon the platform makes the other persons in the audience who do not understand the subject suppose that you know what you are talking about, and most persons in most audiences do not understand any particular subject.

A distinguished Irish orator said that no speaker had ever exaggerated the average ignorance of his audience. There will be persons in the audience who won't speak to you afterwards, because they happened to know what you were talking about and you did not, but they will be an unquestionable minority.

In the time that is covered by my own personal observation the variety of things that the college presidents are asked to do has increased in an extraordinary degree. I believe that it is not because college presidents are supposed to be abler men than the average men who direct affairs of importance, but it is because America feels that she is in an age of difficult questions, and hopes that in college presidents she may find persons who will give disinterested advice,—men who have no axes to grind, men who are supposed to have cultivated a studious habit of examining the subjects they are going to talk about, and a capacity for expression which will enable them at any rate to make intelligible the things that they want to say and the principles they wish to expound. America is very eager just now for disinterested counsel and it is because it thinks that it will receive it from college presidents that they are so often called upon to address audiences of their fellow countrymen.

I do not need to point out how great a moral responsibility that brings to bear upon the college president. I do not need to tell you what a splendid exercise that is for his conscience. I do not need to tell you what a tremendous stimulation it is to his mind that he is expected to be a worthy counsellor among his fellow citizens. He has to counsel them in many ways. He has to show them how public questions and general interests look when held up in the light of those who study questions without regard to the partisan's point of view. He has to try to do [it] in a way that is perhaps uncommonly difficult. There are a great many temptations in the way of the academic mind. Things look very simple or symmetrical in books, but they are neither simple or symmetrical in life. It is very easy for the student to insist upon standards which are Utopian, remote, impossible, and, to borrow a fine phrase from an English writer, "Anything looks black if you hold it up against the light that blazes in Utopia." The clergyman has to be very careful not to hold things up to the light that blazes in Utopia, but to hold them down in the ordinary light of the workaday world and try to expound, so far as he can see them, the relations which those things bear to the moral and material and intellectual interests of the age, reminding them of all the elements of modern life, and particularly of that element for which he is more than others personally responsible,—I mean the element of education.

I believe firmly that nothing more needs explication to the American public at this moment than the real need of education and what it is that it ought to be expected to do for them. The present conception of education in America is that it ought to furnish you with any kind of information that you want. I have never known information to do any man any good at all. I have known some exceedingly well-informed men, some men with memories that hold everything, little and big, that ever touched them, to whom I would never dream of going for counsel or for expert service; and I have known men without any information at all to whose minds I would go just as I would go to hold something up to the mirror of nature itself, knowing that that mind was so made, so perfected by the teachings of education, that it would perfectly and truly reflect the image of the thing the moment it was held up to it. The educated man is the man who has a perceiving and discriminating mind, whose reactions are immediate; who knows what a thing is when he sees it and knows what it means when he sees it.

The modern world not only is a very complex world, but its complexity is woven of things invisible. It is woven of the organization of great corporations; it is woven of the intricate parts and co-ordinations and assemblings of great systems of machinery; it is woven of the intricate, almost untraceable relationships of citizenship, of governing, of philanthropic effort. It is woven of ideas and of processes, and the man who can't grasp invisible things is a man not fitted for modern life. The man who merely has the skill of hand, who merely has the exactness of information to specify items, is merely a tool in modern life. He can be nothing more than a tool, but the man that can conceive organizations that he never will see, who can conceive purposes which have been merely put into words for him, who can understand those moral and spiritual relationships which knit a nation together, is the man who can really serve his country.

The enemies of a country are not the men who consciously purpose its ruin, are not men who consciously do things that are criminal. They have been given to all ages, and the penitentiaries even now are not big enough for them. The real enemies of a country are the men who do it damage and do not know it, but, so far as their consciousness is concerned, are honest men, with righteous purpose, but who are so little aware of the intricate operation and inter-relationship of moral and spiritual relations in this great modern age that they thrust ignorant hands in amongst the fiber and damage the very vital seats of life itself. Men who know the interior secrets of life are the men whom the modern world needs, and this is the function of education. It must be expounded by the college presidents. The pupil must really allow it to be introduced into his system.

I did not know but that Mr. Brownell[1] was poking the same sort of fun at me that some of my young friends who have been students at Princeton University have poked at me, when he seemed to say that I was trying to reduce Princeton to a small college. I and my colleagues have done what Providence threw in our way in that direction. We have made a very large number of young gentlemen realize that a college was not a place for a man who did not desire an education. I remember being very much startled some years ago by a friend of mine who said, that after teaching twenty years he had come to the conclusion that the human mind had infinite resources for resisting the introduction of knowledge. Now, a college is an organized force for overcoming that resistance, and if a man is absolutely impenetrable, why, then he ought to go into some place where his presence will be less of an evidence of dishonesty. That very clever writer, Oliver Hertford, who so delightfully perverts familiar maxims, has this among others, "You can lead an ass to knowledge, but you can't make him think,"[2] and after you lead the ass to knowledge, if you find that you can't make him think, then you ought to release him into a more appropriate sphere.

The only object of an educational institution is intellectual, not its chief object, not its principal task, but its only task. It has no other excuse for existing and not until we all subscribe to that proposition will the process of education in this country take on the force and energy and success which they should have. Not that I mean that young gentlemen can spend their whole time over books or in laboratories and technical tasks, I know they cannot; I know that old gentlemen can't. I do not want to sit down over a book all day. I would not sit down over a book at all if the author were alive and accessible; I would go and talk to him, but most authors are dead and inaccessible. I have to read books. It is the means of getting me into communication with the minds of my fellow men, but I must have some relaxation. I must not go pale; I must keep red blood in my veins; I must keep red blood in my veins to use for the energy of my brain, because the main, the sole object, must be served by these subordinate things, and I must keep an athletic body because I want to have a mind that men will hesitate to tackle. A mind must not hesitate to lay itself along any other mind.

I used to have an old dog to whom I was very much attached. He was a big fellow, and he had a very aristocratic sense of honor. He would not fight any dog smaller than himself and he went blind, and was very unhappy, not because he could not see other things, but because he could not see to fight. Fighting was the end of his existence, and so whenever he perceived the presence of another dog, he would go and lay himself alongside of him to see how big the other dog was, and if he was not as big as he was, he would go sadly away, but if he was, the interesting proceedings would begin at once.

Now, that may be a crude figure, but it is an illustration of what I mean. It is the main object to be of a size that is worth fighting, and then to make it dangerous to be fought. The world needs such men, and the colleges must supply them, and I am happy to believe that Union is one of those colleges that from the first has known the way. There was intimate and personal contact between the teacher and the student. I have delivered a great many lectures, some of them I hope good, but I do not believe that I ever did anybody any particular good by any of my lectures. It is a significant fact that every pupil that has ever thanked me for doing what I did for him mentioned something I did outside the class; and yet I put all the brains I had into those lectures, but the point was that until the lad and I met, he did not know what I was. I did not know what he was, I was not suiting the thing I had to what he wanted. Now, that has been known at Union from the first, that teaching can't be impersonal, wholesale. It must be intimate and personal; intimate by direct contact and personal in its suitability to the individual, not in being laid off in lengths, or elaborated into patterns, but every man fitted to his particular needs. Now, that is, literally speaking, an unsuitable ideal, but it is the only ideal we are considering and it is only approximation to that method that makes an institution an effective instrument of learning.

I congratulate Dr. Richmond for the opportunity into which he has come, as I also sincerely congratulate Union for its having got Dr. Richmond to put in this place, and I want to give him some commiseration for the difficult thing he has undertaken, but also more felicity because, after all, we were put into this world to fight. For my own part I find no more stimulating exercise. Fight fairly, do not abuse the other fellow; keep your mouth shut if he abuses you. Do not indulge in personalities. Be as meek as Moses with regard to yourself, but as dangerous as fire with regard to the subject, so that when a man touches you he will burn his fingers; so that he will realize that you are there to silence any man who can't answer your argument, and that any man who resorts to personalities because he can't answer your arguments will, in any academic community, be laughed off the platform. Come like a gallant knight into the lists, but be sure you have a good horse under you. Be sure that you know the use of the eye and the tilt and do not fail to unhorse the other fellow. It is an age in which we have to recall for ourselves and having recalled for ourselves, recall to others the ideals which made the nation great and one of the central ideals which has served as a sort of structural steel for the making of this has been the idea of a thorough going training of the mind and an open eye to perceive the central, the true, the eternal significance alike of industry, of religion and of force.[3]

Printed in *Union College Bulletin*, II (Aug. 1909), 32-43.

1 Silas Brown Brownell, Union College 1852, lawyer of New York and President of the Board of Trustees of Union College.

2 Ethel Watts Mumford, Oliver Herford, and Addison Mizner, *The Entirely New Cynic's Calendar of Revised Wisdom 1905* (San Francisco, 1904).

3 There is a WWhw outline of this address, dated May 10, 1909, in WP, DLC.

From William Cooper Procter

My dear Dr. Wilson: Cincinnati June 7, 1909

After again visiting last Saturday with Professor West, Mr. Pyne and yourself the several locations considered possible for the Graduate College, my preference still remains with Merwick. If this does not meet with your views and those of the Board of

Trustees, I will accept the Golf Links[1] provided a better approach is secured by the purchase of a broader right-of-way between the Golf links and the Bachelors' Club,[2] covering one or two lots on each side of Canal Street[3] and at least part of the MacDonald property.[4]

As I understand there will be a meeting of the Board of Trustees tomorrow in New York, to provide against the possibility of missing you at Princeton I am sending by Special Delivery a copy of this letter to you in care of Mr. Edwin [Edward Wright] Sheldon.

Trusting that this location may meet with your approval, I am,

Yours very truly, Wm Cooper Procter

TLS (WWP, UA, NjP).

[1] A tract of land of 221 acres with a golf course, located roughly between Alexander Street, what are now College Road West and Springdale Road, and Stony Brook. The tract had been donated to the university in 1905.

[2] About the Bachelors Club, see WW to the Board of Trustees' Committee on the Graduate School, May 30, 1907, n. 5, Vol. 17.

[3] That is, Alexander Street.

[4] The property of James MacDonald, gardener, located at 26 Stockton Place (now part of College Road).

An Interview

[June 9, 1909]

President Wilson's speeches have been so frequently misrepresented that The Weekly took it for granted that the startling statements reported by the newspapers to have been uttered by him in his recent address at St. Paul's School, Concord, N. H., were taken out of their context and made to bear a meaning that was not in the speaker's mind. On his return to Princeton, however, we took the pains to interview the President concerning his address, and he said: "I am extremely mortified that my speech at Concord, which was not radical in any respect, should have been so misrepresented. It was the same old doctrine with which readers of The Weekly have already become familiar. I was simply discussing the problem of the establishment of a proper relation between the studies of schools and universities, and the other activities of student life. The reporter seems to have taken a few whimsical illustrations as the whole substance of the address. I am not afraid that either the schoolmasters or the college men of the country will think that no serious work is being done at Princeton. The contrary has become notorious."

Printed in the *Princeton Alumni Weekly*, IX (June 9, 1909), 551.

To Lawrence Crane Woods

My dear Mr. Woods: Princeton, N. J. June 10th, 1909.

Thank you for your letter of June 5th. I do not know when I have been so shocked or vexed as I have been by the alleged reports of my address at St. Paul's School at Concord. I said absolutely nothing there which I have not been saying for the last four or five years in many forms, and the singular thing is that I said it all over again at St. Paul's in substantially the same form I had used on previous occasions. Some reporter seems with an almost devilish ingenuity to have picked out whimsical illustrations and put together parts of sentences in order to create a sensation and an impression of a radical utterance having been made. His representation that I attacked wealth, for example, is particularly unfounded.

I shall take every proper opportunity to disclaim the opinions I am alleged to have uttered there, but of course these disclaimers will not reach the persons upon whom the initial impression was made. One can only set one's teeth and remember that it is possible to live down these distressing experiences. I quite agree with you that such utterances would, if made, be very unwise and harmful at the present time. I can only comfort myself with the knowledge that I did not make them.

I need not tell you how much I value your constant interest and thoughtful support.

With warmest regards,

Sincerely yours, Woodrow Wilson

TLS (WC, NjP).

To John Watson Foster

My dear Mr. Foster: Princeton, N. J. June 10th, 1909.

Absence from home prevented my replying to your interesting letter of June 1st.[1]

I very much appreciate your suggestion that the $1500 to $2000 which it is likely will remain in the Witherspoon Association treasury after all bills are paid, should be made a permanent fund at Princeton for a prize essay on some American patriotic, historical or political subject, to be called the Witherspoon Prize.

I am not sure that I think that such an application of the money would be wise. Our recent experience with prizes here has not been satisfactory. They do not stimulate as they used to do, and it is possible that the results would be very unsatisfactory.

The best suggestion that occurs to me is that the fund should be applied, so far as its interest will go, to the Scholarship funds of the University. It could be named and kept as a distinct fund, and we are very anxious indeed to add every dollar that is possible to the money by which we are enabled to make the path of worthy fellows without means easier here.[2]

Thank you for sending me the Memorial pamphlet[3] and for quoting what Mr. Bryce was kind enough to say of my address.

Cordially and sincerely yours, Woodrow Wilson

TLS (NjHi).

[1] It is missing.

[2] See J. W. Foster to WW, Dec. 21, 1909.

[3] *The Witherspoon Memorial: Sketch of the Association and Unveiling of the Statue* (Washington, D. C., 1909).

To Granville Stanley Hall[1]

My dear President Hall: Princeton, N. J. June 10th, 1909.

In reply to your letter of May 24th,[2] which has lacked an answer so long only because I have been away from home, I would say that I feel that my acquaintance with available men throughout the country is so limited that I could not venture to speak of any except those with whom I have been personally associated.

One always hesitates to speak of one's immediate colleagues, and yet one's conscience drives him to put in their way the opportunities to which they are entitled. The man who, I think, would be best suited for the place made vacant by the unhappy death of Col. Wright[3] is my own colleague, Professor Andrew F. West. I do not know any man in the country who would be more admirably suited or whose ideals and energy would better fit the place. I have not the least idea whether he would consider such an offer or not. I can only speak my judgment as to his fitness, and outside the circle of my own associates I know no one intimately enough to form a similar judgment concerning him.

With much regard,

Sincerely yours, Woodrow Wilson

TLS (G. S. Hall Papers, MWC).

[1] President of Clark University.

[2] It is missing.

[3] Carroll Davidson Wright, specialist in labor statistics, Commissioner of the United States Bureau of Labor, 1885-1905, and President of Clark College from 1902 until his death on February 20, 1909. The will of Jonas Gilman Clark, who died in 1900, provided for the establishment of Clark College under a presidency separate from that of the university. The college was established in 1902. The college and university shared the same library, campus, and Board of Trustees; however, the college had a separate endowment and its own administration. This unusual arrangement continued until 1921, when the two entities were finally merged.

Notes for an Address

SENIOR DINNER, 10 June, 1909.

THE PROBLEMS OF THE UNIVERSITY.

PREFACE: Appreciation.

Apprehension and embarrassment, because of misrepresentation.

A subject, not a programme: The life and organization of the University.

Neither an attack nor a criticism,—an analysis and a search for an organic, constructive policy.

No American university is what it used to be nor can remain what it is.

Princeton revolutionized within the last ten years.

"Old Princeton"? Where is it? How far back will you go to find and recover it?

Class solidarity will necessarily disappear with numbers and with diversity of study.

Unity and solidarity as a whole gone long ago.

The chief change everywhere, extra-curriculum activities, absorbtion in things which have nothing to do with the main objects of the place.

Reorganization imperative

To recover main aim and restore proportion,

To secure unity and proper interrelationship of interests.

The QUAD. residences:

Their organization

Their freedom

Their integration.[1]

10 June, '09[2]

WWT MS (WP, DLC).

[1] No local newspaper printed a report of this address; however, for a comment on it, see WW to Mary A. H. Peck, June 19, 1909.

[2] Wilson's composition date.

A News Item

[June 12, 1909]

CAMPBELL HALL PRESENTED.

Quiet but appropriate ceremonies marked the presentation of Campbell Hall, the gift of the Class of '77, which occurred to-day at twelve o'clock.

In the presence of the assembled Class of '77 and a large number of visitors, Mr. M. Taylor Pyne '77, in behalf of his class, formally presented the dormitory to the University. President Woodrow Wilson in accepting the gift for the University spoke enthusiastically of the characteristic generosity of Princeton alumni and thanked the Class of '77 for this most acceptable gift to their Alma Mater.

At the conclusion of the ceremonies a huge flag bearing the numerals of the Class of '77 was raised from the tower and the class adjourned to a luncheon served in the dormitory.

Printed in the *Daily Princetonian*, June 12, 1909; one editorial heading omitted.

A Proposed Report by the Committee on the Curriculum

[c. June 12, 1909]

When the resolution of the Finance Committee[1] was received by this committee the President of the University undertook a careful inquiry into the amount and character of the work being done in the several Departments of instruction, with a view to ascertaining whether any decrease or redistribution of the teaching force could be effected which would result in financial saving or a wiser expenditure of money. The result of his inquiry is the earnest conviction on his part that, while one or two of the Departments of the University are undermanned, none is over-manned, and that any change made at present would be very detrimental to the best interests of the University. In that conclusion this Committee concurs.[2]

T MS (WWP, UA, NjP).

[1] See H. G. Duffield to M. W. Jacobus, Jan. 26, 1909, printed as an Enclosure with M. W. Jacobus to WW, Feb. 3, 1909.

[2] As it turned out, Wilson was persuaded not to present this report to the Curriculum Committee. For details, see H. B. Thompson to M. W. Jacobus, June 17, 1909. There is a WWsh draft of this document in WP, DLC, and a WWhw draft in WWP, UA, NjP.

A Sermon

BACCALAUREATE ADDRESS June 13th, 1909.

"We are unprofitable servants: we have done that which was our duty to do." Luke XVII, 10.

Gentlemen: You are now at last full-fledged Princeton men. The four years of your novitiate are over. You have received all that the undergraduate years of the University can give you and will henceforth look upon yourselves as formed upon the Princeton model, of which we are all wont to be proud, and of which men young and old bred in our school of life and learning speak with eager praise.

Princeton is a place, we say, of liberal training. We mean that it is not a vocational school. Students do not crowd here to make their way quickly to professions or to the business callings by which they are to support themselves and advance their material fortunes in the world, but in order to get, first, a general training of the mind and of its perceptions which will make their several occupations more significant to them when at last they have entered them, give the world a more various and comprehensible aspect to their eyes, and quicken their appreciation of its opportunities and its duties.

Not many can draw apart into such a place of vision and of general reckoning with the forces of the world. Most young men, most lads who have not yet grown to be men, must hurry to put their hands to the actual work by which they are to earn their bread and help support those who are too young or too feeble, too delicate or too witless, to support themselves. The world must have workers by the multitude, and they must hasten to their work. Most schools must fit those who resort to them for immediate labour, and many, very many, must labour without the help of schools. Only a few have the leisure or the opportunity or the irresistible instinct to take this slower way of preparation and inquiry and pore upon the map of life and thought a certain while before they traverse it. They seek and obtain a special privilege.

We are not to think of ourselves as in any way essentially distinguished or superior or aristocratic because we have had the privilege of going this special way of preparation and enlightenment. It would be absurd to plume ourselves upon what we have had. It was open and accessible to almost any one who happened to covet it and who had the energy and the persistency to take it. That some of us got it without effort and used it as a matter of course without giving any particular thought to its value or significance merely shows that we were a little duller than the rest and did not know what we were about. It is the use we shall make of what we got out of it that will bring us distinction or else prove us mere negligible items in the great inventory of life and opportunity. If there is any aristocracy of class to be got out of the interesting business, it lies ahead of us, not behind us, in what we shall do, not in what we have done.

The way is longer for us than for others, and beset by greater perils of disgrace and failure. The truth is that this college training we have had has made us in some special sense citizens of a spiritual world in which men are expected to do more than make a living; in which they are expected to enrich the day they live in with something done without thought of pay or material reward of any kind, without calculation of interest,—something given freely from their special store of knowledge and of instructed principle for the service of their neighbors and their communities and for the enlightenment of mankind.

It is a very serious matter to have such opportunities,—an exceedingly serious matter to have had them and neglected them,—perhaps as serious a matter to have had them and profited by them. If they have enlarged the field of our responsibilities, they have increased the field of our duty. We have more to think about, more to strive for, more to do, if we would not be put out of countenance, now that we are Princeton men, than we would have had if we had passed the college by on the other side, gone the usual road, and known no better. The Princeton model is a very gracious model if we live up to it; but, like every other standard, it serves only as a rebuke to us if we do not. Therefore we will. We cannot afford to do anything else. We will set our minds to think the obligation out, and, having determined what it is, will fulfil it to the utmost as strength may be vouchsafed us.

The day and the hour, the immemorial tradition of this service, force the rôle of preacher upon me, and it is not difficult to find a text for my theme. The suitable words are in the tenth verse of the seventeenth chapter of the Gospel of St. Luke. "We are unprofitable servants: we have done that which was our duty to do." Deeply interesting words they are. Like so many other sentences of the extraordinary volume from which they are taken, their meaning strikes beneath the surface of ordinary thought and is hidden from us upon a casual reading, but discloses itself readily enough when once we perceive that we are to look for it deeper than it is our wont to search. Not many servants, of whatever rank or station, do their duty: it is a profitable thing, as the world goes, to have those who will do so much as that; and no doubt the average man who does his duty thinks himself sufficiently serviceable. But there is, nevertheless, a mere judgment of the world itself here in these words of candid Scripture, and no recondite judgment of a spiritual seer. It is the judgment of all the world of affairs that the servant who does only the task set him and no more, volunteers nothing, not so much as an extra minute by the clock, renders the precise service for which he was hired, stops with it and plans nothing more, earning his wages but giving nothing he is not paid for, is in truth a very unprofitable servant, a tool merely, and an indifferent tool at that. He need look for no promotion. He barely earns his present wages.

"Duty" is a very handsome word,—is a very handsome thing,—but let every man look to it that he comprehend what it really means. It conveys an obligation from within, not merely from without. We have not done our duty, we have not even earned our wages, when we have done merely that which was commanded us: we have done our duty only when we have done that which we know completes the service, when we have put the best that was in us into the task, our hearts into the bargain.

You know what the usual standard of the employee is in our day. It is to give as little as he may for his wages. Labour is standardized by the trades unions, and this is the standard to which it is made to conform. No one is suffered to do more than the average workman can do: in some trades and handicrafts no one is suffered to do more than the least skilful of his fellows can do within the hours allotted to a day's labour, and no one may work out of hours at all or volunteer anything beyond the minimum. I need not point out how economically disastrous such a regulation of labour is. It is so unprofitable to the employer that in some trades it will presently not be worth his while to attempt anything at all. He had better stop altogether than operate at an inevitable and invariable loss. The labour of America is rapidly becoming unprofitable under its present regulation by those who have determined to reduce it to a minimum. Our economic supremacy may be lost because the country grows more and more full of unprofitable servants.

But we do not need to turn to the trades unions to illustrate our disregard for the true meaning of duty. You know how some men cheapen their college diplomas by getting them for as little work as possible, and you know that the diplomas they receive mean nothing. I hope that very few of you have that bitter realization today. There are no employers at college in the work of study, but a great many undergraduates assume the attitude of employees and give as little as possible for what they get. They cheat nobody but themselves. The service of study is meant for nobody but themselves. They impoverish their lives and impair their own efficiency by their neglect. They are very unprofitable servants to themselves: they have skimped their services fifty per cent. and make their future associates in business receivers of their bankruptcy, reorganizers of their energy. They will not deceive themselves later about their profit and loss account.

Today, therefore, we look our standards frankly in the face

and plan our programme of regeneration. Intimate domestic life lies ahead of us, exacting professional life, and the wide life of society, in which we may lose or establish an influence, in which we shall win places of honour or fall into obscurity or disrepute. If we are unprofitable servants in any one of these, by a too narrow view of our duty, we shall fall short of both fame and happiness. This, therefore, is our programme: In our domestic relations we will do more than our duty. We will not skimp or calculate or seek to reckon what is the least we are obliged to do, the most we may insist upon receiving. It will be our pleasure,—an increasing pleasure, we shall find it,—to see how much we can give, and to give it with largess of affection. The profit will be ease of heart and the intimate, trusting love of those we serve. Homes are falling to pieces nowadays because men and women, and even children, ask only how much is due them, and not what love and self-sacrifice call upon them to give. Calculations of personal right and of the duty of others eat marriage bonds away like acid and dissolve society.

In our professional and business relations we will measure what we can give by what we have received and will make our thoughts and all our strength, whether of natural gifts or of acquired knowledge, part of our enterprise, will be partners with our employers at heart long before we are partners at law. I know that there are very few partnerships nowadays. We serve corporations, are swallowed up in vast organizations, become the instruments of men we never see and have not access to. I can understand how that might well daunt and confuse an uneducated man, without a comprehending imagination. But we are university men, trained, unless we have cheated ourselves by neglect, to comprehend complex wholes. The very complexity of the thing we are to deal with should challenge us to render corporations the service they most need, the service of men who can understand their organization in all its parts and relations and shape it in operation to the economy, integrity, and success of the whole. Corporations will fall to pieces when they come to consist too entirely of employees rather than of intelligent partners. We will be profitable servants by volunteering an intelligent service not required of us in the bond.

In our social relations we will remember the loyalty and affection we owe our loved ones at home, and the watchful and thoughtful service we owe our partners in business and all who have honoured us with their confidence, but we will add to these things which manifestly bind us the service which no law can exact of us. We will be thoughtful citizens, not for the protection of our families or the benefit of our business, but for the benefit of our neighbors and of the country which nourishes and sustains us all. Here is our field of final and supreme test, in which it will inevitably appear whether we have been bred to the true spirit of our alma mater or not. She has meant us to be men of such kind: we will remember her in all that we do.

There is here a whole philosophy of life. The object, the standard, you set yourself works by a strange alchemy upon the whole spirit of your life. Set out to fulfil obligations, to do what you must and to exact of others what they owe you, and all your days alike will end in weariness of spirit. The road of life will be long and very dreary. There will be no zest in the movement of the day, no refreshment when the night comes and sleep lies heavy upon you. There is no pleasure to be had from the fulfilment of obligations, from yielding to compulsions, from doing what you know you ought to do. Nothing but what you volunteer has the essence of life, the springs of pleasure in it. These are the things you do because you want to do them, the things your spirit has chosen for its satisfaction. They are done with the free spirit of the adventurer. They are the inviting by-paths of life into which you go for discovery, to get off the dusty road of mere duty into cool meadows and shadowed glades where the scene is changed and the air seems full of the tonic of freedom. Your first volunteer service will be your first discovery of yourself, your first intimation of what your spirit is for. It will be your introduction alike into the world of pleasure and into the world of power.

I beg you to look very carefully and very curiously at the world you are about to enter before you enter it, and mark some of its characteristics. I mean the world of business and of the professions here in America. A great deal more light shines upon it now than shone upon it when you entered college. The air has been cleared for you that you might see. An almost unprecedented storm of accusation and inquiry has passed over it, and as the storm draws off it draws many vapours with it; the air grows very sharp and clear. Things stand out about us in very definite outline and evident proportion.

And this is what we see. We have just passed through an era in which men kept their legal obligations as well as usual and yet came near ruining the country, piled up wealth and forgot how to use it honourably, built up business and came near to debauching a nation. It is a very remarkable thing, and should be very interesting to the author of the text I am commenting upon. I need not remind you of the various abuses in the business world which recent legislation has been more or less unsuccessfully attempting to correct, of the vast combinations by which capitalists in this, that, and the other line of enterprise have sought to control the markets of the country, of the special favours the railways have granted to some of their shippers and the manifest injustice and ruin they have imposed on others, of the incalculable values, and lacks of value, given to securities in the stock market by methods of financial manipulation long in vogue unchecked, almost unheeded,—of the thousand and one ways in which what were thought to be the business interests of the country were pushed forward without regard to anything but the profit of those immediately concerned. That profit, stated in terms of wealth, was signally well served. What was intended was accomplished,—and with the results you know.

You have heard the whole story many times, and with many variations, true and false. What has not been sufficiently noticed and emphasized is, that most of those collossal processes of wealth which have now fallen under our condemnation were conducted by honest men who were keeping within the bounds of the law. There were rogues among them, of course, but no more than any age will show, and they were almost always rejected by their comrades when they were found to be rogues. The whole huge game, so far as its success was substantial and lasting, was an honest man's game; no crooks or blacklegs were wittingly admitted into it. Every man served his own particular interest with extraordinary intensity and devotion and with immense success, and could have told you with frank and steady eyes that he had done that which was his duty to do.

But what unprofitable servants they were,—unprofitable even to themselves and to the business enterprises they served: Many of those enterprises are for the time being discredited, their prosperity almost fatally checked by a universal distrust and suspicion, by hostile legislation, by arrested credit. Everything that for their sake should be steady has been thrown out of poise and balance. Their very success has been questionable, if you demand of success that it bring enjoyment and content with it. Success has a heart and you should look into it. It is often of lead, sometimes of gall, sometimes of dry pith, only sometimes a source of living joy.

No mere material object gained ever brought happiness. No man lives with his possessions. He lives with his thoughts, with his impulses, with his memories, his satisfactions, and his hope. I heard a distinguished man say very wisely, the other day, that we must divest ourselves of the idea that men have souls. They *are* souls. They have bodies, and their bodies have material needs which must be supplied. There are bodily pleasures which they may enjoy; but those pleasures will not satisfy them unless they convey to the soul intimations and confirmations of what it desires. They are the mere vehicles of satisfaction, and it is the man himself, the soul, that must be satisfied.

The men who brought disaster upon business by success brought it because they ran with blinders upon their eyes, saw only the immediate task under their hands, volunteered no look around, paid no call of thought or wish upon their fellow men, left statesmanship to politicians and public interests to the censors of public morals, attended wholly to their own business. The business of life is a bigger thing than they thought it. Only the far-seeing eyes are the eyes that descry the real fields of success, the ultimate paths of content and pleasure. The words I have quoted from St. Luke contain nothing less than the secret of what it is to live.

It ought to be an open secret to university men. Indeed, it is evident enough to any man who has looked frankly upon his own life and heeded its plain revelation. If we would have ease of heart, we must first do our duty; but no man glories in the performance of his duty. That is a matter of course. It were dishonour not to do it. What he really looks to to give colour, dignity, distinction, if it may be romance, to his life is what he adds to his duty for his own satisfaction, for the release of the power that is in him.

If you have been set a task, and address yourself to it alert, awake, attentive, you will not watch the clock or begrudge the use of your faculties. You will forget the hours, will find that you have taken hold of the thing as if you were pleasing yourself, not as if you were serving an employer. The thing is upon the instant your own; you are a partner in the business without intention. The thing interests you: you are stretching your faculties upon it: it has ceased to be a task.

If you are a youngster in a law office, and are sent to look up a certain series of cases and the principle involved takes hold upon you as you read, lures you back to the books out of hours, recalls lectures you paid little heed to in the law class and touches them with a new illumination, and sets you at last questioning the very decisions of the court itself, you know what has happened to you. You have begun to become a lawyer. You are thinking out a bit of the processes of society. Your mind has emancipated itself from the office and has become an instrument of the life about you. You are free: you have had your first taste of the excellence of mastery. The zest and the profit are in what it was not your duty to do.

If, after the fatigues of a labourious day, you go home and are struck by something about the attitude of the one you love most there which speaks of sadness or disturbed spirits, and you set yourself to ascertain the cause by some tender art of divination which love has taught you, you will forget that you were fatigued. You will find a new vivacity come into your blood: a weary day will be succeeded by a stimulating, it may be a delightful, evening of light-hearted exertion. When the day is over, if you think about yourself at all, you will wonder what brought the singular refreshment you feel. It will come again whenever you let your thoughts leap away from yourself and do a thing that it pleases you to do, a thing in which you give your heart spontaneous play.

If, on your way to the polls to vote, out of a sense of duty, something brings your mind to attention and suddenly opens your eyes to the significance of what you are about to do; if your thoughts begin to dwell seriously upon the candidates and upon the issues involved, and some image of the community about you, of the action of common purpose between you and your neighbors, forms itself in your mind's eye, you will be aware that the duty you are about to perform is a small and trifling thing if you stop with that,—that your real use consists in the fact that you are a thinking man. At that moment you become a citizen and fill your nostrils with an ampler air.

If a neighbour obliges you to render him a service which you had promised but neglected, and you let the service, though you were obliged to perform it, and the man himself, though he put compulsion upon you, take hold upon you and interest you, interest you so much that you add to the service kindness and a certain thoughtful care in its performance, a volunteered extension even;—if thine enemy oblige thee to go with him a mile and you go with him twain because your thought has been quickened as you walked and you wish his company further, you will have made a friend and gone a whole mile of pleasure.

It is always the same. Whatever you do, whatever comes from the natural fire kindled in you, whatever your spirit willingly undertakes and makes a satisfaction of, that is the thing which profits you. It at once contains and enriches your life. The more you are stimulated to such action the more clearly does it appear to you that you are a sovereign spirit, put into the world, not to wear harness, but to work eagerly without it. You will be a profitable servant indeed when once you have found yourself thus, but it will not be that which interests you. You will be satisfied, you will be loved, you will have life and have it abundantly.

The college man is ready to be the most open-eyed of all adventurers in this inviting field of self-discovery. He knows what the world contains. He knows what he should look for and where he should search to find it. The margins of profit are for him inexhaustible. His opportunities are the measure of his world and of its satisfactions. He may be the king of volunteers.

Gentlemen of the graduating class: It is with real affection and genuine solicitude for your happiness and success that I now address you, on this last day upon which we can take counsel together. I have spoken to you in very simple phrases to-day and have given you only homely and intimate counsel, because I feel very near to you,—as if in some subtle sense, of which I had not before been conscious on like occasions, we were members of one household.

We have said a great deal about the system of instruction which has brought you into close association with preceptors in your daily work throughout the four years of your life here, an association which has grown closer and closer as year was added to year and you were matured by study, but its chief effect, as we all know, has been to draw faculty and students together into a new knowledge of each other. I have felt the effect in the ease and naturalness with which you have approached me and with which I have felt it possible to approach you; and it has culminated at last in the feeling on my part, and I believe on yours, that President and students were, in some real and delightful sense, colleagues in a common life and undertaking.

I have felt very happy in the change; and the simple counsel I have sought to give you to-day has not been the counsel of an officer of the University addressed to his pupils and charges, but the counsel of a friend addressed to younger associates. I have gone further upon the journey of life than you have. I think that I can say that I know what comforts the heart and cheers the will and sweetens all experience. It is contained in this deep saying of our Master: "When ye shall have done all those things which are commanded you, say, We are unprofitable servants: we have done that which was our duty to do." I give it to you as something deeper than the lesson of a seat of learning,—as the lesson of life, which you may learn now at the outset, and be happy to know for the rest of your days. May God bless you and bring you all light and courage and peace.[1]

T and WWhw MS (WP, DLC).

[1] There is a WWT draft of this sermon and a WWsh draft of the charge to the graduating class in WP, DLC.

Woodrow Wilson *et al.* to Robert Randolph Henderson

Dear Bob: [Princeton, N. J.] June 13, 1909

We have all missed you in these delightful days that we have been having together. We have thought about you and talked about you, and rejoiced that you are getting better.

And we want to tell you so, and send you our best love and wishes. Yours always in '79 Woodrow Wilson
C. W. Mitchell
Hiram Woods
Charles A. Talcott
J Edwin Webster
William B Lee
Robert Bridges

HwLS (WC, NjP).

From Charles Monroe Sheldon[1]

My dear President Wilson: Topeka, Kansas, June 14, 1909.

I was very much interested in your recent address on the subject of the college "side shows" monopolising the main feature of college life. Before long I shall have a boy ready for college[2] and I have been wondering whether when the time comes there will be any college in America where the main thing was attended to by the students as a whole. I have been greatly wondering of late years why the authorities in our colleges could not have power enough to subordinate athletics and fraternaties [fraternities] and social functions to scholarship. I had an interesting talk a short time ago with President Eliot of Harvard, in which he expressed himself with great vigor against the game of football, but seemed perfectly powerless to change conditions, although he was President of the University. I am not asking the question to betray either my ignorance or any possible impertinence in seeming to meddle with things which are none of my concern, but I have wondered why the presidents of our great colleges did not have more really to say about athletics and social life so that they could actually shape the college according to their own ideals. Is it because the influence of the alumni is so great that the college authorities themselves have so little to say? When my boy is ready for a college education, I would like to send him to some institution where the President and the professors run the college, and not the students, or at least where the actual heads of departments have some power to say what shall be the main business of the students who attend. As it is now, it seems somewhat of a question when it comes to a choice of an institution where the ideal in the matter of scholarship and real study is actually lived up to.[3] I am glad you spoke as you did and I am confident it will have great weight and I am sure I would not like to be the President of a college today and have my ideas of athletics, fraternities and social life constantly ignored, and subordinated things given first place.

With greatest respect, I am

Very cordially yours, Charles M. Sheldon

TLS (WP, DLC).

1 Pastor of the Central Congregational Church of Topeka, Kansas. Sheldon was, and is, well known as the author of best selling religious novels based upon the ideals of the social gospel movement. His most famous book, *In His Steps: "What Would Jesus Do?"* (first published in Chicago in 1897) became one of the great best sellers of all time: it was translated into some twenty languages, was estimated in 1947 to have sold over 6,000,000 copies in the United States alone, and remains available from several publishers at the present day. See Willard Thorp, "The Religious Novel as Best Seller in America," in James Ward Smith and A. Leland Jamison (eds.), *Religious Perspectives in American Culture* (Princeton, N. J., 1961), pp. 195-96, 233-35.

2 Merriam Ward Sheldon.

3 Young Sheldon was at this time twelve years of age. He attended Amherst College from 1915 to 1917 but received his B.A. degree from Washburn College in Topeka in 1921.

From Job Elmer Hedges

My dear President Wilson: New York, June 15, 1909.

I returned last evening from attendance at the Princeton Commencement and the 25th Reunion of the Class of '84. The impression made upon me by the progress of the university during the past few years, is so marked, that I cannot refrain from felicitating you on the great works accomplished during your administration. The academic atmosphere of the place, is so far in advance of what it used to be, and is proceeding by such leaps and bounds, that I feel a sense of obligation which results in this letter. With renewed congratulations and high regard for yourself, believe me

Faithfully yours, Job E. Hedges

TLS (WP, DLC).

A News Report of An Address at the Alumni Luncheon

[June 16, 1909]

After the Commencement exercises in Alexander Hall on Tuesday, the alumni foregathered by classes on the front campus and marched to the Gymnasium for their annual luncheon. The beautiful decorations of the sophomore dance held the night before were still hanging, and under these the classes were seated at the long tables. The luncheon itself was exceptionally good and promptly served. Adrian H. Joline '70 presided. . . .

The invocation was by the Rev. John Carrington '65, after which Mr. Joline presented President Wilson amid great applause. The President began by expressing the pleasure the assembly had of greeting the distinguished guests of the occasion, saying that he wished particularly to express his own personal feeling of comradeship with President Lowell, a sentiment which was heartily cheered. He went on to say that he did not know of any man whose counsel is more helpful and suggestive than that of President Lowell, and believed that with his accession Princeton and Harvard would be drawn nearer and nearer together. While everyone realizes, he continued, that the educational development of America is now in a transitional stage, and that universities are facing grave problems, this was a time in which he felt he should report on the things in which all could take solid satisfaction. He recalled that since the beginning of his administration the chief development of Princeton had been along scientific lines,–lines on which modern life is based. All life, he said, is being steadily transformed by processes not so much of reflection as of knowledge. Princeton's proof of her connection with modern life is the very noteworthy advance she has made in her teaching staff and in her equipment for the teaching of science. Princeton has pledged herself never to lose her sense of identity with the literary spirit, but any institution which satisfies itself with the literary spirit merely, because [becomes] dilettant[e] and loses vital connection with the service of the age. In a properly coördinated body of studies the power of literary expression should permeate the whole institution and the most effective voice should be given to knowledge. The only way to teach a man to speak or write English is to give him ideas and then challenge him to release them in speech. Your engineer must be a literary man also. In this development of science, which is more characteristic of our university than anything else in recent years, Princeton is coming to an inevitable and proper expression of herself. She is steadily finding herself, finding her task, finding her characteristic place in the modern world, and there will presently come a time when no man shall doubt what Princeton was put into the modern world to accomplish. Continuing, the President emphasized the desirability of variety in universities, each doing its own work efficiently, which is "the enrichment of strength." In conclusion, he said: "It is always a great pleasure and a great privilege to stand in the presence of a body of men like this and endeavor to put into words what I know is their educational and intellectual confession of faith."

Printed in the *Princeton Alumni Weekly*, IX (June 16, 1909), 573-75.

From Edgar R. Laverty[1]

Dear Sir: New York City, June 16, 1909.

In the New York Times of June 14, which purports to give extracts of your baccalaureate address to the students of Princeton University, you are quoted as follows:

> "You know what the usual standard of the employe is in our day. It is to give as little as he may for his wages. Labor is standardized by the trade unions, and this is the standard to which it is made to conform. No one is suffered to do more than the average workman can do. In some trades and handicrafts no one is suffered to do more than the least skilful of his fellows can do within the hours alloted to a day's labor, and no one may work out of hours at all or volunteer anything beyond the minimum."

Now, your reported remarks strike me as being so extraordinary—so different from what I, as a member of organized labor, have found to be the facts—that I feel impelled to ask you if the foregoing paragraph is a correct report of what you said.

If you are correctly quoted, I should like to have you give me your authority for your statement that in labor unions "no one is suffered to do more than the average workman can do." Also give me the names of a few trades or handicrafts where "no one is suffered to do more than the least skilful of his fellows can do within the hours alloted to a day's labor, and no one may work out of hours at all or volunteer anything beyond the minimum."

As a matter of course, a president of a university of the reputed standing of Princeton would not make statements in his baccalaureate address unless he knows, or at least fully believes, that his statements are true. Therefore it ought not be a difficult matter for you to oblige me with the names of those labor unions whose laws, or even policies, bring about the results you specify.[2]

Awaiting your reply with lively interest, I am,

Yours very truly, Edgar R. Laverty.

TLS (WP, DLC).

[1] He was a typographer for the New York *Evening Telegram.*

[2] Wilson's reply is paraphrased and partially quoted in D. L. MacKay to WW, Oct. 13, 1910, Vol. 21.

Henry Burling Thompson to Melancthon Williams Jacobus

My Dear Jacobus: [Greenville P. O., Del.] June 17th, 1909.

I regret that you were unable to be present at the meeting of the Curriculum Committee and the Board meeting.

On Saturday morning, at the close of the dedication of "Campbell Hall," I said to President Wilson,–"I assume you will want to make the meeting of the Curriculum Committee to-day a short one. Is there anything to discuss beyond routine business, and the report on Preceptors, which matter, as I understand, was not concluded at our last meeting; and, with regard to this, I would make the following suggestion:–That the whole matter be referred to a Committee of yourself, Dean Fine and Jacobus; and take six or eight months to examine this question at your leisure." His answer to this was that he would object to Fine, as he felt that Fine acted very badly at the previous meeting. I said that I did not feel Fine should be punished for his action at any meeting, and that his position, as Dean of the Departments of Science, would be of great value on such a Committee, and it put the Committee in such form that the majority was entirely friendly to the views of the President. As time precluded any further discussion, just then, he suggested that I should come to his Library after the ball match. Feeling somewhat annoyed at his attitude towards Fine, before going to his house I met Cleve Dodge and McCormick, and asked their advice in the matter. They stated that they thought my proposition was an entirely reasonable one, but that as Fine's presence on the Committee might be a source of irritation to the President, permit a Committee to be appointed, allowing the President the privilege of naming it,–McCormick taking the view that, no matter what kind of Committee was appointed, its finding would be that present conditions needed reform. Accepting this view, I went to the President's house, and found that he was adverse to the appointment of any Committee, on the ground that the preceptorial system was his own child, and he was entirely capable of taking care of it without the interference of any Committee. He had prepared a resolution, which was virtually as follows:—That after examination of the preceptorial system, the President found the present system adequate, and in this view our Committee concurred.

He was extremely anxious, just at the present time,—for reasons that I cannot explain in this letter, but can give you personally,—that there should be no agitation on the preceptorial question. I told him that, while I was not satisfied to concur with the report, if it produced harmony at this time, I was willing to agree to it.

After leaving him, I met McCormick, Palmer and Jones. Palmer and Jones said emphatically that they would refuse to vote for any such resolution; and McCormick was considerably chagrined that the President refused to consider the appointment of any Committee.

For the sake of harmony, we agreed to suggest to the President that the matter should not be discussed in any form at this meeting, and the resolution was not offered, and there was no discussion,—the meeting being purely one of routine work.

Naturally, such a conclusion is very unsatisfactory to Jones and Palmer, and I am free to say that I share this feeling with them.

It is disagreeable to criticise the President's position, and, while I believe Wilson to be honest in his conclusions, I think he has reached conclusions based on an imperfect knowledge of conditions, which conditions he has not investigated with that thoroughness which the subject demands. I believe, that, in view of the smouldering fire of criticisms on this subject—whether they be just or unjust—it would have been wise on the President's part to have appointed a Committee. If the criticisms are unjust the action of that Committee proves them so; and if reform is necessary it is brought about by the action of an inside Committee, and need not go beyond that.

Unless some definite action be taken on this matter, I am afraid it will become a Board question rather than a Committee question.

I dislike to bother you just at this time, but I feel that it is only just to give you my views of the situation and to keep you posted as to the work of the Committee.

I will say for Fine, that, in the talks I have had with him, he has been reasonable and fair, and shows a disposition to work for harmony, but is convinced that reform is necessary.

Yours very sincerely, Henry B Thompson

TLS (Thompson Letterpress Books, NjP).

To Mary Allen Hulbert Peck

Dearest Friend, Princeton, 18 June, 1909

I was *so* glad to get your letters.[1] I have just passed through the busiest season of the year, when I hardly had time for so much as a thought of myself, but all through it, until your letters came, my thoughts were waiting for word of you and wondering what was happening or going to happen.

Our Commencement season ended, officially, on Tuesday last—and throughout it I had not only my official duties but also a reunion of my class to think of—but it is always term time for me so long as I am in Princeton and even yet I am being rushed from one thing to another, getting the year properly wound up. I am dead tired, but well, very well, and shall clutch the first hour I get in which my head will work to write you a real letter. This is just a line to say that I am alive and all right; that I am grateful to you for your letters and your delightful friendship; and that I am always

Your affectionate and devoted friend,

Woodrow Wilson

ALS (WP, DLC).

[1] They are missing.

To Louis Rinaldo Ehrich[1]

My dear Mr. Ehrich: Princeton, N. J. June 18th, 1909.

I have read this paper with a great deal of interest, but I cannot say that I feel that it is a timely thing that it should be issued. I think that a manifesto in favor of out and out free trade at the present time would only prejudice the advance of the revision policy by which we must some day undertake to approach a better economic condition.

I am very much obliged to you for having submitted the paper to me and need not tell you of my strong sympathy with the cause of tariff reform.

Cordially and sincerely yours, Woodrow Wilson

TLS (de Coppet Coll., NjP).

[1] Art dealer of New York. Ehrich dabbled in politics and wrote many articles and addresses on political and economic questions. The paper he sent to Wilson may have been a copy or a draft of *Free Trade Versus a Revenue Tariff; An Address* (n. p., 1911). He delivered this paper at the annual meeting of the American Free Trade League in Boston on May 20, 1911.

To William Dean Howells

My dear Mr. Howells: Princeton, N. J. June 18th, 1909.

I beg that you will pardon my apparent discourtesy in having left your interesting and important letter of May 13th[1] so long unanswered. I did so only because I was sincerely anxious to find it possible to act upon the very kind suggestion which it contained, namely that I prepare a paper for the meeting of the American Academy of Arts and Letters which is planned for December next at Washington. It was necessary, before I could decide that matter, that I should be near enough the next college year to see what its duties and tasks would be.

I am the more disappointed, therefore, to find that it would be highly imprudent for me to promise a paper for the meeting. I can now pretty plainly see what awaits me next autumn in connection with my university duties, and there are tasks lying ahead of me which put it quite out of the question that I should attempt a paper of any deliberate sort.

I need not tell you how highly I appreciate the suggestion. I should esteem it an honor to be permitted to present a paper at that meeting, and it is with the greatest regret as well as appreciation that I find myself unable to do so.

With much regard,

Sincerely yours, Woodrow Wilson

TLS (W. D. Howells Papers, MH).

1 This letter is missing in the Wilson Papers, and a carbon copy is not extant in the various Howells collections.

To Frank Arthur Vanderlip

My dear Mr. Vanderlip, Princeton, N. J. 18 June, 1909.

I have a young friend who has had to deny himself college and go into business. He is well bred, comes of an excellent family, and is, I think, very intelligent and manly. In spite of a very tender breeding, he also seems willing, and even anxious, to work, as he must, to support himself as soon as possible. His name is Allen Hulbert. He is now serving Dick Brothers of Broad Street at the bottom of their list, because he knew some member of the firm; but the speculative nature of their business makes a connection with them very undesirable. That is not the way in which a youngster ought to be introduced into business.

Will you think it very presuming of me if I ask that you will keep the lad in mind should there be any place on the lower rungs of your ladder where he might have a chance to begin?

I am very much interested in him and it would be delightful to think that he might have an entrance into business where you presided and gave tone to the whole.

He is not literally a lad. He is almost twenty-one.

With warmest regard,

Cordially and faithfully Yours, Woodrow Wilson

TLS (F. A. Vanderlip Papers, NNC).

From Charles Wellman Mitchell

Dear Tommy, Baltimore, June 18th, 1909

I want to thank Mrs Wilson and yourself for the many courtesies and kindnesses shown me during my recent delightful visit to your house. As I told Mrs Wilson, the happiest days of my life are those spent under your roof, because there I can combine the ideal friendship of youth with the pride and loyalty that the mature man feels for his comrade who, in the larger affairs of life, has made good. My social training has been sadly neglected. I am a poor "mixer." I almost hate to meet strangers. My entire capacity for social enjoyment seems to be concentrated into the few glorious days with you and the boys of '79.

Under the present social conditions at Princeton I believe it impossible to reproduce such a class as '79 has proven to be, but of this I am convinced, that in the near future, and under your leadership, many such bodies of men will be graduated. In the meantime, dear boy, be patient. Bide your time. Be assured that the great moral and intellectual forces of the country are bound, by the very nature of things, to stand by you when the problem is fully brought home to them; and that your way will win, because it is the only right way. Spare your strength. Do nothing that you are not compelled to do. Do not even answer this letter. Only remember that added to the Lowells & Garfields and hundreds of other great and good men who are with you in the fight, there is a little chap in Baltimore who yields to no man in his loyalty and devotion. With kindest regards to Mrs Wilson, Miss Axson and Misses Margaret, Nellie & Jessie, I remain

Always affectionately yours C. W. Mitchell

I enclose clippings[1] concerning Dr. S. C. Chew '56[2] which may interest you.

ALS (WP, DLC).

[1] They are missing.

[2] Samuel Claggett Chew, Princeton 1856; physician of Baltimore, Professor of Medicine at the University of Maryland Medical School, and President of the Board of Trustees of the Peabody Institute of Baltimore.

To Mary Allen Hulbert Peck

Dearest Friend, Princeton, 19 June, 1909.

At last there is a little lull in the rush of things and I can turn to you for a little chat. The moment I do so I realize what a dull chap I am and how little that is the least interesting or diverting I have to chat about. My days are full of business, my head goes round with the confused whirl of university politics; I read no books, no, nor anything else that might renew my mind or quicken my imagination; I disperse my powers upon a thousand things scattered and unrelated; how can I be a good correspondent or send you anything that will refresh you? If I had you at hand and could talk to you, I would probably be selfish enough to pour into your ear detail after detail of the politics and contests I am in the midst of, but to write out such stuff is a little *too* deliberate! Even I am above that! A dear old colleague of mine, who is to be married to-day at seventy-six,[1] took me aside yesterday and advised me not to worry: that I was doing everything that could be done and should trust in God for what I could not do. He is so evidently relying on Providence himself that I am sure he is a sincere adviser. It's very funny, by the way. The poor old gentleman has been desperately lonely the last two years since he lost his first wife,[2] desperately in need of some one to take care of him, and all the men in town heartily approve of his marrying again, the woman being of a suitable age, but all the women are horrified and sarcastic. Fortunately there was only one woman he had to consult! He is an impulsive Irishman and will act upon his impulses, God bless him, as serenely in his last year as he did in his first.

We had a very brilliant Commencement, everybody says, and I really enjoyed the reunion of my class. It was delightful to see again the fellows I so love and have so long loved and their affection for me warmed the cockles of my heart. I was a boy again, and a very happy boy, whenever I was with them. And I enjoyed, too, in a still deeper fashion the dinner the Seniors gave me on the Thursday preceding Commencement. I never had such a "send off," and it was not mere shouting and enthusiasm: there was a deep and sober note about it all which meant a great deal,—which may have meant a turning point in my administration. I spoke for an hour and twenty-five minutes, setting before them, as they had asked me to do, my whole thought about the University and what should be done for its betterment and advancement. Every man listened as if to a romance, and when I ended I received a perfect ovation. You may imagine how proud and happy I was. It was worth a great deal of the humiliation I have gone through to have the youngsters turn to me like that. When I get away and can detach myself from the details of the University it will no doubt govern my spirits like a great healing influence.

We shall get away, to Lyme, as I think I told you, on the tenth of July, the day Nellie and Jessie sail for Europe. Lyme is one of the most stately and old-fashioned of New England villages, and we shall be boarding, not with New Englanders, who get on my nerves, but with a jolly, irresponsible lot of artists, natives of Bohemia, who have about them the air of the broad free world. The little world of my winters will assume its proper proportions in my mind; I shall be a citizen of the world once more, and my spirits will brighten with every excursion my thoughts take. My body will take very few. Lyme is a delightful haven in which to sleep, sleep, sleep interminably, as I love to do, and can do, when I am worn out. I shall acknowledge no social obligations whatever, and shall obey the law of inertia as if it were the first canon of morals. When people ask me what my "programme for the summer" is I rejoice to reply that I have none.

It is not fancy, I hope, and the mere wish that it should be so, that enables me to find a note of calmness and of reviving spirits in your last letters. Your garden is having an effect upon your thoughts, as well as your true friends and the quiet homely work of the house and the liberty to think and do as you please that has at last come to you. I am ordering Price Collier's "England and the English" for you to-day, and Ferraro's "Characters and Events of Roman History."[3] I like to think of all you will find in both books for your mind to play upon. I only wish I might share the play with you and hear what you think as you read! The thing of all things that it reassures me most to think about is the delightful freshness and elasticity both of mind and body which is so marked a characteristic of you and so sure an earnest that you will come out triumphant over all the circumstances of your life!

Your devoted friend Woodrow Wilson

WWTLS (WP, DLC).

[1] George Macloskie, who had retired as Professor of Biology at Princeton in 1906, was marrying Lila Mansfield Smith Campbell.

[2] Mary Dunn Macloskie.

[3] Price Collier, *England and the English from an American Point of View* (New York, 1909), and Guglielmo Ferrero, *Characters and Events of Roman History, from Caesar to Nero*, trans. Frances Lance Ferrero (New York and London, 1909).

From Charles Francis Adams

My dear President Wilson: Boston June 19, 1909

I have to thank you not only for the degree conferred upon me last Tuesday, at Princeton, but also for a most agreeable experience in connection therewith.

I frankly acknowledge I went to Princeton, as I always have gone to occasions of that nature, with a sinking heart, wishing myself well out of what I cannot but regard in advance as a doubtful experience. I am glad to say the outcome has with me almost uniformly been of another character; it was especially so last Tuesday.

I cannot refrain, however, from expressing both my surprise and gratification, not only at what I found at Princeton,–the vigor and life, as well as the external surroundings, of the institution,–but also at the state, so to speak, with which the ceremonies were conducted.

When, some sixteen years ago, I received the same degree at the hands of my own University, I remember the form consisted simply of the President uttering my name; I standing up in a mass of spectators and looking at him; and, finally, he and I nodding at each other;–and the thing was over! The form and dignity with which the whole thing went off under your auspices, in accordance with the Princeton program, was, in way of contrast, most suggestive. I hope our friend Lowell will bear it in mind. There is such a thing as over-doing simplicity even; and, in the case of Harvard and the conferring of its Honorary Degrees, this consummation certainly is traditional.

I look back on the occasion of last Tuesday with quite unalloyed satisfaction.

Would you now kindly send me a list of names of your present Board of Trustees? I wish to bear direct, if slight, testimony to each of my appreciation of the honor conferred upon me.

Believe me, Most sincerely, etc, Charles F. Adams

TLS (WP, DLC).

To George Walbridge Perkins[1]

My dear Mr. Perkins: Princeton, N. J. June 21st, 1909.

My Baccalaureate Address has been published in full in our local paper, The Princeton Press.[2] It is not a convenient form in which to handle it, but unfortunately it is the only form I have, and I take pleasure in sending you a copy under another cover.

I thank you sincerely for your interest in it and for what you say of it in your kind letter of the 21st.[3]

With much regard,

Sincerely yours, Woodrow Wilson

TLS (G. W. Perkins Papers, NNC).

[1] Prominent financier, partner in the banking firm of J. P. Morgan & Co. of New York.

[2] It was printed in the *Princeton Press*, June 19, 1909.

[3] It is missing, both in the Wilson and Perkins Papers.

To Charles Francis Adams

My dear Mr. Adams: Princeton, N. J. June 21st, 1909.

I have read your letter of June 19th with a great deal of gratification and thank you most sincerely for your thoughtful kindness in writing it. It is very pleasing to me to think that you enjoyed your visit to Princeton and I can assure you that it gave us all great pleasure to see you here and to have the opportunity of honoring you in the name of the University.

I take pleasure in enclosing a list of the members of the Board of Trustees, as you request.

It would be a great pleasure to see you in Princeton whenever you are passing this way.

Cordially and sincerely yours, Woodrow Wilson

TLS (photostat in RSB Coll., DLC).

From Lawrence Crane Woods

My dear Dr. Wilson: [Pittsburgh, Pa.] June 22, 1909.

You will be amused over the article which has probably appeared more at length in Eastern papers, which I enclose.[1] Fortunately Princeton men know better than this, and I am mighty glad that you anticipated by years just such criticism and that today, no matter what a boy goes to Princeton for—whether it be social prestige, athletic games or anything else—he will either be speedily dropped out or develop to a large extent a trained mind.

Yours very sincerely, [Lawrence C. Woods]

CCL (WC, NjP).

[1] The clipping (from an unidentified newspaper) was a report of an address delivered by the Most Rev. Dr. James Augustine McFaul, Roman Catholic Bishop of Trenton, at the commencement of the College of St. Francis Xavier in New York. McFaul was quoted as stating, among other things:

"The parents who sent their children to the popular colleges like Harvard, Princeton and Yale, where rascality, immorality and a disrespect of womankind are fostered, would attempt to tear down the buildings did they know the grave mistake they were making.

"Such colleges as Yale and Princeton are great factors in the undermining of morality. They do not even study the Bible, which is so much spoken of and so seldom read by their advocates.

"Catholic families are sacrificing faith and morality because they wish to get into society. Actuated by that one dominant and fanatic idea, they send their sons to the large colleges, where they do not even learn the Ten Commandments. . . .

"The professors in these institutions attempt to prove in a learned manner that there is really no difference between right and wrong, and say that no man may show where right ends and wrong begins. Sophistry is at the bottom of their teaching."

The news report indicates that most of the Bishop's speech was centered on the argument that Catholics should adhere to Catholic schools and publications.

From Edward Dickinson Duffield[1]

My Dear President Wilson: Newark, N. J. June 22, 1909.

Ever since the dinner given by the Princeton Alumni Association of Newark last May, I have felt a desire to write, expressing to you my appreciation of the magnificent speech you made on that occasion. I have waited to see, however, whether the impression which you made on me at that time would prove to be lasting. After these weeks I still feel that your speech on that occasion was one of the finest that it has ever been my good fortune to listen to.

So far as it referred to the internal affairs of the University, it presented the whole question to me in an entirely different light from that in which I had viewed it before. I had, what I think others had, a prejudice against the proposed changes, based partly on the ground of a lack of definite understanding as to just what it was proposed to do, but more because of a feeling that what was proposed was to practically obliterate The Princeton that we had known. I am not at all sure now, however, that the preservation of the "Princeton spirit" is not largely dependent upon the adoption in the near future of some such plan as that which you have been advocating, and while the "Quad System," as I understand it, seems to me to have serious objections, nevertheless, I want you to know that your speech made at least one convert to the principle that the undergraduate should be deprived of the right of what you so aptly termed "a selective democracy."

I only wish that a stenographic report of your speech had been made so that it could have had a broader audience than the few who heard you on that evening. The eloquent presentation which you made of the dangers to Princeton, as well as the national dangers resulting from present conditions, was surely entitled to more permanency than a mere after-dinner address. I assume that it would now be impossible for you to reproduce what you then said, but it is a real misfortune that this cannot be done. I want you to know, however, what a really fine thing your speech was and what a deep and lasting impression it has made here.

With kindest regards and best wishes, believe me,

Very truly yours, Edward D Duffield

TLS (WP, DLC).

[1] Princeton 1892, General Solicitor of the Prudential Insurance Company of America of Newark.

To Lawrence Crane Woods

My dear Mr. Woods: Princeton, N. J. June 23rd, 1909.

Bishop McFaul's assault upon the Eastern Universities did appear very much at length in the papers in this part of the country, and I think, from some things that I have heard said, that nobody is more chagrined about it than the Roman Catholics. Such violence, of course, answers and refutes itself. I was called up yesterday over the telephone by Father Leahy, the priest of the Princeton church,[1] who expressed his great chagrin and indignation, and I am sure that, if he dared, he would speak out very vigorously in contradiction of his superior. The real gravamen of Bishop McFaul's charge is that Roman Catholics are beginning to send their sons to Princeton and Harvard and Yale.

He has the reputation in Trenton, I find, of extreme violence and is in the habit of insulting even his own people.

I have very much appreciated your recent letters and shall go on my vacation with very much renewed spirits.

Always cordially and faithfully yours,

Woodrow Wilson

TLS (WC, NjP).

[1] The Rev. Walter T. Leahy, pastor of St. Paul's Roman Catholic Church.

Two Letters to Edward Wright Sheldon

My dear Ed.: Princeton, N. J. June 24th, 1909.

I wish you would be kind enough to read the enclosed letter[1] and give me your judgment in the matter, inasmuch as it is necessary for me to act at once, if we are to secure Professor Littmann.

Probably you know that we have an exceedingly valuable and very unusual collection of Oriental manuscripts here, purchased and placed at the disposal of the University by Mr. Garrett. Littmann was a member of the first Princeton Expedition which went to Syria,[2] an expedition which Mr. Garrett accompanied, and Littmann came to Princeton when that expedition returned. He was here for several years and proved himself an extraordinarily vital and interesting teacher, in addition to winning for himself the greatest distinction in his Oriental field. He is a man of really extraordinary genius, and it is now possible to get him back from Strasburg, to whose university he was called to succeed the most distinguished of the older German scholars in his field. He would feel free now, Howard Butler tells me, to come, but a few weeks later he might not, because they are making efforts to keep him in Germany and unless he gets an offer from America, to which he is very anxious to return, he would feel obliged to accept the new post they would offer him. He feels that America is the best place for him to work, and Princeton the best place in America, and we would be immensely benefitted by his augmented reputation as well as by his direct services.

My own judgment is that it would be safe to act upon the conditions set forth in Mr. Garrett's letter, but I do not feel at liberty to do so before laying the letter before you and getting your own opinion. I might add that Mr. Garrett's personal interest in this matter is very direct and very deep. His intellectual interest in the University lies in this field, and I think he would be greatly disappointed and chagrined if we could not take advantage of this opportunity, which will probably not occur again, to secure one of the first scholars in the world. With your approval I will write to Littmann at once.

Always affectionately yours, Woodrow Wilson

1 It was R. Garrett to WW, June 18, 1909, which is missing.

2 About which, see WW to the Board of Trustees of Princeton University, June 13, 1904, n. 1, Vol. 15.

My dear Ed.: Princeton, N. J. June 24th, 1909.

I enclose this additional sheet to ask if you will not see Pyne and suggest to him that he ascertain when it will be possible to get hold of Cyrus McCormick and Mr. Garrett for a meeting of the Graduate School Committee, to press forward the matter of a site for the Graduate College and the meeting of the other conditions set by Mr. Proctor. I think that it is very important that we should press this business forward before we all disperse for the summer, though I shall be in reach of New York most of the vacation.

Always affectionately yours, Woodrow Wilson

TLS (photostats in RSB Coll., DLC).

To Robert Garrett

My dear Mr. Garrett: Princeton, N. J. June 24th, 1909.

An unexpected rush of business after Commencement has prevented my replying sooner to your letter of June 18th.

So far as my own judgment is concerned, I shall have no hesitation in writing at once to Littmann to invite him to join the faculty again. I think that the suggestions you make in your letter are perfectly safe.

I have not felt, however, on second thought, that I was at liberty in so important a matter to go forward without at least the approval of the Chairman of the Finance Committee of the Board. I have therefore written to Mr. Sheldon, the new Chairman, asking his advice and, at the same time that I ask it, expressing my own strong judgment in favor of the course you proposed. So soon as I can hear from Mr. Sheldon I will write to Littmann, unless, as I do not expect, Mr. Sheldon's judgment should be adverse. In that case I will write to you further in regard to the matter at once.

I want to say how much I admire your interest and generosity in this matter and how earnestly I desire to cooperate in it.

Always cordially and faithfully yours,

Woodrow Wilson

TLS (Selected Corr. of R. Garrett, NjP).

From Edward Wright Sheldon

My dear Woodrow: [New York] June 25, 1909.

I have your two letters of yesterday. With respect to the Graduate School Committee meeting, I have written Pyne to ask whether the meeting could be held before we all scatter for the Summer. I saw in the paper last week that Cyrus McCormick sailed for Europe, and do not know how long it will be before Jacobus will be able to attend. I suppose Garrett and Shea will be available at almost any time.

I return Garrett's letter to you of June 18th. Without having any knowledge of Professor Littmann, I should upon your statement of the case regard it as a decided advantage to the University to secure him. But until provision is made for his salary, I do not quite see how we can incur that additional annual charge. It would be hard to let such an opportunity go, but in the present condition of our finances[1] I think the Finance Committee would be strongly opposed to incurring any fresh obligations. . . . Is there any way in which we can, before you write the Professor, secure a guaranty of so much of the $80,000. as Garrett does not provide? I do not myself see how it can be managed in so short a time. By way of alternative do you think Garrett would be willing in lieu of contributing to the endowment fund to guaranty or to secure guaranties of the $3,000. salary for ten years or until the earlier establishment of $80,000. endowment. It could be understood that the annual contribution should abate proportionately if a part of the $80,000. were obtained. On that basis I should feel justified in approving of Littmann's engagement.

I wish most heartily that I might accede completely to your suggestion. This being a watch dog of the treasury is indeed a canine existence.

Yours sincerely, Edward W. Sheldon.

TLS (WWP, UA, NjP).

1 The problem of a deficit had become somewhat acute since 1907, mainly on account of escalating instructional costs. The deficit was $46,144 for 1907-1908 and $56,085 for 1908-1909. It was made up at the end of the fiscal year by trustees and friends of the university, principally Pyne and Dodge.

From Francis Dundon

Dear Sir: New York, June 25th, 1909.

The New York Times, in its issue of the 14th inst., reporting your baccalaureate address, headed it in part thus: "Woodrow Wilson Hits Labor Unions. Says They Give Least Possible for Wages," and in the report you are quoted as saying that in labor unions, the capacity of the most efficient is regulated by that of the least competent—that no one is allowed to do more than the latter.

The statement is so prepostrously at variance with the actuality that, ordinarily, one might laugh at it; when, however, it is made, on such an occasion, by the head of a great university and is then carried by a great newspaper to its thousands of readers, there is very little humor to be found in it. I wrote to the New York Times pointing out its inapplicability in the cases of the following unions: the printers, the bricklayers, the painters, and the carpenters; but my letter was not published, and no refutation of so very grave, and very unjust a charge was permitted to appear in the columns of that newspaper.

As a member of a labor union, I, therefore, take the liberty to suggest that, in dealing with the question of labor unions, hereafter, you acquaint yourself with the conditions of employment in the above mentioned four unions. You will then understand that in all unions having the 8 hour day, instead of there being such a maximum as you described there is a prescribed minimum; and the man who would fail to come up to that standard would get short shrift.

Yours very truly,

Francis Dundon (Typographical Union)

TLS (WP, DLC).

To Mary Allen Hulbert Peck

Dearest Friend, Princeton, 26 June, 1909.

The story of my days just now is like "the short and simple annals of the poor": it is hard to find anything more than the routine of one day following that of another. There is still routine. So long as I stay here university business will dog me at every turn, and every morning will have to see ten or a dozen letters sent off, about all sorts of uninteresting things. We do not get off till the tenth of July. Nellie and Jessie sail that mor[n]ing for Europe, and that afternoon the rest of us go up to Lyme to settle down for the summer. Next Tuesday Ellen and I go up to Cambridge for the Harvard Commencement. Tuesday and Wednesday nights we are to spend with the Lowells; Thursday I am to deliver the Phi Beta Kappa "Oration";[1] Thursday night we are to spend with old Georgia friends at Milton;[2] Friday we come home again. All through the piping heat of this week I have been hard at work on the "oration," and now that it is finished[3] it sadly shows the effect of the heat. It's a pretty limp affair.

It seems a long, long time since I had a note from you. I keep wondering whether no news is good news or bad. Certainly it is bad in this sense that my mind fills with anxious thought about my friend. Princeton is adorable in the summer. All its beautiful spaces fall quiet: one is suddenly freed from the sense of the world pressing in on all sides and there is everywhere a delightful suggestion of peace and leisure. But by the same token one's dreams are set free. Nothing at hand commands or dominates them and they run where they please. I never long for my friends as I do in these quiet days when the whole scene seems set for peaceful comradeships; when the days run so slowly and lend themselves so perfectly to the choices of the heart as regards what one shall do and think and say. Surely the time and the place were meant for walks and chats and long loafs in the twilight, and strolls in the garden when the moon is up and the fragrance of the flowers seems enhanced in the lighter air. It is all this that gives me a special heart-ache that I cannot see whom I will, cannot have my dearest friends at call, cannot fill the inviting leisure with the pleasures for which it was made. My thoughts, consequently, play constantly about the ones I most miss. It is mingled pain and pleasure. I know of no more delightful thing than to dwell upon the things that give one special delight in those he loves but cannot see, and to recall all the occasions when they displayed them with special grace or piquancy; but there follows inevitably the pang that those days cannot be brought back again or repeated. Admiration is a very pure pleasure: if one could keep the selfish longing from following and displacing it, how pleasant it would be! Apparently both the admiration and the longing are what friendship lives upon in absence.

I hope that someone who has an automobile or a carriage is taking you often to ride these sultry days. One of the things I oftenest think about in connection with you in this beautiful place and at this lovely season is your love of flowers and of everything that is beautiful in nature. I have seen the love of nature in many people, but I never saw it bring so pretty an excitement of the mind in anyone as in you. It is as if it renewed in you some childhood of emotions, when everything is eager and gay and meant for pleasure; and yet there goes with it a poetic thoughtfulness, a play of fancy I never saw even in the most adorable child. It doubles the enjoyment of whoever is fortunate enough to be with you.

And so these quiet days go. I always feel younger in the summer than in any other season, because I then more nearly than at any other time return to the habit of my childhood, when I lived, not in the world actually about me, but in the world of my own thoughts. I find myself unwilling to let any book even or any piece of business invade it or tug me back. For the world of my thoughts is absolutely my own. No man governs me, and no man's opinion; and everything is as I wish it, as it was when I was a dreaming boy. It is delicious, and I believe actually does renew my youth. There is a tinge of sadness in it all, of course, brought out of the real world; but it is a sweet sadness generally, for I am at least with my friends there and no one can separate us.

Am I talking nonsense? Possibly the hot weather has affected my head. But I am a good deal of a salamander. I was born and bred in the South, and would choose the summer out of all other seasons. I am well and hope with all my heart that you are. All join me in love.

Your devoted friend, Woodrow Wilson

WWTLS (WP, DLC).

[1] It is printed at July 1, 1909.

[2] Arthur W. Tedcastle and Agnes Vaughn Tedcastle.

[3] He meant that he had just completed a shorthand draft.

From Adolphus Ragan[1]

Dear Sir, New York, June 26, 1909.

It appears to me to be the duty of Democrats generally, not only to encourage you to accept, but, if necessary, to urge you to quietly seek the Democratic nomination for Governor of New Jersey at the next State Convention.

If nominated there is small doubt of your election, and the nation at large is rather impatiently awaiting the coming of a Jefferson, a Jackson or a Tilden to whom they can feel safe in intrusting the duty of welding together the scattered fragments of our "once glorious union."

A Southern man wrote our immortal Declaration, in defence of which another Southern man carved out this nation with his sword. A Southern man wrote the Constitution, and it was another Southern man whose judicial decisions breathed life into that great Instrument.

It seems that, in view of recent occurrences, our fathers' house has been made a den of thieves; and now we need a Southern man, a real Democrat, to scourge them from the temple. Are we to have him? As I see it, the answer rests very largely with you.

Most Cordially Yours, Adolphus Ragan

ALS (WP, DLC).

[1] An accountant and member of the New York Southern Society.

To Edna Henry Lee Turpin[1]

My dear Miss Turpin: Princeton, N. J. June 28th, 1909.

Your manuscript has come, but amidst the many engagements attending the closing of the college session, I have not even had time to undo the package, and I am now obliged to start for Cambridge to meet a Harvard engagement. But I will take pleasure at the first available hour of leisure in beginning the examination of your manuscript and hope I shall not be too long delayed in it. I know how anxious you will be to get it back and to proceed with your business with the publishers.

I very much appreciate your kind letter.[2] It is a season when I am longing for a rest, but I am sure that I will get pleasure out of reading your chapters.

Cordially and sincerely yours, Woodrow Wilson

TLS (ViHi).

1 A Virginia writer who was at this time engaged in the preparation of *A Short History of the American People* (New York, 1911).

2 It is missing.

Melancthon Williams Jacobus to Henry Burling Thompson

My dear Thompson: Hartford, Conn., June 28th, 1909

When I received from Mr. Imbrie the rescript of the minutes of the Curriculum Committee meeting, I allowed myself for the time being to believe that the impossible had happened, namely that the question of the distribution of the Preceptors among the several Departments, involving an investigation of the whole Preceptorial System, had by common consent been laid upon the table and the Committee was back at its normal and legitimate duties.

Your letter of the 17th instant, however, disallusioned me and placed me in possession of the facts, which, however unpleasant, I am very glad indeed to have.

I have read your letter over carefully more than once, and I am perfectly frank to say that my conclusions are, briefly, as follows:

Whatever may be the reason which the President has for desiring to avoid an investigation of the System, I am quite sure that an investigation will be forced, if not by the Committee then by the Board. I would consider an investigation under these conditions to be, however necessary, an exceedingly unfortunate thing, in that it would be the last straw in breaking the sympathetic relations between the President and the Corporation of the University. It might precipitate the change in the University's presidency which I outlined to you as being at one time seriously imminent, and which I still consider as the most unfortunate thing that could possibly happen to the University at present.

There seems to me, therefore, to be but one single thing to do, and that is to accomplish the thing which I think, if rightly carried through, will either avoid the necessity of an investigation altogether or make the investigation perfectly harmonious an affair. That one thing is to bring Fine and Wilson together in a series of perfectly frank and honest conferences which will get at the points of view held by these two responsible officers of the institution and enable them so to understand each other that the proposition made to the Commitee shall be a proposition which will come from them both and will carry the Committee through its work, whatever that work may be, with a feeling of confidence in the outcome of the situation as it relates itself to the best interests of the University.

It does not seem to me to be a possible thing for any move to be taken as things now are between Wilson and Fine, without a maximum of disturbance and disaster to the University.

Wilson was here, as you may perhaps know, for our Seventy-fifth Anniversary of the Seminary, and delivered to the graduating class one of the most magnificent addresses I have ever listened to from a layman. It carried the large audience by storm and put Princeton University in a position of respect and admiration with thoughtful New Englanders such as it has not been accustomed to have up to this time.

While at my house, I had the opportunity of a few moments' talk with Wilson. It was not the opportunity I should be glad to have, because the time was limited and what we said was only on the surface; but Wilson gave expression to nothing at that time which was not perfectly in accord with what you and I believe to be the fundamental principles governing the Preceptorial System,–principles, I must say, with which I thoroughly agree.

In addition to this, we must remember that president-elect Lowell's eulogy of the Preceptorial System at the alumni banquet at Princeton,[1] which has been widely quoted throughout New England, is likely still more to establish Wilson in his convictions that the System has done for Princeton what nothing else has done for it in the way of giving it leadership in American education.

These things we must reckon with in what we are going to ask Wilson to do, and it seems to me that, apart entirely from the fact that Fine is a subordinate officer to him, we must not expect Wilson to yield the point that he has now taken unless Fine voluntarily comes to him and in such a perfectly patient and reasonable way seeks to accomplish an agreement between his own point of view and that of Wilson as shall make it possible for Wilson to yield whatever may be unreasonable in his position.

Now then, it seems to me that you and I have got to bend our energies to bringing such conferences about. I expect to be home practically all the summer. I have no doubt that you will be up in the Adirondacks very soon, if you have not already left for that delightful resort. Wilson is likely already to have gone from Princeton, and Fine will be away from there as soon as the entrance examinations are an accomplished fact. It is not, therefore, likely that we can get them together now, although it seems to me if any such coming together is possible the sooner it takes place the better; and if you are in possession of any facts as to Wilson's and Fine's plans for the summer that would make this conference practicable now, I would like you to write me at once and we will see what can be done. They must certainly take place if it can be accomplished, before the fall meeting of the Committee and the Board, and nothing could happen of more real benefit to the University than to have these two men come to a settled agreement on this question.

In brief, if Wilson remains possessed of the idea that Fine is out of sympathy with him in the administration of the University, and if Fine becomes established in his conviction that Wilson is arbitrary in his presidential control of that administration, there is nothing but hopeless irritation and final catastrophe ahead of us, and the result of this must necessarily be the sacrifice of Wilson. If that happens, I shall blame no one but Fine. He must clearly understand that he has no right to the idea that because he is Dean he can arbitrarily force his views upon the Committee of the Curriculum without every effort on his part to bring the President of the institution to his way of thinking.

I am perfectly willing, on the other hand, to recognize a certain failure on Wilson's part to handle situations. The very fact that there is a fault on both sides makes it imperative that these men shall come together personally and see the situation as it really is. If this can be accomplished, any investigation that the Committee may undertake or recommend will result in nothing but good. If this cannot be done, it will result in nothing but disaster.

I have just returned from the Berkshires and am writing to you in the hope that, along these lines, we can in some way serve the University which is so dear to us both.

Asking the favor of a prompt reply, and expressing the hope that you may be able in some way to suggest a better method of procedure if this be not satisfactory to you, I am

Yours very sincerely, M W Jacobus

TLS (H. B. Thompson Papers, NjP).

[1] The report of Lowell's speech in the *Princeton Alumni Weekly*, IX (June 16, 1909), 575, was brief. His only remark about the preceptorial system which was quoted was: "Your preceptorial system is universally lauded everywhere I go; it is unquestionably an advance."

Henry Burling Thompson to Melancthon Williams Jacobus

My Dear Jacobus: [Greenville P. O., Del.] June 30th, 1909.

I have yours of the 28th instant, and the shortest way to answer it is to say that I agree absolutely with everything you say. You sum up the whole situation, when you say—"The very fact that there is fault on both sides makes it imperative that these men shall come together personally and see the situation as it really is. If this can be accomplished, any investigation that the Committee may undertake or recommend will result in nothing but good. If this cannot be done, it will result in nothing but disaster." I have felt this from the beginning of the whole trouble, and all of my actions have been governed on these lines. I feel, however, very confident that this can be accomplished. I do not believe that we can get the two men together this summer, and I question whether it is advisable. Time is a great factor in wearing off edges. I think you will have to be the medium to get at Wilson; and, as I have already been talking to Fine on the lines of your letter, I can be of some benefit in that quarter. In any event, the question must not become a Committee matter until a harmonious meeting between these two men can be brought about. On this point I am entirely clear.

There was a better atmosphere at Commencement. The Senior Dinner to Wilson, in my opinion, has done a tremendous amount of good; in fact, Wilson feels he has established his old time relations with the undergraduate body.

Again, I think it is dawning on the majority of our Trustees what Wilson stands for, and how much he is doing for the University. There are some malcontents, to be sure, and always will be.

I expect to be in Princeton about the 8th or 9th of July, and, in all probability, shall see Fine. In that event, it goes without saying that we will drift on to the question at issue.

I go to the Adirondacks on the 28th of next month, and will return about the 3d or 4th of September. My address there is "Beede's Post Office, Essex County, New York." If you want to get at me by letter, and anything develops that needs attention, please let me hear from you.

Yours very sincerely, Henry B Thompson

P.S.,–I do not suppose there is much chance of your coming up with Stephen Palmer, but, in any event, it would be well for you, some time before College opens, to arrange an interview with him. He thinks highly of your opinion and judgment, and I am sure you can do much with him.

TLS (Thompson Letterpress Books, NjP).

An Oration Before the Harvard University Chapter of Phi Beta Kappa

[[July 1, 1909]]

THE SPIRIT OF LEARNING

We have fallen of late into a deep discontent with the college, with the life and the work of the undergraduates in our universities. It is an honorable discontent, bred in us by devotion, not by captiousness or hostility or by an unreasonable impatience to set the world right. We are not critics, but anxious and thoughtful friends. We are neither cynics or pessimists, but honest lovers of a good thing, of whose slightest deterioration we are jealous. We would fain keep one of the finest instrumentalities of our national life from falling short of its best, and believe that by a little care and candor we can do so.

The American college has played a unique part in American life. So long as its aims were definite and its processes authoritative it formed men who brought to their tasks an incomparable morale, a capacity that seemed more than individual, a power touched with large ideals. The college has been the seat of ideals. The liberal training which it sought to impart took no thought of any particular profession or business, but was meant to reflect in its few and simple disciplines the image of life and thought. Men were bred by it to no skill or craft or calling: the discipline to which they were subjected had a more general object. It was meant to prepare them for the whole of life rather than for some particular part of it. The ideals which lay at its heart were the general ideals of conduct, of right living, and right thinking, which made them aware of a world moralized by principle, steadied and cleared of many an evil thing by true and catholic reflection and just feeling, a world, not of interests, but of ideas.

Such impressions, such challenges to a man's spirit, such intimations of privilege and duty are not to be found in the work and obligations of professional and technical schools. They cannot be. Every calling has its ethics, indeed, its standards of right conduct and wrong, its outlook upon action and upon the varied relationships of society. Its work is high and honorable, grounded, it may be, in the exact knowledge which moralizes the processes of thought, and in a skill which makes the whole man serviceable. But it is notorious how deep and how narrow the absorptions of the professional school are and how much they are necessarily concentrated upon the methods and interests of a particular occupation. The work to be done in them is as exact, as definite, as exclusive as that of the office and the shop. Their atmosphere is the atmosphere of business, and should be. It does not beget generous comradeships or any ardor of altruistic feeling such as the college begets. It does not contain that general air of the world of science and of letters in which the mind seeks no special interest, but feels every intimate impulse of the spirit set free to think and observe and listen,–listen to all the voices of the mind. The professional school differs from the college as middle age differs from youth. It gets the spirit of the college only by imitation or reminiscence or contagion. This is to say nothing to its discredit. Its nature and objects are different from those of the college,–as legitimate, as useful, as necessary; but different. The college is the place of orientation; the professional school is the place of concentration. The object of the college is to liberalize and moralize; the object of the professional school is to train the powers to a special task. And this is true of all vocational study.

I am, of course, using the words liberalize and moralize in their broadest significance, and I am very well aware that I am speaking in the terms of an ideal, a conception, rather than in the terms of realized fact. I have spoken, too, of what the college did "so long as its aims were definite and its processes authoritative," as if I were thinking of it wholly in the past tense and wished to intimate that it was once a very effective and ideal thing but had now ceased to exist; so that one would suppose that I thought the college lost out of our life and the present a time when such influences were all to seek. But that is only because I have not been able to say everything at once. Give me leave, and I will slowly write in the phrases which will correct these impressions and bring a true picture to light.

The college has lost its definiteness of aim, and has now for so long a time affected to be too modest to assert its authority over its pupils in any matter of prescribed study that it can no longer claim to be the nurturing mother it once was; but the college is neither dead nor moribund, and it has made up for its relaxed discipline and confused plans of study by many notable gains, which, if they have not improved its scholarship, have improved the health and the practical morals of the young gentlemen who resort to it, have enhanced their vigor and quickened their whole natures. A freer choice of studies has imparted to it a stir, an air of freedom and individual initiative, a wealth and variety of instruction which the old college altogether lacked. The development of athletic sports and the immoderate addiction of undergraduates to stimulating activities of all sorts, academic and unacademic, which improve their physical habits, fill their lives with interesting objects, sometimes important, and challenge their powers of organization and practical management, have unquestionably raised the tone of morals and of conduct in our colleges and have given them an interesting, perhaps valuable, connection with modern society and the broader popular interests of the day. No one need regret the breaking-up of the dead levels of the old college, the introduction and exaltation of modern studies, or the general quickening of life which has made of our youngsters more manly fellows, if less docile pupils. There had come to be something rather narrow and dull and morbid, no doubt, about the old college before its day was over. If we gain our advances by excessive reactions and changes which change too much, we at least gain them, and should be careful not to lose the advantage of them.

Nevertheless, the evident fact is, that we have now for a long generation devoted ourselves to promoting changes which have resulted in all but complete disorganization, and it is our plain and immediate duty to form our plans for reorganization. We must reëxamine the college, reconceive it, reorganize it. It is the root of our intellectual life as a nation. It is not only the instrumentality through which we must effect all the broad preliminary work which underlies sound scholarship; it is also our chief instrumentality of catholic enlightenment, our chief means for giving widespread stimulation to the whole intellectual life of the country and supplying ourselves with men who shall both comprehend their age and duty and know how to serve them supremely well. Without the American college our young men would be too exclusively shut in to the pursuit of individual interests, would lose the vital contacts and emulations which awaken them to those larger achievements and sacrifices which are the highest objects of education in a country of free citizens, where the welfare of the commonwealth springs out of the character and the informed purposes of the private citizen. The college will be found to lie somewhere very near the heart of American social training and intellectual and moral enlightenment.

The process is familiar to every one by which the distintegration was brought about which destroyed the old college with its fixed disciplines and ordered life and gave us our present problem of reorganization and recovery. It centered in the break-up of the old curriculum and the introduction of the principle that the student was to select his own studies from a great variety of courses, as great a variety as the resources of the college and the supply of teachers available made possible. But the change could not in the nature of things stop with the plan of study. It held at its heart a tremendous implication: the implication of full manhood on the part of the pupil, and all the untrammeled choices of manhood. The pupil who was mature and well informed enough to study what he chose was also by necessary implication mature enough to be left free to *do* what he pleased, to choose his own associations and ways of life outside the curriculum without restraint or suggestion; and the varied, absorbing college life of our day sprang up as the natural offspring of the free election of studies.

There went along with the relaxation of rule as to what undergraduates should study, therefore, an almost absolute divorce between the studies and the life of the college, its business and its actual daily occupations. The teacher ceased to look upon himself as related in any responsible way to the life of his pupils, to what they should be doing and thinking of between one class exercise and another, and conceived his whole duty to have been performed when he had given his lecture and afforded those who were appointed to come the opportunity to hear and heed it if they chose. The teachers of this new régime, moreover, were most of them trained for their teaching work in German universities, or in American universities in which the methods, the points of view, the spirit, and the object of the German universities were, consciously or unconsciously, reproduced. They think of their pupils, therefore, as men already disciplined by some general training such as the German gymnasium gives, and seeking in the university special acquaintance with particular studies, as an introduction to special fields of information and inquiry. They have never thought of the university as a community of teachers and pupils: they think of it, rather, as a body of teachers and investigators to whom those may resort who seriously desire specialized kinds of knowledge. They are specialists imported into an American system which has lost its old point of view and found no new one suitable to the needs and circumstances of America. They do not think of living with their pupils and affording them the contacts of culture; they are only accessible to them at stated periods and for a definite and limited service; and their teaching is an interruption to their favorite work of research.

Meanwhile, the constituency of the college has wholly changed. It is not only the bookish classes who now send their sons to college, but also the men of business and of affairs, who expect their sons to follow in their own footsteps and do work with which books have little connection. In the old days of which I have spoken most young men who went to college expected to enter one or other of the learned professions, expected to have to do with books and some of the more serious kinds of learning all their lives. Books were their proper introduction to the work that lay before them; learning was their natural discipline and preparation. But nowadays the men who are looking forward to the learned professions are in a minority at the college. Most undergraduates come out of an atmosphere of business and wish a breeding which is consonant with it. They do not wish learning. They wish only a certain freshening of their faculties for the miscellaneous contacts of life, a general acquaintance with what men are doing and saying in their own generation, a certain facility in handling themselves and in getting on with their fellows. They are much more interested in the incidental associations of college life than in the main intellectual occupations of the place. They want to be made men of, not scholars; and the life led at college is as serviceable for that as any of the tasks set in the class-room. If they want what the formal teaching offers them at all, it is for some definite and practical purpose connected with the calling they expect to follow, the business they expect to engage in. Such pupils are specially unsuitable for such teachers.

Here, then, is our situation. Here is the little world of teachers and pupils, athletic associations, musical and literary clubs, social organizations and societies for amusement, class-room and playground, of which we must make analysis, out of which we must get a new synthesis, a definite aim, and new processes of authoritative direction, losing nothing that has been gained, recovering what has been lost. All the fresh elements we have gained are valuable, many of the new points of view are those from which we must look upon the whole task and function of the college if we would see it truly; but we have fallen upon an almost hopeless confusion and an utter dispersion of energy. We must pull the whole inorganic thing together under a new conception of what the college must be and do.

The chief and characteristic mistake which the teachers and governors of our colleges have made in these latter days has been that they have devoted themselves and their plans too exclusively to the business, the very commonplace business, of instruction, to well-conceived lectures and approved class-room method, and have not enough regarded the life of the mind. The mind does not live by instruction. It is no prolix gut to be stuffed. The real intellectual life of a body of undergraduates, if there be any, manifests itself, not in the class-room, but in what they do and talk of and set before themselves as their favorite objects between classes and lectures. You will see the true life of a college in the evenings, at the dinner-table or beside the fire in the groups that gather and the men that go off eagerly to their work, where youths get together and let themselves go upon their favorite themes,—in the effect their studies have upon them when no compulsion of any kind is on them and they are not thinking to be called to a reckoning of what they know.

The effects of learning are its real tests, the real tests alike of its validity and of its efficacy. The mind can be driven, but that is not life. Life is voluntary or unconscious. It is breathed in out of a sustaining atmosphere. It is shaped by environment. It is habitual, continuous, productive. It does not consist in tasks performed, but in powers gained and enhanced. It cannot be communicated in class-rooms if its aim and end is the class-room. Instruction is not its source, but only its incidental means and medium.

Here is the key to the whole matter: the object of the college, as we have known and used and loved it in America, is not scholarship (except for the few, and for them only by way of introduction and first orientation), but the intellectual and spiritual life. Its life and discipline are meant to be a process of preparation, not a process of information. By the intellectual and spiritual life I mean the life which enables the mind to comprehend and make proper use of the modern world and all its opportunities. The object of a liberal training is not learning, but discipline and the enlightenment of the mind. The educated man is to be discovered by his point of view, by the temper of his mind, by his attitude towards life and his fair way of thinking. He can see, he can discriminate, he can combine ideas and perceive whither they lead; he has insight and comprehension. His mind is a practised instrument of appreciation. He is more apt to contribute light than heat to a discussion, and will oftener than another show the power of uniting the elements of a difficult subject in a whole view; he has the knowledge of the world which no one can have who knows only his own generation or only his own task.

What we should seek to impart in our colleges, therefore, is not so much learning itself as the spirit of learning. You can impart that to young men; and you can impart it to them in the three or four years at your disposal. It consists in the power to distinguish good reasoning from bad, in the power to digest and interpret evidence, in a habit of catholic observation and a preference for the non-partisan point of view, in an addiction to clear and logical processes of thought and yet an instinctive desire to interpret rather than to stick in the letter of the reasoning, in a taste for knowledge and a deep respect for the integrity of the human mind. It is citizenship of the world of knowledge, but not ownership of it. Scholars are the owners of its varied plots, in severalty.

If we recognize and accept these ideas, this conception of the function and the possibilities of the college, there is hope of a general understanding and accommodation. At present there is a fundamental misunderstanding. The teachers in our colleges are men of learning and conceive it their duty to impart learning; but their pupils do not desire it; and the parents of their pupils do not desire it for them. They desire something else which the teacher has little thought of giving, generally thinks it no part of his function to give. Many of the parents of our modern undergraduates will frankly tell you that what they want for their sons is not so much what they will get in the class-room as something else, which they are at a loss to define, which they will get from the associations of college life: and many more would say the same thing if they were equally ingenuous. I know what they mean, and I am free to say that I sympathize with them. They understand that all that their boys get in the class-room is instruction in certain definite bodies of knowledge; that all that they are expected to bring away from their lectures and recitations is items of learning. They have consorted with college men, if they are not college bred themselves, and know how very soon items of knowledge slip away from them, no matter how faithful and diligent they may have been in accumulating them when they were students. They observe that that part of the college acquisition is very soon lost. College graduates will tell you without shame or regret, within ten years of their graduation, that they remember practically nothing of what they learned in the class-room; and yet in the very same breath they will tell you that they would not have lost what they did get in college for anything in the world; and men who did not have the chance to go to college will everywhere be found to envy them, perceiving that college-bred men have something which they have not. What have they got, if learning is to be left out of the reckoning? They have got manliness, certainly, *esprit de corps*, the training of generous comradeships, a notable development of their social faculties and of their powers of appreciation; and they have lived under the influence of mental tasks of greater or less difficulty, have got from the class-room itself, from a quiet teacher here and there, some intimation, some touch of the spirit of learning. If they have not, they have got only what could no doubt be got from association with generous, self-respecting young men anywhere. Attendance on the exercises of the college was only a means of keeping them together for four years, to work out their comradeships and their mutual infections.

I said just now that I sympathized with men who said that what they wanted for their sons in college was not what they got in the class-room so much as what they got from the life and associations of the place; but I agree with them only if what is to be got in the class-room is nothing more than items of knowledge likely to be quickly lost hold of. I agree with them; but I see clearly what they are blindly feeling after. They should desire chiefly what their sons are to get out of the life and associations of the place; but that life and those associations should be freighted with things they do not now contain. The processes of life, the contagions of association, are the only things that have ever got any real or permanent hold on men's minds. These are the conducting media for every effect we seek to work on the human spirit. The undergraduate should have scholars for teachers. They should hold his attention steadily upon great tested bodies of knowledge and should insist that he make himself acquainted with them, if only for the nonce. But they will give him nothing he is likely to carry with him through life if they stop with formal instruction, however thorough or exacting they may make it. Their permanent effects will be wrought upon his spirit. Their teaching will follow him through life only if they reveal to him the meaning, the significance, the essential validity of what they are about, the motives which prompt it, the processes which verify it. They will rule him, not by what they know and inform him of, but by the spirit of the things they expound. And that spirit they cannot convey in any formal manner. They can convey it only atmospherically, by making their ideals tell in some way upon the whole spirit of the place.

How shall their pupils carry their spirit away with them, or the spirit of the things they teach, if beyond the door of the class-room the atmosphere will not contain it? College is a place of initiation. Its effects are atmospheric. They are wrought by impression, by association, by emulation. The voices which do not penetrate beyond the doors of the class-room are lost, are ineffectual, are void of consequence and power. No thought will obtain or live there for the transmission of which the prevailing atmosphere is a non-conducting medium. If young gentlemen get from their years at college only manliness, *esprit de corps*, a release of their social gifts, a training in give and take, a catholic taste in men, and the standards of true sportsmen, they have gained much, but they have not gained what a college should give them. It should give them insight into the things of the mind and of the spirit, a sense of having lived and formed their friendships amidst the gardens of the mind where grows the tree of the knowledge of good and evil, a consciousness of having taken on them the vows of true enlightenment and of having undergone the discipline, never to be shaken off, of those who seek wisdom in candor, with faithful labor and travail of spirit.

These things they cannot get from the class-room unless the spirit of the class-room is the spirit of the place as well and of its life; and that will never be until the teacher comes out of the class-room and makes himself a part of that life. Contact, companionship, familiar intercourse is the law of life for the mind. The comradeships of undergraduates will never breed the spirit of learning. The circle must be widened. It must include the older men, the teachers, the men for whom life has grown more serious and to whom it has revealed more of its meanings. So long as instruction and life do not merge in our colleges, so long as what the undergraduates do and what they are taught occupy two separate, air-tight compartments in their consciousness, so long will the college be ineffectual.

Looked at from the point of view at which I stand in all that I have been saying, some of the proposals made in our day for the improvement of the college seem very strangely conceived. It has been proposed, for example, to shorten the period of general study in college to (say) two years, and let the student who has gone the distance our present sophomores have gone enter at once upon his professional studies or receive his certificate of graduation. I take it for granted that those who have formulated this proposal never really knew a sophomore in the flesh. They say, simply, that the studies of our present sophomores are as advanced as the studies of seniors were in the great days of our grandfathers, and that most of our present sophomores are as old as our grandfathers were when they graduated from the pristine college we so often boast of; and I dare say that is all true enough. But what they do not know is, that our sophomore is at the age of twenty no more mature than the sophomore of that previous generation was at the age of seventeen or eighteen. The sap of manhood is rising in him but it has not yet reached his head. It is not what a man is studying that makes him a sophomore or a senior: it is the stage the college process has reached in him. A college, the American college, is not a body of studies: it is a process of development. It takes, if our observation can be trusted, at least four years for the completion of that process, and all four of those years must be college years. They cannot be school years: they cannot be combined with school years. The school process is an entirely different one. The college is a process of slow evolution from the schoolboy and the schoolboy's mental attitude into the man and his entirely altered view of the world. It can be accomplished only in the college environment. The environment is of the essence of the whole effect.

If you wish to create a college, therefore, and are wise, you will seek to create a life. We have allowed ourselves to grow very anxious and to feel very helpless about college athletics. They play too large a part in the life of the undergraduate, we say; and no doubt they do. There are many other things which play too large a part in that life, to the exclusion of intellectual interests and the dissipation of much excellent energy: amusements of all kinds, social preoccupations of the most absorbing sort, a multitude of activities which have nothing whatever to do with the discipline and enlightenment of the mind. But that is because they are left a free field. Life, at college, is one thing, the work of the college another, entirely separate and distinct. The life is the field that is left free for athletics not only but also for every other amusement and diversion. Studies are no part of that life, and there is no competition. Study is the work which interrupts the life, introduces an embarrassing and inconsistent element into it. The Faculty has no part in the life; it organizes the interruption, the interference.

This is not to say that there are not a great many undergraduates seriously interested in study, or that it is impossible or even difficult to make the majority of them, the large majority, pass the tests of the examinations. It is only saying that the studies do not spring out of the life of the place and are hindered by it, must resist its influences if they would flourish. I have no jealousy of athletics: it has put wholesome spirit into both the physical and the mental life of our undergraduates. There are fewer morbid boys in the new college which we know than there were in the old college which our fathers knew; and fewer prigs, too, no doubt. Athletics are indispensable to the normal life of young men, and are in themselves wholesome and delightful, besides. In another atmosphere, the atmosphere of learning, they could be easily subordinated and assimilated. The reason they cannot be now is that there is nothing to assimilate them, nothing by which they can be digested. They make their own atmosphere unmolested. There is no direct competition.

The same thing may be said, for it is true, of all the other amusements and all the social activities of the little college world. Their name is legion: they are very interesting; most of them are in themselves quite innocent and legitimate; many of them are thoroughly worth while. They now engross the attention and absorb the energies of most of the finest, most spirited, most gifted youngsters in the undergraduate body, men fit to be scholars and masters in many fields, and for whom these small things are too trivial a preparation. They would not do so if other things which would be certain to grip these very men were in competition with them, were known and spoken of and pervasive in the life of the college outside the class-room; but they are not. The field is clear for all these little activities, as it is clear for athletics. Athletics has no serious competitor except these amusements and petty engrossments; they have no serious competitor except athletics. The scholar is not in the game. He keeps modestly to his class-room and his study and must be looked up and asked questions if you would know what he is thinking about. His influence can be set going only by the deliberate effort of the undergraduate himself who looks him up and stirs him. He deplores athletics and all the other absorbing and non-academic pursuits which he sees drawing the attention of his pupils off from study and serious preparation for life, but he will not enter into competition with them. He has never dreamed of such a thing; and, to tell the truth, the life of the place is organized in such a way as to make it hardly possible for him to do so. He is therefore withdrawn and ineffectual.

It is the duty of university authorities to make of the college a society, of which the teacher will be as much, and as naturally, a member as the undergraduate. When that is done other things will fall into their natural places, their natural relations. Young men are capable of great enthusiasms for older men whom they have learned to know in some human, unartificial way, whose quality they have tasted in unconstrained conversation, the energy and beauty of whose characters and aims they have learned to appreciate by personal contact; and such enthusiasms are often among the strongest and most lasting influences of their lives. You will not gain the affection of your pupil by anything you do for him, impersonally, in the class-room. You may gain his admiration and vague appreciation, but he will tie to you only for what you have shown him personally or given him in intimate and friendly service.

Certain I am that it is impossible to rid our colleges of these things that compete with study and drive out the spirit of learning by the simple device of legislation, in which, as Americans, we have so childish a confidence; or, at least, that, if we did succeed in driving them out, did set our house in order and sweep and garnish it, other equally distracting occupants would crowd in to take their places. For the house would be empty. There must be life as well as study. The question is, not of what are we to empty it, but with what must we fill it? We must fill it with the things of the mind and of the spirit; and that we can do by introducing into it men for whom these things are supremely interesting, the main objects of life and endeavor, teachers who will not seem pedagogues but friends, and who can by the gentle infection of friendliness make thought a general contagion. Do that; create the atmosphere and the contacts of a society made up of men young and old, mature and adolescent, serious and gay, and you will create an emulation, a saturation, a vital union of parts in a common life, in which all questions of subordination and proportion will solve themselves. So soon as the things which now dissipate and distract and dissolve our college life *feel* the things which should coördinate and regulate and inspire it in direct contact with them, *feel* their ardor and their competition, they will fall into their proper places, will become pleasures and cease to be occupations, will delight our undergraduate days, but not monopolize them. They are exaggerated now because they are separated and do not exchange impulses with those greater things of whose presence they are sometimes hardly conscious.

No doubt there are many ways in which this vital association may be effected, but all wise and successful ways will have this in common, that they will abate nothing of the freedom and self-government which have so quickened and purified our colleges in these recent days of change, will have no touch of school surveillance in them. You cannot force companionships upon undergraduates, if you treat them like men. You can only create the conditions, set up the organization, which will make them natural. The scholar should not need a statute behind him. The spirit of learning should not covet the support of the spirit and organization of the nursery. It will prevail of its own grace and power if you will but give it a chance, a conducting medium, an air in which it can move and breathe freely without effort or self-consciousness. If it cannot, I, for one, am unwilling to lend it artificial assistance. It must take its chances in the competition and win on its merits, under the ordinary rules of the game of life, where the most interesting man attracts attention, the strongest personality rules, the best organized force predominates, the most admirable thing wins allegiance. We are not seeking to force a marriage between knowledge and pleasure; we are simply trying to throw them a great deal together in the confidence that they will fall in love with one another. We are seeking to expose the undergraduate when he is most susceptible to the best and most stimulating influences of the university in the hope and belief that no sensible fellow fit for a career can resist the infection.

My plea, then, is this: that we now deliberately set ourselves to make a home for the spirit of learning: that we reorganize our colleges on the lines of this simple conception, that a college is not only a body of studies but a mode of association; that its courses are only its formal side, its contacts and contagions its realities. It must become a community of scholars and pupils,—a free community but a very real one, in which democracy may work its reasonable triumphs of accommodation, its vital processes of union. I am not suggesting that young men be dragooned into becoming scholars or tempted to become pedants, or have any artificial compulsion whatever put upon them, but only that they be introduced into the high society of university ideals, be exposed to the hazards of stimulating friendships, be introduced into the easy comradeships of the republic of letters. By this means the class-room itself might some day come to seem a part of life.[1]

Printed in the *Harvard Graduates' Magazine*, XVIII (Sept. 1909), 1-14.

[1] There are WWhw and WWT outlines, a WWsh draft, and a WWT draft of this address in WP, DLC.

To Mary Allen Hulbert Peck

Dearest Friend, 3 July, 1909. Princeton

We got back from Cambridge yesterday afternoon,—and I found no letter from you awaiting me. I am very much disturbed. I feel sure that you would not have let so long a time go by without writing unless there had been some serious reason for your doing so,–illness or some ill fortune of which you did not wish to tell me! It is now a good deal more than two weeks since I had a line from you. Please write, if you can, when you get this, and tell me how things go with you.

I do not know whether I can give you a very coherent account of our visit to Boston and Cambridge or not; my spirits are so much dashed that I cannot think with much interest of it.

We stayed with the Lowells, as I think I told you, we were to, and they were as lovely to us as old friends, very natural and sweet and cordial. They introduced us, besides, to many most interesting people, their relatives and others, and we have brought away a very delightful impression of their whole circle. The whole atmosphere of Harvard seems to us changed by the change of presidents. Mr. Lowell is of an absolutely different type from Mr. Eliot, cordial, natural, friendly, open to all ideas, and very democratic indeed. He has brought Harvard back already into connection with the rest of the academic world. The two days I spent there, therefore, seemed spent among friends, not among strangers.

On Thursday I delivered my Phi Beta Kappa "oration," "The Spirit of Learning," and put into it the whole of my academic creed. To my great astonishment, it was received with enthusiasm (Think of enthusiasm at Cambridge!) and I was made to feel that my audience sympathized with the whole conception I sought to lay before them,–a conception which, if carried out at Harvard, would undo half the work Mr. Eliot has done. Mr. Eliot was in the audience, and showed very plainly that he was disturbed both by what I said and by the reception given it there where he had been king. When the address is printed I will send you a copy of it, of course, and hope that you will find it tolerable reading. If you happen to get hold of a copy of the Boston *Transcript* for July first you will, I believe, find the whole of it printed there. I was stupid enough to come away without buying any copies.

Thursday night we spent out at Milton with some old Georgia friends of Ellen's, and very dear, interesting people they are. Do you remember my telling you once of a lady who once visited us here in Princeton, of Mrs. Hibben's asking whether she was attractive or not, of my replying "Y-e-s,–morally attractive!", and Mrs. Hibben's exclaiming "What a thing to say of a woman!"? Well, this was the lady, this friend at Milton. She is still "morally attractive" and more,–for she seems to me to improve, and her husband is wholly delightful,–just as human, as full of fun, as bub[b]ling with wit as any man I ever knew, and a thoroughly kind and efficient man, besides. He is one of the best companions and one of the truest friends this country contains. We were off early Friday morning, took the ten o'clock train out of Boston, and were at home by half past five in the afternoon, but on the whole that evening with the Tedcastles on a serene hill-top in quiet Milton, with country hills all about us and southern friends to carry us back to happy days long ago stands out in my memory more vividly than the two crowded days in Boston and Cambridge and constitutes the best part of the story. It is very delightful to be in the stir of interesting things and to be cheered and made much of on an "occasion," but the thing that really makes your heart warm is what you are grateful for and keep for your refreshment in the memory.

And so all roads of thought lead back to you. I wonder what my dear friend in Pittsfield is doing. I should so like to have some definite image of what is filling her days, of how she is faring now that she has settled to her quiet life of house-keeping and gardening and reading,—whether she has time to read the books I send her and whether they have the relish she expected; what fortune she is having with her little group of tested friends,—how often she sees them and what they do for her; how Mrs. Allen is; how she stands the heat; in brief, all that the days bring her,—for I am interested in it all. I pray that she will be good and not let me go longer carrying these uncomfortable interrogation points about in my head. They are an uncomfortable shape for carrying in so sensitive a part of one's anatomy!

I shall have to be man of all work for about a week now, till the children get off. Our servants are going one by one, have gone, indeed, one by one, to get summer places (we are staying much later than usual) and their substitutes are very unsatisfactory. They work like other temporary arrangements. The household moves slowly and is hard to steer, like a ship under jury masts. I must leave the quarter deck, therefore, and work like a common sailor. And I am glad to do it. It is a pleasant variety for the nonce. The president business and the orator business grow precious monotonous by the time they have run from September to June. Then I have the refuge of a little reading and a little writing and a little of the other rudiments I have no chance to brush up on during term time. There is an article or two I have promised the publishers (or, rather, the editors), and they will prevent my feeling like a hired man. I vote for the summer vacation over all other seasons!

I am very well. This has, on the whole, been my hardest winter, and yet I have come out of it in really fine shape. Perhaps another season will bring happier things. It is my earnest prayer it may bring you at last real release and peace and settled fortunes. All unite with me in all affectionate messages.

Your devoted friend, Woodrow Wilson

WWTLS (WP, DLC).

To Adolphus Ragan

My dear Sir: Princeton, N. J. July 3rd, 1909.

Absence from home has prevented my acknowledging sooner your very cordial and gratifying letter of June 26th.

I need not tell you that I warmly appreciate it. I feel very keenly the necessity for an effective party of opposition and believe with all my heart that the welfare of the country calls for an immediate change in the personnel of those who are conducting its affairs in responsible political positions.

It is particularly gratifying to me to think that you should think I might myself be of service in this matter. I have thought a good deal about the various suggestions of this kind that have come to me and have been very much in doubt as to what my duty was. I am placed, as you will see, in a very embarrassing position, because it is manifestly undesirable that the head of a University should seek a prominent part in party contests. No serious proposal,–I mean emanating from authoritative party sources,–has ever come to me that I should allow myself to be a candidate for office, except when the minority in the New Jersey Legislature at one time thought of giving me their complimentary vote for United States Senator. If such an invitation should come, I quite agree with you that it would be my duty to give very careful consideration to the question where I could be of the most service, but I feel that my official connection with Princeton precludes me from active candidacy for any political preferment.

With much regard and sincere appreciation,

Very truly yours, Woodrow Wilson

TCL (RSB Coll., DLC).

To Arthur W. Tedcastle

My dear Mr. Tedcastle: Princeton, N. J. July 5th, 1909.

I was stupid enough to leave in one of the small bureau drawers in the room which Ellen and I occupied the other night my copies of the address I delivered at Harvard on Thursday. Could you, without too much trouble, send the clearest copy (it is on somewhat smaller paper than the other) to Professor William R. Thayer, Magnolia, Mass.? I have promised it to him for publication in the Harvard Graduates Magazine. And will you not send the other copy or copies (I have forgotten whether there are one or two) to me here? I am really ashamed that my absent-mindedness should give you this trouble.

Ellen and I enjoyed immensely our little visit to you. It was the only natural part of our trip. Functions and mixing with strangers and making speeches still seem to me artificial, and it was an interval of delightful peace and enjoyment which followed at Milton.

We got home very promptly, every train being on time, and Ellen is now plunged in the business of getting the girls ready for their European trip. She unites with me in most affectionate regards to you both.

Always faithfully and sincerely yours,

Woodrow Wilson

TLS (WP, DLC).

To Edward Wright Sheldon

My dear Ed.: Princeton, N. J. July 5th, 1909.

I received a letter from Momo this morning along with the one from you.[1]

In the circumstances, no doubt it is best not to have a meeting of the Committee on the Graduate School just now. I did not know that Dr. Jacobus had gone to Europe.[2] If Mr. Proctor understands the delay and its causes, I think that that should justify us in postponing the further consideration of our difficult business until the autumn.

It was a genuine pleasure to see you the other day. I do not know when I have more enjoyed a talk. I wish that we both might have leisure for more of the same kind.

Always affectionately yours, Woodrow Wilson

TLS (photostat in RSB Coll., DLC).

[1] Both letters are missing.

[2] McCormick, not Jacobus, was in Europe.

A Letter to the Editor

Princeton, N. J.

To the Editor of The Republican: *July 6, 1909.*

I have read with great appreciation your careful and thoughtful editorial on my recent Phi Beta Kappa address at Harvard, and wish to thank you for the candor and fairness with which it is written.[1] At the same time, I find myself a good deal taken aback by your interpretation of the address in one point. I think that it would produce a very grim smile on the faces of recent Princeton graduates to read an editorial advising me to insist upon hard work by the students of our universities. That insistence I took for granted in my address as a matter of course. Nothing but hard and consistent work can possibly underlie any wholesome or successful college discipline. The point of my address was that there must be something besides compulsion,–that the compulsions of the daily task must be transmuted into something more natural, more spontaneous, more allied with pleasure and the natural instincts of undergraduate nature. You will find in the address itself, I think, an intimation to that effect, where I speak of it being perfectly possible to oblige undergraduates to perform their tasks, but go on to say, what I have just now repeated, that that in itself is not sufficient and does not yield the real life of the mind. My motto would be work, of course, but work translated into the terms of pleasurable life, if possible. I think that it is entirely possible so to translate it.

Woodrow Wilson.

Printed in the Springfield, Mass., *Republican*, July 8, 1909.

[1] A lengthy news report of Wilson's address appeared in the Springfield *Republican* on July 2, 1909. On July 3, the *Republican* printed a long editorial on the address. Much of the editorial was a summary of the contents of Wilson's speech. Toward the end, however, the editorial writer presented both Wilson's solution to the present problem of higher education and his own criticism of that solution:

"From this point onward, we may take the short cut to President Wilson's conclusion. The real life of college students having been separated from the intellectual life of the class-room, he would unite them into one stream again. But how? By forcing the students back into the class-room? No. President Wilson's plan is to have teachers who will reach out to the student and by 'contact, companionship, familiar intercourse,' permeate the student with general culture and the spirit of learning rather than learning itself. . . ."

The editorial writer went on to say that there was a basic weakness in Wilson's scheme: "Nowhere does he preach the gospel of work. Students, in his ideal college, are not to be made or expected to drudge. What they get of 'liberal culture' and 'the spirit of learning' is to be obtained from the ideal teachers 'by the gentle infection of friendliness.' The undergraduate is tenderly to be 'exposed,' like a photographic plate, to the stimulating influences of the higher life. Knowledge and pleasure are to 'fall in love with each other.' . . . College life is to be one grand, sweet song for the students, and the professors are to forever hypnotize their pupils into the Elysian fields of culture.

"Without posing as modern educators, let us not shrink from saying that the scheme of college education that either eliminates or minimizes hard, rigorous work as the basis of achievement in whatever field of activity is sure to be exposed, sooner or later, as a glittering fraud. Nor can one believe that the colleges will ever attain 'the higher synthesis' until they revive the old-fashioned idea that it is work that makes men as well as cities or empires. . . ."

An Article

[*July 6, 1909*]

MY IDEAL OF THE TRUE UNIVERSITY

The word "university" means, in our modern usage, so many different things that almost every time one employs it it seems necessary to define it. Nowhere has it so many meanings as in America, where institutions of all kinds display it in the titles they bestow upon themselves. School, college and university are readily enough distinguishable, in fact, by those who take the pains to look into the scope and methods of their teaching; but they are quite indistinguishable, oftentimes, in name. They are as likely as not all to bear the same title.

But practise is always the best definer; and practise is slowly working out for us in America a sufficiently definite idea of what a university is. It is not the same idea that has been worked out in England or Germany or France. American universities will probably, when worked out to the logical fulfilment of their natural development, show a type distinct from all others. They will be distinctive of what America has thought out and done in the field of higher education. Those which are already far advanced in their development even now exhibit an individual and characteristic organization.

The American university as we now see it consists of many parts. At its heart stands the college, the school of general training. Above and around the college stand the graduate and technical schools, in which special studies are prosecuted and preparation is given for particular professions and occupations. Technical and professional schools are not a necessary part of a university, but they are greatly benefited by close association with a university; and the university itself is unmistakably benefited and quickened by the transmission of its energy into them and the reaction of their standards and objects upon it. As a rule the larger universities of the country have law schools, divinity schools and medical schools under their care and direction; and training for these, the "learned," professions has long been considered a natural part of their work. Schools of mechanical, electrical and civil engineering have of late years become as numerous and as necessary as the schools which prepare for the older professions, and they have naturally in most cases grown up in connection with universities because their processes are the processes of science, and the modern university is, among other things, a school of pure science, with laboratories and teachers indispensable to the engineer. But the spirit of technical schools has not always been the spirit of learning. They have often been intensely and very frankly utilitarian, and pure science has looked at them askance. They are proper parts of a university only when pure science is of the essence of their teaching, the spirit of pure science the spirit of all their studies. It is only of recent years that we have seen thoughtful engineers coming to recognize this fact, preach this change of spirit; it is only of recent years, therefore, that technical schools have begun to be thoroughly and truly assimilated into the university organization.

There is an ideal at the heart of everything American, and the ideal at the heart of the American university is intellectual training, the awakening of the whole man, the thorough introduction of the student to the life of America and of the modern world, the completion of the task undertaken by the grammar and high schools of equipping him for the full duties of citizenship. It is with that idea that I have said that the college stands at the heart of the American university. The college stands for liberal training. Its object is discipline and enlightenment. The average thoughtful American does not want his son narrowed in all his gifts and thinking to a particular occupation. He wishes him to be made free of the world in which men think about and understand many things, and to know how to handle himself in it. He desires a training for him which will give him a considerable degree of elasticity and adaptability, and fit him to turn in any direction he chooses.

For men do not live in ruts in America. They do not always or of necessity follow the callings their fathers followed before them. They are ready to move this way or that as interest or occasion suggests. Versatility, adaptability, a wide range of powers, a quick and easy variation of careers, men excelling in businesses for which they never had any special preparation—these are among the most characteristic marks of American life, its elasticity and variety, the rapid shifting of parts, the serviceability of the same men for many different things, and the quick intelligence of men of many different kinds in the common undertakings of politics and in public affairs of all kinds. If the American college were to become a vocational school, preparing only for particular callings, it would be thoroughly un-American. It would be serving special, not general, needs, and seeking to create a country of specialized men without versatility or general capacity.

The college of the ideal American university, therefore, is a place intended for general intellectual discipline and enlightenment; and not for intellectual discipline and enlightenment only, but also for moral and spiritual discipline and enlightenment. America is great, not by reason of her skill, but by reason of her spirit,—her spirit of general serviceableness and intelligence. That is the reason why it is necessary to keep her colleges under constant examination and criticism. If we do not, they may forget their own true function, which is to supply America and the professions with enlightened men.

I have described the university as a place with a college at its heart, but with graduate schools and professional schools standing about and around the college. The difficulty about thus associating teaching of different kinds is that the spirit of the graduate and professional schools should not be the same spirit as that of the college, and that there are certain dangers of infection to which the college and the schools of advanced and professional study are both alike exposed by the association. Look, first, at the danger to the college. It is in danger of getting the point of view of the graduate and professional schools, the point of view of those who prosecute study very intensively along special lines. Their object, if they be thorough, is technical scholarship. That should not be the object of the college. Its studies, as America has conceived the college (and I am sure she has conceived it rightly), are not prosecuted with a view to scholarship. Scholarship can not be had at the age of twenty-one, at the age at which youngsters graduate from college. They may by that time have been made to see the way, the arduous way, to scholarship and to desire to travel it; but they can not have traveled it. It is a long road. A lifetime is consumed before one reaches the quiet inn at the end of it. The object of the college is a much simpler one, and yet no less great. It is to give intellectual discipline and impart the spirit of learning.

We have misconceived and misused the college as an instrument of American life when we have organized and used it as a place of special preparation for particular tasks and callings. It is for liberal training, for general discipline, for that preliminary general enlightenment which every man should have who enters modern life with any intelligent hope or purpose of leadership and achievement. By a liberal training I do not mean one which vainly seeks to introduce undergraduates to every subject of modern learning. That would, of course, be impossible. There are too many of them. At best the pupil can, within the four years at the disposal of the college, be introduced to them only by sample. He can be, and should be, given a thorough grounding in mathematics, in his own language and in some language not his own, in one of the fundamental physical and natural sciences, in the general conceptions of philosophy, in the outlines of history, and in the elements of correct political thinking; and it is very desirable that he should go beneath the surface in some one of these subjects, study it with more than usual attention and thoroughness, and find in it, if he can, some independence of judgment and inquiry. Students in a modern college can not all follow the same road, and it is not desirable that they should do so. Besides the thorough drill in a few fundamental subjects which they should all have, they should be encouraged to make the special, individual choices of particular fields of study which will give them an opportunity to develop special gifts and aptitudes and which will call out their powers of initiative and enable them to discover themselves. The college should be a place of various studies, alive with a great many different interests.

The common discipline should come from very hard work, from the inexorable requirement that every student should perform every task set him, whether general or special, whether of his own choice or exacted by the general scheme of study prescribed for all, with care and thoroughness. The spirit of work should pervade the place—honest, diligent, painstaking work. Otherwise it would certainly be no proper place of preparation for the strenuous, exacting life of America in our day. Its "liberalizing" influences should be got from its life even more than from its studies. Special studies become liberal when those who are pursuing them associate constantly and familiarly with those who are pursuing other studies—studies of many kinds, pursued from many points of view. The real enlightenments of life come not from tasks or from books so much as from free intercourse with other persons who, in spite of you, inform and stimulate you, and make you realize how big and various the world is, how many things there are in it to think about, and how necessary it is to think about the subjects you are specially interested in in their right relations to many, many others, if you would think of them correctly and get to the bottom of what you are trying to do.

The ideal college, therefore, should be a community, a place of close, natural, intimate association, not only of the young men who are its pupils and novices in various lines of study, but also of young men with older men, with maturer men, with veterans and professionals in the great undertakings of learning, of teachers with pupils, outside the classroom as well as inside of it. No one is successfully educated within the walls of any particular classroom or laboratory or museum; and no amount of association, however close and familiar and delightful, between mere beginners can ever produce the sort of enlightenment which the lad gets when first he begins to catch the infection of learning. The trouble with most of our colleges nowadays is that the faculty of the college live one life and the undergraduates quite a different one. They are not members of the same community; they constitute two communities. The life of the undergraduate is not touched with the personal influence of the teacher: life among the teachers is not touched by the personal impressions which should come from frequent and intimate contact with undergraduates. The teacher does not often enough know what the undergraduate is thinking about or what models he is forming his life upon, and the undergraduate does not know how human a fellow the teacher is, how delightfully he can talk, outside the classroom, of the subjects he is most interested in, how many interesting things both his life and his studies illustrate and make attractive. This separation need not exist, and, in the college of the ideal university, would not exist.

It is perfectly possible to organize the life of our colleges in such a way that students and teachers alike will take part in it; in such a way that a perfectly natural daily intercourse will be established between them; and it is only by such an organization that they can be given real vitality as places of serious training, be made communities in which youngsters will come fully to realize how interesting intellectual work is, how vital, how important, how closely associated with all modern achievement—only by such an organization that study can be made to seem a part of life itself. Lectures often seem very formal and empty things; recitations generally prove very dull and unrewarding. It is in conversation and natural intercourse with scholars chiefly that you find how lively knowledge is, how it ties into everything that is interesting and important, how intimate a part it is of everything that is "practical" and connected with the world. Men are not always made thoughtful by books; but they are generally made thoughtful by association with men who think.

The present and most pressing problem of our university authorities is to bring about this vital association for the benefit of the novices of the university world, the undergraduates. Classroom methods are thorough enough; competent scholars already lecture and set tasks and superintend their performance; but the life of the average undergraduate outside the classroom and other stated appointments with his instructors is not very much affected by his studies; is almost entirely dissociated from intellectual interests.

It is too freely and exclusively given over to athletics and amusements. Athletics are in themselves wholesome, and are necessary to every normal youth. They give him vigor and should give him the spirit of the sportsman—should keep him out of many things of a very demoralizing sort which he would be inclined to do if he did not spend his energy out-of-doors and in the gymnasium. Amusement, too, is necessary. All work and no play makes Jack not only a dull boy, but a very unserviceable boy, with no spirit, no capacity to vary his occupations or to make the most of himself.

But athletics and amusement ought never to become absorbing occupations, even with youngsters. They should be diversions merely, by which the strain of work is relieved, the powers refreshed and given spontaneous play. The only way in which they can be given proper subordination is to associate them with things not only more important, but quite as natural and interesting. Knowledge, study, intellectual effort, will seem to undergraduates more important than athletics and amusement and just as natural only when older men, themselves vital and interesting and companionable, are thrown into close daily association with them. The spirit of learning can be conveyed only by contagion, by personal contact. The association of studies and persons is the proper prescription.

Turn from the college, which lies at the heart of the university, to the graduate and professional schools which lie about the college and are built upon it, and you are discussing an entirely different matter, looking for different principles and methods. Their right relationship to the college, moreover, is a very difficult question to determine. Both the college and the high school are trying to do two things at once—two things not entirely consistent with each other. The majority of pupils in the high school—the very large majority—do not intend to carry their studies any further. They must get all the schooling they are going to get before they leave the high school. They must be given the best training, the completest awakening within the field of knowledge that the school can give them, for that is to be their final preparation for life. A small minority, however, must be prepared to enter college. Majority and minority must be handled, in such circumstances, in different ways, and it is very hard indeed to arrange the courses of study in a way that will be suitable for both. The high school is clearly justified in shaping its policy and its methods to the needs, first of all, of the majority. Exceptional arrangements must be made, if possible, for the minority.

Similarly, in the college the great majority of undergraduates mean to go at once from their courses there into some active practical pursuit; do not mean to go on to more advanced university studies. A minority, on the other hand—a larger minority than in the schools—do intend to go further, will enter the graduate schools to become teachers and investigators, or the technical and professional schools for some calling for which a special training is necessary. The difficulty of the college is to arrange courses and adopt methods which will serve both these classes. It does so, generally, by offering a much larger choice of studies than it is possible or desirable to offer. But the majority must determine its chief characteristics and adaptations. Its chief object must be general preparation, general training, an all-round awakening.

It is evident, therefore, that the college, while it should be the foundation of the professional schools, not only stands below them, as their support and feeder, but also alongside of them; would be necessary if they did not exist; furnishes the only introduction our young men desire or need get to the wider fields of action and experience which lie beyond it. It is, first of all and chiefly, a general fitting school for life. Its social organization and influence are almost as important as its classrooms. It is not a subordinate school, but the chief, the central school of the university. For the professional schools it is, at the same time, an indispensable foundation. That profession is clearly impoverished which does not draw to its special studies men bred to understand life and the broader relations of their profession in some thorough school of general training. In these higher schools the atmosphere is changed; another set of objects lies before the student; his mind has already begun to center upon tasks which will fill the rest of his life. He can not, there, seek the things that will connect him with the more general fields of learning and experience.

What is called the graduate school in our universities is not, strictly, a professional school. As a matter of fact most of its pupils will be found to be looking forward to the profession of teaching; but graduate schools of the higher type do not keep that profession in mind. Their object is to train scholars, whether in the field of literature, or science, or philosophy, or in the apparently more practical field of politics. They carry the college process a stage farther and seek to induct their students into the precise, exacting methods of scholarship. They not only carry the college process farther, they also alter it. Their students are thrown more upon their own resources in their studies; are expected to enter on researches of their own, strike out into independent lines of inquiry, stand upon their own feet in every investigation, come out of their novitiate and gain a certain degree of mastery in their chosen field, their professors being little more than their guides and critics. They are not taught how to teach; there is no professional tone in the life of the school. They are taught how to learn, thoroughly and independently, and to make scholars of themselves.

Schools of medicine, law and theology, on the other hand, while also, when upon a proper plane, schools of scholarship, are professional schools, and have in all their instruction the professional point of view. Their object is not only to introduce their students to the mastery of certain subjects, as the graduate school does, but also to prepare them for the "practise" of a particular profession. They devote a great deal of attention to practical method—to the ways in which the knowledge acquired is to be used in dealing with diseases, with disputes between men over their legal rights, and with the needs and interests of men who should be helped with spiritual guidance. They are frankly and of necessity professional. The spirit of the doctor's or of the lawyer's office, of the pulpit and of the pastor's study, pervades them. They school their men for particular tasks, complicated and different, and seek to guide them by many practical maxims.

Similarly, the technical schools are professional schools, their objects practical, definite, utilitarian. Their students must not only know science and have their feet solidly upon the footing of exact knowledge, but must acquire a very thorough mastery of methods, a definite skill and practise, readiness and precision in a score of mechanical processes which make of them a sort of master-workmen. The practical air of the shop pervades such schools, as the practical air of the office pervades the law school. They are intent upon business, and conscious all the time that they must make ready for it.

In the professional schools of an ideal university nothing of this practical spirit would be abated, for such schools are, one and all, intensely and immediately practical in their objects and must have practise always in mind if they would be truly serviceable; but there would always lie back of their work, by close association with the studies of the university in pure science and in all the great subjects which underlie law and theology, the impulse and the informing spirit of disinterested inquiry, of study which has no utilitarian object, but seeks only the truth. The spirit of graduate study, and of undergraduate, too, would be carried over into all professional work, and engineers, doctors, ministers, lawyers, would all alike be made, first of all, citizens of the modern intellectual and social world—first of all, university men, with a broad outlook on the various knowledge of the world, and then experts in a great practical profession, which they would understand all the better because they had first been grounded in science and in the other great bodies of knowledge which are the fountains of all practise. That is the service the university owes the professional schools associated with it. The parts should be vitally united from end to end.

The professional schools, in their turn, do the university this distinct and very great service, that they keep it in conscious association with the practical world, its necessities and its problems. Through them it better understands what knowledge, what kind of men, what scholarship, what morals, what action, will best serve the age for whose enlightenment and assistance it exists. Our universities should be "ideal" chiefly in this—that they serve the intellectual needs of the age, not in one thing, not in any one way only, but all around the circle, with a various and universal adaptation to their age and generation. America can never dispense with the enlightenment of general study, and should wish to have as many of her young men as possible subjected to its influences. She should demand that her professional schools be grounded in such studies in order that her professional men may see something more than individual interest in what they do. It is best, therefore, that professional schools should be closely associated with universities, a part of their vital organization, intimate parts of their system of study. That very association and inclusion should make them more thorough in their particular practical tasks. They should be the better schools of technical training. The ideal university is rounded out by them, and their roots are enriched by her fertile soil of catholic knowledge and inquiry. The ideal university would consist of all these parts, associated in this spirit, maintained always in this relationship.[1]

Printed in *The Delineator*, LXXIV (Nov. 1909), 401, 437-38.

[1] There is a WWhw outline of this essay, dated June 28, 1909; a WWsh draft dated July 6, 1909; and a WWT draft entitled "The Ideal University" and dated July 6, 1909, all in WP, DLC.

From Ralph Adams Cram

Dear Dr. Wilson: Boston, July 8, 1909

I am deeply indebted to you for going over the draft on the article on "Architectural Princeton."[1] I also sent a copy to Mr. Pyne and he and Mr. Henry made more minute criticisms than you did. All these criticisms have now been adopted and the article goes on [to] the American Architect.

I can assure you nothing would give me greater pleasure than the opportunity of talking with you about the site of the Graduate College. I will come on to Princeton, almost at your convenience, if you want me to do so. I want to see how the Sage buildings are getting on anyhow. On the other hand, if you are to be in Boston at any time during the summer, can you not arrange to come out and spend the night with us at Nahant, where I have the most fascinating old house imaginable and where our wonderful cliffs and the invigorating sea breeze could only give you great satisfaction.

In the matter of the Graduate College site, my interest is increasing and my convictions suffering a sea change. In view of the new possibilities opening out before the Graduate College, I am rapidly receding from my original advocacy of the Prospect site. Just at present I am unofficially studying in detail the golf links property and am working over some maps and plans that serve to convince me, at least, that the potentialities of this same golf links site are really extraordinary. I very much want to canvass the whole matter, and so I will come to Princeton at your convenience unless you can give us the very great pleasure of spending a night with us in Nahant.

Very faithfully yours, R A Cram

TLS (WP, DLC).

[1] Ralph Adams Cram, "Princeton Architecture," *The American Architect*, XCVI (July 21, 1909), 21-30.

To Mary Allen Hulbert Peck

Dearest Friend, Princeton, New Jersey, 9 July, 1909.

This is indeed hard luck! I am to be in New York to-night and shall not find you there! The children sail to-morrow and I go up, beforehand, to-night to carry the luggage and make sure it gets to the steamer. I do not see how I can possibly go in on Sunday or Monday. We go up to Lyme on Tuesday; there are a hundred things to be done before we go which it is my duty to do; it would be selfish and faithless of me to go away when I was most needed. I am more disappointed than I can say. I am most unfortunate.

Thank you for the long letter.[1] I was desperately hungry for news of you. The account of the fire thrilled me,—particularly when I thought of your playing your little stream of water from the hose directly on the glowing electric wires! You must have been holding it by the rubber tubing and not by the metal nozzle. It is terrible to think what might have happened! And how splendidly you behaved,—not only with great courage, but also with singular judgment and presence of mind. You are an extraordinarily capable person, and I am proud to be your friend. I did not wait for the fire to find this out; but even the little account you give of it fills me with enthusiasm.

I wonder of [if] the little brooch ever reached you. I have been corresponding with the Express Company about it, but they are very poor correspondents and have as yet told me nothing definite.

I must not write a letter now. There is everything to do, and everything must be done at once!

With affectionate messages from us all,

In haste,

Your devoted friend, Woodrow Wilson

WWTLS (WP, DLC).

1 It is missing.

Two Letters to Robert Garrett

My dear Mr. Garrett: Princeton, N. J. July 9th, 1909.

I am really distressed at the situation about Littmann. I feel not only the deepest interest in getting him back at Princeton, but I feel there is a certain very real sense in which the University owes it to you, in view of your generosity in supplying so much invaluable oriental material, that someone should be appointed to make use of it in the best way. At the same time, I cannot criticize Mr. Sheldon's action for a moment, because I know how reluctantly he acted (I have seen him since his letter was written), and I know how inexorable he feels the necessity to be of holding me back from adding expenses for meeting which no permanent arrangement can at present be made.

Mr. Butler tells me that Littmann must know before the first of August or he will be obliged to accept a new arrangement which the University of Strassburg is trying to make for him. Would it be possible for you to see Mr. van Rensselaer about this matter? You may remember that at the time Littmann left Mr. van Rennselaer volunteered to say that he would make up any necessary addition to Littmann's salary to keep him. I have no doubt that his interest in the matter has continued.

I hope that if there is anything you think of that I can do or any person you think of that I could go to in the matter, you will let me know, so that I may act with you at once.

Cordially and faithfully yours, Woodrow Wilson

TLS (Selected Corr. of R. Garrett, NjP).

My dear Mr. Garrett, Princeton, N. J. 10 July, 1909.

Thank you most sincerely for your kind letter of the eighth instant.[1] It makes me very happy. I had quite set my heart on getting Littmann back here, where he belongs, and, on the strength of your letter, I am writing to him to-day, very cordially and urgently.

After I wrote you I learned from Pyne that he had been in communication with Mr. Procter and that Mr. Procter would perfectly understand any necessary delay in our committee action. That was the point I was chiefly concerned about, and, that being taken care of, I quite agreed with Pyne that it would be better to postpone further meetings of the Committee on the Graduate School until the early autumn.

I was in New York to-day and was wondering at what pier you were seeing Mrs. Garrett off. I was seeing two of my daughters off, with friends, on the Red Star Line steamer "Kroonland."

Let me again, both personally and officially, thank you most warmly for your great generosity and invaluable aid in the matter of securing Littmann. I always admire the way you do these things.

With warmest regard,

Faithfully Yours, Woodrow Wilson

WWTLS (Selected Corr. of R. Garrett, NjP).

[1] As the following letter reveals, he sent Garrett's letter to E. W. Sheldon.

To Edward Wright Sheldon

My dear Ed., Princeton, N. J. 10 July, 1909.

I forwarded your letter to Mr. Garrett, and here is his reply. It makes me very happy, and I am writing to Professor Littmann by this mail. This is a great stroke for the University, and I am sure will everywhere in the academic world be thought so.

It was a real pleasure to see you the other day. It always seems possible really to *talk* in Princeton; in New York it seems always imperative to *act* and be off.

I saw two of my daughters off for Europe to-day, and on Tuesday next I take Mrs. Wilson and our remaining daughter up to Lyme. My address there will be Care Miss Florence Griswold, Old Lyme, Connecticut.

Always,

Faithfully and affectionately Yours, Woodrow Wilson

WWTLS (photostat in RSB Coll., DLC).

From Richard Spencer Childs

Dear Sir: New York July 10th, 1909.

I have invited the other men who met at the City Club April 22nd to meet there again at 4 o'clock Tuesday, July 20th, and trust that this date will be acceptable to you.

In talking over the matter,[1] Ludington and I thought that it might be a foxy plan in case Mr. Woodruff attended the meeting, to simply appoint the Executive Board consisting of Professor Beard, Binkerd, Ludington and myself, giving to them the power to fill the first memberships in the Advisory Board. This, I think, would remove any possibility of awkwardness at the meeting.

Following the afternoon meeting, I would like to have the Executive Board and yourself, Mr. Ford and Mr. Abbott remain for dinner in the private dining room at the Club. The Executive Board can then create the Advisory Board and hold a joint meeting with them in the evening. I would be very glad also to put you up at the Club for the night.

For your information I am forwarding herewith a copy of the Constitution as we revised it.[2]

Yours very truly Richard S Childs

TLS (WP, DLC).

[1] See A. C. Ludington to WW, April 11, 1909.

[2] A typed copy entitled "CONSTITUTION SUGGESTED FOR THE SHORT BALLOT ORGANIZATION."

To Mary Allen Hulbert Peck

Dearest Friend, Princeton, 11 July, 1909.

The fever of packing and "closing the house" is almost over, and I have a few moments in which I may indulge myself in the pleasure of writing to you.

We start to-morrow morning, in order to catch the one o'clock train at the Grand Central. I was about to say the one o'clock train for Lyme, but, alas! it is not for Lyme. It drops us at Saybrook

Junction, to take the choice of either waiting indefinitely for a local train to take us the one station further or hiring vehicles and going on by way of the road and the ferry, the Connecticut River lying between Saybrook Junction and our destination. I think we shall take the ferry. We should be in Lyme by about five o'clock; and when we are there shall be about as much out of the world as if we had ridden in twenty miles away from the railroad. My address, after this, if you please, will be, Care Miss Florence Griswold, Old Lyme, Connecticut.

The Griswold's have been great people in their time and are still decidedly gentlefolk. Miss Florence has taken artists (for whom Lyme is headquarters in this part of the world) in to board in her her [*sic*] spacious old house time out of mind, and the place is a perfect artistic curiosity shop, the walls and doors of one room, for example, being painted from end to end with landscapes and figures by men of all stamps, most of them now famous, who have lived there the pleasant, informal life they love and she permits. The artists of the Lyme school regard her as their patron saint, and have all in their turns made love to her. In summer all the meals of the singular household are taken out-of-doors on the piazza, the women at one table, the men at another, in order that they may with the less embarrassment come directly from their work to the table, dressed as they happen to be. The men's table is known as "the hot air club," and it I shall very appropriately join. I expect to be quite in my element in Bohemia.

I am sorry, very sorry that your son should look so thin and strained as to distress you. Probably you exaggerate it in your anxiety about his health. Remember that it is his first plunge into business and must necessarily be a strain at first. I believe that in the long run he will thrive on the stimulation and compulsion of it. I was surprised, and I must say not a little disappointed, to learn from my friend in the United States Mortgage and Trust Co.[1] that he had declined to leave Dick Brothers and go to the Company. I do not know what they offered him, but I am very sorry indeed that he is to remain with that speculative concern, of which the regular bankers speak with significant reserve. Perhaps something will open for him at the United States Trust Company or at the National City Bank. If it does I hope he will not decline it unless there is some very imperative reason for his doing so. The habit of mind he is likely to form will render it very hazardous for him ever to have any money of his own. Unless unusually lucky, he will not be likely to keep it. If trained in a house of another kind, on the contrary, it might make it possible for him to use it very safely and very profitably. Why should you blame yourself so bitterly for having made it necessary that your son should go into business at the normal age? It seems to me exactly what you should want him to do in normal circumstances, and the first year or two is sure, if the boy really works and serves his novitiate, to be very trying, a real discipline. It is what every well trained business man has been through.

Please thank Miss Dawes[2] for the invitation to address the Wednesday Club again. I think I had better rest on my laurels. Having made so delightful an impression last year, by reason of some too great kindness on the part of my audience, it would be rash for me to risk a reversal of judgment. I understand strategy better than that! The fact is, too, that I have gone quite stale, as the athletes say, on speaking. I am overtrained. There is no snap or ginger left in me. I feel as if I simply *could* not do it again until, perhaps, the cold weather comes to touch me into life again. It is hard to say No, in view of all that is involved. It is a case of resisting temptation. But I feel that I must. I simply must rest, or I shall not be fit for the tasks of next winter, which are likely to be as hard and exacting, perhaps as anxious, as any I have had. It's a braw world, evidently not meant for pleasure, except as pleasure is to be got out of hard sledding. I do not mean that I am not well. I am only very tired and out of tone. I mean to fill my days at Lyme with loafing and with the kind of mild work that draws the thoughts to itself without taxing one too much.

I wish you would tell me what other books you want. It will give me great pleasure to send them. As for myself I am for the time being reduced to so maudlin a state by the winter's fatigue that I can read nothing but detective stories with zest and comprehension. I suppose my mind will return to me after a little, if there's any left. I've used it like a spendthrift in recent years. Another evidence of my reduced state, I fear, is that I write a portentously stupid letter nowadays. It is not—I assure you, that I cannot write, but only that nothing occurs to me to say! I trust that by autumn I may improve.

It seems a shame to leave this big, cool, comfortable house for a boarding house which has not even a bath in it. We shall have to be very English and very primitive. But, for some reason, it seems always a proper part of a summer vacation to have a certain element of roughing it in it.

It has been suggested that I run for Governor of the State in the approaching campaign, but I put a passage about the trades unions in my baccalaureate address at Commencement which I think will make the politicians who control such matters very shy of me. I have had the labour papers hotly after me: chiefly because what I said was true, that they scale all labour down to a minimum, and seek to give as little as possible for their wages. Our gardener has been championing me against the workmen hereabout.

I will let you know when we get settled in our new quarters. Meanwhile all join me in affectionate messages.

Your devoted friend Woodrow Wilson

WWTLS (WP, DLC).

[1] Cornelius Cuyler Cuyler.

[2] Anna Laurens Dawes, journalist and author of several books on political and biographical subjects, officer or member of various missionary and philanthropic organizations. She was president of the Wednesday Club of Pittsfield, Massachusetts, to which Wilson spoke on October 6, 1908. About this speech, see Mary L. G. Hinsdale to WW, Oct. 8, 1908, Vol. 18.

From Abbott Lawrence Lowell

Dear Mr. Wilson, Cambridge [Mass.] July 14, 1909

It maketh a glad heart and even a cheerful countenance to receive a letter such as yours.[1] I feel as if we might be on the eve of a very great advance in university and especially college organization. I do not feel that we have yet worked out the problem, although you have taken some long strides towards it. I should like to have some talks with you, because I feel that our ideas are very much alike.

Very truly yours, A. Lawrence Lowell.

TLS (WP, DLC).

[1] Wilson's letter is missing in the Lowell Papers.

From Melancthon Williams Jacobus

My dear President Wilson: Hartford, Conn., July 15th, 1909

It is not altogether fair to put into print your most admirable address at our recent Commencement without telling you what we are doing with it, and placing at your disposal such copies of it as you may care to have.

We have been sending out to our alumni a letter to interest them in the young men of their churches and parishes, with a view to the ministry, and with it we are sending to each alumnus a copy of your address.

I think you will approve of the spirit of the letter, a copy of which I enclose herewith,[1] and will feel that what you said so splendidly to the graduating class will be of help and service not only to the alumni themselves, but to such young men as they may be privileged to interest in this great vocation.

I am sending you, under separate cover, a dozen copies of the address; and should you care for additional copies, I should be only too pleased to forward them to you.

I wish I might be able to come down some day while you are still in these parts, and have a talk with you over Princeton matters. I notice that no further discussion of the question of the Preceptorial matters was had at the Commencement meeting of the Curriculum Committee, but I cannot believe that this means that all discussion has ceased. The principles involved in the question are so serious that I am anxious that, when the discussion is resumed, if it is to be, it may be in the utmost harmony and sympathy of action, not only between yourself and Fine, but between both of you and the Committee itself.

Has anything occurred since Commencement that would indicate the development of the situation, or is there anything which you have in mind as likely to help that development towards the best interests of the University before the fall meeting of the Board?

I shall be in Hartford until the latter part of next week, when I shall be absent for a few days, though I expect to return and remain here the rest of the summer.

With kindest regards to Mrs. Wilson, believe me

Yours very sincerely, Melancthon W Jacobus

TLS (WP, DLC).

[1] A form letter to "My Dear Sir," June 25, 1909, urging alumni of the Hartford Theological Seminary to seek out promising young men in their congregations to persuade them to enter the Christian ministry.

To Mary Allen Hulbert Peck

Dearest Friend, Old Lyme, Connecticut, 18 July, 1909.

We have been settled here now *almost* long enough for me to feel as if my vacation had begun; and just as that delightful feeling begins to creep upon me I have to plunge back into what I thought I had left! On Tuesday I go down to New York to attend a little conference on the short ballot (I think I told you about our little "movement" to rescue the voter from the impossible); Wednesday and half of Thursday I must spend in Philadelphia (of all places the worst in summer) to get a delapidated tooth replaced (yes, replaced; I have come to that!); Thursday night I return to New York, and Friday come back to Lyme to complain of all I have had to go through in my expedition out into the world. And happy I shall be to get back! Lyme is certainly a haven. We have the sound of trains often in our ears and motor cars whirr by on the road at our door; but the world which passes by us does not notice us: we are side-tracked at a very quiet rural station where life has hardly changed its pace since the thirties. Certainly it is the same town to a stick that I knew four years ago. I have changed much more than it has. The motors that pass the door (the street in front of us is the main road between New-Haven and New London, New York and Newport) affect my imagination much more than the trains do, not only because they are painfully visible, but also because they contain for the most part, in all probability, specimens of the sort of people I like least, the restless, rich, empty-headed people the very sight of whom makes me cynical. I am glad to have them pass by, but very resentful that I must forever have their dust (and odour) in my nostrils. I would they were indeed dust! They go by with their usual reckless speed, and, in this dry season, fill the air, obscure the very heavens with the dust they stir. They keep me a bit irritated with the consciousness that they are in the world to deepen all its problems and give it nothing at all that it can profit by. They and their kind are the worst enemies of Princeton, and create for me the tasks which are likely to wear my life out. But enough of them,—let them pass and be d— forgotten. I will rest a little in spite of them.

I had many a deep pang of disappointment that I could not see you in New York last week. There was no way to manage it. I thought of you a thousand times. It would have been worth half a vacation for refreshment to see you and spend a few hours in your company. And now, when you are not to be there, I am to be in New York. This is the kind of thing that tries the soul! Does the summer bring any old friends to Pittsfield, like Mrs. Roebling, for example, with whom you can rest your heart and renew your spirits? I hope with all my heart it does. I hope, too, that Mrs. Allen's trouble has not returned to make you anxious. Give her my warmest regard. I have learned to admire her most sincerely. It would make me very happy to have some opportunity to serve her.

Everything goes very normally and pleasantly with us here. I have made friends with the men very easily. They are very easy to make friends with,—and I hope I am. Moreover, they are interesting fellows; and three of them can really paint: Mr. Robinson, Mr. Bicknell, and Mr. Hoffman.[1] Mr. Hoffman is not allowed to paint very much just now, because his fiancee[2] (I am not sure of the spelling) is here and demands all his attention, with an ingenious selfishness which is interesting. He will have to marry her to get rid of her! Mr. Bicknell is a bachelor, and a very whimsical, delightful fellow, who can strike off excellent jests by merely giving his mind its natural play: a man of great charm of personality and very good to look at. I do not see how Madge can have spent a summer with him (last summer) and not fallen in love with him. He is the sort of man I should *think* a woman would fall in love with at once: and I do not often think that of a man. Mrs. Robinson[3] is a slave to her husband, by whom he profits deeply,–and a very charming slave. He has long been delicate and her anxiety about him, the necessity of taking care of him, has brought out in her the mother instinct beautifully. Her loving attentions have made him very selfish, and sometimes I could shake him for his impositions upon her and his ungracious, unappreciative appropriation of everything there is in her (and there is a great deal); but the other evening his real feeling came out very prettily and touched me a good deal, giving me a different feeling about him. They had just received news of the unexpected death of the wife of an artist friend of theirs. Robinson was evidently a good deal affected. "It will break him all to pieces!" he exclaimed, and presently went and sat off apart, very silent, looking across the piazza at his wife. When she moved, to fetch something, he sprang to her assistance and they went off together into the garden, appearing in a moment again, in the twilight, with his arm about her waist. It had evidently come upon him "What if *she* should die!" Thus are men brought to their senses when door-mat wives have become too much a matter-of-course under their feet. Mrs. Wilson says it is all right: that Mrs. Robinson is doing what she ought to do: "They have no children and that is her whole duty, and chief pleasure. That is what a woman ought to do." But the matter seems to me debateable. Whatever women ought to do, men ought to be knightly and chivalrous and lighten the burden for those they love. There are a bevy of women in the house, attached and unattached, but none of them seems to count except Mrs. Robinson and Miss Florence, the resourceful lady who is the mistress of us all, thinking of us and thinking for us, deserving description in a separate letter, like a portrait in its own frame. Behold your friend subdued to the Bohemian habits of the place and eating among the men without his coat, like a lady in her shirt-waist. He tries to wear very pretty ties, and the costume is said to become him. How happy it would make him could a lady he knows who is made for good company and good fellowship look in upon this little world and complete it. It is very interesting and would be worth her while.

All join me in affectionate messages, and I am always

Your devoted friend, Woodrow Wilson

WWTLS (WP, DLC).

[1] Frank Alfred Bicknell, Harry Leslie Hoffman, and William S. Robinson, American landscape artists.

[2] Beatrice Amanda Pope, whom Hoffman married on April 5, 1910.

[3] Lois E. Ball Robinson.

From Harold Bolce[1]

Dear Sir: New York July 19, 1909.

I am pleased that you wrote to me.[2] I am now preparing some material which will discuss the points brought up in your much appreciated letter, and I shall take opportunity to send this matter to you. In the September issue, the side of the church in this controversy will be set forth,[3] and later, there will be expressions from different standpoints. I shall be pleased to have you write me something again.

Clergymen of all denominations have discussed these articles. Rev. John L. Bilford, of Brooklyn,[4] says that "the articles constitute a terrible indictment." On the other hand, Rev. J. Herman Randall, a Baptist clergyman of New York City,[5] welcomes the college philosophy as indicative of what he regards as a saner faith. The final article on these subjects will deal with a study of the soul, and in this discussion, Ernst Haeckel, the German savant, will take part.[6]

Yours very truly, Harold Bolce

TLS (WP, DLC).

[1] Free-lance journalist of New York. His business address at this time was "Care Cosmopolitan Magazine, New York, N. Y." and he used the magazine's letterhead in his correspondence. However, he seems to have had no official connection with the publication other than as a regular contributor.

Bolce at this time was writing a series of articles for *Cosmopolitan* in which he portrayed the teachings of many noted American college and university professors as calling in question all traditional doctrines, especially those of Christianity, but also those of morality, politics, family life and, indeed, all fields of human knowledge and belief. The articles appeared as follows: "Blasting at the Rock of Ages," *Cosmopolitan Magazine*, XLVI (May 1909), 665-76; "Polyglots in Temples of Babel," *ibid.*, XLVII (June 1909), 52-65; "Avatars of the Almighty," *ibid.*, July 1909, pp. 209-18; "Christianity in the Crucible," *ibid.*, August 1909, pp. 310-19; "Rallying Round the Cross," *ibid.*, Sept. 1909, pp. 491-502.

At the beginning of the first article, Bolce stated that he had toured well-known American colleges and universities from coast to coast, had entered some institutions as a special student, and at others had "attended lectures as a visitor, or interviewed members of the faculty, or consulted the typewritten or printed records of what they teach." He specifically listed nineteen of the best known public and private institutions of higher learning of the country, including Princeton, in which he had carried out his investigations. Bolce professed to be impartial in his analysis, even indicating his admiration for the reigning spirit of free inquiry, and he repeatedly stated that the views of the professors he cited should not necessarily be taken as representing their institutions as a whole. However, the content (to say nothing of the titles) of the articles was written up in sensational style, and Bolce frequently quoted brief statements or even single sentences of specifically named professors very much out of context. Moreover, when, as was perhaps anticipated, the first two articles created a furor among religious leaders, neither Bolce nor his editors hesitated to portray the series as representing an irreconcilable conflict between "the colleges" and the Christian church. The series, which was originally to consist of three articles, was extended to include two more, one of which presented the position of those professors who avowedly were attacking the teachings of the Christian church and a final one which presented a rebuttal based on the views of a small number of religious leaders.

2 Wilson's letter is missing. However, it was almost certainly a protest against the presentation of his views in the second article of Bolce's series, "Polyglots in Temples of Babel," which dealt with the teachings of noted American historians, economists, and political and social scientists. Wilson's alleged views were discussed in the second and third paragraphs of the article, pp. 52-53, as follows:

"Eminent college men, among them Pres. Woodrow Wilson, of Princeton, Prof. Barrett Wendell, of Harvard, and Prof. William Graham Sumner, of Yale, hold that the doctrines of the founders of this Republic have long since served their day and should no longer be applied to the needs of the present. . . .

"President Wilson teaches that the world needs a new civilization. America, considering itself free, is enslaved to the past. Everything apprizes us of the fact that we are not the same nation now we were when the government was formed. The minds that prepared the way for the American republic were dominated by Rousseau, the 'apostle of all that is fanciful, unreal, and misleading in politics.' To be ruled by the French economist, says President Wilson, 'was like taking an account of life from Rider Haggard.' He believes in leadership, however, and teaches that we have not made enough of it, quoting with approval an English historian who says that 'Americans are a nation because they once obeyed a king.'"

Moreover, the sentence mentioning Rousseau was used as a caption for a sketch illustration of Wilson on the second page of the article, and it also, together with the sentence mentioning Haggard, was substantially repeated (without mentioning Wilson's name) in an "Editor's Note" which prefaced the article.

Wilson may also have objected to the treatment of the alleged views of Ernest Ludlow Bogart and George Byron Louis Arner, at this time, respectively, Preceptor and Instructor in the Department of History, Politics, and Economics at Princeton, in this and other articles in the series.

However, neither Wilson's name nor any comments by him were mentioned in Bolce's subsequent articles or in the editorial commentary in "Magazine Shop-Talk," although the comments upon the series of numerous other scholars and religious leaders were presented. This fact would seem to lend credence to the theory that Wilson's letter was critical.

3 "Rallying Round the Cross," cited in n. 1.

4 The Rev. John Louis Belford, pastor of the Church of the Nativity (Roman Catholic), Brooklyn.

5 The Rev. John Herman Randall, pastor of Mt. Morris Baptist Church, New York.

6 In "Rallying Round the Cross," p. 501, Bolce referred to "a forthcoming article in the *Cosmopolitan*" by Ernst Haeckel. However, no article by Haeckel ever appeared in the magazine.

From Edward Dickinson Duffield

My dear President Wilson: Newark, N. J. July 23, 1909.

I have been intending ever since the receipt of your letter to write you in reference thereto, and would have done so had I not hoped that I might take advantage of your kind suggestion of a personal talk. It has been impossible, however, for me to get to Princeton, and as I see by the paper that you have now left for the summer I fear that that pleasure will have to be deferred.

It so happens that since writing to you I have been appointed by the Orange Alumni Association one of a committee of three to endeavor to present to the Association some definite information as to just what are the present evils confronting Princeton, and what is proposed in order to obviate them. As I understand it, it is the feeling of the Association that it would prove beneficial at this time to take up the whole matter and endeavor by a clear and definite comprehension of the situation to remove some of the misunderstandings which have arisen since your suggested plan was brought out. Personally, I think I fully appreciate that the problem is largely an educational one, and with which the opinion of a layman will probably be of little value. I have hesitated somewhat to serve on the committee for fear that any action which we might take would possibly tend to complicate rather than simplify the situation, but, after consideration, I have hoped that at least in some small way we might accomplish something toward the solution of the difficult problems which confront Princeton.

I would appreciate it greatly if you would write to me, telling me briefly just what is proposed to be done by the Quad system; the benefits you hope Princeton will obtain by its adoption, and what the evils are which you believe it will help to eradicate. There also seems to be some doubt as to whether the Quad system is offered merely for the purpose of eradicating the present unsatisfactory conditions in student life, or whether it is a proposition entirely independent thereof, and the elimination of club evils is merely incidental to it. I am frank to say that I must confess to ignorance on this point, and will be glad if you will enlighten me. It would be a real pleasure to us all if you could arrange to meet with us informally some time in the Fall, and give us your ideas on the whole situation. I cannot but feel that such a meeting would prove really beneficial.[1]

I sincerely appreciate the very kind tone of your recent note, and am exceedingly glad that if anything I said was of the slightest aid to you in considering the very difficult problems which I know you have to meet. I sincerely hope that at no very distant date I may have the pleasure of talking over these matters with you personally, and again assure you of my very real desire to render any aid to your administration and to Princeton which I can do.

I trust that you are having a most enjoyable vacation, and with kindest regards, believe me,

Very truly yours, Edward D Duffield

TLS (WP, DLC).

[1] See E. D. Duffield to WW, Dec. 28, 1909, and Jan. 3, 1910.

To Mary Allen Hulbert Peck

Old Lyme, Connecticut,
My dearest Friend, Care Miss Florence Griswold, 25 July, 1909.

Will you consider it immodest on my part if I call your attention again to the address at the head of this sheet? Do you not remember what Ole Bull[1] used to say of his practicing? If he omitted to practice for a single day, he said, he noticed the difference in his playing. If he left off practicing for two days, his friends noticed the difference. If he omitted it for three days everyone noticed the difference. If more than the usual period goes by without a letter from my friend, I notice a difference in myself. Before the period grows much longer, those near me notice the difference. If it grows really long, everybody notices the difference. The time is at hand when everybody will begin to notice the difference. Do you think a fellow can really have a holiday if he have not also a holiday spirit? And do you think he can have a holiday spirit if his thoughts are filled with anxious conjecture about those whom he loves? There is no holiday in asking oneself, Can it be illness? Are they away? Can there be anything the matter? Have their spirits ebbed so low that they do not care to write? Do they think of me less often than before? Is it less pleasure than it used to be to write to me? Such questions lead the spirits astray and play havoc with rest and recuperation. Be generous, therefore, and write. Write about yourself: write anything that is uppermost in your thoughts, and I shall be grateful. Only do not forget to write! I am very sensitive to silence, because nothing so disturbs me as conjecture. The world is too full of things that *may* happen to render that endurable.

I carried out my programme last week to the letter, and suffered all things at the hands of the dentists. For they were plural, —before the day was over I should have said that they were legion. To one I went and had gas administered to me and a tooth extracted (a front tooth, at that), and regained consciousness soon enough to enjoy the "trimming" he said he had to do. The other took an impression of my mouth and had a plate made and fitted with a substitute tooth on it. What do you think of that? Your friend has entered the false tooth stage. Does not that sound like old age and dissolution? Do you care to retain the friendship of a decrepit old gentleman from whom you are so far away that you cannot lend him the support of your arm when he tries to walk? Presently his wits will grow dull, and then what a burden his letters will become! Think it over. Do not sacrifice yourself.

Fortunately he still has a certain physical elasticity and vigour. He was no sooner back from the dentist's than he walked two or three miles over hill and dale to a friend's house by the river here, played golf for a couple of hours and walked back again all aglow with the refreshment of mind and body. Until this summer I had not tried golf since the mishap to my left eye. I fancied that the imperfect vision of that eye would prevent my playing. To my great delight I find that it does not! I play as well as ever I did. That is not saying much; but it is saying that I can still get a vast deal of pleasure out of the game, and I am very happy over the discovery. I would not know myself if I were cut off from all games. I shall lose my identity when I can be no kind of a sport whatever. The livest thing in me is the boy that still lingers there, to break out on the slightest provocation. He can still, I find, laugh at even false teeth, and regard his situation as only whimsical and amusing masquerading behind such a damaged person!

I came back to find the make-up of the household here a good deal altered. People come and go. You no sooner get interested in them or fond of them than they are off. It is always the interesting ones that go. The others, to whom you never give a thought and who serve as a sort of filling, are fixed and stationary, as are their counterparts in nature. But, fortunately, even the commonplace ones are not, in this house, of the ordinary boarding house breed. It is, even in its mere ballast, an artists' house. The man who is attracting my attention just now, as something outside my experience hitherto, is a Mr. Albert,[2] who, I am told, is just now the principal theatrical scene painter in the country. Out here he amuses himself painting landscape, and it is immensely interesting to see how histrionic every cloud and hillside becomes under his brush. I never saw natural objects take the stage with more circumstance and action! One scrutinizes the picture closely to see how it is that the trick is played, and comes away without finding out. I dare say it is a mere trick of exaggeration: that just as conversation that is to "carry" from the distance of the stage must be uttered in tones pitched far above the key and force of actual conversation, so the painting that is to carry and give setting to the whole must have a heightened tone, an exaggerated emphasis. I have noticed the same thing in public speech. When I read stenographic reports of speeches that I have made, the emphasis of every sentence seems to me exaggerated. Every statement seems to[o] broad, too unqualified, too much heightened by emphasis. I do not think Mr. Albert notices it now. The dramatic looks to him natural. Perhaps the natural looks tame and untrue.

Speaking of public discourses, I wonder if you will care for the one I am sending you by this mail? It is the address I delivered at the seventy-fifth anniversary of the foundation of Hartford Theological Seminary a few weeks ago. They have liked it enough to send it out broadcast. I am very much more anxious that you should like it. I am sure you will tell me with perfect frankness whether you do or not. The Harvard address is in type (I have just finished reading the proof), but the magazine in which it is to appear has not yet been issued. I will not forget to send you a copy. I mean to spare you nothing of mine!

I am very well, notwithstanding the nerve-racking experiences I have just gone through with with [*sic*] the dentists. I wish that I knew that you could say as much for yourself. I find myself wishing particular pleasures for you,—this sort of sight-seeing expedition, that walk, such and such friends, sight of this or that picture, the amusement of some play I happen to hear of. If thoughts could provide for your happiness and entertainment, how well taken care of you would be! Pray school your own thoughts to take care of your peace and happiness, and be sweet enough to admit me into them occasionally as always and altogether Your devoted friend, Woodrow Wilson

WWTLS (WP, DLC).

1 Ole Bornemann Bull (1810-1880), Norwegian violin virtuoso. Like Niccolo Paganini, after whom he modeled himself, Bull was as well known for his personal eccentricities as for the brilliance of his performances.

2 Ernest Albert, who was just at this time shifting the focus of his interest from theatrical scene designing to landscape painting. Albert had a business address in New York while residing in New Rochelle, N. Y.

From Moses Taylor Pyne

My dear Woodrow: New York July 27th, 1909.

When I saw you last week I did not have a chance to tell you of Procter's visit. He and Mrs. Procter[1] came over in the afternoon and spent the night with us. We drove around the Campus and looked at all the sites again. He expressed the view, which he said was practically the final one with him, that he did not feel that the lower part of the campus down by the Lake, or around Patton Hall, or below the Club houses would be a satisfactory site for the Graduate College as he wished and expected to see it developed, and that he did not feel inclined to make his offer good unless a better site than those were chosen.

It seems to me that we are up against the proposition now as to whether we should accept or decline his offer in toto next October, and in view of the money that seems to be following his money and his tremendous interest in Princeton, I think this should be taken into very serious consideration.

With kind regards to Mrs. Wilson and to Margaret and hoping that you are enjoying your summer, believe me, as ever,

Yours very sincerely, M Taylor Pyne

TLS (WP, DLC).

[1] Jane Eliza Johnson Procter.

Henry Burling Thompson to Melancthon Williams Jacobus

My Dear Jacobus: [Greenville P. O., Del.] July 27th, 1909.

I am enclosing with this statements showing the income and expense accounts of Princeton University for the past five years. As there is a tremendous increase in our expense account you will see that the Finance Committee were justified in asking for statements from the Curriculum Committee and from the Grounds and Buildings Committee as to the possibilities of effecting economies in their departments. There is no question, that, as a Board, we are relying too much on the generosity of two men; viz, Momo Pyne and Cleve Dodge, who have for some two or three years past generously made up the deficiency at the close of the fiscal year. I am thoroughly convinced that this is an absolutely wrong policy to live under, and that this question of deficiency should be met in some other way.

Within the last two weeks,—both at Princeton and New York,— I have spent considerable time with Momo Pyne and with Sheldon, on this business, and we have reached this conclusion: That it is useless to attempt to discuss this question in full Committees, for reasons that must be apparent to you; and we think it advisable that Sheldon, as Chairman of the Finance Committee, should call a meeting for the latter part of September, of the Chairmen of the Curriculum, Grounds and Buildings and Finance Committees, with the President, and then let us take up the question dispassionately and at our leisure.

I have presented a very full statement to Sheldon,–including your letters, as to conditions that obtain in the Curriculum Committee; and my object in writing to you is to advise you in advance of the objects of the meeting which Sheldon will call. We are sure this is the best way to treat the matter, for all the above Chairmen are persona grata to Wilson, and we could discuss the question with him without friction.

Please consider this letter as confidential and not to be discussed, as this idea is to emanate from Sheldon, as Chairman of the Finance Committee.

I should be glad to hear from you as to whether you approve of this idea; and, at the same time, kindly return me the statements mailed with this letter.

My address for the month of August will be "St. Hubert's Post Office, Essex County, New York."

Yours very sincerely, Henry B Thompson

TLS (Thompson Letterpress Books, NjP).

To Mary Allen Hulbert Peck

Dearest Friend, Lyme, Connecticut, 1 August, 1909.

It was such a pleasure, and so delightful a relief to my spirits to receive your letter,[1]–a letter which, somehow, seems to breathe a new air I have not noticed in your letters for a long time–the beginning of a new self-posses[s]ion and self-mastery which is no doubt the result of your freedom and your expected peace and rest. I hope that you will presently find it a pleasure and a means of "finding" yourself to write a good deal of what you are thinking in letters to me. At every crisis in one's life it is absolute salvation to have some sympathetic friend to whom you can think aloud without restraint or misgiving. It is more than salvation: it does more than save the spirits and give strength and serenity. It enables one to understand the crisis itself and one's own thought better, and constitutes a sort of air in which one consciously develops and frees oneself of both doubt and fear, as if growing into a new self. I have proved this for myself more than once; and I would be so proud and happy if I might render you the same service. I *will* understand and I will sympathise as keenly and entirely as your heart could wish. Will you not use me and make me *feel* my use? That is what I am for. I am happy that I was sent to you at such a time. I am glad you sent me that unspeakable clipping from Town Topics, for I am sure I felt when I read it just as you did. It is impossible to put into words the feelings that well up in one's heart when he reads slanderous, malignant, lying paragraphs like that: the anger, the sorrow, the flaming passion of the thought that here is a wrong there is no way to right, a wrong done to a lovely and honourable woman by an anonymous scoundrel![2] Ah! if one could only put one's heel on the vipers that do these things and grind them somewhere into the slime they love! But I suppose to do that would be to go in some degree down into the slime with them, and one would not like to soil even one's shoe with the contact! I can only say that I resented and grieved over it too deeply for words, because I know you, how truly fine and undeservedly unhappy, how like a noble woman worthy of every man's reverence, and how utterly unlike what these low creatures imagine every brilliant and unhappy woman to be. I believe in you because I know you: and I believe in you profoundly, to the bottom of my heart! How thankful I am that your spirit is elastic and can stand these strains. Even the fatigue you speak of, brought on by the packing, the work about the house and the trying trips to New York, are in a way a safeguard and a help: for it is physical fatigue, and part of it comes from the delightful garden. Are you being consumed by drought in Pittsfield as we are here? We have had only one rain worthy of the name in some six or more weeks. The earth is parched, the flowers wan and discouraged, the trees turning to an autumn colour, and the air pallid with dust, which covers and takes the life out of everything. There are signs of an unusually early autumn, the most noticeable of which, and the most interesting is that the swallows are gathering for their migration, quite two weeks sooner than they usually gather, sitting in innumerable companies, in quaint endless rows, on the telephone wires (where there is not current enough, I suppose, to tickle their feet), chirping away in quiet undertones of suppressed excitement. I pass under them every afternoon as I return from the golf course up on the hills by the river.

Nothing happens to us here, of course. I have not even begun the writing I am expecting to do, to keep my mind out of mischief. Yesterday afternoon Ellen and I were whisked out in an automobile, through sandy, uncomfortable roads to a friend's house some three or four miles from here, on a perch high above the Connecticut, to lunch with a lady and gentleman named Williams.[3] He is the propri[e]tor of the famous Williams soap, but an interesting man besides, and she is a charming woman to whom the ladies of Hartford look for all sorts of leadership in things that are worth while, and who acts as a sort of special providence to the school at Farmington, from which she was graduated,—the school made famous as "Miss Porters.'"[4] It was very pleasant; but we were just a field or two away from the golf course, and my heart was there all the time. If I could have decently run away, I would have done so with the shout of a boy let out of school.

A very tragical piece of news came to me yesterday. My classmate and life-long friend, Cornelius C. Cuyler, was killed yesterday, in France, in an automobile accident. He was a member of our Board of Trustees and a very important man in financial circles in New York. It came as a great shock, and will further complicate the situation at Princeton. I have often talked to you of Cuyler, but I doubt if your memory will particularly single him out from the many men I have talked of in telling you about Princeton affairs. He was essentially "a good fellow" and useful and influential in a score of ways. He will be sadly missed, and some stranger will take his place. I shall probably have to make a journey or two to New York in connection with personal and college matters which his death will affect. His body will come back on a steamer which sails on the fourth and reaches New York (I suppose) about the tenth or eleventh.

The circle here changes, I am sorry to say, almost from day to day,—and, as ill luck will have it, it is generally the most interesting members of it who go away; so that just at present I am forced to talk more than I like with a sentimental gentleman from Boston,—one of the writers for the TRANSCRIPT,—who puts as little sound sense into his discussion of public matters as possible. Fortunately he is easily silenced, not seeming to relish controversy, and readily discovers where we cannot hit it off with each other. He is an amateur painter, besides, and is generally off somewhere covering little canvasses with paint. What bores these harmless people can be sometimes: the dangerous fellows are much more companionable!

Please forgive this stupid letter,—a poor return for yours. Read into it what you know I would say if I knew how, and anything else that it would please your humour to have it contain. For it is meant wholly as a message of affection, and for your pleasure. All join me in warmest messages; and I am, as always,

Your devoted friend, Woodrow Wilson

WWTLS (WP, DLC).

[1] It is missing.

[2] The clipping is missing, but it was the following item from the New York *Town Topics, The Journal of Society*, LXI (June 24, 1909), 6:

"Pittsfield, Mass., which always has some amusing *sub-rosa* affair underway, is now devouring with great glee the contents of little notes which Thomas D. Peck has been sending out to tradespeople, carrying the information that he has made Mrs. Peck a liberal allowance and that hereafter she will pay all bills which she may contract. Simultaneously with this titbit for consumption at the lady's inn is a newspaper despatch from Warrenton, N. C., to the effect that Mr. Peck has offered to establish there a wonderful cotton mill under certain conditions. It doesn't state in the despatch that Mr. Peck is going to live there, but that is the Pittsfield supposition, as it is generally conceded that Tom Peck is a much happier man down in Virginia or Carolina shooting wild turkey than in Pittsfield, where his business affairs have not been any too prosperous, and since the rush marriage of one of his daughters in Woonsocket, R. I., and the rather tame wedding of the other at the Homestead, he has little interest in Pittsfield. Mrs. Tom's latest fad is said to be designing new monograms for her cigarettes. Her cable bill to Bermuda must be quite an item, but then she has so many friends and interests there that it may not be unusual."

[3] George Goodwin Williams and Jeannette Hunt Williams. Williams was President of the J. B. Williams Co. of Glastonbury, Conn., manufacturers of shaving soaps and other men's toiletries.

[4] Mrs. Williams had attended Miss Porter's School, founded in 1843, from 1880 to 1884.

An Essay

[Aug. 3, 1909]

THE MAN BEHIND THE TRUST

The corporation has become an indispensable instrument of modern business. We could as little afford to dispense with it as we could afford to dispense with machinery. All commerce and industry would drop back to a very primitive level if we were to put them again in the hands of individual enterprise.

But the corporation is an instrument, a powerful instrument, as well as a very useful one, and is as powerful for evil as for good when misdirected. Moreover, its organization is necessarily so complicated and elaborate that when it is misdirected it is extremely difficult to tell with certainty who misdirected it. Because it is so powerful and can so easily crush the individual and overwhelm alike opposition and all competition, it ought to be held sternly responsible to the law for its actions; and yet it is not a person and cannot be punished. The whole difficulty of the law in controlling it lies in the fact that its organization conceals its parts, and it is very hard indeed to determine whom it is fair to hold responsible for its transgressions.

I heard an excellent illustration used the other day by Mr. Samuel Crothers,[1] which, unlike most illustrations, thoroughly illustrates the whole question. There is, he said, a very strong and just indignation felt by all thoughtful persons against those who take "joy" rides in our powerful modern vehicles, the automobiles; but our indignation is apt to take a very childish form and vent itself upon the machines themselves, denouncing them as enemies of human life and all rational pleasure. Two things are worth observing: first, that automobiles, including the great touring cars which are most often misused, have become not only useful but indispensable; and second, that those who take "joy" rides in them are almost never their owners but generally chauffeurs or other irresponsible persons who are making use of them without their owners' consent or approval. Our anger and the penalty of the law should descend upon these persons: they are our enemies and we should deal with them as such,—as mere outlaws, to whom the law shows her sternest, most pitiless face. The public, in every just conception of the matter, are the owners of corporations, those great machines which can crush men's hearts out and snatch their living from them; those who misuse them, who take "joy" rides in them, to satisfy their own greed for wealth and power, are our enemies, are public enemies, nothing less, and should be dealt with accordingly. We should not seek to check and control them by destroying or injuring the dangerous but indispensable instruments they use but by dealing with them personally and directly as with those who have borrowed the machines for their own unlawful use and run amuck.

The illustration seems to me to illustrate the matter perfectly. It only clears the thought: it does not remove the practical difficulties that surround the successful handling of it. It shows that we are handling it in the wrong way now; but it does not point out the way in which it should be handled.

That we are using the wrong means now in seeking to control corporations and those still greater organizations which we call "trusts" and which are but mightier corporations, is to my mind very clear. We are trying three several ways: (1) fines imposed upon the corporations for illegal actions; (2) its destruction by the withdrawal of its charter; (3) the actual oversight of its operations by government bureau or by commissions such as the "public service commissions" which several states have set up and clothed with extraordinary powers. Fines fine the stockholders, who have not only not sanctioned the illegal act sought to be punished but have actually had no knowledge of it. Fines, moreover, are all taken out of the business and put into the public treasury sums of money which, if very much multiplied, the state would have no use for, and which are very much needed in the transactions of the business from which they are withdrawn. To deprive a corporation of its charter is to destroy the machine for which we have legitimate uses. To control through commissions is to bring the government sooner or later into the actual direction of the business of the country,—a course to which no man who knows anything of the history of government and liberty should permit himself for a moment to consent. All these are methods of hampering or smashing the machine itself. Control by commissions looks very like erecting the government itself into an all-dominating machine.

The immemorial processes of the law are the only effectual ones and the only just ones: they seek out the responsible individual and make him answer personally for the illegal act, to the extent, if necessary, of his life and entire property. A few really responsible individuals made to feel the full weight of the law for the misdirection and unlawful practices of modern corporations would moralize business as nothing else would or ever can. "Corporations," as was long ago said, "have no bodies to be kicked and no souls to be damned"; they are mere instruments; it were silly to try to kick or to damn them; but the modern person, particularly the modern "successful" man, is as unwilling to go to jail as any of his predecessors and can be made very thoughtful of his responsibilities by the liability to lose his liberty and with it all that he has gained and got power by.

This, then, is the problem of the modern reformer: to drive the individual from his cover in the maze of modern business and make him answer the ancient responsibilities of the law. It is a very difficult thing to do: the lawyers and law-makers of our day will have to make a much more thorough and searching and discriminating analysis of modern business than they have yet made before it can be done. But it can be done. The law can oblige corporations to disclose their organization in such a way as to enable those who enforce legal responsibilities to put their hands in every instance upon the man by whom the illegal act was authorized or ordered. If they put dummies in such places of responsibility and seek in that way to shield the real culprits, they will do so but once. When one or two dummies have gone to the penitentiary, no more dummies will be obtainable. The public will find the process worth the price of the punishment of one or two innocent men. The real men will immediately have to disclose themselves. It is by this means we shall discover and moralize the men behind the corporations.

3 Aug. '09 (Lyme)

Transcript of WWsh (WP, DLC).

1 The Rev. Dr. Samuel McChord Crothers, Princeton 1874, pastor of the First Church, Unitarian, of Cambridge, Mass. and author of numerous literary works. Crothers had received an honorary Litt.D. at the Princeton commencement on June 15, 1909, and spoke briefly at the alumni luncheon. Wilson might also have heard Crothers speaking either formally or in conversation during his (Wilson's) visit to Boston and Cambridge from June 29 to July 1, although Crothers is not listed as a participant in the accounts of the Harvard commencement activities at that time.

From Richard Ludwig Enno Littmann

Dear Mr. President: Oldenburg, Gr. [Germany] August 4th, 09.

I have no words to express my gratitude towards you on one side, and my regret on the other side. You know how much I have become attached to Princeton and how dearly I am keeping her in mind all the time. When I received your good letter my wish to return to you and to take up my interrupted work with you again grew stronger than ever. And I did not hesitate to express this feeling to my friends at Strassburg. But when it was known that I had received your call the faculty decided at once to delegate the Dean and two of the older members to try to keep me back. And several of the oldest members of the faculty urged me privately to stay. I did what I had told Professor Butler that I would do in case I should receive from Princeton: I asked that the Government should found an Oriental Seminary in the University, knowing that a Seminar had been refused twice to other Professors within the last year, and I asked also that my salary should be raised at least some four hundred dollars, knowing that the finances of the Government are not in a very good condition. For a while it seemed that the Curator, i.e. the Imperial Commissioner for the University,[1] was not willing to take these demands into consideration at all. Then he told me that he was going to request the Governor of Alsace-Lorraine[2] to grant these demands. There the matter rests now.

I would not have written you about this, had I not seen a notice in the newspapers to the effect that I had received and declined a call from Princeton. I fear this notice may have reached you before this letter. But I wish to say that I have no idea of how this notice came into the hands of the reporters: it must have been a secretary who told what he ought not to have told.

I am exceedingly sorry that a matter of sentiment has partly turned into a matter of business. I can not bear the idea that I might hurt the feelings of my friends at Princeton who have honoured me with their confidence and friendship. On the other hand, I know that it would almost break the heart of Professor Noeldeke,[3] my most highly esteemed predecessor, teacher and friend, if I should really leave Strassburg. However, there is a slight possibility that I shall do so after all. I shall, of course, let you know at once, when I hear from the Governor. With the assurance of my lasting gratitude,

I remain yours very faithfully Enno Littmann

ALS (WP, DLC).

[1] Adolf Stadler.

[2] The *Statthalter*, or Governor General, of Alsace-Lorraine at this time was Karl, Graf von Wedel.

[3] Theodor Nöldeke, Professor at Strassburg, 1872-1906. He was a philologist specializing in Semitic languages and the history of Islam.

From Henry Dallas Thompson

near Plymouth [England]. Dampfer Kurfürst[1]

Dear Wilson: 5 August, 1909

As a citizen of the State of New Jersey I sincerely hope that you will consent to be the Democratic candidate for Governor, if the opportunity offers, next year. I believe you can take the nomination without being bound to either of the rather unpopular factions in the northern part of the State,[2] while neither of those factions will feel that the other can control you, and therefore in secret oppose you. I believe that no other good candidate from your party could stand so well with all factions (except the so called labor vote, which I suppose would be against you)

I am

Very faithfully yours Henry Dallas Thompson

ALS (WP, DLC).

[1] *Kurfürst* was a vessel of the Norddeutscher Lloyd shipping line of Bremen.

[2] That is, the Democratic party political machine in Essex County, headed by James Smith, Jr., and the one in Hudson County, led by Robert Davis.

A Statement

[*c. August 7, 1909*]

METHOD OF UNDERGRADUATE INSTRUCTION

Instruction in Physics, Chemistry, Biology, and Astronomy is given, of course, not only by means of lectures and formal tests upon text books, but also by means of practical experimental work in the several laboratories and in the working observatory. In Mathematics, besides the stated class exercises and occasional lectures, certain hours are set apart each week during which the instructors of the Department are accessible for informal consultation by all students who wish further explanation or discussion of such portions of their mathematical work as most interest them or give them the most difficulty. In Geology, similarly, there is field work and constant informal resort to the geological museum, added to frequent conferences with the instructors in the several courses on the reading assigned.

Instruction in what may be called the reading Departments, Philosophy, History and Politics, Art and Archaeology, and the languages is given chiefly by means of informal conferences on the reading assigned. A "course" consists, not of the lectures given in connection with it or of the study of a particular text book relied on by the lecturer, but of a prescribed body of reading to which the lectures given are supplementary. Each student is made responsible to a particular preceptor for his reading, and reports to him once a week in each course for conference. He reports to the same preceptor throughout for all his reading in the several courses of the special Department in which he has chosen to concentrate his work, and for his reading in the courses outside his special Department to the lecturer in that course or to the instructor who has charge of its formal conduct in the class-room.

At each conference the preceptor usually meets from three to six of the men assigned him. The methods of conference differ, of course, with the character of the subject, but are always informal, being intended, not as a quiz or recitation or drill, not as a method of coaching, but, so far as the preceptor is concerned, as a means of finding out how thoroughly and intelligently the student has done his reading, and, so far as the student is concerned, as a means of stimulation and enlightenment with regard to the study in hand. His work is explained to him where it is obscure, and its scope and implications are extended out of the wider reading and maturer scholarship of the preceptor, whose real function it is to serve him as "guide, philosopher, and friend." Study centres upon these conferences, as in the scientific Departments it centres upon the laboratory. They are meant to supply to study the life which it cannot have in the formal exercises of the class-room and to bring the students into an intimate contact with their teachers which is hardly possible in other methods of instruction.

One object of this method of instruction is to lay the principal emphasis of work upon the constant reading required, upon what is ordinarily called "term work," rather than upon preparation for occasional examinations. In reckoning the "standing" of a student more weight is given to his work with his preceptor than to his performance in examination. Each preceptor is expected to report in Departmental meeting upon the work of the men assigned him, and it is only upon his recommendation that they are admitted to examination. He may recommend the exclusion from examination of any of his pupils who seem to him to have neglected their work or to have done it too indifferently. He makes no formal report to any university officer of their absences from his appointed conferences or of their attendance, but forms his own estimate of their thoroughness and faithfulness and gives his judgment upon the basis of an intimate observation.

All members of the Faculty do "preceptorial" work: those who lecture or conduct the formal class exercises acting as preceptors in the reading connected with their own courses for those students who elect those courses but not the entire work of the Department within which they lie, and those who bear the special title of preceptor taking oversight of all the departmental reading of those students who elect the whole work of their Departments.

Printed in *Catalogue of Princeton University . . . 1909-1910* (Princeton, 1909), pp. 111-13.

To Mary Allen Hulbert Peck

My dearest Fr[i]end, Lyme, Connecticut, 8 August, 1909.

Everything goes with me as usual, except that I have actually put spurs into the old nag, my mind, this week and done a piece of work,—a piece of writing for which I know no proper style. I had to write a page or two for the University Catalogue on "The Method of Undergraduate Instruction." Our famous preceptorial system had never been mentioned in that se[n]tentious annual. What is the proper literary style for a University Catalogue,—what mixture of businesslike explicitness and well chosen phrase, with a flavour here and there, as if somebody in particular, and not the unabridged dictionary, had written it? I admit I do not know. I had never written in catalogue style before, and felt very ill at ease, like a literary person in stays. But what I wrote was, I flatter myself, at least intelligible.

I am to be away from this delectable place where no[thing]

happens, for a[t] least a part of this week. Poor Cuyler's body is expected to reach New York (in charge of that hard featured, worldly wife of his[1] whom I cannot imagine entertaining the real sentiment of love) on Thursday, and will be buried the next day in Princeton, the place he more truly loved than any other in the world. I must run down to Princeton on Thursday afternoon to get the proper clothes to wear (I am to be one of the pall bearers) and be back in New York for the services, which will be held at the Brick Church on Fifth Avenue at two on Friday. Immediately after the services the body will be taken by special train to Princeton for burial. I expect to spend Thursday and Friday evenings in New York, leaving for Boston at midnight on Friday night for a conference with the University architect which has turned out to be desirable. It is hard to analyze my feelings about Cuyler. He has not been a true friend the last two years. He has done and said many disloyal things. And yet I have a stubborn way of loving my friends which has brought me through all these heart-breaking things with very little change. I had a deep, unreasoning affection for him: it would be hard to say why; and, now that he is gone, I feel very tender things stealing into my heart about this friend of my boyhood,—always full of glaring faults, never taken by any of us for anything but what he was, and yet endeared to everybody by many generous qualities and many engaging traits,—a bundle of contradictions, like all the rest of us. It's a queer world, and there are not many unimpeachable people in it. We love generally without justification and there are only two or three whom we admire with entire reverence and perfect faith. All of this sounds very solemn and perhaps a little pessimistic; but I do not mean it pessimistically. I retain a deep faith in people notwithstanding the savage blows that faith has received. But I dare say I must carry this sadness with me all the week, for I must be reminded at every turn of the anxieties and uncertainties that surround me. I have come to feel that the finest word in the language is loyalty and the finest guide in life is certainly courage. We must get our deepest satisfactions and all our strength out of that and make life gallant and true *for us*, whatever happens. To lose heart or loyalty for a moment is to prove recreant and fall irrevocably unhappy.

It has not lightened my spirits that that tariff of abominations has been passed,[2] and just now there is in this very house a man

[1] May (or Mary) Townsend Nicoll Lord, whom Cuyler had married on March 3, 1906.

[2] The Payne-Aldrich Tariff Act was signed by President Taft on August 5, 1909. See G. B. M. Harvey to WW, May 10, 1909, n. 1.

who has been largely responsible for lobbying into it one of the worst abominations of all, the representative of the hosiery men,[3] who have arranged to have us pay a little more than usual to them for the inferior stuff they turn out because the Germans make much better stockings and sell them cheap. I am trying to avoid conversation with him altogether, because I know that I will flare up and say something very plain if I do talk with him. He is full of his triumph at Washington and yet uneasy in his conscience and eager to prove to everybody that he did what was perfectly right. He comes here occasionally because he is an amateur artist and spends the intervals between lobbyings making sketches. The love of nature does not seem to be a very moralizing influence.

Do you recognize what these letters are? They are merely a poor attempt on my part to have the pleasure of an imaginary conversation with you. I like to pour out my thoughts just as they come into my head, as I do when I am with you, and try to imagine what you would say at each pause. What I say does not come as spontaneously as if I had the stimulation of your presence and it were real give and take, and I am a very poor hand at constructing your side of the conversation. You would say much better things,–much more delightful and full of unexpected turns and stray fancies,–than I can make up for you. But there is a sense of companionship, nevertheless, and I love to try. It is thus that we keep vividly conscious of one another throughout long separations and keep alive the delightful impression of travelling the road of life together, not losing sight of one another or straying from the ways the other's mind and spirit pass along.

I am taking in the Springfield Republican this summer, and derive a strange pleasure from reading the letters from Pittsfield. They contain nothing but notes of what the town council is doing, of the trials in the police courts, of the criticisms of the trolley service, of the boat parades on Pontoosac lake and the moonlight bal[l]oon ascensions, with now and then a marriage notice and a personal note; but they give me some glimpse of the town and of what is going on around you, none the less. I knew when you were forbidden to use your garden hose because of the scarcity of water (and felt very sorry), and learned something of the arbitrary temper of your chief of police when he forbade the women to make their speeches for "votes for Women." It's an odd, subtle thing how after a while definite impressions of a place

[3] It has proved impossible to identify this lobbyist among the several spokesmen for the American hosiery interests before the Senate Finance Committee.

are built up out of these trivial items, if one has ever seen it and has any imagination.

I am very well; work just enough for my morale; and play just enough golf and have just enough idle talk with the men in the house to keep the feeling alive in me that I am still a young man. My title during the summer is Colonel Wilson. All join me in warmest messages and I am happy to be

Your devoted friend, Woodrow Wilson

WWTLS (WP, DLC).

To Ralph Adams Cram

My dear Mr. Cram, Lyme, Connecticut, 8 August, 1909.

I will come to Nahant, with pleasure. I am to be in Princeton and New York on Thursday and Friday of this week (Mr. Cuyler is to be buried in the dear old village on Friday, after funeral services at the Brick Church in New York at two o'clock that afternoon), and it is my present plan to take the Friday midnight train out of New York for Boston. I shall try to take the 9.30 boat for Nahant. If I miss it, I will telephone you. I shall look forward to the day with keen pleasure. Saturday evening I must go on to Hartford. Thank you very much for your letter[1] and its detailed information about the boats and trains.

Cuyler's death was indeed one of the profoundest shocks I ever received. He and I were classmates and had been life-long friends. My affection for him was peculiarly intimate and deep. Your letter expresses the common verdict about him.

Mrs. Wilson joins me in warmest regards to Mrs. Cram[2] and yourself.

Cordially and faithfully Yours, Woodrow Wilson

TCL (RSB Coll., DLC).

[1] It is missing.

[2] Elizabeth Carrington Read Cram.

From Edwin William Pahlow

Marblehead Neck, Mass.

Dear President Wilson: August 14/09.

Professor Bourne of Western Reserve University[1] has asked me to consider an opening there for the coming year. Before doing so, however, I would like to know whether my accepting this offer would inconvenience you, and whether or not you have determined upon my retention at Princeton during the year 1910-1911.

I feel in a rather unsettled position in regard to this, because, in the first place, I drew from you an appointment as preceptor which you would not have made of your own free will, and because I realize now that, in my great but awkward zeal to serve you and the University, I ventured into fields beyond my province.

If it is possible for you to inform me on this point, I will appreciate it greatly.[2]

I hope you are having a restful summer.

Yours respectfully, Edwin W. Pahlow.

ALS (WWP, UA, NjP).

[1] Henry Eldridge Bourne, Professor of History at the College for Women, Western Reserve University.

[2] See E. W. Pahlow to WW, Aug. 22, 1909.

An Article

[*Aug. 18, 1909*]

WHAT IS A COLLEGE FOR?

It may seem singular that at this time of day and in this confident century it should be necessary to ask, What is a college for? But it has become necessary. I take it for granted that there are few real doubts concerning the question in the minds of those who look at the college from the inside and have made themselves responsible for the realization of its serious purposes; but there are many divergent opinions held concerning it by those who, standing on the outside, have pondered the uses of the college in the life of the country; and their many varieties of opinion may very well have created a confusion of counsel in the public mind.

They are, of course, entirely entitled to their independent opinions and have a right to expect that full consideration will be given what they say by those who are in fact responsible. The college is for the use of the nation, not for the satisfaction of those who administer it or for the carrying out of their private views. They may speak as experts and with a very intimate knowledge, but they also speak as servants of the country and must be challenged to give reasons for the convictions they entertain. Controversy, it may be, is not profitable in such matters, because it is so easy, in the face of opposition, to become a partisan of one's own views and exaggerate them in seeking to vindicate and establish them; but an explicit profession of faith cannot fail to clear the air, and to assist the thinking both of those who are responsible and of those who only look on and seek to make serviceable comment.

Why, then, should a man send his son to college when school is finished; or why should he advise any youngster in whom he is interested to go to college? What does he expect and desire him to get there? The question might be carried back and asked with regard to the higher schools also to which lads resort for preparation for college. What are they meant to get there? But it will suffice to centre the question on the college. What should a lad go to college for,—for work, for the realization of a definite aim, for discipline and a severe training of his faculties, or for relaxation, for the release and exercise of his social powers, for the broadening effects of life in a sort of miniature world in which study is only one among many interests? That is not the only alternative suggested by recent discussions. They also suggest a sharp alternative with regard to the character of the study the college student should undertake. Should he seek at college a general discipline of his faculties, a general awakening to the issues and interests of the modern world, or should he, rather, seek specially and definitely to prepare himself for the work he expects to do after he leaves college, for his support and advancement in the world? The two alternatives are very different. The one asks whether the lad does not get as good a preparation for modern life by being manager of a foot-ball team with a complicated programme of intercollegiate games and trips away from home as by becoming proficient in mathematics or in history and mastering the abstract tasks of the mind; the other asks whether he is not better prepared by being given the special skill and training of a particular calling or profession, an immediate drill in the work he is to do after he graduates, than by being made a master of his own mind in the more general fields of knowledge to which his subsequent calling will be related, in all probability, only as every undertaking is related to the general thought and experience of the world.

"Learning" is not involved. No one has ever dreamed of imparting learning to undergraduates. It cannot be done in four years. To become a man of learning is the enterprise of a lifetime. The issue does not rise to that high ground. The question is merely this: do we wish college to be, first of all and chiefly, a place of mental discipline or only a school of general experience; and, if we wish it to be a place of mental discipline, of what sort do we wish the discipline to be,—a general awakening and release of the faculties, or a preliminary initiation into the drill of a particular vocation?

These are questions which go to the root of the matter. They admit of no simple and confident answer. Their roots spring out of life and all its varied sources. To reply to them, therefore, involves an examination of modern life and an assessment of the part an educated man ought to play in it,—an analysis which no man may attempt with perfect self-confidence. The life of our day is a very complex thing which no man can pretend to comprehend in its entirety.

But some things are obvious enough concerning it. There is an uncommon challenge to effort in the modern world, and all the achievements to which it challenges are uncommonly difficult. Individuals are yoked together in modern enterprise by a harness which is both new and inelastic. The man who understands only some single process, some single piece of work which he has been set to do, will never do anything else, and is apt to be deprived at almost any moment of the opportunity to do even that, because processes change, industry undergoes instant revolutions. New inventions, fresh discoveries, alterations in the markets of the world throw accustomed methods and the men who are accustomed to them out of date and use without pause or pity. The man of special skill may be changed into an unskilled laborer overnight. Moreover, it is a day in which no enterprise stands alone or independent, but is related to every other and feels changes in all parts of the globe. The men with mere skill, with mere technical knowledge, will be mere servants perpetually, and may at any time become useless servants, their skill gone out of use and fashion. The particular thing they do may become unnecessary or may be so changed that they cannot comprehend or adjust themselves to the change.

These, then, are the things the modern world must have in its trained men, and I do not know where else it is to get them if not from its educated men and the occasional self-developed genius of an exceptional man here and there. It needs, at the top, not a few, but many men with the power to organize and guide. The college is meant to stimulate in a considerable number of men what would be stimulated in only a few if we were to depend entirely upon nature and circumstance. Below the ranks of generalship and guidance, the modern world needs for the execution of its varied and difficult business a very much larger number of men with great capacity and readiness for the rapid and concentrated exertion of a whole series of faculties: planning faculties as well as technical skill, the ability to handle men as well as to handle tools and correct processes, faculties of adjustment and adaptation as well as of precise execution,—men of resource as well as knowledge. These are the athletes, the athletes of faculty, of which our generation most stands in need. All through its ranks, besides, it needs masterful men who can acquire a working knowledge of many things readily, quickly, intelligently, and with exactness,—things they had not foreseen or prepared themselves for beforehand, and for which they could not have prepared themselves beforehand. Quick apprehension, quick comprehension, quick action are what modern life puts a premium upon,—a readiness to turn this way or that and not lose force or momentum.

To me, then, the question seems to be, Shall the lad who goes to college go there for the purpose of getting ready to be a servant merely, a servant who will be nobody and who may become useless, or shall he go there for the purpose of getting ready to be a master adventurer in the field of modern opportunity?

We must expect hewers of wood and drawers of water to come out of the colleges in their due proportion, of course, but I take it for granted that even the least gifted of them did not go to college with the ambition to be nothing more. And yet one has hardly made the statement before he begins to doubt whether he can safely take anything for granted. Part of the very question we are discussing is the ambition with which young men now go to college. It is a day when a college course has become fashionable,—but not for the purpose of learning, not for the purpose of obtaining a definite preparation for anything,—no such purpose could become *fashionable*. The clientage of our colleges has greatly changed since the time when most of the young men who resorted to them did so with a view to entering one or other of the learned professions. Young men who expect to go into business of one kind or another now outnumber among our undergraduates those who expect to make some sort of learning the basis of their work throughout life; and I dare say that they generally go to college without having made any very definite analysis of their aim and purpose in going. Their parents seem to have made as little.

The enormous increase of wealth in the country in recent years, too, has had its effect upon the colleges,—not in the way that might have been expected,—not, as yet, by changing the standard of life to any very noticeable extent or introducing luxury and extravagance and vicious indulgence. College undergraduates have usually the freshness of youth about them, out of which there springs a wholesome simplicity, and it is not easy to spoil them or to destroy their natural democracy. They make a life of their own and insist upon the maintenance of its standards. But the increase of wealth has brought into the colleges, in rapidly augmenting numbers, the sons of very rich men, and lads who expect to inherit wealth are not as easily stimulated to effort, are not as apt to form definite and serious purposes, as those who know that they must whet their wits for the struggle of life.

There was a time when the mere possession of wealth conferred distinction; and when wealth confers distinction it is apt to breed a sort of consciousness of opportunity and responsibility in those who possess it and incline them to seek serious achievement. But that time is long past in America. Wealth is common. And, by the same token, the position of the lad who is to inherit it is a peculiarly disadvantageous one, if the standard of success is to rise above mediocrity. Wealth removes the necessity for effort, and yet effort is necessary for the attainment of distinction, and very great effort at that, in the modern world, as I have already pointed out. It would look as if the ordinary lad with expectations were foredoomed to obscurity; for the ordinary lad will not exert himself unless he must.

We live in an age in which no achievement is to be cheaply had. All the cheap achievements, open to amateurs, are exhausted and have become commonplace. Adventure, for example, is no longer extraordinary: which is another way of saying that it is commonplace. Any amateur may seek and find adventure; but it has been sought and had in all its kinds. Restless men, idle men, chivalrous men, men drawn on by mere curiosity and men drawn on by love of the knowledge that lies outside books and laboratories, have crossed the whole face of the habitable globe in search of it, ferreting it out in corners even, following its bypaths and beating its coverts, and it is nowhere any longer a novelty or distinction to have discovered and enjoyed it. The whole round of pleasure, moreover, has been exhausted time out of mind, and most of it discredited as not pleasure after all, but just an expensive counterfeit; so that many rich people have been driven to devote themselves to expense regardless of pleasure. No new pleasure, I am credibly informed, has been invented within the memory of man. For every genuine thrill and satisfaction, therefore, we are apparently, in this sophisticated world, shut in to work, to modifying and quickening the life of the age. If college be one of the highways to life and achievement, it must be one of the highways to work.

The man who comes out of college into the modern world must, therefore, have got out of it, if he has not wasted four vitally significant years of his life, a quickening and a training which will make him in some degree a master among men. If he has got less, college was not worth his while. To have made it worth his while he must have got such a preparation and development of his faculties as will give him movement as well as mere mechanical efficiency in affairs complex, difficult, and subject to change. The word efficiency has in our day the power to think at the centre of it, the power of independent movement and initiative. It is not merely the suitability to be a good tool, it is the power to wield tools, and among the tools are men and circumstances and changing processes of industry, changing phases of life itself. There should be technical schools a great many and the technical schools of America should be among the best in the world. The men they train are indispensable. The modern world needs more tools than managers, more workmen than master workmen. But even the technical schools must have some thought of mastery and adaptability in their processes; and the colleges, which are not technical schools, should think of that chiefly. We must distinguish what the college is for, without disparaging any other school, of any other kind. It is for the training of the men who are to rise above the ranks.

That is what a college is for. What it does, what it requires of its undergraduates and of its teachers, should be adjusted to that conception. The very statement of the object, which must be plain to all who make any distinction at all between a college and a technical school, makes it evident that the college must subject its men to a general intellectual training which will be narrowed to no one point of view, to no one vocation or calling. It must release and quicken as many faculties of the mind as possible,–and not only release and quicken them but discipline and strengthen them also by putting them to the test of systematic labor. Work, definite, exacting, long continued, but not narrow or petty or merely rule of thumb, must be its law of life for those who would pass its gates and go out with its authentication.

By a general training I do not mean vague spaces of study, miscellaneous fields of reading, a varied smattering of a score of subjects and the thorough digestion of none. The field of modern knowledge is extremely wide and varied. After a certain number of really fundamental subjects have been studied in the schools, the college undergraduate must be offered a choice of the route he will travel in carrying his studies further. He cannot be shown the whole body of knowledge within a single curriculum. There is no longer any single highway of learning. The roads that traverse its vast and crowded spaces are not even parallel, and four years is too short a time in which to search them all out. But there is a general programme still possible by which the college student can be made acquainted with the field of modern learning by sample, by which he can be subjected to the several kinds of mental discipline,–in philosophy, in some one of the great sciences, in some one of the great languages which carry the thought of the world, in history and in politics, which is its framework,–which will give him valid naturalization as a citizen of the world of thought, the world of educated men,–and no smatterer merely, able barely to spell its constitution out, but a man who has really comprehended and made use of its chief intellectual processes and is ready to lay his mind alongside its tasks with some confidence that he can master them and can understand why and how they are to be performed. This is the general training which should be characteristic of the college, and the men who undergo it ought to be made to undergo it with deep seriousness and diligent labor; not as soft amateurs with whom learning and its thorough tasks are side interests merely, but as those who approach life with the intention of becoming professionals in its fields of achievement.

Just now, where this is attempted, it seems to fail of success. College men, it is said, and often said with truth, come out undisciplined, untrained, unfitted for what they are about to undertake. It is argued therefore, that what they should have been given was special vocational instruction; that if they had had that they would have been interested in their work while they were undergraduates, would have taken it more seriously, and would have come out of college ready to be used, as they now cannot be. No doubt that is to be preferred to a scattered and aimless choice of studies, and no doubt what the colleges offer is miscellaneous and aimless enough in many cases; but, at best, these are very hopeful assumptions on the part of those who would convert our colleges into vocational schools. They are generally put forward by persons who do not know how college life and work are now organized and conducted. I do not wonder that they know little of what has happened. The whole thing is of very recent development, at any rate in its elaborate complexity. It is a growth, as we now see it, of the last ten or twelve years; and even recent graduates of our colleges would rub their eyes incredulously to see it if they were to stand again on the inside and look at it intimately.

What has happened is, in general terms, this: that the work of the college, the work of its classrooms and laboratories, has become the merely formal and compulsory side of its life, and that a score of other things, lumped under the term "undergraduate activities," have become the vital, spontaneous, absorbing realities for nine out of every ten men who go to college. These activities embrace social, athletic, dramatic, musical, literary, religious, and professional organizations of every kind, besides many organized for mere amusement and some, of great use and dignity, which seek to exercise a general oversight and sensible direction of college ways and customs. Those which consume the most time, are, of course, the athletic, dramatic, and musical clubs, whose practices rehearsals, games, and performances fill the term time and the brief vacations alike. But it is the social organizations into which the thought, the energy, the initiative, the enthusiasm of the largest number of men go, and go in lavish measure.

The chief of these social organizations are residential families, —fraternities, clubs, groups of house-mates of one kind or another,—in which, naturally enough, all the undergraduate interests, all the undergraduate activities of the college have their vital centre. The natural history of their origin and development is very interesting. They grew up very normally. They were necessary because of what the college did not do.

Every college in America, at any rate every college outside a city, has tried to provide living rooms for its undergraduates, dormitories in which they can live and sleep and do their work outside the classroom and the laboratory. Very few colleges whose numbers have grown rapidly have been able to supply dormitories enough for all their students, and some have deliberately abandoned the attempt, but in many of them a very considerable proportion of the undergraduates live on the campus, in college buildings. It is a very wholesome thing that they should live thus under the direct influence of the daily life of such a place and, at least in legal theory, under the authority of the university of which the college forms a principal part. But the connection between the dormitory life and the real life of the university, its intellectual tasks and disciplines, its outlook upon the greater world of thought and action which lies beyond, far beyond, the boundaries of campus and classroom, is very meagre and shadowy indeed. It is hardly more than atmospheric, and the atmosphere is very attenuated, perceptible only by the most sensitive.

Formerly, in more primitive, and I must say less desirable, days than these in which we have learned the full vigor of freedom, college tutors and proctors lived in the dormitories and exercised a precarious authority. The men were looked after in their rooms and made to keep hours and observe rules. But those days are happily gone by. The system failed of its object. The lads were mischievous and recalcitrant, those placed in authority over them generally young and unwise; and the rules were odious to those whom they were meant to restrain. There was the atmosphere of the boarding-school about the buildings, and of a boarding-school whose pupils had outgrown it. Life in college dormitories is much pleasanter now and much more orderly, because it is free and governed only by college opinion, which is a real, not a nominal, master. The men come and go as they please and have little consciousness of any connection with authority or with the governing influences of the university in their rooms, except that the university is their landlord and makes rules such as a landlord may make.

Formerly, in more primitive and less pleasant days, the college provided a refectory or "commons" where all undergraduates had their meals, a noisy family. It was part of the boarding-school life; and the average undergraduate had outgrown it as consciously as he had outgrown the futile discipline of the dormitory. Now nothing of the kind is attempted. Here and there, in connection with some large college which has found that the boarding-houses and restaurants of the town have been furnishing poor food at outrageous prices to those of its undergraduates who could not otherwise provide for themselves, will be found a great "commons," at which hundreds of men take their meals, amid the hurly-burly of numbers, without elegance or much comfort, but nevertheless at a well-spread table where the food is good and the prices moderate. The undergraduate may use it or not as he pleases. It is merely a great co-operative boarding-place, bearing not even a family resemblance to the antique "commons." It is one of the conveniences of the place. It has been provided by the university authorities, but it might have been provided in some other way and have been quite independent of them; and it is usually under undergraduate management.

Those who do not like the associations or the fare of such a place provide for themselves elsewhere, in clubs or otherwise,—generally in fraternity houses. At most colleges there is no such common boarding-place, and all must shift for themselves. It is this necessity in the one case and desire in the other that has created the chief complexity now observable in college life and which has been chiefly instrumental in bringing about that dissociation of undergraduate life from the deeper and more permanent influences of the university which has of recent years become so marked and so significant.

Fraternity chapters were once—and that not so very long ago

—merely groups of undergraduates who had bound themselves together by the vows of various secret societies which had spread their branches among the colleges. They had their fraternity rooms, their places of meeting; they were distinguished by well known badges and formed little coteries distinguishable enough from the general body of undergraduates, as they wished to be; but in all ordinary matters they shared the common life of the place. The daily experiences of the college life they shared with their fellows of all kinds and all connections, in an easy democracy; their contacts were the common contacts of the class-room and the laboratory not only, but also of the boarding-house table and of all the usual undergraduate resorts. Members of the same fraternity were naturally enough inclined to associate chiefly with one another, and were often, much too often, inclined, in matters of college "politics," to act as a unit and in their own interest; but they did not live separately. They did not hold aloof or constitute themselves separate families, living apart in their own houses, in privacy. Now all that is changed. Every fraternity has its own house, equipped as a complete home. The fraternity houses will often be the most interesting and the most beautiful buildings a visitor will be shown when he visits the college. In them members take all their meals, in them they spend their leisure hours and often do their reading,—for each house has its library—and in them many of the members, as many as can be accommodated, have their sleeping rooms and live, because the college has not dormitories enough to lodge them or because they prefer lodging outside the dormitories. In colleges where there are no fraternities, clubs of one sort or another take their places, build homes of their own, enjoy a similar privacy and separateness, and constitute the centre of all that is most comfortable and interesting and attractive in undergraduate life.

I am pointing out this interesting and very important development, not for the purpose of criticising it, but merely to explain its natural history and the far-reaching results it has brought about. The college having determined, wisely enough, some generation or two ago, not to be any longer a boarding-school, has resolved itself into a mere teaching machine, with the necessary lecture rooms and laboratories attached and sometimes a few dormitories, which it regards as desirable but not indispensable, and has resigned into the hands of the undergraduates themselves the whole management of their life outside the class room; and not only its management but also the setting up of all its machinery of every kind,—as much as they please,—

and the constitution of its whole environment, so that teachers and pupils are not members of one university body but constitute two bodies sharply distinguished,—and the undergraduate body the more highly organized and independent of the two. They parley with one another, but they do not live with one another, and it is much easier for the influence of the highly organized and very self-conscious undergraduate body to penetrate the faculty than it is for the influence of the faculty to permeate the undergraduates.

It was inevitable it should turn out so in the circumstances. I do not wonder that the consequences were not foreseen and that the whole development has crept upon us almost unawares. But the consequences have been very important and very far-reaching. It is easy now to see that if you leave undergraduates entirely to themselves, to organize their own lives while in college as they please,—and organize it in some way they must if thus cast adrift, —that life, and not the deeper interests of the university, will presently dominate their thoughts, their imaginations, their favorite purposes. And not only that. The work of administering this complex life, with all its organizations and independent interests, successfully absorbs the energies, the initiative, the planning and originating powers of the best men among the undergraduates. It is no small task. It would tax and absorb older men; and only the finer, more spirited, more attractive, more original and effective men are fitted for it or equal to it, where leadership goes by gifts of personality as well as by ability. The very men the teacher most desires to get hold of and to enlist in some enterprise of the mind, the very men it would most reward him to instruct and whose training would count for most in leadership outside of college, in the country at large, and for the promotion of every interest the nation has, the natural leaders and doers, are drawn off and monopolized by these necessary and engaging undergraduate undertakings. The born leaders and managers and originators are drafted off to "run the college" (it is in fact nothing less), and the classroom, the laboratory, the studious conference with instructors get only the residuum of their attention, only what can be spared of their energy—are secondary matters where they ought to come first. It is the organization that is at fault, not the persons who enter into it and are moulded by it. It cannot turn out otherwise in the circumstances. The side shows are so numerous, so diverting,—so important, if you will—that they have swallowed up the circus, and those who perform in the main tent must often whistle for their audiences, discouraged and humiliated.

Such is college life nowadays, and such its relation to college work and the all-important intellectual interests which the colleges are endowed and maintained to foster. I need not stop to argue that the main purposes of education cannot be successfully realized under such conditions. I need not stop to urge that the college was not and can never be intended for the uses it is now being put to. A young man can learn to become the manager of a foot-ball team or of a residential club, the leader of an orchestra or a glee club, the star of amateur theatricals, an oarsman or a chess player without putting himself to the trouble or his parents to the expense of four years at a college. These are innocent enough things for him to do and to learn, though hardly very important in the long run; they may, for all I know, make for efficiency in some of the simpler kinds of business; and no wise man who knows college lads would propose to shut them off from them or wish to discourage their interest in them. All work and no play makes Jack a dull boy, not only, but may make him a vicious boy as well. Amusement, athletic games, the zest of contest and competition, the challenge there is in most college activities to the instinct of initiative and the gifts of leadership and achievement,—all these are wholesome means of stimulation, which keep young men from going stale and turning to things that demoralize. But they should not assume the front of the stage where more serious and lasting interests are to be served. Men cannot be prepared by them for modern life.

The college is meant for a severer, more definite discipline than this: a discipline which will fit men for the contests and achievements of an age whose every task is conditioned upon some intelligent and effective use of the mind, upon some substantial knowledge, some special insight, some trained capacity, some penetration which comes from study, not from natural readiness or mere practical experience.

The side shows need not be abolished. They need not be cast out or even discredited. But they must be subordinated. They must be put in their natural place as diversions, and ousted from their present dignity and pre-eminence as occupations.

And this can be done without making of the college again a boarding-school. The characteristic of the boarding-school is that its pupils are in all things in tutelage, are under masters at every turn of their life, must do as they are bidden, not in the performance of their set tasks only, but also in all their comings and goings. It is this characteristic that made it impossible and undesirable to continue the life of the boarding-school into the college, where it is necessary that the pupil should begin to show his manhood and make his own career. No one who knows what wholesome and regulated freedom can do for young men ought ever to wish to hail them back to the days of childish discipline and restraint of which the college of our grandfathers was typical. But a new discipline is desirable, is absolutely necessary, if the college is to be recalled to its proper purpose, its bounden duty. It cannot perform its duty as it is now organized.

The fundamental thing to be accomplished in the new organization is, that, instead of being the heterogeneous congeries of petty organizations it now is, instead of being allowed to go to pieces in a score of fractions free to cast off from the whole as they please, it should be drawn together again into a single university family of which the teachers shall be as natural and as intimate members as the undergraduates. The "life" of the college should not be separated from its chief purposes and most essential objects, should not be contrasted with its duties and in rivalry with them. The two should be but two sides of one and the same thing; the association of men, young and old, for serious mental endeavor and also, in the intervals of work, for every wholesome sport and diversion. Undergraduate life should not be in rivalry and contrast with undergraduate duties: undergraduates should not be merely in attendance upon the college, but parts of it on every side of its life, very conscious and active parts. They should consciously live its whole life,–not under masters, as in school, and yet associated in some intimate daily fashion with their masters in learning: so that learning may not seem one thing and life another. The organizations whose objects lie outside study should be but parts of the whole, not set against it, but included within it.

All this can be accomplished by a comparatively simple change of organization which will make master and pupil members of the same free, self-governed family, upon natural terms of intimacy. But how it can be done is not our present interest. That is another story. It is our present purpose merely to be clear what a college is for. That, perhaps, I have now pointed out with sufficient explicitness. I have shown the incompatibility of the present social organization of our colleges with the realization of that purpose only to add emphasis to the statement of what that purpose is. Once get that clearly established in the mind of the country, and the means of realizing it will readily and quickly enough be found. The object of the college is intellectual discipline and moral enlightenment, and it is the immediate task of those who administer the colleges of the country to find the means and the organization by which that object can be attained.

Education is a process and, like all other processes, has its proper means and machinery. It does not consist in courses of study. It consists of the vital assimilation of knowledge, and the mode of life, for the college as for the individual, is nine parts of the digestion.[1]

Printed in *Scribner's Magazine*, XLVI (Nov. 1909), 570-77.

[1] There is a WWsh draft, dated Aug. 18, 1909, and an undated WWT draft of this essay in WP, DLC.

To Robert Bridges

My dear Bobby, Lyme, Connecticut, 19 August, 1909.

I am sending you the article under another cover. I sincerely hope that you will like it. It contains the full doctrine of the St. Paul's School speech, but is of course not in the form of that address and is developed in another way. I have retained the phrase about "the side shows swallowing up the circus" in order to, so to say, identify the views with those expressed in the address.

I was glad to get a glimpse of you the other day,[1] depressing as the circumstances were. I think the impressions of that sweet and solemn afternoon will remain with me permanently.

I hope that your vacation will bring you all sorts of refreshment. Good luck to you in everything!

Affectionately Yours, Woodrow Wilson

WWTLS (WC, NjP).

[1] That is, at the funeral of C. C. Cuyler on Friday, August 13, 1909, held at the Brick Presbyterian Church in New York and his burial the same day in the Princeton Cemetery.

To Robert Garrett

My dear Mr. Garrett, Lyme, Connecticut, 19 August, 1909.

Here is a serious disappointment. The enclosed letter[1] has just reached me here and I forward it to you at once.

I was careless enough to leave home without your vacation address. I am, therefore, obliged to send this to Baltimore with the request that it be forwarded to you. I regret the delay which this will cause.

Of course there is a chance still that he will come, but it seems exceedingly slim.

I hope th[a]t you are all well, and that you are having a refreshing vacation.

With warmest regard,

Cordially and faithfully Yours Woodrow Wilson

WWTLS (Selected Corr. of R. Garrett, NjP).
[1] That is, R. L. E. Littmann to WW, Aug. 4, 1909.

From Robert Bridges

My dear Tommy: New York, August 20, 1909.

Thank you very much for being so prompt with the article, "What is a College Education For?". I cannot exaggerate the amount of pleasure that it gave me, not only for the opinions expressed but for what I always expect in your writing, the splendidly effective form in which it is put. The article is exactly suited to put the whole question in the proper way before the intelligent public who have, I fear, occasionally gathered wrong impressions from the fragmentary reports. The temper of it is excellent, and the whole manner of it is persuasive. I am sure it will do the cause that is nearest your heart a great deal of good.

Selfishly, of course, we are glad that we can be the vehicle for printing it. Mr. Burlingame[1] has returned from Europe and he has read it and joins in my satisfaction in having it.

It has already gone to the printer and you will receive galleys early next week. Our intention is to put it immediately into the November number which will be made up toward the end of next week.

The question of payment I have never mentioned to you. We want, of course, to meet your wishes in the matter. The article is about 7 pages in length, and we had in mind $400. as payment for it. I hope you will be perfectly frank with me in this matter which is a difficult one to gauge.

With best wishes Faithfully yours Robert Bridges

TLS (WP, DLC).
[1] Edward Livermore Burlingame, Editor of *Scribner's Magazine*.

To Robert Bridges

My dear Bobby, Lyme, Connecticut, 21 August, 1909.

I am delighted that the article pleased you. The subject is so very near my heart that I feel myself a very poor judge of whether I write of it well or ill.

The sum you mention, as payment for the article, is perfectly satisfactory to me. I really had not had that part of it very much in mind. I knew that the Magazine would offer what it thought the piece worth.

I am glad to hear that Mr. Burlingame is at his post again.

That means your release. I hope that you can get business more entirely out of your head than I have found myself able to do this summer and that you will have a jolly good time.

Always, Affectionately Yours, Woodrow Wilson

WWTLS (WC, NjP).

To Mary Allen Hulbert Peck

My dearest Friend, Lyme, Connecticut, 22 August, 1909.

It was so delightful to see you: the impressions of the evening I spent with you and Allen have filled my memory with images to which I can return again and again for refreshment and has added greatly to my content. I am eager to hear whether you went on to Trenton, as you spoke of doing; whether you had an enjoyable time there (I suppose it poured rain there, as it did in these parts, on Monday and Tuesday); and what luck you had in appartment hunting when you got back to New York. Did you go over to Brooklyn and search there, as you said you might? I can fancy that now, with the tunnel and all the other improved connections between the two sides of the river, you might find it pleasanter and freer to live over there than to go to the remote top of Manhattan Island just for the sake of being in New York. I do not know where appartments have been built in Brooklyn, but I know that there are parts of the town which seem most inviting; much quieter and much more homelike than any part of New York that I know.

My own trip was interesting enough. I did not spend Saturday in Boston but out at Nahant, where Mr. Cram occupies an old house which looks in its gray masses like a piece of the little promontory on which it stands, in a sort of dignified isolation, as if it did not condescend to consort with the showy modern houses, the new comers, that seek its neighbourhood on either hand. Though I had come on business, Mr. and Mrs. Cram had arranged to have a few interesting people come in, and so I had to do a lot of misce[l]laneous talking. Fortunately Barret[t] Wendel[l][1] was at lunch. He likes to talk better than I do, even, and talks extremely well: and I was a little out of the running for a very interesting reason. We had been served with mint juleps just before lunch; they were much stronger than I realized; and I had to talk as carefully as I could to talk straight. I felt so unreal that I cannot be sure that I *did* talk straight, and the whole meal seemed to me like a play in which I was engaged without quite knowing what the plot was. I should like to hear

Mrs. Wendell's[2] impressions of me,–for it was with her, chiefly, that I talked. My errand was to make Cram himself see what the development of Princeton was to be if I kept hold, in order that he might understand more perfectly the architectural problems which are to fall to him. I spent the morning, therefore, discoursing as eloquently as I knew how of our whole educational future, as we sat looking out on the broad reaches of Massachusetts Bay, and my thoughts swung off now and again to the crow[d]ing associations of the spot,–the things I like to think of and the things I do not like to think of, the good things and the mean things that Boston stands for; and of New England and the New England character, all the pain and all the amusement it had given you and every free spirit that has come within its touch. I dare say my speech wandered at times and my discourse grew vague! The older I get the more conscious I grow of the network of associations upon which our consciousness is built and our lives woven, the more sensitive to winds of thought from all quarters of the heavens. My friends, and all that they mean to me, in particular, grow more and more a conscious part of my life, a part, I mean, of which I never cease to be conscious, and that gets fused with all my thoughts and purposes. Perhaps I am talking vague nonsense. I must trust to you, with your delightful capacity to comprehend and interpret, to render it into sense, and into poetry: for it is that to me. From Boston I went, on Saturday afternoon, to Hartford, and spent Sunday there with Dr. Jacobus, one of my special conusellors [counsellors], a member of the Princeton Board and a loyal partizan of my schemes. It was a day of perfect airs. I never saw nature more perfect or felt a sweeter air. And the great house in which I stayed has singular dignity and beauty: the beauty of line and space and colour, touched with the refinement of cultivated people, who love books and friends. But the day was necessarily filled with discussions of serious matters, freighted with not a little anxiety, so that even the perfect day and the sympathy and counsel of a genuine friend did not save me from depression and the sense of weight, of burden, which I feel so much of the time, but temporarily escape in the summer. I came back here on Monday, in a downpour of chill rain, and quietly waited for it to clear again. When it did clear my spirits regained their summer tone and I have worked and played since with some approach to serenity.

I did not appreciate while I was with you and thinking of other things the unusual beauty and delightful satisfaction to the touch of this exquisite new binding on my beloved Oxford Book.[3] How can I thank you enough? It will be a constant delight to me, for the book is in my hands every day. Its contents now have a worthy habitation. Will you not send me the name and address of the young binder? I might once and again have a chance to turn a bit of business his way, and might even have a little job for him occasionally. There are books which one feels obliged to invest with unusual dignity sometimes, either for their own sakes or for the sake of the person for whom they are intended.

The summer seems racing towards its end now. We shall be returning to Princeton in less than four weeks: and many a little job I had intended to finish in the vacation still stares me in the face reproachfully. If I play golf every afternoon there is apparently time for little else than the business letters I must get off every day. That's the reason I set apart Sunday for a letter to you. That makes it a day of release and pleasure: a red-letter day. We are all very well and get the best of news from the dear ones on the other side of the water. They seem to be filling their hearts with all the innocent pleasure there is to be found on that play ground. It makes us very happy to read their letters,[4] they are so full of the zest of the thing.

I hope that you did go to Trenton and that you stayed long enough to run over to Princeton after the rain had freshened it. The dear old town has a special charm when its summer drowsiness is upon it. It looked very solemn the other evening when that sad procession filed through it.

All unite with me in sending warmest messages, and I am, as always, Your devoted friend Woodrow Wilson

WWTLS (WP, DLC).

1 Professor of English at Harvard University.

2 Edith Greenough Wendell.

3 *The Oxford Book of English Verse, 1250-1900*, chosen and edited by Arthur T. Quiller-Couch (Oxford, 1900). This book is in the Wilson Library, DLC.

4 These letters from Jessie and Eleanor are missing.

From Edwin William Pahlow

Dear President Wilson, Princeton, August 22/09.

Thank you very much for your cordial letter of the 19th, which reached me at Marblehead. Under the circumstances, I willingly give up the consideration of going elsewhere.

Mrs. Pahlow[1] wishes me to send her warm regards to Mrs. Wilson and you.

Respectfully yours, Edwin W. Pahlow.

ALS (WP, DLC).

1 Gertrude Curtis Brown Pahlow, a writer of short stories.

To Edna Henry Lee Turpin

My dear Miss Turpin, Lyme, Connecticut, 23 August, 1909.

I am thoroughly ashamed that it should have taken me all this time to find the leisure to examine your interesting manuscript, and I beg that you will forgive me. Even more matters of business than I had anticipated, and pieces of writing I knew nothing of when I saw you, have eaten up my vacation, and the delay has been really unavoidable. I do not regret it the less on that account, and sincerely hope that it has caused you no serious loss or inconvenience.

Even as it is I have not been able to read the whole of the MSS. I have confined myself, for the most part, to the portions you were yourself kind enough to indicate, as containing delicate or disputable matter.

My judgment is that the work is excellently done, with moderation, fairness, and good judgment, and I sincerely congratulate you.

My only suggestion is, that you re-write the passage about the Fourteenth Amendment. It reads as if that Amendment conferred the suffrage on the negroes. It forbade discrimination against them, in the suffrage as in other matters, on the ground of race, colour or previous condition of servitude, but it did not confer the ballot.

I hope that the summer has brought you real rest and refreshment.

With renewed apologies and with the best wishes for the book, that it may have the success it deserves,

Very cordially Yours, Woodrow Wilson

P.S. I am sending the MSS. by express, addressed,
Miss Edna H. L. Turpin
Care George W. Cabell, Esq.,
Shipman, Va.

WWTLS (ViHi).

From David Benton Jones

My dear Doctor: Chicago August 24th, 1909.

I want to thank you for your very cordial note of August 19th. I am very glad to be on this side again, and we curtailed our stay in England by only a week, so that we did not seriously change our plans owing to the very rainy season. We had a very delightful visit from start to finish. We all felt, however, that it was longer than it should have been; either that, or we were tired of motoring. Zig-zagging up from Naples to London through four or five different countries has many very delightful elements, but it is also a very, very long journey.

I did not need your assurance that you were still "hammering away" at the present conditions of college life. It is a constant surprise to me to find in the papers of this country such outspoken condemnation of the present conditions and such widespread appreciation of the need of some change. Your work in this matter is not confined to mere leader-ship;—you were, I believe, the first to speak out and to compel general attention to the subject.

You speak of now and then feeling "deep discouragement." I only hope that you are physically taking care of yourself so as to continue the work. I do not fear that your discouragement will be so deep as to induce you to abandon the greatest present need in our university life. I am more than ever convinced that the fundamental conditions repeatedly stated by you indicate the way of redemption.

I expect to visit Princeton some time this Autumn and shall take great pleasure in dropping in to see you for at least a brief visit.

The members of my family are all very well and wish to acknowledge your very kindly remembrances.

Very sincerely yours, David B. Jones.

TLS (WP, DLC).

To Robert Garrett

My dear Mr. Garrett, Lyme, Connecticut, 26 August, 1909.

I am sorry to say the thing has happened, and Littmann has been obliged to stay. I dare say he could not have done otherwise in view of all the circumstances he mentions;[1] but I am deeply sorry that the splendid material you have put at Princeton's disposal should have to wait still longer for its proper utilization.

Cordially and faithfully Yours Woodrow Wilson

WWTLS (Selected Corr. of R. Garrett, NjP).

[1] Littmann's letter is missing.

To Edward Wright Sheldon

My dear Ed., Lyme, Connecticut, 26 August, 1909.

Immediately upon the receipt of your last letter,[1] intimating that Mr. Procter might come over in his yacht from Easthampton and see me, I wrote to him (I knew no more detailed address than simply "Easthampton"), telling what you had said, informing him when I should be away (for a few days, now long since passed), and expressing the very earnest hope that I might have the opportunity of seeing him. He has not replied to the letter. Did I get the wrong address? Letters do not miscarry often, these days. I do not wish to omit anything of my duty, or opportunity, in this matter, but neither do I wish to put the University, through myself, in an undignified position.

I hope that your vacation has been a genuine one and that it has put tonic into every part of you.

Always Affectionately Yours, Woodrow Wilson

WWTLS (photostat in RSB Coll., DLC).

[1] It is missing.

Two Letters to Mary Allen Hulbert Peck

Dearest Friend, Lyme, Connecticut, 29 August, 1909.

A conversation is hard to maintain when one party to it is silent. The person to whom all the speaking is left falls to wondering what the other is thinking about,—especially what she is thinking about what he is saying; whether she is sad or tired or out of spirits or uninterested or absorbed in something else, her thoughts abroad. In brief, it is so long since I had a letter from you that I cannot adjust my thoughts to what you are doing or thinking. I do not even certainly know where you are. Have you disappeared in Brooklyn? Persons have been known to disappear by merely going to Brooklyn. When I saw you in New York your plans were undertermined [undetermined], and I do not know where you may be. My monologue must, therefore, be disturbed and disjointed, interrupted by many silent conjectures, disheartened by the lack of response,—a voice out of the void.

Suppose I should be driven to the dismal expedient of talking altogether of myself,—having nothing else to talk of! A long continuence of such a regime might make of me a hopeless egoist, always analyzing and interpreting myself. That is the danger of vacation. Business stops; one is no longer in the midst of men and affairs; all the day is at his disposal for nothing in particular, and the people about him are as vacant as he. The talk is all personal and trivial. There is nothing to steady one and enlarge his thoughts; and the first thing he knows he is himself looming large in all his moments of reflection. If he has the privilege of writing to some one who is quick to understand and to sympathize, the temptation is complete. The most demoralizing subject in the world creeps into every sentence and he draws upon all the resources of the English language to depict his own frames of mind.

Just now I am going through an experience which perhaps accentuates these tendencies. The Exhibition of pictures by the Lyme artists opens on Wednesday; this house is their headquarters; I sit down with the "hanging committee" at every meal, and hear all the talk of the sensitiveness of this man and the arrogance of that about the place given his picture on the walls of the little library, with its most unsuitable light. The jealousies and personalities of another profession, from which I myself stand entirely detached, are displayed before me in all their detail, in all their consequences. I do not mean that the men display more ill nature than others or that they speak with conscious and intentional unkindness of their fellow artists; but of course I know what men mean when they talk; I can read between the lines very plainly. And because I am not a part of it or in it, it seems to me that these fellows live in a rather petty world,—much more petty than the world I live in (there's where the poison of self-appreciation finds entrance), a very small province of the great kingdom of life; and I feel the condescension of an outsider, who is touched by none of these things! Of course it is not true. There are as many and as small personal jealousies, there is as little generous appreciation of other men's work in mine as in other professions. Only, just now the impression of it is dulled, the sound of it is not in my ears: I am enough removed to remember the big outlines and overlook the ugly details. I can get over feeling big and "superior" only by recalling some of my associates and remembering some of [my] own bad moments. The Exhibition business is very diverting in a way. It is extremely interesting to see thus intimately the inside of another profession. And on Wednesday and the days following we shall have the much more various amusement of seeing the great American public by sample and hearing its comments on art. Our house keeps itself while the Exhibition is on. Miss Florence, as everybody calls her, is at the Exhibition all the time, trying, with many a subtle art of which she is mistress, to sell pictures. She is the warm friend and partisan of every artist of the lot of them, feels herself personally implicated in the success or failure of their work, fills her generous heart with all their hopes and fears, keeps her eyes open for every indication of interest in any picture of the collection on the part of a possible buyer, and is elated or depressed as she succeeds or fails in "landing" them. One would think every mother's son of them was her own flesh and blood! It is really very beautiful and charming.

I meant very seriously and eagerly the suggestion I scribbled at the bottom of the announcement of the Exhibition I sent you. How delightful it would be if Mrs. Brown[1] would bring you in her motor to see Lyme and the pictures! The roads from Hartford down to our ferry are fairly good (those on this side the river, I am told, are not), and the roads from here to New York all that could be reasonably desired (in America). Can you not manage it? I am afraid it would mean only a glimpse of you; but a glimpse is better than nothing,—how much better than nothing! If you are coming of course you will write me beforehand to expect you. I might in some way miss you. If I know beforehand, perhaps I can arrange some way in which to catch more than a glimpse of you,—for example, by having you and Mrs. Brown lunch with us here, if they can squeeze you in, and you do not mind squeezing.

We are expecting to be here until about the eighteenth of September. Madge is just now in bed with a digestive upset, but the rest of us are quite well; and everything goes very smoothly and normally with us. My days consist of a quiet morning of writing, an afternoon of golf (now, alas! of calling, occasionally), and an evening of talk or reading. I am trying to put together a few of my old essays for a companion volume to "Mere Literature." Do you think that worth while? It is my only present means of keeping in the ranks of authors.[2] University affairs wear an unaltered aspect; but I expect to go back to them with normal nerves and a stiffened purpose, while my opponents show signs of weakening if they should be hard pressed a little longer.

Please introduce me to your present confidence by writing me a letter. I can think of nothing that would give me so much pleasure, of nothing that my spirits at this moment more need. Be generous and take me back into favour as a correspondent.

Always Your devoted friend, Woodrow Wilson

[1] The Editors have been unable to identify her.
[2] This volume never came to fruition.

Dearest Friend, Lyme, Connecticut, 5 September, 1909.

I am very much distressed and disturbed. I have not heard from you in more than three weeks; and my mind is full of all sorts of fears: that you are ill, that you are in some new and deep trouble, or that the old trouble has grown worse. I beg most earnestly that you will write or have some one else write as soon as this reaches you, to relieve my distress and anxiety. It possesses my thoughts and goes with me into everything I do. My mind is driven about hither and thither by a thousand conjectures: all of which issue in the same blank anxiety.

Nothing happens to us: not even what we want to happen. There are several important matters of university business which I have hoped to see come into shape to be handled before the term opens and swallows us up in routine; but nothing moves. Everything stands still.

Our present excitement is the exhibition of pictures, which is truly beautiful. The artists being, most of them, now our friends, we find ourselves as much involved in the hopes and fears of the little coterie as to what pictures will be sold, which not, as if our own fortunes and reputations depended on the question. I do not think that it is partiality for this man and that that makes me think the pictures in this year's exhibition particularly fine; and their beauty is enhanced by the unusually tasteful and effective way in which they are grouped in the hanging. Each wall is a perfect scheme of colour as well as a delightful group of pictures. The gallery is the little local library transformed. This house, in which we are lodging, is a sort of additional show. I have told you how uniquely it is decorated, its door panels and the panels of the wainscoting in the dining room painted by celebrated artists, out of gratitude and affection for "Miss Florence." It is really worth seeing as a curiosity, and many of the pictures are worth seeing for their own sake. One or two of them are singularly beautiful. Some member of our variegated household is on hand, morning and afternoon, to show strangers about the house. It might be made an amusing function, if it did not have to be repeated so often. One might "get up" a speech like a Cook's man, and get some sport out of it.

Ellen and I have have [*sic*] fallen more in love than ever with Lyme. It certainly abounds in beauties of all kinds. This has been an unusually fine summer, so far as temperature was concerned, and there have been comparatively few mosquitoes, too. We may be getting sadly deceived by an exceptional season; for three years ago, when we were here, it was oppressively hot and mosquitoes abounded. But we are willing to take our risks, and are diligently looking about for some little house, that we can afford, to buy or some site on which to put one up.[1] It is a paradise for painters; and Ellen is never so happy as when she is here. She has really made remarkable progress with her painting, too, this summer. It would in a way be a relief to have our summer problem permanently settled, and some real home all the year around.

I am deep in an article on the tariff that I am trying to write for the North American Review. It is easy to form the judgment that Congress has put up a big job on the country, but it is difficult, I find, to express it in genteel and parliamentary terms,—particularly when I do not *want* to express it in genteel and parliamentary terms. I am trying to poison every arrow the article contains, subtly enough to conceal the poison but effectually enough to kill. I cannot claim that the thing is getting written in a very judicial frame of mind. I want to hit hard, and if I observe the rules of the game I hope I may be forgiven the zest and enjoyment with which I hit. It is a very complicated subject: I may easily fall into pitfalls and errors; but the fun is worth the risk. This is what I was meant for, anyhow, this rough and tumble of the political arena. My instinct all turns that way, and I sometimes feel rather impatiently the restraints of my academic position. I do not know that anyone will be pleased by this article I am concocting. The Democrats have come out of the discussion and action in Congress with as little credit as the Republicans,—perhaps with less, for they showed themselves hypocrites and cynically indifferent to what the party had promised to do upon this very question. One can only hope that opinion will move in some imperative way in this matter without regard to party lines,—in a way to change those lines somewhat radically. If I have good luck, and that steady mare, my mind, maintains at once her docility and her mettle, I shall finish the writing in two or three days and have about a week of entire vacation before returning to college. I have had piece after piece of work on hand all summer till now. I[t] has not done me any harm, but good, rather; because it has kept my mind out of mischief. Its mischief always lies in the field of worry; and that, until lately, has been driven out. Now I am deeply worried about my silent friend! What can have made her fall so silent?

Vacations seem painfully short when they are just beginning; but, after all, they are quite long enough. By the time they are ended it is high time one should be at work again, for his own discipline and steadying. I do not want to go back to Princeton particularly, but I do want to get back to work and fill my days once more with hard and necessary things. I begin to miss the tonic of it. I feel strange and side-tracked and remote from the movement of affairs of all kinds,–rusticated and in danger of rusting. This is what comes of being obliged to work all your life. You presently cannot do without it. You *want* to be involved and feel the weight of things on your shoulders. After all, work, well done, is the only thoroughly satisfactory thing in the world, and, if done with zest, is the only entirely wholesome thing.

All join me in affectionate messages. I hope that Mrs. Allen is well and that all still goes prosperously and hopefully with your son. Give him my regards, when you write. I am perfectly well; and would give my head to hear from you.

Always, Your devoted friend, Woodrow Wilson

WWTLS (WP, DLC).

1 He took steps to purchase a tract of land in Lyme from David P. Huntley, but difficulties in clearing the title prevented final closing. There are numerous letters from Huntley, dating from September 23, 1909, to April 3, 1910, in WP, DLC, relating to the proposed purchase.

An Article

[*Sept. 5, 1909*]

THE TARIFF MAKE-BELIEVE.

The wrong settlement of a great public question is no settlement at all. The Payne-Aldrich tariff bill, therefore, which its authors would fain regard as a settlement of the tariff question, is no settlement at all. It is miscellaneously wrong in detail and radically wrong in principle. It disturbs more than it settles, and by its very failure to settle forces the tariff question forward into a new and much more acute stage.

It is so obviously impossible to settle the question satisfactorily in the way these gentlemen have attempted to settle it; it is so evident that men of their mind and with their attitude towards the economic interests of the country can never settle it that thinking men of every kind realize at last that new men and new principles of action must be found. These gentlemen do not know the way and cannot find it. They "revised" the tariff, indeed, but by a method which was a grand make-believe from beginning to end. They may have convinced themselves of the intelligence and integrity of the process, but they have convinced nobody else. The country must now go to the bottom of the matter and obtain what it wants.

It has gone to the bottom of it at some points already, and the process will be carried very far before it is through with it. In

THE TARIFF MAKEBELIEVE.

The wrong settlement of a great public question is no settlement at all. The Payne-Aldrich tariff bill, therefore, which its authors would fain regard as a settlement of the tariff question, is no settlement at all. It is miscellaneously ~~ridiculously~~ wrong in detail and radically wrong in principle. It disturbs more than it settles, and by its very failure to settle forces the tariff question forward into a new and much more acute stage.

It is so obviously impossible to settle the question satisfactorily in the way these gentlemen have attempted to settle it; it is so evident that men of their mind and with their attitude towards the economic interests of the country can never settle it, that thinking men of every kind realize at last that new men and new principles of action must be found. These gentlemen do not know the way and cannot find it. They "revised" the tariff, indeed, but by a method which was a grand makebelieve from beginning to end. They may have convinced themselves of the intelligence and integrity of the process, but they have convinced nobody else. The country must now go to the bottom of the matter and obtain what it wants.

It has gone to the bottom of it at some points already, and the process will be carried very far before it is through with it. In the first place, it is the general opinion throughout the country that this particular revision was chiefly pretence ~~makebelieve~~, and that it is the first time that we have had tariff legislation of this kind. The McKinley tariff bill and the Dingley tariff bill, whatever may be thought of their wisdom or of their validity as acts of statesmanship, were unquestionably frank and genuine. There ~~Their~~ was no concealment or makebelieve about either their purpose or their character. No doubt many things were accomplished by them of which the public knew nothing and was intended to know nothing. Not all the advantages gained by this, that, or the other industry from ~~of~~ legislation of that kind could be explained to the public without creating inconvenient comment and starting questions that might cut very deep; but that is true of all legislation which is meant to give particular classes of citizens a special economic assistance or advantage. Private favours will inevitably creep in. But no one was deceived. The men who put those measures through had no doubt that they had the support of the country in doing so. They gave the country what they thought opinion would sustain: gave it what they honestly supposed ~~thought~~ that it wanted. But no one who is capable of assessing opinion ~~opion~~ now can possibly claim that that is what the men who were behind the Payne-Aldrich legislation did. They knew that they were not giving the country what it wanted, and the more thoughtful and statesmanlike among them deeply regretted that they could not. There was a process almost of haphazard in the construction of the House bill, and mere false leadership and chicanery produced the bill which the Senate substituted for it, and which largely prevailed in conference.

First page of Wilson's manuscript of "The Tariff Make-Believe" the first place, it is the general opinion throughout the country that this particular revision was chiefly pretence, and that it is the first time that we have had tariff legislation of this kind. The McKinley tariff bill and the Dingley tariff bill, whatever may be thought of their wisdom or of their validity as acts of statesmanship, were unquestionably frank and genuine. There was no concealment or make-believe about either their purpose or their character. No doubt many things were accomplished by them of which the public knew nothing and was intended to know nothing. Not all the advantages gained by this, that or the other industry from legislation of that kind could be explained to the public without creating inconvenient comment and startling questions that might cut very deep; but that is true of all legislation which is meant to give particular classes of citizens a special economic assistance or advantage. Private favors will inevitably creep in. But no one was deceived. The men who put those measures through had no doubt that they had the support of the country in doing so. They gave the country what they thought opinion would sustain: gave it what they honestly supposed that it wanted. But no one who is capable of assessing opinion now can possibly claim that that is what the men who were behind the Payne-Aldrich legislation did. They knew that they were not giving the country what it wanted, and the more thoughtful and statesmanlike among them deeply regretted that they could not. There was a process almost of haphazard in the construction of the House bill, and mere false leadership and chicanery produced the bill which the Senate substituted for it and which largely prevailed in conference.

The methods by which tariff bills are constructed have now become all too familiar and throw a significant light on the character of the legislation involved. Debate in the Houses has little or nothing to do with it. The process by which such a bill is made is private, not public; because the reasons which underlie many of the rates imposed are private. The stronger faction of the Ways and Means Committee of the House makes up the preliminary bill, with the assistance of "experts" whom it permits the industries most concerned to supply for its guidance. The controlling members of the Committee also determine what amendments, if any, shall be accepted, either from the minority faction of the Committee or from the House itself. It permits itself to be dictated to, if at all, only by the imperative action of a party caucus. The stronger faction of the Finance Committee of the Senate, in like fashion, frames the bill which it intends to substitute for the one sent up from the House. It is often to be found at work on it before any bill reaches it from the popular chamber. The compromise between the two measures is arranged in private conference by conferees drawn from the two committees. What takes place in the committees and in the conference is confidential. It is considered impertinent for reporters to inquire. It is admitted to be the business of the manufacturers concerned, but not the business of the public, who are to pay the rates. The debates which the country is invited to hear in the open sessions of the Houses are merely formal. They determine nothing and disclose very little.

It is the policy of silence and secrecy, indeed, with regard to the whole process that makes it absolutely inconsistent with every standard of public duty and political integrity. If the newspapers published and the public read even the debates, empty of significance as they generally are, the entire country would presently realize how flagrant the whole make-believe is. The committees under whose guidance the bills are put through the Houses disclose nothing that is not wrung from them by members who have made investigations of their own and who insist upon having their questions answered; and there are few enough who have the audacity or take the trouble. But here and there a fact is dragged out, and before the encounters of debate are over enough has been brought to the light to make extremely instructive reading. It is devoutly to be wished,—merely to cite examples,—that every voter in the United States had read, or would yet read, the debates in the Senate on the duty on electric carbons,—the carbons used in the arc-lights in all our cities,—and on the duty on razors. Every detail is a commentary on the whole depressing business.

One extraordinary circumstance of the debates in the Senate should receive more than a passing allusion. The Republican party platform had promised that the tariff rates should be revised and that the standard of revision should be the differences between the cost of producing the various articles affected in this country and in the countries with which our manufacturers compete. One of our chief industrial competitors is now Germany, with its extraordinary skill in manufacture and the handicrafts and its formidable sagacity in foreign trade; and the Department of State, in order to enable Congress the more intelligently to fulfil the promises of the party, had, at the suggestion of the President, requested the German Government to furnish it with as full information as possible about the rates of wages paid in the leading industries in that country,—wages being known, of course, to be one of the largest items in the cost of production.

The German Government of course complied, with its usual courtesy and thoroughness, transmitting an interesting report, each portion of which was properly authenticated and vouched for. The Department of State placed it at the disposal of the Finance Committee of the Senate. But Senators tried in vain to ascertain what it contained. Mr. Aldrich spoke of it contemptuously as "anonymous," which of course it was not, as "unofficial," and even as an impertinent attempt, on the part of the German Government, to influence our tariff legislation. It was only too plain that the contents of the report made the members of the controlling faction of the Finance Committee very uncomfortable indeed. It undoubtedly showed, what independent private inquiries readily enough confirm, that the wages paid to skilled laborers in Germany are practically as great as those paid in the United States, the difference in the cost of living in the two countries being taken into consideration. To have made it public would have been to upset half the arguments for the rates proposed with which the committee had been misinforming the country. It would no doubt have explained, for example, why the skilled grinders of Solingen do not think it worth their while to emigrate to America and oblige almost all razor-makers in other countries to send their blades to them to be ground,–and many another matter left studiously undebated, unexplained, about which Senators had been asking for information. It would have proved that the leaders of the party were deliberately breaking its promise to the country. It was, therefore, thrown into a pigeonhole and disregarded. It was a private document.[1]

In pursuance of the same policy of secrecy and private management, the bill was filled with what those who discovered them were good-natured or cynical enough to call "jokers,"–clauses

[1] This account was not altogether accurate. The report, which consisted of statements collected at the request of the State Department by the German government from local chambers of commerce and similar organizations in the various manufacturing centers of Germany, had been transmitted by the State Department to the Senate Finance Committee on April 3 and 13, 1909. On May 25, in the midst of the Senate debates on the Aldrich bill, Senator Robert M. La Follette, insurgent Republican of Wisconsin, introduced a resolution calling upon President Taft to transmit the report. Taft replied on May 28 stating that it had been sent to the Finance Committee in April. This led to a lengthy debate on May 29 as to whether the document should be printed. Aldrich strenuously opposed publication of the complete document and did make the remarks attributed to him by Wilson. The debate was interrupted for the reading of a second message from Taft, also dated May 28, transmitting the report itself, which Aldrich had just returned to the State Department. The Vice-President then ordered that the report be printed, and, no senator objecting, this was done immediately.

For the report, see 61st Cong., 1st sess., Sen. Doc. No. 68; for La Follette's resolution and the debate on the report and whether it should be printed, see *Congressional Record*, 61st Cong., 1st sess., pp. 2351-52, 2526-37.

whose meaning did not lie upon the surface, whose language was meant not to disclose its meaning to the members of the Houses who were to be asked to enact them into law, but only to those by whom the law was to be administered after its enactment. This was one of the uses to which the "experts" were put whom the committees encouraged to advise them. They knew the technical words under which meanings could be hidden, or the apparently harmless words which had a chance to go unnoted or unchallenged. Electric carbons had been taxed at ninety cents per hundred; the new bill taxed them at seventy cents per hundred *feet*,—an apparent reduction if the word feet went unchallenged. It came very near escaping the attention of the Senate, and did quite escape the attention of the general public, who paid no attention at all to the debates, that the addition of the word feet almost doubled the existing duty.

The hugest practical joke of the whole bill lay in the so-called maximum and minimum clause. The schedules as they were detailed in the bill and presented to the country, through the committees and the newspapers,—the schedules by which it was made believe that the promise to the country of a "downward" revision was being kept by those responsible for the bill, were only the minimum schedules. There lay at the back of the measure a maximum provision about which very little was said, but the weight of which the country may come to feel as a very serious and vexatious burden in the months to come. In the case of articles imported from countries whose tariff arrangements discriminate against the United States, the duties are to be put at a maximum which is virtually prohibitive. The clause is a huge threat. Self-respecting countries do not yield to threats or to "impertinent efforts, on the part of other Governments, to affect their tariff legislation." Where the threat is not heeded we shall pay heavier duties than ever, heavier duties than any previous Congress ever dared impose.

When it is added that not the least attempt was made to alter the duties on sugar by which every table in the country is taxed for the benefit of the Sugar Trust, but just now convicted of criminal practices in defrauding the Government in this very matter;[2] that increased rates were laid on certain classes of cotton

[2] In November 1907, an investigation by the United States Customs Service discovered that the government was being systematically defrauded of a substantial portion of the customs duties on imported sugar by means of scales rigged to underweigh the sugar on the docks of the American Sugar Refining Company in Brooklyn. Henry L. Stimson, then United States Attorney for the Southern District of New York, brought a civil suit against the company in the United States District Court. On March 5, 1909, judgment was rendered against the company in the amount of $134,116.03 for fifty-four specific in-

goods for the benefit, chiefly, of the manufacturers of New England, from which the dominant party always counts upon getting votes, and that the demand of the South, from which it does not expect to get them, for free cotton bagging was ignored; that the rates on wool and woollen goods, a tax which falls directly upon the clothing of the whole population of the country, were maintained unaltered; and that relief was granted at only one or two points,–by conceding free hides and almost free iron ore, for example,–upon which public opinion had been long and anxiously concentrated; and granted only at the last moment upon the earnest solicitation of the President,–nothing more need be said to demonstrate the insincerity, the uncandid, designing, unpatriotic character of the whole process. It was not intended for the public good. It was intended for the benefit of the interests most directly and selfishly concerned.

There was noticeable confusion in the counsels of the dominant party. Some said this, some said that. Many were anxious, probably a majority in the House, to fulfil in entire good faith the promise their party convention had given in its platform and the President had so frankly interpreted and repeated; others were willing, some were eager, to evade it. Their leaders led them by the way of evasion. I do not know whether they were conscious of doing so or not. It need make no difference to the country whether they were or not: it is only the fact that interests it, however the fact may affect individuals. If the leaders of the Republican party were not aware that they were seeking a way of evasion, they have an unusual capacity for deceiving themselves; if they were, they did not deal honestly by the country. Either alternative proves them wholly unserviceable and untrustworthy. We need not stop, therefore, to choose between the alternatives: for we are not discussing their characters, but the present interests of the country with regard to the tariff. The question that interests us is this: How out of this confusion of counsel was an agreement reached, and why was the agreement that which the leaders of the Houses desired rather than that which the rank and file of the party would have

---

stances of fraud between 1901 and 1907. As the direct result of this decision, the American Sugar Refining Company was forced to pay to the government on April 29, 1909, estimated duties due on ten years of sugar shipments in the amount of $2,000,000. Sizable sums were later recovered from other large sugar refining companies, and a number of criminal convictions were secured against officials of the companies and members of the Customs Service involved in the frauds. For a summary of the affair as it had developed as of May 9, 1910, see 61st Cong., 2nd sess., House of Representatives, Document No. 901. See also Elting E. Morison, *Turmoil and Tradition: A Study of the Life and Times of Henry L. Stimson* (Boston, 1960), pp. 103-09.

honestly preferred? What, when its policies are in debate within its own ranks, finally determines the course the Republican party will take in a matter like this?

I know, of course, as every one does, how great the power of the Speaker of the House[3] is, and the great and sinister hold the chairman of the Finance Committee of the Senate[4] has upon the legislative machinery of that body, whatever signs of apparent independence it may show in the open processes of debate. It is matter of common knowledge what Mr. Cannon and Mr. Aldrich would prefer to have the House do when any question of this sort is under consideration. But these men represent forces, they do not constitute them. The forces that control the Republican party lie outside of them. They are only the spokesmen of those forces. Why do the rank and file of the Republican members still, in this day of change, find themselves unable to make an independent choice in a matter like this, of capital importance to their party and to the country? They do not mistake the signs of the times. Why, then, are they impotent?

The question can be answered very frankly, and, I hope, without partisan bias and without offence to honorable men whose principles I would not presume to call in question. The Republican party is old at the business of tariff-making and has established a business constituency. Its leaders feel that they must satisfy that constituency, and they force their followers to follow them by very concrete and practical arguments. It has come to a point where they have grown very stubborn and short-sighted in their loyalty to their constituency, but that is hardly to be wondered at. The loyalty is of long standing and has become a fundamental asset, as it seems to them, of party business.

The business of tariff-making naturally grows more and more complex, naturally comes to involve a greater and greater complexity of interests. Those who conduct it extend their clientage from generation to generation, to make sure that they have clients enough. Whatever principle may underlie tariff-making, and however valid that principle may be, however fundamental to the general development and prosperity of the country, tariff schedules arranged for "protection" are governmental favors. Those who make them, though acting for the nation, are the patrons of the industries favored: they dispense the largess of the Government, and those who receive the favors will be their partisans and followers so long as the favors continue. The relation cannot be avoided. The only thing that can be avoided is

[3] Joseph Gurney Cannon, Republican of Illinois.
[4] Nelson Wilmarth Aldrich, Republican of Rhode Island.

the corrupting influence of the relationship, and that can be avoided only by very strong men. A political party cannot withstand it for many generations together: cannot, I mean, withstand the gradual corruption of its will,—the temptation to make use of the patronage it dispenses for the perpetuation of the power it derives from it, the unfailing support at the elections of the wealthiest and most influential classes of the country.

Here, in a protective tariff, are the entrenchments of Special Privilege, and every beneficiary will of course crowd into them on the day of battle, determined to keep his own. Shall a man not defend what he has?

I am not seeking to point a moral. Neither am I drawing up an indictment of the Republican party. I am merely outlining the natural history of a governmental policy whose prime object is to make particular industries safe against competition. Parties are capital epitomes of human nature; and I dare say that any other party that espoused this principle of legislation would use it for party advantage in the same way. My point is rather how it has been used than who has used it. Its uses and effects are plain,—painfully plain now. Its use is to extend to certain undertakings Government favor and assistance; its effect has been to build up special privilege. No doubt the country will have to hold those responsible who managed the business; but its real interest will not be in punishing them, many of them honest and public-spirited enough, but in getting rid of special privilege. That it has made up its mind to do. It now only seeks the best and most effectual way.

It sees plainly enough, at last, that the place to begin is the tariff. That it saw before the last Presidential election; but Mr. Cannon and Mr. Aldrich have managed between them to make it more evident than ever before. They have executed their purposes, not wisely, but too well. A day of judgment is at hand.

> "The sword of Heaven is not in haste to smite,
> Nor yet doth linger."[5]

The purpose of the people has much the same habit. Perhaps it *is* the sword of Heaven!

It is not a question of schedules. It is possible that by reasonable schedules,—by a minimum of favoritism and make-believe,—the tariff-makers of the special session might have quieted the country,—might have induced it to let the troublesome and per-

[5] Dante Alighieri, *The Divine Comedy*, "Paradise," Canto XXII, lines 16-17. Wilson was quoting from one of the numerous editions based on the English translation by Henry Francis Cary, first published in London in 1814.

plexing subject drop for a decade or two. But it would have been only a stay of judgment. The essential wrong would still have cried out to be righted. And the essential wrong is this: that, except for a few men who have been fairly hypnotized by a system which they have accepted as political gospel since their youth, it has ceased to be a matter of principle at all and has become merely a method of granting favors. The favors are obtained in two ways—by "influence" and by supplication of a kind for which there is no classical or strictly parliamentary designation. In the vulgar, it is called "the baby act."

What "influence" consists of is a very occult matter, into which the public is not often privileged to inquire. It is compounded of various things, in varying proportions: of argument based upon the facts of industry and of commercial interest, of promises of political support, of campaign contributions, not explicitly given upon condition, but often spoken of by way of reminder, of personal "pressure" through the channels of old friendships and new alliances,—of things too intimate to mention,—though not, I believe, even in the minds of the most cynical and suspicious, of direct bribes. There is seldom any question of personal corruption. It is wholly a question of party corruptions, so far as it is a question of corruption at all.

The "baby act" consists in resorting to the Ways and Means Committee of the House and the Finance Committee of the Senate with pitiful tales, hard-luck stories, petitions for another chance, as the hosiery-makers did at the special sessions. It is an act very unpalatable to American pride, and yet very frequently indulged in with no appearance of shame. "Foreigners make better goods," is the burden of its cry, "pay smaller wages, and can add the ocean freights to their price and still beat us in our own markets." It often seems to mean that the foreigner has superior skill, uses better machinery, adapts his patterns more quickly to changing tastes, is more practised in economies of all sorts and is content with smaller profits. And so a handful of American gentlemen go to Congress and beg to be helped to make a living and support their operatives. Some among them do not need the protection: they have perfected their processes and their stuffs, can afford by better organization and more studied economies to pay American wages and still beat the foreigner, if need be, in his own markets oversea. But the rest do need it to make good their failure. American labor is the most intelligent in the world, and when intelligently made use of is worth its extra wage, earns it without affecting the market. But the Government must support those who do not know how to use it as intelligently as their rivals, and the people of the country must be made to buy the goods they make at prices that will support them. This is indeed the "baby act" and these are easily recognizable as "infant industries"!

And so the question comes to be, What will the people say of this new system of the support of favored industries by the Government, now that they have come to understand it? For it is a new system. The principle upon which the system of protection was originally founded was the development of the country, the development of the resources of the continent and the skill of the people. That principle is intelligible and statesmanlike, particularly in a new country, without capital and unprepared for competition in a trading world. The principle now proclaimed and acted upon, with show of patriotic fervor, is that profits must be assured to those who cannot stand competition after development, *after* the accumulation of capital in the country, the perfecting of skill and the full attainment of economic and industrial independence amidst the trading and manufacturing nations of the world. This is indeed a new theory and will not bear examination.

Hamilton's position, the position of those who have intelligently and consistently followed him, is defensible enough. It is idle to bid a new nation on an undeveloped continent to put its faith in the natural laws of trade and production, buy in the cheapest and sell in the dearest market, build up its wealth on the demand for what it has and buy what it has not. For it has not at the outset capital enough to find out either its resources or its capacities. There must be a waiting and a spending time at the first before it finds out what its resources are and what it can do with them. The farmer cannot expect a crop the first season from unbroken prairie or uncleared land. It costs money to put nature into shape to be profitably used. Deposits of ore do not constitute riches until the mines have been opened and machinery has been installed by which the ore can be readily and economically got out. That takes time and money. Even when the mines are opened and can be worked at a profit they produce only ore. The nation that cannot use its ores in manufacture is still a poor nation, however rich its deposits. Only a few men in it will be rich until other men in it get the capital and the opportunity to use the ores in manufacture. That again, takes time and money. South Africa was not rich because a few men owned and worked diamond-mines in it. Taking the world at large and as a whole, how are you to know which is the cheapest market in which to buy or the most advantageous in which to sell, so long as a whole continent lies undeveloped, a whole nation untrained, so long as America or South Africa has not come into the markets with its hidden stuffs and its unschooled peoples?

This is the question for statesmen. Nobody now doubts that the policy of Hamilton put the nation under a great stimulation, gave it the economic independence it needed, immensely quickened the development of its resources and the powers of its people. Protected from the direct competition of those who had already acquired capital oversea, who had already become masters of industry and put hundreds of ships upon the sea, who had the stuffs to work in and the skill to work them, things took on a very different aspect for the enterprising spirits of the young nation from that which they had worn in the old colony days. Those who cared to venture upon enterprise,—and who in America did not?—had the markets of a growing and industrious people to themselves. As the nation grew their trade grew, and their wealth,—with their wealth, their independence and their spirit of enterprise. It was wise,—in the circumstances it was more than wise, it was necessary,—to give the country an opportunity thus to find itself. It was necessary and wise to put it thus economically upon its own feet and make it worth its while to discover and develop its own resources.

It is perfectly consistent with such a policy, moreover, to give to every new enterprise, even in our day of America's abounding wealth and resourcefulness, such protection as it may need to get its start and come to its proper perfection of equipment and operation, provided it be an enterprise suitable to America's soil or resources or capacities. So far as the policy of protection has for its object the diversification and enrichment of American industry, it is admissible, dangerous though it be, because liable to be used in a spirit of favoritism and for party ends. The only thing not consistent with the sound original policy upon which the single defensible theory of the system rests is the encouragement and support by "protection" of industries in their very nature not natural to America, but forced and artificial. Being artificial, not indigenous from the outset, they will need artificial stimulation to the end. Those who undertake them will always have to be supported out of the public purse—by the taxes laid at the ports.

But this original basis and theory of protection, this genuine enterprise of statesmanship, was long ago abandoned or forgotten by the leaders of the party that stood for the system. Its leaders no longer talk of "infant industries" to be carefully nurtured and brought to maturity for the sake of the nation and its development. They know the sort of smile with which such talk would now be received and do not relish the thought of it. They boast, rather, of the economic supremacy of America in the money-markets, the steel-markets, the foodstuff-markets, the implement and machinery markets of the world, and naïvely insist that that supremacy should be maintained by import duties at the ports levied for the sake of those who are conducting our successful enterprises, in order to keep their profits safely up and make them feel that the country (which is, being interpreted, the party in power) will take care of them. It is not a system of stimulation or development; it is a system of patronage. Statesmen need no longer debate it: politicians of very ordinary managing abilities can easily keep it going. Indeed, it is no proper job for statesmen. It is a thing of lobbies and private interviews, not a thing of open debate and public policy.

Even this bad system worked no radical harm upon the country for a generation or two. The continent abounded in every kind of natural riches, individuals were greatly stimulated by the many inviting opportunities for manufacture and trade, the population of the country was growing by leaps and bounds, its domestic markets widening with every decade, its diversified industries enriching one another. The country was generously big and wide and various, its immense stretches extending into every climate of the temperate zone, its hills and valleys and high ascending western slopes inviting to every development of modern civilization. Its vast areas of free trade, trade absolutely without hindrance or restriction, guaranteed exemption from restraint by the interstate commerce clause of the Constitution, made it an incomparable field for rapid and normal development, a development about which, it turned out, there was almost nothing that was artificial and little that was not sound and lasting.

Moreover, those who had undertaken the great industries to which the customs legislation of Congress had given leave had not yet gone into combination. Enterprise was entered upon on individual initiative, was conducted by simple partnerships and small companies. There was a very active and quickening competition within the field of each undertaking that proved profitable. Those who succeeded had no more power than their mere wit at succeeding gave them. Fortunes were made, but upon a modest scale. The rich men of the country had only their local influence and did not determine the industrial processes of a whole continent or the methods of a whole industry. The prosperity of the country wore a generous and democratic aspect and did not set classes off in sharp contrast against one another.

There was favoritism in arranging the system of protection, of course, and individuals were very often thought of rather than the country as a whole. The "log-rolling" in Congress was very often spoken of in the newspapers and with a great deal of asperity. The system had its glaring faults and dangers. But it was at least a game into which almost any one could get. It did not yet wear the ugly face of monopoly or special privilege.

We look upon a very different scene now. It is no longer a scene of individual enterprise, of small bodies of capital embarked upon a thousand undertakings,—a scene of individual opportunity and individual achievement,—able men everywhere, singly or in small groups, making themselves the economic servants of communities and reaping the legitimate profit of many an enterprise their own brains had conceived. It was in that day that the industries of the country were originated and put upon a footing to succeed. In our later day those who control the great masses of capital swept together out of the multitudinous earnings of the last two or three generations have combined together and put at the head of every great industry a dominating corporation, or group of corporations, with an organization and resources which are irresistible by any individual competitor,—by any competitor not supported by a like colossal combination of brains and means. The richest of those who enjoy the favors of the Government have combined to enjoy a monopoly of those favors. Enormous fortunes are piled up for a few, for those who organize and control these great combinations; but they are relatively very few in number and all men in their field of enterprise who are not in their combination are apt to become, first their crushed rivals, and then their servants and subordinates.

It is a very different America from the old. All the recent scandals of our business history have sprung out of the discovery of the use those who directed these great combinations were making of their power: their power to crush, their power to monopolize. Their competition has not stimulated, it has destroyed. Their success has not varied industry, it has standardized it and brought it all under a single influence and regulation,—not the regulation of law, but the regulation of monopoly.

It is easy to exaggerate the iniquity of many of the things that have been done under this *régime* of the trust and the colossal corporation. Most of their methods were simply the old cutthroat methods of private individual competition on a new scale. What made them cruel and disastrous was not their kind, but their scope. Their kind was as old as economic history and rivalry in industrial enterprise, but their scale was new and ominous.

The competition, the underselling, the aggressive canvassing, the rival expenditure and rapid improvement of process possible to these men who had vast capital behind them, who shipped so much that every railroad stood ready to bid for their patronage with lowered rates, who could buy a competitor out at any price and stood always ready to buy at the moment of greatest strain and discouragement, could not be withstood. The field cleared before them. The power was theirs, and smaller men, smaller concerns, went down before them. They had "cornered" the opportunity which the Government's favoring legislation had been intended to create.

Too much moral blame, it seems to me, has been laid upon the men who effected these stupendous changes. They were men of extraordinary genius, many of them, capable of creating and organizing States and Empires. Commercial morals had not been adjusted, by themselves or any one else, to the new and unprecedented scale upon which they did business. Private consciences were pooled and confused and swallowed up in those huge combinations. Men were excited and blinded by the vast object they sought, and pursued it, as it were, impersonally, by means they would not have used had they been dealing simply and face to face with persons and not merely upon paper with complex transactions, involving the business of a continent. It was a process in which commercial morals had again to find themselves, as in the days of treasure fleets and international spoliation.

But my present object is not to assess individual responsibility. I am describing conditions, not drawing up an indictment against those who created them or framing an excuse for them. I am studying a national policy and its effects; and about that, viewed in its present aspects, some things are very plain and ought to be plainly spoken of.

In the first place, it is plain that these new masters of our industry do not need the assistance or the "protection" of the Government. They own or control a preponderant percentage of the resources of the country: of its mines, its forests, its cattle, its railways. They have brought the industries they control to a high state of perfection in equipment and organization, economizing their processes and improving their output. They have invaded foreign markets and sell to all the world, where there is no Government to assist them, where, on the contrary, there are hostile tariffs to overcome. They have made themselves entire masters of the opportunity created for them. Manufacturers engaged in the same lines of industry elsewhere copy their machinery and imitate their methods. All the world is justly jealous of their huge success. Their balance-sheets, on the one hand, and the success and skill of their processes, on the other, show how little they need protection.

In the second place, no political party can afford to be their partners in business. It amounts to that. In the earlier days of protection, when import duties created opportunities for thousands of men, the political party that maintained the system of protection had all the nation for partner. The benefits of the system were widely distributed. Its beneficiaries could nowhere be assembled in a single lobby. Their names could be included in no possible list. They were the people of the country by sample. But now, as compared with the former thousands, they are few. The names of most of them are known everywhere. Their influence is direct, personal, pervasive.

They are doing nothing novel through the lobby. It is just what the beneficiaries of this dangerous system have always done. It would seem the natural process of obtaining protection,—to ask for it and argue its necessity with the figures of the business in hand. But they are so few, so individually powerful, and command so many things that political parties need, or think that they need, for their success: money, widely-extended influence, the gift and the use of business organization national in their scope and control! They have as powerful a machinery ready to their hand as the Government itself. It is highly dangerous for the Government to be in partnership with them in the great enterprise of developing the country: their grip upon it can so easily become too direct and personal! The country cannot afford an alliance of private interest with governmental authority, for whatever purpose originally conceived, however honorably arranged at the outset. No body of business men, no political party, can long withstand the demoralizing influences of the relationship,—particularly no body of men so compacted and unified in interest as those who manage and finance the trusts.

It is not necessary for my argument to claim or to prove that high protection created the trusts and combinations of our time. I believe that it can be shown that it did, though I am ready to admit that they might, and probably would, have arisen in any case, though in a different form and with different proportions. But that is a complicated question which may for the present be put upon one side. Certainly the trusts have now cornered the opportunities created by the system of high tariffs. They no longer need the assistance of the Government; and it is highly desirable that there should be no alliance, and no appearance of an alliance, between them and either of the political parties.

That our industries are still greatly stimulated is evident enough. They are very vital and very prosperous. There is general employment; and when things go well and the money market is not manipulated, or upset by our uncommonly bad system of currency, there is a general feeling of ease and hopefulness. But there is not general prosperity: that is a very different matter. When the great industrial and trade combinations can operate freely and without fear of disturbed prices and a frightened money-market there is always ready enough employment for those who seek it,—at wages forced up and maintained, not by prosperity or the good business of the great corporations, but by the aggressiveness and determination of organized labor. The country is given occupation by those who have cornered the privileges to be had under the favor of Congress, and their success is easily made to look like the reign of unbounded opportunity for the rank and file; but that does not increase the proportion of employers to employees. The initiative and control are still with the few. Their money makes the mare go, and it is they who ride.

It does not do to think of these things with bitterness. It is not just to think of them with bitterness. They came about by natural process, not by deliberate or malignant plan. But it is necessary to point them out in plain language, to discuss them with candor and to comprehend them, when the talk is done, with wide-open eyes. It is easy to fall into exaggeration. Not all the industry of the country is in the hands of great trusts and combinations. Only its main undertakings are, its largest and most lucrative enterprises. But the picture I have drawn is, in the rough, true and tends from decade to decade to represent the the truth more and more perfectly and completely. If the tendency had worked itself out to its ultimate consequences, if it had accomplished its perfect work, it would probably be too late for reform. The body politic is still sound and still elastic enough to work upon; and many of the very men who have profited most by this new and ominous state of affairs are ready to join in the wholesome processes of reformation which will make opportunity general again,—not a monopoly, but a universal stimulus.

The fact which has disclosed itself to us, in these later days of the country's awakening, is this, then. We have witnessed the partial creation, the almost complete creation, on the one hand, of a comparatively small privileged class or body of men, the men who control capital and the uses to which it is put and who have, as the representatives (as all too literally the representatives) of the business of the country, the ear of Congressional committees; and we begin to see, under them, associated with them, on the other hand, a vast unprivileged body ("class" is too definite and formal a word) which forces its way to a share in the benefits of our apparently prosperous conditions only by threats and strikes, and is steadily deprived of a large percentage of what it thus gains by rapidly rising prices which day by day increase the cost of living amongst us. And the rise of prices itself seems to be connected with the system.

There has been a rise in prices in almost all the trading countries. The large recent increase in the supply of gold has had a great deal to do with it, here as elsewhere. Gold, the world's standard of value, having become cheaper because more abundant, more of it is demanded in exchange for goods, whose value has not changed. But this universal phenomenon of the rise of prices has had its special features and vagaries in America utterly dissociated from the price of gold; and it would be easy to prove that those who have managed to get control of the greater part of the output of the mines and factories have, by combination, set the prices to please themselves. They have made the usual use of their opportunity. While the Government has, by its high protective policy, spared them the anxiety of foreign competition, they have, by organization and agreement, spared themselves the embarrassment of any competition at all.

What, then, shall we do? Shall we adopt Thorough as our motto and sweep the whole system away, be quit of privilege and favors at once, put our industries upon their own resources and centre national legislation wholly upon the business of the nation? By no means. The system cannot be suddenly destroyed. That would bring our whole economic life into radical danger. The existing system was built up by statesmanlike and patriotic men, upon a theory upon which even the most sceptical economist must concede it possible to found a valid and effective policy. It is very likely that by slower, sounder, less artificial means the country might have worked its way up to the same extraordinary development and success, the same overwhelming material achievement and power; but that is a question no longer worth debate by practical men. As a matter of fact, the method of artificial stimulation was adopted, has been persisted in from generation to generation with a constant increase of the stimulation, and we have at last, by means of it, come to our present case. It will not do to reverse such a policy suddenly or in revolutionary fashion.

It must in some conservative way be altered from decade to decade, if possible from year to year, until we shall have put all customs legislation upon a safe, reasonable and permanent footing. A process of alteration, steadily and courageously persisted in, will not disturb the business or embarrass the industries of the country, even if tariff act follows tariff act from session to session, if it be founded upon a definite principle by which its progress may be forecast and made ready for. Such a principle must be found. And the nation must find means to insist that, whatever party is in power, that principle shall be followed with courage, intelligence and integrity. The present method and principle of legislation does not keep business equable or free from harassing anxiety. It is based upon no principle, except that of self-interest,—which is no principle at all. No calculable policy can be derived from it. Discussion gives place to intrigue, and nothing is ever fixed or settled by its application.

What, then, shall the principle of reform be which shall hold us steady to an impartial and intelligible process? The old principle of Hamilton, in a new form and application: the very principle upon which the protective policy was set up, but applied for the purpose of reforming the system and bringing it to the test of a single definite object, its original purpose and energy having been fulfilled and spent.

Hamilton's purpose was to develop America, to give her industries of her own; to make it immediately worth the while of her enterprising and energetic men to discover and use her natural resources, the richness and extent of which even he never dreamed of; to enrich and expand her trade and give her an interior economic development which should make her an infinitely various market within herself; and to continue the stimulation until her statesmen should be sure that she had found her full vigor and capacity, was mistress of her own wealth and opportunity, and was ready to play her independent part in the competitions and achievements of the world. That object has been attained. No man not blinded by some personal interest or inveterate prepossession can doubt it. What would Hamilton do now?

In one sense, it is not a question of politics. It does not involve Hamilton's theories of Government or of constitutional interpretation. Some of us are Jeffersonians, not Hamiltonians, in political creed and principle, and would not linger long over the question, What shall we do to return safely to Hamilton? It is not a Hamiltonian question. Constitutional lawyers long ago determined that it was certainly within the choice of Congress to lay import duties, if it pleased, with a view to the incidental benefit of traders and manufacturers within the country; and, if that incidental object has in later days become the chief and only guiding object of the rates of duty, that, I take it, is only a question of more or less, not a question which cuts so deep as to affect the power of Congress or draw it seriously into debate again. As a matter of fact, the policy was entered upon and has been carried—to what lengths we know. The Hamiltonian principle, not a political, but an economic principle, was the only wise and defensible principle upon which it could have been established. It is also the only wise and safe principle upon which it can be modified and in part got rid of. For when you have the general benefit of the country as your standard, you have a principle upon which it is as legitimate to withdraw protection as to give it.

It may seem like a vague principle, affording room for many varieties of contrary judgment; but it will be found to lose its vagueness when stated in contrast with the principle upon which Congress has acted in recent years. In all the recent tariff legislation of the country, in all legislation since 1828, the committees of the House and Senate, when making up the several schedules of duties they were to propose, have asked, not what will be good for the country, but what will be good for the industries affected, what can they stand, what rates of duty will assure them abundant profits? It is true that they have assumed,—it has been the burden of innumerable weary campaign speeches, —that the prosperity of the individual interest considered would be the prosperity of the country; but the poor sophistry of that argument has long been commonplace. By hard, desperately hard, use that assumption has been worn through to the thread. It must be replaced by new and sounder stuff. No doubt you can say to the country, "Feed and sustain these corporations and they will employ you: feed your employers out of the taxes and they, in turn, will give you work and feed you." But no candid student of this great question can now confidently believe that a policy which has the profits of the manufacturers as its main object is likely to promote the impartial, natural, wholesome, symmetrical, general development of the country.

The men who happen to possess the field do not constitute the nation; they do not even represent it when they speak of their own interest. We have taught them, by our petting, to regard their own interest as the interest of the country; but the two are by no means necessarily identical. They may be, they may not be. It is a question of fact to be looked into. Their prosperity and success may or may not benefit the country as a whole. Even if the country be indisputably benefited, it might be still more highly benefited by the promotion of an entirely different interest. What the fact is may depend upon many circumstances. It is those circumstances we are bound to look into, if we be indeed statesmen and patriots, asking not what the protected interests want or can prove that they need, but what it is to the general interest of the country to do: whether some interests have not been too much favored, given a dominance not at all compatible either with honest politics or wholesome economic growth. In brief, we are now face to face with a great question of fact. What part of the protective system still benefits the country and is in the general interest; what part is unnecessary; what part is pure favoritism and the basis of dangerous and demoralizing special privilege? These are the questions which should underlie a tariff policy. No other questions are pertinent or admissible.

"The benefit of the country" is a big phrase. What do you mean by it? What do you mean by "the country"? *Whom* do you mean by it? If you are honest and sincere, you mean the people of the country, its sections and varieties of climate and population taken, not separately or by their voting strength, but together; its men and women of every rank and quality and circumstance; its bone and sinew. If any particular industry has been given its opportunity to establish itself and get its normal development, under cover of the customs, and is still unable to meet the foreign competition which is the standard of its efficiency, it is unjust to tax the people of the country any further to support it. Wherever the advantages accorded by a tariff have resulted in giving those who control the greater part of the output of a particular industry the chance, after their individual success has been achieved, to combine and "corner" the advantage, those advantages ought to be withdrawn; and the presumption is that every industry thus controlled has had the support of the Government as long as it should have it.

There is something more than the economic activities of the country to be considered. There is its moral soundness; the variety, not of employment, but of opportunity for individual initiative and action which the policy of its law creates; the standards of business its trades and manufactures observe and are gauged by; and the connection which exists between its successful business men and its Government. By these significant matters should the tariff policy of Congress be judged, as well as by the tests of successful business.

Only those undertakings should be given the protection of high duties on imports which are manifestly suited to the country and as yet undeveloped or only imperfectly developed. From all the rest protection should be withdrawn, the object of the Government being, not to support its citizens in business, but to promote the full energy and development of the country. Existing protection should not be suddenly withdrawn, but steadily and upon a fixed programme upon which every man of business can base his definite forecasts and systematic plans. For the rest, the object of customs taxation should be revenue for the Government. The Federal Government should depend for its revenue chiefly on taxes of this kind, because the greater part of the field of direct taxation must be left to the States. It must raise abundant revenue, therefore, from customs duties. But it should choose for taxation the things which are not of primary necessity to the people in their lives or their industry, things, for the most part, which they can do without without suffering or actual privation. If taxes levied upon these do not suffice, the things added should be those which it would cause them the least inconvenience or suffering to dispense with. Customs thus laid and with such objects will be found to yield more, and the people will be freer.

There is no real difficulty about finding how and where to lay such taxes when once a just principle has been agreed upon, if statesmen have the desire to find it. The only trouble is to ascertain the facts in a very complex economic system. Honest inquiry will soon find them out, and honest men will readily enough act upon them, if they be not only honest, but also courageous, true lovers of justice and of their country.[6]

Printed in the *North American Review*, CXC (Oct. 1909), 535-56.

[6] There is a WWT outline of this article, dated Aug. 25, 1909, and a WWsh draft, dated Aug. 30 and Sept. 5, 1909, in WP, DLC. The WWT MS is in WC, NjP.

From James Gore King McClure[1]

My dear President Wilson: Chicago September 10, 1909.

I enclose a tentative programme of a celebration that McCormick Theological Seminary expects to hold on November 1st and 2nd, 1909. The celebration means much to the McCormick family and to the Seminary.[2]

As I return from Europe this week, where I have been spending the summer, I find that the Committee having the matter of the celebration in charge have deferred communicating with you, thinking that I was the one to write to you. What we wish is that you should deliver some general address on any theme or phases of thought that bear directly or indirectly on the subject of theological seminary interests. You will notice that definite subjects have been assigned to the speakers who precede the closing speaker of the celebration.

I cannot tell you how eager I am for you to accept this invitation. No one is more assured than myself of the burdens you bear and of the difficulty a man in a position like your own has in responding to the various requests that are made of him. If you can possibly come to us to speak for a greater or less time as you are able, your coming will be hailed with the greatest delight by us all and will be an immense gratification. Very possibly, material that you have used heretofore at Hartford or other places can be used by you now. It will all be fresh for those who gather for this special celebration. Please do come, and please telegraph me at my expense that you will come.[3]

The Seminary is to provide the railway expenses and hospitality of all who take part in the programme.

The only person on the programme that I enclose to you who is unable to come to us is Dr. Mackenzie of Hartford. The others have accepted.

We shall look for some leading Congregationalist in Dr. Mackenzie's place.[4] Most cordially, James G. K. McClure

TLS (WP, DLC).

[1] The Rev. Dr. James Gore King McClure, President of McCormick Theological Seminary. He had received the D.D. degree from Princeton University in 1906.

[2] The enclosure described a series of events to be held on November 1 and 2, 1909, commemorating the eightieth year of the inception of the seminary, the fiftieth year of its location in Chicago, and the centennial of the birth of Cyrus Hall McCormick, Sr. The events included a speech memoralizing the life and work of McCormick by President Walter William Moore of Union Theological Seminary in Richmond, Va., papers on various aspects of ministry and theological education, receptions and toasts, and Wilson's speech, scheduled for the evening of November 2.

[3] Wilson accepted and delivered the address printed at Nov. 2, 1909.

[4] The Rev. Dr. Williston Walker, Titus Street Professor of Ecclesiastical History at Yale since 1901, took Mackenzie's place. He was one of three men who delivered papers on "Theological Education: What Should Be the Ideals of the Theological Seminary for Usefulness in the Coming Half Century?" The other participants were President Augustus Hopkins Strong of Rochester Theological Seminary and Robert William Rogers, Professor of Hebrew and Old Testament Exegesis at Drew Theological Seminary.

Two Letters to Mary Allen Hulbert Peck

Dearest Friend, Lyme, Connecticut, 12 September, 1909

It delighted me more than I can say to get your letters,[1]–not only because they were delightful letters but because almost four weeks had gone by since I had heard from you, and any news of you was as refreshing to me as rain on a parched land. I must admit the letters made me very uneasy, too; for working in that ancient filth is one of the most dangerous things I can think of your doing. It must be full of germs of every sort,–not necessarily from the people who once handled it (most such germs cannot have remained alive so long) but because such stuff naturally houses everything that is morbid and unwholesome, and there is no enemy to the mucous membrane like ancient dust. I hope with all my heart that you have taken no serious harm from the horrid tasks you have been working at.[2]

How *very* clean you must feel: how free from all old trash and impediments of all kinds: how thoroughly your own mistress, with an environment of your own choosing. The effect of it all on your spirits is deliciously evident in your letters. There is evidence of fatigue and disgust, of course, and I cannot help fearing as I read that you have overdone, and carried the cleaning through with a feverish energy that necessarily overtaxes; but underneath it all there bubbles up the joy of freedom, of accomplishment, of release, of purification,–of a return to yourself and to your own natural tastes and thoughts! It is as if you had at last found yourself, after a long nightmare,–at last become vivid and real in your own independent personality,–were just beginning to come to full flower after your own kind. I expect to see you grow more normal, and by the same token more delightful, with every passing month. Now we shall know and enjoy (how deeply!) the real Mary Allen, so long obliged to deny herself more than an occasional peep from behind her masquerade. It will not make as much difference to you as you think that you have so little to get along on. You will have the pleasure of discovering your own resources of skill and character: and I think you will find them inexhaustible. That is the happiness these last letters give me.

I hope that you are not going to be Quixotic enough to go down and work at cabinet making for Miss Darrell.[3] I have the greatest

[1] They are missing.

[2] Wilson was writing to Mrs. Peck in Pittsfield, Mass. As WW to Mary A. H. Peck, Oct. 25, 1909, indicates, she had decided to leave her husband and move to an apartment in New York. Wilson was referring to her preparations and packing for the move, which occurred during late 1909.

[3] The Editors have been unable to identify her.

admiration for her, and would certainly not give you any ungenerous advice; but you cannot give your physical strength to her without withdrawing it from your own proper life and its tasks; and that might be very serious. I am deeply distressed to hear of her trouble, and admire you more than ever for the way in which you are bestirring yourself to help her. I hope with all my heart that it will all turn out well with her.

It pleased me very much to hear of your plan of boarding with your mother in Bermuda. The suggestion that you might go down and be the guest of the Governor[4] made me very unhappy. It could not but be perceived what his object, his chief object, was in wishing to have you with him, namely, to get your aid and counsel in the private enterprise he has so much at heart.[5] Whether you abetted him (as of course *I* know you would not) or restrained him, it would be thought that you were his confederate at heart. It made me very unhappy to think of your running that risk. I am delighted beyond measure that you are not going to take it. The plan you now propose will be perfectly restful and will be full also of a great deal of quiet pleasure and satisfaction for you. How I wish I could hope to be there too!

Ellen feels that it is impossible for us to come up to Pittsfield just now. Her servants have gone back on her; everything is in confusion about her housekeeping plans; and she must go home as soon as possible. And it would be just about as difficult for me to come now. But we both want to come a little later, if it will be convenient for you to have us later. I am to attend Lowell's inauguration at Harvard on the sixth and seventh of October. How would it suit you to have Ellen and me come to you on the eighth and stay, if possible, till the eleventh? Would not the trees then be in their autumn glory (have on the "taudry" dress of which the English lady spoke) at that time, and would it not be a time when we should most enjoy wandering out of doors? Ellen will write you herself, and we want to [*sic*] you to say with the utmost frankness what would suit you best. The next hiatus in my engagement calendar does not come until the middle of November, and that would be too late, would it not? I am to be at Brookline and Boston on the twelfth and thirteenth of November,[6] and we could probably come on the fourteenth. If we come early in

[4] Lieutenant-General Frederick Walter Kitchener, Governor of Bermuda since 1908. He was a brother of Horatio Herbert Kitchener, 1st Earl Kitchener of Khartoum.

[5] That is, to court her. The Governor was a widower.

[6] To speak at the Harvard Congregational Church in Brookline, Mass., and to address the Princeton alumni in Boston. A news report of these addresses is printed at Nov. 13, 1909.

October, it will be almost as good as coming now. How heartily I hope that that will work out![7] It would put me in high spirits to have that to look forward to as I turn my face homeward to put on the harness and shoulder the burden! We start for Princeton on next Saturday, the eighteenth. This is our last Sunday in Lyme. At least for the present. We are so in love with the place that it looks more and more as if we would buy a house or a piece of land here, and make it our regular summer home.

The article on the tariff is finished. It now needs only the finishing touches of correcting and polishing. I shall send it to my editor, Colonel Harvey, within a day or two, and try to forget it. I have promised to address a new Democratic Club in Plainfield, New Jersey,[8] on the twenty-ninth of October on the issues of the day, and I am told, a good deal to my annoyance, that they are announcing the speech as "the opening of the campaign." I suppose they mean the State campaign which is to culminate in the choice of a Governor next year. One can never do a simple thing without its at once beginning to wear the appearance of being something else,—particularly something meant for one's own personal advancement.

Please do not let so long a time go by again without writing. I must keep in constant touch with you, if my spirits are to be steady and my tasks well done.

We are all well, and all unite in the most affectionate messages. My chief message is *Take care of yourself*. That is fraught with more affection, if you will be kind enough to read between the lines, than any other message I could frame. And yet you cannot need that assurance to realize that I am

Your devoted friend, Woodrow Wilson

[7] The Wilsons visited Mrs. Peck in Pittsfield from October 8 through October 11, 1909.

[8] A news report of Wilson's speech is printed at Oct. 30, 1909.

Dearest Friend, Princeton, New Jersey 19 September, 1909.

Here we are in Princeton again. The little journey was ac-c[o]mplished yesterday, very comfortably, for it was a delightful day,—almost as perfect as this wonderful, pure-aired Sunday, with its exquisite distances, at once clear and full of soft, dreamy atmosphere: a day to think poetry in, and, if you cannot think it, to feel it. We spent the morning getting out of our trunks and boxes (those of us who had them. My trunk did not not come) and the afternoon on the side piazza, Stockton Axson, Madge, Ellen, and I, drifting upon a quiet stream of talk and drinking in the heavenly air, while our eyes enjoyed every familiar thing about us, in the garden, in the angles of the house, in the country far away. Our own Margaret had to go to Baltimore a week ago to be with my sister,[1] who had to undergo an operation for one of the many ills women are heirs to and who did not like to leave her young daughter[2] alone in a boarding house. We are therefore a small family. Jessie and Nellie seem to be enjoying their foreign trip to the utmost; we get perfectly charming letters from them; but we miss them dreadfully and all the time.

We are eager to learn whether the time I suggested for our visit to Pittsfield will suit you. If it is going to be an inconvenient time for you to receive us, we shall wish to plan for some other. I hope it will be all right: I am looking forward to the time with such unmixed delight.

It is easy on a day like this to think of you, and to realize what you would think and say, were I near enough to hear and share what was passing through your thoughts. You love nature so genuinely and so simply, respond to it so eagerly and entirely, grow so gay and excited, so like a delightful girl, when it is at its best, its most poignant phases of beauty, that a day like this, so sweet and yet so vivid, so still and yet so quick with life, seems as if it were meant to contain you and to draw out in you all that is sweetest and happiest. You are a veritable child of nature. I mean it in a deeper sense than usual. I mean not only that there is a splendid naturalness and spontaneity about you, which you have never been able to spoil or cover by any self-defensive mask, but that Nature herself calls to you upon the instant, like a mother to her child, and that always in her presence the fine truth of you comes out, radiant, unmistakable. When you walk in the open you are much more easily and transparently yourself, whatever the talk may explicitly run upon, than in any room or any formal company. There is an air about you like the air of the open, a directness, a simplicity, a free movement that link you with wild things that are yet meant to be taken into one's confidence and loved. And so you have seemed part of the day to me ever since morning. There are winter days in Bermuda like this, and I remember them as days when you could not sit still, hearing the call of out-of-doors too loudly, and wanting to be quit of the house and all its thoughts. I can sympathize with you in it all deeply and keenly; but out-of-doors does not, alas! make me so delightful as it makes you.

I wish you could see some of the country about Lyme. It is in some respects incomparable in its beauty. Ellen and I have become so confirmed in our love of it by this summer's vacation there that we shall probably buy a piece of woodland there and put up a simple summer camp on it. No other country accessible to us makes her so happy, and it seems remote enough from ordinary associations, near enough golf and interesting human beings to suit me as well as a restless fellow can be suited anywhere. I wish the roads from it to the Berkshires ran more direct!

We are all well; all send affectionate messages to you; and one of us is Your devoted friend, Woodrow Wilson

WWTLS (WP, DLC).

[1] Annie Wilson Howe (Mrs. George Howe, Jr.).

[2] Annie Wilson Howe.

To Louis Edelman[1]

My dear Sir: Princeton, N. J. September 20th, 1909.

Allow me to acknowledge the receipt of your letter of September 14th.[2]

I wish very much that I could express an opinion that was worth publishing on the future of the American negro in the United States, but though it is a subject to which I have given a great deal of thought, I have never been able to bring my thinking to a satisfactory conclusion. I feel that men resident among the Southern negroes are the only men who can really answer this question with any degree of confidence.

With much regard,

Sincerely yours, Woodrow Wilson

TLS (WC, NjP).

[1] An oculist of Birmingham, Ala.

[2] It is missing.

To Cleveland Hoadley Dodge

My dear Cleve: Princeton, N. J. September 22nd, 1909.

One Sunday last winter you noticed the ragged condition of the hymn books in the University Chapel and were generous enough to say to me that you would pay for a new set.

I immediately obtained the figures as to how many would be necessary, but had hardly done so when other matters came up and crowded the thing entirely out of my mind.

I do not like to go forward with it now without asking you whether you would still be willing to have me do so.

I think about 600 books would be necessary and, if authorized

Woodrow Wilson in 1908

Andrew Fleming West

Howard Crosby Butler

John Grier Hibben

Edward Capps

Edwin Grant Conklin

Winthrop More Daniels

Guyot Hall near completion, 1909

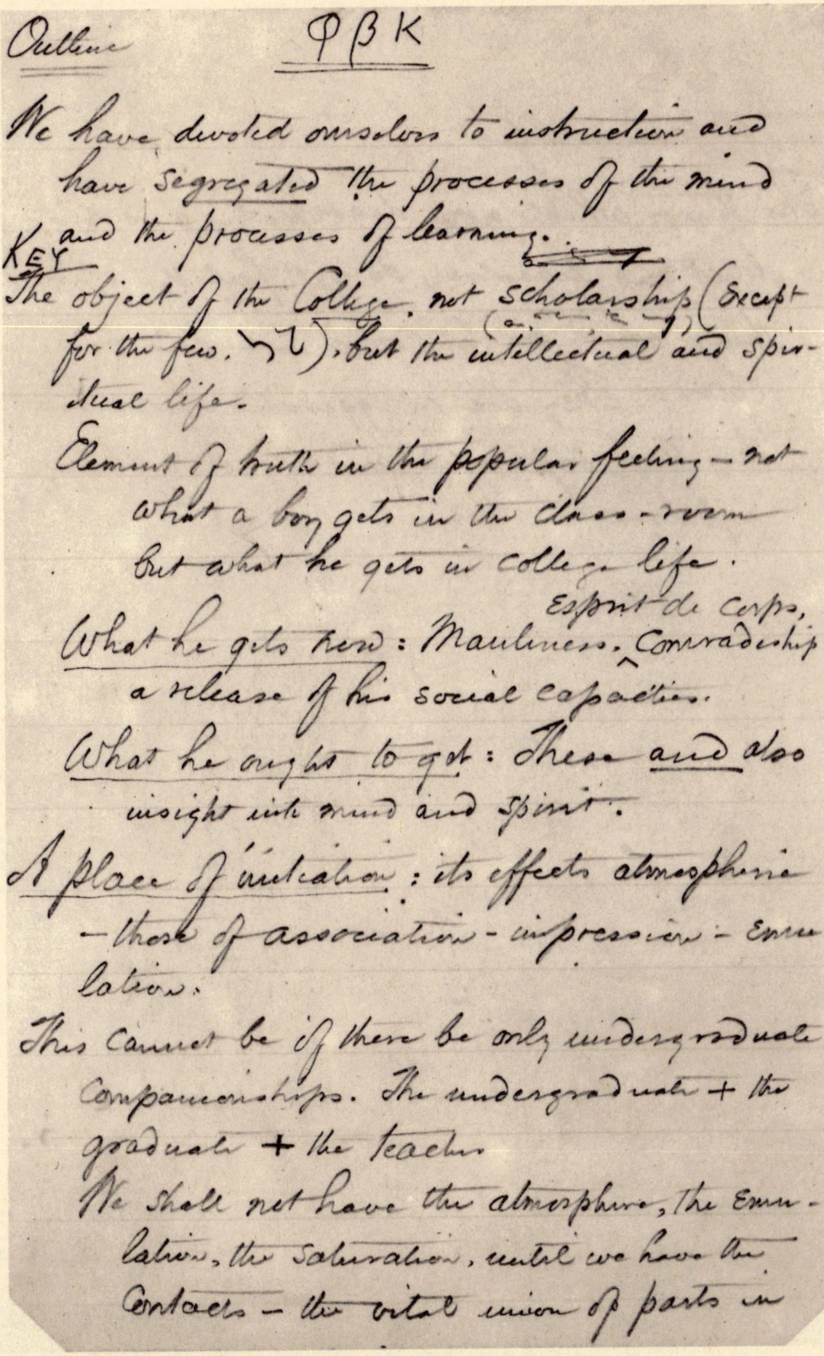
Outline ΦβK

We have devoted ourselves to instruction and have segregated the processes of the mind and the processes of learning.

KEY
The object of the College, not scholarship (except for the few), but the intellectual and spiritual life.

Element of truth in the popular feeling—not what a boy gets in the class-room but what he gets in college life.

What he gets now: Manliness, esprit de corps, comradeship a release of his social capacities.

What he ought to get: These and also insight into mind and spirit.

A place of initiation: its effects atmospheric—those of association—impression—emulation.

This cannot be if there be only undergraduate companionships. The undergraduate + the graduate + the teacher

We shall not have the atmosphere, the emulation, the saturation, until we have the contacts—the vital union of parts in

First page of Wilson's outline of his Phi Beta Kappa address at Harvard

Ralph Adams Cram

Woodrow Wilson and his family on the terrace at Prospect
The daughters, from the left, are Eleanor, Jessie, Margaret

Mary Allen Hulbert Peck

by you to do so, I will ascertain from the publishers what the price would be for them.

I sincerely hope that the summer brought you real rest and refreshment.

Always affectionately yours, Woodrow Wilson

TLS (WC, NjP).

From Ralph Adams Cram

Dear Dr. Wilson: Boston, Sept. 22, 1909

It is a long time since I have heard anything from you, and I am wondering what has happened, if anything, in the case of the Graduate College. When I last saw you, you expected to see Mr. Proctor very shortly, when the question of site was coming up for further consideration. Of course we are hoping against hope that actual construction may begin next Spring, and if this is to be the case, we shall want a good many months in which to prepare preliminary sketches and working plans for a building which, in the very nature of things, must be totally different in its layout and in its design to what we already have done. If there is anything I can do as Supervising Architect to help straighten the matter out, you have simply to let me know, but I should warn you that after the 4th of October, I may be difficult to control, owing to the lamentable fact that I have been drawn on the jury and shall probably have some difficulty in getting excused for any length of time during the six weeks or more that I shall be expected to serve. I could come to Princeton next week, if a consultation were possible, or desirable, at that time, but after that I am afraid most of my visits will have to be on Saturday and Sunday, when the Court will let me off.

Very truly yours, R A Cram.

TLS (WP, DLC).

From Ebenezer Mackey[1]

My dear Dr. Wilson, Trenton, N. J., September 22, 1909.

The New Jersey State Teachers' Association will hold its 55th Annual Meeting in Atlantic City Tuesday, Wednesday and Thursday, December 28th, 29th and 30th. The Association has a membership of approximately 6,000 teachers in this State. The central theme which I have chosen for discussion at the general sessions is "Training for Citizenship." I would like to have first a presentation of true ideals of the mission and function of the state, patriotism, loyalty, obedience to law, the enforcement of law, and other duties of citizenship. Then we should have discussions of education as a means for the prevention of crime and dependency. I am very eager to have you speak at one of these sessions and would like especially to have you make the address of the first evening session of the Convention, Tuesday, December 26th [28th]. Your relation to the cause of education in this state and in the United States, and your special studies in the line of history and civics, make you in my judgment the one man whom it is most important for us to have upon our program on this occasion. I hope you will find it both convenient and agreeable to accept the invitation. I shall be pleased to present the invitation in person if you so desire and will name the time for an interview.[2]

Wishing you the greatest possible happiness and success in your work for the coming year, I am,

Sincerely yours, E Mackey

TLS (WP, DLC).

[1] Supervising School Principal, Carroll Robbins School, Trenton, N. J., and President of the New Jersey State Teachers' Association.

[2] Wilson accepted; his address is printed at Dec. 28, 1909.

To Ralph Adams Cram

My dear Mr. Cram: [Princeton, N. J.] September 23rd, 1909.

I certainly owe you an apology for not having written you sooner. I have had it in mind several times, but my mind has this failing, that negatives pass out of it and only positives are left in occupation.

And it is a negative I have to report. My letter to Mr. Procter miscarried and the result was that we did not have any interview at all. I was very much disappointed, but on the whole I dare say it may work out just as well in the end through the action of the Committee of our Board of Trustees rather than through individual efforts.

I feel as you do the extreme desirability of pushing this matter as fast as possible, but one of the members of the committee of the Board is absent in Europe.[1] Just so soon as he returns we will have a meeting of the committee and put things in motion. For the moment there is nothing to do but to await his return.

It was a great disappointment to Mrs. Wilson and me that we could not visit you in Nahant. I found on my return to Lyme so many things to do which could not be postponed that going away again turned out to be out of the question.

Please give my warm regards to Mrs. Cram, and believe me,

Always faithfully yours, [Woodrow Wilson]

CCL (WWP, UA, NjP).

1 Cyrus H. McCormick.

A News Report

[Sept. 24, 1909]

UNIVERSITY FORMALLY OPENED

Exercises Conducted by President Wilson Start One Hundred and Sixty-Third Session.

The formal opening exercises of the one hundred and sixty-third session of the University were held yesterday afternoon in Marquand Chapel. The academic procession entered the chapel at 3 o'clock.

President Wilson conducted the exercises, opening them with the general confession. A hymn was then sung, followed by a short reading from the Psalms. President Wilson then delivered a very impressive address.

The session opens, he said, with the first thought in the minds of all being one of profound sadness. This sorrow is due to the death of Mr. Cornelius C. Cuyler, of the class of 1879, a man whose services to the University defied description and enumeration. He was a noble illustration of the best that Princeton stands for.

We never cease missing and mourning our dead, but our outlook should be directed toward the future. So every man entering college should ask himself why he came. And though there is no harm in certain childish traits that are purely superficial, yet, having come to college as a man, one should put away childish things. Our age is distinctly a creative one, which will be distinguished for its advances into fields little explored. That which gives mastery in this time is intellectual achievement. Because the University was a means of attaining this power, a student should realize that school days are over, and that the responsibilities of life are at hand. Play is excellent. It should be encouraged, but it should not be made an occupation; a man's occupation is work.

To everyone an opening is a solemnity. It is especially so to the entering man, on account of the strange and new experiences that are before him. Through these happenings, amid every confusion, the new man is at liberty to form opinions favorable and otherwise of the men and customs he meets. But always he should be sure of a respectable opinion of himself.

Princeton cannot give to her sons brains or the desire for work. The destiny for each man is carved out by himself. But Princeton is the place from which men may emerge, men certain of the future because they have conquered the past.

In concluding his address, President Wilson bade the entering men welcome, and extended a still warmer welcome to the faculty and the returning men, better known to him because of at least a year of friendship and comradeship.

The president's speech was followed by a prayer and a hymn, and the exercises were closed with the benediction.[1]

Printed in the *Daily Princetonian*, Sept. 24, 1909.

[1] There is a WWhw outline of this address, dated Sept. 23, 1909, in WP, DLC.

From Charles Scribner

My dear Mr. Wilson: New York Sept. 24, 1909

It will give me great pleasure to replace the Bible for the Chapel and I thank you for giving me the chance. I have asked Mr. Darrow[1] to find out the size and edition of the one now in use and whether it is desirable to make any change, for I wish to have the new copy exactly right.

Before I left for the other side in July Bridges showed me your letter about the article which you hoped to write for us and on my return I am delighted to find it[2] here. I have read it with great interest. It closes almost as abruptly as the old fashioned serial which stopped just when the hero faced the villian [villain].

Also I wish you to know that my son[3] is now one of your undergraduates—that is if the sophomores did not do him up last night. He is from St. Paul's School and thus far has been a source of satisfaction only. Unfortunately my name is in the Social Register and my pile is too close to four figures for you to expect much from him, but I hope he will leave a good record in the University and get here as soon as possible.

Yours sincerely Charles Scribner

TLS (WP, DLC).

[1] Charles Whitney Darrow, Princeton 1903, at this time Business Manager of Princeton University Press and of the Princeton Publishing Co., publishers of the *Princeton Alumni Weekly*.

[2] "What Is a College For?", printed at Aug. 18, 1909.

[3] Charles Scribner, Jr., Princeton 1913.

To Charles Scribner

My dear Mr. Scribner: Princeton, N. J. September 25th, 1909.

Allow me to thank you most heartily for your delightful and gracious letter of yesterday. You are certainly generous, and generous in a very characteristic fashion.

I am very much interested in your comment upon my article for the magazine. I was fully conscious of its abrupt termination, but I did not think it wise at present in a magazine article to plunge into an exposition of my favourite plans.[1] Those plans are receiving very much more favourable comment outside Princeton circles than within, but I am hoping that Princeton men will soon give me leave to make a very clear exposition of them.

It is a pleasure to know that your son is here, and I hope sincerely that college custom will sufficiently relax to allow me to know him better than I am allowed to know most of the undergraduates.

Always cordially and faithfully yours,

Woodrow Wilson

TLS (Charles Scribner's Sons Archives, NjP).

[1] That is, the quadrangle plan.

From Cleveland Hoadley Dodge

My dear Woodrow: New York September 25, 1909.

I have just returned from three weeks in the woods, and I find your good letter of the 22d.

I am very glad that you have not forgotten the ragged condition of the hymn books in the Chapel. It is a small matter, but it looks bad to anyone visiting Princeton and attending the Chapel, and I should be very glad to furnish new books. It might be well for you to advise with the proper people and see if we could secure, possibly, a better book than we have been using.

I sincerely trust that you have had a good rest and that everything in the College is opening up well.

Looking forward to seeing you soon,

Yours affectionately, C H Dodge

TLS (WP, DLC).

Two Letters to Mary Allen Hulbert Peck

Princeton, New Jersey,
My dearest Friend, 26 September, 1909.

I wish very much that I could know how you are. It would make these rather hard days of the opening of the college year seem a good deal brighter and easier. I would have one less thing to worry about, and could go about my business with one less question at the back of my head, to call my thoughts off at the wrong moment. After all, friends whom you love are a great nuisance, when you cannot have them at your side or where you can look them up when you choose, to see that they are all right. When they are at a distance, and *will* not write and one can only fill one's thought with conjectures about them, one always gets hold, perversely, of the wrong, the most disturbing conjectures. Suppose some friend, for example, has just been sorting a lot of old rubbish, dating, undisturbed, from unwholesome times long ago, and had, when she last wrote, a wretched cold, and made a half-playful allusion to germs when last she wrote, germs that might have lingered in the old stuff, it may be, a generation,–those germs poison your thought at every turn of the day, and your mind is sick, even if your friend is not, –particularly if you have a good memory and remember how your friend can carry a cough a winter through.

The University is under way for another session. It's simple enough to open it and set it going. We simply march in procession, in cap and gown, to the chapel, sing a hymn or two, read a passage out of Scripture, and hear the president greet the incoming men with a little homily on work and the opportunities and responsibilities of college men; and then classes assemble and everybody gets to work after his kind. Then the familiar crop of tasks and perplexities, those hardy annuals, spring up immediately, their season having come, and come to blossom with astonishing rapidity. Sophomores are tiresome young fools, and Freshmen are a great anxiety, and hardly worth being anxious about since they are to become sophomores in their turn. Committees meet and discuss the same old cases and questions, in new guises. There are lectures to deliver, and you are plagued by the same old ignorance: I mean your own, not the students'. Parents flock, with the same old delusions about their sons. Trustees tease you with suggestions and oppositions; alumni criticise, and praise as ignorantly and injudiciously as they criticise; invitations which you can hardly decline call you away just when you ought to be at home and "on the job." In brief, you know that you have fallen into the regular routine of your life again, and look around to pick up such scraps of mere pleasure as you can, as the days hurry by.

And yet a good many things wear an altered face this time. There is a new officer, a new dean,[1] taking hold this year, a young man with a very sensible and businesslike way of addressing himself to his duties and a fine idea of thoroughness. Old committees have to be in part changed in their personnel, and that means that new men, recently introduced into the Faculty, are recognized in the new appointments to be made, must be recognized because they deserve it; and the mere change of personnel means a movement forward in many an item of business, a new application of old principles here and there,–even an altered principle of action now and again. I wonder if that is what is the matter? I wonder if some of the older men, who used to feel as if the thing were in their hands, are as restless as they are because they feel themselves slipping out of the game, a new Princeton coming on whose promise of change is to them a threat of unwelcome things, things not of their own choosing. It is a favourite phrase of theirs, that I am doing away with "old Princeton" so fast that it will presently have lost its identity for the "old grad."

By the way, do you know one of our new men, Professor Frank Frost Abbott, the very distinguished classical scholar whom we coaxed away from Chicago? He comes from "somewhere up your way." He has just published a volume of essays and sketches under the title "Society and Politics in Ancient Rome"[2] the dedication of which reads, very simply but very significantly, "To M. A. P." I should very much like to have the full name attached to those initials! They render me deeply curious, and I naturally turn to you for enlightenment. Mrs. Abbott[3] is herself a very fascinating person, but those are not her initials. She could hold her own for charm and piquant interest even against unusual competition; but she is no such map of delights as I have seen laid before me, as if of a dear country in which everything pleased at once the heart and the mind! I wonder if I might ask Professor Abbott as well as you? I might read his face: at this distance I cannot read yours!

I will change the subject, to something less disturbing, but itself disturbing, too. I think that the thing that most strikes me each year at the opening of the University is the number of new

1 That is, Edward Graham Elliott, the new Dean of the College.
2 *Society and Politics in Ancient Rome: Essays and Sketches* (New York, 1909).
3 Jane Harrison Abbott.

faces in the faculty room when we meet after the opening exercises. There is always a sprinkling of young men, just called in to recruit the ranks at the bottom, and their presence makes me feel shy and uncomfortable. I love old, accustomed things and old, familiar faces. I hate the feeling of being at home and yet among strangers, who look curiously at you and sit by with critical mien. And yet, alas! *some* of the old, familiar faces do not wear the old, familiar expression, do not give back the glance as they used to. What a fool I am to go back to that so often! Can my heart *never* be cured of its hurt?

It is Sunday. It has been another of those heavenly days I was trying to describe when I wrote a week or two ago. The preacher[4] stayed with us till early afternoon, and was one of the nobler sort, whose talk puts heart into you, turning so naturally, as it does, to every good and hopeful thing. He seemed a natural companion for so serene and clear a day, with its air of freshness and renewal. I am ashamed to have let in despondent thoughts.

We are all well. Madge has just returned from New York with excited praise of the naval parade yesterday,[5] and news as if of another world. What a day it was for a pageant! At least I suppose the storm had passed with you as it had with us, and that nature had made ready for a holiday in all our eastern country. All join me in affectionate messages, and I am happy in having the right to subscribe myself

Your devoted friend, Woodrow Wilson

WWTLS (WP, DLC).

[4] The Rev. Dr. Floyd Williams Tomkins, rector of the Church of the Holy Trinity, Philadelphia.

[5] She had been to see the Hudson-Fulton Naval Pageant on Saturday, September 25, in which warships from several nations took part. The ships and several buildings in Manhattan were illuminated at night by strings of lights; there were also displays of fireworks.

Dearest Friend, Princeton, N. J. 29 Oct. [Sept.], 1909.

You mistook the date.[1] I shall be at the Harvard inauguration on the 6th and 7th of October. My plan, if it suits your convenience, is to join Mrs. Wilson somewhere *en route* (She is not going with me to Cambridge) on the 8th and reach Pittsfield that evening. We could stay, if you will let us, until the 11th, that is from Friday evening till Monday. You may be sure I am giving you, in this arrangement, all the time there is between engagements which I must respect. What are you going to do with us?—*Not*, we hope with all our hearts, get up *any* sort of entertainment for us! We are coming *to see you* and Mrs. Allen and want nothing else,—hope against anything else!

Why, when your friend's week-end letters are so dull, do you wish for a mid-week letter? Throughout the week my time belongs to any one who chooses to ask for it—and letters into which I wish to put some leisure of mind—some ease of spirit—are out of the question. I am writing now by snatches between conversations with callers, during my business hours ("2 to 4 every Monday, Tuesday and Wednesday in term time"—in the big, formal office you have seen), expecting every moment to hear the door of the outer office open and hear some one for a half hour or so on some matter of difficulty, big or little. Only matters of difficulty come to me—everything ordinary and normal takes care of itself. I am glad that there are delightful persons to think about amidst the questionings and worries! There is a particular delight in thinking often, at every turn of the day, that I am permitted to be

Your devoted friend, Woodrow Wilson

ALS (WP, DLC).

[1] Her letter is missing.

To Cleveland Hoadley Dodge

My dear Cleve., Princeton, N. J. 1 October, 1909.

Thank you most sincerely for your letter. You are generous, as always.

The choirmaster thinks the book we are now using on the whole the most satisfactory that he has seen; and I have given him several later ones to examine.

The book we are now using is "The Chapel Hymnal," published by The Presbyterian Board of Publication. We shall need at least six hundred copies. They agree to furnish them for forty-six cents each, ordered in that quantity. This will make the bill, if my arithmetic is correct, $276.00. On the strength of your letter I am ordering them to-day.

I shall look forward with real eagerness to seeing you. There are always many things to talk over, and I always come away heartened from a talk with you.

Always, Affectionately Yours, Woodrow Wilson

WWTLS (WC, NjP).

From Lawrence Crane Woods

My dear Dr. Wilson: Pittsburg, Pa. October 1, 1909.

We had the first meeting of our Princeton Club Executive Committee last evening and are planning our year's program. While it seems to be almost impossible for us to secure a theatre or hall for the purpose, if at all practicable we hope to arrange to have the Triangle Club here for Friday night and Saturday matinee performance, and then have our great Reunion Saturday night, as is our custom. Any time in March or April would answer our purpose. I presume if we have the Triangle Club, it would be impracticable for us to have our meeting much before the first of April.

I am giving you these suggestions in advance, hoping that nothing will prevent our having the pleasure and privilege and Princeton the profit of your being our honor guest this year. Surely the second or third best Princeton alumni center in the country should have a visit from the President not less than every other year.[1]

Pray appreciate now that I am simply putting this before you in order that you may work it in with your other engagements to the least inconvenience to yourself. I certainly hope that you will not be overwhelmed with general public speaking this year. Just the other day I was approached as president of the club here to see if we would not use our good offices to secure your presence at a dinner here in February, and I told the people frankly that, while appreciating their action, I did not believe that it was a friendly thing to you or to Princeton to be flooding you with requests to speak, and that I hoped you would reduce your engagements this year to those only of the first importance.

I trust you have had a very delightful and restful summer.

Very sincerely yours, Lawrence C Woods

TLS (WP, DLC).

[1] Wilson accepted the invitation. News reports of his address are printed at April 17 and 20, 1910, Vol. 20.

From William Frederick Dix[1]

My dear Dr. Wilson: New York, October 1st, 1909.

At a meeting of the Board of Trustees of this Company held on the 29th ulto. you were nominated to fill the vacancy caused by the recent resignation of Mr. Hugo Baring of London,[2] by Mr. Henry W. Taft[3] and seconded by Mr. Wayne MacVeagh.[4] Both of these gentlemen spoke of the honor it would be to the

Board to have you as a member and there was much pleasure expressed by others [other] members on their being informed that you had signified your willingness to accept election. There were no other nominations and under our By-Laws the nomination must go over until the next meeting of the Board which will occur on October 27th, at which time you will without doubt be duly elected a member. President Peabody[5] has asked me to express to you his personal gratification in the matter and to say that he and all the members of the Board will give you a most cordial welcome.

Please allow me to give you my personal assurance that you will be most pleasantly received as a trustee of this Company.

With cordial regards, I am,

Very truly yours, William Frederick Dix

TLS (WP, DLC).

1 Princeton 1889, Secretary of the Mutual Life Insurance Co. of New York.

2 A partner in the London banking firm of Baring Bros. & Co., Ltd. Actually, at this time Baring was living in New York and managing the bank's New York office, Baring Brothers & Co., Ltd.

3 Henry Waters Taft, a brother of President Taft and member of the New York law firm of Cadwalader, Wickersham & Taft. From 1905 to 1907 he had served as special assistant to the United States Attorney General in the case against the American Tobacco Co.

4 Isaac Wayne MacVeagh, prominent politician, diplomat, and former Attorney General of the United States. At this time he was a member of the Washington law firm of McKenney & Flannery and resided in Bryn Mawr, Pa.

5 Charles Augustus Peabody, President of the Mutual Life Insurance Co. of New York since 1906.

Two Letters from Cyrus Hall McCormick

Dear Woodrow: Chicago 2 October, 1909.

I am deeply regretful that I cannot be at the meeting of the Graduate School Committee which is to be held on Monday. I had set aside business so that I could go, but unfortunately I have a temporarily disabled hand which my surgeon tells me is not well enough for me to travel with.

I understand that Ned Sheldon will not be at the meeting, so it is possible that a final conclusion of the matter may not be reached, altho Pyne advises me that he thinks so much time has elapsed, the matter ought to be settled now.

The first publication of this matter occurred about May nineteenth,[1] so practically only one month has elapsed since this offer in which any work could be done, for it would not be fair to count the summer vacation as time running against us.

I have written Pyne expressing my views as to the order of preference and choice of sites, and he has my personal views;

but I told him also that I would accord to the will of the majority. My order of preference, as explained to Pyne, is as follows:

1. The Olden and Brackett properties.[2]
   I recognize that there are large difficulties in the way of acquiring these properties.
2. The property on the east side of Washington Street, sloping down the hill and fronting on Prospect Avenue by the acquiring of Professor West's old house[3] and the property just south of it.
   I understand that this property has been sold to a club[4] and they are now erecting their building, so this might be a very difficult question; but you can see the strategic advantage of having a gate-way entrance to the Graduate School at the corner of Prospect Avenue and Washington Street, with the rest of the School and the buildings sloping down the hill and spreading out into the open field as far as necessary.
3. The golf ground.

N.B. I leave out entirely "Merwick" because of Mrs. Swan's will; and the location between '79 Hall and the President's House as being too contracted and as being too much in the centre of the University grounds.

I suggested to Pyne that we ought to have the opinion on the question of this location of Messrs. Capps, Abbott and Conklin, who are men we are depending upon to make this Graduate School a success. I also suggested that Mr. Proctor should, if possible, be brot in contact with some of the members of the Graduate School Committee other than Professor West, Pyne and yourself.

I am, Very cordially yours, Cyrus H. McCormick.

[1] That is, the news account of the Procter offer, which appeared in the *Princeton Alumni Weekly*, IX (May 19, 1909), 501.

[2] The Olden property was on the east side of Washington Road, running approximately from Prospect Avenue to William Street. The Brackett property was on the northeast corner of Prospect Avenue and Washington Road.

[3] West's house was on the southeast corner of Washington Road and Prospect Avenue.

[4] The Campus Club occupied West's house in 1901; construction of a new club house was completed on the same site in 1910.

My dear Woodrow: Chicago 2 October, 1909.

I have just learned that you have consented to be in Chicago for November second, to deliver an address at the Historical Celebration at the Seminary here. It is needless for me to say that I expect you to come directly to our house. I would like to know when you are planning to leave, and whether you will have any time for luncheon with some of the Alumni here or to visit any of the schools on November third,[1] or whether you will be here for Saturday or Sunday, the thirtieth or thirty-first of October.

Do not put anything aside in answering this note, but let me know whenever it is convenient for you to arrange your plans.

I am, Very sincerely yours, Cyrus H. McCormick.

TLS (WP, DLC).

1 Insofar as is known, Wilson did not speak at any Chicago school during his visit in November. However, he did speak briefly at a dinner of the Princeton Club of Chicago, as the news report printed at November 3, 1909, reveals.

From Ebenezer Mackey

My dear Dr. Wilson: Trenton, N. J. Oct. 2nd, 1909.

I am very greatly delighted to have your acceptance of our invitation to deliver an address at the meeting of the State Teachers' Association in Atlantic City Tuesday evening, Dec. 28th. You have chosen just the theme[1] which I think is of the utmost importance just now for us to hear you discuss. Atlantic City is a place of many attractions and the Christmas Holiday Season is a time when teachers find it difficult to attend meetings, but I am expecting not only that a large audience will greet you at the meeting, but also that your message will reach a still larger number of teachers and other friends of education through the newspapers and the Annual Report of the Association.

With the most cordial greetings, I am,

Sincerely yours, E. Mackey

TLS (WP, DLC).

1 "The State and the Citizen's Relation to It." This address is printed at Dec. 28, 1909.

From James Edward Shepard[1]

Dear Sir: Durham, North Carolina Oct 2/09

I am in receipt of your kind favor of Sept 28/09.[2] I can appreciate fully the many calls upon you and how you cannot accept all. This movement right now needs all the sympathy and support possible. The idea is new to the American people, so far as the Negro is concerned.

With strong backing from our white friends North and South, we will secure and hold public attention.

I am writing this letter to make a second request, which means a great deal and the granting of which is a contribution and a favor to the race.

The request is will you not write a letter which I could make public showing the advantages of this kind of education for my people. Such a letter would have great weight.[3]

I am asking it because I know you are not in the habit of doing such things.

I am making a copy of a testimonial which I have just received from Supt Joyner of N.C.[4]

Yours very truly James E. Shepard

I am glad to state that Hon H. B. F. Macfarland Commissioner of the Dist of Columbia, Wash. D. C. and Dr. Len G. Broughton, Atlanta Ga.[5] have accepted places on the Board. The number under the Charter to be 29. Two more yet to be chosen.

ALS (WP, DLC).

[1] This distinguished black educator, who left a deep imprint upon higher education in North Carolina, was born in 1875, trained in pharmacology at Shaw University, and was self-taught in theology. He served as comparer of deeds in the Recorder's Office, Washington, D. C., during 1898, and as deputy collector of United States internal revenue at Raleigh, N. C., 1899-1905. From 1905 to 1909, he began his educational work among Negroes as field superintendent of the International Sunday School Association. In 1909-10, he organized and became President of the National Religious Training School and Chautauqua for the Colored Race in Durham, N. C. This institution became the Durham State Normal School, 1923-25, North Carolina College for Negroes, 1925-47, North Carolina College at Durham, 1947-69, and North Carolina Central University in 1969. Shepard was president of this institution under its various names until his death in 1947.

[2] Shepard's papers were destroyed by fire in 1925, hence Wilson's letter is not extant. However, as Shepard's letter soon makes clear, he had asked Wilson to become a number of the Board of Trustees of the National Religious Training School and Chautauqua for the Colored Race.

[3] Wilson probably replied; however, his letter is not extant.

[4] James Yadkin Joyner "To Whom It May Concern," Sept. 27, 1909. Joyner was Superintendent of Public Instruction in North Carolina and also serving at this time as President of the National Education Association. His letter expressed his sympathy for any movement for the education of Negroes and his approval of the National Religious Training School and Chautauqua for the Colored Race. He commended it "to the support of those interested in the moral and religious training of the Negro race in the South."

[5] The Rev. Leonard Gaston Broughton, M.D., founder and pastor of the Atlanta Baptist Tabernacle and founder of the Tabernacle Infirmary and Tabernacle Dormitory for Young Ladies in Atlanta.

To Cyrus Hall McCormick

My dear Cyrus: Princeton, N. J. October 4th, 1909.

Thank you very much for your two letters of the second.

I sincerely hope that there is nothing really serious the matter with your hand. The way you speak of it makes me a little apprehensive.

I feel that we must have a full meeting of the Committee on the Graduate School before the present questions pending are decided, because for my own part I may say that I know of no more important questions connected with the future of the University. It is necessary that we should have a very full and frank conference about the whole matter and discuss the various things which are involved. They are many and of the highest consequence. Perhaps the meeting this evening may help to clear up matters a little.[1]

It gave me great pleasure to be able to consent to speak at the McCormick Seminary. When I learned that the exercises were in celebration of the services of your father, I felt that I could not decline. It would have disappointed me too much not to be permitted to take part.

Always faithfully and affectionately yours,

Woodrow Wilson

TLS (WP, DLC).

[1] The meeting was a standoff. Wilson forcefully presented his case for central location of the Graduate College and argued that he needed the opportunity to try to bring Procter to his point of view. The committee decided to postpone a decision until Wilson had conferred with Procter, which would occur before the meeting of the Board of Trustees on October 21. See A. F. West to W. C. Procter, Oct. 5, 1909, and M. T. Pyne to W. C. Procter, Oct. 5, 1909.

To Lawrence Crane Woods

My dear Mr. Woods: Princeton, N. J. October 4th, 1909.

Thank you very much for your letter of October 1st. I do not see now any reason to doubt my ability to attend the reunion of the Pittsburgh alumni in March or April. If you will be kind enough to keep me apprised of the progress of the plans, I shall try to make the date that is convenient to you convenient also to myself. The latter part of the week which you propose is much the best with me because it does not interfere with my lecture engagements here in Princeton.

It is very pleasant to hear of all the interest the Pittsburgh men are taking in the University. I am sure every one of us here feels the vital influence of the group of devoted men in Pittsburgh.

Please give my warm regards to your brother and his wife[1] and believe me,

Always faithfully and cordially yours,

Woodrow Wilson

TLS (WC, NjP).

[1] Edward Augustus Woods and Gertrude Macrum Woods. He was manager of the Edward A. Woods Co. of Pittsburgh, general agents for the Equitable Life Assurance Society of the United States.

To John Alexander Campbell

My dear Mr. Campbell: [Princeton, N. J.] October 4th, 1909.

Allow me to acknowledge the receipt of your letter of October 2nd, enclosing a letter to be presented to the Board of Trustees[1] proposing that a portion of the income to be derived by the University from Campbell Hall, the gift of the Class of 1877, be devoted to the maintenance of one of the unendowed professorships of the University and that the professorship so supported be called "The Class of 1877 Professorship," under the conditions named in your letter. The proposal seems to me a most reasonable one and I have no doubt at all that the Trustees will be very pleased to adopt it.[2] The class seems to me to have exercised unusual generosity in every respect in connection with this gift, and the suggestion your letter contains seems to me to be clearly in the interests of the University.

Cordially and sincerely yours, [Woodrow Wilson]

CCL (WWP, UA, NjP).

[1] Both Campbell's letter and its enclosure are missing.

[2] At their meeting on October 21, 1909, the trustees created a new chair entitled "The Class of 1877 Professorship." Charles Freeman Williams McClure was its first occupant as Class of 1877 Professor of Zoology. In addition, the trustees ruled that lineal descendants of the Class of 1877 should be given preference for rooms in Campbell Hall.

From Frederick A. Duneka

Dear Mr. Wilson: New York October Fourth 1909

Thank you ever so much for your note of October 2, which brings the cheering information that you have a volume of essays which we[1] may have the honor of publishing.[2]

We should, of course, be delighted to do this book. The terms, I assume, would be the usual royalty arrangements.

It is too late, as you perhaps know, to issue a volume with any expectation of success this Autumn; or did you have Fall publication in mind?

Let me thank you again in the name of Colonel Harvey and of the House, for the opportunity you so kindly give.

Yours sincerely, F A Duneka

TLS (WP, DLC).

[1] Harper and Bros.

[2] The volume was never published.

William Cooper Procter to Moses Taylor Pyne

Cincinnati, Ohio, October 4, 1909

I understand meeting of Trustees held at Princeton today to avoid possible misunderstanding may I ask you to advise them if necessary that I have visited Princeton six times and personally examined every site suggested both on the grounds and on the maps and that only two are satisfactory namely Merwick and Golf Links. Wm. Cooper Procter

TC telegram (M. T. Pyne Coll., NjP).

From John Alexander Campbell

My dear Mr. President, Trenton, N. J., Oct. 5, 1909.

I am much indebted for your letter of October 4th and for the kindly expressions contained in there regarding the Class of '77. Our fellows have always valued very highly your friendship, and have had a great admiration for you personally, and the gift of the dormitory under your Presidency is tangible evidence of this regard and confidence. They will be glad to know that you favor the naming of one of the Professorships "The Class of 1877 Professorship.["]

With best wishes and kindest personal regards to yourself and family, Yours very truly, John A Campbell

TLS (WP, DLC).

Andrew Fleming West to William Cooper Procter

Dear Cooper: [Princeton, N. J.] October 5, 1909.

At a meeting of the Trustees' Committee on the Graduate School held last night in Mr. Pyne's Library, Princeton, the Committee considered the question of the site of the Graduate College in view of your offer, and I herewith send you the following extract from the minutes of the Committee meeting:

"With a view to forwarding the decision of the Committee with respect to its recommendation to be made to the Board of Trustees the Secretary was requested to write Mr. Procter that it was the desire of the Committee that the President should confer with Mr. Procter at as early a date as can be arranged and report to the Committee prior to the October meeting of the Board."

The October meeting of the Board occurs on Thursday the 21st., and President Wilson will communicate with you in the hope of arranging for a conference as soon as possible.

Ever yours, Andrew F. West

TCLS (WWP, UA, NjP).

Moses Taylor Pyne to William Cooper Procter

CONFIDENTIAL

My dear Mr. Procter: [Princeton, N. J.] October 5th, 1909.

I told you last June that I would keep you advised as to what was done at the meetings of the Committee regarding the Graduate School. Your telegram reached me on Monday afternoon in good season before the meeting, and I presented it to the Committee. The whole Committee were present with the exception of Mr. McCormick, who is ill in Chicago, and Mr. Garrett, whose son is dangerously ill in Baltimore.

At the meeting the President brought out very strongly his views as to the interpenetration of the life of the Graduate College with that of the Undergraduate, and suggested another site which he called a new site, but which, in a general way, was considered by us last year. He expressed his views so strongly and also expressed the feeling that you ought to hear them before making your final decision that there was nothing for the Committee to do but to tell him that if he thought so, it was his duty to go out to Cincinnati and lay his views before you. I should say, however, that the views did not impress themselves upon me as of any value, and that while there was no direct vote taken, the matter being left until after his interview with you, I know that he did not have a majority of the Committee with him. If he has this interview with you we are to have a meeting of the Committee immediately upon his return, and it is understood that the matter is to be finally decided on the 21st of October, the date of the meeting of the Board of Trustees.

I regret very much that the matter has taken this course but in view of the fact that the President seems to think it so vital to present this matter to you, it was deemed best to have an adjourned meeting of the Committee after his return from Cincinnati. It, however, does not delay the final consideration of the matter, which must be done on the 21st of October.

With kind regards to Mrs. Procter, believe me,

Yours very sincerely, M. Taylor Pyne.

TCL (M. T. Pyne Coll., NjP).

From John Franklin Jameson[1]

Washington, D. C.
Dear Friend and "Former Student": October 6, 1909

On the evening before my fiftieth birthday I was, not unnaturally, "considering how my life was spent." Without overmuch beating of the breast or tearing of the hair, I was coming rapidly and easily to the conclusion that I had not played my hand nearly so well as I ought, when a letter[2] was brought in which, brief and simple as it was, immediately changed the whole aspect of the matter. I said to myself at once, and have been saying to myself ever since, that if seventy-five such persons, men and women who are doing such work and occupying such positions in the world, could think well enough of me and my twenty-four years of teaching to write such a letter as that, I had no right ever to feel discouraged. I thank you from the bottom of my heart, dear friend, you and your associates, for your kind thought, your affectionate remembrance, your good wishes. You have increased the happiness with which I always think of the best of those whom I taught, and have made my whole life seem to me better worth while.

I should have been more than content with your friendly letter had it stood alone. But when I got back to Washington, a few days ago, I found in my hall a truly magnificent Tiffany clock, one of the handsomest I ever saw—so handsome indeed that I ought immediately to have the hall re-papered, and get a new suit of clothes! But whether I ever succeed in living up to it or not, it will be a source of pride and pleasure to me all my days. I thank you most heartily for your part in this beautiful gift, and cordially hope that you will come soon to see it. It is so placed that it is the first thing I see as I enter my house, and I never see it without grateful and happy thoughts of those who sent it.

With the best of wishes, and especially, if you are teaching, with the hope that you may have such men and women to teach as I have had, I am, as always,

Sincerely your friend, J. F. Jameson.

ALS (WP, DLC).

1 At this time Director of the Department of Historical Research at the Carnegie Institution of Washington and Managing Editor of the *American Historical Review*.

2 WW *et al.* to J. F. Jameson, Sept. 19, 1909, HwLS (J. F. Jameson Papers, DLC). The letter read: "We, your former students, hope that you will accept this birthday present as a mark of our gratitude, appreciation, and warmest regard." As Jameson's letter indicates, the gift was a Tiffany clock. Among the signers of the letter, in addition to Wilson, were Frederick Jackson Turner, Charles McLean Andrews, John Martin Vincent, Westel Woodbury Willoughby, William Franklin Willoughby, Davis Rich Dewey, and Mary Emma Woolley.

William Cooper Procter to Moses Taylor Pyne

My dear Mr. Pyne: Cincinnati. October 6, 1909.

Upon my return to the city I found your several favors and wired you as requested, relative to the locating of the proposed Graduate College.

I received a telegram from President Wilson, asking me to meet him, which I take to mean that no definite conclusion was reached at the meeting. I am sorry that he is so greatly opposed to the selection made as, in my opinion, it is the only one available and I will have to stand for it.

I have wired President Wilson that I will met him in the East about the twentieth and hope that a definite conclusion can be reached at that time and the matter finally settled. I hope I may have the opportunity of seeing you also about that time.

With kind regards to Mrs. Pyne,[1] I am,

Yours very sincerely, Wm. Cooper Procter.

TCL (M. T. Pyne Coll., NjP).

[1] Margaretta Stockton Pyne.

A Statement About the Bible

[Oct. 8, 1909]

"The educational value of a knowledge of the Bible is that it both awakens the spirit to its finest and only true action and acquaints the student with the noblest body of literature in existence, a body of literature having in it more mental and imaginative stimulus than any other body of writings. A man has deprived himself of the best there is in the world who has deprived himself of this."

Printed in the *Daily Princetonian*, Oct. 8, 1909.

From William Cooper Procter

Cincinnati Oct 8 [1909]

Will meet you at Princeton Wednesday morning the twentieth

Wm Cooper Proctor.[1]

T telegram (WWP, UA, NjP).

[1] This was a reply to WW to W. C. Procter, Oct. 5, 1909, quoted in WW to E. W. Sheldon, Oct. 12, 1909.

From Melancthon Williams Jacobus

My dear President Wilson: Hartford, Conn., October 8th, 1909.

In the confusion of these last two days, I failed to ask you whether Wednesday evening or Wednesday afternoon, October 20th, would be the more convenient to you for a meeting of the Curriculum Committee.

A meeting must be called, according to a statement just received from Mr. McAlpin, in order to report to the Board new appointments on the Faculty which have not as yet been acted on by them. For this reason at least, therefore, a day and hour will have to be fixed for the Committee's coming together. Kindly let me know your preference and I will call the meeting accordingly.

Trusting that you are securing some needed rest after the strenuous days we have been having, I am

Yours very sincerely, Melancthon W Jacobus

TLS (WP, DLC).

From David Benton Jones

My dear Doctor Chicago Oct. 8 '09

I cant tell you how it delighted me to see in Lowell's address your name mentioned in a way that clearly indicates your position as leader in the movement to reestablish University life in this country.[1] Only a brief statement appeared in our papers.

There is no doubt of the growing recognition of present conditions. Will Princeton resign her present position at the head of the movement? That is my chief concern.

Very Sincerely David B. Jones.

ALS (WP, DLC).

[1] Actually, Lowell referred only briefly to Wilson in his inaugural address, citing his "luminous Phi Beta Kappa oration" at Harvard (printed at July 1, 1909). In that address, according to Lowell, Wilson "dwelt upon the chasm that has opened between college studies and college life." Lowell stressed that "the undergraduate should be led to feel from the moment of his arrival that college life is a serious and manysided thing, whereof mental discipline is a vital part." *Harvard Graduates' Magazine*, XVIII (Dec. 1909), 220-221.

From Edward Wright Sheldon

My dear Woodrow: New York. October 11th, 1909.

In view of the very serious condition of the finances of the University, the temporary charge of which is now confided to me, I have been examining the possible directions for retrenchment. Among them is the possibility of reducing the number of the teaching force, if an opportunity should present itself. A reduction in any salary is, I assume, impracticable. You have doubtless given this subject most careful consideration, and can let me have your views without any considerable expenditure of time. It is not of course a question of what we should like to do, but what, under the spur of necessity, we must do to bring our finances into better condition. The present situation of being subject for our current expenses to the changing ability or mental attitude of contributing alumni seems to me not only unbusinesslike but intolerable.

If you have a copy of Mr. Proctor's letter of last May in which he made his conditional offer for the Graduate College, will you kindly send me one? I should like to have the precise language before me. Have you been able to arrange any interview with him?

Trusting that your Cambridge visit was most agreeable, and that the journey to Hanover[1] will not be unduly fatiguing, believe me, Yours sincerely, Edward W. Sheldon.

TLS (WP, DLC).

[1] Wilson was to attend the inauguration of Ernest Fox Nichols as President of Dartmouth College and to make an address, the text of which is printed at Oct. 14, 1909.

To Edward Wright Sheldon

My dear Ed.: [Princeton, N. J.] October 12th, 1909.

Thank you very much for your letter of October 11th, which reached me this morning. I am just back from Cambridge, where everything was very interesting, but I am heartily glad to be here again and get once more down to the business which absorbs us all.

I need not say that the question of possible retrenchment, even in our expenditure for teaching, has occupied my thoughts a great deal.

You will remember that the Finance Committee passed a resolution asking the Committee on the Curriculum to take up the matter of any possible reduction of expenses on the teaching side.[1] The committee has had one discussion of the matter which centered chiefly upon the very difficult question of the necessary number of Preceptors in the various Departments. It is so hard to arrive at a standard for determining the necessary number that that discussion resulted in very little, and I am now consulting with the Heads of the various Departments with a view to reporting very fully to the committee on the Curriculum on this matter before the January meeting. Our contracts with the preceptors all run to the end of this year, the close of the original guarantee. This is the year, therefore, when it is necessary to consider the whole matter and see what can be done, Department by Department, to effect a greater economy. Unhappily, all the salaries are so low that reductions in salary seem really out of the question, if we are to expect the men to live here at all, but I am hoping that in one or two Departments it may be possible to reduce the teaching force. To do so will, I am afraid, considerably impair the efficiency of the Preceptorial System, and it is going to be hard to effect reductions without giving the impression that we are returning upon our tracks, but I know the present necessity and shall not hesitate to advise anything that seems practicable.

I foresee this. It is certainly true that in some of the Departments there is a sadly inadequate teaching force. In my own Department, for example, to which something like two thirds of the upperclassmen resort in their choice and which is clearly overwhelmed with teaching, so much so that we have had to resort to the questionable expedient of having preceptorial work done by a number of instructors as well as by men undoubtedly qualified for the preceptorial rank and task. Of course, no one of us would think of remedying the situation by making the teaching inadequate in other Departments, but if it should prove possible to reduce the number of Preceptors in one or two of the other Departments, it will, it seems to me, be our duty to ask ourselves whether we ought not merely to effect a redistribution and relieve the Department which is now suffering most heavily.

I think that you used just the right words when you speak of the present situation as not only unbusinesslike but intolerable. I am ready to enter upon any way of escape except that which should deprive us altogether of our present prestige by seeming to be a deliberate impairment of the system which has given us that prestige. I can tell you what I think practicable just so soon as my present investigation, which is necessarily slow-footed, is completed.

I enclose my copy of Mr. Procter's letter of May 8th making his conditional offer for the Graduate School. On October 5th, the day after our meeting at Pyne's, I telegraphed Mr. Procter as follows: "Graduate School Committee of the Board earnestly desires me to confer with you to set forward our important business. Am officially bound to attend Harvard and Dartmouth inaugurations, but will be free 12th, 13th, 15th, 16th. Would it be possible for me to meet you in the East on any one of those dates or in Cincinnati on the 16th?", to which I added the addresses at which I could be reached. Under date of October 8th I received from Mr. Procter the following answer: "Will meet you at Princeton Wednesday morning, the 20th." You will notice that the 20th is the day just before the Board meets, and Mr. Procter's choice of that date seems to me to create a seriously inconvenient situation. I am at a loss to understand his action and should like very much to know your own judgment as to how the committee ought to act in the meantime. It will, of course, be extremely difficult, if not impossible, to handle the matter with deliberation then, and I am afraid that his choice of the 20th is apt to operate to force our hand.

The exercises at Harvard were very interesting, but Princeton is so engrossing at Present that I can hardly get my mind back to what took place at Cambridge.

With warm regard,

Always affectionately yours, [Woodrow Wilson]

CCL (WWP, UA, NjP).

[1] H. G. Duffield to M. W. Jacobus, Jan. 26, 1909, printed as an Enclosure with M. W. Jacobus to WW, Feb. 3, 1909.

To Moses Taylor Pyne

My dear Momo: [Princeton, N. J.] October 12th, 1909.

On October 5th, the day following our meeting at your house, I sent the following telegram to Mr. Procter: "Graduate School Committee of the Board earnestly desires me to confer with you to set forward our important business. Am officially bound to attend Harvard and Dartmouth inaugurations, but will be free 12th, 13th, 15th, 16th. Would it be possible for me to meet you in the East on any one of those dates or in Cincinnati on the 16th"; to which I added the addresses at which I could be reached. He replied on the 8th that he would meet me here in Princeton on the 20th.

You will notice that this is the date immediately preceding the meeting of the Board of Trustees. I regret this exceedingly, because it gives us no sufficient time for deliberation after the conference.

I am starting for Dartmouth tomorrow morning and shall not be able to get back from the distant place before Friday night or Saturday morning.

I take it for granted that our meeting set for Saturday[1] will be held, but in any case I should like to see you as soon as possible to consult as to what is to be done.

Always cordially and faithfully yours,

[Woodrow Wilson]

CCL (WWP, UA, NjP).

1 Actually, because Procter was unable to meet Wilson until October 20, this meeting of the trustees' Committee on the Graduate School, set for October 16 in New York, was canceled. See M. T. Pyne to WW, Oct. 14, 1909.

To Melancthon Williams Jacobus

My dear Dr. Jacobus: [Princeton, N. J.] October 12th, 1909.

I have your letter of October 8th. Mrs. Wilson and I got back from Massachusetts only last night. It was tantalizing to catch occasional glimpses of you at the exercises at Harvard without being able to talk to you again.

I did not hear from Mr. Procter until after I left Cambridge. He then telegraphed me under date of October 8th: "Will meet you at Princeton Wednesday morning, the 20th." I feel that this choice of date is very unfortunate and that his coming to Princeton on that day will make it impossible to handle the great matter we have in hand in any deliberate or successful way, but I suppose there is no use, after my telegram which I read you, in trying to arrange it differently.

Because Mr. Procter is to be in Princeton during the day, I think it will be best for us, if it suits your convenience, to have the Curriculum Committee meet in my office that evening at say half past eight o'clock. There is very little except routine business to dispose of, inasmuch as my report about possible retrenchment in the Preceptorial System is not to be ready until the January meeting.

I hope that you did not find the affair at Cambridge too fatiguing and that you found it as interesting and amusing as I did.

Cordially and faithfully yours, [Woodrow Wilson]

CCL (RSB Coll., DLC).

To Thomas Duckett Boyd[1]

Princeton, N. J.

My dear President Boyd: October 12th, 1909.

I was absent from home when your kind letter of October 8th reached Princeton and am only just now at my desk again.

It is extremely gratifying to me that you should desire me to make the address on behalf of the endowed universities on the occasion of your approaching celebration of the Fiftieth Anniversary of the establishment of the Louisiana State University, and you may rest assured that I would do it with pleasure, if it were possible. Unhappily, however, I am bound by engagements elsewhere from which I cannot honorably withdraw.

I hope that you will express to all who have united with you in this invitation my warm appreciation and sincere regret, and that you will allow me to express for myself and my colleagues the warmest congratulations upon the completion of a half century of honorable service by the University.

Cordially and sincerely yours, Woodrow Wilson

TLS (T. D. Boyd Papers, LU).

[1] Prominent southern educator and President of Louisiana State University and Agricultural and Mechanical College since 1896.

From William Cooper Procter

My dear President Wilson: Cincinnati October 13, 1909.

I find I have to be in New York early next Wednesday afternoon. May I ask you, therefore, to meet me at the Holland House at 10:15 Wednesday morning instead of my meeting you in Princeton? If you think it advisable for me to go to Princeton, I could meet you there early in the morning, but my time would be very short. Kindly advise me which you prefer.

Yours very truly, Wm. Cooper Procter

TLS (WWP, UA, NjP).

From Edward Wright Sheldon

My dear Woodrow: New York. October 13th, 1909.

I have your letter of yesterday, and earnestly hope that the efforts you are making for a reduction in our teaching expenses may be successful. The Treasurer has sent me this morning a copy of the draft Budget for the year, which shows an estimated deficit of over $71,000, and this will probably be increased rather than diminished. Mr. McAlpin, for example, has just reported to me that the expense of bringing out the General Catalogue and the Alumni Directory shows a considerable balance over the receipts from those two publications.

In view of Mr. Procter's suggestion regarding the time of his conference with you, I see no other path open than to defer the matter until the 20th. Of course, as you say, that leaves the Graduate School Committee little time in which to take up the matter prior to the Board meeting, but I suppose that if you do not succeed in inducing Mr. Procter to change his views the whole matter will have to be thrashed out in the Board. The Committee is not likely to unite upon any recommendation. Does not this render a meeting of the Committee this coming Saturday unnecessary? Should we not postpone it until next Wednesday night? Yours sincerely, Edward W. Sheldon

TLS (WP, DLC).

William Cooper Procter to Moses Taylor Pyne

My dear Mr. Pyne: Cincinnati. October 13, 1909.

Professor West spent part of Sunday with me and advises me quite fully of the conditions relative to the Graduate College.

I have to be in New York by two o'clock next Wednesday and I could meet you that afternoon at half past three either down town or in the Pennsylvania Station, Jersey City. If neither of these are convenient to you, please advise me and will write you immediately after my interview with President Wilson advising you of it.

Mrs. Procter and I thank you for your kind invitation to dine with you in New York Tuesday night, but we have a wedding engagement on Monday night which prevents our leaving Cincinnati before Tuesday.

With kind regards to Mrs. Pyne, I am,

Yours sincerely, Wm. Cooper Procter

TCL (M. T. Pyne Coll., NjP).

An Address at the Inauguration of Ernest Fox Nichols as President of Dartmouth College

[[Oct. 14, 1909]]

It gives me peculiar pleasure to be the bearer of admiring congratulations to the retiring President of Dartmouth, Dr. Tucker,[1] from the institution I represent. We have watched at Princeton the extraordinary progress of Dartmouth under his administration with a growing conception of what the character and power of a single man can do. And also it is most gratifying to me to bear messages of Godspeed to the new man who is assuming this distinguished succession.

1 William Jewett Tucker, President of Dartmouth, 1893-1909.

I would prefer to believe that the honor conferred upon me today by the gracious vote of the Trustees of this College[2] came to me as a representative of Princeton rather than as an individual, for I like to believe that such acts are a recognition of the community of purpose which exists among the colleges of this country, and that we are consciously trying to draw together into a single force the powers, both individual and organic, which lie in the educational institutions of America.

I have been thinking, as I sat here tonight, how little, except in coloring and superficial lines, a body of men like this differs from a body of undergraduates. You have only to look at a body of men like this long enough to see the mask of years fall off and the spirit of the younger days show forth, and the spirit which lies behind the mask is not an intellectual spirit: it is an emotional spirit.

It seems to me that the great power of the world—namely, its emotional power—is better expressed in a college gathering than in any other gathering. We speak of this as an age in which mind is monarch, but I take it for granted that, if that is true, mind is one of those modern monarchs who reign but do not govern. As a matter of fact, the world is governed in every generation by a great House of Commons made up of the passions; and we can only be careful to see to it that the handsome passions are in the majority.

A college body represents a passion, a very handsome passion, to which we should seek to give greater and greater force as the generations go by—a passion not so much individual as social, a passion for the things which live, for the things which enlighten, for the things which bind men together in unselfish companies. The love of men for their college is a very ennobling love, because it is a love which expresses itself in so organic a way and which delights to give as a token of its affection for its alma mater some one of those eternal, intangible gifts which are expressed only in the spirits of men.

It has been said that the college is "under fire." I prefer, inasmuch as most of the so-called criticism has come from the college men themselves, to say that the college is *on fire*; that it has ceased to be satisfied with itself, that its slumbering fires have sprung into play, and that it is now trying to see by the light of that flame what its real path is. For we criticise the col-

2 Wilson had been awarded the LL.D. degree. The citation read: "Woodrow Wilson, lawyer, historian, student of politics, man of great strength of purpose, who is steadfastly forging the college that ought to be out of the college that now is." *The Inauguration of Ernest Fox Nichols* . . . (Hanover, N. H., 1909), p. 81.

lege for the best of all reasons,—because we love it and are not indifferent to its fortunes. We criticise it as those who would make it as nearly what we conceive it ought to be as is possible in the circumstances.

The criticism which has been leveled at our colleges by college men, by men from the inside, does not mean that the college of the present is inferior to the college of the past. No observant man can fail to see that college life is more wholesome in almost every respect in our day that [than] it was in the days gone by. The lives of the undergraduates are cleaner, they are fuller of innocent interests, they are more shot through with the real permanent impulses of life than they once were. We are not saying that the college has degenerated in respect of its character.

What we mean I can illustrate in this way. It seems to me that we have been very much mistaken in thinking that the thing upon which our criticism should centre is the athletic enthusiasm of our college undergraduates, and of our graduates, as they come back to the college contests. It is a very interesting fact to me that the game of football, for example, has ceased to be a pleasure to those who play it. Almost any frank member of a college football team will tell you that in one sense it is a punishment to play the game. He does not play it because of the physical pleasure and zest he finds in it, which is another way of saying that he does not play it spontaneously and for its own sake. He plays it for the sake of the college, and one of the things that constitutes the best evidence of what we could make of the college is the spirit in which men go into the football game, because their comrades expect them to go in and because they must advance the banner of their college at the cost of infinite sacrifice. Why does the average man play football? Because he is big, strong and active, and his comrades expect it of him. They expect him to make that use of his physical powers; they expect him to represent them in an arena of considerable dignity and of very great strategic significance.

But when we turn to the field of scholarship, all that we say to the man is, "Make the most of yourself," and the contrast makes scholarship mean as compared with football. The football is for the sake of the college and the scholarship is for the sake of the individual. When shall we get the conception that a college is a brotherhood in which every man is expected to do for the sake of the college the thing which alone can make the college a distinguished and abiding force in the history of men? When shall we bring it about that men shall be ashamed to look their fellows in the face if it is known that they have great faculties and do not use them for the glory of their alma mater, when it is known that they avoid those nights of self denial which are necessary for intellectual mastery, deny themselves pleasure, deny themselves leisure, deny themselves every natural indulgence in order that in future years it may be said that that place served the country by increasing its power and enlightenment?

But at present what do we do to accomplish that? We very complacently separate the men who have that passion from the men who have it not,—I don't mean in the class room, but I mean in the life of the college itself.

I was confessing to President Schurman[3] tonight that, as I looked back to my experience in the class rooms of many eminent masters I remembered very little that I had brought away from them. The contacts of knowledge are not vital; the contacts of information are barren. If I tell you too many things that you don't know, I merely make myself hateful to you. If I am constantly in the attitude towards you of instructing you, you may regard me as a very well informed and superior person, but you have no affection for me whatever; whereas if I have the privilege of coming into your life, if I live with you and can touch you with something of the scorn that I feel for a man who does not use his faculties at their best, and can be touched by you with some keen, inspiring touch of the energy that lies in you and that I have not learned to imitate, then fire calls to fire and real life begins, the life that generates, the life that generates power, the life that generates those lasting fires of friendship which in too many college connections are lost altogether, for many college comradeships are based upon taste and not upon community of intellectual interests.

The only lasting stuff for friendship is community of conviction; the only lasting basis is that moral basis to which President Lowell has referred, in which all true intellectual life has its rootage and sustenance, and those are the rootages of character, not the rootages of knowledge. Knowledge is merely, in its uses, the evidence of character, it does not produce character. Some of the most learned of men have been among the meanest of men, and some of the noblest of men have been illiterate, but have nevertheless shown their nobility by using such powers as they had for high purposes.

We never shall succeed in creating this organic passion, this great use of the mind, which is fundamental, until we have made real communities of our colleges and have utterly destroyed the

[3] President Jacob Gould Schurman of Cornell University.

practice of a merely formal contact, however intimate, between the teacher and the pupil. Until we live together in a common community and expose each other to the general infection, there will be no infection. You cannot make learned men of undergraduates by associating them intimately with each other, because they are too young to be learned men yet themselves; but you can create the infection of learning by associating undergraduates with men who are learned.

How much do you know of the character of the average college professor whom you have heard lecture? Of some professors, if you had known more you would have believed less of what they said; of some professors, if you had known more you would have believed more of what they said. One of the dryest lecturers on American history I ever heard in my life was also a man more learned than any other man I ever knew in American history, and out of the class room, in conversation, one of the juiciest, most delightful, most informing, most stimulating men I ever had the pleasure of associating with.[4] The man in the class room was useless, out of the class room he fertilized every mind that he touched. And most of us are really found out in the informal contacts of life. If you want to know what I know about a subject, don't set me up to make a speech about it, because I have the floor and you cannot interrupt me, and I can leave out the things I want to leave out and bring in the things I want to bring in. If you really want to know what I know, sit down and ask me questions, interrupt me, contradict me, and see how I hold my ground. Probably on some subjects you will not do it; but if you want to find me out, that is the only way. If that method were followed, the undergraduate might make many a consoling discovery of how ignorant his professor was, as well as many a stimulating discovery of how well informed he was.

The thing that it seems to me absolutely necessary we should now address ourselves to is this—forget absolutely all our troubles about what we ought to teach and ask ourselves how we ought to live in college communities, in order that the fire and infection may spread; for the only conducting media of life are the social media, and if you want to make a conducting medium you have got to compound your elements in the college,—not only ally them, not put them in mere diplomatic relations with each other, not have a formal visiting system among them, but unite them, merge them. The teacher must live with the pupil and the pupil with the teacher, and then there will begin to be a renaissance, a new American college, and not until then. You may have the

[4] **Probably a reference to John Franklin Jameson.**

most eminent teachers and may have the best pedagogical methods, and find that, after all, your methods have been barren and your teachings futile, unless these unions of life have been accomplished.

I think that one of the saddest things that has ever happened to us is that we have studied pedagogical methods. It is as if we had deliberately gone about to make ourselves pedants. There is something offensive in the word "pedagogy." (Applause.) A certain distaste has always gone along with the word "pedagogue." A man who is an eminent teacher feels insulted if he is called a pedagogue; and yet we make a science of being a pedagogue, and in proportion as we make it a science we separate ourselves from the vital processes of life.

I suppose a great many dull men must try to teach, and if dull men have to teach, they have to teach by method that dull men can follow. But they never teach anybody anything. It is merely that the university, in order to have a large corps, must go through the motions; but the real vital processes are in spots, in such circumstances, and only in spots, and you must hope that the spots will spread. You must hope that there will enter in or go out from these little nuclei the real juices of life.

What we mean, then, by criticising the American college is not to discredit what we are doing or have done, but to cry ourselves awake with regard to the proper processes. (Great applause.)

Printed in *The Inauguration of Ernest Fox Nichols . . . as President of Dartmouth College October 14, 1909* (Hanover, N. H., 1909), pp. 143-50.

From Moses Taylor Pyne

My dear Woodrow Princeton, N. J. 14 October 1909

It is too bad that Procter & you could not get together before the 20th. I saw Ed Sheldon yesterday who told me that the conference would not take place until that date & we agreed that, under the circumstances, a meeting would be useless on Saturday afternoon. He also said that he wanted to be away at that time and then, to bring Cyrus & Shea from the West only five days before the Board Meeting and Jacobus & Garrett from a distance and for you, West & myself to go to town, when nothing new could be said or done, was not worth while. So we decided to postpone the meeting until you had seen Procter.

I don't know where you are to be, so am sending this letter to your address here, presuming that Mr Close will open it and advise you. Yours very sincerely M Taylor Pyne

P.S. I have been away from home since Monday–Hence delay in answering your letter. Could you attend a meeting Wednesday evening?

ALS (WP, DLC).

Two Letters from Richard Spencer Childs

Dear Dr. Wilson: New York, October 14th, 1909.

It looks now as if we were going to have a very successful and productive little dinner on the 20th., with about 20 men in attendance representing a good deal of potential strength.

The Executive Board has found it so easy to get men to come in this way, that we want to continue the work along this line, and hold another dinner toward the end of November.

If you can find a date in that season that is convenient for you, I would like to know it, because if we can announce that you are to be there, it will give a different character to the second dinner, so that the same men can be induced to come again and bring their friends.

We might find it more difficult to get them to another dinner that was exactly like the first!

Trusting that you will find this plan feasible, and with best regards I am, Yours very truly, Richard S Childs

Dear Dr. Wilson: New York, October 14th, 1909.

Among the matters which I proposed to bring up at the meeting of the Advisory Board preceding the dinner at the City Club on October 20th, was the election of Mr. Winston Churchill of New Hampshire,[1] and Mr. U'ren of Oregon,[2] as Vice-Presidents. Both of these men have voluntarily taken great interest, and offered us permission to use their name in any way we saw fit.

Mr. U'ren is at present campaigning in Oregon for a short ballot, and proposes to reduce the average ballot from 20 names, to about 5–making the entire administrative department of the State appointive by the Governor, and radically simplifying the County government.[3]

Are those names as V. Pres. satisfactory to you?

We also have an encouraging letter from Judge Lindsay of

Denver,[4] and believe that we can also use his name a little later.

Having Vice-Presidents, it logically follows that we should have a President. Would you be willing to go on the firing line in this way, if the Advisory Board desires it?[5]

Yours very truly, Richard S Childs

TLS (WP, DLC).

[1] Prolific popular novelist who was involved in the progressive movement in New Hampshire. Elected to the New Hampshire legislature in 1903 and 1905, he ran unsuccessfully for governor on the Progressive ticket in 1912.

[2] William Simon U'Ren, Oregon progressive leader, who successfully agitated for the institution of the initiative, referendum, and recall in that state. At this time, he was practicing law in Oregon City and serving as secretary of the Oregon Single Tax League.

[3] Little is known about this campaign; in any event, U'Ren did not succeed.

[4] Benjamin Barr Lindsey, Judge of the County Court of Denver since 1901 and pioneer in the establishment of a juvenile code and juvenile courts.

[5] Wilson accepted. See R. S. Childs to WW, Oct. 25, 1909. Wilson served as president until the Short Ballot Organization merged with the National Municipal League during the First World War.

From James Phinney Munroe[1]

Boston, Massachusetts

My dear President Wilson, October 14, 1909

I thank you very much for your cordial letter of the 12th inst, with its expressions of regret relative to the invitations of the Mass[.] Reform Club and the Boston City Club.

It is superfluous to say, on the one hand, how deeply I and my associates regret your decision, and, on the other hand, how fully we appreciate the conditions which have impelled that decision. The demands upon a college president, and especially upon one of transcendent ability, are enormous, and we would not have ventured to add one had we not been so eager to give ourselves and our associates the rare privilege of hearing you. Hoping that this privilege is only postponed, I am, with highest regard,

Yours very faithfully James P. Munroe

ALS (WP, DLC).

[1] Treasurer of the Munroe Felt and Paper Co. in Boston and President of the Massachusetts Reform Club, 1903-1909. He was active in various educational and social reform organizations.

From Melancthon Williams Jacobus

Hartford, Conn.,

My dear President Wilson: October 15th, 1909.

On my return home this morning I found the following telegram from West:

"Inasmuch as the President and Mr. Procter cannot confer

until October 20th, the chairman asks me to notify the Committee on the Graduate School that the committee-meeting appointed October 16th is postponed."

It does seem to me that the wording of this letter gives you a perfect right to proceed in a personal conference with Mr. Procter, according to the original vote of the Committee, and that West and Pyne understand that this is what you are to do on October 20th before the Committee meeting. I would at all events assume that this is their understanding, and proceed on this assumption.

I trust that you had a comfortable night's rest and were carried safely to the end of your journey, and that you are having at least a chance to get a bit of recovery from these last two weeks, before the meeting of the Board of Trustees.

It was a great pleasure to see you again at Dartmouth, and I cannot soon forget the designation of yourself when you received your degree as one who was forging out of the college that is the college that ought to be. Such a reputation is worth a great struggle.

With kindest regards,

Yours very sincerely, M W Jacobus

TLS (WP, DLC).

From Andrew Fleming West

My dear Wilson: Princeton, N. J., October 15, 1909.

Your note of October 12th.[1] came to me in my mail yesterday, asking me to call a Committee of the Faculty on the Graduate School in regard to the question of the site of the Graduate College, in order that the Committee of the Board may have the benefit of a full and explicit opinion of the Faculty Committee without delay. We are having very frequent meetings, in fact almost daily of late, in order to dispose of the regular business of the Committee, and we shall take up this matter fully and promptly, beginning at our meeting tomorrow.

At the last meeting of the Trustees' Committee on the Graduate School adjournment was taken to Saturday, October 16th., in New York, unless otherwise called by the Chairman of the Committee. In view of the fact that your conference with Mr. Procter was not to be held until October 20th., the Chairman asked me to issue notice that the meeting for October 16th. in New York was off. So I telegraphed this to every member of the Committee, and sent a telegram to you at Hanover, N. H. in care of President Nichols and a duplicate of the telegram to your secretary, Mr. Close.

Ever sincerely yours, Andrew F. West

TLS (WWP, UA, NjP).
[1] It is missing.

To Moses Taylor Pyne

My dear Momo: Princeton, N. J. October 16th, 1909.

I am just back from Dartmouth and find your kind note of the 14th on my table.

I think you were quite right in postponing the meeting of the Committee, in the circumstances. I was really distressed that Mr. Procter could not make connections with me sooner.

The Committee on the Curriculum meets Wednesday evening in my office at half past eight, but the business I have to lay before it is only routine business and will not take the Committee long. I should think it quite possible to have a meeting of the Committee on the Graduate School at nine or half past wherever you choose to appoint it to meet, and I earnestly hope that it will be possible for you to appoint it for that evening. I shall desire the opportunity to report to the committee the result of my conference with Mr. Procter.

Instead of coming to Princeton, Mr. Procter has written me that he is obliged to be in New York on Wednesday afternoon for business and has asked me to meet him at the Holland House at 10.15 Wednesday morning. I will, of course, do so.

Always affectionately yours, Woodrow Wilson.

TCL (M. T. Pyne Coll., NjP).

To Francis Charles Macdonald[1]

[Princeton, N. J.]

My dear Mr. Macdonald: October 18th, 1909.

I have heard with the greatest regret and concern of your doctor's opinion that you have been under too great a strain and need a rest. I hope that if the rest is indeed necessary, you will not hesitate to take it and I can assure you that you are at liberty to do so without any decrease in your salary, to provide for the instruction which would be necessary if you should feel obliged to go away.[2]

I want you to go away, if it should be necessary, with the feeling that we value you here most highly in every respect. I have never before had a proper opportunity for telling you how fully I share the opinion of your colleagues in the English Department that your services and character are of the greatest value to the University. Nothing has given me more concern than the necessity we have been under to keep your stipend at the poor figure at which it now stands.[3] I have watched for an opportunity to increase it and have been prevented only by the extraordinary weight of the deficit which the Trustees of the University have every year to face. I hope with all my heart that this disability will be of only short duration and that the time may soon come when we shall be able to put it upon a par with the men who are doing equal work.[4]

I am writing this with great solicitude for you and for your welfare and hope that everything will go happily with you toward entire restoration and strength.

With warm regard,

Sincerely yours, [Woodrow Wilson]

CCL (WWP, UA, NjP).

[1] Princeton 1896, Preceptor in English.
[2] Macdonald did not take medical leave in 1909-10.
[3] $1,600 per annum.
[4] His salary was raised to the normal preceptorial stipend of $2,000 in 1910.

From Cyrus Hall McCormick

My dear Woodrow: Chicago 18 October, 1909.

I have little to suggest as to how you shall present the matter to Mr. Proctor, for I realize both the difficulty of the undertaking and the fact that you know much better than I just how to treat it.

Two suggestions, however, may be helpful to you in case you are not well acquainted with Mr. Proctor. The *first* is that, having thot of going on my own hook to see him at Cincinnati sometime ago, I wrote to a very dear friend who is one of the businessmen in Cincinnati and who is well acquainted with Mr. Proctor, to ask him to tell me something about his characteristics;[1] and the enclosed letter,[2] which I think you will admit is a very frank and clear analysis of character, is the result. From this you will see that Mr. Proctor is no doubt somewhat obstinate, and having formed an opinion, will be loath to give it up. The regret is that he has formed his opinion without full investigation of all sides of the question.

The *second* suggestion I have, therefore, to make, is that we are likely to make more of an impression upon him by appealing to his best judgment rather than by trying to compel him to accept our opinions; in other words, persuasion is a stronger tack with him, I should think, than pressure or force.

It may not be an inapt illustration of a long-headed view of what is the best reward for investing in a University or branch of a University to cite the case of Rockefeller who, in building up the University of Chicago, was entirely willing that others should have the seeming advantage of having their names on the buildings while he quietly and unostentatiously gave the thing which was most difficult to secure—namely, the endowment, and thereby really gets the *greatest* credit of all!

If we could persuade Mr. Proctor that his name would stand higher in the course of time by supplying money for the teaching force of the Graduate School rather than by piling up brick and mortar, that would be a great object gained; but even if he wishes to contribute the brick and mortar, he might be persuaded that his reputation and the glory of the whole enterprise would be greater if it was built up slowly and modestly rather than on such lines of magnificence as are now being planned.

It may not be unnatural that he should like the flattery and the satisfaction of seeing the Proctor Towers loom up across the country as one approaches Princeton, and perhaps that is one of the reasons for his preference for the golf grounds. Our effort, therefore, should be to try and persuade him to reach the higher point of wishing to help establish a great and growing Graduate School rather than to construct a magnificent architectural design of buildings.

I may be in New York on Wednesday afternoon, as I am planning to meet the '79 Committee, and if I do not do this, my plan was to go up to Princeton on Wednesday afternoon or evening. If there is any way which occurs to you that I can be any help to you with Mr. Proctor in New York on Wednesday afternoon or evening, that might be more important than for me to go to Princeton that evening. Perhaps you might telephone to Wilder any message which you may have for me, and I can telephone his office and find out what it is, as I shall have several other errands there.

Even if I cannot be reached, you may wish to communicate with or see Thomas Jones who will be in New York on Wednesday and who feels about the location of this Graduate School just as I do; and it might be well for you, if you wish to, to have Thomas Jones see Mr. Proctor. I can arrange for Wilder to reach T. Jones

I do not know that any of these thots are practical, and am only suggesting them in turning about the various plans which occur to me for helping to get this matter fairly before Mr. Proctor from the stand-point that he has not yet considered.

It has no doubt occurred to you as a beneficial thing to suggest that Mr. Proctor might wish to get the personal opinions, aside from your own, of either or all Messrs. Conklin, Capps and Abbott, as they are the men who will no doubt be influential as teachers in building up the Graduate School.

Wednesday morning I shall be at the Manhattan Hotel. I am unable to say just how long I will be there in the morning. My train arrives at Twenty-third Street at nine-fifty five, so I would not be available to see you until the afternoon, or at least after your interview with Mr. Proctor.

I am, Very sincerely yours, Cyrus H. McCormick.

P.S. Please keep Mr. Chatfield's letter carefully and confidentially for me.

TLS (WP, DLC).

[1] C. H. McCormick to A. H. Chatfield, Sept. 17, 1909, CCL (C. H. McCormick Papers, WHi), inquiring about Procter's business acumen and personality. Albert Hayden Chatfield was a paper manufacturer of Cincinnati.

[2] A. H. Chatfield to C. H. McCormick, Sept. 20, 1909, TLS (C. H. McCormick Papers, WHi), which Wilson returned to McCormick. In this letter, Chatfield wrote in glowing terms about Procter's skill in managing the affairs of Procter and Gamble and described him as "a man of large vision and great executive ability." However, Chatfield added, Procter was "a very firm man in his opinion" and had "no social instinct." Chatfield advised McCormick that Procter would "resent any discussion of a private benefaction such as he proposes to make, without some favorable circumstance arising to bring about such a conference." He therefore offered to serve as an intermediary to introduce McCormick to Procter and provide a favorable setting in which McCormick could discuss the terms of Procter's offer.

From Moses Taylor Pyne

My dear Woodrow Princeton, N. J. 18 October 1909

In view of your letter I am calling a meeting of the Committee on the Graduate School in the Trustees Room on Wednesday evening October 20th at nine P.M. and hope that the Curriculum Committee meeting will be a short one as these late meetings play the mischief with my nerves, and we cannot begin really until you are through with the first meeting.

I shall be away all day Wednesday as I must go to the marriage in Staten Island of my secretary, Mr Seaman,[1] who has been with me over twenty years.

Yours very sincerely M Taylor Pyne

ALS (WP, DLC).

[1] William I. Seaman, a lawyer and secretary to Pyne, who married Marjorie Luce on October 20, 1909.

To Edward Wright Sheldon

My dear Ed.: Princeton, N. J. October 19th, 1909.

I find that, as I supposed, I turned over all the letters written me by Mr. Procter to Professor West for the files of the Committee on the Graduate School. I am sincerely sorry that I cannot supply you with the letter, therefore, of which you spoke.

The more I think over the subject of our conference yesterday after the committee[1] meeting, the more I am convinced that you have chosen the right course and the more hopeful I am that we may recover out of this situation the real government of the University.

Always affectionately yours, Woodrow Wilson

TLS (photostat in RSB Coll., DLC).

[1] That is, the Finance Committee of the Board of Trustees.

From Andrew Fleming West, with Enclosure

My dear Wilson: Princeton, N. J., October 19, 1909.

Your letter of October 12th. was laid before the Faculty Committee on the Graduate School on October 14th., and I transmit herewith a copy of the action taken by the Committee in response to the request of your letter. With the approval of the Committee I also transmit a copy to Mr. Pyne as Chairman of the Trustees' Committee on the Graduate School.

Ever sincerely yours, Andrew F. West

ALS (WP, DLC).

E N C L O S U R E

Report of the Faculty Committee on the Graduate School on the Site of the Proposed Graduate College, October 19, 1909.

Pursuant to the request of President Wilson the Faculty Committee on the Graduate School held a special meeting on Saturday, October 16. Professor Butler was invited to sit with the Committee and to participate in its deliberations, and to add to this report the expression of his own view. Dean West laid fully before the Committee the question of the site of the Graduate College. At two subsequent meetings, held on October 18 and October 19, the Committee first obtained the individual opinions of each member of the Committee on this question, and then entered into a full discussion. At the close of the discussion the Committee took the following action:

RESOLVED, That the Faculty Committee on the Graduate School expresses unanimously its most urgent desire that satisfactory arrangements may be concluded whereby Mr. Procter's munificent proffer may be accepted by the University.

The Committee however acknowledges that it has been unable to agree upon the matter of the site of the proposed Graduate College. Upon this matter of site the majority and the minority by mutual consent express themselves respectively in the Memoranda appended hereto, said Memoranda to constitute a part of this Report.

MEMORANDUM A

The position of the majority of the Committee is expressed in the following resolution:

> RESOLVED, That taking into consideration the administration of graduate affairs and the intellectual life of the University, we favor placing the new graduate building upon a location, as central as possible, upon the University campus, for the following reasons:

FIRST, because the unity of University administration, with all the accompanying implications of unity of educational ideals and endeavor, could with difficulty be secured by any other than a central location.

SECOND, because the solidarity of University interests which we conceive to be essential to the development of the University, and such a degree of desirable contact between Faculty and graduate students and between graduate and undergraduate students as is essential to a common intellectual life, is only to be obtained by such a central location.

THIRD, because the natural tendency towards separation between graduate and undergraduate interests would be fostered by a distant location of the residential hall. Should the new building not be centrally located, we should fear the eventual emergence of a separate establishment with interests alien to and separate from those of the College. The untoward effects of the isolation of particular schools has been witnessed at Columbia, at Pennsylvania, at Johns Hopkins, and elsewhere; and early mistakes in location have been remedied, where possible, at great expense. We feel that an appreciable distance in intellectual sympathy as well as in social contact already exists, unfortunately, between the graduate students in Merwick and the more numerous body of bona fide graduate students resident in the town.

FOURTH, the accessibility of laboratories, libraries, and seminaries for graduate students who particularly require these facilities at all hours will be immensely greater if the new structure is centrally located. This consideration is much more important in the case of graduate students than in the case of undergraduates. If the daily life of the graduate students should centre about a distant point, the distance itself would become an impediment to their work which would have to be treated as a new problem of administration.

FIFTH, the distant location of the new building would, of necessity, exclude from the benefits of the common rooms and the social life of the place that large section of our graduate students who for financial reasons would be unable to live in the building, unless the University is to assume a part of the cost of maintaining the building and the table. Such a separation of our graduate students into two groups would create among them a situation analagous to the present club situation among the undergraduates. The avoidance of this deplorable cleavage in the ranks of the graduate students could be effected only by a still greater sacrifice. If, by endowment directed thereto, it is attempted to house in the same building not only the well-to-do graduate students but also the larger number of graduate students of lesser means, the evil result would be twofold: First, we should have adopted the policy of uniformly contributing to the living expenses of all graduate students,—a policy which has hitherto been tried mainly in theological seminaries, and which has tended to the lowering of the morale and quality of the recipients: Second, we should have embarked upon a financial policy which would not only prove very expensive but which would also prove a growing lien upon the funds otherwise available for the really essential ends of graduate work, to wit, the adequate provision of facilities for advanced study in the way of instruction and equipment.

SIXTH, the project of a residential hall for graduate students involves an academic experiment which has not yet been fully tested; and in these circumstances we feel that the experiment should be conducted under the safest conditions possible. We should deprecate the unnecessary hazard of indefinite architectural expansion which might attend the location of new buildings at a distance from the present centre of the University.

If the experiment should prove a failure, there would be, under the condition of distant location, no possibility of retrieving the situation thus created.

Signed: E. G. Conklin,
W. M. Daniels,
H. B. Fine,
Edward Capps.

MEMORANDUM B

The undersigned members of the Faculty Committee on the Graduate School respectfully state their opinion as follows:

I The selection of a site for the Graduate College should not be determined solely or even mainly by theoretical or conjectural considerations, but in the light of the best available experience. To obtain evidence as to the best mode of handling the problem of the residential life of graduate students the University has authorized for the last four years and for this current year the establishment and conduct of the Graduate House on a site removed from the campus and affording residential separation, but no other separation from the undergraduates of as many graduate students as the house can accommodate. Before this plan was instituted and tried we were clearly of the opinion that the Graduate College should be located at least in immediate contiguity to the central campus, preferably on what is known as the Olden Tract, for the reason that the choice of a site at some distance raised the question as to whether residential separateness might not tend to separateness in institutional and intellectual development and thus make difficult the maintenance of the integral unity, beneficent interaction and close sympathetic relation of the Graduate College with the University as a whole.

The experience of four years' constant and intimate observation of Merwick has convinced us not only that no such danger now exists or is to be apprehended, but that residential removal at not too great a distance from undergraduate surroundings is highly favorable to the best intellectual life and personal well-being of our graduate students. The proof of this is the unusually fine record in scholarship made by the students at Merwick and their unanimous enthusiasm because of what they have been able to accomplish in such surroundings. They have been so deeply interested in the matter as spontaneously to prepare a petition giving the reasons for their urgent preference for a site separated as Merwick is.[1] An appended statement (marked "Exhibit A")[2] briefly recites the facts as to what they have actually done in scholarship. It is a record of which the University may be proud indeed. That it is due in considerable measure to their residential separation from the undergraduates is not merely a matter of opinion, but of well-evidenced fact. We should be glad if any of the graduate students who have been connected with the Graduate House should be questioned on these matters.

Moreover, the students at Merwick are not in any way detached in interest from the University as a whole. Administratively they are and must be under the sole control of the President and Trustees. Scholastically all their exercises are held in the same libraries, laboratories, seminaries and class rooms as accommodate the exercises of the undergraduates. In every case their instruction and research is under the direction of professors who also direct the studies of undergraduates. No tendency or desire to have this otherwise has appeared. The primary feeling of these students, whether graduates of Princeton or of other institutions, is that they are Princeton men, enjoying the full scholarly benefit of universities studies and considerable undergraduate acquaintance in the places of common resort on the central campus, and the added personal, social, and intellectual benefits of their distinct residential community life as graduate students. They testify to this emphatically and without exception.

Even if the situation were otherwise and any desire to to have separate classrooms, libraries, seminaries and laboratories were to manifest itself, as in our judgment there is not the slightest likelihood, the cost of making such useless separate provision on any adequate scale would be prohibitory.

Because, therefore, of the unusually successful results yielded by the four years of experience at Merwick, which,

1 The petition was M. S. Burt *el al.* to the trustees' Committee on the Graduate School, March 13, 1907, TLS (WWP, UA, NjP). For a summary of its contents, see WW to the trustees' Committee on the Graduate School, May 30, 1907, n. 3, Vol. 17.

2 This appendix, not printed, noted that fifty-seven students had been at Merwick from 1905 to 1909, and that twenty-three of them had received appointment as fellows of the university, "a record not equalled by any other body of graduate students we have ever had." It further described the subsequent successful careers of twenty-four graduate students.

by reason of our neighborhood, we have watched more closely than any other persons, excepting Professor Butler who has lived in the house, we think that the residential Graduate College should not be placed on any part of the campus in close proximity to undergraduate comings and goings, but should be sufficiently removed to make certain the development of a distinct graduate tone by our graduate students in their community of intellectual interests. This by no means interferes with the coming of undergraduates to the Graduate College frequently and in considerable numbers, not only as visitors but as welcome guests of graduate students. So far as the limited accommodations at Merwick permit, this has been done continuously for the last four years, and with excellent results.

Intercourse between graduate and undergraduate students is not determined by propinquity, but by community of interests. The undergraduates who have been guests at Merwick have been attracted thither by their interest in a prospective graduate career.

There appears to be a strong feeling on the part of a majority of our Committee that a residential college placed elsewhere than on the central part of the campus, or close to it, would not be a convenient resort for graduate students who were too poor to live in it, and therefore had to take their lodgings in town. Such students it is thought would thereby be cut off from participation in its social and other advantages, and thus two distinct classes of graduate students would be created. We are thoroughly satisfied that this feeling is without real foundation. Any appearance of this sort today is due solely to the fact that the present Graduate House can accommodate only a minority of our graduate students. Those who have the feeling referred to overlook the following facts:

1 The experience at Merwick proves that with increased numbers in residence the cost per student is inevitably lowered and that, in any event, the number who could not pay the minimum charge in the proposed residential college would be very small indeed. We have already had a considerable number of students of extremely narrow means, men who were obliged to earn in the summer, sometimes by day-labor, the means which enabled them to live at Merwick. Even now, on the present necessarily more expensive basis, the number of students now at Merwick and the Graduate Annex and men who have asked to come

in this year is 42. We know of others who have not come because of their desire to have single rooms—of which there are only two at Merwick. We also know of others who have not come solely because they learned the house was full. These taken together make two-thirds of all our regular graduate students.

2 It needs to be remembered that the Graduate College, properly planned, will be able to take students, without any concessions from the fixed scale of prices for room and table, at rates at least as low as they can obtain in town, except for distinctly inferior board and lodgings, which are only too often injurious to their bodily and mental welfare.

3 Of course the Graduate College should be planned to be capable of accommodating all our graduate students. When this is built and reasonably low rates are charged, which can easily be done, as our present experience daily proves, the difficulty regarding poor students living in it is removed so far as it can be removed under any system whatever, wherever the Graduate College may be placed. We firmly believe that the minimum rate for room, board, light and heat in a fixed scale of charges can be made seven dollars a week, or perhaps even a little lower. Moreover, with a system of fellowships and graduate scholarships sufficiently developed and wisely administered there is no reason why any poor graduate student of real merit should find himself unable to live in the Graduate College.

4 It is of the utmost importance for the sake of their self-respect and happiness that the poorest graduate students shall have the advantages the others enjoy. They cannot all live happily together unless all live together somewhat similarly in decent comfort. To lower the tone or plane of living is not the way to accomplish this.

II We have referred to Merwick solely because it yields the only body of well-tested experience as to the fact that a reasonable distance from the central campas [campus] has not in any degree impaired either the development of the intellectual life of our graduate students or their interest in the University as a whole. We appreciate the fact that in the present situation Merwick as a possible site is out of the question. The only practicable site on University grounds and off the central campus is the Gold [Golf] Links, a spacious and diginified [dignified] site admirably fitted for the Graduate College. It has one great advantage Merwick lacks, namely its visibility from the central campus. Moreover the actual distance can be minimized by the proposed approaches. With the necessary growth of Princeton in the future the Golf Links as an integral part of the campus is sure to be utilized and thus brought into increasingly closer relations with the rest of the campus and its activities. We cannot see that the question of immediate proximity to the central campus can be regarded as so essential as to imperil, by insistence upon it, the securing of Mr. Procter's splendid benefaction. We make this statement because we have learned from the communication of the Chairman of the Trustees' Committee to our Faculty Committee that Mr. Procter's gift is conditioned on the selection either of Merwick or the Golf Links.

Signed Andrew F. West,
John Grier Hibben.

STATEMENT OF PROFESSOR BUTLER

Having been invited by the Committee of the Faculty on the Graduate School to take part in their discussion of the question of the site of the proposed building for the Graduate School, and having been requested to append a statement to their report, I take the liberty of stating that I have shared in the Committees deliberations, have heard read both the report of the majority and that of the minority, and do hereby express my unqualified approval of, and concurrence with the report of the minority.

While many of the objections raised by the majority to a site a little removed from the central campus bore weight with me four years ago, every one of these objections has vanished from my mind under the light of my practical experience as a resident, with the group of graduate students at Merwick.

Signed Howard Crosby Butler.

TCR (WP, DLC).

From Edward Wright Sheldon, with Enclosure

My dear Woodrow: New York. October 20, 1909.

I have your letter of yesterday.

As understood at the meeting of the Finance Committee last Monday, I wrote Mr. Cadwalader a letter with reference to aid from Mr. J. P. Morgan for current expenses. I enclose a copy of this letter, and have just received the accompanying reply from Mr. Cadwalader. In view of this, would it not be well for you to write Mr. Morgan on the subject? Will you kindly return Mr. Cadwalader's letter after perusal?

Yours sincerely, Edward W. Sheldon

TLS (WP, DLC).

ENCLOSURE

Edward Wright Sheldon to John Lambert Cadwalader

My dear Mr. Cadwalader: [New York] October 18, 1909.

Last Spring you and President Wilson I believe had a talk with Mr. J. Pierpont Morgan with reference to securing some financial aid from him for Princeton University. My impression was that you subsequently told me that he, while unable to add to the endowment of the institution, had offered to give $5,000 a year for five years towards current expenses. We still have a substantial deficit for the year ending July 31, 1909. Would it be possible to secure $5,000 now from Mr. Morgan and treat it as a reduction pro tanto of that deficit? Subsequent payments might then be asked in July of each of the next four years.

We were talking over the general subject of the finance of the University at a meeting of the Finance Committee this afternoon and the President confirmed my recollection regarding your report of Mr. Morgan's generous offer. Would it be possible for you to remind him of this, or do you suggest some other method of bringing the matter to his attention?

Yours sincerely, (Signed) Edward W. Sheldon.

TCL (WP, DLC).

William Cooper Procter to Moses Taylor Pyne

My dear Sir: New York. October 20th, 1909.

President Wilson this morning gave me his reasons for placing the Graduate College in close proximity to the other college buildings. I regret that I am unable to agree with him and still think it *essential* for its full development that the Graduate College have a location distinct and apart from the Undergraduate College.

I am sorry if my offer has been inopportune and will withdraw it—with regret—if it is in any way embarrassing to the best interests of our University.

Yours very truly, Wm. Cooper Procter.

TCL (M. T. Pyne Coll., NjP).

From the Minutes of the Board of Trustees of Princeton University

[Oct. 21, 1909]

The Trustees of Princeton University met in stated session in the Trustees' Room in the Chancellor Green Library, Princeton, New Jersey, at eleven o'clock on Thursday morning October 21, 1909.

The President of the University in the chair. . . .

Mr. Pyne, Chairman of the Committee on the Graduate School, reported as follows:

Princeton, October 21, 1909.

TO THE TRUSTEES OF PRINCETON UNIVERSITY,

Gentlemen:

By request of your Committee on the Graduate School I report to the Board on the matter of the site of the proposed Graduate College:

The Committee has held several special sessions on this question in view of Mr. Procter's offer. The substance of his offer is that he will give five hundred thousand dollars toward carrying out the plan of the proposed Graduate College, provided an equal sum is also secured and a satisfactory site chosen instead of Prospect, which had been selected as the site for the building to be known as the John R. Thomson Graduate College.

In response to his proposal the Committee on May 12th. adopted the following minute which was communicated to Mr. Procter:

"RESOLVED: That this Committee has heard read with great satisfaction the letter of Mr. William Cooper Procter, as affording a prospect of the early completion of the scheme for a Graduate School on a permanent and dignified basis;

FURTHER RESOLVED: That a Committee consisting of the President, the Dean of the Graduate School and the Chairman of the Trustees' Committee, with Mr. Cadwalader and Mr. Sheldon, seek an early occasion for a conference with Mr. Procter to discuss and consider certain of the details, prior to the meeting of the Board of Trustees to be held on the 14th day of June."

On June 4th. the sub-Committee met in New York and had an extended conference with Mr. Procter. Next day Mr. Procter came to Princeton and examined all the sites that had been suggested, accompanied by Mr. Pyne, Chairman, President Wilson and Dean West. On his return to Cincinnati he wrote a letter to the President, June 9th., certifying either Merwick or the Golf Links as his preference. He visited Princeton again on the Saturday before Commencement and further examined the various sites.

At the Commencement meeting of the Board, held June 14th., the Board passed the following resolution:

> "RESOLVED: That the hearty thanks of the Board of Trustees be conveyed to Mr. William Cooper Procter for his generous proposal regarding the Graduate College."

On October 4th. the Trustees' Committee met in Princeton and discussed at length the question of the site in view of Mr. Procter's offer. At the suggestion of the President, the Committee expressed its desire that the President should confer with Mr. Procter again as soon as possible and report to the Committee prior to the October meeting of the Board. Mr. Procter came to New York the morning of October 20th. and met the President. This is the seventh visit Mr. Procter has made from Cincinnati to Princeton or New York on the matter of the site.

The Trustees' Committee met last night, October 20th., in Princeton. The minutes of their meeting are as follows:

Princeton, October 20th., 1909.
9 P M

The Committee met in the Trustees' Room. All the members were present. The minutes of the last meeting were read and approved.

President Wilson reported the result of his conference held with Mr. Procter in New York this morning, stating that Mr. Procter adheres to his previously expressed preferences in regard to the site of the proposed Graduate College.

The President also read a report on the site question from the Faculty Committee on the Graduate School.

After extended discussion of the matter of Mr. Procter's offer the following resolution, offered by Mr. Sheldon and seconded by Dr. Jacobus, was put to vote and carried:

> While expressing its urgent desire that satisfactory arrangements may be concluded whereby Mr. Procter's munificent proffer may be accepted by the University, be it
>
> RESOLVED, that this Committee approves the position of the majority of the Faculty Committee on the Graduate School expressed in the following resolution adopted October 19th., 1909:

"RESOLVED, that, taking into consideration the administration of graduate affairs and the intellectual life of the University, we favor placing the new graduate building upon a location as central as possible, upon the University campus."

Five members voted in the affirmative:

President Wilson, Dr. Jacobus, Mr. McCormick, Mr. Sheldon, Mr. Garrett.

The following three members voted in the negative:

Mr. Pyne, Chairman, Mr. Shea, Dean West.

The Committee then requested the Chairman to report to the Board and to propose such action as he might deem advisable.

Adjourned.

(Signed) Andrew F. West, Secretary.

REPORT OF COMMITTEE ON THE GRADUATE SCHOOL ACCEPTED

The report of the committee on the Graduate School was accepted.

OFFER OF MR. PROCTER ACCEPTED

Mr. Pyne offered the following resolution, which was seconded by Mr. Green:

RESOLVED, That the very generous offer of Mr. Procter be accepted.

MR. SHELDON'S AMENDMENT

After discussion, Mr. Sheldon offered as an amendment to Mr. Pyne's resolution the following preamble and resolution which were seconded by Mr. Dodge:

"Mr. William Cooper Procter of the Class of 1883, having in May 1909 offered to give to the University to be expended for such objects as he might designate in furtherance of the plans for the Graduate College, the sum of $500,000. payable in ten equal quarterly installments of $50,000. beginning July 15th, 1910, provided, first, an equal sum were secured for the Graduate College in gifts or responsible pledges by May 1st, 1910, and provided, second, that the site for the JOHN R. THOMSON GRADUATE COLLEGE in the grounds of Prospect selected by the Board of Trustees in April 1908 in accordance with the terms of the will of Josephine A. Thomson Swann be abandoned and that College established either at Merwick on Bayard Lane or on the northerly portion of the Golf grounds near the present Club House, and the Board having carefully considered Mr. Procter's important proposition and having through the Committee on the Graduate

School conferred with him from time to time on the subject it is

RESOLVED, that by reason of its inability to comply with the conditions named by Mr. Procter, the Board has reluctantly concluded that it cannot accept his most generous offer.

RESOLVED, that the Board renews its warm thanks to Mr. Procter for the deep interest in the University which is evidenced by his proffered gift, and records its keen regret that a complete realization of his personal wish in regard to the Graduate College does not seem possible.

RESOLVED, that it would gratify the Board deeply if Mr. Procter could find it possible to yield his personal preference in this regard to the policy in the development and administration of the Graduate College and the physical site therefore to which the Board had already committed itself, and which the Board felt convinced was in the highest interest not only of the Graduate College but also of the whole University.

RESOLVED, that a committee of three to be named by the President be appointed which shall present the foregoing resolutions to Mr. Procter.

REPORT OF FACULTY COMMITTEE ON THE GRADUATE SCHOOL READ

The President of the University read the report of the Faculty Committee on the Graduate School.

RESOLUTION BY DR. MC PHERSON

After further discussion Dr. McPherson offered the following resolution:

RESOLVED, that the further consideration of the Report of the Committee on the Graduate School, the motion of Mr. Pyne and the amendment of Mr. Sheldon be postponed until the next meeting of the Board.

DR. MC PHERSON'S RESOLUTION LOST

The Board voted on Dr. McPherson's resolution and it was lost.

MR. SHELDON'S AMENDMENT LOST

The Board voted on Mr. Sheldon's amendment and it was lost.

DR. STEWART'S AMENDMENT TO MR. PYNE'S RESOLUTION

Dr. George B. Stewart moved to amend Mr. Pyne's resolution by adding "Provided that the legal right to use Mrs. Swann's money in the erection of the Graduate School upon the Gold [Golf] Links be assured, and that Mr. Procter first advise us of his intention in relation to the disposition of his proposed gift."

The amendment was seconded by Dr. Wood.

DR. STEWART'S AMENDMENT ADOPTED

The Board voted on Dr. Stewart's amendment and it was adopted.

MR. PYNE'S RESOLUTION ADOPTED

Mr. John A. Stewart called for the yeas and nays on Mr. Pyne's resolution and the vote was recorded as follows:

YEAS: Pyne, Alexander, G. B. Stewart, Dixon, Henry, McPherson, Green, Wood, Davis, Russell, Shea[,] Imbrie, Palmer, Farrand 14

NAYS: Wilson, J. A. Stewart, McCormick, Jacobus, Magie[,] Dodge, De Witt, Garrett, Thompson, Sheldon 10

ACTION OF APRIL 9, 1908 RESCINDED

Mr. Henry offered the following resolution, which was seconded by Mr. Alexander:

> RESOLVED, that the action of the Board of Trustees taken April 9, 1908, in selecting PROSPECT as the site for the Graduate School be rescinded.

Chancellor Magie called for the yeas and nays on Mr. Henry's resolution and the vote was recorded as follows:

YEAS: Pyne, Alexander, G. B. Stewart, McCormick, Dixon, Jacobus, Henry, Green, Davis, Russell, DeWitt, Garrett, Thompson, Shea, Imbrie, Palmer, Farrand 17

NAYS: J. A. Stewart, Magie, Dodge, Sheldon 4

From Henry Smith Pritchett

Personal

My dear President Wilson, [New York] Oct. 21, 1909.

I have read with great satisfaction and encouragement your address before the Φ.B.K. of Harvard as printed in the College [magazine].[1] I am glad that in addition to making clear your own conception of what the college ought to mean in a democracy you also made clear the fact that those who are today asking hard questions of the college are its friends not its enemies. I was disappointed in this respect in President Nichols' inaugural which seemed to me to resent a little any criticisms of existing conditions. His attitude appeared to me to be that of a teacher in a single branch of science suddenly called on to look at education from the larger human standpoint.[2] I shall miss my count if your service in this matter does not bear large fruit.

Sincerely yours, Henry S. Pritchett

ALS (WP, DLC).

[1] Woodrow Wilson, "The Spirit of Learning," *Harvard Graduates' Magazine*, XVIII (Sept. 1909), 1-14; printed at July 1, 1909.

[2] While admitting the validity of some of the criticisms of college education, Nichols viewed them as shallow and misdirected. "The college is the latest phase of the institutional life of our country to be assailed by the reformer," he declared, "and it cannot be denied that we have been unfortunate in some of those who have hurried in to tell us our faults." Moreover, he argued that "beyond just measure . . . dissatisfaction paralyzes hopefulness and effort; we must keep clear of pessimism, if we are to go forward." *The Inauguration of Ernest Fox Nichols* . . . (Hanover, N. H., 1909), pp. 54, 74.

To Edward Wright Sheldon

My dear Ed., Princeton, N. J. October 22nd, 1909.

I have your letter of the 20th. It reached me yesterday while we were absorbed in the business of the Board.

I am a good deal at a loss to know in what form to cast my reminder to Mr. Morgan. I take the liberty of enclosing a letter. If you approve of it, will you not be kind enough to have it dropped in the mail? I assume that Mr. Morgan is in New York and I have directed it to his place of business rather than to his residence, chiefly because I do not know the exact address of the latter.

I find it hard to resume business after the excitement of yesterday. It seemed to me that your presentation of the case in the Board was in every way admirable. It was full at once of reserve and of strength.

Always affectionately yours, Woodrow Wilson

TLS (photostat in RSB Coll., DLC).

To John Pierpont Morgan

My dear Mr. Morgan: [Princeton, N. J.] October 22nd, 1909.

I take the liberty of writing to you to recall your conversation with Mr. John L. Cadwalader and me at your library last spring, in which you were kind enough to say that you would subscribe $5000 a year for five years to the expenses of Princeton, which we are having so much difficulty in carrying, and to ask what would be your pleasure as to the payment of the subscription.

My excuse for doing this is that this is the period of the year when we are making up our budget. I need not say that I write only in order to assist the business of our Finance Committee and not by way of soliciting the payment of the subscription at any particular time.

With much respect,

Sincerely yours, [Woodrow Wilson]

CCL (WWP, UA, NjP).

To Howard Allen Bridgman[1]

My dear Mr. Bridgeman: Princeton, N. J. October 22nd, 1909.

It was very kind and thoughtful of you to send me the extract from the Congregationalist and Christian World, containing an editorial suggested by my address at Hartford,[2] and I am very much gratified that I should have been of any service to thought in such a matter.

Cordially and sincerely yours, Woodrow Wilson

TLS (de Coppet Coll., NjP).

1 Editor of the Boston *Congregationalist and Christian World.*

2 The editorial was "The Modern Prophet," *The Congregationalist and Christian World,* XCIV (Oct. 2, 1909), 429. It referred to a long quotation from Wilson's address at Hartford Theological Seminary, which was printed on the front page of the magazine and which stressed that "the business of the Christian Church, of the Christian minister, is to show the spiritual relations of men to the great world processes, whether they be physical or spiritual." Using this idea of Wilson's, Bridgman focused on the prophetic role of the preacher as an interpreter of the central importance of the Christian gospel for understanding modern society.

To Henry Smith Pritchett

[Princeton, N. J.]

My dear President Pritchett: October 23rd, 1909.

I am sincerely obliged to you for your letter of the 21st. It gratifies me very much that you liked the Phi Beta Kappa Address and that you think there is a likelihood that such utterances will bear fruit.

I shared with you the disappointment at President Nichols' address and was astonished that after uttering it he should confer a degree upon me as one who was "forging out of the college that is the college that ought to be," for certainly I have been one of the chief critics of whom his address seemed to complain and upon whom it certainly threw cold water. I think the explanation must be that he had other criticisms in mind and did not make his own attitude really clear.

For my own part, I find Boards of Trustees the most difficult persons to instruct in this matter. I am often tempted to appeal to the general public in specific terms, though of course I realize that as yet that would be a foolish and perhaps demagogic course to pursue.

It was thoughtful and kind of you to write.

Always cordially yours, [Woodrow Wilson]

CCL (WWP, UA, NjP).

To Mary Allen Hulbert Peck

Dearest Friend, [Princeton, N. J.] 24 October, 1909.

I felt very badly that I should have disturbed you the other night with a telephone call when you were so weary and so needed the rest and refreshment of a good, long sleep; but I felt uneasy and did not quite dare wait till the morning. I had been out all evening, at a long and important meeting. When I went to my room I found a note on my dressing table, which Madge had put there before going to bed, which said you had called me up on the telephone and had asked, when told that I was not in, that I call you when I returned. I was afraid that something had happened to you, that you needed my advice or assistance at once. Late as it was, therefore, I ventured to put in the call,—with the result that I only awaked you out of a restful sleep and disappointed you by telling you that I could not get into town the next day! The little interview gave me the blues and sent me to bed very sad. You were evidently *so* tired and discouraged, and I was of no use whatever! Of course you understood,—you always do; but that only rendered it the harder to bear that I must say I could not come. Please write me all about what you were able to arrange, and tell me some way I can yet be of service. I shall wait impatiently for a letter.

I promised in that little talk over the telephone that I would write and tell you all about the strenuous and disheartening week that has just passed. This is the first leisure I have had in which to fulfil the promise; and now that I am free to come to you, in thought, for the easing of my mind, I do not know just what to tell to make the whole tiresome business clear without a tedious narrative full of matters no one but a university man, and a Princeton man at that, could understand. Suffice it to say that, after a week-long struggle, the Trustees adopted a plan of that arch-intriguer West's which I and all my colleagues on the Faculty earnestly opposed,—a plan of deep and lasting consequence to the University and its whole development. They adopted it, not because they were convinced of its excellence, but because they wanted the half million dollars he had induced a friend of his to offer them for its carrying out. The money overshadowed all my counsel. They do not trust West any more than I do. They think him a nuisance and would be glad to get rid of him. But they did want the money. It is the second time they have done this. They rejected the plans of mine about which there has been so much debate, rejected them though their judgments approved them, because they feared they would fail to get money from a small group of men who were passionately opposed to them. Twice, therefore, on two questions as important as can arise in my administration, they have refused to follow my leadership because money talked louder than I did. It is really intolerable. I am too angry just now, too disheartened, too disgusted, to think straight or with any sort of coolness about what I ought to do in the circumstances. Of course my instinctive inclination is to resign and leave them to their own devices,–to turn to something that will engage my energies and interest my mind in a new field. But that is the last thing a sport ought to think of. He ought not to leave the field so long as there is any slightest chance to prosecute the fight with self-respect and with true prowess. There seems a fighting chance yet to win, and I must stand by the fine men, in the Faculty and in the Board, who are assisting me to the end. I am proud of the fact that I have an almost solid Faculty behind me and in the Board a minority made up of the strongest, most thoughtful, most influential men of the whole body[.] I must not disappoint them in anything. I shall have to possess my soul in patience, and keep my powder dry, until the battle is finally won or lost, all force and strategy alike exhausted, before I can see what it is my duty to do.

In the meantime I admit, to *you*, that I am very low in my mind, filled with scorn and disappointment, and fighting to hold my tongue from words that might make all breaches irreparable. I have a sharp tongue, I am afraid, when I am excited, and it would be inexcusable to let it spoil an institution, an institution for which I have been made responsible. Fortunately my supporters in the Board are as much roused as I am. I can afford to let them do the strong talking. Some of them are likely to make it very strong.

On the heels of the meeting of the Board came the meeting of the Physical Society (the Society in which the students of physics are associated for reading papers and meeting one another) here, to be present at the opening of our splendid new laboratory. Of course the chief of them had to be invited to be our guests here at Prospect and I had officially to play host to all of them, making an address of welcome[1] and standing by to do the polite in every matter that affected their pleasure or entertainment. To-day I have had to entertain the minister, Dr. Lyman Abbott.[2] To-night I am quite played out and ready for bed.

Why is it, do you suppose, that, no matter how tired one is, one's heart can revive him and make it a deep pleasure to turn even to letter writing, if only it is a beloved friend to whom the letter is to go? It is a very delightful provision of nature, at any rate. Maybe there is a subtle selfishness in it. One is sure of the friend's love, too; and it freshens every power there is in one to think how thought will answer to thought when the letter is read: how every word of disappointment or weariness will draw forth instant and perfect sympathy, how sweet a commerce if spirit is set up by the simple instrument. It is a greater comfort than I know how to estimate to have you with your perfect sympathy and understanding to turn to. I shall have to be careful not to overburden you with my own untoward fortunes, to dwell on them just enough to help you for a little to forget your own. After all, I am in no hard case. Life would be very commonplace if there were no struggle and contest in it,–if it were all smooth sailing. One must have something to whet one's teeth on, something to develop and test one's self by. And I have good health, a very happy home, delightful people to love. I may call upon you for sustaining sympathy, but I should be a churl to complain!

All join me in affectionate messages. I am really much more interested in your fortunes than in my own. A letter, therefore, is the present greatest need of

Your devoted friend, Woodrow Wilson

WWTLS (WP, DLC).

1 A news report of his remarks at the presentation of the Palmer Physical Laboratory is printed at Oct. 27, 1909.

2 Editor of the *Outlook*, who preached in Marquand Chapel.

From Edward Wright Sheldon

My dear Woodrow: [New York] October 24th [1909].

The letter to Mr. Morgan seems to me to cover the ground admirably, and has been posted. If the $5,000 comes, I should like to apply it on account of the last year's deficit, which I should suppose was intended to be so reduced when the gift was made.

I think you handled the Graduate School difficulty with great ability and fineness of spirit last Thursday. What will be the outcome of the two conditions attached to the acceptance of Procter's offer, I cannot foresee. It may take a year or two to determine whether the Thomson College may legally be built on the Golf Grounds, and the requirement of a specification of the uses to which Procter's money is to be put, has in it a possibility of offense. So the Board may not have done as much towards a final disposition of the questions involved as was apparently supposed. However, time will settle this as it will many other of our problems. Yours sincerely, Edward W. Sheldon.

ALS (WP, DLC).

To Mary Allen Hulbert Peck

Dearest Friend, Princeton, 25 Oct., 1909.

I am in my office, there is a lull in the succession of callers, and my thoughts turn to *you*, probably starting in on the labour of packing and getting ready to move,—if you decided on the appartments you spoke of. I find my mind dwelling on that move and the new life you are about to attempt. I dread, for you, the labour of moving and the anxiety about ways and means, but I do not dread what will happen when you are established in New York,—provided the quarters you take are comfortable. The way you bestow your belongings will make them beautiful and I believe that the simple life and domestic work you are planning for yourself will make you well and happy. You will have your boy with you, the little home will be in some new sense your own, there will be work and management enough to accustom you to the new independence, your present restlessness will be quieted, and the city itself will beguile your thoughts. Don't spoil the boy. His work and responsibilities have already begun to make a man of him, and he is apt to grow physically stronger much faster under this daily necessity to work than he would under petting and too much *thinking* of his health and welfare.

26 October.

Forgive me for being so didactic. That last sentence, after twenty-four hours interval (no less), looks very offensive. I am thankful that I can let *any* sentence I may happen to write stand as it was written, with the perfect assurance that you will interpret it as it was meant. I am so anxious to let you have the benefit of *any* contribution I can make to the relief of your anxiety or the increase of your confidence in these days of your experiments and your loneliness,—even if it be only a contribution out of my experience in dealing with adolescent youngsters. My thoughts follow you throughout the day. I hope you are conscious of it and get some little solace from the fact.

My thoughts of myself and my own affairs have cooled off since Sunday, when they were in a whirl—with only one idea constant,—and that, that I had submitted often enough and must now 'ask the Trustees their intentions,' in order to ascertain whether my connection with them is any longer honorable and consistent with self-respect. *That* still stands fast in my mind,—though, to tell the truth, I do not know to just what I would turn or how I could avoid feeling rather cheap stepping down and out,—and rather unfaithful to the fine men in the Board and in the Faculty who still have hope of better counsels and rely on me to lead them in these days of discouragement. What do *you* think? Give up only when I am sure that we have reached a veritable impasse?

I shall never write good letters till I cure myself of writing about myself. I don't ordinarily. The temptation lies in your sweet indulgence and affection for me. I know that you will be as interested as I am, and so I *think* about myself and go over and over the same ground. I wish I could make you know how grateful I am, and how happy all you think of me makes me!

Your devoted friend Woodrow Wilson

ALS (WP, DLC).

From Richard Spencer Childs

Dear Dr. Wilson: New York City October 25th, 1909.

I am very glad to report that the Advisory Board has unanimously elected you President of The Short Ballot Organization, and has been greatly pleased to learn that you are willing to accept. Mr. U'Ren and Winston Churchill were elected Vice-Presidents at the same time.

The dinner was a happy little affair of about 20 people, all of whom either represented power in themselves, or were in close touch with effective men, to whom they can pass the inspiration along. There was considerable debate in which everybody shared. It centered principally upon an effort of the majority to convince the minority of three, of the overwhelming importance of the Short Ballot.

All these men will help us considerably in widening the circle, and it seems to me that by January we will be able to muster a crowd of at least 100 men at a dinner in New York for a formal launching of the Organization.[1]

The most important branch of the work, that of the press bureau, is under way, and you have probably received the first batch of "tainted news" which we are sending out to 700 newspapers.

Yours very truly, THE SHORT BALLOT ORGANIZATION,
Richard S. Childs Secretary.

TLS (WP, DLC).

[1] Wilson's address to the Short Ballot Organization on this occasion is printed at Jan. 21, 1910, Vol. 20.

William Cooper Procter to Moses Taylor Pyne

My dear Mr. Pyne: Cincinnati. October 25th, 1909.

I thank you for advising me so promptly of the favorable action of the Board of Trustees in accepting the Golf Links as the site of the future graduate college and for the kind expressions contained in your letter.

As I thought I had at some time written either to you as Chairman or to President Wilson, stating broadly the purposes towards which I wish the money applied, I delayed answering your letter until my return home, but I now find I am mistaken.

The only building I wish to have the honor of erecting is the dining hall. I prefer that all the balance go towards the endowment of professorships and scholarships. I purposely refrained from making definite statement in my offer, as I felt that it might be easier to raise the additional five hundred thousand dollars if the field were left more open to meet the wishes of others who might contribute. If a definite statement is desired, I am perfectly willing to stipulate that not exceeding $200,000 will be expended on buildings,–I, of course, do not anticipate or favor spending so large a sum on the dining hall alone,–and that the remainder will be applied to endowment as above stated. I, of course, had expected to confer with others as to the best form of endowment, as I feel my need of advice upon the subject very keenly.

I have received no notice of the action of the Board other than yours, which I took as a personal notification rather than official. Kindly advise me if a more formal declaration of intention is desired.

Permit me to congratulate you upon the most excellent manner in which you have handled the entire matter. I feel that it is to your patient interest and tact that I am indebted for the favorable decision of the Board.

Yours very sincerely, Wm. Cooper Procter.

TCL (M. T. Pyne Coll., NjP).

To Cleveland Hoadley Dodge

My dear Cleve: Princeton, N. J. October 26th, 1909.

I hate to trouble you with a bill, but you were kind enough to authorize me to go ahead and order the hymnals for the chapel and here is the reckoning. They let us have 600, which I hope will be enough, at 46 cents each.

There are many things I would like to talk over with you, in view of the last meeting of the Board, and I am going to take the liberty, as soon as I can get in the least foot-loose, to come up and see you.

Always cordially and affectionately yours,

Woodrow Wilson

TLS (WC, NjP).

From Abbott Lawrence Lowell

Dear President Wilson: Cambridge [Mass.] October 26, 1909

Princeton has the Presidency this year of The Association of American Universities, which meets at Madison early in January, and I am writing to inquire whether you could not prepare a paper on the position and importance of the arts course, as distinct from the professional and semi-professional, course, in the future?[1] You, President Hadley, and I, are very much interested in this subject, and I gather that the bulk of the members are inclined to take a different view. Owing to the loss of the Treasurer at Yale,[2] President Hadley is very busy just now, and, moreover, says that he has spoken about this subject until he fears that the Association is weary of him. Harvard has also taken, of late, a large share in the proceedings, and, as a new comer, I do not want to begin by reading a paper; but if you will prepare a paper I should be delighted to back you up in the discussion. Yours very truly, A. Lawrence Lowell.

TLS (WP, DLC).

1 Wilson's address, "Position and Importance of the Arts Course as Distinct from the Professional and Semi-Professional Courses," is printed at Jan. 5, 1910.

[2] Thomas Lee McClung had resigned as Treasurer of Yale University to assume the post of Treasurer of the United States, which he held from November 1, 1909, until November 22, 1912. Hadley was Acting Treasurer of Yale for the academic year 1909-10.

Moses Taylor Pyne to William Cooper Procter

My dear Mr. Procter: [New York] October 26th, 1909.

I telegraphed you the result of the meeting on Thursday afternoon and sent a special delivery letter to the Holland House the same evening. There was no answer required to either telegram or letter and I presume that you received them and took them on with you to Cincinnati on Friday morning. As I have come to town, however, for a couple of days and left before the mail came in this morning, in order, in case the letter and telegram missed you, you would not think that I neglected notifying you, I simply repeat what I said in the letter, that, by a large majority, the Board decided to accept your very generous gift, and to place the Graduate College on the Golf Links. The question having been raised as to the right of the University under Mrs. Swann's Will to place the buildings on the golf links, I was a little afraid that the clergymen on the Board, not understanding business matters, would vote against the resolution, and I accepted that as a provision and that I am now trying to clear up. One of the clergymen[1] objected that he did not know for what purpose the balance of the $500,000 over and above the amount that you expected to spend on buildings would be expended. I answered him that no one could tell now where it would be most needed, and I was satisfied that all you wanted to do would be to expend it to the best interest of the University, but fearing again that the clergymen would be opposed to this question, I allowed him to put in a provision, saying that the vote was upon condition that you would explain what was to be done with this money. It was a foolish thing to raise, but there are six clergymen on the Board and they are trained to put their attention on the details and to neglect general principles. As I understand it, all that is desired is for you to write to me, for example, and say that it is your intention to put the larger part of this half million dollars into endowment for Fellowships and Professorships in such manner as might be decided by you after conference with the Trustees Committee on the Graduate College.

I cannot tell you how relieved and satisfied I am that this matter has been finally determined. You have been so kind and so patient and so delightful in the way in which you took this long delay that I want personally to express to you my deepest thanks and appreciation of your whole attitude in the matter, and to say to you that, having brought this thing through in the way I promised I propose to do all in my power from now on to develop this Graduate College in the strongest and fullest way possible. I should have had this feeling of course in any event but I feel now that I am bound by every principle of duty and responsibility to sacrifice everything else to this one thing.

I have had the architects at work on the plans already, and my purpose is to push it through and to commence work this spring.

You told me that you expected to sail on the 5th of November. I suppose you will be in New York for a day or two before that time. Cannot we arrange for a talk together over the matter, either at Princeton or in New York? We should be delighted to have you stay a day or two with us at Princeton, or I should be glad to come on to New York, and hope that you and Mrs. Procter will dine with Mrs. Pyne and myself there. In any event, I hope that you can now go abroad feeling that the matter has been settled and that we are doing everything we can to carry out your wishes in what you desire, and to raise the balance of the money to meet your condition.

With kindest regards to Mrs. Procter, in which Mrs. Pyne joins me, I am, Yours very sincerely, M. Taylor Pyne.

TCL (M. T. Pyne Coll., NjP).

[1] He was the Rev. Dr. George Black Stewart.

A News Report

[Oct. 27, 1909]

Formal Opening of the Palmer Laboratory

In the presence of a large audience of visiting scientists, members of the Board of Trustees and the Faculty, and other invited guests, the Palmer Physical Laboratory was formally presented to the University on the evening of October 22nd. The ceremony was held in the large lecture room of the building where Professor Howard McClenahan '94 meets his classes, and the room was tastefully decorated with banners and palms. When Mr. Stephen S. Palmer, the donor of the building, entered, he was received with great applause, and a few minutes later when he rose to make the formal presentation, the audience rose with him and cheered enthusiastically. . . .

President Wilson, in accepting the laboratory on behalf of the

University, recalled that the date was the 163rd anniversary of the founding of the University, an occasion on which it was particularly appropriate to receive such a handsome gift. He said that one of the most interesting lines of Princeton's historical development, that of the study of physics, was associated with the illustrious name of Joseph Henry, who stretched the first electric telegraph across the Princeton campus, and with the labors and ideals of Professor Brackett, who by years of patience, hope and perseverance had kept the lamp of research burning. The occasion, he said, marked in a sense the culmination of Dr. Brackett's labors, their crowning and fulfilment.

In expressing the thanks of the University to Mr. Palmer, the President said that it is the distinction of America that there are men of affairs who see such opportunities as this and act upon them with unstinted generosity; that this gift had been made in just the right way, to suit the men and the work for which it was intended. Turning to Mr. Palmer, he said: "I know of no case in which a man has been more unstintedly liberal than you are in providing the means of scientific study."

Referring to David B. Jones '76 and Thomas D. Jones '76, who had provided the endowment for the laboratory,[1] President Wilson said that these benefactors had matched the generosity in a similar spirit, with thoughtful forecast of what would be needed always for the maintenance of the building and of the teaching that was to be done within its walls. It was a happy occasion, he said, when the University could rejoice not merely in the incomparable building, but in the work it is permitted to do and in the character, the devotion, the vision of its friends, to whom Princeton was profoundly grateful.[2]

Printed in the *Princeton Alumni Weekly*, x (Oct. 27, 1909), 70, 72.

[1] Of $200,000, about which see n. 1 to the resolutions printed at Jan. 14, 1909, Vol. 18.

[2] There is a WWT outline of this address, dated Oct. 22, 1909, in WP, DLC.

Notes for an Address of Welcome

New Jersey *Library Association.* 27 October, '09

Sincere pleasure to welcome you to Princeton

Glad to believe this recognized to be place of serious and successful study of library administration.

A place of books.

Our preceptorial system makes it a place of reading: the Library its centre.

Books as sources of information and as *a means of life*
The business of the University to make them so in fact
A plethora of *facts*—a notable rarity of *insight.*
You the servants of those who seek *both.*

WWhw MS (WP, DLC).

Notes for a Talk

Whig Hall Smoker 27 Oct., 1909.

The Hall an instrument of serious opinion
Its characteristic function the debate of questions *on their merits.*
Formation of college opinion on college questions
What you *want* a question for *boys*
What you think you *ought to have* a question for men
The lasting comradeships of *principle* formed in this wise, comradeships which look *forward* to the long experience of life
The association of your mind with books and with the world, of wh. the school has told you nothing, but of wh. the University should be the forecast and epitome.

WWhw MS (WP, DLC).

From Edward Wright Sheldon

My dear Woodrow: [New York] October 27, 1909.

The meeting of the Finance Committee at Princeton was held here, pursuant to my call, yesterday afternoon for the purpose of electing a chairman. Under all the curcumstances [circumstances] I agreed to continue to act as chairman in the hope that some other favorable trustee might be found who could fill the position permanently.

I owe you an apology for not sending you a notice of this meeting. Supposing that you knew of it I had fully expected to see you and to talk over various matters with you. It appears that the stenographer misunderstood my instructions and that no formal notice was sent you. However very little was done besides filling the chairmanship and it would have been hardly worth your while to have come to New York for that.

Yours sincerely, Edward W. Sheldon.

TLS (WP, DLC).

From Cleveland Hoadley Dodge

Dear Woodrow New York Oct 27th 1909

It is a pleasure to enclose check for the new hymn books.

I too am anxious to see you & have a good talk & am at your disposal whenever you are ready[.] If you have to come to town won't you lunch with me or better still come up to Riverdale for the night.

It was interesting to note the attitude of the clergy t'other day. If they after confessing they know nothing of the merits of the case, succumb at once to the bribe of a dubious 500 M[,] query—what would they do if $2000000.00 for your social reorganization, was dangled in their faces. It looks as if the amendments will practically nullify Momo's motion.

John Mott spent Monday night with me. He is a very warm admirer of you & your policies. He knows American colleges better than anyone, & in spite of being a BA Cornell & MA Yale has decided to send his son[1] to Princeton next year. He especially approves of your plans for social reorganization & after we had discussed them & I told him of the need of a large sum of money, he earnestly exclaimed, "I wish Pres. Wilson would let me help him to secure 1 or 2 millions from Mr Rockefeller & if I could only have an hour with him & get thoroly loaded with his ideas I believe I could present the matter successfully." He has great influence with father & son & I am sure could reinforce any efforts of yours in that direction

I shall endeavor to get you & Mott together as soon as possible.

The accounts of his visits to all of the great universities in Europe, especially in Russia, were like a romance.

Hoping to see you soon Ever affly C H Dodge

ALS (WP, DLC).

[1] John Livingstone Mott, who entered Princeton in the autumn of 1910 and was graduated with the Class of 1915.

From John Grier Hibben

My dear Woodrow Princeton Oct. 27/09

I saw Stockton [Axson] today, and he tells me that he repeated to you the conversation which I had with him on Saturday last. It is a matter of great satisfaction to me, that you understand my point of view, as Stockton assures me you do. Therefore, I know that you will appreciate my position in reference to the various committees of the Faculty, of which I am a member. As I told Stockton, it is my wish to resign from the Committee on Non-Athletic Organizations. I hope that Stockton himself will be willing to undertake the Chairmanship of that Committee in my place. He understands the conditions, precedents, & general procedure connected with the work of the Committee & will make an ideal Chairman. If it meets with your approval, I should like to resign also from the Committee on the Course of Study, & from the Committee on Examination & Standing.

I should prefer however to remain on the Committee on Sanitation as I have always been particularly interested in the Infirmary. As to the Committee on the Graduate School, which for me is the most difficult and trying of all, I am sure you will understand that it would be most unwise for me to withdraw from it at present. My future relation, however, to the work of the Graduate School is a subject which I wish very much to discuss with you as soon as a convenient opportunity offers. I trust that you will interpret the spirit & disposition of this letter in the light of all that Stockton has communicated to you.

Ever faithfully yours J. G. H.

ALS (WP, DLC).

From Cyrus Hall McCormick

My dear Woodrow: Chicago 27 October, 1909.

I trust that you will advise me by telegram as to the day and hour of your arrival.

I am securing your tickets to return Wednesday morning by the morning train for Princeton, but I am not sure whether you said you were returning direct to Princeton. Do not trouble to reply to this until you come, unless you wish your return tickets secured for some other point.

I am, Very sincerely yours, Cyrus H. McCormick.

P.S. Will you please bring with you Mr. Chatfield's letter which I sent you a few days ago.

TLS (WP, DLC).

From William Frederick Dix

My dear Dr. Wilson: New York, October 27th, 1909.

I take great pleasure in notifying you that at a meeting of the Board of Trustees of this Company[1] held to-day you were unanimously elected a member of the Board.

I am sending you under separate cover a copy of our Charter and By-Laws and will regularly send you notifications for the monthly meetings which occur on the last Wednesday of each month at 12.30 o'clock P.M. If you find it convenient to attend the meeting next month, I hope you will call at my office a little before the hour of meeting and it will give me great pleasure to show you around a little and have you meet the President and some of the officers.

Please accept my congratulations and assurances that the Trustees are much gratified at the prospect of having you with them in future.

Very sincerely yours, William Frederick Dix.

TLS (WP, DLC).

1 The Mutual Life Insurance Company of New York.

To Edward Wright Sheldon

My dear Ed.: Princeton, N. J. October 28th, 1909.

Thank you very much for your letter of yesterday.

I thought it strange that I did not receive a notice of the meeting of the Finance Committee on Tuesday, but you may be sure that I was not in the least hurt. I knew that there had been some mistake or oversight and would have come on, if I had heard of it in time.

I am more relieved than I can say that you have consented to continue as Chairman of the Finance Committee, at any rate for the present. You have already given an air of business and definiteness to its business which I am sure the whole Board feels, and I do not know of any member of the Board except yourself who could render efficient service in the present circumstances in that position. It gives one a sense of security and confidence to have you in it, and I know that in expressing this feeling I am expressing the feeling of the Board itself.

Always affectionately yours, Woodrow Wilson

TLS (photostat in RSB Coll., DLC).

To Cleveland Hoadley Dodge

My dear Cleve: Princeton, N. J. October 28th, 1909.

Thank you most sincerely for your check, which I am today handing to the Treasurer of the University. It will be a great satisfaction to have the new books in the chapel. Mr. Charles

Scribner was kind enough to give us a very handsome new Bible, and now I feel that we are ready for good society.

What you tell me about John Mott is more than interesting and I shall certainly put myself in a position to see him, with your kind assistance, at a very early date.[1] This is a suggestion which we should follow up with eagerness, praying that it may result in something to relieve us from our present almost impossible position. I cannot tell you how your own interest and support cheer me and keep me in courage.

Always affectionately yours, Woodrow Wilson

TLS (WC, NjP).

[1] Wilson had a long meeting with Mott on November 10, 1909, in which he repeated the salient features of his quadrangle plan. Mott's Hw memorandum of this conversation, dated Nov. 10, 1909, is in the J. R. Mott Coll., CtY-D.

From Melancthon Williams Jacobus

Private

Hartford, Conn.,

My dear President Wilson: October 28th, 1909

. . . It has taken me some time to get over the meeting of the Board of Trustees and the feeling of discouragement which came when I saw how impossible it was to impress some of the men, from whom as educators one would have expected a fine appreciation of the University's ideals, with anything except the money question. Still I was glad to hear what Dodge had to say, and was impressed by the significance of the remarks of Chancellor Magie.[1]

It does seem to me that we cannot be satisfied in the Graduate School Committee until we have had this point that the Chancellor raised definitely and decisively settled. The letter of Mr. Lindabury[2] to Pyne was so contradictory and seemed so clearly to confess the very point for which we are contending that I cannot but believe a fair interpretation of the will of Mrs. Swann will cast the golf grounds out as a legally possible site. Have you any knowledge as to whether Mr. Sheldon is taking steps to follow this out and have it definitely settled? We certainly cannot, as a Committee, make the contract for the Thompson College buildings until we have taken a vote on the interpretation of the will.

I had hoped to receive from McCormick a letter stating the results of a conference which he was to have with Dean Fine regarding Fine's suggestion to me, made just before the meeting, to the effect that if West could be eliminated from the control of the intellectual part of the Graduate work–in other words, if he could retire as Dean–and be relegated to a mere Headship of the Thompson College, it would be quite possible for the Graduate School Committee of the Faculty to attempt the carrying out of the University ideals, even were the site such as the golf course.

I do not know whether you had an opportunity to speak with Fine about this matter, and whether his suggestion impressed you as practicable. I think it has come to the parting of the ways, where the only hope for the University development of the Graduate School, no matter what the site of its buildings may be, lies in the removal of West from the intellectual control of the Department.

I know you are very busy, and it may be asking too much of you to request a word in reply to this letter; but I am so far from the center of things that I have to rely on correspondence for almost all my contacts with these moving situations.

With kindest regards,

Yours very sincerely, Melancthon W. Jacobus

TLS (WP, DLC).

[1] There seems to be no record of William Jay Magie's remarks at the meeting of the trustees on October 21, 1909. However, for his earlier legal opinion in regard to the Swann bequest, see W. J. Magie to G. Cleveland, March 13, 1908, printed as an Enclosure with E. W. Sheldon to WW, March 21, 1908, Vol. 18.

[2] Richard Vliet Lindabury, a prominent Newark corporation lawyer, who resided in Bernardsville, N. J., and had drawn Mrs. Swann's will.

From Pierce Butler[1]

Dear Sir: Saint Paul [Minn.] Oct. 28, 1909.

I am causing the Secretary of our Board of Regents to send to you the printed matter to which reference was made when I called on you on the 19th inst.[2] I trust the same will contain the desired information. Should there be anything that you would like further information about, kindly write me and I will undertake to furnish it.

While, as you know, our conversation was wholly informal, and my suggestion that you consider coming to Minnesota was without authority from the Board of Regents, I am satisfied that an intimation from you that such a proposition would be entertained and, perchance, favorably considered, would be welcomed by the Board and all having the welfare of the University at heart. I will esteem it a favor to have you suggest anything for me to do in order to aid you in speedily acquiring a complete understanding of the situation here, and the opportunity presented.

Yours truly, Pierce Butler

TLS (WP, DLC).

[1] Member of the Board of Regents of the University of Minnesota and of the law firm of How, Butler & Mitchell of St. Paul, Minn. He served as Associate Justice of the United States Supreme Court, 1922-39.

[2] To talk about the possibility of Wilson's accepting the presidency of the University of Minnesota.

To Melancthon Williams Jacobus

My dear Dr. Jacobus: [Princeton, N. J.] 29 October, 1909.

Thank you sincerely for your letter of yesterday. . . .

We have discussed a good deal here the advisability of advocating the partial elimination of West which has been suggested. It is my clear opinion, and the clear opinion of most of the men most nearly concerned, that it must be a total elimination or nothing. His influence upon the graduate students is one of the most serious things of the whole situation. To deprive him of his office of Dean and make him Master in residence of the College, would be to concentrate all his energies and all his powers of intrigue upon activities which would certainly bring an impossible temper into the School. It would only be to try another compromise, face another disappointment, and have to do the thing at last when it would seem a mere personal disgust with the man. I have felt it to be my duty to tell every one who has spoken to me about the subject that the only thing my judgment was perfectly clear about, just at this juncture, was that I could not consent to any further concession of any kind which would not entirely eliminate West from the situation. My judgment did not at all approve of the compromise which set up the present committee of the Faculty. I thought then that just our present disappointment was inevitable. But, out of personal consideration for me, the whole thing had been agreed upon by the men chiefly concerned here before I was approached about it; and I did not feel at liberty to make an issue at the last moment. I was willing to have the experiment tried, but it has turned out just as I expected. The men on the committee themselves declare it an utter failure. So would any other half-way measure be: and the one proposed perhaps more subtly irritating than the present.

Since I am writing this letter myself, on my own machine, and not dictating it, I can say that Mr. Stephen Palmer has become convinced that he not only voted on the wrong side, but that it is his duty to do everything possible to get a reconsideration and put matters right. He is working hard at it and with his characteristic directness there are rays of hope that he may effect something important. He says he will go directly to Mr. Procter, if necessary, to tell him the truth about the whole situation. I am kept out of the negotiations, purposely, and know only in a general way what is going on. There are so many compromises possible that I do not feel at all safe; but, at any rate, there is now a party, consisting of the most thoughtful, influential, honorable men in the Board, which has set its face against what the prevailing influences represent; the situation is no longer the President (apparently) against the Board, but a group of men who cannot be ignored against a somewhat larger group who have neither cohesion nor principle of action, and who must, therefore, sooner or later yield. This fact gives me the feeling, for the first time since the meeting two years ago,[1] that the tide is turning, and that the Board may again rouse itself to make its own independent choice of policy and leadership. Even if nothing gives way now, an eventual collapse of the opposition is inevitable. And something may give way now under Mr. Palmer's eager assaults.

The choice now is between sustaining West and reorganizing the University, on the one hand, and getting rid of his influence altogether and following our own ideals, on the other. It is only by cutting the issue clear in this way that we can accomplish anything.

Fortunately, the provisos attached to the resolution accepting Mr. Procter's offer give us time to see our way to what is possible. We still have a fighting chance, if we fight for what we really want and ultimately must demand, the later the worse for the University and the present administration.

How cheering it is to have your letters and your counsel and sympathy!

With warmest regard

Cordially and faithfully yours, Woodrow Wilson

TCL (Charles Scribner's Sons Archives, NjP).

1 That is, since October 17, 1907, when the trustees withdrew their endorsement of the quadrangle plan.

To Henry Smith Pritchett

[Princeton, N. J.]

My dear President Pritchett: October 29th, 1909.

I have read the portions of your fourth Annual Report with care and, I need hardly say, a great deal of interest.

There is only one part of it which seems to me to call for any comment. For myself I am not at all sure that we have operated the rule for retirement on the ground of twenty-five years service long enough to be justified in forming conclusions as to its influence. I should hesitate to change it just yet.[1] I think we must remember that these first years of the operation of our rules have been years of adjustment merely, during which the universities were finding themselves in their relation to us and during which we had to meet conditions which will probably not recur. I mean conditions as to the personnel of the faculties in accepted institutions. I should expect the next few years to be much more normal and to furnish much safer grounds for forming conclusions.

Personally, I value the service rule as it now stands very highly. I think it very desirable both that men should have the opportunity of retiring before they have lost their full vigor and also that institutions should be permitted to correct occasional mistakes in appointment or retire men who have really in twenty-five years failed to fulfill the promise which in the earlier part of their career justified their appointment and retention. It seems to me that it gives the Foundation a certain distinction to be something more than the Trustees of a fund designed to meet the disabilities of old age and disease.

I know that these considerations will appeal to you and feel sure that you will agree with me that this matter needs very thorough threshing out before we act upon it.

With warm regard,

Cordially and sincerely yours, [Woodrow Wilson]

CCL (WWP, UA, NjP).

1 Pritchett had proposed that the provision that a professor might retire on pension after twenty-five years of service, regardless of age, be changed so that only those teachers who were disabled after at least twenty-five years of service be granted pensions. As Wilson's letter indicates, Pritchett had discovered that some men had retired after twenty-five years of service before attaining sixty-five either because they were pressed to do so by their institutions or they preferred research to teaching. Pritchett's proposed change was adopted by the trustees of the Carnegie Foundation for the Advancement of Teaching on November 17, 1909. See Carnegie Foundation for the Advancement of Teaching, *Fourth Annual Report of the President and Treasurer* (New York, 1909), pp. 61-73, 189-91.

To Cyrus Hall McCormick

My dear Cyrus: Princeton, N. J. October 29th, 1909.

Thank you very much for your letter of the 27th. You have done quite right in securing my return tickets direct to Princeton and I am very much obliged to you for taking the trouble.

I am returning Mr. Chatfield's letter with this, for fear I should forget to put it in my pocket when I start for Chicago. The letter was of real service to me in my interview with Mr. Procter.

I wrote you yesterday the hour of my arrival. I am hoping to reach Chicago on the Chicago Limited at four o'clock Monday afternoon.

Always faithfully yours, Woodrow Wilson

TLS (WP, DLC).

A News Report of a Political Address in Plainfield, New Jersey

[Oct. 30, 1909]

A CHANCE FOR THE DEMOCRATS

Woodrow Wilson Compares Its Stand with that of Party in Power.

WARMS UP ON TARIFF QUESTION

Special Dispatch to the EVENING NEWS.

PLAINFIELD, Oct. 30—"The Democratic Opportunity" was pointed out by Dr. Woodrow Wilson, president of Princeton University, in an address last night in the Plainfield Theatre. Dr. Wilson spoke under the auspices of the local Democratic club, and in his address he hit the party in power by saying that it had "become entangled with all sorts of interests, great and small," while the Democratic party "is free from entanglements."

Dr. Wilson declared that the principle upon which the Aldrich tariff was based was not for the benefit of the country at large, "but for the benefit of those engaged in the protected industries." Speaking of public service commissions he said the method is only in its infancy. Dr. Wilson added that the opportunities it offered for political influence and individual tyranny "every one well read in the government's history could easily perceive."

Dr. Wilson added that it was possible to make all corporations disclose the details of their organization in order to determine responsibility.

He spoke in part as follows:

The Democratic party is now facing an unusual opportunity and a very great duty. The party in power has become entangled with all sorts of interests, great and small: has lost its freedom of choice in a hundred ways, and may be said by reason of its peculiar policies to have allied itself with something less than the nation as a whole. The Democratic party, on the other hand, is free from entanglements and is at liberty to choose policies suited to the national conditions as a whole. It is free to make a program for the general good if it will with perfect candor and simplicity.

But it should do this without allowing itself to be embarrassed by old formulas. Most of the old formulas of our politics are worn threadbare and have lost their significance. Take, for example, the old formulas with regard to strict construction and the old ideal of "as little government as possible." The indisputable fact is that the Federal Government has in recent years been launched into many fields of activity, even the existence of which previous generations did not foresee.

It was inevitable, in our changed conditions, that the Federal Government should come out into many new fields of power. I, for one, am very jealous of the separate powers and authority of the individual States of the Union. But it is no longer possible with the modern combinations of industry and transportation to discriminate the interests of the several States as they could once be discriminated.

The party has always stood for a careful restraint of the powers of government, and the position I am advocating is not in derogation of the ancient principles. But it should, whenever national action is necessary, be shy, not of governmental power, but of its organization in the wrong way and its use to the wrong ends. The debates of our coming campaigns must centre upon the means we are to use in accomplishing ends which the whole country sees that it is necessary to accomplish. The Democratic principle is that government should study not only regulation, but individual liberty and individual responsibility, and that no regulation incompatible with the freedom and development of the individual is tolerable. This principle, rightly interpreted, leads to many interesting conclusions.

Apply these doctrines to the great questions of the day, and see what they will yield you. The original principle of protective tariffs in this country turned at every point upon this single object: The calling out of all the resources and energies of the nation, and their protection against foreign competition, so long as they should be unable to bear competition. The principle upon which the Aldrich tariff is based is a radically different one—not the benefit of the country at large and the careful stimulation of its many and various industries—but the benefit of those engaged in the production industries, the incompetent along with the competent. It is a means of insuring profits to certain bodies of manufacturers, on the plea that what they are doing adds to the wealth and trade of the nation, but without regard to the question whether they are adding to the wealth and trade of the nation in the way which is most wholesome and most suited to the common benefit. The whole system is a system of favors, by which not the country at large is profited, but certain perfectly distinguishable beneficiaries of the government and the party which grants the favors. The demoralization of the whole thing, its corrupting effect upon our politics, its enfeebling effect upon our industries, its sinister effect upon our political principles, is now evident to every man who allows himself to think without obscuring his view by private considerations of self-interest.

It is necessary under our dual system of government that the Federal Government should depend upon indirect taxes for the most part for its support, and that almost all direct taxes should be left to the States for their maintenance and development. And it seems a perfectly consistent and legitimate principle to allow the element of incidental protection to come in, but it must not be brought in as a mere subsidy, cramping the life of ordinary purchasers. There could be no objection in such a policy if it were undertaken by a responsible party and adhered to with courage and consistency. The industries of the country could easily adjust themselves, if proper time were allowed for the process.

Apply our principle to the trust question and observe what it will yield. We are at present trying the very hazardous experiment of regulating trusts in one or other of two ways. In the first place, we are attempting to restrain them from forms of organization, and courses of action which are against the general interest by the compulsion of fines and penalties. These fines and penalties generally fall not upon the individuals responsible, but upon the stockholders, who, under our present extraordinary administration of the law, are without any real power to control the business they nominally own. Fines also operate to take out of legitimate business large sums of money of which the public treasury is not in need, and whose withdrawal embarrasses the general process of trade and manufacture. It is a means of regulation which so far has certainly not accomplished its objects.

The other means by which we seek control is the government of public service corporations, as we have come to call them, through commissions. We have carried this method so far that we have virtually gone the length of dictating their management, which carries us very much beyond the point of mere control. We do not see the significance of this method of control at present because the commissions so far appointed have generally consisted of men of some wisdom and great honesty. But the method is only in its infancy. The opportunities it offers for political influence and individual tyranny every man who is well read in the history of government can easily perceive.

There is only one principle in regard to these matters which the Democratic party can consistently adopt. It is perfectly possible to make all corporations so disclose the detail of their organization as to make it evident to the officers of the law what official, what authority, from its board of directors down to its most subordinate responsible officer, is responsible for the acts of the corporation with which the law chooses to deal. That being done, it is perfectly feasible for the law to punish the person or persons directly who ordered any illegal thing done.

We live in an age in which old things are passing away, in which all things are under scrutiny, in which the renaissance of government by opinion and the general interest is as plainly forecasted by every sign of the times as it was in the period preceding the French Revolution. The world has learned self-control in the time which separates us from that revolution, and America of all countries is not apt to follow the hysterical ways which then set Europe in turmoil. It will use the ordinary instrumentalities of peace and counsel to bring the radical changes about which are now inevitable. The question I wish to leave with you tonight is: Will the Democratic party offer its services in the great enterprise?

The meeting was presided over by Leroy J. Ellis, general passenger agent of the Norfolk and Western Railroad. Seated with Dr. Wilson on the stage were 30 prominent residents of the city, including nearly all its clergymen.[1]

Printed in the *Newark Evening News*, Oct. 30, 1909; editorial sub-headings omitted.

[1] There is a WWT outline of this address, dated Oct. 25, 1909, in WP, DLC.

From Norman Edward Mack[1]

My dear President: Buffalo, N. Y., Oct. 30, 1909

I see by the papers that you made a good Democratic speech before the Plainfield Democratic Club, at Plainfield, N. J., last night. I wish you would be kind enough to mail me a copy of this speech so I can print it in an early number of the National Monthly. At the same time I would like to have you mail me one of your latest pictures to be used in connection with the article.[2]

With kind personal regards, I remain,

Very cordially and sincerely yours, Norman E. Mack

TLS (WP, DLC).

1 Editor and publisher of the *National Monthly*, organ of the national Democratic party; chairman of the Democratic National Committee since 1908; and founder, editor, and publisher of the Buffalo *Illustrated Times* and the Buffalo *Evening Times*.

2 Wilson sent Mack a reproduction of the 1908 drawing by Frederic Yates which is published in the photographic section of Volume 18. Mack published the picture along with Wilson's article, printed as the next document.

A Political Article

[*c. Nov. 1, 1909*]

THE DEMOCRATIC OPPORTUNITY

The Democratic party is now facing an unusual opportunity and a very great duty. The party in power has become entangled with all sorts of interests, great and small, has lost its freedom of choice in a hundred ways, and may be said by reason of its peculiar policies to have allied itself with something less than the nation as a whole. The Democratic party, on the other hand, is free from entanglements and is at liberty to choose policies suited to national conditions as a whole and to all the new aspects of politics which have revealed themselves in recent years. It is free to make a program for the general good, if it will, with perfect candor and simplicity.

It should do this without allowing itself to be embarrassed by old formulas. Most of the old formulas of our politics are worn thread-bare and have lost their significance, having been formulated for another age which had other and very different questions to settle, and which settled them with a sincerity which we can imitate only by translating our principles into new forms and statements.

Take, for example, the old formulas with regard to strict construction and the old ideal of "as little government as possible." The indisputable fact is that the Federal Government has in recent years been launched into many fields of activity even the existence of which previous generations did not foresee. We should not now stop to be pedantic about the way in which we shall construe the fundamental law of our Government or attempt the impossible task of forcing its present activities into the framework of old statements. We should seek the best construction, should direct the activities of the Federal Government toward the objects which clearly lie within its province by means which we are convinced to be just and efficient.

It was inevitable, in our changed conditions, that the Federal Government should come out into many new fields of power. I for one, am very zealous for the maintainance of the separate powers and authority of the individual States of the Union. But it is no longer possible with the modern combinations of industry and transportation to discriminate the interests of the several States as they could once be discriminated. Interests once local and separate have become unified and national. They must be treated upon a national scale, in a national spirit, and by the national Government. The Federal Government must, if possible, be kept to its old temper of restraint and carefully studied constitutional right, but it cannot be kept to a little field when the field is in fact great and must be occupied by some common authority. Our principles are not new, but the forms in which we should express them must of necessity be new. They are so novel, indeed, as often to make the principles themselves bear an appearance of radical novelty. There should be no limitation of the functions of the Federal Government by number, but only limitation by carefully considered principle and carefully adopted instrumentalities of action.

The Democratic party has always stood for a careful restraint of the powers of government, and the position I am advocating is not in derogation of its ancient principles in this matter. But it should, whenever national action is necessary, be shy, not of governmental power, but of its organization in the wrong way and its use to the wrong ends. The debates of our coming campaigns must center upon the means we are to use in accomplishing ends which the whole country sees that it is necessary to accomplish. There are Democratic means which we can conscientiously and earnestly advocate, and there are radically undemocratic means which we should oppose with every ardor and power that is in us.

Undemocratic methods and means are those which serve the interests of parties or of groups of men and which ignore the general interest and the essential rights and opportunities and responsibilities of individuals. The Democratic principle is that government should study not only regulation but individual liberty and individual responsibility and that no regulation incompatible with the freedom and development of the individual is tolerable. This principle, rightly interpreted, leads to many interesting conclusions.

Stated in general terms, our principle should be: Government, not for the sake of success at whatever cost and the multiplication of material resources by whatever process, but for the sake of discriminating justice and a wholesome development as well as regulation of the national life.

Apply these doctrines to the great questions of the day and see what it will yield you. Apply it first of all to the great questions which center in tariff legislation. The original principle of protective tariffs in this country was that laid down by the great statesman who may be said to have originated it. I mean Alexander Hamilton. His argument for protective tariffs turned at every point upon this single object; the calling out of all the resources and energies of the nation, and their protection against foreign competition so long as they should be unable to bear competition. He thought always of the general development and never of the particular interests of those who were engaged for their own profit in furthering it. The principle upon which the Aldrich Tariff is based is a radically different one, as sharply contrasted with the principle of Hamilton as private interest is contrasted with public benefit. The object of that tariff, and of those which immediately proceeded [preceded] it, is not the benefit of the country at large and the careful stimulation of its many and various industries, but the benefit of those engaged in the protected industries, the incompetent along with the competent. It is a means of insuring profits to certain bodies of manufacturers on the plea that what they are doing adds to the wealth and trade of the nation, but without any regard to the question whether they are adding to the wealth and trade of the nation in the way which is most wholesome and most suited to the common benefit.

Again and again there have been instances in previous revisions of the tariff in which when certain duties were lowered the manufacturers directly affected found themselves face to face with certain loss, but turned loss into profit by a reconsideration of their whole business, the institution of neglected economies, the installation of improved machinery, and the careful stimulation of all their business processes. Recent tariff legislation seeks at every point to relieve them of such necessities of vigilance and improvement; seeks to protect those who have not put their business at its best against foreigners who have. The whole system is a system of favors, by which, not the country at large is profited, but certain perfectly distinguishable beneficiaries of the Government and the party which grants the favors. The demoralization of the whole thing, its corrupting effect upon our politics, its enfeebling effect upon our industries, its sinister effect upon our political principles is now evident to every man who allows himself to think without obscuring his view by private considerations of self interest. A day of reckoning upon this matter is at hand, and it will be an unjust reckoning, a mere reaction, unless we determine and insist upon the true principle of correction.

What shall that principle be? Nothing else than the principle upon which the whole system was originally founded, namely a studious attention to the general and public benefits to be conferred by it. It is indisputable that a large majority of our industries have been so developed and perfected as to render them quite independent of governmental assistance, if the gifted men who have developed and now control them will but devote their attention to economy and efficiency. By common consent we rule the markets of the world with the chief industries of which we are so proud, and the further subsidizing of the industries concerned by taxation of the people at large has become not only unnecessary but iniquitous and is manifestly inconsistent with the common good. There are other industries which have been artificially fostered and which apparently do not spring out of the natural conditions and capacities of America which can be maintained, it is said, only by a constant aid or subsidy from the Government. Of these the people must ask themselves the question, Do we wish to maintain them? Can we afford to pay for things not naturally or advantageously produced in America when we could get them as well and much cheaper by importation? Shall we saddle ourselves forever with this systematic charity? There are other industries not yet fully developed, to which protection can honestly and consistently be extended until such time as they shall seem ready for independence. There are resources not yet exploited whose exploitation may take time and may need the covert of tariffs. What we need, in brief, is knowledge of the actual facts in respect of each industry and the honesty to act upon those facts when we have ascertained them.

But how shall we act upon them? Certainly not by rapid and radical changes in our present tariffs, but by such a prolonged and steady change as will bring about an adaptation of the fiscal policy of the Government to the real needs and circumstances of our manufacturing and laboring classes, with a view ultimately to get upon this basis; the taxation for the support of the Government of things for which it will not be a real hardship to pay high prices; if taxes upon these do not suffice, the taxation of those things which it will least burden the people to pay for, things not absolute necessaries, things which they can do without without suffering or privation; and throughout the whole process an honest seeking for the things which will yield the most revenue with the least burden to the people.

It is necessary under our dual system of government that the Federal Government should depend upon taxes of this sort, for the most part, for its support and that almost all direct taxes should be left to the States for their maintenance and development. And it seems a perfectly consistent and legitimate principle to allow the element of incidental protection to come in, wherever it may be brought in without being a mere subsidy and without cramping and embarrassing the life of ordinary purchasers. There could be no injustice in a policy such as I have outlined, if it were undertaken by a responsible party and adhered to with courage and consistency. The industries of the country could easily adjust themselves, if proper time were allowed for the process.

Apply our principle of government for the sake of justice and development to the trust question and observe what it will yield. We are at present trying the very hazardous experiment of regulating trusts in one or other of two ways. In the first place, we are attempting to restrain them from forms of organization and course of action which are against the general interest by the compulsion of fines and penalties. These fines and penalties generally fall, if paid, not upon the individuals responsible, but upon the stockholders, who, under our present extraordinary administration of the law, are without any real power to control the business they nominally own. Fines also operate to take out of legitimate business large sums of money of which the public treasury is not in need and whose withdrawal embarrasses the general processes of trade and manufacture. It is a means of regulating which so far has certainly not accomplished its objects.

The other means by which we seek control is the government of public service corporations, as we have come to call them, through commissions. We have carried this method so far that we have virtually gone the length of dictating their management, which carries us very much beyond the point of mere control. We undertake through commissions to dictate to those corporations the methods and means by which they shall conduct their business and we threaten them with penalties of the severest sort if they do not obey the directions given them. These directions may or may not have regard to the possibilities of the case, may force upon those corporations policies and measures which will render their business unprofitable; and yet the government which dictates consents to no responsibility in the matter and has calmly adopted the policy of rule even if it involves ruin.

We do not see the significance of this method of control at present because the commissions so far appointed have generally consisted of men of some wisdom and great honesty, and public opinion has watched the processes of control with a constant critical scrutiny. But the method is only in its infancy. The opportunities it offers for political influence and individual tyranny, which are the bases of graft, every man who is well read in the history of government can easily perceive. By this method of control we shall presently run into choices we never dreamed of, into nothing less than the fundamental choices of governmental ownership and direction, so that responsibility shall not be divided from power.

There is only one principle in regard to these matters which the Democratic party can consistently or conscientiously adopt. It is this. That control shall not be managed in such a way as to increase the powers and temptations of those who administer government, but in such a way as shall make law supreme through judicial instrumentalities, by making it operate directly upon individuals and emphasizing in every item of legislation the responsibility of individuals. It is perfectly possible to make all corporations so disclose the detail of their organization as to make it evident to the officers of the law which official, which authority, from its board of directors down to its most subordinate responsible officer, is responsible for the acts of the corporation with which the law chooses to deal. That being done, it is perfectly feasible for the law to punish the person or persons directly who ordered any illegal thing done. Such a process would check and correct illegal and unconscientious practices as no fine or corporate penalty ever can, and is as feasible in the case of public service corporations as of those which perform a less direct and obvious public function. Here is something which lawyers can work out and which will clear the whole air of chicane and evasion, which will, moreover, remove from government the burden and the temptation of the actual administration of corporate undertakings. One conspicuous responsible person sent to the penitentiary for ignoring the public interest would do more to correct recent abuses than a thousand fines piled high upon one another or a thousand corporate penalties for disobeying the orders of commissions.

There is one way of keeping such principles in constant vigor and increasing the likelihood of their adoption and operation. That is to put public opinion in control. This can be done in only one way, but can in that way be completely and easily done. It can be done by a few fearless men who will take it upon themselves to give the public full information about everything of which they have any knowledge in connection with the management of parties, the making of laws, and the conduct of every part of the public business, by fearless and consistent candor with regard to everything the Government is handling and with regard to the ways in which it is being handled. It is an absolute dereliction of public duty on the part of anyone responsible for public affairs to regard anything done by governmental authority in the field of law or policy as a private transaction, to be determined by secret conferences upon grounds not disclosed to the public view. One of the most wholesome things that has been suggested with regard to the control of corporations is that there should be the utmost publicity in respect of their operations and obligations. It is strange that we have not seen that this is also the way to purify and control government.

We live in an age in which old things are passing away, in which all things are under scrutiny, in which the renaissance of government by opinion and the general interest is as plainly forecast by every sign of the times as it was in the period preceding the French Revolution. The world has learned self-control in the time which separates us from that revolution, and America of all countries is not apt to follow the hysterical ways which then set Europe in turmoil. It will use the ordinary instrumentalities of peace and counsel to bring the radical changes about which are now inevitable. The question I wish to leave with you is: "Will the Democratic party offer its services in the great enterprise?"

Printed in the Buffalo, N. Y., *National Monthly*, I (Jan. 1910), 249, 253; editorial headings omitted.

A Religious Address at McCormick Theological Seminary

[[Nov. 2, 1909]]

THE MINISTRY AND THE INDIVIDUAL

Mr. Chairman, ladies and gentlemen: I feel that it is a privilege and a responsibility to bring this interesting program to a close, particularly when I know how simple the message I bring to you will turn out to be.

It seems singular that each generation should ask itself for what purpose the gospel had come into the world, and yet it is necessary, if we would understand our own purposes, that we should ask ourselves in our own generation that fundamental question. No doubt Christianity came into the world to save the world. We are privileged to live in the midst of many manifestations of the great service that Christianity does to society, to the world that now is. All of the finest things that have made history illustrious seem to have proceeded from the spirit of Christ. All those things which distinguish modern civilization are things which it has derived from the spirit of the church, which, when it has remembered Christ, has reminded the world of the ideals according to which it should serve mankind, should serve all the ends for which men live together; and in our own day in particular there are a great many notable movements afoot which are manifestly touched—at their root, at any rate—with the spirit of Christ.

But Christianity did not come into the world merely to save the world, merely to set crooked things straight, merely to purify social motives, merely to elevate the program according to which we live, merely to put new illuminations into the plans we form for the regeneration of the life we are living now. The end and object of Christianity is the individual, and the individual is the vehicle of Christianity. There can be no other vehicle; no organization is in any proper sense Christian; no organization can be said itself to love the person and example of Christ. No organization can hold itself in that personal relationship to the Saviour in which the individual must hold himself if he would be indeed one who lives according to the Christian precepts.

You know what the distinguishing characteristic of modern society is, that it has submerged the individual as much as that is possible. In economic society particularly we see men organized in great societies and corporations and organic groups, in which each individual member feels that his own conscience is pooled and subordinated, and in co-operating with which men, as you know, constantly excuse themselves from the exercise of their own independent judgment in matters of conscience. The great danger of our own day, as it seems to me, is that men will compound their conscientious scruples on the ground that they are not free to move independently; that they are simply parts of a great whole, and that they must move with that whole, whether they wish to or not. For they say, "The penalty will be that we shall be absolutely crushed." The organization must dictate to us, if we be members of a corporation; if we be members of a union, the union; if we be members of a society of whatever kind, the program of the society must dominate us. It was easy in a simpler age to apply morals to individual conduct, because individuals acted separately and by a private and individual choice, but we have not adjusted our morals to the present organization of society; and whatever you may say in general terms with regard to the obligation of the individual to exercise his own conscience, you will find yourself very much put to it if a friend comes to you with an individual problem of conduct and asks you how in the circumstances you think he ought to act.

It sometimes seems like a choice between breaking up the program of the organization and subordinating your own conscience. I have had men tell me who were in the profession to which I was originally bred—the profession of the law—that it is extremely difficult to thread their way amidst a thousand complicated difficulties in giving advice to the great bodies of men whom they are called upon to advise, and to discriminate between what is legally safe and what is morally justifiable.

It is in this age that the preacher must preach. The preacher must find the individual and enable the individual to find himself, and in order to do that he must understand and thread the intricacies or [of] modern society.

It was my privilege to speak upon a similar occasion to this, not many months ago, and there to take as my theme the necessity the minister is under to enable the individual to find himself amid the intricacies of modern thought.[1] This is an age of obscured counsel about many fundamental things, and the average individual cannot unassisted know his place in the spiritual order of the universe as it is now interpreted by multitudinous and differing voices. The minister has the very difficult and responsible task of enabling the individual to find himself amidst modern thought. This evening I must call your attention to the fact that it is also his business to enable the individual to find himself amid modern action. There are daily choices to be made, and the individual must make them at the risk of the integrity of his own soul. He must understand that he cannot shift the responsibility upon the organization. The minister must address himself to him as his counselor and friend and spiritual companion; they must take counsel together how a man is to live with uplifted head and pure conscience in our own complicated age, not allowing the crowd to run away with or over him.

[1] At Hartford Theological Seminary, where he delivered "The Present Task of the Ministry" on May 26, 1909. The text is printed at that date.

You know that the law has shirked this duty. Sooner or later the duty must be faced. The law tries nowadays to deal with men in groups and companies, to punish them as corporate wholes. It is an idle undertaking. It never will be successfully accomplished. The only responsibility to which human society has ever responded or ever will respond, is the responsibility of the individual. The law must find the individual in the modern corporation and apply its demands and its punishments to him if we are to check any of the vital abuses which now trouble the world of business. You may pile fines never so high in the public treasury, and corporations will still continue to do things that they ought not to do, unless you check them by taking hold of the individuals who are ultimately responsible for their policy. While the law waits to find this out, the minister cannot wait. He must attempt and must accomplish what the law declines, for men are dying every day. They are going to their long reckoning. They cannot wait for the law to find the way of the gospel. The minister must be present with them while they live, and comfort them when they die, and reassure them of the standards of their conduct.

Every great age of the world of which I have ever heard was an age not characterized chiefly by co-operative effort, but characterized chiefly by the initiative of the indomitable individual. You cannot give any age distinction by the things that everybody does. Each age derives its distinction from the things that individuals choose to be singular in doing of their own choice. Every turning point in the history of mankind has been pivoted upon the choice of an individual, when some spirit that would not be dominated stood stiff in its independence and said: "I go this way. Let any man go another way who pleases."

We die separately. We do not die by corporations. We do not die by societies. We do not withdraw into our closets by companies. Every man has to live with himself privately—and it is a most uncomfortable life. He has to remember what he did during the day, the things that he yielded to, the points that he compromised, the things that he shrugged his shoulders at and let go by when he knew that he ought to have uttered a protest and stood stiff in declining to cooperate. And this lonely dying is the confession of our consciousness that we are individually and separately and personally related to the ideals which we pursue, and to the persons to whom we should stand loyal. Corporations do not and cannot love Christ. Some individuals that compose them do, but those individuals do not love him truly who cooperate in doing the things that those associated with them do that are inconsistent with the law of Christ.

I have heard a great deal of preaching, and I have heard most of it with respect; but I have heard a great deal of it with disappointment, because I felt that it had nothing to do with me. So many preachers whom I hear use the gospel in order to expound some of the difficulties of modern thought, but only now and again does a minister direct upon me personally the raking fire of examination, which consists in taking out of the Scriptures individual, concrete examples of men situated as I suppose myself to be situated, and searching me with the question, "How are you individually measuring up to the standard which in Holy Writ we know to have been exacted of this man and that?"

I am one of those who remember with a great deal of admiration the work of that extraordinary man, Mr. Moody.[2] He was not a learned man, as you know, and the doctrine that he preached was always doctrine which seemed to have inevitably something personal to do with you if you were in the audience. Whenever I came into contact with Mr. Moody I got the impression that he was coming separately into contact with one person at a time. I remember once that I was in a very plebeian place. I was in a barber shop,[3] lying in a chair, and I was presently aware that a personality had entered the room. A man came quietly in upon the same errand that I had come in on, and sat in the chair next to me. Every word that he uttered, though it was not in the least didactic, showed a personal and vital interest in the man who was serving him. Before I got through with what was being done to me I was aware that I had attended an evangelical service, because Mr. Moody was in the next chair. I purposely lingered in the room after he left and noted the singular effect his visit had upon the barbers in that shop. They talked in undertones. They did not know his name. They did not know who had been there, but they knew that something had elevated their thought. I left the place as I should have left a place of worship. Mr. Moody always sought and found the

2 Dwight Lyman Moody, famous American evangelist of the late nineteenth century.

3 This incident, according to Ray Stannard Baker, occurred in Middletown, Conn., when Wilson was teaching at Wesleyan University. R. S. Baker, *Woodrow Wilson: Life and Letters* (8 vols., Garden City, N. Y., 1927-39), I, 315-16. Later, when asked whether this story was fact or legend, Wilson confirmed it, adding, "My admiration and esteem for Mr. Moody was very deep indeed." WW to H. A. Bridgman, Oct. 26, 1914, printed in *The Congregationalist and Christian World*, XCIX (Nov. 12, 1914), 624.

individual, and that is the particular thing which the minister must do.

As I see the opportunity of the church, it is to assist in bringing in another great age. Ministers are not going to assist very much in solving the social problems of the time, as such. Their attitude toward the social problems of the time is always supposed to be a professional attitude, and they are not of as much assistance in that matter as the average serious-minded layman is. But the opportunity of the church is to call in tones that cannot be mistaken to every individual to think of his own place in the world and his own responsibility, and to resist the temptations of his particular life in such ways that if he be central to anything the whole world will feel the thrill of the fact that there is one immovable thing in it, a moral principle embodied in a particular man.

This is an age of conformity. It is an age when everybody goes about seeking to say what everybody else is saying. Winds of opinion creep through the country. Formulas are repeated with all sorts of dexterity in their mere variation. Men have caught the gregarious habit of conscience as well as of mind, and you will find that nothing heartens an audience in a modern age more than to hear an individual, whether he has anything new to say or not, get up and say something that he really means, singly and by himself, without the least care whether anybody else thinks it and means it or not. A friend of mine who was of such a sort was congratulated for his courage in speaking the things that he really thought. He said: "Why, I am not aware of any courage. It would take courage to do the other thing. If I said the things I did not mean, I would say very contradictory things at different times; I would get all tied up, and I should not know how to get out." The only way to avoid that is by echoing everything else that everybody else says. There was a cynical saying of Dean Swift's, "If you wish to be considered a man of sense, always agree with the person with whom you are conversing." That is a very modern, and also, I dare say, a very ancient way of gaining a reputation of being a man of sense. But it is practiced at the peril of your soul, which is a consideration worth thinking of.

I have often preached in my political utterances the doctrine of expediency, and I am an unabashed disciple of that doctrine. What I mean to say is, you cannot carry the world forward as fast as a few select individuals think. The individuals who have the vigor to lead must content themselves with a slackened pace and go only so fast as they can be followed. They must not be impracticable. They must not be impossible. They must not insist upon getting at once what they know they cannot get. But that is not inconsistent with their telling the world in very plain terms whither it is bound and what the ultimate and complete truth of the matter, as it seems to them, is. You cannot make any progress unless you know whither you are bound. The question is not of pace. That is a matter of expediency, not of direction; that is not a matter of principle. Where the individual should be indomitable is in the choice of direction, saying: "I will not bow down to the golden calf of fashion. I will not bow down to the weak habit of pursuing everything that is popular, everything that belongs to the society to which I belong. I will insist on telling that society, if I think it so, that in certain fundamental principles it is wrong; but I won't be fool enough to insist that it adopt my program at once for putting it right." What I do insist upon is, speaking the full truth to it and never letting it forget the truth; speaking the truth again and again and again with every variation of the theme, until men will wake some morning and the theme will sound familiar, and they will say, "Well, after all, is it not so?" That is what I mean by the indomitable individual. Not the defiant individual, not the impracticable individual, but the individual who does try, and cannot be ashamed, and cannot be silenced; who tries to observe the fair manner of just speech but who will not hold his tongue.

That is the duty of the preacher. I have noticed that there is one sort of preaching in simple congregations and sometimes a different sort of preaching in congregations that are not simple. Now there cannot be two gospels. There cannot be two ways in which individuals shall save themselves. And the minister ought to see to it that with infinite gentleness, but with absolute fearlessness, every man is made to conform to the standards which are set up in the gospel, even though it cost him his reputation, even though it cost him his friends, even though it cost him his life. Then will come that moral awakening which we have been so long predicting, and for which we have so long waited; that rejuvenation of morals which comes when morals are a fresh and personal and individual thing for every man and woman in every community; when the church will seem, not like an organization for the propagation of doctrine, but like an organization made up of individuals every one of whom is vital in the processes of life.

I remember attending recently a missionary conference in which we were all heartened with the plans that were being formed for bringing all the denominations in the missionary field together in a common effort.[4] After all the speeches had been made and we had dispersed and I was going home in the night, I thought: "This is a very beautiful thing that is about to happen in the mission field. But I hope that after it has happened there the people who are being evangelized will not come here and see us, because I should not like to have them think we could do that thing away from home and could not do it at home. I should not like to have them think that we are divided in our Christianity where we live and maintain the civilization of a Christian nation, and are united only among those upon whom we look with a certain condescension, as if they could not understand our differences of doctrine, and therefore they were not worthy the explanation." It is, I suppose, a high intellectual plane upon which we think that we live, but we do not live upon intellectual planes at all; we live upon emotional planes; we live upon planes of resolution and not upon planes of doctrine, if I may put it so. And the reason that we differ so is that we hold ourselves too far above the practical levels of life and are constantly forgetting that the whole vitality of Christianity consists not in its texts, but in their translation; not in the things that we set up as the abstract standard, but in the actions which we originate as the concrete examples.

You will see, therefore, that there is a sense in which the minister is set against modern society. Modern society is collectivist. It says "Unite." The minister must say: "Not so. You can unite for certain temporal purposes, but you cannot merge your souls; and Christianity, come what may, must be fundamentally and forever individualistic." For my part, I do not see any promise of vitality either in the church or in society except upon the true basis of individualism. A nation is strong in proportion to the variety of its originative strength, and that is in proportion to the vitality of its individuals. It is rich in direct proportion to the independence of the souls of which it is made up. And so every promising scheme that unites us must still be illuminated and checked and offset by those eternal principles of individual responsibility which are repeated not only in the gospel but in human nature, in physical nature.

You have loved some person very dearly. You have tried to merge your individuality with that person, and you have never succeeded. There is no person linked spiritually so closely to you that you can share his individuality or he can share yours. And

[4] He was referring to the "China Dinner," sponsored by the Annual Conference of the Foreign Missionary Boards of the United States and Canada, held on January 14, 1909. See W. H. Grant to WW, Dec. 19, 1908, Vol. 18.

this inexorable law, physical and spiritual, is the law which must be the guiding fact for the minister of the gospel. He must preach Christianity to men, not to society. He must preach salvation to the individual, for it is only one by one that we can love, and love is the law of life. And the only person living through whom we shall love is our Lord and Saviour, Jesus Christ.[5]

Printed in *McCormick Theological Seminary Historical Celebration. . . .* (Chicago, 1910), pp. 163-73.

[5] There is a WWhw outline, dated Nov. 2, 1909, and a stenographic transcript of this address in WP, DLC.

A News Item About Remarks to the Princeton Club of Chicago

[Nov. 3, 1909]

BOOM WILSON FOR PRESIDENT.

Princeton Alumni Cheer When He Speaks of His College Furnishing "Leader."

With che[e]rs and songs for "old Nassau" and an enthusiastic indorsement of Woodrow Wilson for president, the Princeton Alumni Association held their first beefsteak dinner and smoker last evening at the University club.

"Princeton is being looked to for a leader now," said Dr. Wilson. "Other universities have furnished great public men, and we must do the same. To do this we must live the good sound traditions of the college in our daily life, sobering down to a realization of our duties."

The speaker's remarks about "Princeton's furnishing a leader" were literally interpreted. He had hardly taken his seat when the oldest alumnus present, the Rev. Isaac [Amada] Cornelison, '50, of Washington, Ill., leaped to his feet and proposed him as the "logical successor to Theodore Roosevelt." In the shouts that followed Dr. Wilson hurriedly left the room.

Printed in the *Chicago Daily Tribune*, Nov. 3, 1909.

From George Walbridge Perkins

My dear President Wilson: New York. November 3rd, 1909.

While in Alaska with my family this Summer we did some exploring and located a bay off Prince William's Sound that had never been charted. We found at the extreme end of this bay a very handsome glacier, in action and of considerable size. It never had been visited by white people so far as any one knows and certainly never has been named. Attached to the main glacier were two smaller glaciers.

I am about to file a map of the bay with the United States Government, and my family would like to join me in naming the fiord "Nassau Fiord," the large glacier "Princeton Glacier," and the smaller ones, respectively, "The Tiger" and "The Tiger's Tail." Before doing so, however, I write to ask if there would be any objection on your part? I have spoken to Moses Taylor Pyne and Cleveland Dodge and both seem to think it would be agreeable.

There are glaciers in Alaska that have been named for Harvard, Yale and Columbia, and I think that this one we located compares quite favorably with any of the others.

With best regards, I am,

Very sincerely yours, Geo. W. Perkins

TLS (WP, DLC).

From Henry Smith Pritchett

My dear President Wilson: New York November 3, 1909.

(I am greatly minded to leave off the "President" continually and call you by a less formal title.) I am very glad to have your note of October 29 and appreciate the point which you raise with regard to any change in the twenty-five year rule. I hope this matter will be very thoroughly threshed out at the forthcoming meeting of the trustees, which I think is an important one. I count also that at the meeting of the executive committee which has just been called to precede the meeting of the trustees we shall canvass this situation.

By the way, I saw a newspaper statement the other day to the effect that your Princeton golf ground was to be sacrificed for a location for the new graduate school. This strikes me as a most sacrilegeous proceeding.

Can you not spare the time to take a half day with me at Saint Andrew's[1] some time while the weather still remains good? We might pick up our friend, "The Laird,"[2] as a third man and perhaps make a day of it.

Very sincerely yours, Henry S. Pritchett

TLS (WP, DLC).

[1] Saint Andrew's Golf Club, located in Chauncey, Westchester County, New York.

[2] Andrew Carnegie.

From Anita McCormick Blaine[1]

[Chicago]

My dear President Wilson: Wednesday [Nov. 3, 1909]

I couldn't catch you for a word last night and so I must send one after you, to thank you for your great address. It was tremendous.

I want to know whether it is to be printed. If it is to be with all of the addresses of the celebration I shall hear of that from Dr. McClure. If not, how may I have it? And I wondered as you spoke of it whether I could see the address you alluded to which dealt with the minister, the individual, and the thought that is called modern.

I should be so glad if I could—but if it involves any trouble please dont think about it.

More thanks than I can say for your great contribution to us all. I am Yours sincerely Anita Blaine

ALS (WP, DLC).

[1] Widow of Emmons Blaine, a lawyer who had died in 1892. She was the daughter-in-law of James G. Blaine of Maine and sister of Cyrus Hall McCormick.

Moses Taylor Pyne to Cyrus Hall McCormick

My dear Cyrus: [Princeton, N. J.] November 3rd, 1909.

Thank you for your letter of the 28th of October. There seems to be a general opinion that Parker Handy would be about the best man possible to carry on the work of the Finance Committee, and I hope that at the next meeting of the Board some one will nominate him.

I appreciate very much what you say about the Procter decision. I could not see my way clear to voting any other way for I felt that had we rejected his offer it would be almost impossible for the President to have withstood the storm that would have arisen up, not only from the Alumni but from the whole country. Once we put it out that Princeton was rich enough to refuse half a million dollars because the giver wishes to put a building a few hundred yards one way or the other, it would become almost impossible to collect money in any direction and the Alumni subscriptions would have fallen off woefully.

Having taken that ground I feel, of course, a great responsibility with regard to the Graduate College and shall devote all the time and attention that I can possibly spare to see that it is carried through on the lines that would appeal to both you and me.

Arrangements are being made by which West is to give up his Chairmanship of the Committee on the Graduate School where most of the friction arose. That, I think, can be carried through shortly and, I think, will obviate the questions that arose.

Yours very sincerely, M. Taylor Pyne.

TCL (M. T. Pyne Coll., NjP).

To George Walbridge Perkins

Princeton, N. J.

My dear Mr. Perkins: November 4th, 1909.

Thank you sincerely for your letter of November third.

I am greatly interested in your exploration in Alaska and very much gratified that you should wish to name the fjord "Nassau Fjord," the large glacier "Princeton Glacier," and the smaller ones respectively "The Tiger" and "The Tiger's Tail." I not only have no objection, but am very much obliged to you for the suggestion.

I hope that your visit to Alaska was full of refreshment and that you have come back from it very much rested from business. Be kind enough to present my regards to Mrs. Perkins[1] and believe me, Cordially yours, Woodrow Wilson

TLS (G. W. Perkins Paper, NNC).

[1] Evelyn Ball Perkins.

To Edward Wright Sheldon

My dear Ed., Princeton, N. J. November 4th, 1909.

I have just received from Mr. J. P. Morgan a check for $5000 and the assurance that he will make a similar payment on November 1st for the next four years. I have handed the check to Mr. Duffield and have told him that I would ask you to instruct him what application to make of the money. I see nothing to prevent our applying it to the deficit of the fiscal year ending August 1st last.

I have just got back from Chicago, where I had a very interesting but fatiguing visit.

Always affectionately yours, Woodrow Wilson

TLS (photostat in RSB Coll., DLC).

To John Pierpont Morgan

My dear Mr. Morgan: [Princeton, N. J.] November 4th, 1909.

Had I not been absent from home fulfilling an engagement in Chicago, I would have acknowledged sooner your great kindness in sending me, through your Secretary, Mr. Allen,[1] your check for $5000, your subscription to the funds of the University.

I need not tell you how highly all connected with the University appreciate your interest in it and this substantial expression of your interest.

With warm regard,

Sincerely yours, [Woodrow Wilson]

CCL (WWP, UA, NjP).

[1] The Editors have been unable otherwise to identify him.

From Harry Madison Cutts[1]

My Dear Sir: Brookline Mass. Nov. 4 1909.

The Princeton Alumni Association of New England invites you to address it at the University Club, Boston, on Friday evening Nov. 12 1909.

It is our hope that after your address in Brookline on the same evening that you can & will visit us at the University Club where we expect to have a goodly number of our alumni ready to meet you.[2] Respectfully H. M. Cutts. '80.

ALS (WP, DLC).

[1] Princeton 1880, a physician living and practicing in Brookline, Mass., and President of the Princeton Alumni Association of New England.

[2] A news report of Wilson's address to the Princeton alumni in Boston and to the Harvard Church in Brookline is printed at Nov. 13, 1909.

To Henry Skillman Breckinridge[1]

Princeton, N. J.

My dear Mr. Breckinridge: November 5th, 1909.

It was a pleasure to get your letter of October 31st,[2] to which I would have replied sooner, had I not been necessarily absent from home.

It was very refreshing to see you and the other Princeton men at Cambridge and I am very proud of the record that the Princeton men have been making in the Harvard Law School. What you tell me of the sentiments expressed at the little gathering of 1907 men heartens me not a little. I should feel very much discouraged if these sentiments were not growing among our alumni.

I take real pleasure in enclosing such a letter as you ask for[3] and hope that it will be serviceable to you in the way you desire.

As to a choice between Louisville and Baltimore, I feel that I am hardly in a position to advise. On general principles, however, I should strongly favor Louisville as a place more likely to see future growth and to share in some particular degree the coming influence of the South than Baltimore. I should imagine, also, that you would have there the advantage of having your family connections well known and of making and retaining a very large circle of influential friends.[4]

Always cordially and faithfully yours,

Woodrow Wilson

TLS (H. S. Breckinridge Papers, DLC).

1 Princeton 1907, a student at the Harvard Law School.

2 It is missing.

3 It is also missing.

4 Breckinridge received the LL.B. degree from Harvard in 1910 and from 1910 to 1911 worked in the office of the United States Attorney in Baltimore. From 1911 to 1913, he practiced law in Lexington, Ky., and from 1913 to 1916 served as Assistant Secretary of War.

From Melancthon Williams Jacobus

My dear President Wilson: Hartford, Conn. Novr. 5th 1909

Your letter in reply to my inquiry was one of the most encouraging words I have heard regarding Princeton in many months.

You will pardon me if I seem anxious to know of results; I am not writing for this purpose, however, but to say that if there is anything I can do to help matters to an issue I am only too ready to do it. The issue must certainly come, however it is brought about, and to my mind the sooner it comes the better

With kindest regards

Yours very sincerely Melancthon W Jacobus

ALS (WP, DLC).

From Annie Dixon McClure[1]

My dear President Wilson, Chicago Nov. 5th [1909]

Henceforth I shall regard you as one of the saints of the earth. I knew of your power as teacher, as College President, as author, and have admired and revered, but to have a man like yourself stand at a reception for nearly two hours, greeting, with grace and kindness, the many friends of the Seminary who came into our home on Tuesday afternoon, and not appear like a caged lion, but like a genial host makes me realize that the aureole is about your head forevermore.

How to thank you for your goodness I do not know, but may I tell you that your presence gave to the afternoon its crowning pleasure for all, and will be a memory to our students that will never fade. Mr. McClure and I are inexpressibly grateful to you. I wish that Mrs. Wilson could have been with you. Please tell her that as a wife she must have a remarkable influence. My husband has never stood by me at a reception quietly for more than a few minutes at a time, while you were faithful, in the receiving line, to the last. It was my regret that I could not even tell you that day how glad Mr McClure and I were to have you here. The Celebration has been a memorable occasion for the Seminary: the climax of all was your address on Tuesday evening, so strong, so true, so wise. I wish every student in the world could hear it. May God bless you for it all. Mr. McClure joins me in kindest regards to Mrs. Wilson.

Sincerely, (Mrs. J. G. K.) Annie Dixon McClure.

ALS (WP, DLC).

1 Wife of James Gore King McClure, President of McCormick Theological Seminary.

From Pierce Butler

(Personal)

Dear President Wilson: Saint Paul [Minn.] Nov. 6, 1909.

I hope that you have read the printed matter relating to our University, which was sent to you at my request some time ago by the Secretary of the Board of Regents, and I also hope that you have been given a good understanding of the size, quality and prospects for greatness of that institution. I would like to reiterate and add to the things that I said and referred to when I called on you recently, but I am sure that you will appreciate the situation and opportunity offered without further presentation of the matter.

I write you this letter to ask that you give me permission informally to say to my associates on the Board of Regents that you will favorably consider, or at least be inclined favorably to consider, an invitation of our Board to become the next President of the University of Minnesota. I think I made it clear to you that Doctor Northrop[1] will lay down the work at the end of the present school year. You know the importance of the matter of naming his successor, and will sympathize with the desire of the Board to dispose of the matter as early as possible, consistent with thorough knowledge of the man to be selected. You may be assured that—without your consent—I will do nothing calculated to give publicity to the fact that you are being considered.

I hope your answer may be favorable. I know that some members of the Board feel as I do, and as I expressed myself to you, and I have no reason to suppose that any member of the Board feels differently. Yours truly, Pierce Butler

TLS (WP, DLC).

[1] Cyrus Northrop, President of the University of Minnesota, 1884-1911.

From Henry Skillman Breckinridge

My dear Dr. Wilson: Cambridge, Mass. Nov. 7, 1909.

I cannot tell you how sensible I am of the great honor you do me in writing such a letter, and however little I may know myself to deserve it, I am extremely gratified.

It is neither possible nor desirable to fail to recognize the responsibility incumbent upon one who asks for, receives, and expects to use such an expression of confidence from one in your position. I humbly aspire not to betray that confidence.

With sincere thanks for your unstinted generosity, I am,

With great respect,

Faithfully yours, Henry S. Breckinridge.

ALS (WP, DLC).

To Anita McCormick Blaine

My dear Mrs. Blaine, Princeton, New Jersey 8 Nov., 1909

I don't know when a letter has reassured and cheered me as yours did! I would have written at once to thank you for it, had I not been again called away from home. I left the church that night very "low in my mind," feeling that I had uttered a very commonplace address, full of obvious things to which no phrases I could find had lent the least distinction,—and nothing any one said to me afterwards dispelled the impression. It seemed to me that I had said nothing as I had wanted to say it—and it seemed a shame to go a thousand miles to make a mediocre homily. You may imagine how your letter delighted me, therefore, and put me in heart again. I value and appreciate your praise very highly and thank you with all my heart.

I would have taken the liberty of calling on you the morning I left Chicago if I had not been ashamed of the address,—for I very much want to have a talk with you, and was greatly disappointed that no opportunity for one offered itself. As for my "plan,"[1] I am beginning to wonder whether I would not be more likely to see it realized at some great State university, where I could appeal directly to public opinion and draw upon the taxes than I am in an institution like Princeton where alumni opinion and alumni money hold off from such enterprises.

The address of the other evening already lies before me, as the reporter took it down—and I think they mean to publish it along with the other addresses. I am asking the Secretary of Hartford Seminary to send you a copy of the other address to which I alluded—since you are kind enough to want to see it. I have no copy here.

With warm regard,

Gratefully Yours, Woodrow Wilson

ALS (Anita M. Blaine Papers, WHi).

[1] That is, the quadrangle plan.

To Melancthon Williams Jacobus

[Princeton, N. J.]

My dear Dr. Jacobus: November 8th, 1909.

I have again been away from home for a day or two and am delayed in replying to your letter of the 5th.

I hope that you will not apologize for asking me about the course of affairs. It is always a pleasure to keep you posted, if there is anything to tell. Unfortunately, I am entirely ignorant about what is just now being done and proposed. I know only that Mr. Palmer has become entirely convinced that he voted on the wrong side at the Board meeting and is doing all that he can to set the matter right. I am afraid, from the few intimations which reach me, (for there is again a kind but mistaken effort to keep me out of the negotiations) that the very compromise which was spoken of in my last letter to you is being urged. I feel that it is no solution at all, and I am really very anxious about the whole matter. It really seems to me that we have come to a parting of the ways in many senses as between two theories of university administration, and I am very much perplexed as to what is the best course for me to pursue. I do not mean that I am perplexed as to the choice I should make, but only that I am perplexed as to the wisest way in which to give it expression.

Just so soon as matters assume any form susceptible of definite discussion, you may be sure that I will let you know, for I shall greatly need your counsel.

With warmest regard,

Cordially and faithfully yours, [Woodrow Wilson]

CCL (RSB Coll., DLC).

William Milligan Sloane *et al.* to Moses Taylor Pyne

Dear Sir: Trenton, New Jersey November 8th, 1909.

In reply to your letter stating that the Trustees of Princeton University have voted to put the building of the John R. Thomson Graduate College on that part of the University Campus known as the Golf Links, and asking the opinion of Mrs. Swann's executors as to that location, we would say that, after due consideration and knowledge of the improvements proposed as to the entrance to the property, we are glad to say that this location will be entirely satisfactory to us.

We appreciate your courtesy in offering to show us the plans of the building when completed, and shall examine them with the greatest interest.

Yours very truly, Wm. M. Sloane.
Bayard Stockton
Francis Larkin (Jr.)
Executors of Mrs. J. A. T. Swann

TLS (Trustees' Papers, UA, NjP).

To Winthrop More Daniels

My dear Daniels: Princeton, N. J. November 9th, 1909.

This is the fifth year of the Preceptorial System, and I am anxious to canvass our experience so far as thoroughly as possible. I would be very much obliged, therefore, if you would furnish me, as soon as it can be thoroughly completed, a statement covering the following points:

First: The number of men in each of the four classes who have chosen your Department during each of the last four years and the first term of the present year.

Second: The number who have chosen electives in your Department without choosing the Department itself. I would be obliged if under this head you would state how many have taken one course, how many two courses, etc., during each of the last four years and the first term of the present year.

Third: The system followed in your Department in allotting preceptorial work, whether in the case of those who have chosen the Department or in the case of those who have chosen electives in the Department, as so-called "floaters."

Fourth: How far and in what way the Professors and Assistant Professors in your Department (that is, those who conduct courses) have been participating in the preceptorial work, and how far, in the judgment of the Department, it would be possible to draw those who conduct courses more systematically into the general preceptorial function. I mean how far it would be feasible to include them among those members of the Department who undertake preceptorial work outside the field of their own immediate courses of instruction.

Fifth: In just what way the preceptorial method has been applied in each of the courses given in the Department.

Sixth: How far and by what methods you think experience has shown the present preceptorial method to be applicable and serviceable in the several courses of your Department, and what differences exist in this respect between the several courses.

My object in making these inquiries is to ascertain whether we are organizing our preceptorial work in the most effective way and in the way which will not only make use of the whole teaching energy of the Department but also, so far as possible, draw all the members of the Department into a true preceptorial relation with the students who resort to the Department for instruction.

I would be very much obliged to you if you would see me as soon as possible to arrange a conference about this matter before you have taken more than the preliminary stages towards formulating the statement I have asked for. If there is a committee in your Department on preceptorial allotments and arrangements, I should like to see one or more members of that committee at the same time that I see you, if you would be kind enough to arrange the conference with me.

Faithfully and sincerely yours, Woodrow Wilson[1]

TLS (Wilson-Daniels Corr., CtY).

[1] Wilson sent this same letter, *mutatis mutandis*, to all heads of the non-scientific departments. There will be much subsequent correspondence about the staffing situation in various departments. Wilson finally prepared a report on the non-scientific departments (it is printed at May 13, 1910, Vol. 20), but he apparently did not submit it to the trustees's Committee on the Curriculum.

From David Benton Jones

My dear Doctor: Chicago November 9th, 1909.

I am going to send you a very brief note for the purpose of quoting the last clause of a sentence in a long letter which I have just received from Mr. Cadwalader. He wrote apropos of his coming election to the Board. It was entirely uncalled for, but I none the less appreciated his writing me, and especially what he said. The burden of the note, which is immaterial as to my present purpose, was to make certain that I did not misunderstand his taking a place on the Board after our many conversations regarding it. I think it is very important that Mr. Cadwalader should be a member of the Board, and I shall be greatly relieved and delighted when he takes his place after his election.[1]

The clause which I wish to quote, and which I think is important, is in these words: "I think that Wilson is the best asset they have down at Princeton, and I hope they will adjust it on some terms agreeable to him." That is, the location of the Graduate School.

May I urge upon you the importance of your refraining from formulating an ultimatum on the subject as long as you possibly can. The issue is not of a kind which the country will understand or which you can make clear to outsiders. There may be those who would be glad to have the final issue joined on some such a matter or situation. I am extremely anxious that it should not, in the interests of Princeton as well as your own.

As Mr. Cadwalader requested that his letter to me regarding his coming election to the Board be considered personal and confidential to myself, I trust you will regard this letter referring to it as confidential, though I do not feel that I am violating his confidence in repeating the sentence I quoted. The number of those who feel as Mr. Cadwalader has expressed himself is increasing steadily, and that is my reason for urging that you should not allow yourself to be out-manouvered. The mere location cannot be made to appear to outsiders to involve a vital principle. In time, if the present scheme is carried out, it will, I think, be a mortifying monument to those responsible for it.

Very sincerely yours, David B. Jones.

I thought it would be brief but it is not. I shall feel more at liberty to send you items from time to time if you will not trouble to make any reply, as none is called for. D. B. J.

TLS (WP, DLC).

[1] Cadwalader was elected a Life Trustee at the Board of Trustees' meeting on January 13, 1910. He had served as an Alumni Trustee from 1901 to 1909.

A News Report

[Nov. 10, 1909]

LIVE AND LEARN

President Wilson Addresses Graduate Students' Association.
Ideals for Study Outlined.

President Woodrow Wilson delivered a very instructive talk last night before the newly organized Graduate Students' Association, in which he outlined what he considered should be the ideals of all graduate students. In opening his address, Dr. Wilson said that the formation of these ideals depends in large measure upon our purpose in life. If we approach study with the mere idea of how it may benefit our future profession, we can never become real scholars. Our one wish should be to gain intellectual power, to acquire the ability to deal with a great subject in a masterful way. The speaker then divided graduate study into three stages. In the first place, a student must learn to profit by the study of others, to be able to teach his pupils as much knowledge as he possibly can. But it is not alone necessary for a man to know just as much as he intends to teach; he must strike out into new fields for himself, and resolve not always to be relying on the knowledge of others but to make up his mind to be quit of masters.

Taking up his second point, Dr. Wilson said that a much more important movement in graduate study is that of inspiring men with an unfailing curiosity, for this has led many to some great fact in knowledge. As his last and most important point the speaker stated that the final aim of a graduate student should be to acquire the power of bringing together any knowledge he has gained and of expounding it as part of a great whole.[1]

Printed in the *Daily Princetonian*, Nov. 10, 1909.

[1] For this talk, Wilson used the notes printed at Nov. 7, 1902, Vol. 14.

From Leroy J. Ellis,[1] with Enclosure

My dear Sir: New York, November 10, 1909.

I inclose copy of resolution passed by the Plainfield Democratic Club at its meeting last night, conveying to you some sense of its appreciation of your address in Plainfield, on 29th ult. A resolution was also passed appointing a committee to canvass the practicability of publishing and distributing the address in Pamphlet form.

In our conversation over the telephone last night, I understood you to be willing for us to publish the address and that you might care to revise it as published in the papers, that being an abstract and not the address in full. I therefore enclose the address as clipped from the Newark Star,[2] so that you can revise it if you desire. I consider the address as the best utterance in the cause of sound Democracy that has yet been published, and am determined, with your permission, to publish it in pamphlet form.[3]

You would be pleased if you could hear the numerous expressions of pleasure and satisfaction which come from those of all parties, who heard your address. I was talking to a physician yesterday, who votes the Republican ticket generally, who heard your address, who exclaimed while discussing it, "Well, if the Democrats ever put him up for President I would certainly vote for him." That is a fair sample of the sentiment you created in Plainfield.

You remarked at the apparent absence from the meeting of the mechanic class of citizens. One of these gentlemen, a member of the Club, and talked of as one of the "Old war horses" in the Democratic ranks, when I reproached him for not being present, said "Well I have read his speech over six times and enjoyed it every time, and I believe what he says, but did not go to hear him because he helped to give the nomination to Parker instead of Bryan." He said that was the feeling which is, or was very general, and that Bryans friends were loath to go to hear you. This feeling may have kept some away. There were a number of Bryans friends there nevertheless.

By-the-way, you have been sent, as I was, a clipping from a newspaper in which Mr. Martine[4] and I were quoted as saying, "That we would like to see you made Governor." Now, while I think that would be a consum[m]ation devoutly to be wished, I want to disavow doing any talking of that kind to newspapers, and don't like to be credited with it. It but cheapens the talker and the one talked of. I said nothing of the kind, and don't feel that I would have a right to. With the highest esteem,

Very cordially, L. J. Ellis.

TLS (WP, DLC).

1 New York agent for the Norfolk & Western Railway, who lived in Plainfield and was president of the Plainfield Democratic Club.

2 This enclosure is missing.

3 Insofar as the Editors know, the address was never published in pamphlet form.

4 James Edgar Martine of Plainfield, an indefatigable Democratic candidate for office.

E N C L O S U R E

A Resolution

[Nov. 9, 1909]

RESOLVED

That this club sends greetings to Dr. Woodrow Wilson, and a vote of thanks for the magnificent and instructive address delivered by him, at the Plainfield Theatre, October 29th, 1909, and hereby endorses that address as a sound and conclusive exposition of the Democratic doctrine on the points discussed, and which if adopted by the Democrats of the Nation as their guide would carry them to victory in the next national election, and the Nation to a period of peace and unexampled prosperity.

T MS (WP, DLC).

From Thomas Wilson[1]

Personal

My Dear Dr. Wilson, St. Paul, Minn. Nov. 11, 1909.

I have before me your letter of the 9th inst. to Mr. Butler about the subject matter of his conference with you a few weeks ago; and as a member of the Board of Regents of the University I wish to say that a postponement of your decision for "two or three weeks longer to consider it" is reasonable and will result in no inconvenience to us.

I am greatly pleased to know that you are considering, for, as it seems to me, your election is full of promise to both you and the University. There is no reasonable doubt but that it is to be the prominent institution of learning of the middle northwest. That it will have ample pecuniary support does not seem to admit of the least doubt and while it has numbers it is yet in the formative period when a master can impress himself upon it to his great credit and its great advantage. I hope you may see your opportunity—I had almost said your duty—as I do. We "wont let this matter drop" so long as there is a reasonable prospect of bringing you to our view.

I am, Yours truly, Thomas Wilson

TLS (WP, DLC).

[1] Member of the Board of Regents of the University of Minnesota and General Counsel for the Chicago, St. Paul, Minneapolis and Omaha Railroad. He had served as Chief Justice of the Supreme Court of Minnesota, 1864-69, and in the United States House of Representatives, 1887-89.

From Pierce Butler

(Personal)

My Dear President Wilson: Saint Paul [Minn.] Nov. 12, 1909.

Yours of the 9th inst. is received and I am very much gratified at its contents. I trust that your further consideration of the matter will lead you to a conclusion favorable to acceptance of the presidency of our University. The delay of two or three weeks, which you suggest, will not, I believe, in any way embarrass the Board.

I beg again to assure you that your favorable answer will be most welcome to me, and I believe to every member of the Board of Regents, and that I believe that your selection will give great satisfaction to the people of Minnesota and the entire Northwest.

Yours very truly, Pierce Butler

TLS (WP, DLC).

From Benjamin Franklin Nelson[1]

Dear President Wilson: Minneapolis, Minn. Nov. 12, 1909

I have just been informed there is a possibility of you considering the Presidency of our University. I sincerely hope you will give the matter serious consideration, as in our opinion it is to be one of the greatest institutions of learning and research work in our whole country.

Hon. Pierce Butler had the pleasure of calling on you a short time ago. I have talked with Judge Wilson, Pres. Northrop and others of the Board of Regents, since Mr. Butler informed us there was a possibility of you considering the position which is to be made vacant on account of Pres. Northrop's resignation as soon as we can secure his successor. I can assure you of the hearty co-operation of the members of the Board of Regents.

It is with great pleasure that I recall a short visit at Princeton some two and one half years ago with my friend Mr. Sensenbrenner,[2] who at that time had a son in Princeton College; the very pleasant visit at your office and my expressing a desire to once more call on Grover Cleveland. I hesitated on account of so many people, in all probability, taking up his time by calling out of mere curiosity to see the great man and you urged me to call before leaving Princeton, assuring me of the pleasant reception that I would receive and which was more than fulfilled at the time I called on who I considered then and do now one of the greatest men America ever produced.

I expect to be in the East soon after Dec. 1st and if agreeable to you would be glad to visit Princeton again and take the matter up with you personally. I sincerely hope you will not dispose of the matter before that time unless you decide to take the Presidency of our great State University.

Yours truly B F Nelson Regent

TLS (WP, DLC).

[1] Member of the Board of Regents of the University of Minnesota and a financier and manufacturer of Minneapolis, with interests in paper, lumber, insurance, and banking companies.

[2] Frank Jacob Sensenbrenner of Neenah, Wisc., at this time General Manager and First Vice-President of Kimberly Clark Corp. His son was John Stephen Sensenbrenner of the Class of 1909.

From Cleveland Hoadley Dodge

Dear Sir: New York November 12, 1909.

Recognizing the great importance of the work of the Philadelphian Society, in the moral and religious life of Princeton University, and the necessity of providing each year at least one good man to act as Secretary of the Society:

In order that proper compensation may be always available for the salary of such Secretary, I hereby give to the Trustees of Princeton University twenty bonds of the denomination of $1000 each, bearing interest at 5% per annum, the income of which shall be used to pay the salary of the Secretary or Secretaries of the Philadelphian Society which is the Young Men's Christian Association of Princeton University, in such manner as shall be determined by the President of the University, on consultation with the Graduate Advisory Committee of the Philadelphian Society:

With the understanding that if the Philadelphian Society should cease to exist, or for any good reason the services of a paid Secretary should not be required, the Trustees shall devote said income to such purposes as shall best promote the religious and moral life of the University.

Very truly yours, Cleveland H. Dodge

TLS (WWP, UA, NjP).

From Abbott Lawrence Lowell

Dear Mr Wilson: Cambridge [Mass.] November 12, 1909.

Mr Castle,[1] our Assistant Dean, in special charge of the freshmen, is going to Princeton, to make some inquiries about the working of your preceptorial system, just after Thanksgiving; and I write to say that any information you can give him, or any way you can help him to get information, will be a kindness to us.

Yours very truly, A. Lawrence Lowell

TLS (WP, DLC).

[1] William Richards Castle, Jr., Assistant Dean of Harvard College and Instructor in English.

Notes for a Lecture at the Harvard Church, Brookline, Massachusetts

Brookline, Mass., 12 November, 1909.

RELIGION AND CITIZENSHIP.

The exaltation of citizenship in Greek times and in our own contrasted.

The religious feeling, historically considered: its connection with ancestor worship, etc. "Pious."

Religion as a *social* nexus and principle.

Has not been fruitful of change: therefore not of improvement.

Progress began when religion began to look for its object away from society to God, and men began to conceive religious obligation in terms of individual, other-wor[l]dly responsibility.

This the principle of purification and of the incorruptible will which has made modern history what it has been, a struggle towards perfection.

"Christian Socialism" an inconceivable thing, if put in terms of *organization* and not merely of *motive*.

"Scientific anarchism" much nearer the truth.

The individual conscience the energy and the salvation of the modern world.

The citizenship of our Lord and Saviour.

Obedience, and utter purity of life and will

2 Nov. '09[1]

WWT MS (WP, DLC).

[1] Wilson's composition date.

A News Report of Addresses to the New England Alumni in Boston and at the Harvard Church in Brookline, Massachusetts

[Nov. 13, 1909]

PRESIDENT WILSON URGES DEMOCRACY

Tells Princeton Alumni Association Revival
Is Essential Before the Colleges Can Have
the New Learning.

"The air is full of criticism of the colleges today," said President Woodrow Wilson of Princeton, speaking on the American college and university, last evening, before the Princeton Alumni Association at the University Club. "What is particularly to be deplored," he continued, "is that this criticism should be misunderstood; that it should be taken for hostile criticism, where, in reality, it is but the criticism of affection, the criticism of friends.

"We need a renewal by the prosperous part of the community of sound democracy. We don't prove that a college is democratic when we say that men from humble conditions can rise to positions of prominence. That is not real democracy. True democracy is a community organized on the principle of involuntary and unselected contact. Whether you are thrown into close relations with men and whether or not you like your fellows is the true spirit and test of democracy.

"Every society has been renewed from the bottom and not from the top, and is in this respect is [*sic*] like a tree. I have told many of you in the class-room that the Roman Catholic church kept political society alive in the middle ages. It was a democracy in which there was no peasant who could not become a priest and no priest who could not become a pope. Society would have died of dry rot had it not been for this rich soil. It is in a similar way that the colleges are the fountains for the renewals of the nation.

"There is coming into our colleges a revival of learning, but we can not have it until there is a revival of democracy.["]

Speaking at Harvard Church, Brookline, President Wilson said:

"I believe that the essence of religion is disturbance, the absence of weak conformity, and that a church that is not a church militant is a church decadent.

"The relation of religion to citizenship is the relation of Christ and his example to individual conscience. A church that does not go out to wage war, in a Christian way, against existing evils, has forgotten its Christian obligations."

Printed in the *Boston Herald*, Nov. 13, 1909.

A Report of an Address at the Phillips Exeter Academy

[Nov. 13, 1909]

CHRISTIAN FRATERNITY.

President Wilson, of Princeton, the Speaker.

Last Thursday evening the Christian Fraternity was addressed by one of the best known college presidents in the country, Mr. Woodrow Wilson, of Princeton University. Mr. Wilson's address was exceedingly powerful, and it produced a strong effect upon his hearers. In substance he spoke as follows:

When I was asked to come here and speak before a religious meeting I accepted after some hesitation. Religion is such a private matter that it is very difficult to talk about. However, I never felt a[t] liberty to decline an invitation like this one.

The passage that kept running through my head when I thought of what I was going to say to-night is found in the book of Ecclesiastes, "He that observeth [the wind] shall not sow; and he that regardeth the clouds shall not reap." Most of you having finished college will go into business, not individually, but as employees of some great corporation. You form a very little piece in a very big machine. The trouble is that most of them are not men enough to resist the bad part of the machine, but let the machine run them. They look at it in this way. "What will happen to me if I do the right? Will I lose my job or keep it? Is it not impertinent for me, inexperienced, to make suggestions to these men who have been at it all their lives?"

Therefore, I think that the words I have just quoted are very keen and cut very deep. If we say "I won't do this thing," or "I won't do that thing," it's all right. We don't have to, but we must pay the penalty. There is no court in which they may be excused. The only word I can think of that I think fits this case exactly is opportunism.

I do not mean to depreciate prudence or caution, but they ought not to think of themselves. Never mind what effect this will be on me, it is right and I will stick to it. If anything happens to them, if anything happens to me, it will not affect the world. It will keep running just the same. But if one lets the right go, and takes the wrong simply to save himself, think of the difference it will make to the world.

What I have urged to you to-night is a regular contempt of opportunism. The great trouble is at school and in college, that the boy forgets what he is sent there for. He is sent for intellectual mastering, that doesn't mean by books alone, but also by athletics. The boy who doesn't know what he is sent there for is disgracing himself, his family and his race.

In the world choose courses which Mr. A. or Mr. B. can't change. One of the highest things in the world is to be unafraid. I think the words I recently heard in a play are right: "The real curse is not poverty, it is fear of poverty."

How do I know, however, that my principle will always hold water, I have made many mistakes, I have changed my mind many times, it is a connection with a divine providence establishing a firm conviction that in following the principle I am doing right. The old live by experience, but the young live by counsel. The youngsters know nothing of our experience and must accept our counsel. Be a genuine sport, play the game lively but like gentlemen and according to the rules, remember honor, and that everything one does shows him to be either a cad or a sportsman. The Bible is the book of rules for that great game.

Printed in the Exeter, N. H., *Exonian*, Nov. 13, 1909.

From James Monroe Taylor[1]

Poughkeepsie, N. Y.
November 13, 1909.

My dear Dr. Wilson,

Pardon me for troubling you a moment, but I have been much interested in your statement about Governor Hughes's proposed Primary Law.[2] You claimed, you may remember, that under it the favorable results obtained in the New York elections could not have happened.[3] I raised the question with a young friend of mine, a professor at Hobart, who was here last year and who is very active in working for this, and he answers that under the present provisions of the proposed law Mr. Hearst and his associate could have been nominated under direct nominations just as they were under the present system. Of course, he says, Gaynor and Bannard could have been nominated as they were, and so he is unable to see why the victory could not have been gained under the proposed law as it was in fact.

Now I am not trying to draw you into any controversy, and I do not propose to go any further in this matter. It is *for my own enlightenment* that I raise the question because I was much interested in your assertion, as I have been weakening somewhat in my own favor for a Primary Bill. A few words from you will be all that I ask, if my friend is wrong in his suggestion. He says that the section of the New York State Primary Law concerning independent nominations is inserted unchanged in the Hinman-Greene Bill. My friend tells me further that he has it at first hand, from one of the conference, that at a small conference, Timothy Woodruff[4] and a few others, arranged for Bannard's nomination and that it was accomplished "just as sure" before the convention met as it was by the convention. Of course that raises the issue again whether it is safer to trust the few, and hold them responsible, than the many. In general theory I think I am with you in feeling that the democracy needs restraint. I am no believer in a referendum. Sincerely yours, J M Taylor

TLS (WP, DLC).

[1] President of Vassar College.

[2] About Hughes's proposed primary law, the Hinman-Green bill, introduced in the New York legislature on March 14, 1909, see A. C. Ludington to WW, Feb. 4, 1909, n. 6. Wilson's statement was made in a conversation with President Taylor about November 5 or 6, probably at a meeting of the Round Table Club (about which see WW to C. H. Marshall, Dec. 26, 1902, Vol. 14) in New York on November 5. That they had a long talk on or near this date is revealed in J. M. Taylor to WW, Nov. 8, 1909, TLS (WP, DLC).

[3] That is, the election on November 2, 1909, of the reform Democratic New York mayoralty candidate, Judge William Jay Gaynor, over his Republican opponent, Otto Tremont Bannard, a banker, and William Randolph Hearst, the publisher, who ran on the Independence League ticket. Gaynor enjoyed the reluctant support of the Tammany Hall organization headed by Charles Francis Murphy. Republicans and independents, known as Fusionists, captured all but one of the other major city and borough offices. See Lately Thomas [Robert V. P. Steele], *The Mayor Who Mastered New York: The Life & Opinions of William J. Gaynor* (New York, 1969), pp. 145-93.

[4] Timothy Lester Woodruff, Chairman of the New York Republican State Committee, who had served as Lieutenant Governor of the state from 1897 to 1903.

From Francis Fisher Kane[1]

Dear Doctor Wilson: Philadelphia, Nov. 14th [1909]

I write to remind you that you are to be my guest for the night of next Thursday.[2] I herewith enclose a time-table. I suppose you will arrive by the train that I have marked and I shall be on hand to meet you. But if you can get away earlier I hope you will do so, as it would be a great pleasure to me to have more of your company than taking you to my house and to and fro the City Club is likely to afford me.

Yours sincerely, F. F. Kane

ALS (WP, DLC).

[1] Princeton 1886, at this time practicing law in Philadelphia. He had served as First Assistant United States Attorney for the Eastern Pennsylvania District, 1896-1900; Wilson appointed him United States Attorney for the same district in 1913.

[2] When Wilson was to speak to the Philadelphia City Club on political reform. His address is printed at Nov. 18, 1909.

To Cleveland Hoadley Dodge

My dear Cleve: Princeton, N. J. November 15th, 1909.

I have already told you what I think of your thoughtful generosity in providing for the support of a Secretary to the Philadelphian Society. It is a most opportune gift and will be of very great service, I believe, to the University as a whole. I want to thank you for it, not only officially but also personally, and I am sure that everybody concerned will be very grateful.

I will, of course, respect your wishes about not making your name public in connection with the gift, though of course I shall have to report the name—and I am sure you will not object to this —to the Board.

I am inexperienced in these matters, but no doubt Ed. Sheldon can tell you how to put the bonds in due form into the possession of the University.

I certainly enjoyed my talk with Mott. His manliness and intelligence are splendid, and I devoutly pray that something may come out of the interview.

Always affectionately yours, Woodrow Wilson

TLS (WC, NjP).

To Edwin Sidney Simons[1]

My dear Mr. Simons: Princeton, N. J. November 15th, 1909.

I am very sorry that you feel as you do about the suspension of your son.[2] As a matter of fact, we have never winked at any of the "rough-housing" by the freshmen. Whenever we have learned of any case of it, we have punished it. The trouble has been that the boarding-house keepers are so in terror of the vindictive action of the students, in case they are informed upon, that it has proved almost impossible for us to learn of cases of this sort. In the particular instance now under consideration the "rough-housing" seems to have been of a peculiarly aggravated and long-continued character and, so far as I can see, was utterly without excuse.[3]

Perhaps we have been mistaken,—I sometimes think that we have been—, in permitting the "horsing" of the freshmen.[4] We have done so because it seemed to us justifiable in view of the fact that it released the freshmen from the rougher and secret kind of hazing. We have tried from year to year to reduce the "horsing" both in time and in extravagance and feel that we are making very slow but perceptible progress. We entertain the hope that some day we may get rid of the whole silly and distressing practice. As a college man, you must know how difficult these things are to handle and how difficult it is to choose the truly wise course.

I know of no case in which "rough-housing" has been overlooked or excused when we knew of it, and it seems to me necessary that we should check it whenever our attention is drawn to it, with a very firm hand. I am sure, from what your letter contains, that you sympathize with that purpose.

I am particularly sorry that the discipline should have fallen upon your son and that it should cause you distress and annoyance, but I do not see how in the circumstances I could be justified in intervening to change the action of the committee. I think the lads concerned must have misinterpreted the personal attitude of the committee towards them. It could hardly be sympathetic in the circumstances, but I am sure that it was not intended to be harsh, for I know the men of whom the committee consists and am sure that there are no juster men in the faculty.

With much regard,

Sincerely yours, [Woodrow Wilson]

CCL (WWP, UA, NjP).

[1] Princeton 1882, Vice-President of Simons Bros. & Co., silverware manufacturers of Philadelphia. His letter to Wilson is missing, as are many of the letters to Wilson about the episode described in n. 3.

[2] John Farr Simons '13.

[3] This incident, which took place during late October or early November 1909, involved ten members of the Class of 1913. Eight of these freshmen were suspended from November 10 to December 8, 1909. They were Charles Dabney Baker, Samuel Dennis Bell, Ferdinand Eberstaat, Ralph Tilden Holsapple, De Witt Clinton Jones III, Lawrence Plummer Naylor, Jr., John Farr Simons, and Warren Ridgeway Smith. Two of the freshmen—Charles Louis Auger, Jr., and Stanley Matthews Moffat—were suspended from November 10 to November 24, 1909. All were residents of the boarding house maintained by Mrs. F. C. Easton at 47 University Place. The Faculty Committee on Discipline, which was headed by Dean Edward Graham Elliott, decided that they should be suspended for "disorderly conduct." University Faculty Minutes, Nov. 15, 1909. The exact nature of their conduct is in doubt, but it appears that the ten were involved in considerable "rough-housing" at their place of residence. The crowning blow, so to speak, occurred when an empty chamber pot, thrown by one student at another, narrowly missed Mrs. Easton. As subsequent documents will reveal, the parents of the suspended students as well as some of their friends were offended by the seeming harshness of the punishment, particularly when measured against the more flexible disciplinary procedures taken against students who were intoxicated for the first time. In class annals, the incident became known as the case of Elliott's Ethics or the Tragedy of Forty-Seven, and the campus humor magazine, *The Princeton Tiger*, xx (Dec. 1909), 3, commented, "The menace to society is not John Barleycorn, but Bill the bouncer. . . . Thus it is that happy homes are broken up and tender infants rendered desolate not by Licker but by man's ungovernable longing to holler."

For an account of the episode by one of the participants, see De Witt C. Jones, Jr. [III] (comp.), *Thirteen for Good Luck*, 2 vols. (n. p., 1958-59), I, 10-11.

[4] "Horsing" is described in H. E. Fisk to WW, Jan. 9, 1909, n. 1, Vol. 18.

To Caroline W. Guppy Smith[1]

My dear Mrs. Smith: Princeton, N. J. November 15th, 1909.

I am sincerely distressed that the discipline of your son[2] should have brought you pain and inconvenience and I wish most sincerely that there were some proper way of relieving you of your distress in this matter by allowing your son to return to the University at an earlier date than that set by the Committee on Discipline. But, unhappily, among so large a number of boys we have to treat these cases in a very legal temper, as courts would treat them. The way the boys in Mrs. Easton's house acted seems to me to have been quite inexcusable and to have gone very much beyond the point even of the rough conduct sometimes characteristic of the first year men in their boarding-houses. We have never allowed such actions to go unpunished when we have been able to learn of them. The trouble is that most of the boarding-house keepers are in terror of retaliatory action of some kind on the part of the men boarding with them in case rough conduct is reported to the University authorities, and we do not often learn of the misconduct of the students in such houses. It happened that the misconduct in this case was open and flagrant and could not escape notice, and we have deemed it absolutely unavoidable to inflict a very noticeable punishment. This rough and ready way of dealing with such matters seems, unhappily, the only way available in dealing with large bodies of men.

I hope that you will not think that our action casts, even in our own minds, any reflection upon the character of your son. We know how boys of excellent principle and of steady character are betrayed into misconduct of this sort by example and infection of their classmates. I am sure that, as you say, the action was not characteristic of your son and have every confidence that when he returns to the University he will justify this estimate of him.

With much regard,

Sincerely yours, [Woodrow Wilson]

CCL (WWP, UA, NjP).

1 Mrs. Charles R. Smith of Paterson, N. J. Her husband was President and Treasurer of Samuel Smith and Son, boiler manufacturers of Paterson.

2 Warren Ridgeway Smith.

To Robert Bridges

My dear Bobby, Princeton, N. J. 16 November, 1909.

The article I wrote for you last summer[1] has attracted much more attention than I expected: indeed, it seems to have been everywhere commented upon, and generally very sympathetically.

When Mr. Scribner wrote me about it (a very cordial, pleasant note)[2] he said very truly that the article seemed to him to stop very abruptly "just as the devil entered." It plainly needs a supplement of constructive suggestion. I wonder if the Magazine would like to accept such a supplement?

It would, of course, contain my plan for quads, as carefully and as sanely treated as I knew how, but very frankly and explicitly advocated as the best organization of our college life (I mean the life of all our colleges). Would Mr. Scribner approve of such an article from me and would it be acceptible [acceptable] to the editors?[3] The time seems to me to have come to speak out, constructively, and I must do it somewhere. Scribner, I am convinced, would be my best platform. I hope I could write so as to offend nobody.

Always affectionately Yours, Woodrow Wilson

I w'd call it "The Reorganization of Our Colleges."

WWTLS (WP, DLC).

[1] That is, "What Is a College For?", which had just appeared in *Scribner's Magazine*, XLVI (Nov. 1909), 570-577. It is printed at Aug. 18, 1909.

[2] C. Scribner to WW, Sept. 24, 1909. Scribner's actual words were: "It closes almost as abruptly as the old fashioned serial which stopped just when the hero faced the villian [villain]."

[3] See R. Bridges to WW, Nov. 22, 1909.

To James Christy Bell[1]

My dear Sir: Princeton, N. J. November 16th, 1909.

Allow me to acknowledge the receipt of your letter of November 15th and to express my sincere regret that you should think the punishment inflicted upon your son[2] and his classmates unjust.

Mrs. Easton did not notify the parents of the boys, I take it for granted, because she knew only too well from the experience of other boarding-house keepers what the probable result would be in respect of her deepened unpopularity with her lodgers. Our greatest difficulty in all matters of this kind is to get any information at all from the lodging-house keepers. In this particular case we never should have known of what was going on, if it had not gone to extraordinary lengths and practically forced Mrs. Easton to resort to the Dean of the College for assistance.

We find it difficult, because of the circumstances I have spoken of, to learn of things of this kind, but we never let them pass without punishment when we do learn of them. I cannot agree with you that freshmen observe actions on the part of older men in the University which justify such conduct as this which we have been obliged to punish. It was no ordinary case of "rough-housing." It had lasted for a number of days and had been carried to lengths which the young men concerned must have known to be intolerable.

I greatly regret that the circumstances surrounding such cases render it impossible for us to communicate with the parents of the boys in time to correct these abuses. It seems to me absolutely necessary that they should be checked, and I do not see any other adequate way in which to check them.

I hope and believe that your expectation that Mrs. Easton will be rendered ugly in her treatment of the boys after their return will not be verified by the facts. I believe that Mrs. Easton will be only too glad to get on pleasantly with the lads and forget the circumstances of this offence. I know very little about her and am sorry to hear that you think her unsuitable to deal with college boys. I dare say that there often is an element of this kind in these cases, and if there is anything specific which we ought to know about her treatment of the men in her house, I should be very much obliged if you would let the Dean of the College, Professor Edward Elliott, know of it, for I am sure he would be prompt to correct it, if it were susceptible of correction.

With much respect,

Sincerely yours, [Woodrow Wilson]

CCL (WWP, UA, NjP).

1 Vice-President of the Nassau Bank of New York.

2 Samuel Dennis Bell.

From David Douglas Metcalfe[1]

Dear Doctor Wilson: St. Louis November 16, 1909.

As you know, the Western Association of Princeton Clubs will meet in St. Louis in 1910, and we are looking forward to your being present at that time.

We have just been advised by the Management of the Triangle Club that they could come out to St. Louis during their Easter vacation, and if that is the case, we would hold the meeting of the Western Association at the same time, namely, Saturday, March 26, 1910.

Could you make your arrangements to attend the meeting of the Western Association at that time?

We are very anxious, indeed, that you be present and we believe that an occasion of this sort will be of great value to Princeton and a source of much pleasure to those members of the Western Association who could not, otherwise, see the Triangle Club's performances.

Will you kindly, at your convenience, let me know whether it would suit you to come to St. Louis for the meeting on March 26th?[2]

With kind regards, I am,

Yours very truly, David D. Metcalfe

TLS (WP, DLC).

[1] Princeton 1904, at this time associated with the insurance agency of J. E. Lawton & Son of St. Louis. He was also Secretary of the Princeton Club of St. Louis and of the Western Association of Princeton Clubs.

[2] Wilson's address to the Western Association of Princeton Clubs on March 26, 1910, is printed at that date in Vol. 20.

A News Report

[Nov. 17, 1909]

NATIONAL ACADEMY MEETS

Scientists Welcomed by President Wilson

The program arranged for the first day of the convention of the National Academy of Sciences was carried out most successfully yesterday and there was a large attendance at each session. President Wilson delivered the address of welcome in the Faculty Room of Nassau Hall. . . .

In welcoming the prominent visitors, the President referred to the historic atmosphere of the room in which the Academy was meeting, for it was in this same Faculty Room that Washington received the thanks of the Continental Congress for his services to his country. He mentioned the marked encouragement which the late President McCosh gave to scientific work at a time when many prominent educators were scoffing at the advantages of the new study in a college curriculum. Princeton was one of the first American colleges to recognize science as an integral part of culture, and this was due in a large measure to the kindly interest taken in the new study by Dr. McCosh. In closing, President Wilson said that he used to feel that the friends of the University were rather slow in supplying her needs for increasing scientific equipment and facilities, but with the gift of the splendid new physical and biological laboratories, he saw that the advantages had come at a time when Princeton could use them best, at a time of wonderful scientific investigation and discovery.[1]

Printed in the *Daily Princetonian*, Nov. 17, 1909; one editorial heading omitted.

1 There is a WWT and WWhw outline of these remarks, dated Nov. 16, 1909, in WP, DLC.

To Louise Whitfield Carnegie[1]

My dear Mrs. Carnegie, Princeton, New Jersey 17 Nov., '09

I am very much disappointed that I am not going to have the pleasure of attending your reception. We are entertaining the National Academy of Sciences at Princeton and, so soon as the meeting of the Trustees of the Carnegie Foundation is over, I must hurry back home to the reception Mrs. Wilson and I are to give to the members of the Academy at the close of their sessions. I am under the obligations of a host.

Mrs. Wilson joins me in warmest regard to you and Mr. Carnegie and in genuine regret that we are thus deprived of the pleasure of seeing you.

Sincerely Yours, Woodrow Wilson

ALS (NN).

1 Mrs. Andrew Carnegie.

From De Witt Clinton Jones, Jr.[1]

Dear Sir: [New York] Nov. 17, 1909.

In reference to the matter of the suspension of my son, De Witt Clinton Jones, 3rd, of the Class of 1913, together with nine other students lodging at #47 University Place, and concerning which I understand you have already received communication from Mr. Edwin S. Simons, the father of one of the suspended students, I, herewith, beg to enclose a copy of letter I have today written to the Dean[2] in connection with this matter which expresses my own feelings and those of the fathers of the other students implicated, with whom I have conferred. I beg that you will give your attention to this matter, if it is possible and in accordance with the rules and regulations and if it is not inconsistent with your views, that it may be arranged to have the sentence of suspension materially reduced.

Thanking you in advance for your courteous attention to this matter, I am,

Yours very truly, [De Witt Clinton Jones, Jr.]

TCL (received from D. C. Jones III).

1 Secretary of the American Dyewood Co. in New York.

2 The enclosure is missing.

From Samuel Archibald Smith[1]

Copy.

My dear Sir: Elizabeth, N. J., Nov. 17, 1909.

I write to you on a matter which is causing misgivings among many friends of Princeton. I refer to the one month suspension especially of De Witt Clinton Jones, 3rd, Lawrence P. Naylor, and John F. Simons. These young men, graduates of the Pingry School, I have known for eleven years, during the greater part of which time they were pupils of mine in Pingry. They come from homes in which refinement, scholarship, and high Christian character are the first things, and their conduct in the Pingry School and in Elizabeth has always been absolutely above reproach. If they had, upon going to Princeton, suddenly developed into drunkards, gamblers, and libertines, I could not protest the severest discipline on the part of the University; but I learn from reliable sources that not a card or a drop of liquor has this year been used in the house where the trouble arose. I do not wish to excuse the boisterous and barbarous conduct of the young men in their "rough-house" play, nor would their parents wish to excuse it; but I am persuaded that to stigmatize these boys as worse than drunkards and that too without the slightest warning to them or to their parents by depriving them for one month of the associations of the college, is most ill-advised and hasty, and I am sure could not have been done with your sanction.

I repeat that I do not wish to excuse any part of their rough and ungentlemanly play, but I know them and their parents well enough to know that the entire business could have been effectually stopped within five minutes if the parents had been previously advised of what their sons were doing and the young men themselves had been warned.

They could hardly have surmised that a thing which had been going on for years without serious discipline or remonstrance should suddenly sink, in the opinion of the college authorities, to the level of debauchery, and result in branding the offender for life.

Cannot something be done, with dignity to the University, to relieve the suffering and manifest injustice of the situation?

Very respectfully yours, S. Archibald Smith.

ALS (received from De Witt C. Jones III).

[1] Headmaster of the Pingry School, Elizabeth, N. J.

An Address on Political Reform to the City Club of Philadelphia[1]

[[Nov. 18, 1909]]

I am sincerely obliged to this Club for the invitation they have extended to me to address them this evening. I think it an honor to be permitted to speak to a body of men of such serious and definite purpose. I believe that clubs like this show one feature of American character more than any other, and that is our inveterate hopefulness.

There are a great many reformers in this country, gentlemen; the only embarrassment is their variety. I have said, in regard to the Socialistic movement in this country, that I am not in the least afraid of the Socialistic spirit, for it is an admirable spirit, I am only afraid of the Socialistic program; but that as yet I am not disturbed even about the Socialistic program, because there is none, there are so many. So long as every group of Socialists develops violent divergencies of opinion, we are safe from Socialism; and I am afraid that so long as reform bodies develop extravagant divergencies of program we are safe from reform.

Of course, it is a hopeful and encouraging circumstance that the spirit of reform has been so manifestly growing in this country in recent years. I have the privilege of going to a good many parts of the United States, and everywhere I find an increasing interest in political betterment, and in no field more noticeably than in the field of municipal reform.

We do not in any direction, therefore, lack the motive which should carry us to better things, but there is the machine, that *bete noir*[*e*] of American Politics; that thing which we have, with an ingenuity of which we have hardly been conscious, made absolutely necessary for the conduct of our politics. We are in the singular position of rebelling against the thing which we have made an absolute necessity. For my part, I do not have the feeling towards the political boss that I find most of my compatriots have. I could not get along without the political boss, neither could you. Just think of what you have done; you have made it necessary to elect so many persons in this country that nobody who does not make a profession of it can possibly make up a workable ticket.

To show you how hopeful I am, I will tell you that I belong

1 Wilson spoke at the annual dinner of the City Club, held at the Hotel Walton in Philadelphia. The other principal speaker was Frederick Albert Cleveland, Director of the Bureau of Municipal Research of New York. The City Club was an organization devoted to civic improvement and municipal reform.

to an organization, as yet contained in very small membership, which calls itself the organization of those interested in a short ballot; and the first time we got together to discuss this question we had a great pile of specimen ballots lying on the table before us, collected from all parts of the country. The one that interested me most was from one of the northwestern states which thinks that it has made the greatest progress in ballot reform. This ballot was larger than the sheet of an ordinary newspaper, printed in columns like a newspaper, and containing at least seven hundred names. There is no man in the United States, not a professional politician sitting up at nights, who could possibly understand the ins and outs of a ballot containing seven hundred names. I vote in a little borough, and yet the ticket that I am ordinarily asked to vote contains from twenty-five to thirty names. It is impossible for me, having some other things to do, to find out what I should know about twenty-five or thirty persons scattered all over the County of Mercer. This County contains some interesting places; among them, it contains the very complicated community known as the City of Trenton, as well as a rural community, known as the Borough of Princeton, and these gentlemen are scattered all over and take covert in the communities that cover the County. I would have to get out a search warrant to discover the character of some of these men. If I wanted to substitute another ballot for that which I am asked to vote upon, I should have to get together a great many persons, and go through a great many difficult combinations, in order to draw the various elements of Mercer County together in a ticket which would be acceptable to the County. In order to do that, I should have to undertake the work of the politician and inasmuch as there must be a division of labor in this country, and as I have enough to do in other occupations, I am very grateful that there should be certain persons who take the time to be professional politicians; otherwise, there would not be any ticket to vote for, and our whole government would go by the board.

What I am trying to illustrate, gentlemen, is that you have made the electoral business of the United States so complicated that you have to have a permanent organization to attend to it; that it cannot be attended to occasionally; that it cannot be attended to successfully by amateurs; that it must be attended to, to be successful, by professionals; and, therefore that you have no right to complain that there are professionals.

Then, what is it that we do, in our periodical throes, to get rid of this incubus? We make things more complicated yet; we say, "Go to, we will have a direct primary," which means that we will have another election. We are not satisfied with one election, one complication, we want two; and we want the first to be harder to manage than the second, by making it more informal than the second, for a complicated thing informally conducted is more difficult to do than a complicated thing formally conducted. Well, the people of any of our communities, if awake and angry, can make almost any piece of machinery work, but ordinarily they are not awake and they are not angry; they are going about their business, and in all ordinary seasons it is just as easy for the professional politician to manage the direct primary as the formal election which follows the direct primary.

I say this because I have inquired into this matter in various parts of the country where the direct primary is in use. The direct primary does not get rid of the machine, but it gives the machine an opportunity to increase its business.

I am one of those who are urgently in favor of everything that will put politics in this country directly back into the hands of the people. My objection to the direct primary is not that it is an attempt to put the affairs of the country back into the hands of the people, but that it does not accomplish that object in all ordinary seasons. Then, I am in favor of various forms of ballot reform, but most forms of ballot reform get us only further into trouble. For example, you may say, we will dispense with all party signs at the heads of the columns on these complicated ballots that we are printing now-a-days, and that means that the ordinary man is more perplexed than ever, for he does not know which column to begin to study. He who has not any rudimentary skill is expected to study all the persons in every column.

Then, you say, in order to be perfectly fair, we will print the names under each office in alphabetical order. Well, so far as I can ascertain, almost every person who is ignorant of the names as a whole, takes his chances and marks the top, or sometimes, if he is a person of peculiar modes of thought, he will mark the bottom of the ticket, but almost never does he mark the middle. So that Mr. A. will probably get elected, Mr. W. may get elected, but Mr. M. has not the slightest chance.

And then, not satisfied with all this complication, we say that we must give the whole business up. At any rate, we cannot elect anybody in the sense of selecting anybody, so let us vote it a bad business and say we will let the electing go on as it is now, only we will insist that when our representatives get together and pass any motion, they shall send it back to us, through the referendum. The referendum can be just as easily managed by the professional politician, to all intents and purposes, as the direct primary and the main election. Go into the State of New York, for example, and take that very interesting organization which we call Tammany. Tammany is, properly understood, a social organization, not a political organization. It is an organization for the private benefit of its members. The district leader in Tammany makes it his business to see that the men who vote his way get all the chances of employment and all the assistance in life that it is possible to give them. The average man, not understanding political questions, not being particularly interested in them, simply wants to know how the men who help him and whom he believes in, vote, and he will vote that way. When the referendum comes in, therefore, he will follow his district leader with just as implicit confidence as when he goes to him in the regular election, for he understands the regular election just as well as he understands the complicated questions which are likely to be submitted to him in the referendum.

If there is no delegation of power the people are helpless in the hands of those who have time and training in political lines, and all the remedies suggested simply throw a more complicated burden upon the voter.

I was talking the other day with a citizen of this country who was born in Switzerland. He said that if he went back to Switzerland, where there was the old-fashioned belief that America is the place where all political processes are developed with the utmost intelligence, and were to tell his former Swiss acquaintances how we manage our elections, he would get nothing out of it except the reputation of being a colossal liar. He said they simply would not believe it because we are the one free people of the world and we would not do it in this impossible way.

I say the present method is downright impossible and the only pathway of reform that is practicable is the pathway of simplification. We have got to turn right face about, and make all our processes so simple that busy men will have the time and opportunity to perform them. That is the way to reform.

So that when your committee complimented me by asking me to come here to-night, I said, "I am going to talk to these people about The Short Ballot, and I am going to talk about nothing else.[")]

I was riding in a railway carriage not long ago with a very interesting member, one of the younger members, of the New Jersey Legislature. At that time they were contemplating the passage of the bill creating the Railway Commission in New Jersey,[2] and we fell to talking about the bill. I said, "How is the Commission to be made up, by what process?" He said, "We will leave that to the people." I said, "What do you mean, that they should be elected?" "Yes," he said. "Well," I said, "do you think that is leaving it to the people?" "Why, certainly," he said. "Now," I replied, "Let us get down to business. There is no reporter present, so let us talk this thing in the terms in which we understand it. I know where you come from. Were you elected by the people in the sense of having been selected by the people? I know the boss who obtained you your present position." "Well," he said, "Professor, I see you know something about politics." I said, "That is my business; I would be ashamed if I did not know something about politics since I try to teach the subject to a number of men younger than myself." I said, "As a matter of fact you were put upon the people of your county, somewhat to their advantage, perhaps, but you were put upon them by the choice of a single person whom both you and I can name without any difficulty; and what I want to know is whether the Governor who is elected by all the people of this Commonwealth, is going to appoint these Commissioners, or whether the Commission is going to be made up by the private agreement of a number of persons whose names most of the voters do not know, but who can arrange the whole thing." "Well," he said, "At present, putting it in those terms, it is the purpose to allow them to be appointed by private agreement." "Very well," I said, "Now, we understand each other. I am opposed to the bill."[3]

We have had a series of Governors in New Jersey, good, bad and indifferent, they need not be specified by name. They have all, without exception, made admirable judicial appointments, because under the arrangement of the New Jersey Constitution, nobody in New Jersey has any part in appointing a Judge except the Governor.

There is an old cartoon of Thomas Nast's,[4] which is often reproduced, and which I am sure you have all seen. It represents the members of the old Tweed Ring standing in a circle. Each man has his thumb pointed at his neighbor, and the title of the

2 About this measure, adopted in 1907, see Ransom E. Noble, Jr., *New Jersey Progressivism before Wilson* (Princeton, N. J., 1946), pp. 100-104.

3 Actually, the measure provided for the appointment of the members of the commission by the governor.

4 Famous nineteenth-century (1840-1902) cartoonist. He began his career with *Frank Leslie's Illustrated Newspaper* but became prominent through his long association with *Harper's Weekly*.

picture is "T'want me." The cartoon was a correct representation of American City Government which is arranged by complex charters so that each man connected with the government can very easily disclaim any responsibility for what is done by handing on the responsibility to the next man in office.

Let me for one moment consider the Commission plan of city government which is coming so much into favor. I doubt whether a Commission of five persons is a large enough body to be made responsible for the government of any considerable city, for the reason that it is not fair to make a man responsible for business which he cannot thoroughly digest, and all parts of which he has not the time or the opportunity to master. I would rather see a body large enough to do what is done in all the well governed cities of the world. It is a very significant fact to my mind, that all the well governed cities of the world have certain features in common and none of these cities is situated in the United States. Take one of the best governed cities in the world, the city of Glasgow, Scotland. This city has a municipal council, which is not divided into two houses, so that there is no hiding as to which house is responsible. It consists of a single house, presided over by a chairman who has the title of Mayor, but who has no independent executive powers whatever. He is merely the presiding officer, and has a small jurisdiction as a Justice of the Peace, but no independent authority or executive power. This municipal body is divided into as many committees as there are branches of the city government and each committee is absolutely responsible for that branch of the city government. It makes all the appointments and conducts all the business of the department.

No voter in the city of Glasgow votes for more than one person, the councilman from his Ward. Every morning after there has been a meeting of the council, or a meeting of one of the committees, the Glasgow Herald contains an account of the business and of the way each member of the council or committee voted upon that business. Every morning, therefore, you can see what your man was about the night before. You know exactly what he did. If it does not suit you, when the next election comes along, you have so simple a thing to do that there is absolutely no necessity for the intervention of a machine. You can simply get together a small group of your neighbors and nominate one person whom you are willing to trust as your representative in the conduct of the affairs of the municipality. There is no confusion as to what you are doing. There is no division of authority. There is no complication of forces. There are no agents. There is an absolutely simple system upon which you apply strictly your own civic will. The result is that the members of the municipal council of Glasgow are constantly attentive to the public mind of the city of Glasgow. They are consciously under scrutiny, and it is a very extraordinary character that is not straight under public scrutiny. If you want to find out the effect of such responsibility, apply it in the case of men you know in office who are not straight—put the meanest man you know into office and there will be such a sudden change in the apparent character of the man that you will think he has undergone a Christian revolution.

Now, I say that these features, the selection of a very few persons by the voters and concentration of authority in these few persons, are characteristic of every well governed city in the world, whether it be in Scotland, England, Denmark, France or Germany, and that this is the only country which does not organize its municipalities upon such a principle. I say, therefore, that the first principle of reform is to lodge authority not in a single person, not in a Mayor who, not having any more hours in the twenty-four than we have, cannot master the whole business of the municipality; but to lodge authority in a body numerous enough to master the business, making it fully responsible for its conduct. Then, in the second place, concentrate in that body all the power. In the third place, give to each individual voter, if possible, only one member of such a body to vote for, and the process of simplification is complete. So that what I mean by the short ballot is not a mere question of space on a piece of paper, it is a question of practicability. It is a question of simplifying the whole relationship of the citizen to his government.

I suppose, gentlemen, that those of you who have not minutely studied the machinery of government in the United States have no idea how complicated it is. I remember going into the office of the county clerk in one of the counties of Tennessee, where I happened to be detained between trains with nothing better to do, circumstances under which I generally go to some such place to see what I can pick up. The clerk was busy, so I sat down with a volume of the revised statutes of the State. Turning them over, I came upon some of the provisions about the Comptroller of the State, who was directed to prescribe the manner in which returns for taxes throughout the State were to be made up, and to send these out to the clerks of the various counties, the clerks in turn being directed to fill in these returns and to send them to the Comptroller. When the clerk had leisure—and clerks in

Tennessee have a good deal—when he had lighted his pipe, and we were comfortably seated near the stove, I said, "Suppose that you did not fall in with the ideas of the Comptroller when he sent you the blank returns, and were to make up some blanks of your own in what you considered better form, what would happen?" He said, "I would not do that." "Of course," I said, "I know you wouldn't, but we are dealing with a hypothetical case. Suppose you made up blanks of your own, what would the Comptroller do?" "Well," he said, "I don't know as the Comptroller could do nothin'." "Well," I said, "who could?"

To make a long story short, we figured it out between us that the District Attorney of the County could indict the clerk among his neighbors; that is to say, he could lay an information against him before the grand jury, which would be composed of his own neighbors. They, if they thought the charge sustained, might find a true bill against him, and send him up to trial by the petit jury, which would also be composed of his neighbors and, indeed, the very persons who voted for him. If the petit jury thought the thing serious and proven against him, they could punish him under the terms of the statute, which was a nice little neighborly business. It goes without saying that the District Attorney, having been arranged for by the local boss on the same ticket with himself, would not lay an information against him before the Grand Jury. It goes without saying that in that homogenious [homogeneous] community where nearly everybody at that time voted the same ticket, it would not be thought a serious offense and nothing would be done by the Grand Jury. And when you come to figure out the processes of our government, it amounts to the fact that many of our officers may be each a law unto himself, for the statutes are so complicated that there is no simplified process of responsibility and consequently there is no placing of responsibility.

Suppose you had all the information and had comprehended all the information which so admirable a body as the Bureau of Municipal Research could supply you with concerning the public business and you found that the public business was not being properly conducted and you knew how it could be better conducted—for I quite agree with Mr. Cleveland that it is just as important to know how the thing should be done right as it is to know when it is being done wrong—what would you do, now? You would get together a reform Committee, or a Committee of 100, or a City Party, and you would make up a ticket; and how would you make up the ticket? Here are scores of offices, how do you make the nominations? You know you must make them by pleasing every group by the nomination of one of the members of that group and parcelling out the independent offices accordingly. Suppose you carried your ticket, where would you be? You would have a body of officers independent of each other, for the most part representing different groups, many of them of varying factions, and not disposed to co-operate. I say all that would be the result, because that always has been the result. You would have combination without co-operation on such a ticket. But, suppose you had only one person to nominate? You could not, perhaps, please all the different groups by a single nomination, so you would have to make a nomination that represented some kind of common counsel, the judgment of the whole community; and when you got that single representative he would know exactly what he was expected to do, and you could hold him responsible for doing it.

Just now, when there is so much interest in improving the means of government, I am hopeful that some practical reforms will be accomplished. I am so constituted, however, that while I am interested in reforms, I am interested only in those reform principles that have a means of practical operation. I must accomplish my business by workable methods. Now, this principle of simplification is such an absolute reversal of all the things we have been attempting, that I find it is the first instinct of every body of men to whom I have ever presented the idea, to say that it is undemocratic. Well, it is undemocratic in this sense, that you elect a smaller number of persons; but it is decidedly democratic in this, that the small number of persons you elect are directly related to the action of public opinion, whereas the present large number of persons you elect are not in any way related to the action of public opinion. I am not interested in the forms of democracy, I am not interested in going through the motions; I am interested in the substance. What I really want to do is to give public opinion a means of operating upon the conduct of government. If I believe that certain means are a means to that end, I do not care what the superficial appearance of the means may happen to be. I know, and you know, that under our present organization we do not obtain democratic results, and that we must change our methods in order to obtain democratic results. The moment that the man you put in office is aware of his responsibility, that he cannot shift it, and that you know that he cannot shift it, that moment will the politics of this country be clarified and purified. The present situation is that of a great, right thinking, right purposing people, looking at the processes of their own politics with a feeling almost akin to despair. Where is the practical spirit that we have boasted of in the past? Where is that spirit of which De To[c]queville spoke in almost moving terms when, in sentences that are warm with admiration, he speaks of the way in which the people that had lately been the subjects of Great Britain, after they had made an imperfect government in the confederation, turned, as he expressed it, "an eye of examination" upon themselves, saw that their processes were mistaken and inadequate and altered the whole character of their government "without," in his fine phrase, "having drawn a tear or a drop of blood from mankind"; and were men enough to be equal to working out a great revolution by processes of peace and deliberation. That is the original credit and majesty of America—her power to scrutinize herself and to go back by direct processes to the realization of her own ideals. And so, when we argue about programs of reform, let us remember that programs are fatal without processes; and that what we want is not to set up masters amongst us, not to concentrate executive authority, but to bring about a veritable representative government in bodies sufficiently numerous to do the business, and so directly related to us that they cannot mistake their responsibility.

The concentration of responsibility in this country is a very interesting thing. Have you never reflected upon the extraordinary power which the President of the United States can exercise? The Constitution has nothing to do with it. I remember that, some years ago, when one of the Presidents[5] was claiming all the power that anybody had ever had anywhere, a witty gentleman said that we need not get excited about it, because he had not exercised it; and he cited in illustration the story of an old negro, recently married, who complained of his wife's extravagance:—'She is the most extravagantist woman ever I seen, wants money in the mornin', wants money in the middle of the day and wants money at night.' 'But John, what does she spend it all on?' 'Why nothin' Boss, I ain't given her any yet.'

Now, in a certain sense, we haven't given the Executive the power yet, but just look at the power he claims and already can exercise, and see how extravagant he can be! I remember meeting one of the Senators of the United States when he was in a very peevish mood and how he said that the Constitution had not given the President the right to send so many messages to Congress. "Why, Senator," I asked him, "what is the matter?" He said the President was bombarding Congress with messages

[5] Theodore Roosevelt.

about everything you could think of and was confusing the whole public business. I said, "Senator, I think you are troubled about the Constitution unnecessarily; the Constitution has not got anything to do with it. The point is not that the President sends the messages to you, but that he publishes them to the country; and if the country happens to agree with him, it does not wait to hear what you have to say. That is the gravamen of the difficulty."

One of the interesting circumstances about our government is that we have all of us taken part in electing only one officer of the country, namely the President, and centered all our attention upon him, knowing that anybody else in the national government represents only some little piece of the United States, and is listening as intently as he can to the opinion of that particular part of the country against the next election. Everything that the President says is printed in every newspaper in the United States, entire, if they have room for it. There is no other officer of the government whose utterances are printed in half the papers of the United States. See what a very simple advantage the President has, therefore: he has the whole nation for an audience and nobody else has. Therefore, his impressions can be made in the mass and entire, instantaneously, and, of course, those gentlemen whose voice does not reach the same distance are unusually cross on the publication of his opinions. But what does that mean? It means that having a person in sight whom we all regard as our representative, we delight to agree with him whenever it is possible, to back him up whenever in [it] is possible, and rejoice when he carries our wishes against the miscellaneous aggregation that we have called a representative body.

In other words, the people of the United States are constantly looking around for this simple, direct, energetic means of exercising all the force of their desires and opinions. And the most interesting thing to me about the influence which a man like the President of the United States can exercise is that it is greatest when it is in the field of moral impulse. It is greatest when the things which he proposes seem obviously to rest upon some great principle of equity and justice. A very astute President could do very extraordinary things, provided he could make it appear that they rested upon the common moral impulse of the country. And this moral impulse is, so to say, unused, going to waste, except as it may here and there be concentrated upon a single individual; and wherever it is concentrated upon a single individual, it finds freedom and expression.

I do not know how, under the present structure of our government, to reform its business. I understand some parts of its business with some detail. I consider myself a competent critic of these parts, but I have not the means, as a voter, to draw together my neighbors for the purpose of realizing in action the changes in its business which my knowledge of the government might suggest to me as necessary.

Now, I am a confirmed optimist. I believe with all my heart what more than one of the gentlemen who have spoken to-night have said. I believe that the right will prevail; but our responsibility is to see that it be afforded reasonably convenient means of prevailing.

The idea of spending all the righteousness that there is in this country in this way—always running its head into a noose—seems to me a fatal exercise of political energy; hence, I recommend simplification. You observe I can no further explain it, because it is so simple it does not need exposition. All I can do is to insist upon the single point I came to make to you, that simplification is the key to the present situation of rule by the machine, and that only simplification can put the machine out of business. If the present machine were to go out of business to-night, under some universal impulse of righteousness, the consequence would be that we would have to make it over again in the morning. Making it over again, we might put new blood into it, new men into it, and for a little while it would run in a way that would please us very much; but put any man's conscience in a place where it can exercise, or fail to exercise, its power under cover and the process of demoralization will set in.

I want you to ask yourselves this question: Are you as careful of your personal morals in distant places where you are not known, as at home where you are known? Have you noticed any subtle effect of the place where you are not known upon your conduct or thought? Now, make all the processes of government private, and then undertake to govern yourselves, and would you trust yourself in a dark room? I shrewdly suspect that I, if I were in the position of some of the men in office whom I criticize, would do exactly what they do. There is nothing more demoralizing than power without responsibility; and there is nothing more sobering and ennobling than power with responsibility.

Let any man know that his neighbors trust him, believe him, and are willing to put their affairs in his hands, and you will see a process of reformation which will astonish you.

In a certain city, which, under the circumstances, I will not name,[6] they set up a commission system of government. They concentrated the whole power in the hands of five persons. Being in a hurry, they selected five persons who had been very questionable politicians; and these gentlemen suddenly became perfectly trustworthy public servants, and have been so for years together. There is a cold air that goes in with responsibility; all sorts of vapors blow away and you see things as they are. You see things as they are because you see things as other people see them, and do not let your own preferences and interests and propositions come in between you and them.

And another very serious aspect of this matter, when you widen it and give it national scope, is this, that when you get a complicated system of government like ours, and then get vested interests dominant in that complicated system, you do not know how to change the thing successfully, for the minute you touch it the vested interests will say, "Let the old order alone, the whole business of the country will go to smash if you don't."

A very witty writer, Mr. Chesterton, has said that it is true that an eminently successful man cannot be bribed; the fact is, he has been, in the sense that the existing order of things has made his success possible. Therefore, he is for the existing order of things, and it has bribed him. It says, "I made you, now stand by me." Therefore he stands by the existing order. It made him, and he does not know what his success or failure might be under a change; and therefore he is more absolutely and successfully bribed than would be possible under other circumstances;[7] because if a man will bribe you in the ordinary vulgar sense by giving you money, he is rogue enough to go back on you. It is not "honest bribery." But the existing order of things says, "you just keep me up and I will keep you up. Don't do anything without first consulting your grandmother, or the New York Tribune." So every successful man wants the status quo.

I was saying to a company of gentlemen the other night, and they did not seem to like it, that I thought the business of a

6 It was Galveston, Texas, which Wilson identified in later speeches.

7 Wilson was paraphrasing a passage from the chapter, "The Eternal Revolution," in Gilbert K. Chesterton, *Orthodoxy* (London and New York, 1908). The relevant passage, which is found on page 219, reads: "For the whole modern world is absolutely based on the assumption, not that the rich are necessary (which is tenable), but that the rich are trustworthy, which (for a Christian) is not tenable. You will hear everlastingly, in all discussions about newspapers, companies, aristocracies, or party politics, this argument that the rich man cannot be bribed. The fact is, of course, that the rich man is bribed; he has been bribed already. That is why he is a rich man. The whole case for Christianity is that a man who is dependent upon the luxuries of this life is a corrupt man, spiritually corrupt, politically corrupt, financially corrupt."

college was to make the young men of this generation as unlike their fathers as possible.[8] I added that I did not mean any disrespect to the fathers. I meant that, generally, by the time a man is old enough to have a son at college he takes more interest in his particular business than in the welfare of the nation; that each new generation should be originals, should be taken away to the general platform of American life; taken away from the atmosphere of their fathers' business, and told to look at America as a whole, and not from the point of view of a particular business; and that I believe the business of the college to be to renew this common impulse and common point of view with each generation.

And so, you see what I mean by the necessity for having an order so simple that it will work without regard to whether our consciences are aroused. We will then know that we can work intelligently and make progress for that noble basis of reform which beats with so strong impulse, I believe, throughout all the country that we love.[9]

Printed tearsheets (T. N. Pfeiffer Scrapbook, NjP).

[8] Wilson had made such remarks in several speeches during the preceding months.

[9] There is a WWT outline of this address, dated Nov. 9, 1909, in WP, DLC.

From Henry Eckert Alexander[1]

Dear Dr. Wilson: Trenton, N. J. November 18, 1909.

I am anxious to go over to Princeton some day when it will be convenient to give me half an hour and have a talk with you. We made our recent local campaign on the theory that the people wanted a "change."[2] I believe that the people of New Jersey are in a like mood. At all events there are opportunities for an educational campaign such as you are initiating with your speeches. By the way, you lose a large constituency when your secretary sends advance copies of your speeches *exclusively* to the Associated Press. The New York Sun through the Laffan Syndicate reaches a large number of newspapers and so does the Publishers Press, now known as the United Press, I believe. With best wishes, I am,

Sincerely yours, Henry Eckert Alexander.

ALS (WP, DLC).

[1] Editor and publisher of the Trenton *True American.* Alexander was soon to become a strong supporter of Wilson's campaigns for the governorship of New Jersey and the presidency of the United States.

[2] In the recent municipal election, Trenton Democrats had campaigned for the overthrow of the long-term Republican majority on the Common Council,

which controlled the appointment of some three hundred office-holders. In the election on November 2, 1909, Democrats managed to capture four new seats, reducing the Republican majority to two. The new division on the Common Council of fifteen Republicans and thirteen Democrats was the closest in several years.

From Henry Moffat[1]

My dear Sir: Yonkers, N. Y. November 19, 1909.

I understand that my son, Stanley Moffat, of the class of "'13" has been suspended for a period of two weeks for "rough-housing."

Having received no specific statement of the charges upon which this action was based, I determined to investigate for myself, and, therefore, with several other gentlemen, whose sons were in the same predicament, I visited Princeton last Monday evening and interviewed the Dean and also the land-lady of the house.

As far as I could make out, the case was one of a simply aggrevated [aggravated] "roughhouse." To my direct question to the land-lady, as to whether at any time any of the boys had uttered to her an insulting word, she answered "No." In fact, as to my own son, the only charge that I have yet been able to find, was that he shouted and yelled. He was not present upon several occasions when the worst "rough-housing" was indulged in and at no time was he guilty of any act of violence to the property, and yet, he is given two weeks suspension.

While recognizing the necessity of putting down these practices, and admitting the propriety of punishment in such cases, I feel justified in protesting against the severity of the one inflicted here, for the following reasons:

1st. That a custom, which has been in existence to my personal knowledge for more than ten years, had not been distinctly forbidden to these boys and that no warning had been given.

2nd. That some consideration should be given to the fact that in the case of my son, at least, his previous conduct had been exemplary and his attention to his studies had warranted his standing in the first group of his class.

3rd. That while any punishment, which is recognized as within the bounds of justice, is of benefit to the culprit, an excessive one is liable to make him lose sight of his fault in his indignation at the injustice inflicted upon him. In his own sight, at least, he becomes a martyr and not a culprit. The whole benefit of the punishment is lost.

This punishment, according to your own regulations, and

according to the words of the Dean, as expressed on Monday evening, is worse than for drunkenness. Against this view of the case, I decidedly protest.

I have further been informed, unofficially,–for as yet nothing has come to me officially except a statement that he had been suspended–that he is to be placed on final probation.

Now I have counselled my son to take his punishment quietly, go back and make good in his work, but I feel that it would hardly be fair that for this offense, he should be a marked boy all through his college life.

I feel deeply grieved over this whole matter and cannot believe that one who has been, throughout the whole of his life, a most enthusiastic son of Princeton could receive anything but a fair and just hearing.

I therefor leave this case with you, feeling confident that your sense of justice will point out the proper course.

Very sincerely yours, Henry Moffat.

TLS (WP, DLC).

[1] Princeton 1875, a physician practicing in Yonkers, N. Y.

To Ralph B. Merritt[1]

My dear Sir: Princeton, N. J. November 20th, 1909.

In reply to your questions with regard to the Honor System of Conducting Examinations, I take pleasure in making the following replies:

First: The method is very simple. Every student who observes anything irregular in the conduct of a fellow student during an examination is expected to report the irregularity to a committee of undergraduates made up as indicated in the enclosed Constitution. The members of the Faculty do not observe the conduct of the undergraduates in examination further than to preserve general order. They are present at the examination chiefly for the purpose of answering questions. The system covers all written tests of any kind. There is a set of written rules, which I enclose.

Second: The system was inaugurated at the request of the undergraduates after a very brief canvass of undergraduate opinion by a small group of upper-classmen.[2] The period covered by the canvass was hardly more than two or three weeks.

Third: There has never been the slightest indication of the existence of any minority inclined to refuse to abide by the rules of the system.

Fourth: Its success has been complete. There was from the

first a very cordial attitude towards it on the part of the faculty, and the few members of that body (never more than two or three) who were at first inclined to doubt the wisdom of it very quickly altered their opinion completely. Among the students it is a special subject of pride, and it has not only operated with success but has undoubtedly affected the whole standard of student life in dealings with the faculty and among themselves.

Fifth: In the period of fifteen years during which the system has been in operation amongst us there have been a number of cases reported. There has never been the slightest indication of any disposition on the part of the general student body to criticize adversely those who reported on their fellow students. The report is made, you will understand, to a committee of undergraduates, their judgment is accepted as final by the faculty, and the whole matter, therefore, is a matter of self government.

Sixth: The system was inaugurated at Princeton in 1894[3] and has, therefore, been in operation fifteen years. The interest in it has increased from year to year rather than lessened, though it is difficult to express an opinion about that, inasmuch as there has been complete acquiescence and support of it from the first and it has now become one of the established institutions of the place.

Seventh: We have no formal student self-government aside from the Honor System in Examinations. There is, however, a Senior Council[4] to which the authorities of the University frequently resort for advice and assistance, and which upon many occasions acts voluntarily as the spokesman of the undergraduates in matters which require to be dealt with. The relations of the college authorities with this council have always been of the most cordial and confidential sort.

Very truly yours, [Woodrow Wilson]

CCL (WWP, UA, NjP).

1 The Editors have been unable to identify him.

2 About the establishment of the honor system, see the Princeton University Faculty Minutes, Jan. 18, 1893, n. 1, Vol. 8, and subsequent documents in that volume.

3 Actually, the honor system was inaugurated in 1893.

4 About this organization, see WW to the Board of Trustees of Princeton University, Dec. 14, 1905, n. 2, Vol. 16.

To Henry Moffat

My dear Dr. Moffat: [Princeton, N. J.] November 20th, 1909.

Allow me to acknowledge the receipt of your letter of November 19th and to say that I am genuinely distressed that the discipline of the University in the case of your son and other members of his class should appear to you in the light it does. It would gratify me very much if I were able to put it before you as it lies in our own minds.

It is true that a certain amount of "rough-housing" has been the very bad custom here for a number of years among the freshmen. It is a custom which has grown up simply because the University authorities were unable to check it. They were unable to check it because most of the boarding-house keepers are so constantly in terror of unpopularity and some form of boycott that we cannot induce them to keep us informed of anything irregular that may happen in their houses. We have never failed in any instance of which we were informed to check the thing very sharply, and in this instance I can assure you that it went very much beyond the bounds of any possible custom. It was long-continued and deliberate and extreme. Your son, I am happy to say, had only a minor part in it, and I am sorry that he should have been involved in any way.

I am bound to say that the fact that your son and his companions were in all other respects exemplary boys both in their attention to their studies and in their general conduct seems to me to make it the more inexcusable that they should have departed from their usual standards in this case. I think that boys of that sort should be held to the very high standard which they have always recognized in their lives, and that it is entirely wholesome that they should be treated as the men they have proved themselves to be. My own experience in dealing with boys is that this is the only wholesome standard for discipline. I do not mean that boys whose previous records were unsatisfactory should not be as severely punished, but that exemplary character renders the offence all the more clearly inexcusable.

I had not understood that these young gentlemen were put upon final probation and I am sure you will find that nothing of the sort is contemplated. What they have interpreted in that way is probably a warning that they are to regard themselves as under special obligations, when they return, to behave themselves with order and propriety.

Having been associated with the administration of college discipline almost from my first connection with the faculty here, I feel that no one outside university administration can realize the difficulties and perplexities of it. One of the things that has been most impressed upon me is the necessity of treating all cases in a way which will be as nearly as possible based upon the merits of the case and which will exclude personal considerations. It is impossible to make special allowances in individual cases without seeming to the general body of the students, who cannot be informed of particular cases, to be guilty of favoritism. College discipline is at best an unsatisfactory matter, but I am sure that from my knowledge of my colleagues, the Dean of the College and the members of the Committee of the Faculty on Discipline, I can assure you that you are dealing in this matter with men of the greatest probity and justice.

Let me say again that I am genuinely distressed that you cannot agree with us in this judgment, and I hope sincerely that in the long run you will feel that you have no reason to resent our action in the case of your son. It would grieve me very much to have a Princeton man entertain that feeling.

Cordially and sincerely yours, [Woodrow Wilson]

CCL (WWP, UA, NjP).

To Samuel Archibald Smith

My dear Sir: Princeton, N. J. November 20th, 1909.

Absence from home has prevented my replying sooner to your letter of November 17th.

The authorities of the University have very thoroughly considered the cases of the young gentlemen about whom you write and are of the opinion that no injustice has been done, but that the punishment visited upon them was both necessary and suitable. The disorderly conduct of which they were guilty was carried to a most unusual length and was directed against two women. We cannot think that there are any considerable extenuating circumstances. If offences of this sort were passed over when we were able to ascertain them, the demoralization of discipline would be complete, and I am surprised that you do not realize this.

That disorders of this kind, though much less deliberate and extended than in this case, has often occurred, we understand to be true, but the boarding-house keepers are in such fear of unpopularity that it has proved impossible to induce them to report them. It is only when the disorder becomes unusually aggravated, as in this case, that the authorities are able to learn of it. We have never allowed a case of this sort of which we had knowledge to go unpunished.

You suggest that the parents should have been previously advised of what their sons were doing. Of course, this was impossible. We had no previous knowledge of the disposition of these young gentlemen to conduct themselves as they did, and when the offence had been committed it was no remedy for it to apprise the parents of the conduct of their sons.

You are entirely misinformed when you say that what these young gentlemen did was something "which had been going on for years without serious discipline" and that in this case it was punished "suddenly without warning." What these young gentlemen did went far beyond anything we can learn of having been done before and, as I have already stated, we have invariably punished conduct of this sort whenever we knew of it.

Very truly yours, [Woodrow Wilson]

CCL (WWP, UA, NjP).

To De Witt Clinton Jones, Jr.

My dear Mr. Jones: Princeton, N. J. November 20th, 1909.

Absence from home has prevented my acknowledging sooner your letter of November 17th.

I am sincerely distressed that you and the other gentlemen whose sons were involved in the discipline visited upon the young men at 47 University Place should feel about the case as you do. The University authorities have never failed to punish conduct of this sort whenever they were able to learn of it. Only in extraordinary cases does it come to their attention, because the boarding-house keepers are in such fear of unpopularity and some sort of boycott that they cannot be induced to report disorderly conduct to the University authorities.

In the case about which you write the disorder went so far beyond the usual point and became so unbearable to the two women involved that it inevitably became public property and the University authorities were afforded the opportunity to act as they always must act in such circumstances.

I am sincerely sorry that you should regard the punishment imposed as excessive, but after the most careful conference with the Dean of the College and his associates in the Committee on Discipline, I cannot agree with that conclusion. I believe that any different treatment of the case would lead to the general demoralization of discipline.

We are very conscious of the distressing circumstances of this case, the most distressing being the good scholarship and excellent character of the young men involved. I must say, however, that these very circumstances render it to us the more extraordinary that these young men should so have forgotten themselves and the more necessary that they should be dealt with as entirely responsible men.

With much respect,

Sincerely yours, Woodrow Wilson

TLS (received from D. C. Jones III).

From William Williams Keen[1]

My dear President Wilson: Philadelphia, Nov. 20th, 1909.

Whenever you have decided the month when you will favor us with an address before the Contemporary Club, I shall be glad to know it.[2]

It will give my daughters and myself great pleasure if you will stay with us, and still more if Mrs. Wilson can come with you. I should like to invite some friends to meet you at dinner before the meeting.

Yours very truly, W. W. Keen

TLS (WP, DLC).

1 Prominent surgeon of Philadelphia, at this time Professor of Surgery Emeritus at Jefferson Medical College.

2 Wilson spoke to the Contemporary Club of Philadelphia on March 14, 1910. A news report of his address is printed at March 15, 1910, Vol. 20.

From G. McArthur Sullivan[1]

Hon. Sir: Lynchburg, Va., Nov. 20, 1909

I want so much to come to your School at Princeton. I am a poor Southern colored man from South Carolina, but I believe I can make make [*sic*] my way if I am permitted to come.

Please Sir, send me a catalog and information as to whether a colored man may enter there.

Yours sincerely G McArthur Sullivan

ALS (UA, NjP).

1 A student at Virginia Theological Seminary and College, Lynchburg, Va., owned and operated by Negro Baptists.

From John Nevin Sayre[1]

My dear Dr. Wilson, New York Nov. 21, 1909.

I want to write a word of personal thanks for your talk to us at the Charter Club last Friday night. When the "Quad" idea was first proposed, at the time of my graduation from college, I was not altogether favourably disposed to it; largely because I did not grasp the *whole* significance of what you were trying to accomplish, and thought that evils in the clubs could be reformed, and some arrangement devised to take care of men who did not get elected to clubs.

Since then, however, I have come to wish that more of my time in college had been given to thorough study and the reading of non required books; for I feel the need of it now. I say this in spite of the fact that the training and experience which I got as president of a club, seems to me still to have been most valuable. But I do begrudge some of the time which went in adding up bills, and "sophomore bicker sessions,"[2] and attending countless meetings of the Inter Club Treaty. This is a conclusion which I had come to quite independently of anything you said Friday night. But your talk illuminated the subject for me in other ways, and made the whole plan seem practical. I am convinced that the "virus" is working in many others whom I know.

I would like you to feel that if I could ever be of any assistance to you in this matter, I would gladly use whatever influence I may possess in my own club and elsewhere.

Very Sincerely yours, John Nevin Sayre.

ALS (WP, DLC).

[1] Princeton 1907, at this time a student at Union Theological Seminary in New York. During the 1930s and 1940s he became a prominent pacifist associated with the Fellowship of Reconciliation.

[2] "Bicker" is the term used to describe the period of time, usually a week or two in length, during which sophomores are chosen for membership in the upperclass clubs.

From Robert Bridges

My dear Tommy: New York, November 22, 1909.

I rather expected that I should see you in town Friday or Saturday and so I did not answer your note of the 16th.

I need not tell you how much we are all interested in your proposal and we shall of course be very glad to have for the Magazine your article on "The Reorganization of our Colleges." We note with pleasure that you mean that the article shall be of general application to "all of our colleges." From all points of view, it would not be wise that it should be in any sense a discussion of Princeton conditions alone, because of course we are not in a position to print a discussion from other points of view. This I know is not your intention. I have the greatest faith in your own view of the matter, and my only personal anxiety is that you shall not be misinterpreted or put in a wrong position by those who do not agree with you. I believe that the first article did a lot of good and I know that that is the aim which you have in mind for this supplementary article; on large lines of general application, I believe that its effect will be to enlighten the right people. I appreciate very much that you should have brought the proposal to us.[1] Faithfully yours Robert Bridges

TLS (WP, DLC).

[1] See n. 1 to Wilson's outline for this article, printed at Nov. 29, 1909.

From Henry Moffat

Dear Sir: Yonkers, N. Y. November 22, 1909.

Your letter of November 20th, was received today, and I wish to thank you for your kindness in writing so fully, on the subject, and to express my appreciation of your consideration in this whole matter.

While still unconvinced, due probably to my Scotch ancestry, I am willing to admit your greater experience in these matters and acknowledge your better judgment in dealing with such cases. Your statement that there was no intention of placing my son on final probation gives me great comfort, and I am sure that the boy will take thoroughly to heart the lesson he has learned.

My son returns to Princeton today, thoroughly impressed with the necessity of making good in every way, both in his studies and in his general conduct, and I sincerely hope that you will not have any cause for anxiety in the future, in regard to anything which he may do. Thanking you again, for your kind letter, I am, Sincerely yours, Henry Moffat.

TLS (WP, DLC).

From Roland Sletor Morris[1]

My dear Dr. Wilson: Philadelphia, 22 November 1909.

I want to acknowledge your note of November 20 and tell you how much we appreciate your acceptance of the invitation to address the Contemporary Club and note that you have selected March 8 as being most convenient to you, which date is entirely satisfactory to the Club.

I have no doubt that the meeting on Monday, March 8 will more than meet the expectations of the Committee and members of the Club.

With kind regards,

Sincerely yours, Roland S. Morris

TLS (WP, DLC).

[1] Princeton 1896, a member of the Philadelphia law firm of Duane, Morris and Heckscher. Morris served as Ambassador to Japan during the Wilson administration, 1917-21.

From William James Mayo[1]

Rochester, Minn.

My dear President Wilson: November 23, 1909.

It has come to my knowledge that there would be a possibility of your considering the presidency of the University of Minnesota, which is about to become vacant by reason of the resignation of the valued and honored head, President Northrop. I want to assure you, as one of the Board of Regents, of my sincere approval of any course which would bring about so desirable a result for our university.

Under the able administration of President Northrop our state university occupies a commanding position with over 5,000 students, and is thoroughly equipped with professional schools who number their alumni in the thousands. In many respects this university, which is practically the only one of importance in the state, and from the western border to the Pacific Coast, is capable of a larger field of usefulness and of occupying a preeminent position. It has the entire population of a great and growing state behind it, and has endowments in state lands and other assets which assure its financial future.

Yours very truly, W. J. Mayo

TLS (WP, DLC).

[1] One of the Mayo brothers, founders of the Mayo Clinic in Rochester, Minn. He had been a member of the Board of Regents of the University of Minnesota since 1907.

From James Monroe Taylor

Poughkeepsie, N. Y.

My dear President Wilson, November 23, 1909.

. . . Thank you also for what you say about the direct primary. Your position is a very suggestive one to me, and I am inclined to give full assent to it. The direct primary appealed to me originally, as I read upon it and studied it somewhat, as a possible weakening of the machine. I have not been so confident of that as the months have gone on, and I have great fear that it would result after it became a settled method in about the same domination of bosses that we have at present. My chief hope has been, I confess, in the fact that the bosses did not seem to want the plan. Your point, however, it seems to me, goes far below any of these systems of reforms and strikes at the foundation. It is along the line, of course, of what you said years ago upon democracy,[1] which then won my prompt and hearty assent.

Thanking you for the trouble you have taken in making this statement to me, and with hearty regard, I am

Sincerely yours, J M Taylor

TLS (WP, DLC).

1 When Wilson delivered his lecture, "Democracy" (printed at Dec. 5, 1891, Vol. 7), at Vassar College on Dec. 9, 1892.

To Moses Taylor Pyne

My dear Momo: Princeton, N. J. November 26th, 1909.

I have been studying the sketch of the tower by Mr. Cram[1] and must confess myself disappointed in it. It is too closely upon the lines of the tower we are to have on Nassau Street.[2] My feeling is that, considering the architecture of the place as a whole, it would be a mistake to have two towers so nearly alike. Before coming to any final conclusion in this matter, I would like very much to know how you feel on this particular point.

Always faithfully yours, Woodrow Wilson

TCL (M. T. Pyne Coll., NjP).

1 That is, the proposed Cleveland memorial tower. As R. A. Cram to WW, Dec. 7, 1909, reveals, Wilson and Pyne, members along with Senator John Fairfield Dryden of a subcommittee of the Cleveland Monument Association to suggest a plan for the Cleveland monument, had by this time agreed that the monument should consist of the tower of the proposed Graduate College.

2 A tower planned to be adjacent to what is now Holder Hall. The Class of 1884 had offered to supply the funds for this project. As it turned out, Margaret Olivia Slocum (Mrs. Russell) Sage gave the money for Holder Tower.

To Hamilton Wright Mabie[1]

My dear Mr. Mabie: Princeton, N. J. November 26th, 1909.

Thank you for your letter of November 23rd.[2] I shall look forward with pleasure to seeing you on the ninth of December[3] and accept the invitation you so cordially extend me on behalf of Mrs. Mabie[4] and yourself, with a great deal of Pleasure.

I should like your counsel in the matter of the choice of the subject. There are three amongst which I would be very much obliged if you would make your choice: First, "Our Country and Our Day," an attempt to analyse the general mixture of bloods and processes which now constitutes America; Second, "Political Reform," a general discussion of its present embarrassments and processes; and, Third, "Patriotism," a general analysis of its nature viewed from the point of view of a man who rather likes to think in concrete processes.

My own preference would be for the subject of "Political Reform," but I should hesitate to undertake its discussion before the Athenaeum Club unless you yourself think it appropriate.[5]

Cordially and sincerely yours, Woodrow Wilson

TLS (H. W. Mabie Papers, DLC).

[1] Associate Editor of *The Outlook* and author of numerous literary works.

[2] It is missing.

[3] When Wilson was to speak to the Athenaeum Club of Summit, N. J. A news report of his address is printed at Dec. 10, 1909.

[4] Jeannette Trivett Mabie.

[5] Wilson spoke on the first of the topics mentioned.

From Stephen Baker[1]

My dear Sir: New York, November 26, 1909.

I have not written you regarding the suspension of my son, Charles D. Baker, of the Class "1913," for four weeks, for "rough-housing," as I felt, after an interview with Dean Elliott on November 15th, the Committee on Discipline would not review their action, and I did not see how you could go over the heads of the Committee, and reverse their decision.

I cannot, however, allow the incident to close without entering a protest against the action of the Committee, and the severity of the punishment, as unjust and likely to work injury to the students, in making them lose sight of their fault in their indignation at the injustice of the punishment they have received.

Seven of the fathers of the students had an interview with Dean Elliott on Monday evening, November 15th, and we then stated to the Dean that we believed the boys should be punished, but we took exception to their being suspended, and for so long a period of time. We stated that we understood that for drunkenness, a student was warned for the first offence, and for the second, was suspended for two weeks. Dean Elliott said that was true, and that it was one of the rules of the Committee on Discipline, and when asked if he considered the offence which these students had committed worse than drunkenness, he said "Yes," and when pressed still further, he stated that he "would rather see his brother drunk than engaged in such actions as these students had been guilty of." Am I therefore to understand that this represents the feeling of the Faculty, and that Princeton University is prepared to place itself on record to the effect that the offence committed by these students was more than four times as great as a first offence of drunkenness?

Since our interview, Dean Elliott has sent me a statement of the case, dated November 15th, and after reviewing the various disorders which took place, he adds these two sentences which I wish to quote, not because they refer to my son, but because I believe they represent the attitude of all the young men engaged in this "rough-housing."

> "Your son participated in the disturbance on Thursday, Tuesday and Wednesday night. The conduct of your son before the Discipline Committee was very manly and straightforward, and he expressed himself as being ashamed of the part he had taken in it.
>
> ["]I wish to add that during the whole of this disorder, and in fact during the whole year, the occupants of the house assure me that there has been no drinking among them."

I cannot tell you how much I have been disturbed over this whole matter, as I have another son[2] who is preparing for Princeton and who expects to enter a year from next Fall, but if this action represents the attitude of Princeton University towards the relativity of such an offence as these students have been punished for, to the great moral question of drunkenness, I do not know whether I have any right to send him there.[3]

With kind regards,

Yours very truly, Stephen Baker

TLS (WP, DLC).

1 President of the Bank of the Manhattan Co. in New York.

2 John Stewart Baker.

3 He entered Princeton in the autumn of 1911.

To Stephen Baker

My dear Mr. Baker: [Princeton, N. J.] November 27th, 1909.

Allow me to acknowledge the receipt of your letter of November 26th and to say that I have read it with real distress. I am sincerely sorry that the discipline visited by the University upon your son and his comrades should have made the impression on you it seems to have made, and I hope that before your son's course is completed the whole matter will wear a different complexion in your thought.

We have never in any circumstances allowed offences of this sort to go unpunished. Again and again we have felt ourselves at a disadvantage because unable to learn of offences of this sort, and we know that conduct of this kind has often gone unpunished, but never when we could get authentic accounts of it, and the punishment imposed in this case was not unusual.

I think that you are laying too much stress upon the conversation you had with Dean Elliott. I think that you must realize that a considerable degree of excitement must have accompanied such an interview with seven of the fathers whose sons were concerned and that many things may have been said which were said only under the stress of such an interview. Dean Elliott enjoys our entire confidence, and I am sure from long association with him that he would wish always to handle these matters with entire equity and fairness.

I value your opinion and approval so highly that I take the liberty of again expressing the hope that as this affair is seen in perspective it will wear a different aspect to you. You may be sure that it does not involve disgrace to your son and that the penalty was inflicted only because we must, whenever possible, check disorder of the kind involved in this case.

With much respect,

Sincerely yours, [Woodrow Wilson]

CCL (WWP, UA, NjP).

An Outline of an Article

29 Nov. 1909.

THE REORGANIZATION OF THE UNIVERSITY (For *Scribners*)

Look back to former article: Absorption in non-university interests. Lack of *consciousness* of university aims and influences.

A *play* life.

The *desideratum*: A community life

(*a*) From wh. non-university motives (social rivalry etc.) will be as much as possible excluded

(β) In which the influence of older men and more permanent interests will be constantly felt

The means:

A preceptorial method of instruction—or, rather, of association and counsel in studies.

A residential organization in which

1) With small enough numbers, { Dine together / All essentials together }

2) All classes of the university and all grades, from the President down to the greenest Freshman, will be constantly associated upon a footing of natural familiarity.

3) Artificial (elective) distinctions will be excluded.

Suggestions:

No governing, but only a presiding, 'master.'

Self-government by Committee, within general rules

Impartial assignment and safe-guards against cliques

No segregation of teaching—the unity of the university body jealously preserved.

Wherein does democracy consist?

Not in catholic boyish tastes, but in

Unselected, unavoidable contacts

Not within the choice of any institution that would be national and serve the nation to permit an undemocratic organization.

The fundamental democracy that of the mind: the democratic organization always the richest in ability and achievement.[1]

WWhw MS (WP, DLC).

[1] Wilson's article, "The Country and the Colleges," is printed at Feb. 24, 1910, Vol. 20. For reasons which will become apparent, he decided not to publish it.

To Moses Taylor Pyne

My dear Momo: [Princeton, N. J.] November 29th, 1909.

Thank you for your letter about the [Cleveland] Memorial Tower and the '84 matter. . . .[1]

I am glad that you agree with me that the tower Cram has designed is hardly suitable. The fundamental difficulty I find in forming my own judgment is that we have no drawing of the group of buildings with which it is to be associated. This tower, as Mr. Cram has designed it, seems to me, as you say, heavy and without any soaring quality such as straight lines would give it and such as it cannot have with buttressed corners.

I will act upon your suggestion and return the drawings to Mr. Cram (I suppose to his New York office) with a letter embodying our criticisms.

Always cordially and faithfully yours,

[Woodrow Wilson]

CCL (WWP, UA, NjP).

[1] Pyne's letter is missing.

To Ralph Adams Cram

My dear Mr. Cram: [Princeton, N. J.] November 29th, 1909.

Mr. Pyne and I have conferred about the drawing you were kind enough to submit as a suggestion for the Cleveland

Memorial Tower, and we agree in thinking that the tower is too much like that which will be connected with Mr. Day's group of buildings on Nassau Street and that its buttressed corners and narrowing width as it rises give it an appearance of heaviness. It does not seem to us to soar quite enough. I know how generous you are and believe that you will be willing to think the thing over again for us.

It has occurred to both Mr. Pyne and me that, since Mr. Day's tower is like a slender edition of the central tower of Canterbury, this one might be more nearly an adaptation of the tower of Magdalen. My own feeling is that it should be as simple as possible. I dare say that it is necessary that it should rise rather high, but my own choice would be something broad and solid, like the Founders tower at Magdalen. I know, however, that we can trust your taste and judgment in this matter.

Since I saw you this summer we have done everything that seemed possible to change Mr. Procter's preference with regard to the Golf Links, but to no avail, and it now seems as if we were doomed to put the Graduate College in that very inappropriate place.

Always cordially and faithfully yours,

[Woodrow Wilson]

CCL (WWP, UA, NjP).

From Stephen Baker

My dear Sir: New York, November 30, 1909.

I have received your letter of the 27th inst.

I cannot agree with your suggestion that probably Dean Elliott was laboring under a considerable degree of excitement when he made the remark which I quoted in my letter of November 26th. He made the statement quoted, and after a few moments of desultory conversation, I referred again to the matter, stated that I considered it a very serious statement, that I did not wish to make any mistake or misquote him in any way, and wanted to know whether he wished us to deliberately understand that he would rather have seen his brother drunk than engaged in such actions as the students had been guilty of, and he said "Yes." I then said that I was very much surprised at his attitude and he then asked each father present, one after the other, whether they agreed with what I said, and each one said "Yes." I cannot feel that his views were expressed under stress at any time, but were the deliberate conviction of a man after having been given an opportunity to withdraw his statement if he had so desired.

I am very sorry that you have not answered the question in my letter regarding the University's attitude as to the relativity of this offence to drunkenness. If the Committee on Discipline have made a mistake they should be manly enough to acknowledge it. If the Faculty acquiesce in their action, they admit that this offence is more than four times as great as drunkenness. If, as you suggest, the Dean was speaking under excitement, I think that we parents are entitled to know from you the attitude of the University on this question.

With kind regards,

Very sincerely yours, Stephen Baker

TLS (WP, DLC).

From Wilton Merle-Smith[1]

My dear Dr. Wilson: [New York] November 30th [1909]

I am distressed beyond measure at the action taken by the Dean of the University in regard to the students at 47 University Place. All the papers in the matter have been put before me and it seems to me that the resolution of the Senior Council declaring that the action taken by the Dean was unjustifiable[2] will be endorsed by every Alumnus who knows the facts. The declaration also of the Dean that he considered the offense worse than drunkenness and would rather see his brother drunk than engaged in such actions seems to me unexcusable and his attitude generally promises all sorts of difficulties in the future for the University.

I have talked with undergraduates, with Trustees, with Alumni about this matter and I have not found a single one who upholds the Dean in his extremely severe discipline. I feel that such things work great harm for the University and I regret exceedingly that the change in the Deanship has placed a man in that important position who seems to have so little fitness for the post.

Many of these students will leave Princeton and it will work great injury to the College. It was a similar mistake of discipline and an act of injustice some twenty-five years ago which punished Robert Todd,[3] which prevented Princeton from being remembered in the Will of Mr. John S. Kennedy, as I have been told by his family.[4] Columbia is to receive nearly Four Millions of Dollars from Mr. Kennedy.[5] As many of his family graduated at Princeton and not Columbia, this money, except for that act of injustice might have gone to Princeton.

I wish something could be done to make the families of these students feel that the action of the Dean in this present case did not represent either the feeling or the future policy of Princeton.

Very sincerely yours, W. Merle-Smith

TLS (WP, DLC).

[1] Princeton 1877, pastor of the Central Presbyterian Church of New York.

[2] The Senior Council, at a meeting on November 16, 1909, after having thoroughly investigated the entire affair, resolved that the culprits "were at fault and deserving of reprimand," but that the Discipline Committee's punishment was "unjustifiable." *Daily Princetonian*, Nov. 17, 1909.

[3] Robert Elliott Tod, who, along with another sophomore, had been expelled from Princeton on September 22, 1885, for hazing a freshman. Princeton conferred the B.S. degree as of the Class of 1888 upon him in 1913.

[4] John Stewart Kennedy, Scottish-born banker and philanthropist of New York, who had died on October 31, 1909. Robert Elliott Tod was his nephew.

[5] Newspaper reports of his bequest to Columbia were exaggerated. He left $1,600,000 to that university, having already given Columbia $500,000 to build Hamilton Hall.

Two Letters from Moses Taylor Pyne

My dear Woodrow New York November 30/09

I was very sorry to miss you yesterday and have made several efforts to find you while in Princeton as I wanted to assure you that the differences of opinion we have held, in two matters only, during your administration have made no chang[e] in the friendship and affection I have for you and that I trust your feelings towards me have not changed.

I should not have even thought it necessary to say this, but some of our friends do not seem to realize that the friendship of over thirty years and the intimate association and companionship of fifteen or twenty years cannot be broken by difference of opinion as to the manner of carrying on a work as to the result of which we are entirely at one.

I hope that you appreciate that I am just as much behind you & ready to support you in every way that I can consistently with my oath as Trustee and that I do not & never will allow any personalities to enter into my work. So much idle rumour has gone about that I do not know what you have heard said, but I trust that you will not believe that I have done or said anything that I should not repeat to your face

Affectionately M Taylor Pyne

My dear Woodrow New York Dec 1/09

Cram has sent his plans for Thompson College. I suppose that we should have a committee meeting in the near future, as soon as may be, to consider them and I am writing to ask you to tell me what time would be most convenient for you.

I presume that New York will be the best place to hold the meeting as most of us are here or apt to be here & Jacobus can get here much easier than to Princeton.

With kind regards I am

Yours very sincerely M Taylor Pyne

ALS (WP, DLC).

From Cyrus Hall McCormick

My dear sir: Chicago 1 December, 1909.

You may remember that last spring, when the debating teams were preparing for their contests, I secured the assistance of James H. Gore, Professor in the George Washington University,[1] Washington, D. C., who went to Princeton and coached the members of the team for one or two days. Professor Gore had already been to Yale and had coached the Yale team on the same subject.

I just learn that the Yale Faculty have asked Professor Gore to come to Yale to teach Corporation Economics and Insurance, but as he does not wish to tie himself up to any one institution, he has declined the call but has agreed to give Yale a course of lectures on "Anti-Trust Legislation and its Effects." I believe that no one in Washington is more acquainted with this subject than Professor Gore, and if it should be desirable for the Princeton boys to have such a course of lectures, I shall be very glad to provide the means if you wish to arrange it with Professor Gore. In writing about the matter, he says:

> "I feel that it is most important that our young people should be impregnated with sane ideas on this subject. We are liable to have for a few years considerable 'backing and filling' on this subject and the coming generation may have the final settlement in their hands."

If you and the Faculty think favorably of this, you can write to Professor Gore yourself and arrange the terms with him *without telling him that I have any connection with the matter* except to say that I have brought it to your attention. If you do not care for such a course of lectures, please let me know and I will write to Professor Gore, dropping the matter where it is.[2]

I am, Very sincerely yours, Cyrus H. McCormick.

TLS (WP, DLC).

[1] About Gore, see H. B. Fine to WW, April 1, 1909, n. 1.

[2] About Gore's lectures at Princeton, see C. H. McCormick to H. B. Fine, March 24, 1909, n. 2, printed as an Enclosure with H. B. Fine to WW, April 1, 1909.

From Carl Gustav Schulz[1]

Dear Dr. Wilson, Saint Paul [Minn.] December 1, 1909.

The President of our State University, Dr. Northrop, will retire at the end of this school year. The Regents, in choosing his successor, desire to secure the man who can best continue to build upon the splendid foundation that Dr. Northrop has laid. We have not, as a board, considered any individuals. Several of the regents, with myself, are very firm in the conviction that there is no other man who would so fully meet the situation as yourself.

Our State University is a splendid institution, and its possibilities of growth and usefulness are great. Its permanent endowment at present is somewhat more than three million dollars. There are still unsold lands which will very largely increase this sum. The legislature is unusually liberal in its support, both as regards the current expense fund and for buildings and improvements.

The relations between the State University and the puvlic [public] schools of the state are noth [both] close and friendly. Our public schools constitute a correlated and closely united and at the same time perfectly elastic system. The state high schools number 210; graded schools of four and six departments make another total of 165; the rural schools enroll about 35,000 pupils.

Next to Dr. Northrop, no other college or university president in the country commands so great a share of the confidence, respect, and admiration of the public school men in Minnesota as do you.

These, however, may not be considered as vital reasons for you to consider an acceptance of this position, if tendered. The chief reason would lie in the possibility of large and useful service. No greater impetus or uplift could be given to public education in Minnesota and the Northwest than your election to and acceptance of the presidency of our State University. I trust you will not consider that I am presumptuous in bringing the matter before you in this way. Some of the regents, I think, will call upon you in person.

I am sure that you will give the matter that careful and deliberate consideration which is characteristic not only of yourself, but one of the distinguishing traits in the training which has made Princeton famous.

I enclose the educational directory of the state,[2] which will indicate the membership of the Board of Regents, as well as the fact that the president of the University is *ex officio* a member of the State High School Board, and is thus brought into closer relationship with the secondary schools of the state.

Yours very truly, C. G. Schulz.

TLS (WP, DLC).

1 Superintendent of the Department of Public Instruction of the State of Minnesota and member of the Board of Regents of the University of Minnesota.

2 The enclosure is missing.

From Adolf Frederick Schauffler[1]

My dear Sir: New York City. Dec. 1st, 1909.

I have learned of the difficulty that has arisen in Princeton with ten Freshmen, owing to their "rough housing," and I desire to ascertain from you as an authoritative source the facts in response to the following questions.

1st. Is it a fact that when a student in Princeton is found intoxicated, he is warned?

2nd. Is it a fact that if the student is intoxicated a second time he is suspended for two weeks?

3rd. Is it a fact that some ten Freshmen were suspended for "rough housing" not in any way connected with the use of intoxicating drink for four weeks?

If the above three statements call for an affirmative reply, is it a fact that you consider the discipline enforced on the Freshmen as mentioned above equitable and just in comparison with that meted out for intoxication?

You may possibly ask yourself what reason I have to ask for a reply to the above. My answer is, that I have been asked more than once to recommend colleges for bequests, and have been asked to do so in two different cases within the last three weeks, and I desire, light, therefore, on the attitude that you take as the head of Princeton University with regard to the matters referred to above.

I may add that I have read the correspondence between the Dean and Mr. Stephen Baker.

Yours very respectfully, A. F. Schauffler

TLS (WP, DLC).

1 Congregationalist minister, at this time President of the New York City Mission and Tract Society.

Moses Taylor Pyne to Joseph Bernard Shea

My dear Joe: [Princeton, N. J.] December 1st, 1909.

Messrs. Cram, Goodhue & Ferguson have sent me the Ground Plan drawings for the Graduate College and I have written to the President asking him to arrange a date for a meeting in New York. I cannot tell yet, of course, what time he will set but I shall telegraph you as soon as I hear from him, as I am anxious that you shall be present at the meeting if it can be arranged.

Matters are going on quietly and I hope that the final determination as to the site made by the Board at the last meeting will stand. I have a strong approval in legal form signed by all Mrs. Swann's executors.

Yours very sincerely, M. Taylor Pyne.

TCL (M. T. Pyne Coll., NjP).

From William Henry Grant[1]

My dear Dr. Wilson, New York, N. Y. Dec. 2, 1909.

In connection with the Seventeenth Conference of Foreign Missions Boards of the United States and Canada, which meets in the Chapel of the Marble Collegiate Church, 29th Street and Fifth Avenue, New York, January 12-14, 1910, it is proposed to devote the afternoon of Wednesday, January 12th, to a special conference on Christian Education in China. Several of the New York members of the Committee of Christian Education in China, of which you are a member,[2] have assented to the calling of a meeting of the Committee at five o'clock Wednesday, January 12th, immediately following the session of the conference of Foreign Missions Boards, and if it can be arranged, to continue in session after dinner.

We will have with us in this connection Professor Ernest DeWitt Burton, one of the "Commissioners of the University of Chicago Oriental Educational Investigation."[3] I have written Dr. Burton that the laymen on the China Educational Committee, which is composed of very busy men with very large problems in administrative lines, feel the need of a comprehensive presentation of the situation in China, including the status of the present Christian institutions: That from this ground they can better proceed inductively to lay out their own course of procedure, rather than to have a formulated plan immediately laid before them for approval: That it is a most critical time, and that the representatives of the Boards are ready to discuss the subject and develop a policy of advance as never before, and, yet, that we need to have ourselves and the Committee impressed with the personal and national call to meet a personal and national reciprocal crisis in America and China.

Doctor Burton will occupy the time immediately following the reassembling of the conference after lunch, say, at three o'clock, in the Chapel of the Marble Collegiate Church.

We trust that these arrangements may suit your convenience and lead you to lay aside your other burdens for the time being to give attention to this most important matter. Kindly state whether you can attend on the afternoon of January 12th, and also an evening session if one is found practicable.[4]

Sincerely, W Henry Grant

TLS (WP, DLC).

1 Gentleman of independent means who was deeply involved in foreign missionary work. See W. H. Grant to WW, Dec. 19, 1908, n. 1, Vol. 18.

2 See A. J. Brown to WW, March 17, 1909, and the notes thereto.

3 The Oriental Educational Commission was established by the trustees of the University of Chicago in April 1908. There were only two "commissioners": Burton, Professor and Head of the Department of New Testament Literature and Interpretation, and Thomas Chrowder Chamberlin, Professor and Head of the Department of Geology. Rollin Thomas Chamberlin, Instructor in Geology, and Horace Garner Reed, a recent graduate in law, were appointed secretaries to the commission. The work of the commission was financed by John D. Rockefeller, who was at this time considering the possibility of establishing a university in China modeled on the University of Chicago, a scheme which was soon abandoned as impractical. The principal activity of the commission was a year-long trip to the Middle East, India, China, and Japan, with brief stops in other countries along the way, carried out between August 1908 and August 1909, to study educational conditions and opportunities for Orientals. A manuscript report in six volumes was prepared and submitted to the President and Board of Trustees of the University of Chicago in November and December 1909. It was never published. An indirect result of the work of the commission was the decision of the trustees of the Rockefeller Foundation in 1914 to concentrate their efforts in China upon medical work and education. See Raymond B. Fosdick, *The Story of the Rockefeller Foundation* (New York, 1952), pp. 24-25, 80-82, and "The Oriental Educational Commission," *University of Chicago Magazine*, II (Nov. 1909), 24-29.

4 Wilson may well have attended, but there is nothing in the proceedings of the *Seventeenth Conference of Foreign Missions Boards in the United States and Canada at New York January 12th, 13th and 14th, 1910* (New York, n. d.) to verify that supposition. There was very little coverage of the conference in the New York newspapers and no lists of those in attendance.

To Stephen Baker

My dear Mr. Baker: [Princeton, N. J.] December 3rd, 1909.

A brief absence from home has delayed my reply to your letter of November 30th.

I certainly did not intend to evade the question put to me in your former letter. I thought that it answered itself. I very cheerfully, therefore, answer it now.

I can say with the utmost emphasis that we do not regard the offence against college order committed by your son as in any way comparable in moral gravity with the offence of intoxication. We agree with all Christian men in thinking intoxication one of the most demoralizing and ominous offences, I mean ominous for the young man's future, that an undergraduate can be guilty of. I can think of only one other offence which seems to have wider moral significance, and that is sexual impurity. We have never intended to draw any comparison between offences of disorder and the offence of drunkenness.

But it does not at all follow, it seems to us, that the two offences should be treated upon any scale of comparative values in the matter of such a thing as the length of suspension. The offence of intoxication is, so to say, a private and individual offence. It carries with it a particular social discredit. Many a lad is drawn into it almost unconsciously and is taken by surprise by it when he thought himself careful. To suspend a man for drunkenness is to send him home for an offence which cannot be explained to his friends without bringing upon him a peculiar kind and degree of discredit which does not attach to the offence which your son committed. That is an offence which does not go to the root of moral principle and which, therefore, while deserving of punishment, does not involve disgrace. We have sought to deal with all cases of intoxication in a way which would be most likely to save the lad from further yielding to temptation.

That we have not been wholly mistaken in our method of dealing with it is shown by the very great and encouraging decrease of drunkenness in recent years in the college. Nothing has gratified us more than the fact that drinking is coming to be more and more rare amongst us as compared with the earlier years with which many of us are familiar. We join with all Christian men in regarding the use of intoxicating liquors as one of the most serious things in the life of young men. I beg that you will not misjudge us in this very fundamental matter.

The disorder in which your son took part was concerted, persistent, and directed against two women[1] who were particularly distressed by it and terrified because, in common with other women in their circumstances, they feared to report to the college authorities. The disorder went very far and constituted a very serious breach of college discipline. We may have been mistaken in our judgment as to the proper length of punishment, but we cannot have been mistaken in thinking that the punishment inflicted was of the right sort and that it was necessary. Very sincerely yours, [Woodrow Wilson]

CCL (WWP, UA, NjP).

[1] That is, Mrs. Easton, owner of the boarding house at 47 University Place, and perhaps a woman in her employ, whose identity cannot be determined.

To Adolf Frederick Schauffler

[Princeton, N. J.]

My dear Dr. Schauffler: December 3rd, 1909.

I very cheerfully reply to the questions contained in your letter of December 1st.

First: It has been our usual practice, when a student was found intoxicated, to warn him that any repetition of the offence would be followed by severe discipline.

Second: When a student is found intoxicated a second time, after being warned, he is generally suspended for a minimum of four weeks. The suspension is often longer.[1]

Third: It is a fact that ten freshmen were recently suspended for extreme disorder which was not in any connected with the use of intoxicating drink, and that most of them were suspended for the period of four weeks.

I consider the punishment imposed in this case both just and necessary. It was no ordinary rough play on the part of boys. It was persisted in for several days very systematically and was directed against two women who were particularly helpless in the circumstances because they had reason to fear that, if they took any action in the matter, they would put their house upon a black list and would be prevented from making their living. The disorder went very far beyond the bounds of such occasional outbursts of roughness as might be attributed to the thoughtlessness and high spirits of young men just out of school. The University has never winked at matters of this kind and has always punished them when it has come under its observation.

The implication of your question, however, namely that the University regards the offence of these young men as worse than the offence of drunkenness, is in no way justified. I am confident that I speak, not only for myself but for my colleagues, when I say that we look upon the offence of drunkenness as all Christian people must look upon it. I can think of only one offence characteristic of young men which would be more demoralizing or more ominous for a man's future, and that is the offence of sexual impurity. We have never instituted any comparison between offences such as your questions would intimate.

It seems to us very obvious, however, that offences should be dealt with according to their nature. Intoxication is generally, with us, an individual offence committed against morals and against the boy's own better nature and seems to us susceptible at the outset of being dealt with by moral suasion rather than by putting upon the boy what would be considered an open disgrace. We do not regard suspensions for other offences not moral in their nature as involving disgrace, because all friends of the boys concerned can be frankly told what the offence was, without throwing a doubt upon the boy's future.

We are encouraged to believe that we have not been mistaken in the way we have dealt with intoxication by the fact that intoxication has greatly decreased in recent years at Princeton. Indeed, nothing has gratified me more than the steady decrease of the drinking habit among our undergraduates. You would be putting upon the University a very unmerited stain if you supposed for a moment that we did not regard that offence in the light in which it should be regarded by all men who care anything for the welfare of their fellowmen.

With much respect,

Sincerely yours, [Woodrow Wilson]

CCL (WWP, UA, NjP).

[1] A reading of the Princeton University Faculty minutes for 1908 and 1909 leaves no doubt about the accuracy of this statement.

To Wilton Merle-Smith

My dear Dr. Smith: [Princeton, N. J.] December 3rd, 1909.

You assume a very grave responsibility when, upon an ex parte statement of the case, you condemn the University upon a matter carefully considered and conscientiously acted upon by the constituted authorities. The offence was not of an ordinary character. It seems to me to be all the more grave because persistently and systematically engaged in by young gentlemen of the highest breeding, who should have felt specially bound to behave differently. No example could be more demoralizing to their classmates than the example of men of their sort.

You do a very grave injustice to the very fine man who has assumed the duties of Dean of the College. He enjoys the admiration and confidence of his colleagues and, I am sure, has acted in this matter as in others with the sincere desire to serve the best interests of the University.

I am very much surprised that any question of our judgment with regard to intoxication should have entered into this case. Certainly in any scale of comparative values we should all agree with Christian men everywhere in ranking intoxication as one of the most serious and demoralizing offences young men could commit. We have always regarded it so, but it does not follow that it should be treated in the same manner in which other offences are treated. It is the result, oftentimes, of private and individual temptation. To send a young man home for it is to make it necessary to explain to his friends that he has been guilty of what involves social discredit of a kind not at all involved in the offence committed by the young men at 47 University Place. It is often possible to assist a youngster to pull up in a matter of this sort at once by proper consideration for him. That we have not been unsuccessful in the administration of justice in this matter is evidenced by the very great decrease in drinking in the college and the steady continuance of that decrease from year to year. You would put a most unmerited stain upon your Alma Mater by assuming that our attitude in this matter was different from that of men of honor and thoughtfulness everywhere.

And I must protest, my dear Dr. Smith, most earnestly and solemnly against your intimation that the pecuniary interests of the University are not served by action of this sort. Nothing could be more demoralizing to the administration of the University than to admit considerations of that sort, and when they are admitted in the matter of the administration of discipline in Princeton, it will not be under my presidency.

I hope that you will appreciate the very great shock which your letter gave me and my earnest desire that you should know the real attitude of the University in matters of this kind.

Very truly yours, [Woodrow Wilson]

CCL (WWP, UA, NjP).

To Moses Taylor Pyne

My dear Momo: [Princeton, N. J.] December 3rd, 1909.

I wish that you would be kind enough to send Mr. Cram's plans to Mr. Capps, the Secretary of the Faculty Committee on the Graduate School, in order that the committee and I may go over them before the Committee of the Board takes them up for consideration. It is very necessary indeed that this should be done, in order that the plans should be adapted at the outset as carefully as possible to the purpose they are to serve.

I am sending this letter, though I hope to see you today at or after the Cuyler memorial service.

Always faithfully yours, [Woodrow Wilson]

CCL (WWP, UA, NjP).

To Charles Richard Van Hise[1]

Princeton, N. J.

My dear President Van Hise: December 3rd, 1909.

Thank you sincerely for your kind letter of November 30th.[2] It will give me great pleasure to be the guest of Mrs. Van Hise[3] and yourself when I come to Madison next month.[4] I am afraid that I shall be obliged, because of other engagements, to cut my cloth rather close in the matter of time, but I shall certainly wish to avail myself of your great kindness in asking me to come a little earlier than the date set for the opening of the meeting.

With much regard,

Cordially and sincerely yours, Woodrow Wilson

TLS (Presidents' Files, WU).

[1] President of the University of Wisconsin.

[2] It is missing.

[3] Alice Bushnell Ring Van Hise.

[4] To attend the meeting of the Association of American Universities.

A Draft of a Letter to G. McArthur Sullivan

[c. Dec. 3, 1909]

Regret to say that it is altogether inadvisable for a colored man to enter Princeton. Appreciate his desire to do so, but strongly recommend his securing education in a Southern institution perhaps completing it with a course at the Princeton Theol. Sem., which is under entirely separate control from the Univ. For information about Sem. apply to Rev Paul Martin, Secretary P. T. S.[1]

WWhw MS (UA, NjP).

[1] Sullivan did not attend Princeton Theological Seminary. For the letter sent to him, see C. W. McAlpin to G. M. Sullivan, Dec. 6, 1909.

From Charles Grosvenor Osgood

My dear Dr. Wilson: [Princeton, N. J.] December 3, 1909.

You will, I feel sure, be personally interested and pleased to learn that I am engaged to be married to Miss Bella Owen.[1]

I think Miss Owen has told Mrs. Wilson, but the announcement is not to be made until Saturday afternoon. Could I ask you not to mention it to others until then?

Believe me, always with warmest regard,

Faithfully yours, Charles G. Osgood

ALS (WP, DLC).

[1] Isabella Sheldon Owen. They were married on January 29, 1910.

A News Report

[Dec. 4, 1909]

A FITTING TRIBUTE

Services in Memory of C. C. Cuyler '79
Rendered Impressive by Their Simplicity.

The memorial services in honor of Cornelius C. Cuyler '79, held yesterday afternoon in Marquand Chapel, paid a fitting tribute to the life of a man who devoted so much of his time to caring for the interests of Princeton. The large crowd of friends and relatives assembled in the Chapel heard impressive addresses by President Wilson, the Rev. Dr. Thomas C. Hall[1] and Dr. Henry van Dyke, and during the service well chosen musical selections were rendered.

In speaking of Mr. Cuyler, President Wilson referred to his many-sidedness, saying that it was impossible for one man to know him in all his characters. Not only was he a great man of business, as the ordinary world believed, but he was influential in many organizations which were not connected with his business. Mr. Cuyler's work as a trustee of Princeton University was a labor of love and of service as an enthusiastic son. As trustee of the School of Classicial Studies in Rome, he was the moving force and enthusiasm to which the school owed its existence. Again, as president of the Musical Art Society,[2] it was his spirit that gave impetus to the newly founded society. He had a genius for friendship, with the true spirit of service which went beyond the mere matter of pleasing the heart in its deep sympathy. He carried into his maturity the abounding life and unquenchable vivacity of his boyhood, with its constant joy of action. In the hour of sorrow and deep recollections we can remember that the spirit is permanent and that a life which contains it can never wholly lose that spirit.[3]

Printed in the *Daily Princetonian*, Dec. 4, 1909.

1 Class of 1879, Professor of Christian Ethics at Union Theological Seminary in New York since 1898.

2 Cuyler had been President of the Board of Trustees of the Institute of Musical Art since its founding in 1905. See n. 1 to Wilson's remarks at the opening exercises of the Institute, printed at Oct. 31, 1905, Vol. 16.

3 There is a WWT outline of this address, dated Dec. 3, 1909, in WP, DLC.

To Henry Fairfield Osborn

Princeton, N. J.

My dear Professor Osborn: December 4th, 1909.

Thank you most sincerely for your very kind letter of yesterday.[1] I am very glad indeed that you thought the memorial service to Cuyler so satisfactory. I was myself surprised at the absence of the undergraduates. They were apprised of the service and invited in every way we knew how to use, but they always prove shy in matters of this sort, particularly when they think the company likely to assemble one of unusual dignity. There was a considerable number of representative undergraduates present, however, I am happy to say.

It is very kind of Mrs. Osborn[2] and you to invite me to address the Thursday Evening Club[3] and I wish most unaffectedly that I were free for the evening of January 6th, but unhappily I must attend the meeting of the Association of American Universities in Madison, Wisconsin, on the fourth and fifth of January and on the sixth shall be on my way to Lancaster, Pa., to attend the inauguration of the new President of Franklin and Marshall on the seventh.[4]

I know that I am missing a real pleasure.

Always cordially and faithfully yours,

Woodrow Wilson

TLS (WC, NjP).

1 It is missing.

2 Lucretia Perry Osborn.

3 Founded in 1878 with the intention of bringing together the "intellect of Columbia College and the society of Washington Square," the club came to include many "kindred spirits interested in the arts, literature, music and science." Meetings were held on the first and third Thursdays of each month, from December through April, no meetings being held during Lent. See Frank L. Baker, "Club of Famous Wits Rounds Out 50 Years," *New York Times*, Feb. 5, 1928.

4 Wilson's address at the inauguration of Henry Harbaugh Apple is printed at Jan. 7, 1910.

To Charles Henry Marshall[1]

My dear Mr. Marshall: Princeton, N. J. December 4th, 1909.

I have received your circular of December third containing the names of Major General Leonard Wood and the Hon. George W. Wickersham as having been nominated for membership in the Round Table Club and am glad to express my own opinion as entirely favorable to their election.

I have been very unfortunate in being unable to attend the dinners of the club, but I hope to give myself that pleasure later.

Very cordially yours, Woodrow Wilson

TLS (Round Table Dining Club Scrapbook, NHi).

1 Chairman of the New York board of the Liverpool & London & Globe Insurance Co., Ltd., and Secretary of the Round Table Club of New York, about which see WW to C. H. Marshall, Dec. 26, 1902, n. 3, Vol. 14.

To Charles Grosvenor Osgood

My dear Mr. Osgood, Princeton, N. J. 4 December, 1909.

I congratulate you with all my heart, and rejoice in your happiness. There is no one in Princeton whom Mrs. Wilson and I esteem and admire more than Miss Owen, and our warm admiration for you and our sincere desire that you should find happiness and contentment here combine with our feeling for her to make the news you so kindly send me delightfully welcome.

Cordially and faithfully Yours, Woodrow Wilson

ALS (Selected Papers of C. G. Osgood, NjP).

From Richard Spencer Childs

Dear Dr. Wilson: New York Dec. 4th, 1909

In connection with the enclosed plan for the Short Ballot Banquet,[1] may we ask you to set a date in the last part of January or the first part of February when you could preside over the banquet and speak at length upon The Short Ballot principle?[2]

Yours very truly, Richard S. Childs Secretary.

TLS (WP, DLC).

[1] Enclosed was R. S. Childs to the Advisory Board of the Short Ballot Organization, Dec. 4, 1909, TLS (WP, DLC), together with a typed invitation form. In the letter, Childs explained that the Executive Board of the Short Ballot Organization proposed to hold a banquet inviting as free guests about one hundred men of "power and influence," with as many more as possible of "ordinary individuals," who would be charged for their dinners. The "central feature" of the program was to be an explanation of the short ballot principle by Wilson.

[2] See R. S. Childs to WW, Dec. 9, 1909.

From Stephen Baker

My dear Sir: New York, December 4, 1909.

I beg to thank you for your letter of the 3rd inst.

In justice to myself, I must ask you to kindly submit our correspondence to the Meeting of the University Faculty, which I understand is to be held on Monday, the sixth of December, and I shall trust to hear at an early date of their action in the premises.[1] Very sincerely yours, Stephen Baker

TLS (WP, DLC).

[1] Wilson did not submit his correspondence with Baker to the faculty. However, see W. F. Magie to D. C. Jones, Jr., Dec. 8, 1909, and its Enclosure.

From Job Herbert Lippincott[1]

My dear Mr. Wilson: Jersey City, N. J. December 4, 1909.

Your letter of the 3rd inst. received. It is with great regret that the Committee learned of your inability to be present on the 11th inst.[2] I am writing to you in the hope that it may be possible in some way to arrange matters so that you may be able to attend the dinner and speak. The dinner will commence about 6:30 o'clock, and as Princeton is very near, we could arrange it so that your speech could be at any time during the course of the dinner most convenient to yourself. I do not think that the dinner will be over much before eleven or half past, so that if it were possible for you to come during the evening be assured that you would have a large and interested audience waiting for you. Would it not be possible for you to arrange to be with us for at least a brief time, as you are doubtless aware, your tariff speeches have created a wide impression, and the State Committee are very anxious that the party organization should have an opportunity to hear your address.[3]

With kind regards, I am

Very truly yours, Job H Lippincott

TLS (WP, DLC).

1 A bank teller at the Commercial Trust Company of New Jersey; President of the Board of Excise of Jersey City; and Chairman of the Democratic State Auxiliary Committee.

2 A conference of leaders of the Democratic party in New Jersey was to be held in Trenton in the afternoon of December 11, 1909, to discuss prospects for the gubernatorial campaign during the coming year. The conference, which was arranged by the Democratic State Auxiliary Committee, was to be followed by a dinner at which major party leaders in the state would speak.

3 As late as the day of the conference itself, the *Trenton Evening Times* reported that Woodrow Wilson was to be one of the featured speakers at the dinner and printed a picture of him on its front page. However, in its account of the affair in the issue of December 13, 1909, the *Evening Times* reported that a letter of regret from Wilson had been read at the dinner.

A News Report of an Address to the Philadelphia Teachers' Association

[Dec. 5, 1909]

SCHOOLS ARRAIGNED BY WOODROW WILSON

Dr. Woodrow Wilson, president of Princeton University, speaking last night before the annual meeting of the Philadelphia Teachers' Association at the William Penn High School, arraigned the system of public education in force in this country in a fashion that was characteristically incisive, and dismissed it as a process that is bound ultimately to perish of its own futility and thus make way for a more rational and effective method.

In the course of his address Dr. Wilson sharply differentiated between instruction—which he deemed the adequate definition of the present system of teaching in the public schools—and education. Instruction as it is practiced, the packing into the pupil of a vast quantity of miscellaneous information which has neither his interest or sympathetic understanding, is, he said, not worth paying out the public money for.

Education he deemed an entirely different matter and a priceless attribute, once attained. The fault with the present system of instruction, the speaker said, had grown out of the ambition of the scho[o]ls to cover the entire broadening field of human knowledge in the curriculum, without regard to the fact that the field was constantly widening and that the capacity of the human mind remains unchanged.

The common error is in the belief that knowledge is the object of education when it is, instead, the mere raw material, and when the best efforts of the schools should be directed to training the minds of the pupils properly to wield it after they leave the schools.

Dr. Wilson began his address with a word about the common assertion that the schools of the country are under fire under a prompt necessity of readjustment to the needs of society, which supports them. He pictured the pupil as subjected in the schools to the action of a stupendous stream of what he classified roughly as "information," which is caused to pass over him, depositing, possibly, a thin stratum of knowledge which rarely, however, penetrated to his inner consciousness.

As a result the pupil is thrown out into the tide of affairs in an age which the speaker characterized as the most difficult that this world has known in which "to hold one's self-possession," and is compelled in his own fashion to discern and to use the powers of his mind to keep afloat.

Instead, Dr. Wilson said the schools should teach the mind to feel[,] to explore, to be curious. He prophesied the early readjustment of the present system, and said this is a necessity.

With the evils of the system under which they are teaching, he continued, the instructors have to fight the evil of outside interests which frequently leave the pupil in anything but a receptive state of mind. Speaking of athletic and other interests in the schools and colleges, Dr. Wilson repeated his famous assertion that "the side show has swallowed the circus"—that education in the schools wasn't in its proper place on the front of the stage, but had a place in the wings, to appear occasionally between the acts.

He closed with a hope and a prophecy for the time when schools and colleges would again become places for education primarily.

Printed in the Philadelphia *North American*, Dec. 5, 1909; some editorial headings omitted.

To Thomas Nelson Page

Princeton, N. J. December sixth [1909]

Mr. Woodrow Wilson accepts with pleasure and appreciation the kind invitation of Mr. Thomas Nelson Page, to dine with him on Tuesday evening,[1] December fourteenth, at eight o'clock, to meet the members of the American Academy of Arts and Letters.

HwL (T. N. Page Papers, NcD).

[1] At his home in Washington, D. C.

To Abbott Lawrence Lowell

[Princeton, N. J.]

My dear President Lowell: December 6th, 1909.

I have entertained for a good many years the feeling expressed in a paragraph in the current number of Harpers' Weekly,[1] namely that the Presidents of Harvard, Yale and Princeton could, if they were to agree upon a principle of action and insist upon it, very largely and perhaps completely control the methods of the game of football, and I am taking the liberty of writing to you to ask if it would be agreeable to you to have an informal conference on the subject, to see if we could come to any wise or practicable decision.

It seems to me very clear that the game as at present played is unnecessarily dangerous and contains an unnecessary number of temptations to brutality. It would be a very delightful thing if we could meet public opinion half way in this matter and effect some reform that would save a very noble game. I have no doubt that I am merely anticipating your own thought in this matter.

I am writing to this effect also to President Hadley.[2]

With cordial regard,

Faithfully yours, [Woodrow Wilson]

CCL (WWP, UA, NjP).

[1] An editorial, "Three Doctors Who Can Cure Football," *Harper's Weekly*, LIII (Dec. 4, 1909), 5, described the apprehension of a mother as she awaited news of her two boys who were playing in a football game in Washington. One of the boys suffered a broken neck and died. The editorial continued: "Dr. Hadley, Dr. Lowell, Dr. Wilson, don't you think football, as it was played this year, is a little rough? There had been twenty-seven deaths up to November 21st, gentle-

men, and a multitude of injuries, and the dying was not all done at that time. Many of the deaths had come from injuries received in previous years. Many injuries received this year will kill in a little time.

"You could stop this kind of football if you chose, you three men. The mothers can't, poor souls. . . . But you, if you thought it wise and were agreed, could stop the kind of football that has been played this year, and that has trebled the death-rate. . . ."

2 WW to A. T. Hadley, Dec. 6, 1909, TLS (A. T. Hadley Papers, Archives, CtY).

From Winthrop More Daniels

My dear Wilson: Princeton, N. J. Dec. 6, 1909.

On the 4th. inst. I received from Mr. Close the enclosure of Mr. McCormick's letter, and a request to forward my opinion upon the project.

I am in favor of having the lectures given provided we can be sure of three things;–first, that he (Prof. Gore) is to give under the auspices of Yale University the course of lectures on "Anti-Trust Legislation." I assume that this is the case from Mr. McCormick's letter, but we ought to be sure that he comes properly accredited. Second, the lectures would have, of course, to be optional, i.e. outside the regular curriculum which is sufficiently exacting as it is. Third, the success of the course would depend somewhat on their number. Ten or twelve lectures well-bunched, would be best. I suggest that we go about it on a modest scale at first,–take a small lecture room, and then if occasion calls for it, move up into a larger one. In this expression of opinion I am influenced in some considerable measure by what I think would be of benefit to the Graduate students of whom we have 12 in our Department. We could very readily utilize additional lecturers and lectures for the graduate students, if we could only promise in advance in our Programme of Courses the prospect of such lectures as those contemplated in this course. Very sincerely yours, W. M. Daniels.

(Enclosure of Mr. McCormick's letter of Dec 1/09)

TLS (WP, DLC).

Charles Williston McAlpin to G. McArthur Sullivan

My dear Sir: [Princeton, N. J.] December 6, 1909.

Your letter of November 20th to President Wilson has been referred to me and while appreciating your desire to enter Princeton I regret to say that it is altogether inadvisable for you to consider doing so.

I would strongly recommend you to secure your education in a Southern institution or, if you wish to attend a Northern institution I would suggest that you correspond with the authorities of Harvard, Dartmouth, or Brown; the last named being, as you undoubtedly know, a Baptist Institution.

Yours very truly, [C. W. McAlpin] Secretary.

CCL (UA, NjP).

From Ralph Adams Cram

Dear Dr. Wilson: Boston, December 7, 1909

I beg to acknowledge the receipt of your letter of November 29, in which you take up the question of the proposed Cleveland memorial tower. This letter should have been answered before, but I am just back from Texas, where I had to go in connection with the proposed buildings for the Rice Institute. You, of course, know of these, since Dr. [Edgar Odell] Lovett, the President, was formerly a member of the Faculty at Princeton. I am glad to say that our drawings and visit were successful, and the work has been definitely placed in our hands. This involves a general scheme for the whole layout, with its development for the next century, a million dollars worth of buildings to be constructed next Spring, and more to follow yearly until the whole project is carried out.

I confess, I feel sorry, in a way, that our first sketch for the Cleveland tower should not have appealed to you; not that we are in the least averse to revising our ideas and trying one or more new schemes for this same tower. It is a matter of such vital importance that, as I wrote Mr. Pyne, it should be studied and restudied until we are quite sure we have the right thing. That the sketches we sent you indicated this same "right thing," we are not disposed to hold. Personally, we like them as a beginning, but only as a beginning. We had hoped, however, they might serve for the Sub-Committee as sufficient material on which they could report to the full Committee, that the proposed memorial should take the form of a tower to be built in connection with the Graduate School, and that the full Committee might then report back to us that the recommendation of the Sub-Committee had been adopted and that we should proceed at once to study and restudy the tower, both in the shape of drawings, and models, until we were sure we had the right thing. If I read your letter aright, you do not consider that even these sketches we sent you are adequate for the purpose indicated above and that you want us to make another attempt before you make your report to the full Committee.

This, of course, we are perfectly willing to do, but we are a little in doubt as to just what lines the Sub-Committee feels we ought to follow. You say, for instance, that in your opinion our tower was too much like Mr. Day's. This we do not quite understand. We made every possible effort to differentiate our design from the Sage tower in every conceivable way. We chose a different proportion, a different fenestration, a different corner treatment and, finally, different details. It doesn't seem to us that the two designs have anything in common, except the fact that both are towers. Again, you say that it seems to you that our design has "an appearance of heaviness," that it doesn't seem to you "to soar quite enough." You also say that it seems to you and Mr. Pyne that we might come closer in the case of the Cleveland tower to Magdalen, but also that your own choice "would be something broad and solid like the Founders tower at Magdalen."

There seem to be a good many different ideas here, and I am a little at a loss to know which line we had better follow, that is, whether we had best try for a tall, soaring tower like Magdalen, or a low, powerful mass like the Founders tower. Personally, it seems to me that if the Graduate College is to be built on the golf links site and the Cleveland tower is to form its dominating feature, the tower itself should be lofty and imposing, rather than low and powerful like the Founders tower; in other words, a very tall mass which may be seen from a long distance. Such a tower as the Founders tower would, of course, hardly be seen at all, as it rises not much more than a story above the roof level.

Any ideas you may have on the subject, I beg you will send to us at your earliest convenience, and I would ask also that you return to us, as soon as you can, our first sketches for this same tower, as we have no copies of them and should need them as a basis for our new study. Very truly yours, R A Cram.

TLS (WP, DLC).

Moses Taylor Pyne to Edward Capps

My dear Prof. Capps: [Princeton, N. J.] December 7th, 1909.

I am sending by this mail the Ground Plan of the proposed Graduate College as prepared by Mr. Cram, regarding which I spoke to you yesterday. The President has complained about the Breakfast Rooms, but under Mrs. Swann's Will it is expressly provided that the Thompson Building shall contain kitchens and *dining rooms* for the residents. In that case it will be impossible to substitute any outside building for a dining room.

I hope that there will be no delay in the matter, as it is really vital for several reasons to have the buildings begun this spring. . . . Yours very sincerely, M. Taylor Pyne.

TCL (M. T. Pyne Coll., NjP).

To Winthrop More Daniels

My dear Daniels: Princeton, N. J. December 8th, 1909.

I think that I can say very confidently that there can be no doubt about the bona fides in the case I consulted you about concerning asking Professor Gore to lecture here. Cyrus McCormick vouches for him very directly and I know that it is true, as McCormick says, that he is particularly thoroughly versed in the matter about which he would lecture. Your own suggestions about the arrangements for the lectures strike me as eminently wise, and I am writing to ask if you would be willing to invite Professor Gore here in the name of the Department. I think this would be the best method of proceedure [procedure], and if you would be kind enough to write to Professor Gore asking him if the arrangements you suggest would be satisfactory to him and what fee he would expect, I would be very much obliged to you indeed.

Perhaps you and I can consult as to the best dates and time of year. I hope that in writing you will say that you do so with full authority from me.

Cordially and faithfully yours, Woodrow Wilson

TLS (Wilson-Daniels Corr., CtY).

Notes for an After-Dinner Speech

8 December, '09.

SENIOR COUNCIL DINNER

Reorganization of Princeton not a private or Princeton question, but a national question.

Princeton for the nation's service

What *ought* Princeton to be?

Why are the colleges under examination?

Their atmosphere and objects unsatisfactory to the country.

Once magnified schools, now places of self-pleasing, sport,

and play-life in too large a degree, with no conscious and vital organization for serious business.

The class-room not serious business, under present conditions.

This the ground of recent proposals: to make incidentals and non-essentials less absorbing, and to do this by some natural, creative means which may furnish a life

a) which shall *include all elements* of the University

b) which shall at least *set men free* to concentrate themselves upon permanent objects

c) which shall *remove what is inconsistent* with right university ideals: an inevitable *social ferment* and a deadening *standardization.*

The organization which would be most likely to do this.[1]

8 Dec., 1909.

WWT MS (WP, DLC).

[1] A news report of this address is printed at Dec. 10, 1909.

From Arthur Twining Hadley

New Haven, Connecticut.

My dear Mr. Wilson: December 8th, 1909.

Mr. Lowell and I were both exceedingly glad that you were disposed to take the matter of football reform up so strongly.

The situation is a delicate one. These matters have to be handled by personal conference rather than by letter. Could you arrange to meet me at the Century Club in New York on Friday of this week at any time between the hours of 1 and 8 P.M.? If you could come at 1 I should hope for your company at luncheon; if at 6.30 or 7, dinner. I am sorry to fix the limits so narrowly; but on account of the action of the United States Government in taking away our Treasurer I am more than usually busy, because I am filling two offices. I am occupied on both Thursday and Saturday, and Monday and Tuesday I have Governor Hughes and the President of the United States as visitors.

If Friday is an inconvenient day, and the journey to New Haven is not too overwhelmingly long, I could arrange to see you at almost any time between 3.30 Saturday and 12 Monday except between 1 and 3 Sunday noon. We should be charmed if you could dine with us Saturday evening. You can get to New York easily after dinner; or, if you could spend the night with us, so much the better. If none of these hours is available, I do not suppose that any great harm will be done by letting the whole matter go over till the middle of next week.

If you can find time to go to New York on Friday, I should be glad to have you telegraph me the hour.

Faithfully yours, Arthur T. Hadley

TLS (WP, DLC).

From Abbott Lawrence Lowell

Dear Mr. Wilson: Cambridge [Mass.] December 8, 1909

Your letter about football came yesterday morning, just before President Hadley came up here with Mr. Camp[1] to confer with Mr. Haughton[2] and me, with a view to changes in the rules of football that may diminish the amount of injuries. There is a general movement on the part of the New England College Presidents in this direction, and a few of the biggest colleges could probably get together and agree upon changes in the rules better than a larger number. They could probably make them far more easily than the Rules Committee[3] could. Your letter came, therefore, at a most opportune time, and Mr. Hadley and I hope that you will meet us at some time and see if we cannot agree upon a workable plan. Knowing next to nothing about the rules, I yet know enough to recognize the difficulties that arise when it is proposed to change them; but I think that if our three Universities can get together and agree on a change, the rest must follow us, at least in the East.

As yet we have done nothing but listen to the suggestions of Mr. Camp and Mr. Haughton. We have not framed anything like a plan of changes. Mr. Hadley expects to see you in New York shortly and explain the matter to you more fully.

Very truly yours, A. Lawrence Lowell.

TLS (WP, DLC).

1 Walter Chauncey Camp, football coach at Yale and Treasurer of the Yale Field. In addition, Camp was a prolific author of books on athletics and was President, Treasurer, and General Manager of the New Haven Clock Co.

2 Percy Duncan Haughton, head football coach at Harvard and Assistant Secretary of the Old Colony Trust Co. of Boston.

3 That is, the Intercollegiate Rules Committee, about which see n. 1 to the announcement printed at Dec. 18, 1905, Vol. 16.

From Williamson Updike Vreeland

[Princeton, N. J.] December 8, 1909.

The number of men who chose the Modern Language Department during each of the last four years and the first term of the present year is as follows:

Germanic section, Class of 1906, 4
" " " " 1907, 4
" " " " 1908, 2
" " " " 1909, 0
" " " " 1910, 3
" " " " 1911, 2

Romanic section, Class of 1906, 8
" " " " 1907 4
" " " " 1908 3
" " " " 1909 5
" " " " 1910 9
" " " " 1911 5

FIRST TERM 1905-1906

		SENIORS	JUNIORS	SOPHO-MORES	FRESH-MEN	SPECIALS	
Ger.	43	7				2	9
"	41	10				4	14
"	31	1	29	3		5	28
"	23		2	51	19	6	80
"	13		7	4	173	2	186
"	11	5	8	29	48	4	94
Fr.	43	4				1	5
"	41	14				3	17
"	31		34				34
"	23		8	60	14	4	86
"	13	2	8	9	142	9	170
"	11	12	17	30	72	5	136
Span.	47	18		1		1	20
"	37	4	29			6	33
Ital.	45	5					5
"	35	1					1
Totals		83	149[142]	187	468	52	939[918]

Taking two courses: Seniors 4
" " " Juniors 4
" three " Seniors 8

SECOND TERM 1905-1906

		SENIORS	JUNIORS	SOPHO-MORES	FRESH-MEN	SPECIALS	
Ger.	44	8					8
"	42	10				2	12
"	32		24	2		6	32
"	24		5	46	20	6	77
"	14		3	3	159	6	171
"	12	2	6	24	38	5	75
Fr.	44	6				1	7
"	42	16					16
"	32		21				21
"	24	1	7	50	13	4	75
"	14	1	6	8	130	7	152
"	12	7	12	27	67	4	117
Span.	48	16		1		1	18
"	38	3	23			6	32
Ital.	46	4					4
"	36	1	4				5
Totals		75	111	161	427	49[48]	823[822]

Taking two courses: Seniors 11
" " " Juniors 3
" three " Seniors 4

FIRST TERM 1906-1907

		SENIORS	JUNIORS	SOPHO-MORES	FRESH-MEN	SPECIALS	
Ger.	43	13					13
"	41	12	1				13
"	31	2	32	10		1	45
"	23	2	4	63	20	4	93
"	13	2	6	3	115	6	132
"	11	2	4	21	49	1	77
Fr.	41	12				1	13
"	31	1	21	2			24
"	23	8	8	54	18	5	93
"	13	4	7	13	146	14	184
"	11	3	16	17	53		89
Span.	47	13				6	19
"	37	4	40				44

		SENIORS	JUNIORS	SOPHOMORES	FRESHMEN	SPECIALS	
Ital.	45	2					2
"	35		20			1	21
Totals		80	159	183	401	39	862

Taking two courses: Seniors 5
" " " Juniors 6
" three " Seniors 4

SECOND TERM 1906-1907

		SENIORS	JUNIORS	SOPHOMORES	FRESHMEN	SPECIALS	
Ger.	44	9	1			1	11
"	42	9	1			1	11
"	32		23	10		2	35
"	24	1	2	60	20	5	88
"	14	1	6	3	112		122
"	12		2	18	42	2	64
Fr.	44	2					2
"	42	9				1	10
"	32		14				14
"	24	8	5	54	16	2	85
"	14	4	4	9	161	8	186
"	12	2	12	17	50	3	84
Span.	48	10					10
"	38	3	27				30
Ital.	46	2					2
"	36		11				11
Totals		60	108	171	401	25	765

Taking two courses: Seniors 4
" " " Juniors 2
" three " Seniors 4

FIRST TERM 1907-1908

		SENIORS	JUNIORS	SOPHOMORES	FRESHMEN	SPECIALS	
Ger.	43					1	1
"	41	2	1			1	4
"	33	4	18	5			27
"	31		14	5			19
"	23	1	8	40	35	3	87
"	13		5	3	106	6	120
"	11	3	4	8	56		71

		SENIORS	JUNIORS	SOPHO-MORES	FRESH-MEN	SPECIALS	
Fr.	43	3					3
“	41	10	1				11
“	31	1	32	5		1	38
“	23	2	9	75	23	6	115
“	13	3	13	13	155		184
“	11	5	26	20	83		134
Span.	47	14	1			3	18
“	37	13	35	2		3	53
Ital.	45	4					4
“	35	3	10				13
Totals		68	177	176	458	24	903[902

Taking two courses: Seniors 7
“ “ “ Juniors 8
“ three “ Seniors 3

SECOND TERM 1907-1908

		SENIORS	JUNIORS	SOPHO-MORES	FRESH-MEN	SPECIALS	
Ger.	44					1	1
“	42	2	1			1	4
“	34	3	15	3			21
“	32		10	5			15
“	24		7	36	35	1	79
“	14		2	3	96	6	107
“	12	3	4	7	48		62
Fr.	44	4					4
“	42	11	1	2			14
“	32	1	14				15
“	24	1	5	62	21	8	97
“	14	3	12	11	155		181
“	12	4	25	15	84		128
Span.	48	9				3	12
“	38		28				28
Ital.	46	3				1	4
“	36	3	7				10
Totals		47	131	144	439	21	782

Taking two courses: Seniors 4
“ “ “ Juniors 5
“ three “ Seniors 3

FIRST TERM 1908-1909

		SENIORS	JUNIORS	SOPHO-MORES	FRESH-MEN	SPECIALS	
Ger.	41	8	2				10
"	33	3	6	3			12
"	34	2	14	8		1	25
"	23	2	4	28	25	6	65
"	13	1			111		112
"	11	5	8	15	9	1	38
Fr.	43	5					5
"	41	11	2				13
"	31		26	9		5	40
"	23	9	5	64	23	1	102
"	13	1	8	22	121		152
"	11	2	15	25	31		73
Span.	47	9	1				10
"	37	2	14				16
Ital.	45	2					2
"	35	5	6				11
Totals		67	111	174	320	14	686

Taking two courses: Seniors 6
" " " Juniors 9
" three " Seniors 5
" four " " 1

SECOND TERM 1908-1909

		SENIORS	JUNIORS	SOPHO-MORES	FRESH-MEN	SPECILAS [SPECIALS]	
Ger.	42	6	2				8
"	34	2	8				10
"	32	2	13	8		2	25
"	24	1	4	26	23	5	59
"	14	1		5	99		105
"	12	5	5	17	7		34
Fr.	44	5					5
"	42	11	2				13
"	32		22	8			30
"	24	7	5	63	23	1	99
"	14	1	7	21	111	1	141
"	12	4	18	16	35		73

		SENIORS	JUNIORS	SOPHO-MORES	FRESH-MEN	SPECILAS [SPECIALS]	
Span.	48	7					7
"	38	1	11				12
Ital.	46	1					1
"	36	3	7				10
Totals		57	104	164	298	9	632

Taking two courses: Seniors 0
" " " Juniors 11
" three " Seniors 4
" four " " 1

FIRST TERM 1909-1910

		SENIORS	JUNIORS	SOPHO-MORES	FRESH-MEN	SPECIALS	
Ger.	43	4					4
"	41	8				1	9
"	33	2	13	5			20
"	31		9	13			22
"	23	2	3	71	45		121
"	13	1	1	8	80	9	99
"	11	3	7	30	9	3	52
Fr.	43	10					10
"	41	17	2			2	19
"	31	4	25	11		1	41
"	23	3	15	96	37	4	154
"	13	3	7	29	116	13	168
"	11	6	5	60	31	4	106
Span.	47	7					7
"	37	4	27				31
Ital.	45	5					5
"	35	11	5				16
Totals		90	119	323	318	35[37]	885[884]

III

With the exception of French 31 the Junior and Senior classes in the Modern Language Department are very small, ranging from two or three to fifteen or twenty men in each course, and the instructor in charge of the course usually does the preceptorial work in his own course. For "floaters" this method is, I think, clearly the best, particularly since only a negligible number take more than one course, and even for the departmental men in our Department we believe it is the most advantageous. The number of men electing the Department is very small, and even those who do elect the Department do not, in many cases, follow the same courses. Some men take Senior courses in their Junior year, having entered with the advanced requirement, and do pro-seminary work in their Senior year; and, in the Romanic side, though all who elect the Department are required to take Old French, they have a choice of three other subjects, French 41, Italian, and Spanish.

In the Freshman and Sophomore courses, where the numbers are larger, most of the instructors (I use the term "instructor" to include all those giving instruction) in the Department have some class teaching to do, and everyone, almost without exception, does some preceptorial work. Most men do either class or preceptorial work in at least two of the three elementary courses.

IV

No. IV is, I think, already treated in III. There is no one in the Department who does only class teaching, and no one who does only preceptorial work. It is a rare exception when a man does not do preceptorial work outside his own course.

V

In treating No. V I shall follow the order of courses followed in the University catalogue, and shall describe the application of the preceptorial method in the various courses as I find it described in statements I have received, on request, from the various instructors in charge of courses. Owing to the increased number of students this year and the resulting heavy schedules, the beginners' courses in both German and French are carried on by the class method, no preceptorial work being done with them.

GERMAN 13, 14. Dr. [Alfred Ernest] Richards.

In this course the B.S. and Litt.B. men have two hours of class work and one hour of preceptorial work, while the A.B. men alternate two hours of class and one of preceptorial the following week.

The class work consists of reading modern German authors (such as Keller's "Kleider machen Leute," Arndt's "Deutschen Patrioten," and Nichol's "Modern German Prose").

The preceptorial work consists almost entirely of exercises in

German composition and grammar. Occasionally we have time for practice in sight translation. This kind of work continues throughout both terms. The text for the composition work is Thomas' "German Composition."

GERMAN 23, 24. Professor Priest.

German 23, 24, an introduction to German Literature in the Eighteenth and Nineteenth Centuries, consists of two classroom recitations and one preceptorial conference per week. At the present time the classes are conducted by Professor Thayer and myself; we are assisted in the preceptorial work by Dr. [Robert Mowry] Bell and Dr. [Harold Herman] Bender. In class we read selections from an anthology of Classical and Romantic German literature, the aim of which is to make the student acquainted with the most famous German poetry and prose. The third hour of the course, the preceptorial conference, is devoted, first, to a discussion of the literature read in class. The personal knowledge of an author's literary work which the student gains in recitation, and the criticism in the history of German literature which he studies, afford a starting-point for the discussions of the preceptorial conference. The history of the literature gives the student also the main facts in the lives of the authors. Paragraphs in a political history of Germany are assigned from time to time, so that the student may see connections between the literature and life of the period. During each term one or more fairly easy German stories, about two hundred pages, are read privately by the student. He is expected to read these stories rapidly, approximately as he reads English, and occasional reliable reports of his progress are required.

GERMAN 31, 32. Professor Hoskins.

In German 31 the ordinary methods of interpretation have been used. The students come prepared with usually an act of a drama and have read outside the criticisms in the collateral reading reserved in the library. The play is then taken up act by act and interpreted along the lines of the action, the characterization, etc. with a discussion of the technical, philosophical and social conceptions upon which the play may be said to rest. At the conclusion a résumé is attempted to fix as far as possible form [from] the present point of view its value as an interpretation of human life.

GERMAN 33, 34. Dr Richards, in the absence of Professor Blau.

In this course the men have two hours of class work and one

of preceptorial. The course is devoted to the life and works of Goethe, and consists of lectures and reading. During the first term the students read in class Goethe's "Götz von Berlichingen," selections from Goethe's poems and "Hermann und Dorothea." The second term class work consists entirely of reading Goethe's "Faust." The preceptorial work during the first term has for its subject matter the reading and discussing of Sime's "Life of Goethe"; "Die Leiden des jungen Werthers," and "Iphigenie." In the second term the hour is devoted entirely to the intedpretation [interpretation] of "Faust." The lectures delivered during the course are five in number during the first term.

GERMAN 41, 42. Professor Thayer.

The course covers the literature of the Nineteenth Century, one lecture and two preceptorial hours each week. The lectures give the prevailing political, social, religious and philosophical thought of the times, the relationship of the authors to their times and their chief characteristics. For detail of the lives of the authors the student is generally referred to a history of literature, save as this detail is conspicuously related to their works. The purpose of the lectures is to supply preliminary guidance for the student's own reading; but the opposite method is also used, that is, the student reads in pursuit of the leading ideas of a work without specific information beforehand as to what he will find there, then the lecture becomes a resume of important points. The plan of the preceptorial hour is to illustrate by readings assigned the essential features of the literary movements and the characteristics of the individual authors. The student thus obtains his knowledge, or confirms and deepens it, by first hand contact with the works. Significant passages are read for the sake of form or content but the major part of the preceptorial conference is occupied with a discussion of the works which the students have read, their literary form and the fundamental ideas which they exhibit, particularly as illustrative of the thought of the time; the differentiating characteristics of the authors are brought out by analysis and comparison. The student reads for the preceptorial hour a far larger assignment of German than could be covered by a recitation method. In addition to the works of the German authors, readings are required in the various histories of literatures, essays and other works to round out the acquaintance with author or period.

GERMAN 43, 44. Professor Priest.

The small number of students electing German 43, 44, Middle High German Lyric and Epic Poetry, has made it possible to hold all three hours in the instructor's study, and thus to give each hour the character of a preceptorial conference. In this way the work consists regularly of reading Middle High German literature, and of discussing it from every point of view which may occur to the instructor and each individual student.

FRENCH 13, 14. Professor Buffum.

In intermediate French the preceptorial conference is given up mainly to composition work and drill in the syntax. In addition the students read rapidly a short story which is reported on, usually in French, during the preceptorial hour.

FRENCH 23, 24. Professor Vreeland.

In French 23, 24, the course of which I have charge, and in which Professors [Alfred Austin] Moore and [Régis] Michaud and myself are doing the class work, assisted in the preceptorial work by Professors Critchlow and Koren, Dr. [Charles Engley] Mathews and Mr. [Donald Clive] Stuart, is introductory to the literary courses of Junior and Senior years. For the class work we use an anthology of French prose and poetry covering the last three centuries. We give short assignments in this, and go over the work with the utmost care, thus giving the student an intensive study of the language, and also of the best selections of the best French writers.

For the preceptorial appointment the students are required to read each week all or part of some representative work of the period covered by the anthology. By the combination of these two methods the student is trained to appreciate accurately some of the most delicate points of the language, and is also enabled to acquaint himself first hand with some of the best things in French literature. During the hour of the preceptorial appointment the structure of the text assigned is discussed, its place in literature or the authors ideas, the character of the discussion depending upon the character of the text.

FRENCH 31, 32. Professor Koren.

I have tried reading plays or longer selections by the author under consideration, as a whole (finishing the play in one hour), and also tried reading selections from minor authors belonging to the same period as that treated of in class through the greater authors. I have also tried keeping the preceptorial work entirely apart from the class work. I find that I now use all three methods as the nature of the course demands it: 1. giving a rapid reading of a whole book; 2. supplementing the class work, through the reading of letters, memoires, etc.; 3. studying a special author apart from the class.

FRENCH 41, 42. Professor Gauss.

In French 41, on account of the larger number of students than in Italian 45, the work is here divided more rigorously into class and preceptorial periods, though the teacher believes that this distinction should be minimized as far as possible. Two hours are given to the class's meeting together, the students meeting the instructor preceptorially for the third. The instructor tries to coördinate as far as possible the lectures with the assignments of reading. The lectures are given primarily to paint in the background of the period covered and treat the authors in their general setting and significance. The instructor chooses a representative work of each author which is read in the same week. He avoids discussing that particular work in the lecture, though he tries to suggest a method of approach, attempting merely to whet the appetite of the student and leave him the satisfaction of discovering the truth for himself. This articulates the preceptorial conference with the lecture but keeps it from degenerating into a mere memory exercise or quiz. The subjects treated in the preceptorial hour are thus kept new and fresh and the student's expression of individual opinion is not hampered by the previous expression of opinion by the lecturer. The teacher, believing profoundly in Epicurus' definition of the process of education as "friends seeking happiness together" tries to take out of the relation of teacher and student all professional taint. He tries to make it the relation of friend to friend and not that of physician to patient. To do this it is necessary to disabuse the student of the idea that two days (the class hours), the lecturer does the work, and one day (the preceptorial) he does it. For this reason the students are frequently given reports which are not merely handed in to the teacher but which are read in the regular class hours; and the teacher tries where possible to utilize their knowledge of their more special field or department. What is meant can perhaps best be shown by example. The past week we were just finishing Chateaubriand and Obermann and the post-revolutionary disillusion in France. Instead of telling the students that the movement was European the instructor assigned subjects in English litedature [literature],–Byron's "Childe Harold," Wordsworht [Wordsworth], and Matthew Arnold's poems on Obermann,–to three men in the English Department; Leopardi and Foscolo's "Jacopo Ortis" were given to students of Italian; "Werther" to one in German; and the Greek and Latin world-weary attitude to a classical honours man. They do not merely write these assignments up, but at a meeting of the class we have these reports read. The students and teacher thus feel that they are engaged in a joint enterprise and take a more serious interest in their work than if they were merely preparing a report to be "handed in."

ITALIAN 35, 36. Professor Koren.

Owing to the heavy schedules in the Department this year the preceptorial work in Beginners' Italian has been omitted, a class hour taking its place.

ITALIAN 45, 46. Professor Gauss.

In Italian 45, the class is so small, this year only six, that practically all the work is preceptorial. The class preferred to meet in the instructor's study for each of the three hours and this plan has been adopted. The recitation is very informal. The plan of meeting regularly in the instructor's study has one prime advantage; the books of reference are always immediately at hand. In the course of an hour a man is occasionally delegated to look up some point. The students thus learn almost unconsciously and without effort to use these books of reference and to find their way around in the more important Dante literature. When possible, each man is given some larger field in which he is to coödinate [coordinate] the scattered data. One student, for instance, has Dante's relation to English literature. He is supposed to point out and pick up scattered references and quotations, and these he works up into a presentable report as part of his responsibility in the course.

SPANISH 37, 38. Professor Norhtup [Northup].

In the beginners' course in Spanish the preceptorial method has enabled the instructor to give the student a more efficient drill than is possible under the old system, the same as in the elementary courses in French and German.

SPANISH 47, 48. Professor Northup.

I have for three years conducted my Senior course in Spanish with a view to making my students "reading men" in that subject. I have turned the class into a seminar during the preceptorial hour. The different members of the division are assigned selections from various authors, to be read and reported upon. The results of this method have been on the whole very satisfactory. A number of the best men have formed the habit of reading books in the language and some to my knowledge have kept it up after leaving the university. The preceptorial system seems to have worked splendidly in all our courses with the exception of the Academic divisions of Freshmen Intermediate French, where we find that one preceptorial conference in two weeks is not sufficient for good results.

VI

In discussing VI it is necessary, I think, to differentiate between the more elementary courses (French and German 11, 12, 13, 14) in which the main idea is to give the student a knowledge of the grammar and structure of the language and a certain facility in reading, and the more advanced courses in which the student is expected to become acquainted, first hand, with the literature and thought of the nation. The preceptorial method is clearly more applicable and serviceable to courses of the latter class.

However, for courses of the elementary kind too, especially for French and German 13, 14, the preceptorial work is extremely valuable. Individual needs can be much more carefully looked after than in groups of twenty or thirty, and the student feels much freer to ask about his difficulties. The whole spirit in fact between the instructor and his men is changed. Through free discussion about the grammar and composition the principal points are made much more emphatic and are fixed in the men's minds. The student is given not only what the instructor may think he ought to need, but what he does in reality need, as brought out by the student's questions and work. Through meeting the men in small groups too it is possible to obtain far better results in pronunciation, and even in some cases to speak to some extent the foreign language.

In regard to the more advanced courses, i.e. the courses from Sophomore year on, the preceptorial method is indispensable. Under the class system it was never possible to give the men an appreciative understanding of the foreign literature and thought. They read the texts prescribed, and heard some lectures or read some handbook about them or about the history of the literature; but I believe it was only by exception and rarely that a man really got beneath the surface of what he read, or really intimately connected the text with a just appreciation of it. Since the introduction of the preceptorial method the students have read two or three times as much as before, with increased interest and with a far broader and deeper understanding of the vital meaning of foreign literature and thought.

It will be seen from section II of this report that the number of students taking courses in the Department last year was very much smaller than in any of the other years. The number of hours of teaching done by the various instructors was correspondingly smaller. Therefore it is much fairer to consider the teaching schedules of this year, which is a normal year, rather than the schedule of last year. It will be seen that this year the agerage [average] number of hours per week is 13.4, if the teaching fellow, Mr [George Samuel] Spohn, is not included, and 13, if he is included. I therefore submit below the detailed report of schedules for this year.

	Class hours	Preceptorial hours	Graduate
Professor Vreeland	4	10	
" Gauss	4	6	3
" Hoskins	8	3	3
" Buffum	6	6	3
" Collins	7½	6	
" Crithclow [Critchlow]	8½	4	
" Koren	4	8	
" Moore	4	8	
" Northup	9½	2½	
" Priest	10	7	
" Thayer	3	10	3
" Michaud	4	7	
Dr. Mathews	5	9	
" Richards	5½	8½	
Mr. Stuart	6	7	
Dr. Bell	6½	8	
" Bender	3½	9½	
Mr Spohn, teahcing [teaching] fellow	3½	3½	

Respectfully submitted, W. U. Vreeland

TRS (WWP, UA, NjP).

William Francis Magie to De Witt Clinton Jones, Jr., with Enclosure

Dear Sir: Princeton, N. J. December 8, 1909.

At the meeting of the University Faculty held December 6th., 1909, your letter of December 1st. was presented and read.

The question raised in your letter was also raised by a similar letter from Mr. E. S. Simons. The Faculty considered these communications carefully and directed me as Clerk in acknowledging receipt of them to transmit a minute to be prepared by the Committee on Discipline. I accordingly enclose a copy of this minute herewith.

While no formal action was taken on the second question raised by you as to the meaning of "probation," I was asked by the Dean to explain that the old significance of that word as indicating that any further offense committed by the student would lead to his dismission, no longer obtains, and that all that is meant is that if a student should be guilty of any further offense he would not be shown the consideration which is ordinarily shown to those who offend for the first time but would be more severely discilpined [disciplined] than if he had not been previously involved in another offense. Yours truly, W. F. Magie Clerk

Enclosure.

TLS (received from D. C. Jones III).

ENCLOSURE

[c. Dec. 8, 1909]

MINUTE FROM THE COMMITTEE ON DISCIPLINE

The Committee on Discipline feels that the first case of intoxication may occur, and almost always does occur by accident, and without premeditation. Second and subsequent cases of intoxication cannot be ascribed to accident or ignorance and therefore are punished severely.

The seriousness of the disorder of the recent socalled "rough housing" lies in the fact that there was a deliberately planned agreement to harass and annoy two women. The Committee therefore thinks that such premeditated disorder should be punished more severely than a condition of intoxication which occurs without premeditation.

T MS (received from D. C. Jones III).

To Arthur Twining Hadley

My dear Mr. Hadley: Princeton, N. J. December 9th, 1909.

Thank you most sincerely for your letter of December 8th. I was a good deal embarrassed when I found, as I did immediately after posting my letter to you, that you and Mr. Lowell had already arranged a conference upon this matter. I feared that my suggestion must, just at that moment, have seemed like a self invitation to be included, but I was sure, upon second thought, that I could count upon you to understand that I was in complete ignorance of your arrangement.

Unhappily, I am tied up for the present week and it seems impossible for me to avail myself of any of the opportunities for a conference which you are kind enough to suggest. Are you not intending to be present at the sessions of the National Academy of Arts and Letters in Washington next week? I am going down and am to be in Washington on Tuesday and Wednesday. If you are going, we could arrange very easily and delightfully for a talk there. If you are not, I will take the liberty of writing again to see if we cannot arrange a talk in the near future.

With much regard and appreciation,

Sincerely yours, Woodrow Wilson

TLS (A. T. Hadley Papers, Archives, CtY).

To Abbott Lawrence Lowell

My dear Mr. Lowell: [Princeton, N. J.] December 9th, 1909.

I had hardly posted my letter to you the other day when I learned of the conference you and Mr. Hadley were holding with Mr. Haughton and Mr. Camp. It embarrassed me a good deal to feel that I had thrust myself in, but I know that you will understand that I knew nothing of this conference at the time.

Let me thank you for your letter and its cordial response to my suggestion. I am hoping that I may be able to see Mr. Hadley next week and that after I have seen him, as you suggest, I may have the pleasure of a talk with both of you about this matter which has grown so important.

With warmest regard,

Faithfully yours, [Woodrow Wilson]

CCL (WWP, UA, NjP).

From Moses Taylor Pyne

My dear Woodrow New York Dec 9 1909

. . . I was very glad to have had the talk with you on Saturday and I felt that we were very close together in our ideas, differing principally on matters of detail in which we ought to be able to get together by mutual compromise and by threshing out the questions together.

Yours very sincerely M Taylor Pyne

ALS (WP, DLC).

From Richard Spencer Childs

Dear Dr. Wilson: New York Dec. 9th, 1909.

It seems to me that January 21st is the best date for our dinner that comes within the period you mention; and if satisfactory to you, we will settle it that way.

The dinner will probably be held at the Lotos Club.

My idea is that you are to do the bulk of the speaking in explanation of The Short Ballot Idea and the purposes of our Organization.[1] If Mr. Winston Churchill comes, we will hear from him more briefly; but otherwise we will probably announce no toast list.[2] At the conclusion we can invite questions and suggestions, giving preference in recognition to men whom we are most anxious to hear from. I do not feel that we ought to allow it, however, to become an open debate, or to give to the assemblage any power of passing resolutions.

We will get up a list of guests and show it to you later, and no doubt then you will find it easier to indicate which are the men you feel most anxious to have present.

Yours very truly, Richard S. Childs Secretary.

TLS (WP, DLC).

[1] Wilson's address is printed at Jan. 21, 1910, Vol. 20.

[2] For a list of speakers, see n. 1 to Wilson's address just mentioned.

A News Report of a Talk to the Senior Council of Princeton University

[Dec. 10, 1909]

WHEREIN UNIVERSITIES FAIL

Standardization and Elective Element in Social Life Discussed by President Wilson.

The address which President Wilson delivered at the Senior Council Dinner on Wednesday evening, clearly indicated the reasons for some of the defects which admittedly exist in American universities. They exist not in one but in almost every one; the problems Princeton is trying to solve are before many other institutions. This fact is frequently overlooked in discussions bearing upon the points in question.

After remarking on the fact that Princeton is apt to be self-centered, President Wilson proceeded as follows: "Princeton should frankly take stock of herself, and set an example along wider lines in addition to the example she has set on narrower ones. . . .[1] We ought not to ask what we want Princeton to be for our enjoyment, for our satisfaction and for the mere continuation of those customs which we have all learned to love, but we should ask rather what *ought* Princeton to be, whether it suits us or not. It is from that point of view that we must approach our future.

"What impresses me most in traveling about through the country is that the country is radically dissatisfied with the colleges. It is universally felt, not by the little coteries of men who love the place and cannot therefore be critical, but in those larger circles on whose view our very life depends, that the colleges have lingered at a past point of view and are trying to do something for which the country no longer has any use. . . .

"I want to have the men who are engaged in the various organizations realize the relativity of things—what relation sport bears to intellectual effort, what relation things in which you are interested bear to those in which we are interested; how there is something admirable, beautiful, enticing in the things ahead of you which are not of the same kind as the things which you are interested in now.

"For that reason I have suggested that we take out of our lives here only the undesirable things. The first of these is social ferment, social anxiety, the doubtfulness of what is going to be the fortune of a lad when he enters the university; whether he will have the field of university life thrown wide open to him or whether he will be shunted onto a side track, and made to play a minor part where he will feel, if not mortification, at least that there is something that he missed, not by reason of something that he has done or that he has not done, but because somebody did not *choose* him into the greater privileges.

"What is worse than social ferment is what I can find no better expression for than 'standardization.' The student says, not what *can* I make of myself, but what *must* I make of myself in view of the expectations of the place? The great danger he is under of 'queering' himself by doing something which would be perfectly normal outside, but which he is expected here not to do. . . . So he goes about seeking what he is not expected to do. That is the very negation of university life. The first principle of university life is individual freedom and individuality. If you reduce men to a single standard you impoverish the nation, you deprive it of all particular genius, of all originative action. . . . If you have a social order the chief characteristic of which is to standardize men, you have what no university can afford to retain. I do not know of any means of removing this incubus of standardization except to take out of it this one thing: that a man has to be elected to these privileges.

"That is not the American spirit. America will lose her prestige when she takes on something like that. And therefore she does not like her colleges. . . . We must have an organization which gives us the university consciousness from the time we enter the university until the time we leave it, and upon no other basis can we develop. . . .

"I want you gentlemen to think and believe that whether I suggest the right means or not for the realization of the purposes we have in mind, I have in mind to do a thing which will make you as proud and as happy twenty years from now as I pray God it will make the rest of us."

Printed in the *Daily Princetonian*, Dec. 10, 1909.

1 This and the following elisions are in the original text.

From Winthrop More Daniels, with Enclosure

My dear Wilson: Princeton, N. J. Dec. 10, 1909

I have just completed the somewhat voluminous Report accompanying this note. You will find a considerable amount of "dynamite" at the end, but will know how to handle it, when apprised in advance of its character.

I am, Ever sincerely yours W. M. Daniels.

ALS (WWP, UA, NjP).

E N C L O S U R E

From Winthrop More Daniels

My dear President Wilson: Princeton, N. J. Dec. 6, 1909.

Herewith I beg to make formal acknowledgment of your letter of inquiry dated Nov. 9th. 1909. The Report following is drawn so as to cover as completely as possible the matters in question. In accordance with your advice given our Departmental Committee at our recent interview we have compiled statistics of the number electing courses in our Department which while not covering every one of the nine terms of the Preceptorial system, afford a typical view of the tendencies operative.

1. The first of the queries in your letter of inquiry is as follows: "The number of men in each of the four classes who have chosen your Department during each of the last four years

and the first term of the present year." In reply I would state that our Department offers no courses in Freshman year, and only one course in Sophomore year,–the course in Sophomore History now given in the second term. Omitting Sophomore History for the present, (the number of men taking the course appears in a subsequent Table) the number of Juniors and Seniors electing our Department (including therein Specials assimilated to regular Department men) is as follows. The Table in question was furnished by the Registrar, and affords a comparison of the number of Juniors and Seniors electing other Departments of the University.

Table showing number electing the
Department of History, Politics, and Economics.

	Class of 1906	1907	1908	1909	1910	1911
Hist. Pol. & Econ.	95	116	140	150	124	134
Philosophy	18	11	9	9	9	3
English	44	46	26	28	13	8
Art & Arch.	2	3	2	2	1	3
Classics	5	6	3	2	12	9
Germanics	4	4	2	0	3	2
Romanics	8	4	3	5	9	5
Mathematics	1	14	9	6	14	12
Physics	11	7	14	12	8	3
Chemistry	7	14	3	4	3	4
Geology	21	12	1	6	4	1
Biology	10	16	6	8	4	9
	226	253	218	232	204	193
Percentage in Dept. of His. Pol. Econ.	42.0%	45.8%	64.2%	64.6%	60.9%	69.4%

In addition to the increasing percentage of the two upper classes which is registered in this Department, the work of the Department is also increased by the numbers of men in other Departments who elect one or two courses in the Department of History, Politics, and Economics. At the present time these outside the Department augment the instruction required to be given to those in the Department by 16 per cent. This is wholly exclusive of the instruction in Sophomore History.

2. The second query on your list is the "number who have chosen electives in your Department without choosing the Department itself &c." In reply I append the following table.

	1905-6	1906-7	1907-8	1908-9	1909-10
Sophs. in History	214	—	—	177	—
Jrs. outside Dept. electing 1 course	68	—	45	38	40
Jrs. outside Dept. electing 2 courses	15	—	12	10	13
Jrs. electing Dept. 3 courses each	110	—	142	112	135
Srs. outside Dept. electing 1 course	64	—	36	30	21
Srs. outside Dept. electing 2 courses	30	—	17	4	19
Srs. electing Dept. 3 courses each	53	—	67	110	75
* Srs. electing Dept. 4 courses each	26	—	48	25	34
* Srs. electing Dept. 5 courses each	4	—	22	0	3

In explanation of this Table it should be said that out of the 9 terms we have taken 4,—this on account of the time that would be required for a complete inventory. Soph. History comes only on one of the two terms. We have taken from the Examination Records and the Elective Slips the record of Soph. History for the *first term* of 1905-6 and for the *second term* of 1908-9. For the other courses of Sr. and Jr. year we have taken from the same sources 4 out of the 9 terms; and have so arranged the selections as to give the figures for *two first terms*, to wit, 1907-8 and 1909-10, and for *two second terms*, to wit, 1905-6 and 1908-9. The figures are therefore thoroughly representative. In cases where the figures do not coincide exactly with the Registrar's figures cited in the preceding pages of this Report, it should be borne in mind that the Registrar has taken as the basis of his figures the status of each student at graduation or at leaving College. We have taken the actual enrolment, term by term.

3. In reply to the third query of your letter which asks about "the system followed in your Department in allotting preceptorial

* These items are not included in the number electing 3 courses; that is, the totals 75, 34 and 3 are mutually exclusive.

work, whether in the case of those who have chosen the Department or in the case of those who have chosen electives in the Department, as so-called "floaters," I beg to report as follows: The Preceptors in the Department and the Instructors doing Preceptorial work are divided into two equal groups. At the beginning of the academic year the Juniors who have elected the Department are assigned to one of the two aforesaid groups of Preceptors, and the Seniors in the Department are assigned to the other group. The whole number of Seniors is subdivided as near equally as possible among the group of Senior Preceptors; and the Juniors as nearly as evenly as possible among the Junior Preceptors. The year following there is an [a] change-about in the two groups of Preceptors, those who previously had to give instruction in Junior courses now taking Senior courses and ordinarily having the same students under their special instruction as the year previously. The Preceptors who had Senior courses one year give instruction in Junior courses the following year, thus being assigned to a new lot of men whom the Preceptors will normally have under their charge for the next two years.

This is the general rule underlying the system. There are however a number of special adjustments an understanding of which is necessary to a complete knowledge of the system. Of these, perhaps the most important concerns the assignment of Non-Departmental men who may have elected one or two courses in the Department. Such students are assigned for preceptorial instruction to the Professor who lectures in the courses in question. The Professors divide such students into small groups and meet these groups for the same kind of preceptorial conference as the students registered in the Department receive at the hands of the regular Preceptors. In Junior Jurisprudence the men outside the Department electing the course are numerous, and as the Professor (President Wilson) has not time to do the preceptorial work, a special Instructor is allotted this work to the exclusion of all other work in the Department. Another peculiar arrangement is due to the fact the course in Junior Economics is not given under the Preceptorial system, but in regular recitation Divisions. There are six Divisions* in the class, each meeting three times a week. The Preceptors who take part in this work of regular class instruction in Junior Economics are exempted from doing similar work of class work instruction in Sophomore History, the instruction in the latter course (which falls only in second term) being given by the other Preceptors (in the Junior group of Preceptors) assisted by the Professors of History. There

* Average number per division is 25.

is also one other arrangement relating to the Senior group of Preceptors which deserves mention. No Preceptor in this group is required to give instruction in more than three different Senior courses in the same term. In consequence, where necessary, by a series of interchanges of their Preceptees in particular courses, this result is attained.

4. The fourth query in your letter reads as follows: "How far and in what way the Professors and Assistant Professors in your Department (that is, those who conduct courses) have been participating in the preceptorial work, and how far, in the judgment of the Department, it would be possible to draw those who conduct courses more systematically into the general preceptorial function. I mean how far it would be feasible to include them among those members of the Department who undertake preceptorial work outside the field of their own immediate courses of instruction."

The inquiries here are twofold, first, as to the extent that those conducting courses actually participate in preceptorial work; and second, as to securing from those who now conduct courses more extended preceptorial work in fields outside their own immediate provinces of instruction.

Under No. 3 *supra* I have described in theory the extent to which those conducting courses participate in preceptorial work. They are charged with the preceptorial instruction of all non-Departmental students who elect their courses. They are also charged with the preceptorial instruction of Departmental students who elect 4 or 5 courses in the Department in Senior year to the extent of the courses so elected in excess of 3. The number of hours which they severally devote to this preceptorial work per week was given in the Report submitted to you last year, and has been stated more recently in the returns submitted to Dean Fine this term. While there may be individual exceptions, the amount of instruction on the average which they give, taking into account their participation in the graduate instruction, seems to me to be as much as can fairly be required, if they are to be expected to do any fair amount of study and research, and if Professorships here are to be fairly eligible posts that will command the quality of service that is to be desired. Without attempting any invidious comparisons, I venture to think that the weekly schedule of class room and other instruction given by those conducting courses in the Department of History, Politics, and Economics will compare favorably with the corresponding items in the schedules of the Departments most nearly akin to ours in the general character and nature of the work.

As regards the second point, the securing more extended participation in preceptorial work from those now conducting courses, the plan seems to me impracticable. It is so in the first place, where the weekly schedule of instruction of those giving courses is already full. This is the usual case. Of the eight men in the Department who conduct undergraduate courses regularly two,—the President of the University and the Dean of the College,—have administrative work on their hands, and are clearly not available for further preceptorial work. Another member of the Department, Prof. Paul van Dyke, is absent on leave, abroad. And while this is exceptional so far as the individual Professor is concerned, it not uncommonly represents a percentage of absenteeism on leave which is to be expected. Of the eight men conducting courses there remain then only five at present, from whom the increased participation in preceptorial work is theoretically possible. I do not see a single case among the five where the omission of a weekly lecture in order to participate more fully in preceptorial work would not create more work than could be supplied. The omission of a single weekly lecture attended by 50 men seemingly makes necessary the provision for ten additional preceptorial hours' instruction weekly. The Preceptors have not far from 12 hours of instruction per week already. In some few cases their weekly schedule amounts to 16 hours,—an excessive quantity, certain to impair the efficiency of the work or the vitality, mental or physical, of the Preceptors. In this connection there is another point to be noted. I assume that the increased participation in preceptorial work outside the field in which lecturers are now giving courses would be optional,—in at least some respects. It could hardly be exacted as a matter of right that one who has been elected to a chair of History, for example, should be required to teach Jurisprudence or Economics. Even if no objection were raised by the individual professor, it is questionable how efficient a Preceptor he would prove in a field alien in some degree to that of his chosen study.

5. The fifth inquiry in your letter is as follows: "In just what way the preceptorial method has been applied in each of the courses given in the Department."

In reply, I would say that in general the weekly preceptorial conference in each course has been the rule except in Sophomore History and in Junior Economics. The class in Sophomore History has been so large that it has been impracticable to subdivide it into small groups of 5 or 6, each one of such groups to have one hour weekly with the Preceptor. As a consequence the class has been subdivided into sections of from 15 to 30 each. Each of these divisions has had 2 recitations weekly, and the entire class has met once a week for a lecture. This is only one illustration of the inability of the present staff in the Department to provide the requisite amount of preceptorial instruction. If the staff can not be immediately enlarged, possibly the assignment of a competent Instructor to this work exclusively would make for economy of effort and real efficiency in the Department. In Junior Economics also the preceptorial system has not been applied. In some respects this is not to be regretted. In a subject that in its preliminary stages is mainly analytic, classes of from 15 to 20 can be readily handled; and subdivisions into smaller groups are not desirable on the ground of efficient instruction or on grounds of economy. On the other hand, in the second half of the Junior year the smaller subdivisions might conduce to greater efficiency in the matter of instruction. It is practically impossible under the present system in this course to single out the ablest men and to give them the advantages they might obtain under the preceptorial system proper.

In other courses in Junior and Senior year it has occasionally been necessary to make the groups for preceptorial instruction much larger in point of size than they should have been. As instances of this I may cite Jurisprudence where the number of non-Departmental men has sometimes been so great as to convert preceptorial groups into small recitation classes. The same thing has happened when, in the absence of a lecturer, the course has been put in charge of one of the Preceptors who, in order to meet weekly all of the men who fell to his charge, has had to enlarge the number of men whom he met at a single appointment.*

6. The sixth query upon your list reads as follows: "How far and by what methods you think experience has shown the present preceptorial method to be applicable and serviceable in the several courses of your Department, and what differences exist in this respect between the several courses."

In a general way, it may be said that the present preceptorial system has secured a much greater degree of application to study on the student's part than prevailed before its introduction. It is however to be acknowledged that the ideal of the system has not been reached except in imperfect measure. The transforma-

* In general, when a lecturer is absent on leave, his substitute in conducting the course should lecture in the absentee's place. The present arrangement through no fault on the part of the students or the Preceptor in charge is an ineffectual makeshift. Instead of the student having two lectures a week and an hour's conference with his Preceptor, the student goes with ten or twelve others *once a week* to the Preceptor. The result is wholly ineffectual. The student complains with perfect truth that he is "short suited" in the course.

tion of the student body generally into a set of reading men touched with some noticeable degree of intellectual maturity and enabled by close and constant association with their Preceptors to become intimately interested in great subjects of study has not been attained. There still persists unfortunately altogether too much of a juvenile attitude upon the part of many students, of "getting up" material for an examination which the student too often regards as marking the end of his personal concern with or interest in the subject matter of the courses.

In very considerable measure this unsatisfactory result has issued from causes only remotely connected with the curriculum or the system of instruction. I omit more than a passing reference to this important fact as not lying within the province of this report.

Our present preceptorial system fails particularly to develop strongly enough the bond of intimate personal knowledge and mutual interest between Preceptor and preceptee. In general the student does not meet his Preceptor in our Department until the student's third year in college. During Junior year the student meets his Preceptor in our Department but two hours a week.* In Senior year the student at the best will not meet the same Preceptor more than three hours a week, often not more than two hours a week. This is not sufficient to develop the desired relationship of intimacy and close personal association.

Subject to the limitations noted above, the present preceptorial method has proved serviceable in the courses where it has been applied. Experience has demonstrated that better results could be obtained, if with the present staff of instruction (which in number is quite inadequate) the following changes were made:

FIRST, Lessening the total courses carried by the student from five to four. In general, the student now has to undertake more work than can be done thoroughly.

SECOND, Abolishing the mid-year examinations, and having a final examination in each large subject at the end of the college year. The mid-year examination lessens by fully three weeks the amount of instruction given in class room and in preceptorial conference. This is the largest single item of waste so far as the services of the teaching staff is concerned. (Delay at the beginning of the academic year by reason of the lax enforcement of the prior registration of electives causes a similar waste of time,—often amounting to an entire week.) The prospect which the student would face of an examination at the year's end upon

* There is a partial exception in the cases of students whose preceptor in Junior year happens to be their Instructor in class in Junior Economics.

large subjects would aid him to view his studies in a truer perspective, and impress him with the obvious futility of deferring work until close upon the examination period. I venture to hope also that eventually an examining board for the Department may be constituted to set and conduct all of these examinations, and to provide different tests for pass-men and honor-men.

THIRD, Increasing the amount of written reports to be required of students in the Department. The time for the preparation of such written work would be found in part by reducing the courses of study carried from five to four, as suggested above.

FOURTH, Reducing the amount of required reading in certain courses, particularly Jurisprudence and Constitutional Law, unless the number of courses carried by the student can be reduced from five to four, or unless additional Preceptors can be added to the Department staff. I am not inclined to believe that the amount of reading now required in the History courses, or in the Senior year courses generally, is excessive, although it can not be adequately canvassed in the time now available for preceptorial conferences. The reading in History now exacted lends itself more readily to the capacity of the student than in such courses as Jurisprudence or elementary Economics where the fundamental concepts are new to the beginner and often difficult for the untrained student to grasp and apply. A single, authoritative, well-balanced text-book in such subjects supplemented by such illustrative material as may be requisite, as, for example, selected leading cases in Jurisprudence, would attain better results than those obtained from the reading exacted at present. All of these suggestions for lessening the quantity of reading prescribed at present would be weakened, if the student carried but four courses instead of five; and would be quite pointless, if the time for weekly conferences were doubled.

The two main desiderata, if the preceptorial method in the Department is to succeed, is to secure time for the student to do more reading and study by lessening the number of courses he simultaneously attempts; and to increase the number of hours weekly to be spent in conference with his Preceptors. Instead of two hours per week thus spent as at present in Junior year, there should be not less than four hours so utilized; and even more hours per week thus employed, if possible, in Senior year.

It is, of course, obvious that these changes,–or changes approximating thereto,–can not be effected except by a notable augmentation of the teaching force in the Department. Such an increase is clearly warranted, in my judgment, if due account be taken of the relative amount of instruction in Senior and

Junior years now falling to the Department of History, Politics, and Economics. According to the Registrar's statistics, of 399 students in the two upper classes (exclusive of C.E. students), there are 258 now registered in this Department. Each student carries five courses a term. Of a total of 1985 courses there are given at present 1011 by this Department. This is wholly exclusive of Sophomore History. In other words, of all Senior and Junior courses (exclusive of C.E. courses) certainly one half are now given by the twenty-one men (including the President of the University and the Dean of the College) now in the Department. Unless and until ample reinforcement can be made to the Department staff, any far-reaching betterment of the system of preceptorial instruction is obviously impossible.

It is, of course, apparent upon inspection that some of the changes recommended are quite radical in character, involving additions to the teaching staff, changes in the curriculum, and in the administration of the work of the Committee on Examinations and Standing. Inasmuch however as the eventual arrangement of the college curriculum as it is likely to exist ten years hence is now, as it seems to me, fairly predictable; and inasmuch as the teaching staff ought to be recruited and enlarged with this eventual constitution of the curriculum in view, I venture to add the following suggestions.

The subjects taught in our Department are never likely to be presented to the maximum advantage until the introductory courses occupy their proper place in Sophomore year. Chemistry and Physics which formerly were scheduled in Senior and Junior years have been put in Freshman and Sophomore years. A similar eventual disposition will have to be made of elementary Jurisprudence, Economics, and General History.

Our experience and the experience of many other colleges and universities is only too clear that the "new Humanities" embracing the studies concerned with human society have displaced or are rapidly displacing from the central position in the curriculum the old humanities, speculative Philosophy, *Belles Lettres*, and the non-technical pursuit of the natural sciences. Some there will always be in the student body of a large college who will adhere in their devotion to these studies. It is perhaps to be regretted that their number is not larger; and it is clear that provision should be made for the most complete instruction possible in these branches. But the trend of the tide is unmistakable, and in the long run it will prevail. We now attempt at Princeton to relegate the studies concerned with society to the last two years of the college course. Instead of laying broad the proper foundations early in the course, we spend Junior year in breaking the students in to a new kind of intellectual exercise. The time thereafter is too short really to lay hold upon their deeper intellectual interests, or to take them far afield, if we do succeed in engaging their positive adherence to the study of society. If elementary Jurisprudence, elementary Economics, and General History were taught throughout Sophomore year in small classes and with effective class-room drill, the success in advanced work in the two upper years would be reasonably assured. At present the results in the best cases are suggestive of unfinished products largely for the reason that our curriculum is avowedly a compromise between the claims of a day largely past and one that is all but here. I realize that this aspect of the question reaches quite to the roots of our entire curriculum, and that it will not have its day in court, perhaps for some years to come. But in the recruiting of the University staff of instruction, it seems to me absolutely essential that teachers be added for whose services in future there is certain to be such an increasing demand.

I am, Mr. President,

Yours most respectfully, W. M. Daniels

TLS (WWP, UA, NjP).

From Frank Frost Abbott, with Enclosure

Dear President Wilson: Princeton, Dec. 10, 1909

Perhaps a word of explanation is needed on two points in the accompanying report.

I inferred from our conversation a few days ago that you wished for your immediate purpose only a brief statement of the way in which the preceptorial system is being applied in the several courses, supplemented by any general conclusions or suggestions which might have come out of the experience of the last five years. Consequently I have confined myself to these subjects, and have said nothing about suggestions made by some members of the Department concerning particular courses.

There is a second point on which I ought to say a word. In our conversation you expressed a desire to have a statement of facts which would enable you to answer properly the question, raised in the Committee on the Curriculum, if the Classical Department was making the best use it could of its present corps of instructors. I have taken up this topic under no. IV. To see how the hour-schedules of the Department compared with those of other departments seemed to me the simplest way to get light on the matter. The comparison will, I hope, not seem invidious to you. I have set the figures down because they furnished the information which you desired in answering the implied criticism of the Department.

Very sincerely yours Frank F. Abbott

ALS (WWP, UA, NjP).

E N C L O S U R E

From Frank Frost Abbott

Dear President Wilson: Princeton, N. J., December 9, 1909.

I beg to submit the following statement in answer to your letter of inquiry concerning the application of the preceptorial system in the Classical Department:

I, II. To take up in order the points mentioned in your letter the accompanying table, (A) furnishes the statistics asked for in the first and second questions.

III. In most of the Junior and Senior courses the instructor conducting the course carries the preceptorial work also. For Junior and Senior subjects where help is needed, and for Freshman and Sophomore preceptorial groups, choice is made of the men who seem specially qualified by their training, experience, or personal qualities for the task in hand. The necessity of not burdening a particular preceptor with too many hours and subjects, and of avoiding a conflict in hours of course limits the application of this principle in some cases.

The final responsibility for the allotment of preceptorial work rests with the Secretary of the Department, who makes an assignment after consultation with the instructor conducting the course, and, usually, after conferring with the preceptor concerned. In some cases other members of the department also are consulted.

IV. The preceptorial work of the Professors in the Department who are conducting courses has been limited in the main to the courses of which they have charge. It seemed desirable to give this allotment precedence over all others because of the acquaintance which the Professor in question already had with the members of his class, and because his instruction was likely to be most valuable in the field in which his special training lay. The class work and the preceptorial assignments just mentioned, taken together, bring the number of hours offered by Professors of the Department to such a high point that additions would be likely to diminish their efficiency as teachers or their productivity as scholars. To ascertain if the Classical Department was economizing its resources as carefully as other departments in the University, an examination was made of the hour schedules of the members of the Classical Department and of the corresponding statistics for the other ten non-professional departments of the University. In the Classical Department, this term, the average number of hours for the older men is 9, which is ½ hour per week greater than the combined average of the corresponding officers in all the other departments.

In connection with this group it may be noted that their hours include 24 given to graduate courses, that is 4 of the 9 hours which each of the 6 men concerned gives are in the Graduate School. The amount of work required in these subjects is in the nature of things far greater than is needed in undergraduate courses. Upon this group also falls the direction of students who are writing their theses for the Doctor's degree, and since there are four graduates at present engaged upon their dissertations, with two, or possibly three, more who will soon be at work upon them, this group of men is probably giving more time to students than any corresponding group of classical men engaged in advanced work in any other large university. The average number of hours per week for the classical preceptors this term is 15, or 4 more than the general University average, the average 15 being found in only one other department. The combined average for all the members of the Classical Department is 13, or 3½ hours more per week than the departmental average elsewhere in the University. The pressure upon the Department is likely to be greater rather than less as the Honors Courses and the Graduate Courses develop.

V. The accompanying table (B) gives the classical programme which is being followed this year with Freshmen and Sophomores.

Latin:

Freshmen, first term. The preceptorial hour is given up to Latin Composition.

Freshmen, second term. The preceptors cover about two plays of Terence, discussing with their students such subjects as the construction of the plot, the portrayal of character, and stage setting.

Sophomores, first term. The two authors mentioned here are read in the class and the preceptorial hour respectively because they were contemporaneous and were friends. The topics chosen have to do with the life of their times.

Sophomores, second term. Besides reading the Satires of Horace the members of the preceptorial groups memorize some of the poems of Horace and Catullus, and write upon a topic connected with their reading.

Greek:

Freshmen, first term. The preceptorial hour is devoted to Greek composition.

Freshmen, second term. The aim of the preceptorial work is to give the students "an individual training in the language."

Sophomores, first term. The connecting link between the class work and the preceptorial is furnished by the fact that the *Frogs* of Aristophanes is a parody and criticism of Euripides and Aeschylus. The groups study the spirit of the Greek drama, the staging and production of Greek plays, etc., so far as the time allows.

Sophomores, second term. "Extended and sight reading" in all the groups, supplemented in a group of selected men by the reading and discussion of a chosen prose piece of literature.

Some general difficulties experienced in the application of the true preceptorial method in the first two years, which have been noted by several members of the Department, may be mentioned here:

1. Three-fourth[s] of the time which a student spends in outside work in Freshman year, and two-thirds in Sophomore year, is given to preparation for the class-room. The hour, or the two hours, in which he prepares for his meeting with a preceptor does not in the opinion of several men provide a sufficient basis for profitable discussion.

2. There is a lack of books written in English and suitable for Freshmen and Sophomores, in several fields which we should like to cover. Many instructors find that the Freshmen particularly lack a background of general information to such an extent that the discussions in which they engage are sometimes, almost, if not entirely, futile.

4. The examination and "dropping" system is thought by many to interfere with the perfect working of the preceptorial method. If the hour with the preceptor is not represented on the examination paper, these men think that it will be neglected by the students. If it finds a place on the paper, there are two

possibilities: (a) Preceptors may be allowed great latitude in following their lines of individual preference, in which case special papers must be set for each group. It has been thought that this plan is too complicated and that it may result in the use of examination papers of varying degrees of difficulty for members of the same class taking the same subject, and has been adopted only in a limited way in a few courses. (b) The other alternative is practically the same programme for all the groups.

The difficulties just mentioned have a tendency to reduce the preceptorial work in a subject to a one-hour course, and the discussion to an informal recitation. Against this tendency the Department is constantly struggling. It is so hard to overcome some of the obstacles, however, that several members of the Department would favor the introduction of small divisions in some courses, at least. It might be desirable to try this plan with some course in one of the two lower classes. If it should seem wise to make the experiment, probably our present corps of instructors would allow us to divide the class into sections of 12 or 15 men. On the other hand the feeling is general in the Department that "intimate relations are established between the preceptor and the student," that "there has been a marked change in the attitude of the average boy toward the study of the classics" during the last five years and "an improvement in the intellectual life of the two lower classes."

Suggestions have been made by members of the Department looking to certain changes in the sequence of Freshman and Sophomore courses, and in the subject matter and method of treating certain courses, but, as I understand from our recent conversation that they are not needed for the matter in hand, they are passed over now.

There are twenty classical courses offered in the Junior and Senior years, and detailed descriptions of the way in which the preceptorial method is applied in them have been prepared, and will be submitted for examination if desired, but, for the sake of brevity, they are omitted here.

The plans of work in these subjects are admirable, and all agree that the system is working well.

Very sincerely yours, Frank F. Abbott

A. Men Electing the Classical Department

		1905-06		1906-07		1907-08		1908-09		1909-10
		1st Term	2nd Term	1st Term	2nd Term	1st Term	2nd Term	1st Term	2nd Term	1st Term
	Juniors	9	9	3	3	2	2	14	14	7
	Seniors	4	4	6	6	3	3	1	2	11
	Men taking electives in the department (but not [of] the department)									
1 course	Sophomores	66	67	57	56	46	53	57	75	114
	Juniors	32	17	22	18	18	15	18	15	5
	Seniors	5	7	18	10	26	26	21	40	8
2 courses	Sophomores									
	Juniors	0	1	2	2	1	1	1	2	0
	Seniors	1	1	0	0	0	1	2	1	3

Sophomores

year	First Term		Second Term	
	Latin.	Greek.	Latin.	Greek.
1905 & 1906	71	153	223	27
1906 & 1907	57	174	242	18
1907 & 1908	85	138	190	26
1908 & 1909	57	123	201	25
1909 & 1910	104	151	—	—

Freshmen

year	Latin.	Greek.
1905 & 1906	293	187
1906 & 1907	229	139
1907 & 1908	234	132
1908 & 1909	293	148
1909 & 1910	310	151

Freshmen and Sophomores in the Classical Department

F. F. Abbott

B

FRESHMEN.

	1st term	2nd term
Class Subject	Lysias & Plato's Apology	Herodotus & the Odyssey
Precept. Subj.	Greek Composition.	Herodotus
Class Subject	Sallust & Livy	Plautus
Precept. Subj.	Latin Composition	Terence

SOPHOMORES.

	1st term	2nd term
Class Subject	Alcestis of Euripides	Lucian
Precept. Subj.	Frogs of Aristophanes	Rapid Reading
Class Subject.	The Agricola and Annals of Tacitus	The Odes of Horace and Catullus
Precept. Subj.	The Letters of Pliny and Topics	The Satires of Horace and Memorizing, etc.

TLS with Hw tables (WWP, UA, NjP).

From Robert Scott Walker[1]

Dear Sir New York. Dec 10/09

I hope you will read Albert Shaw's article on "College Reform" in the Dec Review of Reviews.[2] It expresses very forcibly & fully my own convictions, (& doubtless also of many other parents) on this important subject formed largely from my own observations during my son Edward's[3] course at Princeton. Foot Ball, & the Upper Class Clubs, are, in my opinion, both very serious evils, and should be either radically reformed or eliminated altogether. The former occupies the foremost place in the thoughts & ambitions of too many, (I think I may safely say the majority) of the students, especially of the younger classes, to the detriment, if not exclusion, of the studies, & intelectual training, which are the primary objects for which Colleges & Universities are established & maintained. The Clubs tend to breed a spirit of exclusiveness & snobishness, which should be foreign to the cosmopolitan spirit that ought to pervade all the classes from the highest to the lowest. They cultivate & encourage in their members a taste & habit of luxurious & extravagant living far beyond what most of them have previously enjoyed in their own homes, or would be able to maintain after graduation.

I have not forgotten your earnest efforts to overcome these evils & trust you will continue them until successful.

Very sincerely yours Robt S Walker

ALS (WP, DLC).

[1] A retired stockbroker of New York.

[2] Albert Shaw, "College Reform—And Football," New York *Review of Reviews*, XL (Dec. 1909), 724-29. Shaw called for correction of the many evils that he said were attending the "topsy-turvy, Alice-in-Wonderland college development in this country." Enrollment was expanding too rapidly, and college leaders were finding it difficult to maintain discipline. "Colleges," he went on, "are allowing themselves to be invaded by aggregations of social clubs and luxurious cliques." One evil of "great magnitude" was the "craze for intercollegiate athletics," that "furor for exciting public contests that makes the muscular athlete the worshiped idol of college life, and obscures the leader in brains and scholarly work." Football, in particular, needed drastic reform. Over-commercialized and professionalized, the game had degenerated into "unseemly gladiatorial contests in the pretended name of a friendly competition." Not only was it likely to produce serious injury, but it fostered a kind of "factitious heroism" and encouraged unsportsmanlike conduct. It was high time, he concluded, for parents and the general public to rise in protest.

[3] Edward Washburn Walker, Princeton 1907, who was at this time attending the Columbia Law School.

From Charles Elvin Hendrickson, Jr.,[1] with Enclosure

My dear Dr. Wilson: Jersey City, N. J. Dec. 10th 1909.

I have received your letter of the 8th inst. yesterday morning and communicated the contents thereof to the Dinner Committee of our Board of Trade. The Dinner Committee were so pleased at the prospects of having you that they immediately busied themselves to change the date. Only one other speaker had previously promised to speak at the Dinner and after communication with him and explaining to him the situation he was likewise delighted to have the change made, os [so] that the Dinner will be held on January 14th.[2] I telegraphed you as soon as I received this information yesterday and I presume that the telegram was duly received by reason of the fact that I have just received a telegram from Mr. Close advising me that you will be out of Town to-night.

We intended to come down to Princeton to-day and call on you and advise you on any matter in connection therewith about which you might wish to inquire.

Our Alumni is young and we are very glad to have you come here this winter and we shall make this Board of Trade Dinner quite a Princeton Affair. Mr. Dear[3] who is the President of the Alumni Association of Hudson County, wishes to have you spend the night with him at his home and I am enclosing you a letter which he gave me yesterday afternoon to be delivered to you. If you will advise either Mr. Dear or myself of the time of your arrival in the City we will meet you at the Pennsylvania Station and take charge of you here.

Thanking you for your letter of the 8th inst. and for your willingness to favor us, I remain,

Very sincerely yours, Charles E. Hendrickson Jr.

1 Princeton 1895, a lawyer of Jersey City who had served in the New Jersey Assembly in 1907 and 1908. In the latter year he was appointed a member of the New Jersey State Board of Assessors and served as president of that body from 1912 to 1915.

2 For an unknown reason, Wilson was unable to fulfill this engagement.

3 Joseph Albert Dear, Jr., Princeton 1893, Editor of the Jersey City *Jersey Journal* and President of the Evening Journal Association, publishers of the *Jersey Journal*.

ENCLOSURE

From Joseph Albert Dear, Jr.

My dear Doctor: Jersey City, N. J. Dec. 9th., '09.

Owing to another engagement, I am unable to go with the Committee from the Princeton Alumni Association of Hudson County to help extend our invitation to you to come and speak at the Board of Trade dinner in January. You may be sure that all Princeton men in Hudson County will turn out to do you honor and give you a hearty wlecome [welcome] on that occasion. Your presence here will certainly give a boom to our newly organized Alumni Association.

I should deem it an honor to have you be my guest on that evening. Mrs. Dear joins me in inviting you to stay over night at our house. Yours sincerely, Joseph A Dear

TLS (WP, DLC).

A News Report of an Address in Summit, New Jersey

[Dec. 10, 1909]

"TO MAKE MEN UNLIKE SIRES"

That, Perhaps, Says Woodrow Wilson, Is Effect Colleges Should Have.

Special Dispatch to the EVENING NEWS.

SUMMIT, Dec. 10.—Discussing "Our Flag and Our Day" before the Athenaeum last night Dr. Woodrow Wilson asserted his belief that the problem and duty of the day are the resolving into a compact national program a national purpose of the present complex and diverse forces in our national life. Perhaps the most important effect colleges should have upon young men, he thought, was to make them unlike their fathers, so that progress might not be hampered by complacent adherence to the existing order of things. Nevertheless, he explained, the sinews of law are what hold us together, and these sinews are being loosened by those newcomers, who have no restraint but reason. Our safety, therefore, is in making this century, this generation, a century and a generation that can provide itself with a constitution. The danger was, he said, that through specialized interests growth would mean, not progress, but the sapping of the strength of the whole.

The entire address was a most stirring one, and there were frequent demonstrations of sympathy and enthusiasm. Dr. Wilson opened his address by referring to the peculiarity of our nation, in that it cannot be generalized, varying so greatly as it does in its different parts.

He then spoke of our national history as dividing naturally into periods of centuries; one problem being disposed of in each century since the discovery of our land. The first century was given to the establishment of English sentiments [settlements], the second to disposing of governments other than English, and the third to the setting up of a strong, individual government. "And now," Dr. Wilson said, "the problem of this century is what to do with this force we have created and established. This problem is complicated by the mixture of elements in our land."

This mixture of bloods—the importance of which is the resultant mixture of thoughts and motives—brings about an economic and social complexity very difficult to make compact in national life. When trying to state to himself the most important effect that colleges should have on young men, Dr. Wilson said he had thought it would be to make them unlike their fathers, not because of any disparagement intended to the lives and conduct of the fathers, but because the country cannot afford to have the sons give themselves again to the same special interests of the fathers, but rather to broader patriotic aims. "The successful man," said the speaker, "does not want change because his success grew from the existing order of things. This is the negative of progress. To solve the problem of the century, therefore, we must go to men less tied down to the existing order, who can throw off the past generation and going back over the past centuries look far away in the light of past aims to the goal ahead.

"Those bound to special interests, to prepossessions, are like the man in the desert, who is said to have lost himself when in reality that is the only thing he has not lost, and who, if left to himself to find his way would go round in a circle, following his heart. The men of the present time, far from being disgusted by the state of affairs, should be glad that there is a complication, that there is work to be done worth the doing. Theirs it is to form such a combination of interests that there will be a national program, a national purpose. We of the older order talk still in terms of things that do not exist.

"The newer blood does not. It says, 'We cannot stop for the Constitution, if the Constitution does not fit our needs.' These newer bloods are none the less true lovers of our country, but the sinews of law are what holds us together, and these sinews are being loosened by these newcomers, who have no restraint but reason. Our safety, therefore, is in making this century—this generation a century and a generation that can provide itself with a Constitution.

"To keep alive things must grow, but the danger is that there may, through specialized interests, be over much growth in one place which will sap the life of the whole. We must therefore give up our prepossessions; we must find out the new ideas that we never thought of before. We must join the procession. We must bring out the most wholesome ideas and form a newer, stronger generation, more full of aspiration to lift a world—a generation of American men capable of living well in their own day and of playing the prophet of days to come."

Printed in the *Newark Evening News*, Dec. 10, 1909; some editorial headings omitted.

From Frank Arthur Vanderlip

Dear Dr. Wilson: New York, December 11, 1909.

The Bankers of New York City hold their annual banquet at the Waldorf on January 17th. It is the unanimous wish of the Committee having the matter in charge that you will be our guest and speak to us that evening. I want to add to the official invitation my most earnest personal wish that you will see your way clear to accept this invitation. I happen to be Chairmen [Chairman] of the New York City Group of the Association this year, and it will be a personal favor that I shall appreciate in the highest degree if you will come.

Senator Aldrich will speak and Secretary MacVeagh[1] will also make a brief address. There will not be over four speakers, and it will be an early dinner. Your accom[m]odations will, of course, be arranged for and everything done that can be to make the task as pleasant a one as possible. The audience, I hardly need to tell you, is the most representative gathering of financial men of the year. They will listen to you with the greatest interest.

Please do not disappoint me.

Faithfully yours, F A Vanderlip

TLS (WP, DLC).

[1] Franklin MacVeagh, formerly a wealthy wholesale grocer of Chicago, at this time Secretary of the Treasury in the Taft administration.

From Arthur Twining Hadley

New Haven, Connecticut.

My dear Mr. Wilson: December 11th, 1909.

I am sorry to say that I cannot go to Washington for the National Academy of Arts and Letters, on account of the visit of Mr. Taft to New Haven; and during the latter part of the week I have to go to Washington to make a return visit at the White House.

I do not want to try to arrange for a conference on my return from Washington if I can possibly help it—partly because I shall not be alone on the journey, and therefore not fully free to consult my own convenience; but still more because events are moving so rapidly at this end that I do not want to have a conference on my way home from Washington, and then find that things have happened while I was at Washington which put a different face on the whole situation.

Still less do I want to try to arrange things by letter if it can possibly be helped.

I very much hope that things will take such shape that you and Lowell and I can take identical action in the interests of public safety; and I shall do everything that I can toward that end. On the other hand, it will be impossible either to antagonize or ignore the efforts of Harris[1] and others for a New England conference on the twentieth. These are minor difficulties, but they create a rather perplexing situation.

Faithfully yours, Arthur T Hadley

TLS (WP, DLC).

[1] George Harris, President of Amherst College since 1899.

From Howard Houston Henry[1]

Dear President Wilson: Fort Washington. Pa. Dec 11th '09

To-day I saw Mr. Percy Haughton in New York and he told me that President Lowell of Harvard had written or was about to write you a letter refer[r]ing to a suggestion that Princeton, Yale and Harvard should meet with the idea of reforming the foot-ball rules and asking that Mr. Parke Davis[2] be sent to represent Princeton.

This to my mind is a mistake, as I do not think Mr. Davis a man best suited for this position, and I feel confident that you have the same opinion.

There are some very vital and important points that I should like to talk to you about in reference to this meeting of the three universities, therefore I ask, if I may come to see you next Thursday, at any time that will be convenient to you, if you think there is any need of haste I can of course come sooner.

The position that Princeton takes at this time will be a tremendous influence on our future in foot-ball and I should very much like to see you before we commit ourselves to any agreement, even to meet with them.

I should like very much to explain myself more clearly, but it is a very complex situation, which would be foolish for me to try and explain by letter.

Very sincerely yours Howard H. Henry

ALS (WP, DLC).

1 Princeton 1904, former member of the Princeton football team, and son of Bayard Henry. At this time H. H. Henry was in delicate health and lived as a gentleman farmer in Fort Washington, Pa.

2 Parke Hill Davis, Princeton 1893, at this time a lawyer in Easton, Pa. Davis had played for Princeton and later achieved prominence as an historian of football.

From Cyrus Hall McCormick

My dear Woodrow: Chicago 11 December, 1909.

It was not my intention that the lectures of Professor Gore should be for the public so much as for the students. I do not think a public lecture amounts to much in the way of instruction. My only thot was that his address should be primarily for the students and might include such of the Faculty as would wish to hear it. I intended to have covered this idea when I said: "if it should be desirable for the Princeton boys to have such a course of lectures, I would be very glad to provide the means."

It gives me pleasure to know that you and the Faculty approve of this and will communicate with Professor Gore. Whenever you wish the funds for paying Professor Gore, ask the Treasurer to write to Mr. F. A. Steuert[1] at my office, and the matter will receive prompt attention.

I am, Very sincerely yours, Cyrus H. McCormick.

TLS (WP, DLC).

[1] His confidential secretary, Frederick A. Steuert.

To Frank Arthur Vanderlip

Princeton, N. J.

My dear Mr. Vanderlip: December 14th, 1909.

Your letter of the 11th reached me yesterday afternoon and I am going to state to you very frankly my difficulty in replying to it.

No man in public life irritates me and repels me more than Senator Aldrich of Rhode Island, except Mr. Joseph G. Cannon, the Speaker of the House, and I am frankly afraid that I would not behave myself properly if I were to speak after I had heard Mr. Aldrich speak. Moreover, it would be distasteful to me to be on the same programme with him.

You may laugh at me because of my extreme feeling in this matter, but it is very genuine, and I want your opinion as to whether in such circumstances it would be advisable for me to accept the otherwise very attractive invitation you send me. I am sure that, as you say, I could have no finer audience than would be afforded me by the bankers of New York City at their banquet, but I am a more or less excitable and explosive individual and I must not take the risk of marking the occasion by an unpleasant incident.

I do not mean, of course, that I would forget my manners, but I would be likely to say very plain and perhaps unpalatable things, unless I played an extremely demure and unnatural role and confined myself to abstract principles and educational themes, which would hardly be suitable for the occasion.

I know that you will understand and appreciate my difficulty.

With warm regard,

Cordially and faithfully yours, Woodrow Wilson

TLS (F. A. Vanderlip Papers, NNC).

To Winthrop More Daniels

My dear Daniels: Princeton, N. J. December 14th, 1909.

Thank you for your letter of the 12th.[1] Professor Gore's full name is James Howard Gore. His address, as given in Who's Who in America, is 2210 R St., N.W., Washington, D. C.

I return the letter from West. I should like, if possible, to avoid saying what I would have to say in Faculty if West carried out his present plan in the consideration of the matter of Teaching Fellows. I would be very much obliged to you, therefore, if you would be kind enough to let him know in some way that the method he is using is entirely illegal.[2] This might save us from an embarrassing incident. The letter, by the way, fills me with amazement.

Always cordially and faithfully yours,

Woodrow Wilson

TLS (Wilson-Daniels Corr., CtY).

[1] It is missing.

[2] The archival materials on the Graduate School do not fully explain the situation to which Wilson referred. However, the Faculty Committee on the Graduate School, on December 6, 1909, had recommended to the University Faculty that the title of teaching fellow be discontinued. Their report was at that time laid upon the table pending further study, but on March 7, 1910, the University Faculty did resolve to discontinue the title of teaching fellow; it further resolved that no officer of instruction in the university except an assistant or instructor on half-time appointment, or an instructor who had fulfilled the residence requirement of the Graduate School prior to his appointment as an instructor, could be a candidate for any degree. Clearly, Wilson believed that West's proposals and/or actions were not in accord with this proposed policy of the Faculty Committee on the Graduate School.

From Benjamin Franklin Nelson

Dear President Wilson: Minneapolis, Minn. Dec. 15, 1909

Yours of the 13th inst. just received. While we regret exceedingly that you could not see your way clear to accept the Presidency of our State University, we all appreciate your high sense of duty to your Alma Mater and on that ground alone we have consolation in our great disappointment. I will forward your letter to Gov. [Adolph Olson] Eberhart and Judge Wilson.

With best wishes for your success, I am,

Yours truly, B F Nelson

TLS (WP, DLC).

From William Williams Keen

My dear President Wilson: Philadelphia Dec. 15th, 1909.

I am very sure you will not misunderstand me in what I am going to write. The other day at the Contemporary Club, I met Mr. Francis Fisher Kane and he was so enthusiastic about the brief visit that he had from you and begged that he might have the opportunity of entertaining you himself when you came here in March for the Contemporary Club meeting that I had not really the heart to tell him that I had already invited you and

Mrs. Wilson to stay with us, but acquiesced entirely in his wish that he might have the privilege and pleasure of entertaining you.

If it is agreeable to you, therefore, I will let this arrangement stand without telling him that I had already invited you. I gave up the pleasure very reluctantly, I grant (that is to myself), but it is always a pleasure to oblige a friend and also it helps the Club along by one's being generous rather than selfishly getting all he can for himself.

Please present my kindest Xmas greetings to Mrs. Wilson and your daughters. Yours very truly, W. W. Keen

TLS (WP, DLC).

From Albert Shaw

My dear Wilson: New York December 15, 1909

Thank you very much for your letter. In my jocose remark the other day, that you might disagree with my article, I remembered two things: First, that you have always been very fond of the game of football; and, second, that you are at the head not only of an important university but of what I regard as a vastly overgrown college. It is not in the least due to your methods that the college is overgrown. If your plans for bringing order and method into undergraduate life were carried out my criticism of Princeton as numerically too large would quite wholly disappear. I think that the freedom of the elective system at Harvard, together with the great number of undergraduates, is not the best system for boys of eighteen.

I was glad to see you looking so strong and well the other day, and appreciate the importance of the work you are doing and the greatness of the problems you are helping to solve.

Faithfully yours, Albert Shaw

TLS (WP, DLC).

To James Howard Whitty[1]

My dear Mr. Whitty: Princeton, N. J. December 16th, 1909.

It was very pleasant indeed to hear from you, and I am very much interested to hear of the definitive edition of Poe's Poems which you have nearly completed.[2] I shall look forward to examining it with a great deal of pleasure.

I wish very much that I had some special knowledge of Poe or of material which would be of assistance to you, but my particular attention has never been drawn in that direction.

I have inquired at our University Library and find that they have only a few numbers of one volume of the Columbian Magazine, the volume for 1788.

With much regard,

Cordially and sincerely yours, Woodrow Wilson

TLS (WC, NjP).

[1] General Manager of the Improved Mercantile Agency of Richmond, Va.

[2] *The Complete Poems of Edgar Allan Poe*, collected, edited, and arranged with memoir, textual notes, and bibliography by J. H. Whitty (Boston and New York, 1911).

From Frank Arthur Vanderlip

Dear Dr. Wilson: New York, December 17th, 1909.

Your letter interests me very much; but if that were possible, it redoubles my desire that you be a guest of the Bankers at their dinner in January. I will say that in times past I have shared your feeling. I believe, however, that the Senator has been doing very intelligent work in the present instance, and if we are to have any adequate financial legislation within the next few years, it has got to come largely through his efforts. Even feeling the way you do, however, I do not see that there is any need at all for that feeling to deprive us all of what we very much want. We all want to hear you speak and to speak your mind. I could say with most sincere feeling a great deal along the lines of what the country has come to look for when you do speak your mind, but I will content myself with merely saying that nothing will suit the men who have this matter in charge so much as to have you present at this dinner, and as a matter of course, you will come with perfect freedom as to what you will have to say. We sincerely want you. I know perfectly well that it means more to the success of the dinner, (and by success I mean a dinner that enables men to carry away something in their minds as well as in their stomachs), to have you speak than all besides that there is on the programme. I want you to come. Please try to look at it so that it will be possible.

Sincerely yours, F A Vanderlip

TLS (WP, DLC).

Notes for an Address to the Princeton Alumni Association of Northern New Jersey

Alumni at Englewood, 17 Dec., '09.

Congratulations of [on] formation of Nor. N. Jersey Association

Enthusiastic love and organized support of her alumni the breath of life to the University.

These simple enough if Princeton had only to consider old-fashioned progress; but she is now at an intermediate age of the world when a reconstruction of university life has to be considered, and the searching question asked, 'What ought it to be?'

It *is* not what most of you remember. Those who merely visit the place, those who do not live there, *cannot* know what it is.

Is it worth while to send a boy to college for four years of miscellaneous distraction and the ferment of an unreal and mimic world?

The college must be (α) A place whose main interest is intellectual and moral discipline

(β) A place of individual development, the original forces released

(γ) A place, by the same token, of free democratic contacts, where the essence of the life is to be enjoyed without being *elected* to enjoy it.

Princeton has ideas on these subjects: those who have not must fall into the background and cannot serve her.

The alumni of every great college must have in their minds a programme of academic statesmanship. Let Princeton be first in this as in every other element of thoughtful alumni support.[1]

17 Dec., 1909.

WWhw MS (WP, DLC).

[1] There was a brief garbled account of Wilson's address in the *Newark Evening News*, Dec. 18, 1909.

Moses Taylor Pyne to Joseph Bernard Shea

My dear Joe: [Princeton, N. J.] December 18th, 1909.

President Wilson came in to see me today with a new and very astounding proposition. He states that in his mind there is still some doubt as to the legality of building the Thomson

College on the Golf Links, therefore he proposes that we shall divide the Graduate Colleges and have two, one to be built with Mrs. Swann's money on the site of University Hall,[1] and the other to be Procter's college, to be built on the Golf Links. When I said that Procter's gift for building purposes consists simply of a dining hall and that we had nothing in addition to put there except the Cleveland Memorial Tower which would not, of themselves, create a very satisfactory residence college, he said that if the matter were properly presented to Procter he would, no doubt, allow the $300,000 which he intended to put into Endowment to go to the building of dormitories and common rooms.

This strikes me as such a ridiculous solution of the question that it does not seem to me worth considering. At the same time he said that Sheldon and others would approve this settlement of the matter and that it would be very satisfactory to him.

It is so clear to me that this will simply mean the loss of Procter's money and what money could be brought to meet it, and the turning of the Thomson College into a small quad, that I thought I would write to you at once about it. While it seems impossible on the face of it, nevertheless, we must bear in mind that it will probably be brought up and attempted to be put through the Board, and before that will be brought before the Committee on the Graduate School and that a majority would probably favor it.

You said some time ago that you would probably be in Chicago and take a chance to see McIlvaine. I cannot see how he could take this view of the matter, although I should not be surprised if Cyrus McCormick and Jones would approve of it.

I am simply writing this to keep you advised.

Yours very sincerely, M. Taylor Pyne.

TCL (M. T. Pyne Coll., NjP).

1 On the corner of Nassau Street and University Place.

To Frank Arthur Vanderlip

Princeton, N. J.

My dear Mr. Vanderlip: December 20th, 1909.

Thank you very much for your letter of December 17th. I cheerfully yield to your judgment in the matter of the Bankers' dinner, though I must say that I do so with a good deal of diffidence and a good deal of serious doubt as to my ability to come up anywhere near your expectations. You are so kind and so urgent in the matter that I cannot decline, and I sincerely appreciate the compliment of your urgency. I will come and do my best to be both candid and discreet.[1]

Cordially and faithfully yours, Woodrow Wilson

TLS (F. A. Vanderlip Papers, NNC).

[1] Four news reports of Wilson's address are printed at Jan. 18, 1910, Vol. 20.

From Moses Taylor Pyne

My dear Woodrow New York 20th December 1909

I have been thinking over the suggestion made by you on Saturday. There are some difficulties from which I have not, as yet, been able to get away.

I understood you to say that it was your idea to place the Thomson Graduate College on the site of University Hall and to ask Mr Procter to so change his gift that all the half million shall go into buildings, which, with the Cleveland Tower, shall be placed on the Golf Links, so that we shall have two graduate colleges, and to remove the University Dining Halls to the Nassau Inn.

Will you kindly let me know if I have correctly grasped your idea?

I have not the figures nor the ground plan here, but are you sure that the Swann gift will build the whole of the quad (except the Tower) or would it cover only a part? And could we get 800 men in the Nassau Inn without having to make very expensive enlargements and alterations.

It seems to me that it would be rather awkward to again ask Mr Procter to change the terms of his offer at this late day.

Yours very sincerely M Taylor Pyne

ALS (WP, DLC).

From Winthrop More Daniels

My dear Wilson: Princeton, N. J. Dec. 20, 1909.

Here's Prof. Gore's reply to my letter of invitation.[1] Shall I say to him that we accept his offer at twenty five dollars ($25.00) per lecture for a course of six lectures, to be given either two or three at a time, i.e. upon the occasion of a single visit, in March or April, the specific dates to be arranged later?

Yours ever sincerely W. M. Daniels.

ALS (WP, DLC).

[1] Wilson returned it to Daniels.

To Moses Taylor Pyne

My dear Momo: Princeton, N. J. December 21st, 1909.

I realize very keenly the awkwardness of asking Mr. Procter to change the plans he has had in mind, but I feel at the same time that we have come to a point where it is absolutely necessary that some arrangement should be made which will render it possible for me to exercise my authority as President in some satisfactory and efficient way and to arrange the organization of the University under me in such a manner that I can conscientiously be responsible for it. The suggestion I made the other day is central to the consideration of all the things which concern the immediate future of the University. It was for that reason that I took the liberty of laying it before you so earnestly and that I now venture to say again that I think it necessary to do this, or something like it, unless obstacles which I do not now see should arise.

I had a conference with Mr. Imbrie yesterday in order to put the whole proposal upon a definite estimate of income and cost and all the rest, and he hopes in a few days to have the figures ready for me. So far as we were able to get at the figures yesterday by data already in his possession, it was his judgment that the plan could be carried out.

My proposal is this. That we build the quadrangle at the corner of Nassau Street and University place with Mrs. Swann's money. It seems probable that for the $330,000 now available from her bequest it would be possible to pay for the three dormitory sides of the quadrangle and one half of the dining hall side. It is possible that we might need as much as $20,000 more, but Mr. Imbrie informs me that there is no such limitation on our use of the Alumni Fund[1] as would exclude our using a portion of it for a portion of the graduate quadrangle, provided, only, the portion of the building to which it was applied should be put upon the same income-bearing basis as an undergraduate dormitory. Imbrie is confident that the number of men now being provided with meals at University Hall could be taken care of in the other half of the dining hall portion of the quadrangle, plus accommodations such as could be provided at the Nassau Inn. Mr. Day estimates that one half of the dining hall portion of the quadrangle would cost $100,000. We have not yet looked into the cost of making the necessary changes in the Nassau Inn, but, assuming those changes made, there seems to be no doubt that one of the classes could be accommodated there on a basis which would be a paying basis to the owners of the Nassau Inn.

My proposal was that it be suggested to Mr. Procter that he spend, not the whole $500,000, but $400,000 of it for the erection of a suitable graduate hall of residence on the Golf Links, with which, of course, the Cleveland Memorial Tower would be connected, making the total cost for the group, including the tower, $500,000. This would leave a margin of $100,000 for endowment.

I think that if you knew the interest that these suggestions have excited and the enthusiastic approval they have met with in the minds of such men as Capps and Daniels, you would realize how important an element their consideration should constitute in the accommodation of interests here.

I hope that no consideration of haste will prevent our exhausting the possibilities. So far as I can ascertain without definite estimates, the quadrangle at the corner would, after the payment of the interest on the University Hall mortgage, yield sufficient income for ten or twelve Thomson Fellowships.

Let me remind you, also, that we already have graduate students enough to fill, and probably more than fill, one of the proposed establishments, and that, if we can keep the men we now depend upon for graduate instruction enthusiastic in the promotion of our interests, there is no reason to doubt that by the time these buildings were completed we should have men enough to fill both.

I will be very glad indeed to come in and talk this plan or any other phase of the matter over with you whenever you suggest.

Always affectionately yours, Woodrow Wilson

TCL (M. T. Pyne Coll., NjP).
[1] See M. T. Pyne to WW, July 23, 1904, n. 2, Vol. 15.

To Henry Burling Thompson

[Princeton, N. J.]

My dear Mr. Thompson: December 21st, 1909.

There is a Dr. Lewis R. Cary here, who is at present Fellow in Biology, whom Conklin is very anxious to retain at an increased stipend as his Assistant during these strenuous days of the rearrangement of the biological work in the new laboratory and during the second term, when he (Conklin) is to be away. If this is to be done, we shall need an extra $400. I am taking the liberty of writing to ask if you would be willing to contribute to that sum, inasmuch as I really dare not at present go to the Finance Committee for additional sums of money and inasmuch as this should not, I take it, be a permanent charge. If the income of the endowment Cleve Dodge contributed to the work of the Department is ever freed from other charges and made available, I suppose that a portion of it could be used to meet such additional charges as this.

I hope that you will not think that I am taking too great a liberty in making this suggestion.

It would not be necessary, I take it, that this money should actually be paid in for several months.

I hope that you are expecting to be in Princeton some time soon, because there are matters I should very much like to discuss with you which concern the general policy and success of the University.

Always cordially and faithfully yours,

[Woodrow Wilson]

CCL (WWP, UA, NjP).

From Winthrop More Daniels, with Enclosures

My dear Wilson: Princeton, N. J. Dec. 21, 1909.

Enclosed herewith are papers and letters handed to me today by Mr. Shipman, with the hope expressed that I would forward them to you. He said that Mr. Adriance had read the document signed by four of the Preceptors, and was expected to sign it; also that the signatures of other Preceptors were expected, and among them he mentioned Mr. Pahlow and Mr. Myers. If desired, I shall be ready to discuss the matter at any time.

Very sincerely yours, W. M. Daniels.

TLS (WWP, UA, NjP).

E N C L O S U R E I

Charles Worthen Spencer to Winthrop More Daniels

[Princeton, N. J.]

My dear Professor Daniels, 10 December, 1909.

Further reflection inclines me to take advantage of your general invitation yesterday to communicate individually views on any feature of the Report,[1] and writing seems the less time-consuming method.

Concerning greater participation in preceptorial work by men giving courses, I understood the Report to recommend adversely. Were the whole teaching force more nearly adequate in numbers

I should agree that the average number of hours carried by the men giving courses was sufficient, regard being had to the circumstances that you mention. But with the situation as it is, or even improved within the limits of reasonable hope, it seems to me that the contrast between the position of the men carrying seven hours and that of those carrying from eleven to fifteen hours is deserving of attention. Of the burden-grievous-to-be-borne which the Department is carrying, a disporportionate share is laid on the shoulders of the latter group of men. The present situation affords a contrast not merely in the number of hours carried. Attention to several courses on the one hand, and to only one on the other, means a greater absorption of time and energy in the former case, with much less opportunity to carry on special work or writing. In this last-mentioned kind of work the interest of the preceptors is as keen as that of the men carrying seven hours in but one course, but their opportunity is very much reduced.

It seems to me that this has a bearing on the matter of the possible recruiting of the strength of the Department in the future. With the situation as it is, men of the kind we want for the preceptorial function are not likely to find that career sufficient in itself, unless an opportunity for the pursuit of one's own work, more reasonably comparable to that of the men giving courses[,] is afforded. There is too much likelihood of simply adding to the force, Instructors with preceptorial duties, which policy is in my judgment undesirable.

I may say that, for myself, I have had for some time a pretty vivid consciousness of the contrast in the matter of position and opportunities between the seven-hour men and those carrying eleven to fifteen hours. It seems to me that the latter class of men were making a sacrifice in order that so far as their exertions could assist in making it possible the new methods of instruction should have a good chance. You see I have relied on the genuineness of your invitation to communicate views on the subjects mentioned in the Report to express myself freely. May I take this opportunity to express my great satisfaction with the R[e]port generally & with nearly all, if not all, its recommendations.

Very sincerely yours, Charles W. Spencer

TCLS (WWP, UA, NjP).

[1] That is, W. M. Daniels to WW, Dec. 6, 1909, printed as an Enclosure with W. M. Daniels to WW, Dec. 10, 1909.

ENCLOSURE II

Winthrop More Daniels to Charles Worthen Spencer

My dear Professor Spencer: Princeton, N. J. Dec 12, 1909

Your letter reached me yesterday morning, just after I had made personal delivery of my report to Mr. Close, the President's Secretary. With your permission, I shall be glad to forward your letter as a supplement to my Report to the President.

I am still of the opinion that increased participation of Professors in preceptorial work outside of their courses affords a negligible margin of teaching energy to supplement what is already engaged in preceptorial work.

There are but two professors—Ford and Coney—who have a 7 hour schedule. Coney's would have been 10 hours, except that by reason of his illness of last Summer, he was excused by the President this year from giving his 3 hr-per-week graduate course. Prof. Ford carries not one course but two,—one being a graduate course. McElroy and Meeker both carry 9 hours per week,—each carrying two courses, and each will probably have a larger weekly schedule next term. Each will then also carry two courses. The average of weekly hours occupied by Preceptors (exclusive of McCabe[1] & Whittlesey whose schedules I do not know) is exactly 11½. The Junior preceptors this term (except Persons[2] and McCabe) carry but 2 courses first term, and three, second term.

While there is some force in your contention that a Preceptor who simultaneously gives instruction in 3 courses must cover a wider range than a professor who gives but 1 course, the ordinary contrast is between the professor who simultaneously carries 2 courses as against the Preceptor who carries 3. We should both agree, I think, that sometimes a Preceptor may confine himself to the required texts in a given course, while a lecturer giving a course can hardly avoid, in preparing his lectures, digesting a larger number of sources. Still, if the "old barrel" is simply tapped every year, the scrutiny of material may, of course, be *nil*.

As a practical problem, the thing seems to narrow to this: would the obtaining of 4 additional preceptorial hours weekly from Prof. Ford both terms—(I omit Coney, on score of health) and 2 more each from McElroy and Meeker *for one term*; or a net addition of 6 hours per term per year be worth the cost,—or afford the equalization of work and the consequent relief of the preceptors which we desire?

I will hold your letter a day or two, until I hear whether I am at liberty to forward it to Pres. Wilson.

Yours very sincerely W. M. Daniels.

ALS (WWP, UA, NjP).

[1] David Aloysius McCabe, Instructor in History, Politics, and Economics.

[2] Charles Edward Persons, Preceptor in History, Politics, and Economics.

E N C L O S U R E I I I

Charles Worthen Spencer to Winthrop More Daniels

[Princeton, N. J.]

My dear Professor Daniels, 13 December, 1909.

As to forwarding my letter to you to the President in supplement to the Report, I should prefer that it should not be done if it seems to present invidious comment on individual members of the Department. I did not intend it thus—did not know what persons were carrying seven hour schedules. I should of course heartily agree with the special course taken in view of special circumstances to relieve Professor Coney this year. Likewise I do not cavil at the expediency of the arrangement by which Professor Ford carries seven hours.

It does not appear clearly to me whether the average of eleven and a half hours per week carried by Preceptors includes the graduate courses given by them, as the nine-hour, two-course schedules of Ass't. Professors Meeker and McElroy do. If they do not, this matter would be in point, because I understood the President last Spring to say that the giving of graduate courses must be considered to be outside the normal functioning of Department arrangements for the carrying on of the undergraduate work.

If I remember the President's question on this point correctly, I am not prepared to say that your opinion that "increased participation of Professors in preceptorial work outside of their courses affords a negligible margin of teaching energy to supplement what is already engaged in preceptorial work" is not adequate, as a specific reply to a specific question. The point I desired to make in my letter to you was that on the basis of Department arrangements as conceived in the preceding paragraph a distribution of Department burdens is actually in effect which bears more heavily on the preceptorial portion of the force in the matter of opportunities for individual work, as compared with the men carrying seven to nine hours. Here is where the scattering of attention over more undergraduate courses on the one hand, and the reckoning of graduate courses in the weekly schedule on the other, come in.

If you think it desirable that views on the matter I bring up be presented to the President in addition to the R[e]port, it would seem to me that this whole correspondence, or a minute on the subject in a different form, should be sent in. I would rather leave the judgment as to the expediency of such proceedings to you. While the matter is not specifically called for by the President's questions, it seems to me that any changes based upon reply to them should involve consideration of this matter.

Very sincerely yours, Charles W. Spencer

ENCLOSURE IV

Charles Worthen Spencer *et al.* to Winthrop More Daniels

Dear sir: [Princeton, N. J.] December 20, 1909.

We address the following communication to you in response to your general invitation to present views on the subject matter of the report read at the department meeting last week. Being aware of the correspondence between yourself and Mr. Spencer, we enclose copies thereof in order to refer more at length to subjects there mentioned. Admitting that the President's questions do not immediately call for views on the specific matters here presented, nevertheless it seems to us that these matters are at least indirectly germane. It is of course understood that invidious comment or personal animus are not in any way intended or felt. Nor do we wish to tithe mint anise and cummin [cumin] in respect to the comparative amount of effort put forth in attempting to serve the interests of the University. It is merely that you may be aware in a fuller manner than was possible on the day the report was read, of our views on these matters, at a time when the general arrangements of the department are being considered. The question of presenting these views to the President, we wish, of course, to leave to your discretion.

Our purpose, generally stated, may be said to be to communicate the observation that the actual distribution of hours of undergraduate instruction obtaining at present bears more heavily on the preceptors than upon the lecturers, particularly as affecting the opportunity for individual research or writing.

In the first place, our recollection coincides with that mentioned by Mr. Spencer in the enclosed correspondence, viz: that at the department meeting last spring it was the understanding that the giving of graduate courses was to be considered as outside the normal functioning of departmental arrangements for the carrying on of undergraduate work.

Second, surmising that your data for the figures of eleven and one-half hours per week as the average schedule carried by preceptors this term might be based upon the returns to the questionnaire sent around by the Dean this autumn, we made a personal canvass of the preceptors on this matter, with the following results (The figures for the lecturers are based on the facts in your letter to Mr. Spencer.):

For first term 1909-10

Average number of undergraduate hours, Preceptors (Mr. Baxter[1] excluded), 10 12/13

Average number of undergraduate hours, Lecturers (Dean Elliott excluded), 7

Average number of hours both graduate & undergraduate, Preceptors, 12 2/13

Average number of hours both graduate & undergraduate, Lecturers, 8 2/5

It is worthy of note in this connection that the number of undergraduate hours varies in the case of preceptors from class to class, which is not the case with lecturers. Also, it is to be observed that at present the number of students to be provided for is smaller than in some preceding years, and smaller than it is likely to be soon. Further, this year, in the case of preceptors having charge of seniors, they have been obliged to arrange their men in groups somewhat larger than is desirable, in order to carry graduate courses. However the burden as measured in hours of undergraduate instruction carried by the lecturers here may be deemed to compare with the situation elsewhere, it is submitted that there is a substantial margin between the number of hours of undergraduate instruction carried by the group of preceptors and that of the rest of the department. However practically necessary each step in this direction may have been, we believe that the resulting present situation presents a margin worthy of consideration. We believe that this observation has particular force in view of the assumption that the positions of preceptor and assistant professor are in all respects equal. The existence of this margin, for example, we hold to be significant if, as has been done for the last few years, the participation of the preceptors be called for in giving the course in history in sophomore year. The addition of two to a weekly schedule of eleven hours means much more than the addition of the same number of hours to a seven to nine hour schedule. Relief in the matter of the sophomore history course as was indicated in the report would be most welcome. Whether, however, any members of the department outside of the group of preceptors can with advantage be called upon to carry more hours than at present, is not in our view, so much the question, as whether, by any means, the share of the preceptors in the hours of undergraduate instruction may not be lightened so that they may have equality of opportunity for individual work.

Charles W. Spencer
C. H. McIlwain.
Edward S. Corwin
Henry R. Shipman.

TLS (WWP, UA, NjP).

1 Edgeworth Bird Baxter, who was Instructor both in Philosophy and in History, Politics, and Economics.

From Cleveland Hoadley Dodge

Dear Woodrow: New York December 21, 1909.

When Major [Henry Lee] Higginson presented Princeton with $10,000 four years ago, to found the Harvard Fellowship,[1] I registered a private vow that I would some day do the same for Harvard. I wrote to him the other day that I was now ready to give $10,000 to Harvard, if the University authorities would accept the Princeton Fellowship, and I have received a very pleasant letter from President Lowell, a copy of which I enclose,[2] as I think you ought to know about this, although I have requested President Lowell not to mention my name in connection with the gift and I know that you will also consider the matter confidential.

I suppose you will be at the Lowell reception next week at the University Club, but if not, and I do not see you before, let me wish you all the Compliments of the Season.

Yours affectionately, C H Dodge

TLS (WP, DLC).

1 About this fellowship, see the Minutes of the Board of Trustees of Princeton University printed at June 12, 1905, Vol. 16, and C. W. McAlpin to WW, Oct. 11, 1905, n. 1, *ibid.*

2 A. L. Lowell to C. H. Dodge, Dec. 20, 1909, TCL (WP, DLC).

From John Watson Foster

My dear Doctor: Washington, D. C. December 21, 1909

On June last I consulted you as to the disposition of a small balance of the Witherspoon Memorial Fund, and you advised its appropriation to the Princeton scholarship funds.

By the contributions of Mr. Carnagie [Carnegie] and others the amount has been increased to four thousand dollars ($4,000), which I have been instructed by the Board of Trustees to remit to you for investment as a permanent fund, to be known as the John Witherspoon Scholarship.

A check on New York for $4,000 is herewith enclosed, payable to your order. I have to request that you will endorse it over to the proper treasurer, and ask him to send me a receipt for the same *in duplicate*. Very truly, John W. Foster.

TLS (WP, DLC).

To Moses Taylor Pyne

Jersey City Station P. R. R.

My dear Momo: 5 P.M. Dec. 22 [1909].

I spent an hour and ten minutes with Mr. Procter this afternoon. He is unwilling to adjust the terms of his offer to my suggestion.

The acceptance of this gift has taken the guidance of the University out of my hands entirely,—and I seem to have come to the end. Affectionately yours, Woodrow Wilson

TCL (M. T. Pyne Coll., NjP).

From Thomas Davies Jones

My dear Mr President Chicago Dec 22, 1909

When I saw you the other day I did not know that you expect to attend the Madison Meeting. Will your arrangements permit of your stopping over in Chicago either coming or going, and if they will, for how long? We shall like you to be our guest while here (unless Mr McCormick feels that he has prior claims upon you) Very Hastily Yours Thomas D Jones

ALS (WP, DLC).

From Henry Burling Thompson

Greenville P. O. Delaware

Dear President Wilson: December 22d, 1909.

I have your letter of the 21st instant, relative to the retention of Dr. Lewis R. Carey. I shall be glad to contribute $100.00 towards the additional $400.00. Ordinarily, I would be willing to do more, but next month I have to pay my final subscription to the Campbell Hall Building Fund. If Dr. Carey is working on the re-arrangement of the Laboratory, I should think part of his income could properly be taken from the endowment fund.

I shall be in Princeton on the 30th instant. Our meeting[1] is called for 2:00 o'clock, but I expect to arrive in Princeton by 11:00 o'clock A.M. Robert Garrett expects to meet me at that hour, at the Curator's office, and go over his report. I could arrange to see you, say, at 12:00 o'clock, if agreeable to you.

Yours very sincerely, Henry B Thompson

TLS (WP, DLC).

[1] Of the trustees' Committee on Grounds and Buildings.

Howard Crosby Butler to Moses Taylor Pyne

Dear Mr. Pyne: [Princeton, N. J.] Dec. 22nd, 1909

I don't know if West is writing you about our recent Graduate School doings; but, as I wanted to send you my holiday greetings anyhow, I decided to give you an account of yesterday's and today's progress.

Last night Mr. Procter arrived, and West invited most of the Faculty to meet him; about forty came, representing all "sides," schools, kinds and colours I was going to say. It seemed like a real harmony meeting to see Dr. Patton and West, Fine and Hibben, Daniels and Magie, Prest. Wilson and everybody else gathering about the beer and sandwiches and all having a good word for Procter.

It was a delightful party, and I should have said it promised well for the future, if my once simple mind had not learned, in these last months, to look for a "nigger in every woodpile": but I hope and trust there may be none in this one.

Today at three our Committee[1] met again to consider the plans. Daniels was pleasant and said little but left after the first half hour. Fine did not come in until after we had adjourned and then heard of our doings and grunted his approval.

The five who attended the meeting throughout, West, Hibben, Capps, Conklin and myself, had a most agreeable conference and were unanimously agreed on all but two points, the number of baths and the breakfast rooms. The first we could have carried but did not press the point as Capps and Conklin both said it was in their minds a matter of economy, and if the architect could show no considerably greater outlay in having a bath to two men than in a bath to four, they had no objection; for they approved of making the men as comfortable as we could afford. The other point will settle itself, since Mrs. Swann's will and Procter both demand the breakfast rooms, and indeed the opposition to this is not great on the part of Capps or Conklin.

I was amazed and delighted to see how the five men got along together, and how much more rapidly and satisfactorily we could do business without our two professional obstructionists. We expect to have a conference with Cram early in January: and I anticipate no trouble at all unless some new wind blows.

I am doubly convinced that men in the Faculty Committee who are *not* in sympathy with the scheme of Graduate residence and who strongly oppose the settlement should be invited to resign. As a simple alumnus and a member of the Faculty I would not dare to suggest that the same procedure be followed in the Trustees' Committee.

Let me wish you and Mrs. Pyne a very Merry Christmas and the happiest and most prosperous of New Years.

Always sincerely yours, Howard Crosby Butler.

TCL (M. T. Pyne Coll., NjP).

[1] The Faculty Committee on the Graduate School.

To John Watson Foster

My dear Mr. Foster: Princeton, N. J. December 23rd, 1909.

Allow me to acknowledge with the highest appreciation your letter of December 21st, containing a check on New York for $4000, the balance of the Witherspoon Memorial Fund increased by Mr. Carnegie and others, and which you direct, by order of the Board of Trustees of the Fund, to be devoted to the maintenance of the John Witherspoon Scholarship in Princeton University.

In the name of the Trustees I accept the gift with real gratitude, not only because of its value to the University but also because of its testimony to the good will of the Trustees of the Witherspoon Memorial Fund and because of its association with the great name of John Witherspoon. I am sure that my colleagues in the Board of Trustees will regard it as a particularly acceptable and appropriate gift.

I will request the Treasurer of the University to send you a receipt in duplicate, as you request.

Mrs. Wilson joins me in warmest regards to Mrs. Foster[1] and yourself, and I am

Always faithfully and sincerely yours,

Woodrow Wilson

TLS (de Coppet Coll., NjP).

[1] Mary Parke McFerson Foster.

To Cleveland Hoadley Dodge

My dear Cleve: Princeton, N. J. December 23rd, 1909.

You are always doing things which excite my admiration and this gift of yours to Harvard, to which you refer in your letter of December 21st, is certainly altogether admirable. The letter from Lowell in which the gift is acknowledged is just what it ought to be, and I am sure from my knowledge of him that it comes from the heart. I do not like to regard beautiful things of this kind as confidential, but of course I will since you ask it.

I have many things to talk over with you, but they must not invade your Christmas season. I wish you, my dear fellow, the happiest possible Christmas season and a New Year full of everything that you desire.

Always faithfully and affectionately yours,

Woodrow Wilson

TLS (WC, NjP).

To Arthur Twining Hadley

Princeton, N. J.

My dear President Hadley: December 23rd, 1909.

It will give me pleasure to cooperate with you and President Lowell in the arrangement you suggested yesterday: namely, that we each appoint a representative to confer with regard to changes in the rules of the game of football, it being understood, as you then suggested, that you and President Lowell and I shall have an opportunity, if we desire, to discuss with these representatives the changes they suggest before they reach a final conclusion, and that when a final conclusion is reached we shall be bound for the next football season to play under the rules thus reformulated and amended.

The representative I shall appoint is Mr. Howard H. Henry of Philadelphia. Sincerely yours, Woodrow Wilson

TLS (A. T. Hadley Papers, Archives, CtY).

To Abbott Lawrence Lowell

My dear Mr. Lowell: [Princeton, N. J.] December 23rd, 1909.

I had a conference yesterday in New York with Mr. Hadley, in which he laid before me what he understood to be your desire and expressed as his own desire with regard to the method we should follow in trying to secure amendments to the football rules. I have just written him a letter, of which I herewith send you a copy, in which I agree to the plans which he then suggested. I hope that I have correctly understood your purpose in the matter and shall take the greatest pleasure in cooperating with you to the utmost.

My own feeling is that we ought to impress upon our representatives in this conference the absolute necessity of changes sufficiently radical to alter the present character of the game so that mass playing may be eliminated. Nothing else, I am sure, will satisfy the reasonable demands of the public in this matter, and nothing less is needed.

At the same time, I enter this arrangement with a sincere willingness to abide by the results, at any rate for the season proposed, in which those results may be tested.

I have just heard from Mr. Cleveland H. Dodge of his gift of a Princeton Fellowship to Harvard. This pleases me immensely. Mr. Dodge was a classmate of mine in college. I have known and loved him all my life, and he constantly proves by new actions how admirable he is.

Always cordially and faithfully yours,

[Woodrow Wilson]

CCL (WWP, UA, NjP).

To Henry Burling Thompson

[Princeton, N. J.]

My dear Mr. Thompson: December 23rd, 1909.

Thank you very much for your generous offer to contribute $100 towards the additional $400 necessary to retain Dr. Lewis R. Cary. I am sincerely obliged to you and hope that this sort of thing will not often be necessary.

I expect to be in Princeton all of the thirtieth and would be very much obliged if you could meet me, as you suggest, at noon on that day. If you will be kind enough to come to Prospect, I would very much appreciate it.

Always cordially and faithfully yours,

[Woodrow Wilson]

CCL (WWP, UA, NjP).

Melancthon Williams Jacobus to Henry Burling Thompson

My dear Thompson: Hartford, Conn., December 23d, 1909.

Nothing but pressure of administrative work has delayed my answer to your letter of the 14th instant, which I have read with great interest and not a little instruction.

I am reading Professor Hoskins' articles in the "Alumni Weekly," and feel that it is quite impossible for the Curriculum Committee and the Board of Trustees to avoid taking under consideration some at least of the points which he raises.[1]

On the docket for the next Committee meeting will be placed the items which you suggest, namely the C.E. entrance requirements in mathematics and a statement showing the number of students in the various elective courses for Junior and Senior years.

The second item calls for some preliminary investigation, and I am going to suggest that these statistics be prepared in advance of the Committee's meeting so that they can be placed before us then.

Your postscript to the effect that matters have become more satisfactory between the President and Pyne is a great relief and leads me to the following suggestion:

When we were last in Princeton, I had a talk with Wilson, most satisfactory in its character, urging him to that patience which is absolutely indispensable to the working out of his ideals, and encouraging him to embrace in every way he could such opportunities as offered themselves to him for strengthening friendships on the Board and establishing points of contact with the undergraduates, especially in such ways as he did with the Charter Club. He was surprised and naturally delighted to know the effect of his talk at the latter Club, and is even more anxious than you and I are to gain the ear of those who are willing to be informed on the University's policy and life.

Now, in view of his satisfactory talk with Pyne, and also in view of the delicate and embarrassing decisions which may come up before us (in which, of course, he will be more or less involved) regarding the final disposition of the Graduate School discussion, what I want to suggest is that sometime before the next meeting of the Board, which is on the 13th of January, we shall get Wilson and those who are his friends among the Trustees together in New York for a conference, the object of which will be to come to a better understanding between ourselves and him so that there may be some sort of sympathy and unity of action in the meetings; and having decided upon what is for the present the wise policy to pursue in the University's administration, to be able to carry that through without the constant irritation of uncertain discussion and debate in the sessions of the Board.

Now, this policy pertains, first of all, to a reduction of expenses until we shall secure a balancing of accounts that will free us from this unnatural and demoralizing dependence upon one or two liberal pocketbooks to carry the University along; secondly, the management and disposition of the Graduate Department with its Graduate School; and, thirdly, the development of the internal administration of the University which shall assure Wilson that in developing the policy of Deanships we are not setting him aside but recognizing his official rights while we are trying to increase the educational efficiency of the University.

It seems to me if we can come to an understanding on these three important points there will be a harmony of action and a consequent progress in things such as we have not yet been conscious of.

In this connection may I say that I wrote to MacAlpin the other day to secure from him a rescript of Dr. Stewart's motion in amending Pyne's resolution regarding the site of the Graduate School. Stewart's amendment is as follows:

"Provided that the legal right to use Mrs. Swan's money in the erection of the Graduate School upon the Golf Links be assured, and that Mr. Proctor first advise us of his intention in relation to the disposition of his proposed gift."

I think it is necessary that we keep clearly in mind what this amendment involves in any future action we may be called upon, in Committee or Board, to take regarding the erection of the buildings.

Have you heard anything more about Mr. Palmer's endeavors to effect a compromise in the matter of West's connection with the School?

Thanking you very much for the enclosure, which I read with interest and return herewith, I am, with kind regards,

Yours very sincerely, Melancthon W. Jacobus

P.S. I would like your opinion as to the wisdom of the conference I suggest, and if you think well of it, when it might be held and who might be asked to take part in it. J

TLS (WP, DLC).

[1] John Preston Hoskins, Princeton 1891, Assistant Professor of German at Princeton, had recently published four "papers," as he called them, under the title, "The Princeton Entrance Requirements, As Compared with Those of

Harvard and Yale," which appeared in the *Princeton Alumni Weekly*, x (Nov. 24, Dec. 1, Dec. 8, and Dec. 15, 1909), 134-38, 151-55, 167-70, and 187-90. A note in *ibid.*, Nov. 24, 1909, p. 131, indicates that Hoskins had undertaken the series at the request of Edwin Mark Norris, editor of the *Princeton Alumni Weekly*. The comparison of the three institutions was very detailed and complex, and Hoskins concluded that, for a variety of reasons, the entrance requirements for Princeton were considerably harder to meet than those for Harvard and Yale. In a number of specific instances, Hoskins indicated his belief that the Princeton requirements were unduly restrictive and tended to prevent many desirable students from entering Princeton.

From Moses Taylor Pyne

My dear Woodrow: New York December 24th, 1909

I trust that what was evidently a hasty note pencilled by you in the Jersey City Station does not represent your well considered conclusions, and that you will withdraw it upon further consideration. Yours affectionately, M Taylor Pyne

TLS (WP, DLC).

From Abbott Lawrence Lowell

Dear Wilson, Cambridge [Mass.] December 24, 1909

You have expressed exactly my views about the conference, and I think we have undertaken it under conditions and in a way that is most likely to lead to a real improvement in the game of football. I shall appoint as our representative Percy D. Haughton. I understand that the three on the Committee will have some surgeon well acquainted with football to advise them with regard to the nature of the injuries. I have told President Hadley that I shall be perfectly satisfied with Dr. Murphy,[1] who was at one time Captain of the Yale Football team, and is now instructor in the Harvard Medical School.

I was delighted with the gift of Mr. Cleveland H. Dodge of a Fellowship to Harvard. That and Mr. Higginson's gift for a similar purpose to Yale and Princeton, seem to me to be among the most delightful things in American college life.

Looking forward to seeing you next week in New York, and wishing you a very merry Christmas, I am,

Very truly yours, A. Lawrence Lowell.

TLS (WWP, UA, NjP).

[1] Fred Towsley Murphy, M.D., at this time surgeon to outpatients, Massachusetts General Hospital, and Visiting Surgeon to the Clinic, Harvard Medical School. In 1910, he became an Assistant in Surgery at the Harvard Medical School, and the following year he left to become Professor of Surgery at Washington University.

From Arthur Twining Hadley

New Haven, Connecticut.

My dear Mr. Wilson: December 24th, 1909.

Your note of December twenty-third troubles me greatly, because it is evident that I did not make my position at all clear. The proposal is not that each appoint a representative. The proposal is that the colleges invite jointly representatives of the different institutions which are agreeable to them all. I doubt very much whether we had better try to go ahead to do anything until after I have seen Mr. Lowell, which I shall certainly do on next Tuesday, and until after we have the conference, which I hope may take place on Wednesday. Pray do not in any event say anything to Mr. Henry which will intimate that his name has been under discussion in this connection. I am all the more anxious that nothing should happen which would place both him and me in a false position, because I have a great personal regard for Mr. Henry, and have no reason to doubt that he would make a good representative.

Faithfully yours, Arthur T Hadley

TLS (WP, DLC).

To Moses Taylor Pyne

My dear Momo: Princeton, N. J. 25 December, 1909.

Thank you sincerely for your letter of yesterday. I know that it came from the heart, and value it accordingly. You need never fear that I will doubt your affection for me or your entire devotion to the University, no matter what happens.

The note I wrote from the Jersey City Station *was* written under deep excitement, but I am sorry to say that the judgment it expressed was not hastily formed. It had been taking shape in my mind for some time, and subsequent reflection has only served to confirm it.

The graduate establishment on the Golf Links cannot succeed. The Faculty has never believed in a graduate establishment which did not constitute the geographical and spiritual centre of the University. A Graduate College which lay in every sense at the heart of things was West's first idea, and the modification of his views and purposes has played no small part in depriving him of the confidence of his academic colleagues. He has now lost their confidence completely, and nothing administered by him in accordance with his present ideas can succeed. Indeed, nothing administered by him can now succeed.

When, at my first interview with Mr. Procter, shortly before the October meeting of the Board, I urged upon him the judgment of the Faculty in this all-important matter, and my own clear judgment, in view of all the circumstances, that a Graduate College removed from close neighbourhood to the existing life of the University would be a reversal of our whole policy hitherto and of our whole academic conception and hope, he replied that he was sorry, but that he could not agree with the Faculty and with me, or with the majority of the Trustees' Committee on the Graduate School, and must insist that his gift, if accepted at all, must be used only on condition that the college provided for by Mrs. Swann's bequest be removed to a distance from the present buildings of the University.

I tried, after the meeting of the Board in October, to accommodate myself as loyally as possible to its decision, in view of Mr. Procter's wishes, to carry out his ideas rather than those of the leading graduate teachers of the Faculty, but I found it against my conscience to assent to the use of Mrs. Swann's money to build on the Golf Links because of the conviction that the directions of Mrs. Swann's will could not be complied with either in letter or in spirit, a) because she directs that the building shall be placed "upon the grounds" of the University and serious doubts exist as to the legality of placing the building on the Golf Links at all, b) because she directs that the rooms in the building shall be rented "at the best prices they will command, to Graduate, Senior and Junior students of the University," c) in order to produce an income which shall be devoted to the maintenance of as large a number of fellowships as possible.

I therefore proposed to Mr. Procter, on Wednesday last, that his gift and purpose be separated from Mrs. Swann's; that we carry out her will exactly by erecting Thomson College in close association with the present buildings of the University, and that as much as necessary of his proffered gift be devoted to the erection and maintenance on the Golf Links of such an establishment as he favours. This suggestion meets with the hearty concurrence of my colleagues here. I explained to him that there are already graduate students enough to fill one of these establishments, and that by the time our building operations could be completed there would, at our present rate of growth (certain to be accelerated under a proper policy), be enough to fill both; that the judgment of the Faculty was strongly against Professor West's ideas in this matter; and that it was likely that such a compromise would make it possible to try both experiments under favourable auspices. He replied, again, that he was sorry to differ with me, but that he did not approve of dividing the graduate students into two separated groups or of associating graduate life with the undergraduate life of the University. He made it much clearer than before that his views were exactly those of Professor West and Mr. Butler, and that if his gift was accepted, he would insist upon the use of Mrs. Swann's bequest in connection with it in accordance with those ideas.

You will see, therefore, what I meant when I said in my note from Jersey City that the acceptance of Mr. Procter's gift had taken the guidance of the University out of my hands entirely. Its acceptance by the Board means its acceptance upon the terms prescribed, terms which govern the use of Mrs. Swann's money as well as the use of Mr. Procter's. It has reversed the policy of the Faculty, and the leading conception of my whole administration, in an educational matter of the most fundamental importance. I am not willing to be drawn further into the toils. I cannot accede to the acceptance of gifts upon terms which take the educational policy of the University out of the hands of the Trustees and Faculty and permit it to be determined by those who give money.

I do not wish even to imply a criticism of Mr. Procter. He is in no way at fault. I admire him very much. He has been very generous to the University and in all his dealings with me has acted with the greatest courtesy and kindness. But his attitude means that we must accept his wishes not only with regard to the manner in which his money is to be spent but also with regard to the way in which Mrs. Swann's money is to be expended and the purposes to which it shall be devoted. I cannot consent, if the gift is deliberately accepted on such terms, to remain responsible for the direction of the affairs of the University, or for the development of her educational policy.

This is a very solemn matter, my dear Momo, but the issue is clear. Neither my conscience nor my self-respect will permit me to avoid it. There is only one position I can take. I take it with real grief that it should be necessary, and with unabated affection for yourself. I know that you have been convinced that you were acting for the best interests of the University. But I must now ask the Board to consider it in a new light. I must ask them to give the University, at whatever cost, its freedom of choice in matters which so nearly touch its life and development.

Always, Affectionately yours, Woodrow Wilson

P.S. In order to correct any hastiness on my part in a matter of so great importance, I laid it in detail before Chancellor Magie, on Thursday last. He said that he thought my judgment in the matter entirely right. He emphasized again, also, his views as to the legality of the proposed use of Mrs. Swann's money.

W. W.[1]

TCL (WP, DLC).

[1] There is a WWsh draft of this letter, dated Dec. 24, 1909, in WP, DLC.

To Cleveland Hoadley Dodge

My dear Cleve., Princeton, N. J. 27 December, 1909.

I hate to send you the enclosed letter to Pyne, for I know it will distress you: but it became my clear duty to write it. Mr. Procter wishes his money to be used in ways against which the whole Faculty,–except a small group which their colleagues would now follow in nothing,–is in rebellion against. It would be mere folly for me to consent; and the principle involved is clear and tremendous.

What I have said to Pyne in the letter means, of course, that West must be absolutely eliminated, administratively. It also means that we must somewhere find the money with which to purchase health and freedom again. It is our turning point. It could not have been postponed.

I am none the less distressed that you should have the worry of such a crisis. I would not have brought it on if I could have in conscience avoided it; and I am with all my heart

Gratefully and affectionately Yours, Woodrow Wilson

I am sending copies of the letter also to Mr. Jno. A. Stewart, Cyrus McCormick, Dr. Jacobus, Mr. Garrett, Mr. Thompson, Ed. Sheldon, Mr. Palmer, and Mr. Jones (to be read also to his brother and to Mr. McIlvaine).

WWTLS (WC, NjP). Enc.: WW to M. T. Pyne, Dec. 25, 1909, WWTCLS (WC, NjP).

To Cyrus Hall McCormick

My dear Cyrus, Princeton, N. J. 27 December, 1909.

I am afraid that the enclosed letter to Pyne will distress you; but the circumstances which it details and the whole situation here made it necessary. We cannot keep our present Faculty or go forward with the present purposes of the University if West or his ideas are to obtain another twelvemonth: and if to the carrying out of those ideas that Mr. Procter's money would be devoted. That I now know, and that knowledge has forced me to act. The letter means that we must get rid of West altogether from any position of authority or post of administration.

The absolute necessity of the moment is that our friends should find the money with which to buy our freedom; but we must have it at any cost, whether it can be supported by funds immediately or not. I am deeply distressed; but my judgment is clear and final. I cannot take part in the present programme or in any programme resembling it.

Affectionately and gratefully Yours Woodrow Wilson

I am sending copies of the letter also to Mr. Jno. A. Stewart, Dr. Jacobus, Cleve. Dodge, Mr. Garrett, Mr. Thompson, Ed. Sheldon, Mr. Palmer, and Mr. Jones (to be read to his brother and to Mr. McIlvaine).

WWTLS (WP, DLC).

To Edward Wright Sheldon

My dear Ed., Princeton, N. J. 27 Decembar [December], 1909.

I was greatly disappointed when I learned that you had been in Princeton on Christmas and that I had not seen you. I wanted to show you in person the enclosed letter and to take counsel with you about it.

I found that I had no choice in conscience but to write it. The situation had become such that to have avoided the issue, feeling as I do, would have been mere weakness. Even had there not been a vital principle involved, vital to the whole morale of the University, the mere duty of keeping our present Faculty and making its work possible would have obliged me to take this stand. I have thought it over long and seriously: the conviction upon which it rests forced itself to the front in spite of every consideration of convenience or experiency [expediency], and I must now abide by it.

My affection for you, my trust in your judgment, my knowledge of your sound wisdom in all matters of duty make me hope with all my heart that you will approve.

Affectionately Yours, Woodrow Wilson

I am also sending copies of the letter to Mr. Jno. A. Stewart, Cyrus McCormick, Dr. Jacobus, Cleve. Dodge, Mr. Garrett, Mr. Thompson, Mr. Palmer, and Mr. Jones (to be read also to his brother and to Mr. McIlvaine).

WWTLS (photostat in RSB Coll., DLC).

To Robert Garrett

My dear Mr. Garrett, Princeton, N. J. 27 December, 1909.

I did not wish to take the important decision indicated in the enclosed letter to Mr. Pyne without letting you know at once. I am indebted to you for so much valuable counsel and such loyal support in respect of every interest of the University that I feel myself bound to you [by] very special ties.

I hope with all my heart that you will approve of the letter, and the principle which it states. The course of events and the very strong feeling of the Faculty in this matter made it necessary that I should make my decision and state it unmistakably. If the next meeting of the Board had been further off, I might have felt at liberty to delay; but every day has added to my conviction, and it had become irresistible. I wished very much that I might have had a talk with you: but I am sure of your own conception of duty in such matters.

With warmest regard,

Faithfully Yours Woodrow Wilson

I am also sending copies of the letter to Mr. Jno. A. Stewart, Mr. McCormick, Mr. Dodge, Dr. Jacobus, Mr. Tho[m]pson, Mr. Sheldon, Mr. Palmer, and Mr. Jones (to be read to his brother and to Mr. McIlvaine).

WWTLS (Selected Corr. of R. Garrett, NjP). Enc.: WW to M. T. Pyne, Dec. 25, 1909, WWTCL (Selected Corr. of R. Garrett, NjP).

To Thomas Davies Jones

My dear Mr. Jones, Princeton, N. J. 27 December, 1909.

Since I saw you I have been forced to make my decision as to what I must do; and it is embodied in the enclosed copy of a letter I sent to Mr. Pyne on Saturday last. Will you not be kind enough to show the letter to your brother and to Mr. McIlvaine?

I hope most sincerely that it will meet with your approval. As I look back to our conversation on the train I feel that I have reason to believe that it will. I should feel very much disturbed to think that I had done anything that did not commend itself to yoor [your] and your brother's judgment as for the best interests of the University.

I found myself in the grip of a conviction which I could not escape, and which I could not delay obeying. A decision made now may possibly save the University from demoralization: a delayed decision might come too late, when everything had crystalized against it. To come to any other conclusion would have been to risk the loss of some of the most valuable men in the Faculty and an impossible situation under West, who must now be entirely eliminated, administratively.

I am also sending copies of this letter to Mr. Jno. A. Stewart, Mr. McCormick, Dr. Jacobus, Mr. Dodge, Mr. Garrett, Mr. Thompson, Mr. Sheldon, and Mr. Palmer.

With warmest regard,

Cordially and faithfully Yours, Woodrow Wilson

WWTLS (Mineral Point, Wisc., Public Library).

To Moses Taylor Pyne

My dear Momo: Princeton, N. J. 28 December 1909.

I am sorry to say that I am obliged to be away from home on the dates you suggest for the meeting of the Committee on the Graduate School. The Association of American Universities, of which Princeton is this year President, meets at Madison, Wisconsin, on the fourth and fifth, and I must start on the second to get there in time. On my way back I have promised to attend the inauguration of the new President of Franklin and Marshall, at Lancaster, Pa., on the seventh.

No doubt we can find another date when I see you at the meeting of the Grounds and Buildings on Thursday. I am just now taking a train to meet the New Jersey State Teachers Association at Atlantic City tonight. There is another blizzard coming, I understand, and I may stay there!

Affectionately yours, Woodrow Wilson

TCL (M. T. Pyne Coll., NjP).

To Thomas Davies Jones

My dear Mr. Jones, Princeton, N. J. 28 December, 1909.

Thank you very warmly for your note of the twenty-second. I am not sure whether I shall have time on my trip to Madison to stop over in Chicago or not. I am afraid I shall not. I am crowding the trip in between other engagements which I cannot set aside. But if it is possible, I shall try to get into communication with you and at least get a glimpse of you both. It was kind of you to think of it.

With warmest regard,

Faithfully Yours, Woodrow Wilson

WWTLS (Mineral Point, Wisc., Public Library).

To Andrew Carnegie

My dear Mr. Carnegie, Princeton, N. J. 28 Dec., '09

I have just learned, from the morning paper, of your painful accident in the Park.[1] I am very sorry. I hope sincerely that the injury has proved to be only a slight one and that you will soon be quite free from any inconvenience from it. The country cannot afford to have an invaluable man even temporarily "laid up."

With warmest regard and sympathy

Faithfully Yours, Woodrow Wilson

ALS (A. Carnegie Papers, DLC).

1 Carnegie had suffered an injury to his left knee when he slipped on ice and fell in Central Park on Monday afternoon, December 27, 1909.

To Carl Russell Fish[1]

My dear Sir, Princeton, N. J. 28 December, 1909.

Allow me to acknowledge your very kind note of the twenty-second,[2] and to say that it will give me pleasure to comply with the wishes of the committee which has charge of the arrangements for the dinner to be given by the Faculty of the University to the visiting representatives attending the meeting of the Association of American Universities. I am very much complimented that they should wish me to be one of the speakers on that occasion.[3] Very truly Yours, Woodrow Wilson

WWTLS (C. R. Fish Papers, WHi).

1 Professor of American History at the University of Wisconsin.

2 It is missing.

3 No Madison newspaper printed a report of this affair.

An Address in Atlantic City to the New Jersey State Teachers' Association

[[Dec. 28, 1909]]

THE STATE AND THE CITIZEN'S RELATION TO IT.

Mr. President, Ladies and Gentlemen:

I esteem it a privilege to speak to this assemblage, and yet a temerity to attempt to speak to you upon so great a subject. The advantage of the subject is, of course, that there is plenty of sea-room in it in which to manoeuver; and I may possibly, for that reason be able to conceal from you the fact that I shall not give it a thorough discussion.

I suppose that every one of us has a somewhat artificial conception of the State. I have found in my classes at the University that almost every one of my pupils thinks of the State in some particular form; thinks of it, naturally, in an American form, and has not got the conception that, though the American form of the state may be characteristic of this country, the object of the State in America is not different from the object of the State anywhere else; that while one form may be better suited than another to enable us to attain the object of the State, that object is, nevertheless, always and everywhere the same.

The only brief and adequate definition of the State that I have been able to find, is that which describes it as "a people organized for law within a definite territory."[1] It seems to me that that is an enlightening definition; because it states so clearly and succinctly what the object of the State is. The object of the State is institutions, is law, is those arrangements upon which we can all agree, in which we can all be ranked and harnessed in order to accomplish some common object.

I know that in modern times it is fashionable to speak of the State as having a great many objects which cannot be embodied in the form of law; but what I want to emphasize at the outset is, that nothing is a proper object of the state which cannot be embodied in law. I find that one of the most useful ways in which to test the thinking of my acquaintances, particularly of my acquaintances who are ardent reformers, is to ask each one of them who has a great sweeping reform in mind to be kind enough to reduce it to a statute[,] to be kind enough to write it down in the definite form which he thinks it ought to have as law and to embody in the law the method of its enforcement. You will find that that is a very excellent way of getting rid of most reformers. After they have been given an immaculately clean sheet of paper and a good pen, and ink that will write, they find that the reform cannot get written in the form of definite law; that they cannot think in statutes; that the trouble is not that they cannot state what they want done, but that they cannot state how they except [expect] to attain it. For the first requisite of a law is that it should be applicable, that it should *work*, that there should be some obvious way of giving it efficacy and authority.

I remember once, for example, I had a very engaging neighbor at dinner. Learning that I was connected with the administration of a college, she said to me, apropos of the habits of undergraduates, "If I had anything to do with a college, I would

[1] See Wilson's notes for the second lecture, "Nature and Objects of Political Society," in his course, the Elements of Politics, printed at March 5, 1898, Vol. 10.

absolutely forbid the undergraduates to drink." "Yes," I said, "and have you ever thought how you would enforce the prohibition?" "Why, no, no!" she said. "But I would have them watched." "Oh!" I said, "how many persons do you suppose it would take to watch (say) a thousand students?" Well, she had never thought that out. I conjecture it would take about a thousand, and that they would get fooled most of the time; that the very way in which not to enforce such a prohibition, was to set the young wits to work how to escape surveillance. If the ardent are to continue to believe that you can stop things by forbidding them, you must insist that they go on to say how you are going to make the prohibition effective, or else you have not produced a law; you have expressed a desire, you have written a moral judgment, you have written merely a wish as to what society should do.

The object of the State is not to express in written form handsome desires, but to put in workable shape certain imperative commands; and it is necessary, in order that we should do that, that these commands should have back of them our general agreement. We find that certain laws, for example, work in some communities and do not work in others; and we find that back of this difference lies the difference in the desires and opinions and judgments of the population: that you can not follow men's habits up with a policeman's club or with the bayonet; that you must first establish an attitude of mind which will give the law the support of the major part of the population before you can make it a law at all. There must lie back of the law, as there must precede the law, a certain general conviction that these things are necessary, a conviction which is so definite that the great bulk of the population is ready to stand behind the command of the law. The law rests for its vitality upon obedience; it does not rest upon the desires of the lawmaker or the will of the lawmaker.

We constantly speak in a very vague way of certain governments as being autocratic,—absolute. But there is in real truth no absolute government in the sense that there is any man anywhere, or any body of men, who can carry out their own private desires with regard to what their subjects or their fellow citizens shall do. Moreover, every tyrant, every autocrat, has just as few hours in the day as every other man has. There are only twenty-four hours for him, as there are only twenty-four hours for you; and if he undertakes to look into the detail of a great empire, he will find that there are not hours enough. He must depend upon others for the execution of his wishes; and in the last analysis he must depend upon all his subjects and all his fellow citizens for their disposition towards him in respect of obedience; for if that disposition grows weak enough, it will presently thwart him; if it grows passionate enough, it will presently produce revolution.

You work in the stuff of the human mind when you conduct a State; and you can not make out of a State what the stuff of the human mind is not ready to produce. You must work in prepossessions; you must work in convictions; you must work in universal perceptions, or else you can not work at all. That is the reason why there has been a steady advance from stage to state [stage] in lawmaking, that generation after generation has been convinced of new purposes, of new ideas, of new necessities, and, because of that conviction, has stood by laws that were new and has given them their obedience.

There are also persons who speak as if this great organic process of the human mind were something that is artificial. The process of the life of the State is a great organic process of the human mind; and the most substantial part of our thinking is the part that we do not derive from our own private meditations but take out of the air, the part that is created by the minds about us. Any individual mind, no matter how rich in its contents or in its power, would be impoverished if it were isolated. It takes the vital processes of its life, like the plant itself, from the atmosphere, from the intellectual and moral atmosphere in which it lives; and this whole process of life in the state is an organic process, a process in which the parts are not separable, and in which the parts can not subsist singly and apart.

Therefore, it seems to me that it is perfectly evident that the State is not an artificial arrangement. It is not created because somebody happened to think of it as a happy arrangement. No body of men have ever been found anywhere, in any state of development whatever, without a State, without a political organization, without a coherence such as we would call a body politic. Moreover, the things that we think, the highest creations of the human mind, the highest exercises of the human mind have come out of this organic and common life. I do not hesitate to say that religion has come out of the life of the State, out of the associated life of men together. The great religious conceptions which move us are not conceptions which have come to men as they sat separate, isolated and apart from their fellow men. All the sweetest images of religion are images drawn from the family, from society,—"Our Father," "Our King," "Our Ruler,"—every term of majesty or of dignity or of sweetness that we have for our Creator, is a term drawn out of our associated life and not out of our individual life.

It is obvious, too, that it is the associated life of men together that has produced art, has produced the visionary creations of the human spirit; those things which no man ever saw except as the brains of other men had created them. The great creations of the painter, of the sculptor, of the architect,—all of these come out of our associated life, particularly that finely artistic expression of national genius which is embodied in architecture. One of the things, Ladies and Gentlemen, which is a visible proof to everybody that America has not yet got her final national consciousness, is that America has not yet got any final characteristic form of architecture. I was walking along the residential streets of a far western city the other day; and it seemed to me as if I were walking through a colossal world's fair exhibit of all the possible forms of domestic architecture. You have only to walk down the residence street of any one of our eastern cities in order to see, cheek by jowl, almost every sort of architecture that the world has produced. Here and there in some skyscraper, in some singular adaption of the form of the tower to the uses of the edifice, you see something that is characteristically American: but whether it is admirably adapted to express our national character or not, I think only time will determine. We are very proud of the soaring sky lines of some of our cities. They are all very novel and exceedingly various in their form but underneath that we all feel making, making, making like a tide, something that will presently express an American spirit in the form of the houses we use and dwell in.

And so it has always been. The great periods of art have been the periods of ardent social and religious feeling, of ardent political feeling. The great age of the renaissance in Italy was the greatest political age that Italy has ever seen, the age of the most vital political passions; this political spirit expressed itself in certain sensitive minds and souls as great art; and ever since we have recognized this as Italian, that as French, that as German; because these great peoples have come to consciousness in a characteristic art.

And so it goes without saying that education is produced by our organic life, though not necessarily the education which we now attempt; for everywhere that I observe education nowadays, I find that it is confined to the processes of imparting information. If you can find somebody to talk to, you can impart information, I dare say, in a desert; but you cannot educate if there are only two persons there, isolated.

Education has to information only the relation that the clothes I wear have to the fields in which the stuffs were grown out of which the clothes are woven. Information, I dare say, is the raw material of education; but it is not education; and no amount of information can constitute education. Some of the best informed men I ever knew were among the most useless men I ever knew, and among the most inconvenient; because they were always throwing at you some chunk of information which you could not deny and by which you felt floored, but which you knew in your heart was perfectly irrelevant to the matter you were discussing. These men who go about carrying encyclopaedias in their heads are just about as useful as encyclopaedias. They are useful to be referred to upon occasion for out of the way pieces of information; but they make very poor reading, and lack sequence entirely. You know the famous remark of the old lady who said the dictionary was very interesting, but it changed the subject very often; and that it is the characteristic of information. It is also the characteristic of most of our school processes,–that they change the subject about every forty minutes, and are just about as disconnected and just about as unlike anything but information as you could well make them.

Now, education is a process of association. Education comes from the association of an immature mind with a mature mind. It is a process which has to do with training minds how to handle themselves; and nothing trains a mind how to handle itself so much as association with a mind that already knows how to handle itself,–as the close and intimate daily association with masters of the mind. That constitutes education, and that is evidently social. Part of the education which I am rejoicing to get from month to month, comes to me from the necessity I am under, by the present dispensations of Providence with regard to college presidents, to travel all over the country. One of the things that I feel has more than anything else to do with forming my opinions, forming my nature, disciplining my mind, is the contact with people all over this country, living under different conditions, in different situations, standing at different points of view, correcting the provincialism of my mind. It has been too much trained in particular regions,–particular regions of the land and particular regions of thought. Education consists in getting out of people this narrowness, this localization, this pettiness, this provincialism of the mind. Obviously that is a function of society.

What I am trying to illustrate is that the State is not merely an artificial arrangement which we have thought convenient. It contains in it almost all the vital processes of the human mind, all the stimulations, all those things which quicken the mind to be something big instead of something little, all those things which enable men to think in terms of masses, in terms of movements, in terms of great moral advances, in terms of great intellectual conceptions. The State is a vehicle of all of that; the State supplies the atmosphere without which none of that could breathe.

But the danger of the State is its exaggeration; the danger of political organization and of social organization is that it will be too powerful and dominate the variety and crush the spontaneity of the individual. I have spoken, up to this point, entirely of the social processes; but I need not tell you that there are also individual processes, and that the ultimate centers of vitality are individual centers. The use of the State is to put you in touch with the general intellectual and spiritual capital of other individuals; but the source of vitality is not in the State; it is in yourself. The richness, the vigor of every State, of every community, consists in the variety and power of the individuals which it contains. There is a point beyond which you can carry social organization to the detriment of the individual, to the danger of the State itself. The glory of human history is the independence and integrity of the individual. The finest spectacle in human history is some man who has insisted upon becoming an insurgent against the race, standing up with his single puny might and bidding defiance to the forces of opinion, saying "These are the things that I think; and, before God, I will not be duressed into saying anything else." I say that that is the handsomest spectacle in the world. The world has gone forward by the force of moral insurgents; the world has gone forward because individuals here and there, little devoted groups here and there, caring nothing for their reputations and nothing for their lives, have denied the leading views of their own generation, have said, "Men and brethren, you are wrong; the thing that is righteous is not contained in your doctrine; the thing that is righteous lies another way; and until you see it, you are on the road to destruction."

These voices can, so far as they are physically audible, be hushed; but they can never be hushed in any other wise. There is something that is indestructible in the human spirit; and the individuality of the human spirit is its only integrity. No human spirit can allow itself to be submerged and swallowed up and all its standards dictated to it.

See what a fine antithesis you have, therefore: the State,—the necessary medium of all altruistic motives, the necessary atmosphere in which all visions must make themselves visible; and yet the individual, not submitting to the mass,—the individual, insisting upon the use of his own faculties, the use of his own perceptions, the use of his own conscience, and becoming, upon occasion, when a great spirit arises, an insurgent against the world!

We have boasted of political liberty. Political liberty will have gone out of the world when everybody shall have conformed. Political liberty is the apotheosis of insurgency. Political liberty is the negation of conformity. It is the upsetting of nicely devised arrangements and tacit understanding. The men who kick over the traces are the men who keep political liberty alive; not the men who conform. The men who won't go with the organization are the men who save the organization itself, by reminding it that it must always square itself with principle or else lose the allegiance of those who try to square their lives and their hopes by principle. When we come to speak of the relationship of the individual to the State, no matter what our image of the State may be, no matter how indispensable we may deem it, no matter how admirable we may conceive it to be, we must nevertheless perceive that the relation of the individual to the State is this: he must lend it his loyal allegiance, just so far as he can do so without doing violence to his own individual integrity of soul and mind. Where he begins to feel that he is doing violence to them, he must stop. The salvation and purification of society depends upon his stopping there.

The interesting thing to me about our modern society is, that it never was before quite so difficult for the individual to do that as it is now. Think of our organic society! Think of the way in which men are bound together in great organizations which we call corporations; and think how difficult it is for any man who forms one little part of a great corporate organization to feel that he has any freedom for the exercise of his own judgment, or the exercise of his own conscience. Think what modern economic society means; it means the pooling of men's judgments and of men['s] consciences. And yet modern economic society is going to be saved, if it is saved at all, by the insurgence of individuals, by the rising up of men who will say, "I am indeed a part of this organization; but I will not allow my moral consciousness to be crushed by it. I say that this thing that has been commanded me is wrong, and I will not do it." There are not many brave enough. Think what it means! Think what it means for almost any man! It means being thrown out of employment; being thrown out of employment means want, and perhaps starvation, for those whom he loves and who are most dependent upon him. All life turns blank and looks impossible when you are thrust out of employment. It might be simple enough in most cases if you alone had to face starvation; that is not where the pinch comes.

The pinch comes because others have to starve as well, and you compromise, you compound with your conscience, you go on with your corporation, you consent to do the thing which you know is wrong. That, Ladies and Gentlemen, is the greatest threat that there is to modern morals.

The prime necessity of modern society is that the individual should find himself morally, should assert himself morally, in despite of the consequences, not stopping to count the cost, simply saying "The thing is wrong and I will not take part in it." It would not take a great many men to do that to stop the things that are wrong. Most of the things that go on in modern economic society, I take leave to believe, are not wrong. It is very convenient to have these great combinations of capital and of industry; I am willing to admit that it is necessary to have them if modern society is to be conducted with success, if the modern material supports of civilization are to be maintained. I do not believe that the wrongs that inhere in these processes are essential to the processes. If I did, I would be against the processes. I believe that most of our great modern corporations (if I am to judge by the men I know who are concerned in them) are honestly conducted. But some of them are not; and there are scores of men all over this country who could break the game up who are nevertheless consenting to take part in it. From the point of view of our present economic circumstances, therefore, the thing we should exalt is the individual conscience, and not the corporate obligation.

Then, take the field of politics. You know what the subtle temptation of politics is,–it is to obey the organization. Every one I ever knew who was versed in politics said that the organization was necessary; and I know, from my own political studies, that the organization is necessary. You cannot do things like a crowd. You must do things organized like an army, if you want to accomplish anything on the confused and complicated modern stage. I have no quarrel with parties; I have no quarrel with political organizations; they are absolutely necessary. But it is also necessary that they should be afraid of the individuals who compose them. It is also necessary that they should recognize that there is a moral law of dissolution; that there are constant dangers of absolute disintegration, and that those dangers lie in the consciences and principles of the individuals who make them up. You know who it is who keep the politics of this country pure. It is the independent voters. The men who always and as a matter of course vote with their party we are under no obligations to whatever. They do not help the country in the least, in respect of reform and progress. The men who help the country are the men upon whom the parties have to have their eye with watchful anxiety, for fear they are not going to vote with them. They are the men who can oblige the parties to do what they want them to do; they are the men who make the changes in our politics and the progress in our legislation.

If you want to be one of the trustees of the national safety, politically speaking, never let the political managers be sure how you are going to vote. Then you have elected yourself one of the board of directors of the country.

So that in every aspect of this complicated question, what you see in it all is this nice balance: here the organized and necessary force,—there the recalcitrant individual; here the law of cohesion, —there the law of dissolution; the law of accumulated tradition here,—there the isolated voice of the reformer crying out that the tradition is wrong. And so a constant alternation: this general movement, that disturbance of the general movement; this co-operation and that refusal to co-operate. Such is the law of life in the whole body politic,—until you come to the field of education.

What particularly interests me about the whole relation of the State to education, is that the obligation of the State to educate is an obligation to drill. I can see no obligation on the part of the State to give each individual what he separately wants in the field of education; but I do perceive a very distinct law of self-preservation, which says to the State, "If you want traditions to be continuous, if you want the habits of the people to be stable and reliable, as a basis upon which your affairs may be conducted, you must see to it that your whole population gets a certain common drill and grounding in fundamental matters."

That is the only sort of education, so far as I can see, that the State is interested in. The State is interested in drill, in discipline, in producing types, in standardizing generation after generation. Did you ever think how amusingly egotistical the process of education is? Each generation looks with sternness upon the generations coming on and says, "My dear children, it is necessary for your salvation that you should be made exactly like ourselves! We are going to tell you what is so, because we know it is so; and we are going to make you swallow it; and we are going to make you repeat it, are going to make you keep on repeating it until you can't get it out of your constitutions." It is the most tremendous, drastic process of standardization that you can imagine. You say to the next generation that they are not at liberty to find out what nature is like. You will tell them what nature is doing; and they must believe it, or else be kicked out of school.

They are not at liberty to question whether these are truths or not; these *are* the truths. You do not give them reasons for it. They are not big enough to understand; they must simply swallow what they are given, and swallow it whole, no matter what gulping it may take to do it.

I took the liberty of saying the other day to a number of gentlemen who rather provoked me by looking exceptionally complacent, that I understand it to be the duty of a college to make the young gentlemen who resorted to it just as unlike their fathers as possible,—by which, I explained to them, I did not mean any discourtesy to the fathers, but simply this: that by the time a man is old enough to have a son at college he is immersed in some particular undertaking and interest and everything that comes up, every question, he looks at from the point of view of that particular interest. We can not afford to let the son be like that; we must take the youngsters and regeneralize them,—draw them away from this too concentrated attention to a particular interest and show them the stage at large, so that they will start, not where their fathers are but where their fathers started or should have started,—so that they will see the interests combined, united, generalized, instead of looking at them separately and it may be selfishly because of a particular and private absorption in them.

Now, that is a socializing process. That is as if we took the young people and said to them, "Your father has been very useful in his time; but he has individualized himself too much; we are going to ask you to look at life from the general point of view of society, from the point of view of the established canons of knowledge; we are going to reduce you to type again before you specialize and produce the individualistic forms of which the older people contain so many specimens." It is a process of drill; it is a process (to repeat the word which best describes it) of standardization.

You will observe, therefore, that the salvation of society, if I am right in the analysis which has preceded, is not going to come from that process. I think that as teachers we ought to remind ourselves that society is not made progressive by education; it is made conservative by education. What education does is to knit the fabric together, not to prepare the impulses which are to change it. They must come from the individual, not from the type; they must come by way of the departure from type, or else there would not be any change at all.

The processes of education are processes of inbreeding: they are processes by which you cut out what is irregular and produce what is regular and up to pattern. That is a necessary process.

But it is a process which is only preliminary: it is to give every individual a training which will prepare him to be himself after he has escaped from the training. In other words, all the great men will have to escape from you before they become great—and from me, also. (Laughter.) They will have to escape from the college and from the school before they can become the individual types of force. Many a youngster goes through the school and through the college who is constantly declining to support its discipline and he gives us no end of trouble; but it may turn out that he, after all, is the most serviceable citizen of the lot. Youngsters,—I would not dare say this at home; but the youngsters who do the irregular things are the youngsters who are apt to keep on doing things all their lives; and the youngsters who do the regular thing day in and day out are apt to be merely the hewers of wood and the drawers of water. I hope it won't be repeated too far away from here (Laughter); but that is my conviction. And yet what most attracts my attention about modern education is, that we are not really doing our job at all. For the particular characteristic (as I just now intimated) of our present processes of education is that they do *not* constitute drill. They constitute an attempt to impart a miscellany of information. We do not finish anything. We give a taste of nearly everything. I have never been at an educational meeting of any kind that I did not hear it eloquently insisted that half a dozen new things should be put into the curricula of the schools and of the colleges. I never meet an earnest person upon a train or any where else that he does not suggest to me that there is something that ought to be taught that Princeton is not teaching; and if I took all the suggestions which are made to me, Princeton would be trying to impart every kind of information that has been heard of in the modern world. If it did undertake that, it would of course not educate anybody; it certainly would discipline nobody.

Discipline consists in subjecting the mind to processes which are continued and continued and continued, until the mind has formed a habit from which it cannot escape. If you were to take a pupil, for example, and subject his mind to the discipline of one language not his own from the time he enters school until he graduates from college; if you subjected his mind to the discipline of some part of mathematical training from the time he entered school until he left college; if you took him by constant reiteration over the field of history, not once but again and again and again, until the movement of human affairs became to him common matter of recollection, common matter of reflection; if you took a few processes and continued them inexorably from the time the process of education began until it ended, then you would have educated men. You could within the program of our schools and colleges select processes enough to constitute samples of the modern intellectual life,—abundant samples of the modern intellectual life.

But what do we do? We prepare just as various a bill of fare as possible and allow the pupil just as great freedom as possible; we jump from part to part of it, which is the negation of drill, the negation of discipline, and therefore no business of the State's. If that is education, then the State has nothing legitimately to do with it. The business of the State, if it is going to pay for education, should drill the minds of each generation in the leading processes that are characteristic of the intellectual life of that age and the leading conceptions which are characteristic of the life of the nation. If private individuals wish to enjoy other more individualistic process, nobody need quarrel with them; but it is no business of the State's to indulge them. I think that one of the most dangerous and explosive things that a man can contain is information. Information seems to contain ideas; but if you don't organize it, it doesn't contain them at all; and if you allow a man to be full of disconnected germs of ideas contained in disconnected unorganized bodies of knowledge, why, you simply make his mind explosive here, there, and elsewhere. You touch it there, he has got a piece of information and he reacts, he explodes; you touch him there, he has got another piece of information there,—he reacts, he explodes. But when you put him out into the field of action, then the explosions are not symmetrical enough to form a motive force (laughter); they don't form a series; and therefore they are not to be considered an analogue, at all, to the modern motive force upon our roads. The explosions there are disagreeable enough; but they at least produce motion. The explosions in these minds do not even produce motion—at any rate, not motion in any one direction, but produce motion in many opposite directions.

That is merely to create disturbers of the public peace, men who are informed at haphazard and will give you a great deal of trouble at a great many disconnected points, but who have no momentum, no apparatus, no concentration, no such training of their intellectual muscles as will make them formidable along a definite line,—men who question everything, men who doubt most things, men who will argue anything. These are not the motive forces of society. The slightest words of the man whose eyes have seemed to contain things that no one else has dreamed are the forces of society. Men who think in terms that run in long sequences, that are rooted in the past and spring toward the future, those are the men to look out for.

And so when we come to look at our country as a whole and to wish for her the things that are best, we ought to hope for America that she should be a place where men love the State, are ready to lay down their lives for it; but are also ready to lay down their lives for the integrity and independence of their own souls and minds, and know that that the best service of humanity is to have a brave mind, a fearless thought, a purpose which cannot be put under duress, a vision which insists upon looking over the heads of the mass and seeing the road that lies and climbs in the distance. America enjoys her freedom because she was once full of revolutionists, because she was once full of men who insisted upon realizing their own ideals; because the ideas which they entertained came out into the field full armed and militant, because she would submit to no wrong and contained men who would proclaim wrong wherever they saw it. When she ceases to contain such men, when she affirms that all her devotion is to the united strength, then she will have ceased to be America. We, of all nations, ought to know how to keep the balance between the combined force and the individual courage, between the things that we must do in common and the things that we will essay alone. (Applause).[2]

Printed in *Annual Report and Proceedings of the 55th Annual Meeting of the New Jersey State Teachers' Association . . .* 1909 (n.p., n.d.), pp. 32-42.

[2] There is a WWhw outline of this address, dated Dec. 28, 1909, in WP, DLC.

From Melancthon Williams Jacobus

Hartford, Conn.

My dear President Wilson: December, twenty eighth [1909]

I was distressed at the evidence presented in your letter just received of the serious stage at which the Graduate School discussion has reached.

It seems to me that some such Conference as we spoke of when I was last in Princeton is almost imperative now, and that it should be held at as early date as possible.

What time will be possible for you to be in New York before the meeting of the Board (excepting January 10th & 11th)?

We can meet as we did before at the Hotel Belmont, either for a 1 or 2 o'clock lunch, in a private room—or informally in the afternoon.

Let me hear from you, by return mail, if possible, naming those to be invited. Yours faithfully M. W. Jacobus

ALS (WP, DLC).

From Cleveland Hoadley Dodge

Dear Woodrow New York Dec 28th 1909

Don't worry about me old man—I am very fit & only worry for your sake

I am glad that you have at last taken the bull by the horns & forced the issue. I knew it must come & don't see how you could have done anything else. I wish you had sent copies of your letter to some of the other members of the clerical contingent who never know anything

Sheldon feels that the matter will be solved in January by the impossibility of complying with the terms of Stewart's amendment & that any guarantee by Momo is not practicable

Your letter will bring us all up standing & clear the air most decidedly & I think you will now sleep better

Anyhow rest assured that I am with you all the time

Hoping to see you at the Lowell reception

Affly C H Dodge

ALS (WP, DLC).

From Henry Burling Thompson

Greenville P.O. Delaware

My Dear President Wilson: December 28th, 1909.

I have received your letter of the 27th instant, with enclosure of copy of letter to Momo Pyne, under date of the 25th. The questions raised are so grave that it is unnecessary for me to even discuss them at this time. I hope to see you on Thursday of this week, at your house, at 12:00 o'clock. The situation is a distressing one, but you know you have my sympathy, and my views coincide largely with your own in this matter.

Yours very sincerely, Henry B Thompson

TLS (WP, DLC).

From Edward Wright Sheldon

My dear Woodrow: New York. December 28, 1909.

Your letter of yesterday with its enclosed copy of your letter to Momo Pyne dated December 25th, reached me this morning and has received my most earnest consideration. I wish very much that I might have had a chance to talk with you on the subject when I was in Princeton. Leaving there though, as I had to do in the middle of the afternoon, I had not more than enough time for my family. Besides, Christmas is so much of a family day that I should have felt reluctant to intrude upon your household.

It is a great disappointment to me that we cannot solve the difficulties about the Graduate School, and I still hope that some satisfactory solution will yet be found. I appreciate your position and knowing how you feel cannot see how you can escape the conclusion to which you have come, calamitous though it might be to the University. What I am directing my best efforts to now, is arranging some settlement of the matter which will make it unnecessary for you to take that stand. I have already talked with Mr. Stewart and Cleve Dodge, who both heartily approve of your decision, and expect to take up the matter seriously with Pyne tomorrow. Incidentally I wish to avoid, if possible, a heated discussion of the subject at the next meeting of the Board. As the question now stands, no compliance with the first condition attached to our acceptance of Mr. Procter's gift can be shown. So far as I know, there has not been even an attempt to comply with the condition, that the legality of placing the Thompson College on the golf grounds be assured.

After I have had a talk with Momo I will let you know the result, but meanwhile wish to assure you of my most cordial sympathy.

Believe me,

Yours affectionately, Edward W. Sheldon.

TLS (WP, DLC).

From James Waddel Alexander

My dear Dr. Wilson, [New York, c. Dec. 28, 1909]

I thank you for sending me the copy of your letter to Pyne. The situation is a lamentable one & puts consciencious members of the Board into a most distressing predicament. My own state of mind is that I must study the pros & cons up to the last minute & whenever called on to vote to do so according to my best judgment, without prejudice.

No matter what I feel called upon, under my oath of office to do, I hope you know in what high respect I hold you and your talents & how genuine my personal regard for you is.

There is one thing I cannot understand, & that is how it comes that West, who has been encouraged & endorsed, & prevented from accepting desirable offices in other institutions, is now regarded as unfit to administer anything.

I think he should be heard before he is condemned.

Hoping that some reasonable solution will be found for a difficulty so painful to all of us who have a hereditary right to love Princeton, & with my best wishes for the New Year.

Yours faithfully James W Alexander

ALS (WP, DLC).

From Edward Dickinson Duffield

My dear President Wilson: Newark, N. J. December 28, 1909.

Ever since last September I have been intending writing you with the hope that I could arrange for a personal interview with you in connection with our correspondence last summer.

Various things have prevented the Committee[1] from doing much this Fall beyond a very interesting interview with Dean Elliot[t]. I suppose that your engagements now are so heavy that it will be difficult for us to get together, but we have thought possibly you might be in New York some time shortly after the first of the year when, if you would advise us, we would try and arrange to meet you there, either at the Princeton Club or elsewhere. Will you be good enough to let me know the possibility of some such arrangement or, if this is not practicable, whether we could arrange to see you in Princeton some time in the comparatively near future.

I also want to write to you on another matter that I have very much at heart. I have been honored with the election as President of the Lawyers' Club of this county which is the actual Bar Association. I think you have been asked to speak at a number of dinners which we have had from time to time, but have found it impossible to do so. This year in addition to the dinner, we are endeavoring to arrange for three or four informal meetings during the winter at which some address on current topics not necessarily of a legal character, but one of general interest, shall be made, and I am exceedingly anxious that you should speak to us on one of these evenings. You would be the only speaker, and I think I could promise you a good attendance of the Bar of the County, and an enjoyable evening. If you are willing to do this for us you could practically select your own time as we have no hard and fact [fast] dates made.

I hesitate to ask you to add to what I know to be numerous engagements, but I really am most desirous that we should, if possible, have the pleasure of hearing you. As I say, you can talk on almost any topic of current interest, and if you have not time to prepare any new remarks, a talk along the lines of your address to the Newark Alumni Association would be most appreciated.

I sincerely trust that you will be able to give us some evening during the winter or early spring.[2]

With kindest regards and the Season's greetings, I am,

Very truly yours, Edward D Duffield

TLS (WP, DLC).

[1] Duffield had been appointed to a committee of three by the Princeton Alumni Association of the Oranges to confer with Wilson about the quadrangle plan and report back to the association. See E. D. Duffield to WW, July 23, 1909.

[2] As future letters from Duffield will reveal, there was some difficulty in setting a date for Wilson's speech to the Lawyers' Club of Newark. However, Wilson did speak on May 20, 1910; a news report of his address is printed at May 21, 1910, Vol. 20.

From Arthur Twining Hadley

My dear Mr Wilson, New York Tuesday Dec 28, 1909.

I tried to see Lowell today with reference to our getting together tomorrow. He has a Harvard reception in addition to his other functions, and this takes up the time which I had rather hoped to use for our talk. His whole day seems pretty full. I am glad to say however that he heartily approves of the choice of Henry, so that the main reason for conferring has fallen away.

If you were going to be in town anyway I think it would be worthwhile to try to get together; but if, as I understand, you did not originally intend to come, I do not think you ought to do so. The chance of our finding time for any satisfactory talk is so small, that we can probably arrange our business better by letter.

As soon as I get home, I will try to suggest a draft of a form of call for the three of us to sign. I wish you would draft one too, for I am am [*sic*] not at all sure that mine will be quite right, and I think it quite possible that I make [might] like yours or Lowell's better. Faithfully Yours Arthur T Hadley

ALS (WP, DLC).

William Cooper Procter to Andrew Fleming West

My dear West: Cincinnati December 28, 1909.

I would have written to you at once about my interview with President Wilson, but was so crowded with Christmas shopping upon my return that I was unable to do so.

President Wilson began by saying that he had thought of another obstacle in Mrs. Swan's will, in that she provided for a building with dining room and kitchen, which meant duplication and unnecessary expense not only in the first cost, but also in the maintenance and operation if her bequest were used in connection with my gift. I replied that the terms of her will were complied with in providing the breakfast room but, dinner being a much more formal meal, I thought a more dignified dining hall was necessary and could not consent not to give it. So far as the operation was concerned, Professor Butler had told me that the separate dining hall with the smaller breakfast room could be operated more economically than by having one large hall, in which all the meals were served. Wilson then stated that Mrs. Swan's will provided, if all the rooms in the Graduate College were not occupied by graduate students, that the building was to be filled with under-graduate students and the surplus income from the buildings paid to the University. It was therefore evidently Mrs. Swan's intent, he said, to provide an income for the University and as the proposed charge to the graduate student, as fixed by you, was so low, there would be no income, and, therefore, the intent of Mrs. Swan's will would not be carried out. He also thought that as soon as the Graduate College was completed, the number of students would immediately reach 125 to 150, so the building as proposed—which he stated provided for 56 students or at the most, if a third story were added, 75 students—would be inadequate to furnish accommodations for them. In consideration of these facts he wished to know whether I would object to having Mrs. Swan's money applied to building another Graduate College and all the expense of the buildings as at present considered, be borne by the money I gave and the equal amount raised from other subscriptions. I replied I was opposed to applying such a large proportion of the money, coming through my offer, for buildings and the corresponding reduction in endowment. He argued that there would be enough money, considering the additional $500,000 to be raised, to do this and I, assuming he already knew of it, foolishly mentioned that the $100,000 for the Cleveland Memorial Tower would not be directly revenue producing. He was very much surprised and very indignant at the idea that such a contribution should be considered a portion of the $500,000 to be raised and wished to know what I thought about it. I told him that the proposition had not been formally presented to me; that, first, the trustees would have to consider whether they wished to consider it as applicable in this way and then it would be my place to say whether I would accept it as a portion of the money to be provided. I stated further that, if he felt the demand for the advantages of the Graduate College would be so great, it would be better to enlarge the scope of the present plans to provide for 125 students. He stated he did not agree to this, but thought there should be a separate group of buildings. I then asked him if it were in his mind that the buildings should be erected on the golf links. He said, "Oh no, they should go upon the Campus among the under-graduate buildings." His first argument for this was, that by having a group of buildings distinct and distant from the other, he could charge a higher rate for the rooms and–by implication at least–such a high rate that they would not all be taken by graduate students and the rooms then left vacant could be rented to members of the junior and senior class, who could afford to take them. In this way he claimed he would obtain revenue for the University and so live up to the intent of Mrs. Swan's will. Such a suggestion was so bad, I contented myself by replying that it would be unsatisfactory to me and I would not for a moment consent to it. He then sai[d] he had hoped he would not be forced to make the argument he was going to make, but the fact was, that a very serious condition had developed in the faculty over the whole question of the Graduate College; that where originally the sentiment, in favor of your plan for the Graduate College, was practically unanimous, now not ten per cent of the members of the faculty were in favor of it and he was working for some compromise arrangement that would meet the views of those opposed to you; that unless this could be done, he could not foresee the outcome. I was surprised at the statement of the sentiment of the faculty, as a great many of the professors, whom I met the night before, had spoken to me so favorably of the whole plan and I could not realize the feeling was so strong as he stated; but that anyhow I did think it was not a matter that could properly [be] presented to me, the Board of Trustees having decided upon the location and having accepted my offer, I had nothing to do with the difficulties within the faculty. He then rose rather abruptly from his chair, saying he was in despair over the situation, that he was worried to death about it and could see no solution. I told him he had no right carrying the burden himself, that he had presented the matter and arguments to the Board of Trustees and that the responsibility was theirs. He made some remark, which I can't quite remember but which prompted me to say, "You had better change your Board of Trustees then," to which he replied, "No, I think they had better change their President."

I have given you the conversation in detail and in sequence nearly as I can remember. I did not have an opportunity to see Pyne and only had a moment's talk with him over the 'phone. I dislike very much to do anything to add to his worry about the difficulty and have not written him the details and would prefer your not showing him this letter. I expect to be in New York before the Trustees meet and will tell him in person enough to advise him of the general situation, which has become pretty acute but, I think, very nearly settled. Please let me hear what you think of it. Yours sincerely, Wm. Cooper Procter

TLS (UA, NjP).

From Moses Taylor Pyne

My dear Woodrow: New York December 29th, 1909.

I am very sorry that you expect to be away all the first week of January, and regret very much that you did not let me know of it before, as we could have had the meeting at an earlier date. As it is now we will have to have it either Tuesday or Wednesday, January 11th or 12th. Ed Sheldon is very anxious to hold it in New York. Will you kindly tell me which day would be the more convenient to you? I have a meeting at 3 o'clock on Wednesday, which makes it rather awkward but I suppose I could cut that if necessary.

I have your other letter regarding our conversation and can assure you that I am giving it my very deepest and fullest consideration. Yours very sincerely, M Taylor Pyne

TLS (WP, DLC).

From Edward Wright Sheldon

My dear Woodrow: New York. December 29, 1909.

After going up town last night it seemed to me important if possible to arrange an early interview with Momo Pyne. The result was that Cleve Dodge and I went to his house late in the evening and spent two hours with him discussing the Graduate School situation. I think it was a wise thing to have had such a conference. Cleve spoke throughout with great force and in admirable temper. We both advised Momo strongly to have the Graduate School Committee report, that the legal difficulties in the way of constructing the Thompson College on the golf grounds were such that it was impracticable to comply with the condition attached to the Board's acceptance in October of Mr. Procter's gift. When we left Momo it was with the understanding that he would give our proposition most careful consideration and let us know whether he could accept it. Cleve feels hopeful.

Yours sincerely, Edward W. Sheldon

TLS (WP, DLC).

From David Benton Jones

My dear Doctor: Chicago December 29th, 1909.

My brother has just shown me a copy of your letter to Mr. Pyne. The reading of the letter quickened my pulse and the outcome cannot be a matter of doubt. It is a stroke which will rescue Princeton from an intolerable position. A position of self-abasement inconsistent with self-respect, not only for you, but for the Board, at least as I see it. I may be absurdly hopeful for Princeton's redemption, but all the larger elements are with you and you are sure to win.

Very hastily, but very sincerely yours, David B. Jones.

TLS (WP, DLC).

From John Aikman Stewart

My dear President Wilson, New York. Decr. 29th, 1909

I have received your letter of the 27th inst. and in reply must say that I cannot take any exception to your position in reference to the Proctor offer. As the matter now stands it is out of the question for the advocates of the Golf Course site to comply with the action of the Trustees at our last meeting, *unwise as I consider that action to have been* and incorrectly stated as news in the newspapers.

At our coming meeting I think we should decline the Proctor proposal on the ground of our inability under Mrs Swan's will to accept it with the conditions imposed by Mr. Proctor.

If any other course be pursued I think the University runs the risk of losing more through changes in wills already made than it will ever receive from Mr Proctor.

Always sincerely yours John A. Stewart

ALS (WP, DLC).

To Moses Taylor Pyne

My dear Momo: [Princeton, N. J.] December 30th, 1909.

I am sorry. I thought that I had spoken to you before of my engagement to go out to Madison, Wisconsin, and that it had slipped your memory.

I am afraid that the twelfth of January is impossible for me because that is the day of several committee meetings here, but I could meet with the committee on Tuesday, the 11th, if the meeting were put early enough for me to meet an evening engagement here in Princeton. I am sorry to say that this is the best I can do.

Always affectionately yours, [Woodrow Wilson]

CCL (WWP, UA, NjP).

To Melancthon Williams Jacobus

[Princeton, N. J.]

My dear Dr. Jacobus: December 30th, 1909.

Thank you most sincerely for your letter of the 28th, which came yesterday when I was obliged to be away from home. I am replying by the earliest possible post.

I am distressed to have disturbed you so much about the situation in regard to the Graduate School. I hope most sincerely that something serviceable for the University may come out of the position I have felt obliged to take. It really was not possible to conduct the administration of the University wholesomely, so far as the Faculty were concerned, so long as we were stumbling from compromise to compromise in that matter.

It is generous of you to suggest a conference. What I would like to suggest in reply is that perhaps it would be best to hold such a conference without me. Such meetings cannot be kept from notice and comment altogether, and I fear to have the impression created that a separate party in the Board is drawing about me and forming plans with me against the majority of the Board. My feeling is that such a conference as you suggest, however, might be very profitable in order to produce a concurrence of views. I am only afraid that the number of men who should be included would make it difficult to hold it unless you waited until the very eve of the meeting of the Board.

I suppose that you will agree with me that the men who should be included are Mr. John A. Stewart, Mr. McCormick, Chancellor Magie, Mr. Dodge, Dr. DeWitt, Mr. Garrett, Mr. Thompson, Mr. Sheldon, Mr. Thomas Jones, and Mr. McIlvaine.

Mr. Stephen Palmer is in the South and, I understand is not at all well. I sent a copy of my letter to Pyne to his New York address with the request that it be forwarded to him, but his son called me up over the phone and said that his father was in such bad shape as yet that he would venture to take the responsibility of not sending it to him.

Perhaps you would like also to include in the conference Mr. David B. Jones. These, however, are only suggestions on my part.

I can only thank you with all my heart for your loyalty to the interests of the University and your desire to take active means to conserve them, and beg you to believe that I am myself not so much distressed as cleared in my mind and judgment and therefore relieved by the present posture of affairs. The issue is so clear and so large that the whole matter has taken on another aspect.

Wishing you every good thing for the new year,

Faithfully and cordially yours, [Woodrow Wilson]

CCL (RSB Coll., DLC).

To Edward Wright Sheldon

My dear Ed., Princeton, N. J. December 30th, 1909.

Thank you heartily for your letters and for what you tell me of the conference you and Dodge have had with Momo. I hope and pray that matters may turn out in a way that will serve the University.

Always affectionately yours, Woodrow Wilson

TLS (photostat in RSB Coll., DLC).

To Charles Henry Marshall

My dear Mr. Marshall: Princeton, N. J. December 30th, 1909.

Allow me to acknowledge the receipt of your notice of the 28th of December that President Henry Smith Pritchett and the Hon. Henry White[1] have been nominated for membership in the Round Table Club and to say that, so far as I am concerned, the election of these gentlemen would be wholly agreeable.

Very sincerely yours, Woodrow Wilson

TLS (Round Table Dining Club Scrapbook, NHi).

[1] Prominent diplomat, who had recently resigned as Ambassador to France.

From Thomas Davies Jones

My dear Mr. President: Chicago December 30th, 1909.

I have your note of the 27th instant enclosing copy of your letter of the 25th to Mr. Pyne. While I have grave doubts as to the wisdom of raising the issue at the time and in the precise form in which it is raised in your letter to Mr. Pyne, now that the lines are drawn it is scarcely necessary for me to say, after what I said to you when I last saw you,–that I am entirely and heartily with you upon what is really the central issue, namely, the necessity to eliminate West and all that West stands for. I think the other issues raised, such, for instance, as the exact location of a particular building, are really collateral issues and I probably would feel forced to differ from you upon the importance of some of them, but as to the central issue, I have no doubts or reservations.

I have read and re-read your letter to Mr. Pyne, with care. I think it is important that no ambiguity whatever shall surround the issue actually raised, and I think your letter does leave matters in a somewhat ambiguous state. Let me explain this somewhat in detail, as I think it is important: I was not at the last meeting of the Board and had some difficulty in ascertaining exactly what was the action taken, and I therefore wrote to Mr. McAlpin asking him to send me a copy of Mr. Procter's letter of May 8th and also of the proceedings of the Board at the October meeting relating to that gift. The same mail which brought me your letter brought Mr. McAlpin's reply. Mr. Pyne's resolution as amended by Dr. Stewart, accepts the offer of Mr. Procter "provided that the legal right to use Mrs. Swann's money in the erection of the Graduate School upon the golf links be assured, and that Mr. Procter first advise us of his intention in relation to the disposition of his proposed gift." The second of these provisos carries with it the clear implication that the "intention" of Mr. Procter when disclosed, shall meet with the approval of the Board of Directors. This is clearly not an absolute acceptance of the offer; neither the Thompson College nor any other building can be erected on the golf links or elsewhere, without further affirmative action by the Board. If the Board receive satisfactory assurances upon the two branches of Stewart's amendment, it can scarcely be said with entire accuracy, that the Trustees would be dealing unfairly with the Swann estate or that in accepting conditions which have been stated to the trustees and which meet with their approval, the trustees, in accepting the Proctor gift, would be accepting it "upon terms which take the educational policy of the University out of the hands of the trustees and faculty and permit it to be determined by those who give money."

Now what I want to ask you is this: Are we to understand from your letter to Mr. Pyne, that unless the Board shall rescind the action taken, as above defined, you decline "to remain responsible for the direction of the affairs of the University"? If you do, then West and his followers will have considerable justification for insisting that you resign because the residential Graduate College is built on the golf links rather than upon the college campus. While it may be your opinion that the action which you have taken would be justified by that issue alone if there were no others, you are even better aware than I am that you would not have on that question alone, anything like the united support of the members of the faculty. They are doubtless in substantial agreement with you as to the unwisdom of building upon the golf links. But I have serious doubts whether, in the opinion of a large number of the trustees, the faculty and the alumni, you would be justified in forcing an issue on that ground, which is not unlikely to divide the friends and supporters of the University to such an extent as to bring real disaster upon the University.

I understand that Mr. Pyne is now convinced that West must be eliminated from the actual work of the Graduate School and only insists upon his being some sort of a head to the residential Graduate College. I take it that West has also yielded a reluctant consent to this arrangement, though it is not unlikely that his assent is coupled with designs not yet disclosed. It would not be fair to Mr. Pyne or to Dean West to assume that West's connection with the Graduate School is to be so profoundly modified, after Procter's offer is made and before it's acceptance becomes actually operative, unless the full scope of the proposed change in the organization of the Graduate School has been fully and frankly stated to Mr. Procter. Good faith absolutely requires a full explanation to Mr. Procter of the entire situation, and while I cannot assume that there has been any deliberate concealment from him, I do not think that he understands the situation fully, and I think it highly probable that when the situation is explained to him, as it must be explained, his offer will be withdrawn and the whole controversy settled in that way. The elimination of West will then become comparatively easy.

My sole purpose in writing to you at this length and in considerable haste, is to urge upon you the importance of so defining the issue as to carry with you all of the friends of the University who are really with you on what I believe to be the main issue, namely, the elimination of West.

Faithfully yours, Thomas D. Jones.

TLS (WP, DLC).

From Richard Spencer Childs

Dear Dr. Wilson: New York Dec. 30, 1909

I nominate William Allen White of Emporia Kansas, and Ben. B. Lindsay of Colorado, as Vice-Presidents of The Short Ballot Organization. I have reason to believe that both of these men will be willing to accept, and I think that they would both be valuable to us.[1]

If you have no objection to either of these men, simply file this letter and make no reply. If for any reason you do not approve, or wish the matter help [held] up, kindly let me hear from you within ten days.

Yours very truly, Richard S Childs Secretary.

TLS (WP, DLC).

[1] Both White and Lindsey were elected vice-presidents and served.

John Lambert Cadwalader to Moses Taylor Pyne

My dear Pyne: New York. 30 December, 1909.

I return to you the President's letter.

I refrain purposely from any extended comment upon it. It is a rather sad admission, from my point of view, of his incapacity for working in a team and of his expecting to convert people who may differ from him to his way of thinking upon a subject where a full interchange of opinion is necessary and as to which the opinion of no person not supported by his co-workers is of any moment whatever.

It has too, an amusing phase–namely, that if the Board of Trustees in any essential point shall differ from the President the Board of Trustees is to give way. Of course, it is unnecessary to comment on any such proposition. On the whole, the letter calls for very serious consideration.

Of course, you are absolutely right in your intention not to insist upon your scheme unless the Board of Trustees as a whole, by a very large vote, shall determine that that scheme ought to go forward and you are perfectly right in not squabbling and skirmishing over the edges of the business.

Yours faithfully, John L. Cadwalader.

TCL (M. T. Pyne Coll., NjP).

From Thomas Davies Jones

My dear Mr. President: Chicago December 31st, 1909.

I wrote you yesterday in great haste and before I had opportunity to discuss the situation with McCormick, McIlvaine or my brother. I believe that all here agree with me that it is not clear from your letter to Mr. Pyne just where you draw the line. Did you intend to state that the conditional acceptance by the Board in October of Mr. Procter's offer had made your position impossible, or that your subsequent conversations with Mr. Procter had convinced you that his exactions will be such that if the Board should accede to them your position will become impossible. The inference is almost irresistible from the paragraph of your letter beginning "You will see, therefore," that you mean to insist upon a rescission of the action already taken; and, if that be correct, your action must, I fear be followed by disastrous consequences. And I therefore fervently hope that the second interpretation above suggested is the correct one.

I am strongly inclined to believe that if Mr. Procter is encouraged to develop his whole mind–his "intention" as the Stewart amendment puts it–his conditions will be such as even Mr. Pyne will concede to be impossible, and that the close alliance between Mr. Pyne and Dean West will, in this way, be broken up, and the elimination of the Dean will then easily follow. I said to you when I saw you last, that further affirmative action by the Board at the January meeting could, in my opinion, be prevented, and that this would throw the whole matter over to the April meeting, when both Mr. Cadwalader and Mr. Palmer will, I hope, be present, and when the exactions of Mr. Procter will be better known than they are now. Time is what we most want to gain just now, and the more I think about it the more I deplore the fact that you have, as it seems to me, forced an issue prematurely.

Faithfully yours, Thomas D. Jones.

TLS (WP, DLC).

From Melancthon Williams Jacobus

Hartford, Conn.,
My dear President Wilson: December 31st, 1909.

I take for granted that there will be need of a meeting of the Curriculum Committee previous to the coming session of the Board, even though no report is called for from the Committee to the Board at this time.

My reasons are, first, that you contemplate making at this time a report on the possibility of economies in the Faculty budget, as stated by yourself at the October meeting of the Committee; and also that Mr. Thompson wishes a discussion by the Committee on two points, (a) the C.E. entrance requirements in Mathematics, and (b) the distribution of students in the elective courses of Junior and Senior years.

I do not know whether the Faculty is ready to present to the Committee any proposals regarding the reconstruction of the C.E. courses of study. If so, these might come before the Committee also at this time, or be deferred until the April meeting.

I am also somewhat in doubt as to whether there is anything to be reported to the Committee regarding the mode of appointment in the Stafford Lectureship course. If I recall rightly, there was some confusion regarding this mentioned last October, but I am uncertain as to whether it was decided to clear this confusion up or to let the matter go as it now stands.

In any case, there would seem to be a call for a meeting of the Committee for the consideration, within itself, of these other matters to be brought before it, apart from any report to be made to the Board.

I am awaiting a letter from Mr. Thompson, which he said he would write me today after he had seen you yesterday in Princeton, regarding the proposed conference in New York. I do not know what his personal opinion may be, but I am strongly of the conviction that you should be present at the conference and state clearly to those who are gathered the clear issue which you feel has been made in the matter of your responsible management of the affairs of the University. For such a purpose as this I should hope that that others besides those who are already avowedly and actually with you in your opinions should be asked to be present at the conference. Those who stand with you do not need further persuasion as to the rightness of your position; but those who do not hold your opinion I think can be brought over to a very different view of affairs by the clear, lucid and convincing statement which I am sure you will make on this vital question.

Personally, I do not care at all whether the opinion gets abroad that there is a party which is gathering around you in opposition to the majority of the Board. I wish very decidedly that this majority would come to just exactly such an opinion. It is, in fact, the very thing I want them to realize. They do not know what they are doing, and the sooner they realize it the better. It is, in my opinion, no time at all for hiding ourselves, but rather the time for showing where we stand and for what we stand, and I should be glad to have such a conference before the Board meets, even though it be the day previous to the meeting.

On the 10th and 11th of next month I am obliged to be here for public functions in which I must take part, but I could be in New York either on the 9th or on the 12th. If you think the latter date is preferable, we can call the meeting early enough to get back to Princeton for a meeting of the Curriculum Committee that night.

I trust you have talked the matter over fully with Mr. Thompson, and I will be glad to have by return mail your judgment in the case.

With best wishes for the new year, which I am sure is going to be one of great things for the University, I am

Yours very sincerely, Melancthon W. Jacobus

TLS (WP, DLC).

From Alexander Thomas Ormond

Dear Sir [Princeton, N. J.] December 31st 1909

In reply to your letter dated November the Ninth I beg leave to submit the following report:

Questions First & Second

In answer to the first two questions I herewith submit a chart in which the information sought is given in convenient form.

Third.

The Preceptorial reading in each subject is decided on in a conference of the Preceptors concerned and the Professor in charge of the subject. This is the rule in the Department which is departed from only in exceptional cases. Considerable latitude is allowed to individual Preceptors in the choice of reading, though in practice the method in this respect varies with different subjects and Professors.

In selecting the reading the Department during the first two years made a difference between the Regulars and Floaters requiring more of the former, but this policy has been largely abandoned since it has been found from experience that the needs of the two classes of students are practically the same. This [is] particularly true in Junior year when all are practically beginners, while in Senior year the Pro-Seminary supplies the demands of department men who require a different quality of work.

In preparing the data for the examination the Professor in charge ascertains in conference with the Preceptors the kind and amount of reading conducted by each Preceptor, the aim of the examination being to test the student's mastery of the matter he has been over rather than his ability to reproduce what he has read or heard.

Fourth.

The statistics of the Department show that it has been the rule rather than the exception for the Professors to take part in the Preceptorial work. For example the present term all the Professors who conduct classes of Juniors or Seniors precept their own floaters, the only exception being that of the Head of the Department who has charge of the Pro-Seminary and a considerable body of graduate students. Without exception the Professors in the Department are ready to do Preceptorial work and also to Precept in subjects other than their own courses. In this connection a scheme of work has been drawn up by a member of the Department which is submitted as a part of this report. (This scheme has not as a matter of fact been laid before the Department.)

Fifth

It has been found that in Philosophy it is *intensive* reading rather than *extensive* reading that counts most with our students. The amount of reading in Philosophy for which undergraduates can reasonably be held responsible is limited and therefore, to a degree, special. The chief importance of the lecture consists, therefore, in treatment of the subject as a whole, dealing with large continents in a general survey, leaving for the Preceptorial work a more detailed treatment of portions of the territory. For example in the History of Philosophy a Junior subject covering both Ancient and Modern Philosophy the lecturer aims to accomplish two things (1) to give a geographical or topographical outline of the great movements as a whole, (2) to interpret the several schools and systems of thought in the light of their leading ideas and their broad historical bearings. The most effective Preceptorial work in connection with this has been found to consist in the reading of some of the great Philosophical classics: in Ancient Philosophy some of the Dialogues of Plato or selections from the works of Aristotle; in Modern Philosophy, characteristic works of Hobbes, DesCartes, Locke, Berkel[e]y, Hume and Kant. It has been found very stimulating to the student to be thus brought into immediate contact with the mind of a great master

The practice in the other subjects of the Department, varying as it does with the character of the subject can be briefly indicated. Preceptor Johnson[1] in connection with Advanced Psychology reads with his Preceptees parts of Piersons Grammar of Science, Paulsen's Introduction to Philosophy and James's Psychology.[2] Professor Patton in connection with his lectures reads such works as Mills' Utilitarianism and Sedgwicks Methods of Ethics.[3] In the course in the Outlines of Philosophy the students read with the Preceptors Watson's Selections from Kant;[4] or in place of it Kants Critique as a whole, and Foundations of Knowledge. On the whole, the two factors in the system have worked harmoniously, though not without a degree of friction caused by what seems to have been a failure on the part of some of the members of the Department to realize the true import of the Preceptorial System.

Sixth

The Preceptorial method has proved itself to be about equally practicable in all the courses of the Department, its unsatisfactory working, wherever it exists, being due to failure of adjustment, not to any intrinsic difficulty in the method itself. The general experience of the department is highly favorable and the trend of the system has been decidedly in the direction of promoting higher and more scholarly ideals in both students and instructors. Taken as a whole the experience of the Department of Philosophy justifies the conclusion that the Preceptorial system

[1] Roger Bruce Cash Johnson, Earl Dodge Preceptor in Philosophy.

[2] Karl Pearson, *The Grammar of Science*, 2nd edn. (London, 1900); Friedrich Paulsen, *Introduction to Philosophy*, 2nd American edn. from the 3rd German edn., tr. Frank Thilly (New York, 1898); and William James, *Psychology* (New York, 1892).

[3] John Stuart Mill, *Utilitarianism* (London, 1863, many later edns.), and Henry Sidgwick, *The Methods of Ethics*, 7th edn. (London and New York, 1907).

[4] Immanuel Kant, *The Philosophy of Kant as Contained in Extracts from His Own Writings*, selected and translated by John Watson, new edn. (London and New York, 1901).

has made good and that rational progress for Princeton in the future will lie in the direction of perfecting its method and more completely incorporating it with the other parts of our system of teaching.

Suggestions

In furtherance of this end the following suggestions are ventured:

1. That in order to secure a larger measure of of [*sic*] co-operation among the Departments, a committee be constituted composed of one member from each of the Departments in which Preceptorial work is carried on; the province of this committee being to consider the working of the Preceptorial system as a whole with a view to making any suggestions or recommendations to the Departments they may think advisable, it being understood that the function of such committee shall be purely advisory.

2. In view of a feeling that prevails among the Preceptors of the Department of Philosophy and perhaps in other Departments as well; to wit, that it is felt as a hardship to be debarred from lecturing to undergraduates, the following tentative suggestion is ventured: that this feeling might be met and the interests of a more complete organization be conserved, by opening up to the Preceptors a limited use of the lecture function. Of course different subjects might involve the use of different methods of reaching the end in view, and it might not be found either practicable or advisable in all cases. The following method would seem to be practicable for most of the subjects in the Department of Philosophy. The Professor in charge of the subject to continue as at present, dealing with the subject as a whole, leaving to the Preceptor the privilege of selecting some special part of the field on which he may deliver from six to eight lectures a term. The question of hours would have to be settled; also that of the relation of the Preceptorial lectures to the other parts of the system. But the difficulties in the way do not seem to be insuperable, while the introduction of such a feature, aside from the advantage the student would derive from it, would give an additional impetus to the men who are doing Preceptorial work, as well as contribute to the further consolidation of the system of instruction as a whole.

Respectfully Submitted Alexander T. Ormond

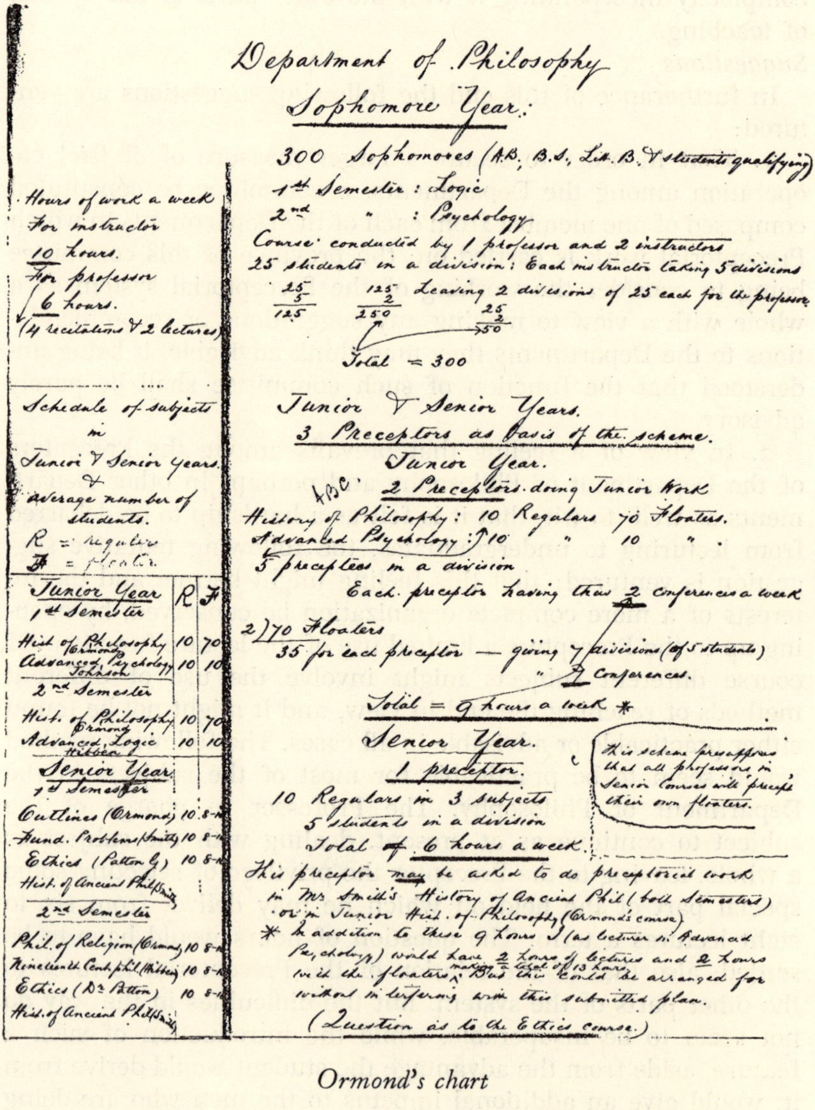

Department of Philosophy

Sophomore Year.

Hours of work a week
For instructor
10 hours.
For professor
6 hours.
(4 recitations & 2 lectures)

300 Sophomores (A.B., B.S., Litt. B. & students qualifying)
1st Semester: Logic
2nd " : Psychology
Course conducted by 1 professor and 2 instructors
25 students in a division: Each instructor taking 5 divisions
25 × 5 = 125 125 × 2 = 250 Leaving 2 divisions of 25 each for the professor 25 × 2 = 50
Total = 300

Junior & Senior Years.
3 Preceptors as basis of the scheme.
Junior Year.
ABC 2 Preceptors doing Junior Work
History of Philosophy: 10 Regulars 70 Floaters.
Advanced Psychology: 10 " 10 "
5 preceptees in a division
Each preceptor having thus 2 conferences a week
2)70 Floaters
35 for each preceptor — giving 7 divisions (of 5 students)
" 7 conferences.
Total = 9 hours a week *

Senior Year.
1 preceptor.
10 Regulars in 3 subjects
5 students in a division
Total of 6 hours a week.

This scheme presupposes that all professors in Senior courses will precept their own floaters.

This preceptor may be asked to do preceptorial work in Mr Smith's History of Ancient Phil (both Semesters) or in Junior Hist. of Philosophy (Ormond's course)
* In addition to these 9 hours I (as lecturer in Advanced Psychology) would have 2 hours of lectures and 2 hours with the floaters, making a total of 13 hours. But this could be arranged for without interfering with this submitted plan.
(Question as to the Ethics course.)

Schedule of subjects in Junior & Senior years. & average number of students.
R = regulars
F = floaters

	R	F
Junior Year		
1st Semester		
Hist of Philosophy (Ormond)	10	70
Advanced Psychology (Johnson)	10	10
2nd Semester		
Hist. of Philosophy (Ormond)	10	70
Advanced Logic (Hibben)	10	10
Senior Year		
1st Semester		
Outlines (Ormond)	10	8-10
Fund. Problems (Smith)	10	8-10
Ethics (Patton G.)	10	8-10
Hist. of Ancient Phil (Smith)		
2nd Semester		
Phil. of Religion (Ormond)	10	8-10
Nineteenth Cent. phil. (Hibben)	10	8-10
Ethics (Dr Patton)	10	8-10
Hist. of Ancient Phil (Smith)		

Ormond's chart

Department of Philosophy

Sophomore Year.

Hours of work a week For Instructor 10 hours.
For professor 6 hours. (4 recitations & 2 lectures)

300 Sophomores (A.B., B.S., Litt.B., & students qualifying)
1st Semester: Logic
2nd " : Psychology

Course conducted by 1 professor and 2 instructors

25 students in a division: Each instructor taking 5 divisions

25	125	Leaving 2 divisions of 25 each for the professor
5	2	25
125	250	2
		50

Total = 300

Junior & Senior Years

Schedule of subjects in Junior & Senior years & average number of students.

R = regular
F = floater

3 Preceptors as basis of the scheme.

Junior Year.

1st Semester	R	F	2nd Semester	R	F
Hist of Philosophy Ormond	10	70	Hist. of Philosophy Ormond	10	70
Advanced Psychology Johnson	10	10	Advanced Logic Hibben	10	10

2 *Preceptors* doing Junior Work

History of Philosophy: 10 Regulars 70 Floaters.
Advanced Psychology: 10 " 10 " .

5 preceptees in a division
Each preceptor having thus 2 conferences a week

2) 70 Floaters
35 for each preceptor—giving 7 divisions (of 5 students)
" 7 conferences.

*Total = 9 hours a week**

* In addition to these 9 hours I (as lecturer in Advanced Psychology) would have 2 hours of lectures and 2 hours with the floaters making a total of 13 hours. But this could be arranged for without interfering with this submitted plan. (Question as to the Ethics course).

Senior Year

1st Semester	R	F	2nd Semester	R	F
Outlines (Ormond)	10	8-10	Phil. of Religion (Ormond)	10	8-10
Fund. Problems (Smith)	10	8-10	Nineteenth Cent. phil. (Hibben)	10	8-10
Ethics (Patton G)	10	8-10	Ethics (Dr. Patton)	10	8-10
Hist. of Ancient Phil. (Smith)			Hist. of Ancient Phil. (Smith)		

1 preceptor.

10 Regulars in 3 subjects
5 students in a division
Total = *6 hours a week.*

This scheme presupposes that all professors in Senior Courses will 'precept' their own floaters.

This preceptor *may* be asked to do preceptorial work in Mr. Smith's History of Ancient Phil (both Semesters) or in Junior Hist. of Philosophy (Ormond's course).

Schedule of Professors' Hours.

First Semester

Ormond — 9 hours

Hibben
(a) 4 recitations in Logic } 6 hours
(b) 2 Lectures " "
(c) Graduate course (am unable to say how many hours[)]

Smith
(a) 4 hours of lectures (2 courses Fundamental Problems & Hist. of Ancient phil.)
(b) Preceptorial work in these 2 courses: Am unable to say how many hours are given to this preceptorial work.

Patton G.
(a) 2 lectures on Ethics
(b) Precepts floaters in this course &
(c) Conducts graduate course in Ethics

Second Semester

Ormond — 9 hours.

Hibben
(a) 2 lectures in Advanced Logic.
(b) 2 " in 19th Century philosophy.
(c) 2 preceptorial hours probably (1 in each course)
(d) graduate course (am unable to say how many hours[)]

Smith
(a) 4 recitations in Sophomore Psychology
(b) 2 lectures to Sophomores.

(c) 2 lectures on History of Ancient Philosophy
(d) Preceptorial work in course on Hist. of Ancient Phil

Patton G. No lectures. Dr. Patton lectures 2nd Semester
(a) 'Precepts' floaters in his father's course.
(b) Conducts a graduate course.

Department of Philosophy[5]
Distribution of Students in the Department.

Juniors

First Term	1906	1907	1908	1909	1910
Regulars	11	9	9	9	7
Floaters	56	67	50	74	71
No. taking *two* subjects	0	0	0	1	2
Adv. Psychology	19	13	12	23	16
History of Philos.	58	72	56	70	78
Total	67	76	59	83	78
Second Term					
Regulars	9	8	8	9	
Floaters	58	43	40	53	
No. taking *two* subjects	0	1	1	0	
Adv. Logic	35	16	18	13	
History of Philos.	46	39	34	56	
Exp. Psychology	4	4	4	2	
Total	57	51	48	62	

Seniors

First Term	1906	1907	1908	1909	1910
Regulars	17	11	9	9	11
Floaters	10	21	14	4	8
No. taking two subjects	4	3	0	0	4
Ethics	22	30	16	9	17
Exp. Psychology	23				
Fundamental Problems (started in 1907)		11	15	10	14
Outlines of Philosophy	20	13	10	12	14
Total	27	32	23	13	19

[5] To make possible the typographical reproduction of Ormond's charts, some columns have been rearranged.

Second Term				
Regulars	17	11	9	9
Floaters	9	6	5	1
No. taking two subjects	4	0	0	0
Ethics	22	15	11	9
18th Cent. Philos.	22	11	11	9
Outlines of Philos.	20	13	10	10
Total	26	17	14	14

ALS (WWP, UA, NjP).

From Arthur Twining Hadley, with Enclosure

New Haven, Connecticut.

My dear Mr. Wilson: December 31st, 1909.

I am enclosing herewith a draft of a letter regarding football accidents and football rules. I am by no means prejudiced in favor of the result that I have achieved, and think it not impossible that either you or Mr. Lowell may suggest a better one.

Faithfully yours, Arthur T Hadley

TLS (WP, DLC).

ENCLOSURE

Arthur Twining Hadley *et al.* to Walter Camp *et al.*

Gentlemen: [New Haven, Conn., c. Dec. 31, 1909]

We desire you to act as a committee to advise the authorities of Harvard, Princeton, and Yale Universities concerning the causes which have led to the serious injuries at foot-ball during the season which has just closed and concerning the changes in the rules which are necessary in order to make the game safer.

CCL (WP, DLC).

Henry Burling Thompson to Moses Taylor Pyne

Dear Momo: Wilmington, Del. December 31st, 1909.

Our meeting yesterday was largely routine work, and the minutes of the meeting and Imbrie's report on appraisal,—which takes up the installation of Freshmen in Dormitories,—will give you full information as to just what we did.

I saw the President at his house, by appointment, and went over the situation with regard to Dean West and the Graduate School. To boil the whole question down, we have reached a point which I was afraid, as far back as two years ago, we would ultimately come to, and that is, the President and Dean West cannot maintain a permanent relationship in the work of the University. I said to Cleve Dodge, at the time of the Institute of Technology offer,[1] that it would only be a question of time when we would reach the point that we have arrived at now. The President has apparently made up his mind absolutely on the lines of the letter which he has written you. He shows no excitement, but feels that he has gone to the limit on his handling of West, and says, with entire frankness, that if the Trustees are not satisfied with his position, he is entirely willing to accept the result, but he wants it absolutely understood that this attitude is not taken as a threat or as a hold-up, but that his position is intolerable, and, unless he has relief, he cannot maintain the Presidency of the University. I am entirely satisfied with the sincerity of his position, and I am free to say that I believe he has the sympathy of the majority of the Faculty and of the leading men in the Faculty. It goes without saying that there are strong men like van Dyke and Hibben who do not agree with him, but the bulk of the men whom we are dependent on in the Faculty are really in sympathy with him. I do not say this, based on my knowledge of what the President tells me, but from what I gather from others. Now, that we have reached the point that I have anticipated, I do not propose to worry over it. I shall vote to sustain the President, and am entirely willing to meet the consequences of that action. I am aware that it is going to make a row, and it is going to hurt us in certain quarters with West's friends and with Wilson's enemies. We are going to lose certain of our subscribers to the Committee of Fifty Fund, but we might as well meet the issue now and adjust our future course to meet the new conditions. The situation is an unfortunate one, but, frankly, I do not believe that we can continue to temporize over this question any longer. It has been a sore point for two years, and we have now reached the parting of the ways, and must come to a final decision.

I have not attempted to go into details in this letter, but have simply tried to confine it to the main point at issue.

As I stated to you on Wednesday night, I shall be very glad to talk this matter over with you and Sheldon at a time that is mutually convenient.

Yours very sincerely, Henry B. Thompson.

P.S. Do not understand I commit myself to University Hall for Graduate School site. This I did not discuss, only the bigger question.

TCL (M. T. Pyne Coll., NjP).

[1] That is, when West had been offered the presidency of the Massachusetts Institute of Technology in 1906.

To the Board of Trustees of Princeton University

[Princeton, N. J.] 1 JANUARY, 1910.

GENTLEMEN OF THE BOARD OF TRUSTEES:

I have the honour to submit my annual report for the year 1909.

The year which has elapsed since my last report was prepared has been marked by the resignation from this Board of our colleague Mr. DeWitt Clinton Blair and by the death of Mr. Cornelius Cuyler Cuyler, who had been an active member of this Board since 1898.

Mr. Blair was elected a member of this Board in 1900, had served upon its Finance Committee, had contributed generously to the support and equipment of the University, and had enjoyed throughout his nine years of service the just appreciation of his colleagues. He resigned his seat because he felt it no longer possible to give the business of the University the attention he knew it to deserve without putting too great tax upon his strength, if he attempted any longer to add that to the duties which devolved upon him as the head of the great financial business over which he presided. Our regret at his withdrawal is united with the hope that he may enjoy increased health and strength with his greater freedom from responsibility.

The death of Mr. Cuyler was most tragical and has affected our whole university community very profoundly. He lost his life on the thirty-first of July, 1909, in an automobile accident in France, while in the full enjoyment of health and in the full zest of a delightful summer vacation. He was a man of so many sides, so various in his activities, so full of vigour, so interesting and so delightful in his gifts and character, that it is difficult to characterize him adequately. He was a remarkable man of business who yet devoted his energies in an extraordinary degree to the promotion of enterprises which lay remote from business, enterprises of the mind, of Christian missions, of art, of sport, undertakings that represented every side of life and which drew him into the companionship of men of every sort and interest; and he was a friend always, in business and out of it, to scores of men who had reason to bless him for the thoughtful and always generous aid and sympathy he gave them, lavishly and graciously, with unfailing loyalty. All sides of him were made manifest in his service of the University, which began long before he was made a member of this Board. He served her as a man of business, as an experienced man of the world, conversant with a hundred aspects of life, and as a loving son, an unfailing friend, spending the best powers of his heart and mind to advance her welfare.

Professor William Alfred Packard, Professor Emeritus of Latin in the University since 1905 and for thirty-five years previous to the time of his retirement one of the most active, efficient, and distinguished members of its faculty, died at his home in Princeton on the morning of the second of December, 1909, in the eightieth year of his age. Dr. Packard was born on the twenty-sixth of August, 1830; came of a family of distinguished scholars and men of science; and brought to the service of the University, when he was at his prime, an influence of genuine culture and refinement, of exact scholarship and schooled literary taste, and of elevated personal character of which scores of his pupils will retain the pleasant flavour and feel the gentle stimulus so long as they live. He was a teacher of unusual parts. It would be difficult to say just what were the elements of the power which he exerted in the class-room. A force burned in him which never flared or made any noise, but which every man who sat under him felt and was submissive to. Every one was aware at once, upon coming into contact with him, of the high standards of personal conduct and of self-respecting performance he stood for: he seemed in some subtle way to embody them. His pupils felt obliged by some force they could not reckon with to attempt, at least, to deserve his respect and approbation. He did not display in the class-room the quality of gentleness which endeared him to the colleagues and friends who knew him more familiarly. We loved the man as well as revered the scholar and the scrupulous gentleman. We mourn his loss with a deep and genuine sense of bereavement.

Since my last report there have been the following resignations from positions upon the teaching staff of the University filled by election by this Board:

Professor James Hopwood Jeans, the distinguished mathematician, has returned to England to prosecute his studies privately, without formal university connections.

Mr. Junius Spencer Morgan, by whose intelligent service and fruitful suggestions the administration of the University Library has so much profited, and who has been in so many ways one of the most thoughtful, helpful, and generous friends of the University, has resigned his post as Associate Librarian in order to be free to concentrate himself upon other duties.

Mr. Adam LeRoy Jones, Preceptor since 1905 in the Department of Philosophy, has resigned to accept responsible administrative duties at Columbia University.

Mr. Wilmon Henry Sheldon, Preceptor in the same Department, has resigned to accept a professorship in philosophy at Dartmouth College.

Mr. Ernest Ludlow Bogart, Preceptor in the Department of History, Politics, and Economics, has resigned to accept an appointment as Professor of Economics at the University of Illinois.

Mr. Edgar Dawson, Preceptor in the same Department, has resigned to assume the headship of the Department of History at the Normal College maintained by the City of New York.

Mr. Andrew Runni Anderson, Preceptor in the Department of Classics, has resigned to accept an appointment at Northwestern University.

Mr. Donald Cameron, Preceptor in Classics, has resigned to become Professor of Classics at Boston University.

Mr. Harold Ripley Hastings, Preceptor in Classics, has resigned to prosecute his studies as teaching fellow at the University of Wisconsin.

Mr. Donald Alexander MacRae, Preceptor in Classics, has resigned to devote himself to secondary school work, which so much needs recruiting by men of his stamp and scholarship.

Mr. Leroy Carr Barret, Preceptor in Classics, has resigned to accept a position at Dartmouth College.

Mr. Carl Eben Stromquist, Preceptor in Mathematics, has resigned to join the teaching staff of the University of Wyoming.

Since my last report to the Board the following promotions and additions have been made in the teaching staff of the University:

Dr. Edward Elliott, since 1905 Preceptor in History, Politics, and Economics, was last June elected Professor of Politics and Dean of the College. The deanship of the college is an office which was at that time created and which deals chiefly with undergraduate discipline.

Dr. Luther Pfahler Eisenhart, since 1905 Preceptor in Mathematics, was at the same time made Professor of Mathematics. As Vice-chairman of the Committee of the Faculty on Examinations and Standing he is charged with the direct administration of the rules regarding scholarship.

Dr. Edwin Plimpton Adams, since 1905 Assistant Professor of Physics, was, at the same meeting of the Board, elected Professor of Physics, to take the place made vacant by the resignation of Professor James Hopwood Jeans.

Dr. George Augustus Hulett, since 1905 Assistant Professor of Physical Chemistry, was at the last meeting of the Board, in October, elected Professor of Physical Chemistry.

Dr. Philip Howard Fogel, Instructor in Philosophy, was in June last advanced to the rank of Preceptor in Philosophy. Dr. Fogel was graduated Bachelor of Arts from Ursinus College in 1901, A.M. from Princeton University in 1903. In 1904 he received from Princeton the degree of Doctor of Philosophy. The years 1904-1906 he spent as Instructor in Philosophy at Princeton; during the year 1906-1907 he was a student of philosophy at the universities of Berlin and Heidelberg; and during the years 1907-1909 was again Instructor in Philosophy here.

Mr. Charles E. Persons, elected Preceptor in History, Politics, and Economics in June 1909, was graduated Bachelor of Arts from Cornell College, Iowa, in June 1903, A.M. from Harvard University in 1905. He was a graduate student in the Department of Economics at Harvard University during the years 1904-1905 and 1906-1908, having in the intervals served as instructor in the high schools of his native State. During the academic year 1908-1909 he was Instructor in Economics at Wellesley College.

Dr. Henry Lamar Crosby, elected Preceptor in Classics in June, 1909, was graduated Bachelor of Arts from the University of Texas in 1901, Master of Arts in 1902; and in 1903 took the degree of Master of Arts from Harvard University. In 1905 he received the degree of Doctor of Philosophy from Harvard. During the year 1905-1906 he was Instructor in Greek at the University of Pennsylvania, and from 1906 to 1909 was Assistant Professor of Greek at the University of Missouri.

Mr. Charles Hodge Jones, in June elected Preceptor in Classics, was graduated Bachelor of Arts from Princeton University in 1900, after which he was for five years Instructor in Classics at Tome Institute, at Port Deposit, Maryland. From 1905-1907 he was Instructor in Classics at Princeton, at the same time pursuing graduate studies. From 1907-1909, when he returned to the University, he was a student in classics at the University of Halle.

Dr. George David Birkhoff, elected Preceptor in Mathematics in June 1909, was graduated Bachelor of Arts from Harvard

University in 1905, Master of Arts in 1906. In 1907 he received the degree of Doctor of Philosophy from the University of Chicago. From 1907-1909 he served as Instructor in Mathematics at the University of Wisconsin.

Dr. Joseph Henry Maclagen Wedderburn, elected Preceptor in Mathematics in June, was graduated Master of Arts, with high class honours, from the University of Edinburgh in 1903. During the academic year 1902-1903 he was assistant in the physical laboratory at Edinburgh; during the winter of 1903-1904 studied at Leipzig, and during the summer of 1904 at Berlin. The academic year 1904-1905 he spent as a graduate student of mathematics at the University of Chicago. In 1905 he was appointed Lecturer in Mathematics at Edinburgh, an appointment which he held until he came to Princeton. In 1908 he received from the University of Edinburgh the degree of Doctor of Science.

Dr. Elijah Swift, chosen Preceptor in Mathematics at the meeting of the Board in June last, was graduated Bachelor of Arts from Harvard University in 1903, Master of Arts in 1904. From 1904-1907 he studied, as a Fellow of Harvard University, at the University of Goettingen, from which University he received the degree of Doctor of Philosophy in July, 1907. When promoted to the rank of Preceptor he was Instructor in Mathematics here.

The following have received appointments as Instructors, Assistants, or Teaching Fellows in the University:

In Philosophy: Edgeworth Bird Baxter, A.B., Princeton University, 1890; Elliott Park Frost, A.B. Dartmouth College, 1905, A.M. Dartmouth College 1906, Ph.D. Harvard University 1908; Henry Clay McComas, A.B. Johns Hopkins University 1897, A.M. Columbia University 1898.

In History, Politics, and Economics: Edgeworth Bird Baxter, A.B. Princeton University 1890; Francis William Coker, A.B. University of North Carolina 1899, A.B. Harvard University 1902; David Aloysius McCabe, A.B. Harvard University 1904, Ph.D. Johns Hopkins University 1909; John Mabry Mathews, A.B. Johns Hopkins University 1906, Ph.D. Johns Hopkins University 1909; and Conyers Read, A.B. Harvard University 1903, A.M. Harvard University 1904, Ph.D. Harvard University 1908.

In Classics: Charles Christopher Mierow, A.B. Princeton University 1905, A.M. 1906, Ph.D. 1908; John Nevin Schaeffer, A.B. Franklin & Marshall College 1903, B.Litt. Oxon. 1908; and Henry Bartlett Van Hoesen, A.B. Hobart College 1905, A.M. Princeton University 1906.

In English: Radcliffe Heermance, A.B. Williams College 1904, A.M. Williams 1906, A.M. Harvard University 1908, A.M. Princeton University 1909.

In Modern Languages: Robert Mowry Bell, B.S. University of Minnesota 1883, M.D. Harvard University 1890, Ph.D. University of Leipzig 1907; and Harold Herman Bender, A.B. Lafayette College 1903, Ph.D. Johns Hopkins University 1907.

In Mathematics: Harris Franklin MacNeish, B.S., University of Chicago 1902, M.S. University of Chicago 1904; and Louis Serle Dederick, A.B. Kenyon College 1905, A.M. Harvard University 1907, Ph.D. Harvard University 1909.

In Physics: Bartholomew John Spence, B.S. Northwestern University 1905, Ph.D. Princeton University 1909.

In Chemistry: Garrett Davis Buckner, B.S. State University of Kentucky 1908; James Llewellyn Crenshaw, A.B. Central University of Kentucky 1907, A.M. Central University of Kentucky 1908; and Guy Fleming Lipscomb, B.S. Alabama Polytechnic Institute 1907.

In Mineralogy: John Cooke Beam, B.S. Princeton University 1909.

In Civil Engineering: William Edgar Baker, Jr., C.E. Princeton University 1909, Instructor in Graphics; Milton Argyle Campbell, A.B. Westminster College 1906, C.E. Princeton University 1909, and Edward Davis Townsend, C.E. Princeton University 1905, Instructors in Geodesy; and Crowell Marsh Dennis, C.E. Princeton University 1909, Instructor in Civil Engineering.

Arnold Guyot Hall.

Guyot Hall was opened for instruction on the 11th of October, 1909. Its plan and arrangement are the result of close coöperation between the architects and the faculty committee appointed in January, 1907, to formulate plans for a building designed to house the various geological and biological laboratories. I am indebted to my colleague, Professor Gilbert van Ingen, for the following description of the completed building.

The interior dimensions of the main building are 288 feet in length by 56 feet in width, and of the extension, 63 feet in length and 35 feet in width. The central section has a basement and four stories and the wings and extension have three and two stories respectively. With a cubical content of about 1,250,000 cubic feet it has a serviceable floor area of 85,146 square feet, or nearly two acres.

The approved features observed in buildings of this class recently erected in the eastern States have been incorporated, such as simplicity and dignity of design, stability, economic utilization of cubical content, fire-proofing, abundant fenestration, adjustability to changing requirements of different laboratories through use of soundproof, though removable, partition walls, and a generous provision of electrical illumination and power, and of gas and water.

The general illumination is provided by the alternating current system, and a 30 kilowatt motor-generator set furnishes direct current for the projection and photo-illuminating apparatus. Abundant gas supply is at hand for secondary illumination and as a source of heat on laboratory tables. Natural ventilation is relied on to a large extent, almost entirely in the west end of the building. A ventilating plant furnishes a tempered forced draft and exhaust for the corridors, museum, lecture room, library, and certain laboratories in which noxious fumes and odors may be generated. Additional independent minor exhaust systems care for the proper circulation of air through the photographic darkrooms.

The Departments of Biology and Geology occupy approximately equal portions of the building, Biology having the eastern end and Geology the western. Certain rooms, the museum, lecture room, and library, are shared in common. An executive committee attends to all business bearing upon the inter-relations of the departments, while each department maintains its autonomy in purely intra-departmental affairs.

The Natural Science Museum occupies the entire first story of the building and, with its gallery along the south side of the central section, has about 19,300 square feet for exhibition space. Here will be installed exhibits selected from the material heretofore contained in the E. M. Museum of Geology and Archaeology in Nassau Hall, the Biological Museum on the top floor of the School of Science, the Morphological Museum in the 'Seventy-seven Laboratory, and the Mineralogical Museum in the Chemical Laboratory. It will be the duty and object of the curators to build up a museum of exhibits illustrating the subjects taught in the building and the lines of investigation carried on by the members of the instructing staff and the graduate students, so exposed and labelled that each will explain itself to the uninitiated visitor as well as to the beginning student. The museum is placed on the first floor in order that all persons entering the building must pass it and come within its influence.

The only lecture room in the building is centrally placed in the basement and has a seating capacity of 210. It has abundant natural and unusually satisfactory artificial indirect illumination and is to be fitted with all appurtenances needed for the conduct of lecture courses and meetings of scientific societies. The library, centrally placed on the second floor, has a large reading room with lateral stacks having a shelf capacity for 20,000 volumes, and will contain the working libraries of the Geological and Biological Departments.

The fundamental principle followed in the arrangement of the upper stories was to provide a separate suite for each distinct branch of the sciences to be housed there that is at present taught or is in immediate prospect of being taught in the building. The plan was designed not only to give independence to the different lines of investigation and instruction so far as this might be consistent with a carefully correlated scheme of subjects, but also to permit the proper handling of students in small groups in close association with the instructors. To this end, each suite consists of a laboratory-lecture-room with its adjoining office for preceptorial conference, a private laboratory for the instructor in charge of the work, preparation and store-room for the elaboration and storage of the crude collections. In order that this ideal may be realized in its entirety, it is necessary that each laboratory shall have its full equipment of collections and apparatus requisite to the proper conduct of its particular courses of instruction. The general plan has been realized in a satisfactory manner in respect of the arrangement of the rooms, and the resulting independence of the different laboratories as well as the absence of confusion of classes and materials is a source of gratification to the instructing officers.

The private laboratories provided for the instructors are designed to afford them opportunity to carry on their investigations in undisturbed freedom and security. In planning the building ample provision was also made for the work of graduate students and specialists. It is our earnest hope and belief that, when the necessary equipment is secured, work of this character will be very largely developed.

The manner in which the different parts of the building have been distributed among the departments may be indicated by giving the number of rooms with their floor area and the uses to which they are put:

Eighteen laboratories are provided. The Department of Biology has nine,—for Physiology, General Zoology, Graduate Zoology, Histology, Comparative Anatomy, Botany, and Biology, with an aggregate area of 7216 sq. ft. The Department of Geology has also nine laboratories, accommodating Blowpipe Analysis, Experimental Geology, Structural Geology, Petrology and Economic Geology, Mineralogy, Physical Geography, Stratigraphy and Invertebrate Palaeontology, and Vertebrate Palaentology, with an aggregate area of 6944 sq. ft. The Department of Biology has, in addition, eight offices, sixteen research rooms, six preparation rooms, and eleven store rooms, a total of 33 rooms for instruction, with 13,452 sq. ft., and 17 rooms for curatorial purposes, with 9424 sq. ft. To Geology are devoted, in addition to the laboratories, nine offices, sixteen research rooms, five preparation rooms, and ten store rooms, a total of 34 rooms, with 13,772 sq. ft., for instruction, and 15 rooms, with 5921 sq. ft., for curatorial work. The rooms shared in common are the Museum with 19,300 sq. ft., the lecture room with 2340 sq. ft., and the library-reading room with 1534 sq. ft. Adding these to the others mentioned above, shows a total of 50,389 sq. ft. devoted to instruction and 15,345 sq. ft. to curatorial work. The balance, of 19,403 sq. ft., is taken up by the halls, corridors, toilets, heating and ventilating plants and janitors' quarters. Thus, about 76 per cent of the total floor space is devoted to the scientific work of instruction, investigating, and preparation therefor, a very satisfactory solution of the problem presented.

We have in Guyot Hall a building adapted to the peculiar needs of the scientific departments occupying it in far higher degree than is the case with most laboratories erected for similar purposes. The Committee on Grounds and Buildings, the Faculty Committee in charge of operations, and the architects, are to be congratulated on the highly successful result of their coöperation, and our gratitude to the generous friends of the University who presented the building is confirmed and deepened by the results.

The Vivarium.

By the generosity of the friends who gave Guyot Hall the equipment of the University for biological study is being made complete by the addition of an unusually well equipped Vivarium.

The study of living animals and plants is a most important part of Biology, and the Vivarium, planned by Professor Conklin, provides exceptional facilities for such work. It is a separate building placed in the field south of Guyot Hall and is now nearly completed. It measures about 62 by 40 feet, is one and one-half stories high, and is constructed of brick, with glass roof and concrete floors. It contains fourteen large aquaria, constructed of concrete, with an aggregate area of nearly 400 square feet and a capacity of nearly 10,000 gallons. Half of these aquaria are to contain sea water, the other half fresh water. The water will be pumped from two large cisterns under the building, each of which has a capacity of 10,000 gallons, and, after circulating through the aquaria, will return to the cisterns through filters. A great variety of animals and plants of both marine and fresh water forms, may thus be kept under conditions favorable for observation and experiment. In addition to the aquaria the Vivarium contains rooms, with suitable cages, for insects, amphibians, reptiles, birds, and mammals. It also contains two research rooms, a photographic room, and rooms for pumps and filters. A greenhouse, 30 by 33 feet, adjoins it on the west, and a bit of swampy ground, nearby, has been converted into a pond for biological uses. It is hoped that we may be able in the near future to develop the extensive grounds south of Guyot Hall as a botanical garden and arboretum.

Additional Dormitories.

The dormitory provided for by Mrs. Sage's generous gift of two hundred and fifty thousand dollars is now entirely under roof, and work on the interior is being rapidly pushed forward. There should be no difficulty in having it ready for occupation by the opening of the next academic year. Additional entries, built by the generosity of the classes of 1881 and 1885 and other friends among our graduates, have been added to the northern portion of the building on Nassau Street, and are also under roof. With these additional entries the building should accommodate one hundred and fifty men. Additional money, from the Alumni Fund and other sources, being now available, your Committee on on Grounds and Buildings has authorized the letting of contracts for four other entries, to constitute a southern extension of the great group of which the building already erected will form the chief part, and it is hoped that ground may be broken for this extension early in the year, so soon as weather conditions permit. The construction of the building is in every way satisfactory. The native stone used in its walls has proved both serviceable and beautiful, and each step in the completion of the group increases our gratitude for Mrs. Sage's generosity, as well as our appreciation of the work of the architects and of the builders working under their supervision.

REGISTRATION.

The following table shows the number admitted to the University as undergraduates this year, as compared with last:

	1908	1909
Freshmen admitted without conditions	157	154
Freshmen admitted with conditions	235	234
New qualifying students not yet admitted to regular standing	40	51
	432	439

Of the applicants admitted in 1908 thirty, for one reason or another, did not come. This year the number admitted who did not come was forty-one. The following is a summary of the figures, stated in another way:

	1908	1909
Total number of students admitted who did not come	30	41
Total number of freshmen admitted	392	388
Total number of freshmen admitted who actually entered	362	347
Examined, but not admitted	75	86
Preliminary and partial examinations	468	446

Of the Freshmen now enrolled 151 qualified as candidates for the degree of Bachelor of Arts, 159 as candidates for the degrees of Bachelor of Science and Bachelor of Letters, and 37 as candidates for the degree of Civil Engineer.

It is interesting to note the steady increase in the number of students entering from other colleges, the so-called "qualifying" students, and that this increase is taking place notwithstanding the new regulations which recently went into force with regard to such admissions. It is now our rule that "a candidate coming from another college to which he was admitted by certificate" will be admitted only when he has passed "the Princeton Freshman entrance requirements in each subject in which his standing in his former college was not in the upper half of his class. Such of these requirements as are not satisfied by examination at the time of admission must be satisfied in accordance with the rules which apply to students regularly admitted upon examination." Such a rule is made necessary in fairness to men admitted on examination. It has not diminished the number of admissions from other colleges,—an indication, among other things, that the students who come to us from other colleges are of an excellent kind and quality.

"Of the entering students",—I quote from the report of the Dean of the Faculty,—"38% are Presbyterians, as against 37% last year, and 30% Episcopalians, as against 27% last year. There are thirty Methodists (last year 27), sixteen Congregationalists (last year 11), fifteen Roman Catholics (last year 25), thirteen Hebrews (last year 11), ten Baptists (last year 9), six Dutch Reformed (last year 5), five Quakers (last year 2), three Lutherans (last year 8), two Unitarians (last year 5), one Universalist, one Christian Scientist, and one Disciple of Christ, as last year." Last year there was one Independent and one United Presbyterian, but this year no entering student connected with either of these denominations is registered. More than one-half of the entering students are communicants of the churches with which they are connected. The average age of the Freshmen at entrance is this year eighteen years and eleven months, as against eighteen years and nine months last year.

The total undergraduate registration of the University is this year 1253, and was last year 1223, an increase of thirty. The increase of last year over the year preceding was thirty-five. The total student enrollment is this year exactly 1400, as against 1314 last year, an increase of 86, there being this year thirteen students in the School of Electrical Engineering, as against ten the year before, and 134 graduate students, as against 91 last year, besides an increase in the number of students entering from other colleges.

This registration is larger than that of any previous year except the year 1903-4, when the total registration was 1431. The following comparative table shows where the difference lies. It lies in the fact that we have almost eliminated the anomalous class of "Special students." The few "special students" now admitted to the University are admitted under genuinely exceptional circumstances. All others not admitted to regular standing are required to show such qualifications as justify us in enrolling them as candidates for degrees who are merely awaiting the application of particular tests which will presently put them upon the regular rolls. We class them as "Qualifying students," and they are subjected to our full tests, as the old "Special students" were not.

	1903-4	1909-10
Graduate students	114	134
Electrical engineers	7	13
Candidates for Bachelors' degrees	1202	1248
Special students	108	5
	1431	1400

The Graduate School.

The increase in the number of graduate students is especially noticeable. It is unquestionably due to the new impulse and distinction given to graduate studies here by our recent notable additions to the Faculty of the University, to our recent reorganization of graduate studies, and to the splendid facilities we have recently been supplied with for teaching and investigation in the fields of Physics, Biology, and Geology by the erection and equipment of the Palmer Laboratory and Guyot Hall. Last year there were ninety-one graduate students, this year there are, as just stated, one hundred and thirty-four. Last year forty-seven of those pursuing advanced studies were devoting their whole time to those studies, while forty-four were combining graduate study in the University with work in the Princeton Theological Seminary or with the work of teaching. This year there are seventy-six regular graduate students (as I may, perhaps, be allowed to call them), including 44 Fellows, 5 Graduate Scholars, and 27 others without appointment, while the number of graduate students pursuing graduate studies in connection with other work is fifty-eight. There is thus an increase in both kinds.

Of the regular graduate students, 14 are in residence at Merwick; 14 not in residence take their meals there; and ten are in residence at what we have come to call the Graduate Annex. It will thus be seen that one-half of our present regular graduate students are not connected with the graduate house,—with our provisional system of residence.

The University Faculty recommends to you, through your Committee on the Graduate School changes in the scope and method of study for the degree of Doctor of Philosophy which I hope that you will approve. Heretofore we have not had a satisfactory method of admission either to the Graduate School or to candidacy for the degree of Doctor of Philosophy, admitting to the School with too little systematic scrutiny of the applicant's fitness to undertake advanced studies and to candidacy for the degree with too little preliminary knowledge of the applicant's work or preparation. It is recommended that, hereafter, applicants for admission to the School whose undergraduate course is regarded as unsatisfactory or deficient may, with the permission of the Faculty Committee on the Graduate School, be admitted to graduate standing while making up their deficiencies by undergraduate work, or may be required to enroll themselves as undergraduates in the class for which they may prove prepared. With regard to the terms of admission to candidacy for the degree of Doctor of Philosophy and the studies to be required of those who desire to qualify for that degree, the recommendations of the Faculty contemplate very material, very interesting, and very desirable changes.

They recommend,—and the recommendation has my cordial endorsement,—that hereafter admission to the Graduate School shall not necessarily imply admission to candidacy for a higher degree; but that a graduate student who desires to become a candidate for the doctor's degree must make formal application to the Faculty Committee on the Graduate School to that effect at least as early as the beginning of the academic year in which he purposes to present himself for the final examination; that he must designate in his application the subject in which he purposes to do his work; that the application must be endorsed by the Department in which that subject lies and must include a satisfactory certificate of the applicant's ability to use French and German as instruments of research; and that the application, thus endorsed, must be approved by the Faculty Committee on the Graduate School and reported to the University Faculty.

It is further recommended, with regard to the studies of the candidate, that our present practice of requiring the choice of one chief subject of study and "two suitable subsidiary subjects," one of which "must be logic, psychology, ethics, or the history of philosophy," be abandoned, and the study of the candidate be concentrated upon some one great field of study, to a portion of which the more particular and original work of his thesis must be devoted. This change is stated in the following terms in the formal action of the Faculty:

"Before offering himself for the final examination the candidate is expected to have acquired a broad general knowledge of the subject he has chosen and a comprehensive and detailed knowledge of some one main division of it. In certain cases, however, the candidate may, on the recommendation of the Department in which his subject lies, and with the approval of the Committee on the Graduate School, substitute for a main division of his subject a like division of a germane subject; or he may be required to take additional work outside his subject.

"Candidates for the doctor's degree are also required to take at some time during the period of their graduate study a series of twenty weekly lectures on the general trend of philosophical and scientific thought, to be given, with assigned collateral reading, by a member of the Department of Philosophy.

"The candidate shall present to the Department in which his work chiefly lies a thesis on some topic in the special field of his study. If the thesis is accepted by the Department, as giving evidence of high attainment and the power of independent research, the candidate will be recommended by the Department to the Committee on the Graduate School for admission to the final examination. This recommendation must be accompanied by a statement of the amount and character of the graduate work done and by the formal approval of the thesis."

"It is recommended also that the three-year plan of conferring the degree of Master of Arts be discontinued." This refers to the conferring of the degree of Master of Arts "upon a Bachelor of this University who shall have submitted to the Faculty a satisfactory dissertation on some literary, philosophical, or scientific subject previously approved by the Faculty, not earlier than the third year after graduation"; a practice which has yielded very unsatisfactory results, very few graduates having been stimulated by it to do literary, philosophical, or scientific work of importance, and the few dissertations submitted having been for the most part very disappointing.

These changes constitute an adoption of the French, rather than the German, system of study for the higher degrees. They will, we believe, produce thoroughness and comprehensiveness of preparation for the higher degrees, particularly among students made ready for the more advanced studies in the haphazard way in which most American college men are made ready,—not under a German, but under a very different system of preliminary training,—such as has never been produced under our present practice. I heartily recommend them to you for your approval.

In May last Mr. William Cooper Procter, of the class of 1883, generously offered the University the sum of five hundred thousand dollars upon the conditions set forth in the following letter, addressed to Professor Andrew F. West, the Dean of the Graduate School:

CINCINNATI, OHIO, May 8, 1909.

DR. ANDREW F. WEST,
Princeton University,
Princeton, N. J.

My dear Professor West:

I have read with much interest the book prepared by you outlining the scheme of the Proposed Graduate College of Princeton University. Believing in its great value to Princeton, provided the scheme is carried out on these lines, I take pleasure in making the following proposition for acceptance by the Board of Trustees.

I will give the sum of Five Hundred Thousand Dollars to be expended for such objects, in furtherance of the plans, as I may designate, provided an equal sum is secured for the Graduate College in gifts or responsible pledges by May 1st, 1910. I do this on the understanding that my subscription is to be paid in ten equal quarterly installments beginning July 15th, 1910, and that the money for the other subscriptions or gifts shall be paid into the Treasury of the University not later than October 15th, 1912.

I have visited and examined the proposed site at Prospect, and beg to say, that in my opinion, it is not suitable for such a College. I feel, therefore, obliged to say that this offer is made upon the further understanding that some other site be chosen, which shall be satisfactory to me.

Yours very truly,
WM. COOPER PROCTER.

The acceptance of this generous gift, deeply appreciated by the Board and by all friends of the University, was embarrassed by obligations which the Board had undertaken in accepting the recent bequest of Mrs. Josephine Thomson Swann. Mrs. Swann left to the University the whole of her residuary estate, to be used, in memory of her husband, Senator John R. Thomson, to construct a building for the use of the graduate students of the University, which she directed should be called "The John R. Thomson Graduate College of Princeton University," which she directed should be erected upon the grounds of the University, and with regard to the use of which her will makes certain definite stipulations. In October, 1909, however, the Board, believing that some arrangement might be made by which both gifts could be used without conflict or breach of existing obligations, accepted Mr. Procter's gift, with the proviso that it should find it possible to make use of it without conflicting with legal duties already assumed.

The difficulties are these. (a) Mrs. Swann's will directs that the building for which her bequest was meant to provide shall be erected "upon the grounds of the said University," and there is considerable difference of opinion among the legal advisers of the Board as to the legality of placing it upon a site so distinctly separated from the grounds upon which the present buildings of the University stand as the present golf links are, the site selected by Mr. Procter as the site of his preference. (b) Mr. Procter contributes his great gift for the purpose of promoting a plan for providing a place of graduate residence which shall be set apart exclusively for graduate students, while Mrs. Swann's will explicitly directs that the rooms in the John R. Thomson College are to be rented "at the best prices they will command, to Graduate, Senior and Junior students of the University." (c) Mrs. Swann's gift is made for the purpose of producing a sufficient revenue from the rental of rooms to provide for the maintenance of a number of fellowships, and it is very doubtful whether any building set apart for the exclusive occupancy of graduate students could be administered upon an income-bearing basis.

Five Years of the Preceptorial System.

This is the fifth year of the preceptorial system. We can look at it and assess it now in the light of experience. It has passed the experimental stage, but the period of experiment through which we have carried it has taught us many things with regard to its proper use and application which should enable us to employ it hereafter with greater confidence and intelligence.

It is not, primarily, a system of instruction. Its chief object is not efficient teaching. It is not an improved class-room method or a new way of drill to keep the pupil up to his tasks. It is a system of *study*, primarily intended for the reading courses, to give to them means of work as direct, as simple, as individual as those long employed in the laboratories of the sciences. It has been too commonly supposed by observers, even by admiring observers, of the system outside Princeton that it is its characteristic feature that teachers meet their pupils informally in very small groups for intimate instruction. That is not the fundamental matter. The essence of the system is that "classes" and class-rooms are done away with, except for purposes of drill. A "course" does not consist in following a certain teacher's lectures or in "getting up" certain texts to be recited in class. It consists in a body of reading such as any mature man would naturally undertake, whether he had the advantage of experienced guides and teachers or not, if he wished to make himself master of a certain subject. The men read subjects; they do not get up courses. Lectures are supplementary, explanatory, illustrative, are an excellent means of stimulation and additional exposition, but could be dispensed with, often have been dispensed with, without materially affecting the processes of study or in any way robbing them of their reality and vitality. Grown men who have ceased to be schoolboys are systematically reading great subjects. That is the essential and central fact of the system. It is not a new method in pedagogics.

The "conferences" with their preceptors to which the men are periodically summoned are immensely important, but they are not recitations and the preceptors are not coaches. They are not teachers meeting their "classes" in small "divisions." They meet their men to discuss the reading they have done and to draw out its various significance, by comment, by amplification out of what they themselves have read, by mental exchanges of any kind that may prove natural and serviceable. Their object is, of course, to see that the men have actually done the reading that is to be discussed; but it is also to see that they have understood it, to render them counsel, assistance, and stimulation; and many of them have told me with great pleasure how they have seen their men grow under the process, begin to think for themselves, and insensibly learn to use books naturally, for the sake of their contents, and not for the sake of making a creditable show of diligence and intelligence at the "conference." In brief, these conferences between preceptors and small groups of men assigned to their guidance (the groups range in number from two to six men) is a method of associating older students with younger upon as natural a footing as possible.

The system is a method of study, but also a method of close association between pupil and teacher. Intimate association, informal, unforced, natural, is the only certain means of intellectual contagion. A rare occasional man here and there may spread the contagion of mind and spirit which is the real power of the teacher by means of lectures and formal class-room exercises, if he be a man of exceptional genius and possess a personality which only his presence and speech are needed to interpret; but the rest of us must be known and sampled in some everyday fashion of constant intercourse to be felt as comrades of the mind, to be recognized as persons whose influence cannot easily be shaken off or forgotten. The method of the preceptorial system is not so much a method of instruction as a method of association and influence. This, and no formal matter of the numbers in a conference group, is the conception which is of its essence.

It is a process of study which is meant to be a means, not so much of instruction, as of intellectual development. If it fails of becoming that, it is a mere improvement in pedagogic method, worth while, no doubt, but no great matter. It has not failed of becoming a means of intellectual development among us. Our preceptors are, almost without exception, men of unusual parts and of unusual personality. They make themselves felt as men, as intellectual guides, as original thinkers and independent students of their subjects, and often also as friends and enjoyable companions. If they were not such men, vitality and reality would go out of the system at once and it would have no real significance except as a means of keeping men at their tasks, of keeping them at work between examinations. If I had not had what seems to me conclusive testimony to the effect that the preceptorial conferences have served these genuine and highest purposes of education, I would feel that I must report them useful, indeed, but a great disappointment.

It is evident, however, that this full and satisfactory use of the system is not possible in all studies or at all stages of study. At the outset we attempted to apply it somewhat indiscriminately all along the line, in studies of every kind that happened to lie outside the laboratories, wishing rather to ascertain its limits by actual experience than by premature theory. And we have ascertained them. That is exactly the service our five years of experience has rendered us. We now see pretty clearly where it is applicable and where it is not, where it can be applied in full and where it should be applied only in part, or only in a modified form. That is what entitles me to say that it has passed its experimental stage.

There are various courses given, particularly in Freshman and Sophomore years, which are elementary and which consist in a uniform drill in certain fundamental principles and processes: the courses in elementary mathematics, for example, through which all the younger men are put, and the courses in Greek and Latin composition. Here conferences are meaningless and unsuitable. It is, of course, desirable that the men should meet for drill in small classes, in order that the drill may reach each man at each exercise; but it is not necessary that the classes should be as small as preceptorial groups. They may be two or three times as large without loss of efficiency and particularity in the teaching and may be conducted by the older and more familiar class methods. Most of our Freshmen come in very meagerly provided with vocabularies in Greek and Latin, and a great deal of the teaching of the first year must be devoted to familiarizing them with a large enough number of the words most used in the writers they are to read to enable them to use their texts with some freedom and pleasure. This teaching is also obviously of the nature of drill and can, my classical colleagues believe, be undertaken in some simpler way than we have hitherto used under our new system. All such courses fall necessarily under the head of instruction, not under the head of education,—of intellectual stimulation or development or of initiation into great subjects.

There is a training, too, in the fundamental general principles of a subject like Economics which can be given in classes. It requires only clear and precise definition and exposition, deals in definitely stated propositions which constitute the general and undisputed ideas of the subject, need not be based upon excursive reading, and is suitable to be handled by lectures and fixed in the minds of the students by formal recitation. Here, again, large lecture classes and small "divisions" for recitation afford as suitable and efficient means of teaching as can be employed. It is instruction and must be systematically organized as such.

There is still another function of teaching which may be called explanation. It is best illustrated by an example taken from the Department of Mathematics. Certain members of the teaching staff of that Department keep definite hours in easily accessible rooms, usually in the public buildings of the University, where it is understood that they may be consulted by any student who wishes to have his mathematical work more fully explained to him than it has been explained in class, difficult points cleared up, processes made plain to him which he has not fully comprehended, or the reason of which he has not seen at all; and the students avail themselves of the opportunities thus afforded them very freely, without formal appointment. The classes in the higher mathematics are for the most part small enough to make the relations of teacher and pupil very direct, personal, and informal, a veritable preceptorial relationship; and in the more elementary classes the accessibility of the instructors at certain fixed office hours suffices to accomplish all that preceptorial conferences could accomplish in so formal and exact a science.

It is outside the fields of drill, formal training, and occasional explanation that the preceptorial system has its proper application and its most noticeable and admirable results. In the reading subjects, and after the elements of a great subject have been mastered, it serves to bring out by its intimate and informal processes all the most natural and fruitful methods of study; serves as a means of teaching men how to read and think for themselves, how to approach great subjects, not like boys, but like men; throws lads as they grow more thoughtful into close association with men who are older and more mature and whose studies have touched them with an enthusiasm for the subjects they are teaching; makes for independence, maturity, and intellectual development. This is what we have desired and what we are accomplishing. This is the preceptorial work proper, to which other, earlier processes are fundamental and preparatory.

Much, of course, remains to be desired. The system has accomplished no revolution in human nature; and it has not overcome the very serious impediments which exist in the present competitive social structure of our universities or in the extraordinary development among our undergraduates of activities of every sort which absorb their attention and divert their energies from their university work. Teacher and pupil do not live in the same atmosphere. Their lives are separated and contrasted alike in kind and in interest. The undergraduate lives in a world in which other things than study take precedence of it as if of course. He turns aside from the things which chiefly engross him to have a brief conference with his preceptor about reading which lies remote from the ordinary courses of his thought. And his preceptor cannot be his companion in the matters which constitute his life. The one lives in one world, the other in another. They are not members of the same family or of the same social organism; and the rivalry between the life and the work of the student generally results in the victory of the life. If that life does not actually absorb the greater part of his time it does absorb the greater part of his thought and of his ambitions. Under our present university organization the preceptorial system can be carried only to the borders of the life of the place, not to its centre; and so long as this is the case its results, admirable as they have been, must disappoint us.

There are other things, too, which stand in the way. If you look into any one of the Departments of study, you will find readjustments of the curriculum needed, better assignments of reading, a larger staff necessary to do the work readily and well and in its true spirit and freedom from artificial restraints. But these difficulties are chiefly administrative and can be gradually overcome as we study the matter. The system has approved itself and has had admirable results. We can by degrees give it better subject-matter, better means, and full ranks of teachers. As soon as possible we must give it also an atmosphere to breathe.

Respectfully submitted, WOODROW WILSON.[1]

Printed document (WP, DLC).

[1] There is a WWsh draft, a WWT draft, and a heavily emended typed draft of this report, all dated Jan. 1, 1910, in WP, DLC.

To Thomas Davies Jones

My dear Mr. Jones, Princeton, N. J. 1 January, 1910.

Thank you for your letter of the thirtieth, to which I hasten to reply.

My letter to Mr. Pyne must be read as a letter to Mr. Pyne, who knows the whole interior of this question. As a general exposition of this difficult matter it is no doubt unsatisfactory, though I had hoped that it was not ambiguous. I would, of course, have put my case for general scrutiny in other terms.

The case lies, in my mind, in this analysis:

First, As to our execution of Mrs. Swann's will, there is involved both the letter and the spirit. The Board in its action at the October meeting safeguarded the one but not the other. It asked to be reassured with regard to the legality of the proposed use of Mrs. Swann's bequest; that is, it reserved judgment until it should be satisfied that it would not be liable to a successful suit at law by Mrs. Swann's heirs; but it made no further reservation in that matter. Mrs. Swann's will plainly directs that such a use be made of the building as will make it yield an income for the support of fellowships, and it is conceded that it could not be made to yield such an income if erected on the Golf Links. That may not be illegal, but it is certainly wrong, and has not been safeguarded. The object is made plain by the pains Mrs. Swann took to show the means by which it should be attained, namely, the admission of Seniors and Juniors, as well as Graduates, to the building who could pay the requisite rents.

Second, The other question involved is, Whether, if we were to accept Mr. Procter's gift on the terms he prescribes, we should be taking the educational policy of the University out of the hands of the Trustees and Faculty. I maintain most distinctly that we should be. The Trustees make no reservation at all as to the wiidom [wisdom] of the policy proposed. We now know that Mr. Procter's gift means West's policy. That policy every thinking element in the Board and in the Faculty rejects. We give up our judgment entirely in the most essential matter of all in order to get the money. Even if West were eliminated, we would still be agreeing to do what a majority of the Trustees' Committee, all but a majority of the Board itself; and a very large majority of the Faculty think radically unwise. That is giving up the government of the University for the sake of the money. I am confident that the majority of the Board would decide the policy differently if the gift were out of the way. I think that we should decline the gift because it is not offered for the advancement of a policy of which we approve.

To put the matter explicitly upon the ground of our disapproval of West and what he stands for, would, it seems to me, be to make it appear a personal matter, which the friends of the University would certainly misinterpret greatly to our discredit. We have the authority to eliminate West at any time. If he is at fault, it would be asked, why not retire him? Why decline the gift to get rid of him, if the gift would be acceptable and advantagious [advantageous] to the University without him? We now know, indeed, that Mr. Procter's gift is made to put West in the saddle, but we cannot make that a matter of public discussion. We can make it public, however, that we do not feel at liberty to accept gifts for purposes of which we disapprove.

In reply to your question, I would say that I do not at all demand that the Board rescind the action of October. I agree with you that that action leaves it free still to decline the gift in its present form without bad faith to anybody.

I would like you to feel that I am not demanding anything. I feel, merely, that the Board is in danger of adopting a policy into the carrying out of which I can put neither enthusiasm nor any kind of planning will; and that I should cease to be serviceable to the University if it did.

I am not at all sure that Mr. Pyne has accepted the necessity of eliminating West. He distinctly reserved judgment when I talked with him about it. And he has not at all consented to his entire elimination, the only practicable remedy. I am quite sure, too, that West does not comprehend or accept the situation. He made that plain at the last meeting of the Faculty Committee on the Graduate School, where his tone was higher than ever. It is absolutely necessary that he should be eliminated altogether, administratively. To put him in residential charge of the building of the Graduate College would create a situation almost as impossible as if he were to remain Dean of the Graduate School.

Any further compromiie [compromise] in the matter would simply throw us into another period of hopeless futilities.

I am looking forward with pleasure to the opportunity of seeing you and Mr. McCormick on Monday evening; but I thought that your letter was entitled to an immediate and explicit answer, without waiting for that interview. I thank you for putting the matter so distinctly and for giving me the opportunity to make this further explanation.

With warmest regard and the best wishes of the season,

Cordially and faithfully Yoors [Yours]

Woodrow Wilson[1]

WWTLS (Mineral Point, Wisc., Public Library).

1 There is a WWsh draft of this letter, dated Jan. 1, 1910, in WP, DLC.

To Melancthon Williams Jacobus

My dear Dr. Jacobus: [Princeton, N. J.] January 1st, 1910.

Your letter of yesterday has reached me this morning.

I wish I could give you a definite report of Mr. Thompson's judgment about the matter of a conference, but unfortunately our talk the other day when I saw him was so entirely upon the merits of the questions involved that we spoke only incidentally of the conference, inasmuch as I understood that he was writing to you about it. I gathered that his feeling was that which I expressed in my former letter to you, but your present letter seems to me to put a different face upon the matter. I was thinking of such a private conference as we once held before, but the matter, as you explain it more fully in the letter that reached me this morning, wears a different aspect. For my own part, I should be very happy to meet with such a conference and to explain matters as fully and clearly as I know how, and I like your idea very much of including others besides those who voted with us at the last meeting of the Board. The only difficulty will be the delicacy involved in leaving anybody out, as if we were marking them as matter of course opponents, and yet to invite everybody would be to have an informal meeting of the Board.

As you will know by this time, I have called a meeting of the Committee on Honorary Degrees for four o'clock on the afternoon of the 12th and have suggested to you a meeting of the Curriculum Committee on the evening of the 12th. Of the two dates you suggest, therefore, the 9th seems to me would be the better, provided we can get the men from a distance on at that time.

In the meantime, matters seem to be clearing a good deal, the chief cause of anxiety at present being that Mr. Pyne is holding off and does not say what his attitude in the case will be. One member of the Board who voted with the majority in the October meeting, namely Mr. Imbrie, seemed yesterday, when I had a conversation with him, to be convinced that it was necessary to withdraw our acceptance of the offer, on the ground that it was impossible to comply with the provisos embodied in the action of the Board. Indeed, he seemed to be converted to the view of the matter expressed in my letter to Mr. Pyne, and I think it quite certain that he would vote with us.

Since I wrote you I have sent copies of my letter to Pyne to Dr. George B. Stewart, Mr. John D. Davis, Mr. Joseph B. Shea, and to Dr. DeWitt. I am leaving home on Sunday evening to attend the meeting of the Association of American Universities at Madison, Wisconsin, and have arranged to see Mr. McCormick and Mr. Thomas Jones when I pass through Chicago on Monday evening. On my way back I must attend the inauguration of a new President at Franklin and Marshall College on the 7th, so that I shall not be in these parts again until the eithth [eighth].

To return to the matter of the conference, it seems to me now to be largely a matter of feasibility. If we can get the proper men together, I think it might serve a very useful purpose, and I am very grateful to you for suggesting it. I think it might be serviceable for you, if you find the time, to write to Mr. Thompson again, stating the matter just about as you have stated it in the letter I have received this morning. I think that statement would put it in a new light before him and that he would be very likely to feel that we might gain more certain concert of action in that way than we would otherwise have.

Dodge and Sheldon spent an evening with Pyne recently, going over the whole matter and urging upon him this form of action: that the Committee of the Board on the Graduate School report to the Trustees a recommendation that in view of the fact that it was not possible to comply in full with the directions of Mrs. Swann's will, if Mr. Procter's gift were accepted in the terms in which it was offered, they therefore recommend that it be declined, in view of the circumstances, with great appreciation and regret. In other words, that Mr. Pyne stand out of the way merely and let the original judgment of the Committee be the only recommendation made to the Board. Pyne merely promised to take the matter under very careful consideration. Sheldon, in reporting the matter to me, closes his letter with the sentence,

"Cleve is hopeful." I was afraid, when I read the sentence, that it meant that Sheldon was not.

My own chief anxiety is to avoid any excited discussion in the Board which might bring out some bitter utterances. I am sending you, for your information, letters from Sheldon and Mr. Thomas D. Jones. Letters from Mr. John A. Stewart and Cleve Dodge which I have received are merely very delightful out and out endorsements and discuss no part of the business.

With warmest regard and gratitude,

Faithfully yours, [Woodrow Wilson]

CCL (RSB Coll., DLC).

To Arthur Twining Hadley

My dear Mr. Hadley: Princeton, N. J. January 1st, 1910.

Thank you for submitting to me the proposed draft of our letter to Messrs. Camp, Haughton, and Henry.

My own feeling is that it is too restricted in the scope of its suggestions. I should think that it would be better to make the commission a little broader and to say something like the following:

We desire you to act as a committee to advise the authorities of Harvard, Yale, and Princeton Universities concerning the best method of altering the manner in which the game of football is at present played in American colleges, in order to eliminate from the game the more serious forms of danger to the life and health of those who participate, and in order to give it more attractive character as a sport.

What I am afraid of is that the inquiry will be too technical and microscopic and that the remedies proposed will be aimed at the elimination of particular dangers rather than at the general improvement of the game. The wording that I have employed is not particularly happy, but the idea, I trust, is clear.

With much regard,

Sincerely yours, Woodrow Wilson

TLS (A. T. Hadley Papers, Archives, CtY).

To Abbott Lawrence Lowell

My dear Mr. Lowell: [Princeton, N. J.] January 1st, 1910.

I dare say that Mr. Hadley has sent you a draft of the letter he suggests as a form of commission to the gentlemen we are to ask to advise us in respect of the alteration in the rules of football.

I have written to him to say that it seems to me the form he suggests hardly constitutes a broad enough commission. I am afraid that if we used it, we should be confining inquiry to a rather narrow technical field, in which specific dangers would be more considered than the general object of improving the game. I have therefore written to suggest to him the following form:

> "We desire you to act as a committee to advise the authorities of Harvard, Yale, and Princeton Universities concerning the best method of altering the manner in which the game of football is at present played in American colleges, in order to eliminate from the game the more serious forms of danger to the life and health of those who participate, and in order to give it more attractive character as a sport."

which, whether very happily worded or not, at any rate conveys the idea which seems to me to be essential. The public is really very much displeased with football as at present played as a sport, and I think that our representatives should consider the matter very broadly and not wholly with a view to the mere exclusion of the present forms of extreme danger to the spine and specific parts of the anatomy.

It was a great disappointment to me that I could not be in New York at the reception given you by the University Club. I had hoped to pay my respects to you then and wish you, as I do now, the very best and happiest fortunes for the new year.

Always cordially and faithfully yours,

[Woodrow Wilson]

CCL (WWP, UA, NjP).

From George Brinton McClellan Harvey

Deal Beach, N. J. January 1, 1910.

May the New Year treat you kindly, best wishes to you and yours from entire Harvey family. George Harvey.

T telegram (WP, DLC).

From John DeWitt

My dear Dr. Wilson, Princeton, N. J. 1st January 1910

I have received and read with great care the copy of your letter addressed to Mr Pyne, and enclosed to me in a letter in which you express the hope that I shall be able to approve of the position which you felt obliged in your letter to Mr. Pyne to take.

Briefly stated this position I suppose to be as follows: Should the Board of Trustees not reverse its vote to accept Mr. Procter's proposal to give $500,000.00 to the Thomp[s]on Graduate School on condition, first, that $500,000.00 be raised within a given period, and, second, that the school building be placed on the "Golf-Links" property of the University, you will retire from the Presidency.

This position I could not approve of and continue to be your friend, supporter and well-wisher. Had you done me the honor before sending the letter to Mr. Pyne, to ask my advice about it, I must have strongly advised you not to send it. Now that, having sent it, you express the hope that I shall approve of your having done so, I am bound to reply that it is impossible for me to approve of a course which before it was taken I would have strongly deprecated.

Since your election to the Presidency, I have been deeply interested in the educational ideals you have been trying to realize. I have sympathized with your efforts to raise the intellectual level of the students. I have rejoiced in your success in initiating the preceptorial system. I heartily agree with you and your colleagues in the belief that the essence of a graduate school is adequate graduate courses and not a building housing a secluded student community. Beside all this, I have regarded it as my duty as a Trustee, when in doubt about a particular measure to give my vote to the Administration in charge; and it was largely on this ground that I voted with the minority against accepting Mr. Procter's proposal in which he reserved the right, without naming the objects to the Board, to spend the money he proposed to give for objects which he should designate.

The Board voted to accept the gift and to confer with Mr. Procter. Meanwhile, Mr. Procter has made known the objects for which his gift is to be used. They are first a dining hall for the Thompson School on the Golf-Links property and secondly such uses as shall be determined on by the Board. If he has imposed any other limitations I have not heard of them. The relation of the Graduate School to the University is not changed. Its administration is still under the supervision of the Trustees. The President is still *ex officio* a member of the Trustees' Graduate School Committee; and the Faculty is still to appoint its own Committee on the School. So that the only obstacle in the way of developing a graduate school on lines approved by the Faculty and Trustees is the fact that the school building is to be placed not on the present campus but on the Golf-Links property.

This mere question of location your letter raises to a question of principle; and of principle so radically important that you express your determination to suspend the continuance of your present relation to the University on its determination. And you hope that I shall approve of your position.

Now, my dear Dr. Wilson, I cannot do so. The question of location is not a question of radical importance. It is a question of detail, a question of instrument. That the placing of the building on the Golf-Links property will prove an insuperable or even a serious obstacle to the development of the Graduate School along the lines approved by the Faculty I do not believe. Perhaps the location is not ideal. But in a large and complex institution like a University the ideal instruments cannot always be obtained.

I cannot resist saying that you will be taking a great responsibility on yourself by retiring for the reason and on the occasion you mention. No doubt retirement is inviting. Your great position involves great labors, great burdens and many perplexities. But you are in it, and its responsibilities are yours. Have you considered among these, those which are due to your colleagues in the Faculty who have given you the most loyal support and whom your resignation now would leave without support? Then there is the preceptorial system which is so closely associated with your administration. Have you carried it beyond the point of danger? Is it not probable, too, that your resignation under these conditions will bring about a grave division in the Board of Trustees, and deprive the University of the support of gentlemen whose support is in a high degree important?

No doubt, should you choose to do so you could find an occasion for severing your relations with the University which would not seriously harm it; though I should deeply regret your resignation. But this is not such an occasion.

I am, dear Dr. Wilson,

Most sincerely yours John DeWitt

ALS (WP, DLC).

To Cleveland Hoadley Dodge

My dear Cleve, Princeton, N. J. 2 January, 1910.

Bless you for your note! It put tonic into my heart and brain! You are certainly a perfect friend and colleague.

I hope for the best; but I am afraid that a victory will, in our present circumstances, be barren enough if we cannot find the money to give us real independence. Has any breaath [breath] of hope come your way from Mott? A big gift just now would redeem and liberate us!

I have now sent copies of my letter to Momo to the following members of the Board, in addition to those I mentioned before: Dr. Geo. B. Stewart, Chancellor Magie, Dr. DeWitt, Mr. Shea, and Mr. Jno. D. Davis. I am going to send one also to Dr. Frazer.

I hope that you will send copies to any others you may think it wise to send them to. I have had a most satisfactory talk with Mr. Imbrie, and think that he now thoroughly agrees with us. It occurs to me that Mr. James W. Alexander is thoroughly worth informing. We must do the work this time!

With warmest gratitude,

Affectionately Yours, Woodrow Wilson

WWTLS (WC, NjP).

To Charles Williston McAlpin

My dear McAlpin, Princeton, N. J. 2 Jan'y, 1909 [1910]

In the absorption of recent days, over the critical business about which I wrote you, I have forgotten to thank you for the beautiful copy of Boccaccio's Life of Dante[1] you were generous enough to send me! Forgive me. It was not because, even amidst such anxieties, the gift passed unnoticed. It gave, and gives, me a great deal of pleasure, both in itself and as an evidence of your thoughtful affection. I am off for Madison to-day, and send you, with warm affection, this good-bye and this greeting for the New Year.

Our warmest regards to Mrs. McAlpin

Faithfully Yours, Woodrow Wilson

ALS (photostat in RSB Coll., DLC).

[1] Giovanni Boccaccio, *A Translation of Giovanni Boccaccio's Life of Dante*, tr. George Rice Carpenter (New York, 1900). The publisher was the Grolier Club. This volume is in the Wilson Library, DLC.

To Mary Allen Hulbert Peck

Dearest Friend, North Phila. 2 Jan'y 1910

While I wait here a few minutes for my train to Chicago, I must scribble you a line or two. I have just been talking to you over the telephone, but I could hear you very indistinctly. The only comfort of it was to hear your voice and to gather that you were well.

I am off to preside over the annual meeting of the Association of American Universities at Madison, Wisconsin, on Tuesday and Wednesday. On my way back I must attend the inauguration of a new president (poor devil!) at Franklin and Marshall College, at Lancaster, Pa. I ought to get home by Saturday, the eighth.

My "crisis" goes merrily on! I am glad to get off for a little and look at it from arm's length and get my poise and sense of humour back. Next week the Board of Trustees and the final test!

I am a good, a philosophical traveller. I have a compartment all to myself in which to meditate my address, and smile at my adventures in life, and think much of my dear friends.

Take care of yourself. May the New Year bring you in all things your heart's desire! All the most cordial greetings of the season to Mrs. Allen and your son.

Think of me always as

Your devoted Friend, Woodrow Wilson

ALS (WP, DLC).

From Howard Houston Henry

Dear Doctor Wilson, [Fort Washington, Pa.] Jan 2,'10

While in New York last Wednesday, where I went for the Advisory Committee[1] meeting, I happened upon Mr. Percy Haughton, who said that he had a copy of a letter sent to President Lowell, in which you had named me as the Princeton representative to work with you in relation to the changing of the football rules.

I think I understand pretty well the situation especially the attitude that Yale will take and it seems very important that we must all three be absolutely bound to abide by the rules decided on by the majority and approved of by a majority of the three Presidents. Camp I am sure wants very few changes, and he will want to leave a loop hole to jump back to the decision of the Intercollegiate Rules Com. should they be less radical than what we propose. Haughton has told me his suggestions are all impossibilities, which he knows we will not accept, or else a game in which the scoring will be done by mass plays, from the 25 or 15 yard line. Camp is afraid to have a meeting until he has seen me for he wont commit Yale to radical changes if he can help it, and he wants my ideas first. I dont see the use of this nor do I approve of decieving [deceiving] him, so I think the best thing is for me to keep away until Yale is definitely committed to stand by what is done at the final voting of the three universities.

Haughton and I have gone over the game pretty carefully, he having spent the last three days with me in Phila and I think we have gotten pretty definite changes in mind. The hard part is to make the proposed change and then be sure of how the rule is going to be taken advantage of, for we cannot have loop holes of escape.

This Friday I am going to stop over in Boston on my way to Quebec and do a little more work on the rules, and if you should want me for anything at any time send word to me at Fort Washington and I can come immediately, for the butler here will be in touch with my whereabouts each day.

Very sincerely yours Howard H. Henry

ALS (WP, DLC).

[1] The Graduate Advisory Committee of the University Athletic Association, about which see J. L. Williams to WW, Sept. 25, 1891, n. 2, Vol. 7.

Henry Burchard Fine to Henry Burling Thompson

My dear Thompson, [Princeton, N. J.] Jan. 2. 1910

At the request of President Wilson I am writing to you of a difficulty which has arisen and which he felt at a loss to meet himself. I am writing because he did not realize the existence of the difficulty until just as he was about to go west to the meeting of the Association of American Universities at Madison, Wis. A meeting of the Faculty Com. on the Grad. School with Mr. Cram has been arranged for the afternoon of Saturday, Jan. 8, to go over the question of plans for the Graduate College. Wilson feels that since these plans are for a Graduate College situate on the Golf Links, Jan. 8 is a very unfortunate time for such a discussion to take place, especially as it was a part of the program that he should be present. One set of plans prepared for the Graduate College by Mr. Cram has been discarded already, and were Mr. Cram to know what the present situation is, it is hardly likely that he would think it wise to make the journey to Princeton until a later date. Wilson feels that if nothing is said to Mr. Cram and he takes the trouble to come on, only to find a little later that everyone present at the conference except himself knew at the time that the discussion might prove to be purely academic, he will think that he has been trifled with and be indignant. And clearly it needs no argument to show that in fairness to Mr. Cram he should be informed. But the meeting was arranged by West in response to a request from Pyne that the Faculty Com. be got to act on the plans with the least possible delay (the arrangement was made 10 days ago.) Wilson is afraid that if he sends word to Mr. Cram, his action will be interpreted by those now opposed to him as an assumption on his part that the Board will support him in the position he has taken. It therefore suggested itself that you, the Chairman of the Com. on Grounds and Buildings, might be able to think out some way of communicating with Mr. Cram that would bring about a postponement of the meeting—a way that would not involve Wilson or be open to the objection of interference with a plan related as this one is to Pyne. You will know better than I can whether Mr. Cram is a person to whom it would be wise to reveal the fact that the question of the site of the Graduate College may be reopened at the next meeting of the Board. But apart from that, I have thought that there might be business ahead for the Com. on Grounds and Buildings which could be used as a reason for requesting Mr. Cram's presence in Princeton at a date later than next Saturday but near enough to that date to make a postponement of the meeting with the Faculty Committee necessary to save Mr. Cram's making two visits to Princeton. But you are much more likely to think of a way out of the difficulty than is anyone to suggest it to you.[1] If you can think of no way that approves itself to you, you will be the best judge as to whether it is best to act at all. Cram's having to make an unnecessary visit to Princeton would be much less calamatous than the occurrence of anything at this time which would cause embarrassment to Wilson. If you wish to communicate with Wilson, you can reach him on Tuesday and Wednesday at Madison, Wisconsin (care of the University of Wisconsin.) I am uncertain whether or not he is to be there on Thursday also. He expects to reach Princeton again on Saturday morning.

With best wishes for the New Year,

Sincerely yours, H. B. Fine

ALS (H. B. Thompson Papers, NjP).

[1] See H. B. Thompson to R. A. Cram, Jan. 4, 1910.

From Cleveland Hoadley Dodge

Dear Woodrow New York Jan 3/10

Happy New Year. Thanks for your letter. Mott has been so absorbed by the great Rochester Convention[1] that he has not had time for anything else, but I hope to see him soon & trust that his interest has not cooled.

Ed Sheldon & I spent two hours with Momo the other evening & I think that things are going to work out all right

Poor old Momo. I am very sorry for him but I believe that he has seen a great light Affly CHD

ALS (WP, DLC).

[1] The Sixth International Convention of the Student Volunteer Movement for Foreign Missions, held in Rochester, N. Y., December 29, 1909-January 2, 1910. More than 3,700 persons attended the convention, including 2,500 student delegates who heard reports and appeals for foreign missionary work. The addresses were published as *Students and the Present Missionary Crisis* (New York, 1910).

From Joseph Bernard Shea

Dear Mr. President: Pittsburgh. Jan. 3, 1910.

Yours of the 31st received this morning when I reached my office.

I am utterly at a loss to know how to answer it. It is most distressing to me that we should apparently be so unable to understand each other's positions in this matter, and if there is any possibility of my being able to stop off at Princeton before the next Board Meeting, I shall certainly do so, as I would welcome the opportunity to talk it over. If I should find it possible to do this, I will telegraph you in advance.

I sincerely trust that a way out may be found.

Ever sincerely and faithfully yours, J B Shea

TLS (WP, DLC).

From William Jay Magie

My Dear Mr. President, Elizabeth, N. J., 3d Jany 1910

Your letter to Mr. Pyne, with a copy of which you favored me, —states the whole case with accuracy.

Much as it grieves me I feel bound to say that I adhere to the view I expressed at our interview. If I were in your place I [would] have sought to discover some other course than that you have taken that I might adopt & advise you to adopt, but I have not been able to discover any.

In our interview I naturally emphasized my view of the dereliction of duty involved in our using the Swan fund in opposition to the directions of the will. But I was not insensible of the other objections to the acceptance of Proctor's gift with a condition requiring a change in the educational policy of the University.

I do hope there may be some change of view before our meeting. Very sincerely yours, W. J. Magie

ALS (WP, DLC).

From Arthur Twining Hadley

New Haven, Connecticut.

My dear Mr. Wilson: January 3, 1910.

I am very glad you have brought up the point about the scope of the suggestions so clearly and definitely.

I am quite free to admit that my own letter was restricted in its scope. I want to eliminate certain specific dangers. Whatever tends toward that end, no matter how technical or microscopic, seems to me of importance. Whatever is aside from that end, whether it will make the game more attractive or not, seems to me outside the sphere of the Yale Corporation.

I am sorry that Lowell is at Madison. I wish we might have the chance to talk the situation over together at once. I fear that we shall have to do so before anything can be given to the public.

Faithfully yours, Arthur T Hadley

TLS (WP, DLC).

From Edward Dickinson Duffield

My dear President Wilson: Newark, N. J. January 3, 1910.

I was very glad to receive your letter of December 30th. It seems to me that the afternoon of the 14th in Newark would be entirely satisfactory for us, and, if you are agreeable to the plan, I would suggest that you arrange to take lunch with me on that day, spending the afternoon in talking the matter over[1] and going from here to Jersey City. I think I can get Mr. Allen[2] without difficulty, and, probably, Mr. Hagemayer.[3] In any event, I would be exceedingly glad if you could arrange to lunch with me and give me some light on the subject, even if I cannot procure the other members of the Committee, although, as I say, I will do my best to see that they are both here.

So far as the Lawyers' Club goes, if you could give us some time the latter part of March, it would be entirely satisfactory. I am obliged to go to New Orleans early in March, probably not returning before the 10th, or, possibly, a little later, so that you had better fix on some date after the 15th. I think any date between the 15th and 30th that would suit your convenience would be perfectly agreeable to us, and I am delighted that we can look forward to having you at that time. We are all proud of the Bar of the County, and it will be a real pleasure to us to have you meet with us. I will talk the matter over with you a little more in detail when I see you, as I hope to on the 14th.[4]

With kindest regards, believe me,

Very truly yours, Edward D Duffield

TLS (WP, DLC).

[1] That is, to confer about the quadrangle plan.

[2] Andrew Jackson Allen, Princeton 1890, Principal of Public School No. 1 in Hoboken, who lived in East Orange, N. J.

[3] Arthur Herbert Hagemeyer, Princeton 1897, stockbroker in the firm of Halstead & Hagemeyer of New York, who resided in South Orange, N. J.

[4] As has previously been noted, Wilson spoke to the Lawyers' Club of Newark on May 20, 1910, and a news report of his address is printed at May 21, 1910, Vol. 20.

Melancthon Williams Jacobus to Henry Burling Thompson

My dear Thompson: Hartford, Conn., January 3rd, 1910.

Your letter of yesterday has just been received, and I shall try to get Cleve Dodge on the 'phone tonight and ask him what he thinks is best to do, if anything, before the meeting of the Board of Trustees, to secure concerted action on this matter.

I am most anxious to avoid heated discussion and debate in the open meeting of the Board. With this end in view, I think some sort of understanding should be had before the Board meeting as to what action shall be presented to the Trustees regarding the Graduate School location.

I received a letter from Wilson yesterday, enclosing letters received by him from Sheldon and David Jones and Thomas Jones, to whom, as you know, he sent copies of his letter to Pyne.

Wilson seems to think that the thing to be done is to get Pyne to consent to allow the Graduate School Committee to recommend to the Board, without opposition from himself, that, in view of the fact that it was not possible to comply in full with the directions of Mrs. Swann's will under the conditions imposed by Mr. Proctor, it be declined with thanks.

Wilson's letter, as you see by the enclosed copy,[1] shows that he was somewhat converted to the idea of a conference in which he should be present to persuade certain men of the opposition to his views. However, I am convinced that if Pyne will feel irritated by any such "town meeting," it is certainly the thing we do not desire to do. It is worse than useless to ask men to come to a conference who have announced beforehand that they would be irritated by any conference.

I am sending you in this same mail a call for a Curriculum Committee meeting on the evening of Wednesday, January 12th, to consider the President's report on possible economies in the Faculty budget and, if we have time, your items on the C.E. entrance requirements in Mathematics, and the distribution of students in the elective courses of the Junior and Senior years.

I do not think that anything more is needed than the cordial assent of Pyne to the proposed action on the Graduate School matter, which practically eliminates West as far as any future handling of that School on his own lines of development is concerned. Pyne's following in the Board is distinctive and definite, and if he concurs with the Committee in this matter there will be no opposition.

There remains, however, the always present question of the elimination of West, and I cannot see how this will ever be accomplished short of his departure from the University, or certainly his resignation from the Deanship of the Graduate School.

He will certainly never come to be persuaded that he is not wanted. He knows that already, and yet it is a serious thing to ask for his resignation, even from his Deanship. It is a square issue between the President and the Dean as to where the College shall be located, but even the deciding of this does not, unless I greatly mistake the character of the Dean, eliminate him from the situation. It is, of course, of immediate need that we shall decide upon a recommendation to be made to the Board regarding the location of the Graduate School, and secure united action on the recommendation. But we are still confronted with the other personal issue, and we will not have settled the matter until some action on this point be also decided on and carried.

I will let you know what advice I get from Cleve Dodge.

Yours very sincerely, M W Jacobus

P.S. I find it is not going to be possible for me to be present at the meeting of the Graduate School Committee. A telegram from Pyne informs me that [at] the President's request it is called in New York for 3 PM on Tuesday. You will see from my letter to Wilson that I told him I would be detained in Hartford, unvoidably, through Monday & Tuesday MWJ

TLS (WP, DLC).

[1] WW to M. W. Jacobus, Jan. 1, 1910, TCL (WP, DLC).

Henry Burling Thompson to Cleveland Hoadley Dodge

Dear Cleve: [Greenville P.O., Del.] January 3d, 1910.

I have been talking over the telephone with Sheldon this morning, and we are trying to meet Momo at Sheldon's house at dinner either to-morrow or Wednesday evening. If we can get Momo once settled the rest is easy, for men like Stewart, Wood and Davis would then be with us. It will be useless to waste any time on men like Bayard [Henry], MacPherson, Shea, Farrand, etc.

It is important to convert Archie Russell to our way of thinking, and I think it is up to you to talk the matter over with him and get him straightened out, as you did Stephen Palmer.

A big conference does not seem advisable. Jacobus, I think, can attend to Stewart, if you can attend to Russell. Of course, the difficult problem will be to get Momo to come down off his perch, and get him down in a dignified way.

In the language of the late Mr. Quay,[1] burn this letter.

Yours sincerely Henry B Thompson

TLS (Thompson Letterpress Books, NjP).

[1] Matthew Stanley Quay (1833-1904), senator from Pennsylvania 1887-89, 1901-1904, and prominent in national Republican politics.

To Various Trustees of Princeton University

My dear – [Jan. 4, 1910]

I feel it to be my duty to send you a copy of a letter I wrote to Mr. Pyne after my last interview with Mr. Procter. I wrote it after very serious consideration, without the least personal feeling, and with the most earnest desire to serve the best interests of the University

Sincerely Yours, Woodrow Wilson

Mr. Close: Please send above, with copy of my letter of Dec. 25 to Mr. Pyne, to Mr. J. W. Alexander, Rev. Dr. Jno. Dixon, Hon. Bayard Henry, Rev. Dr. S. J. McPherson, Mr. H. W. Green, Rev. Dr. Chas. Wood, Mr. A. D. Russell, Mr. Alex Van Rensselaer, and Mr. Wilson Farrand

WWhw draft LS (WP, DLC).

To Wilson Farrand

My dear Mr. Farrand: Princeton, N. J. January 4th, 1910.

I feel it to be my duty to send you a copy of a letter I wrote to Mr. Pyne after my last interview with Mr. Procter. I wrote it after very serious consideration, without the least personal feeling, and with the most earnest desire to serve the best interests of the University. Sincerely yours, Woodrow Wilson

TLS (W. Farrand Coll., NjP).

From Andrew Fleming West

Princeton, N. J., January 4, 1910.

On request of the President a meeting of the Trustees' Committee on the Graduate School is hereby called by Mr. Pyne, Chairman, for three o'clock Tuesday afternoon January 11th., in Mr. Pyne's office, 30 Pine Street, New York City.

Andrew F. West

TLS (WWP, UA, NjP).

Henry Burling Thompson to Ralph Adams Cram

Dear Mr. Cram: [Greenville P. O., Del.] January 4th, 1910.

I am informed that a meeting of the Faculty Committee of the Graduate School with you has been called for Saturday, January 8th. Circumstances have arisen in connection with this unfortunate question of the Graduate School which will make it embarrassing for President Wilson to be at that meeting; consequently, I am going to ask you to have sufficient confidence in my judgment to do the following: Please telegraph to the Chairman, or Secretary, of the above Committee that you will be unable to be in Princeton on Saturday, and to postpone the meeting; also, telegraph President Woodrow Wilson, care of the University of Wisconsin, Madison, Wisconsin, that the meeting has been postponed. I shall be in a position within a few days to explain my action, and, if necessary, will assume all responsibility of any criticism that you might possibly be subjected to. In the meantime, please consider the above entirely confidential.

I shall be glad to know if you see fit to carry out my request.

Yours very truly, Henry B. Thompson. Per M. E. B.

TLS (Thompson Letterpress Books, NjP).

An Address in Madison, Wisconsin, to the Association of American Universities

[[Jan. 5, 1910]]

POSITION AND IMPORTANCE OF THE ARTS COURSE AS DISTINCT FROM THE PROFESSIONAL AND SEMI-PROFESSIONAL COURSES

It is my privilege this morning to present for Princeton a paper on the position and importance of the arts course as distinct from the professional and semi-professional courses. I say that I present this for Princeton University. I think I may be reasonably sure that the opinions I am about to express are those of Princeton University, but I should prefer that you should regard the details of these opinions as my own.

I was in some doubt when I began to think this paper out—for I have not had the time to write it—as to the meaning intended to be conveyed in the title. There are many meanings that might be derived from it, but I shall take the natural meaning. I shall assume that the subject means, "What do we think of the arts course, and what is the object of the arts course, as contrasted with the professional and semi-professional courses?"

I think that it is best to start out with certain ideas that seem to be preliminary to the whole discussion. It seems to me that all specialism—and this includes professional training—is clearly individualistic in its object. I mean that the object of professional training is the private interest of the person who is seeking that training. He is seeking to prepare himself for a particular profession. He is seeking to make himself ready for a particular performance in the world which will be the means of his own support, and, it may be, of his own private distinction. His point of view, therefore, is centered in himself. His purpose is to make himself efficient for the life which he wishes to lead; and I suppose that that is the object of all special training, whether it be called professional or not.

There is a very interesting and suggestive passage in Mr. Chesterton's book on *Orthodoxy* which seems to me to illustrate a portion of this subject. He says that it is not true to say of a man who has won success and position in the world that "you can't bribe a man like that." He says it is true only in this sense, that he has already been bribed. He has won his success by particular processes supplied him by the world as it stands. He is therefore bribed to see that the world as it stands is not changed, for fear the conditions of his success should be altered. He is under bonds to stand by the *status quo*. The *status quo* is his opportunity. To change it would be to alter his opportunity, and his whole point of view, centered as it is upon one special interest, is the point of view of that special interest.

You do not need to be told how practically all the difficulties of our national life, all the difficulties in the field of statesmanship, I mean, arise out of the jealousies and the competitions of special interests and the lack of understanding between them or of a common object. My own experience in conversing with distinguished lawyers or distinguished bankers or distinguished manufacturers is that with each one of them I have to approach the subject we are discussing from a special point of view, namely, his own, and try, if it be possible, to draw his thought and vision out to the broader field which he has for the time being overlooked and forgotten, but which, nevertheless, is the field with which he must relate himself successfully if his business is not to draw him into courses which will be against the general interest. It is this specialization of interest which constitutes the danger, I mean the intellectual danger as well as the economic danger, of our times.

I took the liberty of saying to a body of gentlemen whom I was addressing not long ago, who provoked me by the exceeding complacency of their appearance, very well-to-do men, that I thought it to be the object of a college to make the young gentlemen who resorted to it just as unlike their fathers as possible. I hastened to explain that I did not mean any disrespect to the fathers, but merely this: that by the time a man was old enough to have a son at college he had become so immersed in some one special interest that he no longer comprehended the country and age in which he was living, and that it was the business of a college to regeneralize each generation as it came on, to give it a view of the stage as a whole before it was drawn off to occupy only a little corner of the stage and forget the rest, to forget the plot as a whole in the arrangement of its portion of it. And I believe that that is the preliminary thought with which we must approach the subject assigned to me for discussion this morning. We must realize the fact that all professional and semi-professional, all special training is individualistic in its object.

The question we have to ask, therefore, is as to the relative value, on the one hand, of a discipline whose object it is to make the man who receives it a citizen of the modern intellectual and social world, as contrasted, on the other hand, with a discipline whose object is to make him the adept and disciple of a special interest. I think that that is not an unfair statement of the subject that is to be discussed.

When you come to a discussion of the special terms of the subject, there is an initial difficulty. There is no arts *course*, if you use the term in the singular. If you look our colleges over, you will find that there is nowhere an arts course—almost nowhere. There is a miscellany of courses whose object is not professional or semi-professional. This miscellany of courses is not arranged with any organic connections. It is not arranged in any fixed sequence. It is not organized with regard to any particular congruity between its several parts. And therefore we are in the position of those who would ask, "Is it possible to have an arts course? And if it is possible, is it desirable? If it is desirable, upon what grounds is it desirable?"

Notwithstanding the fact that we have no arts course, I suppose that when we use that term we have substantially the idea which I have tried to outline already. I suppose we mean a body of studies whose object is not individualistic, but whose object is a general orientation, the creation in the mind of a vision of the field of knowledge, in some degree, at any rate, as a whole, the development of a general, catholic, intellectual sympathy, the development of a power of comprehension. I do not believe, for my own part, that the object of an arts course is knowledge. If it were, we would have to acknowledge a practically universal failure, for we all recognize the fact that a graduate of any one of our colleges, after he is ten years out, has practically forgotten all he studied as an undergraduate. If it is the knowledge that was valuable to him, he has lost it, and the value has gone out of it. What he was taught to do with his mind in receiving the knowledge, however, what he was taught to see, what he was taught to discriminate, what he was taught to sympathize with, what he was enabled to comprehend, is what he has got out of it. And if he shall have got that out of it, he has got everything out of it; for the knowledge itself is the mere material upon which these habits are formed, the habit of looking facts so steadily in the face that the atmosphere disappears from them and you see them cold as they are; the habit of stating things with precision, of reasoning with exactness, of reasoning with fearlessness, of moving from premises to conclusion like those who desire to see the truth and desire not to be deceived: these are some of the things that a man gets out of this kind of discipline.

I heard it said very wittily the other evening that it was a very rare man who could state a fact without also stating an opinion, and I believe that the most desirable discipline for the rising youth is that he should by education be able to acquire the habit and the discrimination which must underlie the habit of stating a fact without stating an opinion.

Moreover, it seems to me that this orientation has in it a moral content as well as an intellectual. I believe that the object of the kind of discipline which we mean when we speak of an arts course is to cultivate in those who receive it a correct moral appreciation, a correct appreciation of moral values; so that they must not be allowed to confine themselves to the field of the exact sciences, for example, where sympathy is neither here nor there, where moral perceptions are involved only in so far as the student divests himself of prejudice and sincerely seeks the truth. There the subject-matter itself is non-moral, whereas the subject-matter of life is saturated with moral imputations, and all those studies which concern themselves with life should constitute a training in moral perception. The facts of history may escape our memory, but the morals of history, the operations of character, the play of motive, the distinction of integrity, may leave their lasting impression upon us.

I shall assume that, at any rate for my conception, this is the basis of the discussion we undertake this morning. It seems to me, therefore, that we have been pursuing elusive things, and are now of necessity about to return to the obvious things, the things which have been all along obvious, but of which we have been impatient because they were obvious and we were seeking the curious, the unusual, the original.

There is of course a debate as to the best means of orientation. I understand orientation to mean an ability to know the east from the west, and by that means to know where you are. I have often thought it was an extremely inaccurate expression when a man had lost his way in a desert or a jungle to say that he had lost himself. That is the only thing he has not lost. What as a matter of fact he has lost is the rest of the world. If he knew where any other thing of definite position was in the rest of the world, he would have something to steer by and he could get out. Orientation I understand to be illustrated by that. A man has found where he is in relation to the intellectual and moral content of the world, and, having ascertained his relations to other things and to other persons and to other forces, he knows more accurately where he himself is located.

I admit that it is an open question as to what the best means of orientation are. If we found upon the classical studies, we found upon the past, where unquestionably the springs of modern thought lie, but where you cannot find a very large part of the modern intellectual subject-matter. The great suggestions, the great processes, the great anticipations of all intellectual action are to be found there, but modern thought is not to be found there. If, however, we build entirely upon modern thinking and upon the modern subject-matter of thought, we have only the short, modern view, and our connections with the past upon which it rests come only, it may be, indirectly, through the fact that modern literature of necessity and unconsciously reflects the older history of the mind. In order to get your complete orientation, therefore, in order to have the map of modern life laid before you in its entirety, it is not sufficient to build upon either of these disciplines, either the older or the newer. Each is incomplete without the other.

We have to ask ourselves then, "What are we to do in this field of almost unlimited choice?" For, while it is true that you can name a definite content for the older curriculum and a definite, though miscellaneous, content for the varied newer curricula, it is not true that it is possible to combine out of the two a single curriculum which will give you the discipline which you need in order to be a citizen of the modern intellectual and social world. We have, therefore, to resort to a choice of elements, rather than to a choice of subjects, and we have to remind ourselves before we make that choice what it is that we are seeking to do.

In the first place, we are seeking to impart discipline; and for my part, it seems to me that that is the particular thing which in our modern schemes of study we have forgotten and neglected. We have sought with a diligence which was pathetic the best means of information, but we have not sought with any degree of intelligence the best means of discipline. We have not sought to subject the mind to the processes which it needed for its undeveloped powers, but we have sought to indulge it in the use of its developed powers or of those powers the instinct and beginnings of which were already appreciated by those who possessed them. We have not sought, in other words, to find out in any systematic way whether the mind had received the proper intimations and acquired the proper habits with regard to the processes of the modern intellectual world.

Those processes are quite distinguishable, quite susceptible of being catalogued; and the discipline which the man in the modern world needs is plain enough. It is the discipline which will prepare him to act, not along a single line, but either in this direction or in another as life may lead. We are not now speaking, mind you, only of the training of scholars; we are speaking of the training of men who are to be prepared for life in general; and when you think of modern life, particularly of modern American life, you will at once appreciate the circumstance that a man must not in that life be narrowed to any one thing. If he is, he is sure all his life to be a mere servant, and he may at any moment become an unprofitable servant by the circumstance that the particular thing which he knows is cast aside and has gone out of date. Just as modern machinery is constantly being rejected and absolutely new plants substituted for the old because of new inventions, the necessity for new processes, so minds mechanically adapted to certain processes are being constantly cast aside, cast aside in a way that renders life hopeless for them, because they have no adaptability, no resource, no further outlet. They are worn out and discarded pieces of machinery. Modern life is of all things else changeable. Because it is progressive it is changeable, and because changeable it requires minds that are changeable, that are interchangeable as between processes, as between enterprises. The minds that are to be successful must be the minds ready to turn this way or that in a varying and almost distracting world of change.

The discipline, therefore, that the modern man needs is the discipline of general preparation for the difficult tasks of our own day. And this discipline can be imparted in this general way only in its essential forms. It cannot be the discipline of process, it must be the discipline of principle. For example, it was once possible to teach most of the chemical processes employed in modern manufacture—teach them by rule of thumb, I mean. But there are so many now that it is impossible to teach them by rule of thumb, and we are, happily, driven to the necessity of teaching chemistry as pure science, the necessity of making the student drink at the fountain instead of merely searching out the lower courses of the stream—which recalls the old remark of Coke about the law, that it is better to search out the fountains than to tap the streams. Fortunately, the streams have branched into so many provinces of a great world that it is absolutely necessary that we should go back and test the waters at their fountain-head and trace them thence, if we would follow them and map them as they are.

That is what I mean by saying that all the general discipline of the modern world must be at the sources, must be fundamental, must be a process of the mind, and not a mere process of practical application, in order to be a real discipline, a process of intellectual action rather than a process of drill and information. It must set the mind in the way of doing certain things for itself, rather than put it in the position merely of learning how other persons have done them and imitating the processes that others have used.

But that is not the only thing that is fundamentally necessary. It is also necessary that there should be something for which I can find only a very big word, namely, the word enlightenment. The object of general learning is surely enlightenment. We want to come out of our provincial intellectual habit and know what the world at large is thinking and doing, what the impulses are that are moving it, what the conditions are which it must act upon if it would continue its life successfully and progressively. I do not know of any smaller word that would express the idea. And if our objects of discipline are summed up in the word enlightenment, then it is perfectly legitimate to set as our object this further purpose of giving a man the freedom of the modern world so that he will not bury his head in a particular interest, but will stand high enough to survey the field and see where the tides move, know what the general interests of society are as well as the particular interests of portions of society.

Very well, then, if these be our objects, to communicate discipline, to afford enlightenment, to make a man free of the modern world so that he will not be a yokel and a provincial and will really come out upon a stage where he can look about him and see, we must select the things that will give him the characteristic discipline of the modern world. That leads us to the point where we seek to pick out the elements of an arts course—I mean the fundamental elements. I do not mean the particular subjects and studies, but the fundamental elements, and they seem to me to be only four—unless I have been led very much astray in my analysis.

In the first place, you must give the mind a thorough drill in some part of pure science. I use the word pure, of course, as contrasted with professional science or applied science. You must give the mind the discipline which is so characteristic of the modern world, which enables it to follow the processes and appreciate the results, and produce the results, of modern scientific thinking, in the realm of nature; the elements of pure science, not elaborated, but dwelt upon in their essential elementary conceptions and processes so long, so intensively, so insistently, that the mind can never afterward shake off the prepossessions of scientific inquiry.

It is possible to do that, I dare say, with a single science. I am not schooled in science as I should like to be, but I assume that a central science like physics, if you kept the mind at its processes long enough and intimately enough, would be a sufficient schooling, a sufficient discipline in modern scientific method and modern scientific thinking, and that a man after that drill, if he chose to move out into other fields of science, could do so, not like a stranger but like a man who knew how to enter a new country and to follow its paths with intelligence. It is not necessary, indeed it seems to me futile, that you should introduce the student to half a dozen sciences and give him a glimpse of each. The thing that you want is not information on his part with regard to what the several sciences contain and are doing, but the scientific habit of mind fixed and ingrained by the splendid discipline of a single science that, so far as its elements and its real processes of thought are concerned, has been really mastered by the pupil.

Then it seems to me that you must have the elements of pure philosophy, by which I mean an explanation of nature and human life which seeks to include all the elements. That is a large order, and so far as my reading goes I do not know where to look for such a co-ordination and explanation; but I do know that a very interesting thing has been happening in our day, something which has its indirect influence upon the administration of universities. It used to be possible for men, without any twinges of conscience, to devote themselves exclusively to a particular science. They cannot do so any longer, because the frontiers are being obscured. I cannot now find anybody who can trace a scientific frontier between mathematics and physics, between physics and chemistry, or between chemistry and biology. It is clear enough in the center of the province where you are, but not clear on the frontiers where you are, whether you are in chemistry or physics, whether you are in physics or in mathematics; and as these boundaries disappear, you observe what is happening. Our mind is sweeping through an organic whole. We do not know when we cross from one province to another; which means that there are no natural boundaries, that the boundaries are artificial, boundaries of convention, agreed upon by treaty and not arranged by nature. There is no mountain range piled there, no great river has dug its pathway there. There is no natural, obvious boundary. You do not know, except by convention and if you carry a map in your hand—and then you are not certain—when you have crossed from one to another.

And when you have swept this apparent circle through, you find that there is a segment lacking, a segment the lack of which all men of science are becoming aware of, and that is the spiritual segment. There is something inexplicable in it all unless you insert into this circle the segment of philosophy, in the broad sense in which I have tried to indicate it here. Until you have explained the universe in terms of spirit, you have not explained the universe at all. You may have catalogued it, you may have arranged it, you may have made a museum of it, you may have enabled us to employ the processes of it and understand how nature does this, that, and the other particular thing, but you have not explained it. That is the task, the tremendous task, of the philosopher. The modern philosopher is not trying to think merely in terms of metaphysics; he is trying to think also in terms of physics, he is trying to think in terms of the physical universe, interpreted by the human spirit. Science will be impoverished as a body of thought until that is accomplished.

It seems to me, therefore, that it is indispensable, in this general discipline which we are seeking to outline theoretically, that the mind should be led at any rate to perceive the lack of an explanation, and to understand the main attempts which have been made to explain. That is what I mean by pure philosophy: the fact that there is something to explain, the definite appreciation of just what it is that is to be explained, and so much of the history of philosophy as is necessary to know what attempts have been made to explain it. You cannot be a citizen of the modern world of thought unless you have an introduction, and something more than an introduction, a familiar companionship, with aims of that sort, and there cannot be familiar companionship unless the process is continued for a long time. If you simply go into a lecture room and hear a few lectures on the history of philosophy and come out again, you have got nothing except an impression as to the lecturer, and, it may be, a few interrogation points stirred in your mind; and the average undergraduate is not apt to have interrogation points stirred in his mind. He must have things brought to his mind again and again to have it stirred at all. He is interested in more important matters! He is interested in modern life; but he is not interested in understanding modern life, or mastering modern life. If, however, you once get him imbued with these fundamental ideas, and make these questions hold him, then his mind will lie awake at nights and think of these things, and he cannot get rid of them until he answers them. That is all I want—to get him wide awake; not to furnish him with a ready-made solution, but to get him wide awake, and to impress upon him the grim necessity that there must be a solution if he is going to live in the world at all.

Then I should say that there must be the elements—always the elements; you do not have to cover the wide field; you must go by a single road in each of these cases—the elements of pure literature. The only delight in literature, so far as I can see it, is the delight of enlargement. I suppose we read books of travel because we cannot travel thither ourselves. If we could, I would very much prefer to go than to read another man's travels. I suppose we venture into fields of reading which are not distinctively our own because we would like to be so many things that we are not, because the world is so narrow in our little piece of it, because we want the adventures of life and cannot have them all, because we want to experience the thrills which have stirred other minds than our own, and have moved within the spirits of other men but not within our own. We want to take the walls down from the room and sweep the horizon and know what airs are astir that we did not originate, and have as yet never breathed.

And these visions of the mind, the whole realm of poetry and creative prose, the realm of insight and interpretation, are the regions in which we refresh ourselves and breathe an upper air which keeps our lungs fit for the more sedate and mundane things we have to do. I pity the man who cannot get this dissociation and removal from the actual world occasionally, this refreshment on the uplands, which are ready to his mere desire, if he only entertain it. For my own part, I must say that in my own studies, in the field of politics, I have found more true political interpretation in the poets than I have ever found in the systematic writers on political science. The systematic writers on political science will tell you a great many interesting things, but they interpret almost nothing for you, and some sudden light flashed in a single line of poetry will sometimes interpret more politics to you than you can find in the bound volumes of the political science library; because the poet has suddenly seen what the human heart is striving for out there in the field of politics, has uncovered that; and after you have seen it you know what the significance of your study is.

The field of pure literature is the field of the interpretation of the human spirit apart from those explicit problems of explanation which lie in the field of philosophy; and of course, as you know, in writers like Browning the fields are hardly distinguishable. The poetry is philosophical and the philosophy is poetical. You feel all the unseen forces of a great world stirring there, and a great mind feeling after them, not with the perception of a scientist, but with the instinct of a seer. How could a man be a citizen of the modern world unless he felt all of these things?

And then, I dare say, we would all admit that the field of history and politics is a necessary part of a lad's introduction into the modern world. I shall not dwell upon that, because perhaps it is my own prepossessions which lead me to think that that is one of the necessary elements, but I dare say that is obvious enough.

Now, if these be the elements, if our object be discipline, enlightenment, orientation, and our means pure science, pure philosophy, pure literature, and the facts of history and politics, all of which can be accomplished simply and by uncomplicated courses of study—not the same for every man, but nevertheless with the same elements in every arrangement—then we have to ask ourselves what the method shall be.

In the first place, the method, it seems to me, obviously should include a definite choice of studies. I am assuming that, while each man will be directed to discipline of each kind, there will be a variety of choice by which he can get each kind of discipline. There ought, therefore, to be a definite choice of studies, a systematic sequence of studies, and a systematic combination of studies. Faculties must establish the sequences and the combinations. The student must make the definite choice, definite within the range of his prepossessions and instinctive apprehension as to his own powers, his own tastes, if you will, but nevertheless not a miscellaneous, haphazard, dispersed choice, but a definite choice, a choice guided and limited by the systematic sequence and the systematic combination arranged for him before he makes it. It seems to me that these constitute the necessary characteristics of the method by which we must seek this discipline. I do not want to tire you with more of this, because it seems to me obvious.

I want to go on. If that is what we mean—and that is what I mean—by an arts course, I want to speak of the relationship between it and the professional or semi-professional studies.

I hardly think it worth arguing that a man needs this sort of training before he becomes a special student in any field of scholarship. After all, one of the most significant things about any subject is the way it is related to other subjects. The only field in which I have had experience with advanced students is the field of history and politics, and the most noticeable thing about that field and what is going on in it in advanced study is the number of mares' nests that are daily discovered by advanced students, the number of things that are discovered that were discovered also a great many years ago, and most of which have been discredited and disproved a great many years ago.

A one-time colleague of mine undertook the very ambitious task of drawing all the arts together under a common set of categories and principles. He wrote a book on the subject and carried it to a colleague of his, who was not supposed to be read in the field of art particularly, but who was generally read in the field of knowledge, and asked him to read it and tell him what he thought of it. He read it and then said, "Why, my dear fellow, the trouble about this is that it has been exploded ever since Aristotle." If you do not know the things that have been exploded ever since Aristotle, you are going fruitlessly to retraverse the fields that lie between us and Aristotle; and in the field of history, particularly, most of our advanced students, not knowing the general field of history, and seeking to cultivate little pieces of it, are constantly misinterpreting the facts which lie within those little fields, because of their inability to understand the relationships, to understand the things already known, already established, the conclusions already set up, and the facts which must lie neighbor to these and condition their whole significance. I say that it seems too obvious for argument that no man can afford for his own intellectual safety to specialize in any field until he has traversed enough of the general field of knowledge to know the relation of his special field to the general field and to check his processes by the established intellectual processes of the world.

The constant trouble with literary study, the constant trouble, more conspicuous than elsewhere, perhaps, with philosophical study, is that the men who cultivate those special fields have not been trained and made familiar with the fields which are of an entirely different character but which, nevertheless, so intimately relate to modern thought that every field must take cognizance of them. I mean that a psychologist who does not know science is an incompetent psychologist; that a man who tries to cultivate literature without knowing what are the hard substances upon which the modern mind bites in the whole field of the physical universe will merely pursue shadows, merely fall in love with fancies and phantasms. And so it is dangerous for a man to be at large without a guardian who does not know his whereabouts and consequently the dangers amidst which he is walking in the modern field of knowledge.

When you carry this into the professional field, take for example the lawyer and the engineer. The engineer, in a degree which few persons who are not engineers realize, deals with modern life as well as with structural and constructive processes, and unless he can deal with men and understand circumstances, he cannot be a successful engineer in the higher ranks of the calling. Modern manufacturers, for example, of the structural parts of bridges, are just as likely as not to have an order placed for a bridge to be erected somewhere in the heart of India, and they are asked to send out their own engineer, understanding their own methods of construction, to put the bridge up; and if they send anybody out who is ignorant of India, not only as a climatic condition, but also as a labor market, and doesn't know the motives and the impulses and the singularities of coolies, he might as well stay at home. The modern engineer must know the modern world in order to undertake the principal tasks of his profession. And the modern lawyer, clearly, must understand the modern world, because he is dealing with a larger variety, perhaps, of modern circumstances than the man of any other profession, except the minister; and the minister does not have to deal with it in a way that can get men into jail. The modern minister does deal with all the difficulties of the human mind, but so does the modern lawyer deal with the difficulties of modern business, and a man merely schooled in the principles of the law as divulged in the textbooks and cases is not prepared for his profession.

I was myself bred for the law, and as long as I could stand it, followed it as a profession, and therefore I know something about law and something about lawyers. I was led, therefore, not long ago, in addressing the Cleveland Chamber of Commerce,[1] to make some disagreeable remarks. I was talking about the modern trust problems and the ignorant attempts of modern legisla-

[1] Wilson's address to the Cleveland Chamber of Commerce, "The Ideals of Public Life," is printed at Nov. 16, 1907, Vol. 17.

tion to correct the evils that we all wish to see corrected, and I said that I had no doubt that there were a large number of lawyers who were the trusted advisers of corporations among the company that was listening to me, and that I had something to say to them. I said, "You complain that the legislation now being attempted against corporations is ignorant and mistaken, and may be ruinous, and I agree with you; but if I wanted to formulate a different sort of legislation which would be effective and beneficial, I would have to ask you what sort it ought to be, because you know what is going on, and you know how it could be corrected. If, therefore, you want really to serve the corporations which employ you, and to save them from ruin, you will take charge of the processes of reformation and advise the reformers. If you do not, the day of reckoning will come, which will be a day of ruin, and you only will be to blame. Now, having said this," I added, "and being a lawyer myself, I know you won't have sense enough to do it." It is as Burke long ago said; the study of law is one of the best of mental disciplines, but it does not in the same degree liberalize the understanding; and so the lawyer merely sticks to the processes which stand in the way of progress. He cannot think in any other terms; and yet the modern lawyer, if he is really to live, must confess himself, come out in the world, and be ready to aid in the processes of that world. He cannot do it ignorantly; he cannot do it unless he knows what they are. In most cases he has hurried through a miscellaneous arts course, or skipped it altogether, and has gone from the high school into the law school, and there has saturated himself in the stiffest and most conservative side of social life, the side which goes by formula, the side which goes by rule, the side which goes by precedent and thinks it impiety to make breach of a precedent; whereas the progress of the world makes havoc with precedents, and necessarily so. If you are going to have an unschooled, untried, uninitiated rustic—speaking only in terms of the mind—going into the legal profession, you have condemned him to be an insufficient instrument of the great profession which he has joined.

When we speak, therefore, of the relation of the arts course to the professional courses, we are speaking of the relation of the foundations to the edifice, we are speaking of the relation of the understanding to the career. It is the relation between comprehension and action, and you cannot establish this relationship successfully in any other way.

I of course recognize the fact, as everybody does, that there are exceptional individuals who need no formal training, no exact, definite introduction, who have the genius to perceive and to perceive in large terms the moment they are put into the midst of circumstance; but these are the exceptional men, and these are not the men for whom our arts courses are provided. They are generally the men for whom our arts courses are often intolerable, because it is, for them, like harnessing Pegasus; there is nothing that you can teach him in the way of aerial locomotion.

I would conclude by this suggestion, that professionalism in learning has the same effect upon the intellectual world that professionalism in sport has on the world of sportsmanship. The minute professionalism enters sport it ceases to be sportsmanlike. The minute professionalism enters learning, it ceases to wear the broad and genial face of learning. It has become a commodity; it has become something that a man wishes to exchange for the means of support. It has become something that a man wishes to use in order to get the better of his fellow-men, to enhance his fortunes, to do all the things that center in and upon himself. It is professionalism that spoils the game, the game of life, the game of humanity, the game of co-operation in social undertakings, the whole handsome game that we are seeking to throw light upon by the processes of education.

This, then, seems to me the position and the importance of the arts course as distinct from the professional and semi-professional courses.[2]

Printed in Association of American Universities, *Journal of Proceedings and Addresses of the Eleventh Annual Conference* . . . (Chicago, 1910), pp. 73-84.

[2] There is a WWT outline of this address, dated Dec. 31, 1909, and a stenographic report, emended by Wilson, in WP, DLC.

From Cleveland Hoadley Dodge

Dear Woodrow: New York January 5, 1910.

I have a letter from your Secretary informing me that you have sent copies of your letter of December 25, to all of the members of the Board, and I am very glad you have done so.

Poor Momo is laid up with a bad cold and I hope he is not going to be sick.

I understand that your Graduate School Committee meets on Tuesday, and I sincerely hope you will be able to get Cyrus on to attend the metting [meeting], as I think it most important that he and Jacobus should be there. Harry Thompson has written to Jacobus but I should think it would be a good thing for you to write Cyrus. I think everything is coming out all right.

Yours sincerely, C H Dodge

TLS (WP, DLC).

From Simon John McPherson

Lawrenceville, New Jersey

My dear Dr. Wilson: Jan'y 5, 1910.

I have received your note enclosing the circular copy of the letter which you recently sent to Mr. Pyne.

Your opinion has weight with me, but I regret very much that it is so uncompromisingly stated and, still more, that it is accompanied by the intimation that by virtue of the action of the Board you "seem to have come to an end." Is not the situation in some respects similar to that created at Yale by the discussion over the Hillhouse property?[1]

The matters quoted from Mrs. Swann's will are most important. The intimation that rooms should be rented to undergraduates has not, I think, been much considered by the Board. My own feeling is that the phrase "upon the grounds," &c., might be judicially determined without much difficulty and so lifted out of the realm of personal opinion, however high. I feel too that we have probably failed, or up to the last meeting of the Board had failed, to obtain any formal or official approval of any site for the Graduate School from Mrs. Swann's executors.

I hope that, whatever is decided finally, the question will not be allowed to start personal controversies within the Faculty or outside of it. For that would be not only unpleasant but more or less dangerous to the fundamental welfare of Princeton. I am still convinced that everybody is wiser than anybody, and am hoping to see the whole issue determined with right feelings.

Sincerely yours, S. J. McPherson.

ALS (WP, DLC).

[1] McPherson's comment referred to a controversy then raging at Yale University over the uses to be made of the recently acquired estate of the Hillhouse family. The property lay to the north of the existing campus, not far from the buildings of the Sheffield Scientific School but between one half and one mile distant from the dormitories and recitation halls of Yale College. President Arthur T. Hadley and University Secretary Anson Phelps Stokes, Jr., wished to build laboratories for physics and zoology on the Hillhouse site, which would serve the entire university and thus end some of the existing duplication between the college and the Scientific School. Unfortunately for Hadley and Stokes, these proposals stirred up and intensified the long-standing rivalries between the two schools. The faculty of the college feared that the removal of some of its activities to the distant Hillhouse site would destroy the old unity and spirit of the college and ultimately lessen its importance

as the traditional center of the university. The members of the Scientific School, on the other hand, were determined to maintain its semi-autonomous status and strengthen its hold on the scientific research and teaching of the university. The debate over the matter had gone on within the university since the spring of 1909 and had been extensively discussed in the *Yale Alumni Weekly.* Metropolitan newspapers picked up the subject in January 1910 when it was announced that Margaret Olivia Slocum (Mrs. Russell) Sage had given $650,000 to pay for the Hillhouse property (previously held by a group of private underwriters assembled by Stokes). The *New York Times,* for example, had articles on the controversy in its issues of January 2 and 4, 1910, and editorials in those of January 2 and 5. Eventually, both the originally proposed laboratories and additional ones were built on the Hillhouse site. See George Wilson Pierson, *Yale College: An Educational History, 1871-1921* (New Haven, Conn., 1952), pp. 369-86, 653-59.

From Charles Wood

Dear President Wilson, Washington, D. C. Jan 5/10

Your letter to Mr Pyne, which you kindly sent, I have read with very painful interest. I had no thought that the condition was so strained & critical. It would seem that when all are only anxious for the good of the university there must be some point from which they could see "eye to eye." It might be well if a good part of the coming meeting of the Trustees were spent in Prayer, which Sir Oliver Lodge[1] asserts may sometimes be the surest & most scientific means for obtaining "light & leading"

I am

In deep sympathy Sincerely yours Charles Wood.

ALS (WP, DLC).

[1] Sir Oliver Joseph Lodge (1851-1940), British physicist and student of psychic phenomena; at this time Principal of the University of Birmingham.

From Richard Spencer Childs

Dear Sir: New York January 5, 1910.

I went over yesterday to the New Jersey Civic Federation meeting in the Newark City Hall, to a discussion of a proposed Commission Government Law in Jersey. There were present delegates from the boards of trade of several cities where the commission plan is now being agitated. Passaic has a draft of a bill practically finished, but in the other cities, matters seem to be somewhat in the air. The meeting degenerated into a lecture by myself, as I seemed to be the only one present who had much general information.

There is to be another meeting later, which will have the proposed Passaic Charter as a basis of discussion. Sentiment seemed to be in favor of a state-wide permissive bill.

I told them that you were on record as opposed to the commission plan for large cities, on the ground that five persons were too few to represent the varied elements of a big town and too few to take hold of the elaborate administrative problems, with the little preparation which an elected officer usually has. I told a few of the members privately that you were opposed to the Initiative, Referendum and Recall.

There is a splendid opportunity here to start an illuminating state-wide discussion of some of the fundamental principles of democratic government. The Commission Government movement, despite its faults, is doing an enormous service in breaking up the crust of provincial conservatism that has so long balked progress. This is just the time to get new ideas heard on their merits. I think it probable that I shall have opportunity to work with the committees of the New Jersey State Civic Federation on this matter and will be able to influence them a good deal. My own ideas are represented in the enclosed bill,[1] except that for large cities such as Jersey City and Newark, election should be by wards instead of at large, and the number of commissioners would be increased in proportion to the population.

If you find me unsound in this proposal for a commission government bill, I hope you will stop me now while things are still in a formative stage. If you are willing to come out with an endorsement of the whole proposal of Commission government in Jersey, it will of course be very helpful.

I propose, with your permission, to keep you in touch with the situation privately.[2]

Yours very truly, Richard S. Childs Secretary.

TLS (WP, DLC).

[1] It is missing.

[2] Wilson's reply is missing, and R. S. Childs to WW, Jan. 11, 1910, sheds no light on it.

Edward Wright Sheldon to Cyrus Hall McCormick

My dear Cyrus: [New York] January 5, 1910.

I have been doing what I could during the past two or three weeks to reach some satisfactory adjustment of the Graduate School situation at Princeton. I suppose you received a copy of the President's letter of December 25th to Pyne. Since then I have had two serious talks with Pyne on the subject; the first last week with Dodge, and the second yesterday with Thompson. I think Pyne is very much disturbed at the condition of affairs. At the same time he is very firm in the opinion that the Graduate College should be fixed upon the golf grounds. We have urged him to acquiesce in a report by the Graduate School Committee to the effect that it had been found impracticable to comply with the first condition attached to the acceptance of Mr. Procter's gift by the Trustees in October. This acceptance was, as you will remember, in the following form:

"RESOLVED, that the very generous offer of Mr. Procter be ascepted [accepted], provided that the legal right to use Mrs. Swann's money in the erection of the Graduate School upon the golf links be assured, and that Mr. Procter first advise us of his intention in relation to the disposition of his proposed gift."

Pyne says that he would fulfill this condition if he personally guaranteed the University against loss in case the Swann heirs should succeed in charging the University with a breach of the trust created by the will. And Pyne says that it is a "quibble" to attach to the resolution the meaning that there must be either a general agreement on the part of competent counsel, or an adjudication by some prominent court, before the "legal right" to build upon the golf links is "assured." Just what conclusion Pyne will reach I do not know. It seems to me it depends entirely upon him as to whether we shall have another hot debate in the Board upon the question. If you have a chance to communicate with Mr. John W. Davis,[1] could you ascertain what his position is? I certainly gathered that he favored our placing the College on the golf links only in the event of our being able to do so without any violation of the trust imposed upon us by the will.

I have just heard that there is to be a meeting of the Graduate School Committee in New York next Tuesday afternoon, the 11th, at three o'clock, and think it very important that you should attend this meeting.

Yours sincerely, Edward W. Sheldon.

CCL (E. W. Sheldon Coll., UA, NjP).

[1] He meant John David Davis of St. Louis.

From Henry Burling Thompson, with Enclosure

Dear President Wilson: Wilmington, Del. January 6th, 1910.

. . . I enclose copy of a letter which I have just written to Jacobus, which I think explains itself. I do not believe that Momo will oppose a resolution on the lines of the one suggested in the letter to Jacobus. With his opposition removed, the matter is settled. This is the desirable thing to do. It is difficult for Momo to adjust himself to this position, but I think that he will ultimately land there. If he does not, it is necessary to get sufficient votes without him.

You have doubtless received a telegram from Mr. Cram,[1] postponing the meeting for Saturday. This is, as I understand, as you wish it. I have taken the responsibility of ordering Mr. Cram to cancel the meeting, without any explanation to him,–simply asking him to trust to my judgment in this matter.

I have spent some three or four hours in discussion with Cleve and Sheldon over present conditions, and think that we are all of one mind as to the correct procedure, which is that your Committee on Graduate School will offer the resolution as mentioned in the letter to Jacobus. If this resolution goes through we must start de novo on the question of site. Whether it will complicate the question to discuss site at the next meeting I am not prepared to say. My natural feeling is that if we can do one thing we can do another, but it is well to be diplomatic just at this time. I am convinced, however, that the most likely site now would be the Brackett-Young Observatory property. There is sufficient room to start there, and the Olden property is bound, sooner or later, to fall into our hands. I am very sure that all hands could be united on this site. I do not take kindly to the University Place development. You have cramped yourself for all time at that point. Yours very sincerely, Henry B Thompson

TLS (WP, DLC).

[1] Cram's telegram is missing.

E N C L O S U R E

Henry Burling Thompson to Melancthon Williams Jacobus

Dear Jacobus: [Wilmington, Del.] January 6th, 1910.

Your letter of the 3d instant, with copy of letter from the President, under date of the 31st of December, and copy of your letter to the President, under date of the 1st instant, received.

Doubtless, you have received a letter from Cleve Dodge, from New York, explaining the situation.

Sheldon and I met Momo, by appointment, Wednesday afternoon, and discussed the situation for an hour. Unfortunately, Momo's physical condition,–due to an attack of the grippe,–was such as to make the meeting unsatisfactory; at the same time,

I do not believe that he will oppose a resolution from the Graduate School Committee to the effect that it is not possible to comply in full with the directions of Mrs. Swann's will under the conditions imposed by Mr. Proctor, and that Proctor's offer be declined with thanks. Momo realizes that he is up against the active working forces of the Board, and that he is bound to lose their support unless this resolution goes through. I do not believe that any conference will help the situation now. If Sheldon and Cleve Dodge cannot convince Momo no one can. Cleve feels that it is important, however, that you should talk to Momo.

It seems unfortunate that you cannot be present at the meeting of the Graduate School Committee next Tuesday afternoon in New York. It seems almost vital that you and McCormick should be on hand to support the President.

The important thing is to get Momo to act in such a way that we will not lose his support for the future. His present condition is distressing; and I must say that we should do everything in our power to let him down easily, provided he proposes to let himself down.

I should say that it was up to you to convert Stewart and to hold DeWitt. It is just as well to have the vote with us, even without Momo, and with the support of Stewart, Wood and DeWitt, we would have enough votes to carry our resolution through. Palmer will probably not be present at the Board meeting, but would be with us if there.

Yours very sincerely, Henry B. Thompson.

TCL (WP, DLC).

From John David Davis

My dear Dr. Wilson: St. Louis Jan. 6th, 1909 [1910].

I wish to thank you very much for your letter of the 31st ult., and the copy of your letter to Mr. Pyne which accompanied it. I appreciate the grave import of the situation which has unfortunately developed, and I am glad to be advised of conditions before reaching Princeton. When in the hurry of a Board meeting we are apt to determine certain matters without the fullest consideration. I am not prepared to express my views before the matter is fully discussed at our Board meeting, but I do hope that there is some way in which we can all unitedly continue our work for the development of the University upon the lines which you have so successfully marked out for us during the period of your administration. This ought to be possible, and I am sure that, in the opinion of all the members of the Board, it would be most unfortunate for a question like that now presented to prevent our unitedly continuing to work out the great educational problems for which Princeton is now standing and in which she has so rapidly become a leader. Is it not possible to keep an open mind upon the subject until we can all meet and fully consider all sides of the question?

I sincerely hope nothing will prevent my attending the meeting next week. The only thing now that I see may prevent my attending would be the death of Mrs. Isaac H. Lionberger,[1] which is almost hourly expected.

Princeton in my judgment cannot afford to lose the loyal support of either Wilson or Pyne, and to me it would be inconceivable that she should ever be put in such a situation.

With my very warmest personal regards, and a sincere hope that all will still work out to the entire satisfaction of my very dear friends, I am Faithfully yours, Jno D Davis

TLS (WP, DLC).

[1] Louise Shepley (Mrs. Isaac Henry) Lionberger died in St. Louis on January 8, 1910. Davis attended the meeting of the Board of Trustees on January 13, 1910.

From David Benton Jones

My dear Doctor: Chicago January 6th, 1910.

I am so convinced that the matter we spoke of this morning at breakfast is the one thing necessary to insure your *progressively* successful administration of the University, that I am going to take the liberty of citing an illustration of my meaning.

The notice from Dr. Jacobus of a meeting of the Curriculum Committee, states that the chief matter to be considered is the report to be made to the Finance Committee concerning possible economies in the carrying out of the Preceptorial System (I am giving it from memory).

Now, any report you outline to the Curriculum Committee should, on the theory we spoke of, be passed through the "Process," *which would carry with it in some form the approval in conference of such men in the faculty as would satisfy the Committee and ultimately the Board, that on that subject you had submitted it to the best Cabinet scrutiny available*, and that as a consequence, *the report embodied not only your individual judgment, but the combined judgment of those members of the faculty most competent to pass judgment upon it.*

This will enable you to successfully bring before the various committees and ultimately before the Board, matters which otherwise they would not be willing to entertain without making such inquiry as the "Process" would involve. By securing this in advance, it would not only bring it under constitutional forms, but it would save delay and avoid almost inevitable criticism of procedure. If you establish the "Process" method of reaching conclusions,—in other words, establish a constitutional regime, and then if freedom from financial domination be secured, you will have the two conditions necessary to success. In my judgment both conditions are essential elements. If both can be established, I believe Princeton, in the next ten years, will realize the dreams that some of us have entertained regarding it.

Most sincerely yours, David B. Jones.

TLS (WP, DLC).

From Melancthon Williams Jacobus

My dear Wilson: Hartford, Conn., January 6th, 1910.

I regret exceedingly that the Graduate School Committee meeting has to be called for Tuesday afternoon at 3:00 o'clock, since this is one of the days on which I am detained at Hartford—in fact, at the hour of the Committee's meeting I am supposed to be making an anniversary address, an obligation which I had accepted long before the call for the meeting came.

But I can not have any doubt as to the outcome of that Committee meeting. Sheldon, Garrett and McCormick, if he is present, must all vote together as against Shea and the Dean of the Graduate School, and your vote is also to be counted, so that my presence is not imperative as far as votes are concerned.

I trust you had a conference with Jones and McCormick as you were passing through Chicago, and made the matter perfectly clear to them both—especially so to Jones, whose letter to you (which you were kind enough to enclose to me and which I will hand you again) does not seem to take fully into consideration the clear issue of the present moment. This issue is not as to the site of the College *qua* site, but as to the site of that College as an expression of West's idea as to how that College is to be run and an opportunity for him to develop it along the lines of his idea. This issue is met in the acceptance or the rejection of the Proctor gift, which not only insists upon the golf links site, but insists upon it as an opportunity for the West idea and its development.

With the gift rejected, the legal difficulty is still before us as to the golf links, and I do not see how the golf links can be accepted in view of that legal difficulty. Mr. Jones, therefore, must not get confused as to what is now to be done and the reason why it is to be done; and he must be clear and strong, if he wishes to support you against West, to vote against the acceptance of the Proctor gift. The remaining steps can be taken at their time, but I do not see how they can stop short of a complete elimination of West from the entire Graduate Department, if not from the Faculty.

I am writing to President [George Black] Stewart of Auburn to arrange for a half hour's talk with him either in New York or in Princeton before the meeting of the Board. I am anxious to see that he understands it and realizes that the issue is clear between West and yourself.

With kind regards and best assurances that things are coming all right, I am Yours very sincerely, M. W. Jacobus

PS Thank you for the kind invitation to take Dr. Mackenzie's place on the list of University preachers, but in the present burden of administration duties I am declining all pulpit opportunities, however I may regret the need of so doing

MWJ

TLS (WP, DLC).

From Wilson Farrand

My dear President Wilson: Newark, N. J. January 6, 1910.

I have received the copy of your letter of December 25th to Mr. Pyne, and thank you for it. I need not say how deeply I regret the unfortunate situation that has arisen, and the serious possibilities to the University. It is a situation that calls for the most serious and candid consideration on the part of all of us.

Sincerely yours, Wilson Farrand

TLS (WP, DLC).

From Frank Frost Abbott

Dear President Wilson: Princeton, N. J. Jan. 6, 1910

I am sorry not to have been at home when you came to see me a few days ago. I was working with a graduate student on his thesis, and spent a longer time with him than I had intended.

If Mrs Abbott[1] understood your two questions, you were interested in knowing what saving could be effected by increasing the size of the groups in Greek and Latin composition, and what the situation would be in the matter of hours on the return of Professor Westcott.

In the Freshman class the preceptorial groups this year contain 5, in some cases 6 men. If a division of 25 students should be made next year into two groups of 8 men and one of 9, during both terms, we estimate that 3 less preceptors would be needed than are required with our present arrangement. If an economy is effected the first term by increasing the size of the groups, it would be necessary, would it not, to carry the plan through the year? The estimate is made on that assumption. I need not say that the Department will accept loyally this increase in the size of the Freshman groups, if it seems unavoidable, and probably most of the classical instructors would feel that the change had better be made in the Freshman, than in the Sophomore work. At the same time in their replies to my questionnaire a few weeks ago many of the preceptors expressed the opinion that a group should not number more than 6. Probably they would be very sorry, therefore, if it should prove necessary to make the increase mentioned above.

To pass to the second point, Professor Westcott's graduate courses are not being given this year. Of his courses with upper-class men one (Roman Law) is omitted and the other (Roman History) has been taken on as an extra by one of the men. In the past Professor Westcott has usually given 6 hours to the Freshmen and Sophomores. This part of his work this year has been divided among the other men. They have been very glad to coöperate, although it has made the preceptor's average of hours 15 per week. One other disturbing element has entered into our calculations this year. You may remember that by a recent change in the curriculum Sophomores who are candidates for the degree of B.S. or Litt.B. may now elect Latin *or* Mathematics. The result of this change has been that whereas 57 Sophomores took Latin last year, this year there are 104 members of that class in the Department. This has meant an increase of 15 or 16 hours class and preceptorial work, or to put it in another way, the work of one man has been added to the Department, and, so far as we can see, the addition is likely to be permanent.

To put the result in figures, if we compare the situation last year with that of next year, the case would stand somewhat as follows:

I Assuming no change in size of Freshman groups

	Gain	Loss
By Westcott's return	6 hrs	
By increase in number of Sophomores		16
Net loss		10

II Assuming an increase in the size of the Freshman groups

	Gain	Loss
By Westcotts return	6 hrs	
By increasing groups	45 "	
By increase in number of Sophomores		16
Net gain	35 hrs = 2½ men	

May I add one point in this connection? As soon as the situation permits it, we should like to see the work of the preceptors lightened. So long as they carry 15 or 16 hours a week, they will not be able to do as much in the way of scholarship as we want them to do. The intellectual stimulus which will come from an opportunity to do more as scholars will be reflected in the improved quality of their teaching. I am aware that it is quite unnecessary to mention this point to you, but my strong conviction that we have a unique opportunity to develop a group of brilliant young scholars here, and that the man who is advancing in his chosen subject makes a better teacher than one who is standing still leads me to speak of the subject.

Faithfully yours Frank F. Abbott

ALS (WWP, UA, NjP).
[1] Jane Harrison Abbott.

From Ebenezer Mackey

My dear Dr. Wilson, Trenton, N. J., January 6, 1910.

I wish to place upon record for our State Teachers' Association as well as for myself, some expression of our keen appreciation of your very able and inspiring address of Tuesday evening, December 28th and of your great kindness in consenting to take a part in our program.

The entire program was very acceptable to the members in attendance and received high commendation. Your address was spoken of in the most enthusiastic terms of praise and I received personal congratulations on the part of a great many different members upon having secured you as one of the speakers. We had this year an unusually large number of the leading school men of the State in attendance and it was just such an address as yours, they say, that made it most worth while for them to come. I feel that you have done a very great deal to lift up the meetings of the Association to a distinctly higher level.

With the most cordial greetings, I am,

Sincerely yours, E. Mackey

TLS (WP, DLC).

Henry van Dyke to Moses Taylor Pyne

Dear Momo: Princeton, N. J. Jan. 6, 1910.

I would have come in to see you today if it had not been for the storm. It looks as if our hopes of an era of peace for poor Princeton had vanished, and a sharp and prolonged strife seems to be at hand. A copy of the letter that was sent to you has come to me. It has amazed and grieved me. I want you to know that I feel with you and for you, and have not wavered a bit from the views expressed in the last talks we had together. The body of the alumni trust you as they trust no other man. You will walk, as you have done, in the path of duty for Princeton's sake, and they will be behind you.

Personalities count for little. The thing that we care for is the interest of Princeton, her steady progress, her stability and her future.

The real point at issue is whether it will hurt *Princeton* to put the graduate college anywhere except on the Prospect site. On this point I have looked up a few figures. The measurements were taken in a direct line and on such maps as I had here. They give a general idea of the geography of the subject. In Cambridge I believe the distances are about the same. St. John's College and the FitzWilliam Museum are at opposite ends of the city. I have no map, but I should say they were at least three-quarters of a mile apart. The *Fondation Thiers* in Paris, for graduate students in residence, is nearly three miles from the University and a little further from the *Collège de France*. Ignorance is not wicked, but half-knowledge ought not to talk.

Keep well and steady in these trying days. The tempest will subside, and when the teapot is at peace we shall have some tea.

Faithfully your friend Henry van Dyke

TCL (M. T. Pyne Coll., NjP).

An Address at the Inauguration of Henry Harbaugh Apple as President of Franklin and Marshall College

[Jan. 7, 1910]

Mr. President, Ladies and Gentlemen: I feel it a real privilege and honor to stand here, as a representative of the other educational institutions of the country, to convey to you our hearty greeting and congratulation. This fellowship of universities and colleges, represented in a company such as now sits about me upon this stage, is a very pleasant thing and a very hopeful thing. It means that we recognize, and are glad to recognize, our close association in the common enterprise to which we have devoted ourselves; and it is a very pleasant thing that, whenever an audience like this gathers to greet a new officer of the institution which they know best, the rest of us are privileged to come from our several places of hope and of undertaking to convey cordial messages of congratulation.

If I were speaking to you in private, Sir, and with the candor which one permits himself in private, I should also extend to you my sympathy and condolence. You have come into a singular company, Sir,–the company of college presidents. Their career is a very prominent one, and, I dare say, is regarded as a very happy one; but there is one circumstance of peculiar responsibility which it is almost impossible for them to meet,–they are expected to go everywhere and talk about everything; and I am afraid that it must be admitted that most of the things they talk about they do not understand. I admit that this gives them a certain oratorical freedom which they would otherwise not possess. One is able, in discussing subjects that he knows nothing about, to throw off all the trammels of natural restraint which he feels when he understands the difficulties of the matter with which he is dealing.

But, to turn from jest to earnest, it is a very interesting circumstance of our day that college presidents are called from their individual and local tasks, to address companies of their fellow citizens on so many different sorts of occasions. For my part, I do not regard it as a personal compliment to them, but as the attitude of our country toward those who represent learning and who may be assumed also to approach great questions of public interest without selfish pre-possession. I believe that college presidents are called upon for counsel in our day because it is assumed that they will give unprejudiced advice. There is nothing for a college president to gain by the attitude he may take upon public questions. It is the honorable character of all our institutions of learning that they leave their members free to think as they choose to think as honest men. There is nothing to gain and nothing to lose by the position we take upon questions of the day. There is no absorption, on the part of the men in the college faculty, in any one of the many special interests of our day.

I was saying to a company of gentlemen, not long ago, that it seemed to be the duty of a college to make young gentlemen as unlike their fathers as possible; by which I did not mean any disrespect to the fathers, but merely this, that by the time a man is old enough to have a son in college he has become absorbed in a special undertaking, saturated with all the considerations of a particular business, and, therefore, stands at a single point of view; and it is necessary for America that each generation of young men, as they come on, should be re-generalized, should be shown again the general map of the public interest, not prejudiced by special considerations of particular undertakings; and that, before they serve America in some single harness, they should see America as much as possible as a whole, undivided, not allotted to provinces, not scattered amongst contending interests. And so I suppose that that is the natural point of view of the college president, in looking at the various questions which he is called upon to discuss.

You are called, Sir, as we all are, to preside over the training of young men, and the great questions which we have been facing in the academic world in recent years are questions which go directly to the heart of the inquiry: What constitutes a proper training for young men? I mean, what academic training is it that we wish and desire to give them? It is not an easy question to answer; and you know that the country, in recent years, has grown very audibly critical of the existing programmes of the colleges of the land. It is being perceived that there is something lacking in what the colleges are now doing, whatever it may be that they profess to do; and I, for my part, regard that discontent and that audible criticism as a very wholesome thing for the college itself. I do not think that the difficulty lies so much in the programmes of the colleges as in their performance, and I do not think that their performance falls short of their professions because of any lack of assiduous work on their part or conscientious effort to do the thing which they set out to do. I think that it is because of the students; I think that it is because college life, in our day, has become so absorbing a thing and so interesting a thing, that college work has fallen into the background.

I still give myself the pleasure and privilege of lecturing to classes at the university to which I am attached, and I am constantly aware, on Monday mornings, when I meet my class, that things have happened on Saturday which make it very unnatural for a body of young gentlemen, at nine o'clock on Monday morning, to think seriously of the subject of jurisprudence. I feel very often, like a man snapping his fingers for attention, bound to do something in particular to wrest their thoughts away from the absorptions of their life, and bring them into some quiet place, where those great trade winds of doctrine which blow through the world of business may be felt. And I dare say, indeed I know, that all of my colleagues feel the same contest,—a contest almost between the atmosphere they breathe and the words they speak. The atmosphere is not a conducting medium, because it is the atmosphere of a great many admirable and entirely innocent things, but extremely absorbing things,—sport, all sorts of social engagements, all sorts of undertakings of amusement, all sorts of undertakings which are of a semi-intellectual nature, but only a *semi*-intellectual nature. And so, what we get, in this atmosphere surcharged with the energy of these other things, is the small residium [residuum] of their attention. The tables, therefore, are entirely turned upon us. We are occasionally resorted to, but we do not occupy the front of the stage.

That, it seems to me, is the real danger and the real difficulty of modern college training, and I think, for my part, that it arises, in part at any rate, from the circumstance that our social life has invaded the college. The college is no longer a place set apart; it is just a little section of the world, where certain young gentlemen are professing to do certain things and really doing other things, and those things are what all the rest of the world is doing,—except its business. If it included its business, I should see very valuable training in it; but it is everything *except* the business; the business that goes on there is only make-believe business. Certain young gentlemen think they get business training in going out and soliciting advertisements for the college publications; but I wish you would examine those advertisements. One of our college publications is a literary journal[1] that has a very small circulation (though I think, for my part, that its contents are excellent), and in this journal, circulating only among

[1] The *Nassau Literary Magazine*.

college boys, there is a very large advertisement of the Baldwin Locomotive Works. Now, that clearly is not business. Nobody at the Baldwin Locomotive Works can possibly have supposed that any under-graduate was going to buy a locomotive. We know perfectly well that some officer, paying for it out of his own pocket and not out of the funds of the company, presented that advertisement to this young gentleman as an encouragement. I say that that is not practical business, to solicit advertisements which are given to you because of the interest in you of the persons who give them to you. And so with the rest of the so-called business that invades college life. It is supported, not by success, but by taxation,—for the most part, by taxation on the freshmen. The under-graduates are assessed, and are expected, by the opinion of the college, to yield to the assessment. That, again, is not business. It is not upon the financial foundations which business must really rest upon, namely, of successful management.

And so we are in the case of those who must recapture the strategic positions which are necessary in order that we should be the real purveyors of knowledge. And if social impulses, social ambitions, social arrangements, which pervade the rest of the community, invade the college, what is going to happen? The college is going to lose its democratic feeling, infallibly; and if the college loses its democratic feeling and its democratic character, it shall have ceased to serve the nation. For the peculiarity of all the vital force of history is, that it has come from the bottom, and not from the top. I have again and again said, to my own students, that what saved the Middle Ages,—saved the Middle Ages from dry rot,—was the existence of the Roman Catholic Church; because the Roman Catholic Church supplied the great states of the Middle Ages with the men who were their successful administrators. It did so because it was itself an absolutely democratic organization. There was not a peasant so humble that he could not become a priest, nor a priest so obscure that he might not rise to be Pope of Christendom; and, through these open channels of promotion and of learning, the Middle Ages were supplied with their administrative capacity, not by the aristocracy, but by the democracy that was common to them all. And so, in every state in every age, the renewal has come from the bottom,—from the roots, not from the branches. Men of culture, men of achievement, may be the flower of a civilization, but the flower does not supply the plant with its power; it is the mere expression of what has come from the dark and silent processes of the obscure earth. When our colleges, therefore, cease to be the open channels for this renewal, they will have ceased to be worthy of the patronage of the nation,—they will have ceased to supply her with the things that are necessary for her renewal and for her wholesome life.

It seems to me to be a very happy historical circumstance which united in the name of this college the two names of Franklin and of Marshall. It has always seemed to me that Franklin was, perhaps, the most typical American of all,—the man, who, without much formal assistance from any kind of school (going to school to life itself, but upon a free stage, where capacity told), went from achievement to achievement, until it seemed as if the common man were placed upon a throne, because of his native capacity. And Marshall, the embodiment of the old traditions of order, of historic principles, that structural iron of the law about which all our edifices must be built! It has interested all students of the legal decisions of Chief Justice Marshall that they are singularly lacking in what almost all other decisions bristle with, and that is, references to specific cases or decisions. Marshall seems always to be drawing out of the springs,—seems always to be reasoning out of something inherent in the law and inherent in all political life,—seems to be drawing, consciously or unconsciously, upon the historical experience of the race. Now, a lad like Franklin, in his origin, put in the atmosphere in which Marshall's mind moved, is the typical educated American. The man of the people, who has submitted himself to the processes of the ages, is the man we should seek to make typical of all our educational processes.

I do not belittle, I do not under-estimate, the great advantages of generations of culture. I think that a man who comes of a family which, for generations together, has breathed this air of the old world as well as the new, enjoys an incalculable advantage. There is the more shame upon him if he does not go a longer journey than the other man with less advantage than he. But I do mean that the colleges are not so much for such a man as they are for the others, because such men come from homes where there is an education to be had by those who merely breathe, by those who merely listen, by those who merely converse. They are put into touch with the resources of the intellectual world.

I believe that we are engaged in our profession in a sort of minor statesmanship,—a statesmanship which has nothing to do with parties, but which does have everything to do with the life of the nation; that it is our function to think, not so much of the individual nor so much of the individual's profession, as of the country he is going to serve; and that our prime object in all cases ought to be, to give him such a training that, whether he follow this calling or that, he will serve America as America should be served, by enlightened and disinterested men. That, I say, is, in my view, a minor sort of statesmanship. It is our very solemn duty to see that the things that interfere with the sort of saturation which a man must get and which constitutes his education must be absolutely removed, in order that our processes may have leave to work their perfect work.

Knowledge, ladies and gentlemen, is not education. No amount of information makes a man educated. Some of the best informed men I ever knew were the crudest thinkers I ever knew. Some men who can throw chunks of information at you big enough to floor you throw them in chunks, and they do not know how to dissect or to discriminate their parts. Some of the men absolutely full of knowledge are so full that they cannot move; their minds are so crowded that they cannot see what it is that they contain; and if you will give me the man who has passed knowledge through his brain and forgotten it all, but retained every habit, every capacity, every impulse, that it gave him, I would prefer him in every instance to the man who has retained it, but has not known what to do with it. Education consists in the establishment in the mind of certain habits and powers, that are established by long use, by constant practice; and it does not consist in the accumulation of knowledge. If we regard ourselves, therefore, as mere purveyors of knowledge, we have thought of ourselves in the light which is the least of all the lights in which we should think of ourselves. It is the characteristic of some of the most distinguished graduates of our colleges, the men distinguished for their achievement, that they have forgotten, ten years after they graduated, everything they were taught when they were under-graduates; but they have not forgotten how to use their minds, and so it does not make any difference whether they have cast away the old stuff they used them on or not. It does not do a baby any harm, after its teeth are out, to have thrown away the gum that it used to chew on. The point is, that the teeth are out and that he knows how to chew things that are worth chewing. It is all in knowing how to eat and how to digest. It is not that you have eaten certain cataloguable things. I know persons who come back from Europe and talk of nothing except the food that they had at this, that and the other hotel; which is evidence that food was all they got in Europe, and they could have gotten food just as comfortably and sometimes better cooked if they had stayed at home.

That is, to my thinking, a type of the mind that has had plenty of information, but no education,—through whom the information has passed innocuous. You know, for a long time, for a whole generation, we ate whole wheat, being told, by those who knew what whole wheat contained, that there was more nitrogen in whole wheat than in the wheat with the husks taken off; so for a whole generation we gulped whole wheat. And then some kind gentleman came along and told us that it was quite true that it did contain more nitrogen than the other, but in such a form that it could not enter the system, and that all that it did was to go a procession through us; and so we were delivered from the necessity of eating whole wheat. And so much with of the information that passes through a man's mind. It is good information, it is excellent stuff, if he would only let it enter into the color and texture of his mind; but he does not, and, therefore, he might as well not pass it through his mind, which would give the mind less labor and would do it no harm.

We are bent upon the undertaking, therefore, of releasing the faculties of men, making them serviceable in whatever they undertake; and it is the characteristic of modern American life that occupations do not hold steady in their processes. Their processes change very rapidly, and that man is the best equipped man for American life who can change his process over night. If he has been taught only the process, he cannot; but if he is taught to use his mind upon any process, he can. And that is the educated man.

I congratulate you, therefore, Sir, upon having come out into a field of battle, where the weapons are the harmless weapons of speech, but where there is a great deal to do and a great deal to fight for; and in my opinion, the best weapon is absolutely candid speech, having no secrets from anybody. This is not private business; it is public business. I have always entertained the private opinion that the way to conduct the public business was to tell the public all about it. I know that some politicians do not agree with me; but I know that the most formidable president we have recently had[2] made things very lively by following that idea. Now, I believe that that is the way to reform what there is to reform in the college. They are not vices; they are simply destructives. The way to reform what there is to reform in our modern college life is, to let the people know what the actual facts are in the colleges,—not facts that might make them fear for the morals of their sons, but facts merely that give them reasonable fear that their sons will not get educated; and then we

[2] Theodore Roosevelt.

shall ask their co-operation in the removal of these obstacles, for we must remember, Sir, that a man may gain the whole world and lose his own soul, and I am afraid that that is what we (I mean, the members of faculties) are trying to do, gain the whole world and are in danger of losing our own souls,—gaining the whole world by calling great groups of students about us, but losing our own souls by not having any atmosphere to breathe which is the real communion of thought, the real academic spirit. If these be real dangers and not fallacies of my own, then you, Sir, have come into a difficult task at a very strategic moment.

T transcript (PLF).

From John Dixon

My dear Dr. Wilson: New York January 7, 1910.

I am greatly distressed over the situation which has resulted from the offer of Mr. Proctor. I earnestly hope that you and Mr. Pyne can agree upon some proposition which may be submitted to the Board at its meeting on the thirteenth inst.

It seems to me that the general discussion of the issue as outlined in your letter to Mr. Pyne—a copy of which you kindly sent me—will be fraught with gravest peril. Would it not be much more satisfactory to avoid such discussion and refer the whole matter to a committee representing the various views involved? This committee might privately discuss the situation and reach a judgment which they could submit to the Board later.

With warmest personal regards, and profound appreciation of your splendid services as President of the University, I am,

Very sincerely yours, John Dixon

TLS (WP, DLC).

To Moses Taylor Pyne

My dear Momo: [Princeton, N. J.] January 8th, 1910.

I have just returned from my attendance on the Association of American Universities at Madison, Wisconsin, to learn that you are ill with the grippe. I am sincerely distressed to hear it and beg that you will take the very best care to get well promptly. It would break us all up if you were to be seriously ill, and I cannot help feeling that the action I have recently felt bound to take may have had something to do with your illness by making you worry unduly. I hope that you will not worry. There is no danger of any feeling being stirred in this matter which will interfere with any friendship or affection, and I am sure that we will all work out together some solution that will be to the best interests of the University, whether I remain President or not. We are not working to keep any man in office but merely to solve a very difficult question.

While in Chicago I saw Cyrus McCormick and gathered from what he said that it would be more convenient for him if the meeting of the Graduate School committee of the Board could be held on Tuesday evening instead of Tuesday afternoon. Since I have learned of your indisposition, it occurs to me that it might in every way be more agreeable to you to hold it in the evening at your home, so that you would not be obliged to go out of the house. That would be entirely agreeable to me and I have no doubt would suit the rest of the committee. I hope sincerely that you will do it if you can get your Secretary to arrange it with the members of the committee in time.

But whatever happens, take care of yourself and believe me,

Always affectionately yours, [Woodrow Wilson]

CCL (WWP, UA, NjP).

From Bayard Henry

My dear President Wilson: Philadelphia. January 8, 1910.

Your favor of the 4th inst., enclosing copy of letter sent Mr. Pyne, received. I regret exceedingly the situation which has been developed, but feel, unless Mr. Proctor withdraws his offer, the action of the Board taken at the last meeting should not be reversed.

I am, Yours very truly, Bayard Henry

TLS (WP, DLC).

From Theodore Whitefield Hunt and Gordon Hall Gerould

Dear President Wilson: Princeton, N. J., Jan. 8, 1910

In answer to your questions with reference to the working of the Preceptorial System in the Department of English, we should like to present the following statements:

1 and 2. The numbers of students taking work in the Department during the past five years are shown in the following table:

Term ending:	Seniors			Juniors			Soph.	Fresh.	Total
	Dept.	One	Two	Dept.	One	Two	One	One	
Feb. '06	44	117	21	46	128	7		385	866
June '06	44	106	9	46	136	8	162	385	1013
Feb. '07	46	119	29	26	102	5	196	322	951
June '07	46	110	9	26	114	3		322	714
Feb. '08	26	101	22	28	84	7	168	328	847
June '08	26	139	15	28	129	0		328	734
Feb. '09	28	121	17	13	78	1	180	362	887
June '09	28	129	11	13	88	2		362	715
Feb. '10	13	112	15	8	85	6	247	353	894

3. We have aimed consistently to secure both for students electing the Department and for those electing courses in the Department continuity of preceptorial instruction through the four undergraduate years. Because of the fact that the work in Freshman year is required of all students, and in Sophomore year is taken by about two thirds of each class, the instructors carry through these two years a large number of men, who are transferred to the care of professors and preceptors at the beginning of Junior year. This causes the most considerable break in the ideal continuity. Another break of less importance is due to the existence of the Freshman Hall courses,[1] which necessitates the transfer of many students to new preceptors or instructors at the beginning of Sophomore year. It may be remarked that, if Freshman English were a three hour course, there would be less difficulty than at present in establishing proper relations between students and their preceptors.

At the beginning of Junior year students are assigned to the professors or preceptors who are to meet them for conferences in all of the courses that they may elect as upperclassmen. Each preceptor makes the nucleus of his upperclass groups the men whom he has taught as Freshmen and Sophomores, adding his share of the men who have been taught by instructors during their first two years. Thus, as a matter of practice, the individual

[1] The "Hall courses," initiated in 1906-1907, were courses in public speaking and debate and were open to members of the American Whig and Cliosophic Societies. The courses could be substituted for the required freshman English course in composition and rhetoric. Since their inception, Hardin Craig had taught the students of Whig Hall, Harry Franklin Covington, those of Clio Hall.

preceptor has known and taught the majority of his students in each graduating class through four years, and has taught them in all the courses that they have elected in the Department. By means of a committee on the allottment of students, which keeps a careful record of each individual, it is possible to ascertain to whom, in our parlance, any undergraduate 'belongs,' even though he may not have taken work in the Department for one or two years. In making its assignment of students to preceptors, the committee often has occasion to consider personal preferences or needs, and honors them as far as possible. No essential difference is made, it will be seen, in arrangements for departmental students and for the so-called 'floaters.' An economy of labor, with no loss of continuity in instruction, has been effected by the division of the preceptors into two groups, each of which in any given year teaches Freshmen and Juniors or Sophomores and Seniors.

4. In the courses of Junior and Senior years we already have in operation a plan which to a large extent includes the professors and assistant professor[s] in the general preceptorial function. All of them, in fact, now do preceptorial teaching in the courses which they conduct and all of them, with a single exception or two, in one or more of the other (literary) courses. There are four upperclass courses in which assistance is now given in the preceptorial work by one or more professors besides the one professor who is conducting the course: 32 (Shakespeare); 41 (18th Cent.); 43 (19th Cent.); 44 (19th Cent.). In the opinion of our Department, the plan we are now following is successful; but its efficiency may be increased by more consistent application.

5. Freshman English, 2 hours a week, both terms. The class is divided into divisions of about twenty men each, and these divisions are assigned to instructors and preceptors who meet them for a class-room recitation for three out of every four hours. For the fourth hour (i.e. one hour every other week) the students go in groups of five or six for a preceptorial conference to the same instructor who conducts their class-room exercises. The preceptorial hour is devoted to discussion of assigned reading which further illustrates the authors read in class, and to criticism of written themes. Freshmen taking the Hall courses receive individual instruction in debating and speaking, as well as in the preparation and criticism of their work, but have no preceptorial conferences in the stricter sense of the word.

Sophomore English, three hours a week, first term only. One lecture, and two recitations in divisions of about twenty-five men each. The preceptorial method has not been applied to this course, though individual preceptors and instructors have, when their schedules have not been too heavy, substituted on their own initiative preceptorial conferences for one of the recitations.

Junior year, first term, 31 and 33. Two lectures and one preceptorial hour in each course. Second term, 32 (Shakespeare). One lecture and two preceptorial conferences. 34 (Elementary Old English). Three preceptorial hours and no lectures.

Senior year, first term. 41 (18th Cent.) and 43 (19th Cent.). Two lectures and one preceptorial hour. 45 (Advanced Old English). One lecture and two preceptorial hours. Second term. 42 (Milton) and 44 (19th Cent.). Two lectures and one preceptorial hour. 46 (Chaucer). One lecture and two preceptorial hours.

In Junior and Senior years the entire direction of the student's reading is in the hands of the preceptor. In the linguistic courses (33, 34, and 45) the preceptorial hours are ordinarily used for the interpretation of assigned text in Old and Middle English, and are virtually informal recitations with very small divisions. In the literary courses the preceptorial hours are ordinarily given to a free discussion by the students and preceptor of the books which have been assigned for reading. At the discretion of the preceptor, additional individual conferences are held for the criticism of written work.

6. The Department feels that the present preceptorial method has been in the highest degree successful in the courses of Junior and Senior years. It looks forward to an extension of this method, as soon as there shall be a sufficient teaching staff, to the Sophomore course, where from the peculiar conditions of Sophomore year a closer relation between teacher and student is particularly desirable. It also wishes that the Freshman course might have a schedule of three hours a week instead of two, so that the Freshmen might receive preceptorial instruction one hour each week instead of every other week.

Respectfully submitted,

T W Hunt
Head of the Department
G. H. Gerould
Chairman of Allotment Committee

Department of English
Students enrolled during the years 1906-1910.

Term ending:	Seniors			Juniors			Soph.	Fresh.	Total*
	Dep.	One	Two	Dep.	One	Two	One	One	
Feb. '06	44	117	21	46	128	7		385	866
June '06	44	106	9	46	136	8	162	385	1013
Feb. '07	46	119	29	26	102	5	196	322	951
June '07	46	110	9	26	114	3		322	714
Feb. '08	26	101	22	28	84	7	168	328	847
June '08	26	139	15	28	129	0		328	734
Feb. '09	28	121	17	13	78	1	180	362	887
June '09	28	129	11	13	88	2		362	715
Feb. '10	13	112	15	8	85	6	247	353	894

* This total represents the number of students of all classes receiving instruction in one course. A student taking two courses is counted twice, etc.

TLS (WWP, UA, NjP).

From Edward Wright Sheldon

[New York]

My dear Woodrow: Sunday night January 9th [1910]

How would it do to postpone the Graduate School Committee meeting to Wednesday morning at 10 oclock at Momo's office. He has just come back from Washington and says that time would suit him. Tuesday evening he has a dinner engagement. Will you telephone or telegraph my office in the morning what you think? I will then let Momo know the result.

Yours sincerely, Edward W. Sheldon.

ALS (WP, DLC).

From Moses Taylor Pyne

My dear Woodrow New York 10 Jan 1910

Thank you for your kind letter. I have been pretty badly hit by the grippe & went to Washington for a couple of days to try to break it up. It went off leaving me with a sore throat & bad toothache—a mean combination—so I must squeeze in what time I can at the dentist's.

I *have* worried very much over this matter. I want to meet your wishes and at the same time my views are so strong as to the danger & unwisdom of refusing Procter's gift that I have been torn almost in two. I hope that some solution may be found that will satisfy us all—in part at least.

At Ed Sheldon's suggestion I have altered the date of the Grad School Com meeting to Wednesday morning at ten o'clock[.] It is too bad to always hold these meetings on the eve of the Board m't'g but I could not help this.

Yours most sincerely M Taylor Pyne

ALS (WP, DLC).

From Charles Wood

My dear President Wilson, Washington, D. C. Jan 10.10

Thank you very much for writing me so fully of present conditions. Your letter has helped me to realize, at least in some degree, even from this distance, the difficulties of which you speak. If the irenic spirit in which you write prevails in the Board meeting, that harmony which is absolutely essential for the prosperity not only, but for the very life of the university, must result. I should be very glad indeed, as you kindly suggest, to talk the matter over with you for a few minutes, if you have any time between 9.30 and 11. Thursday morning. Praying that we may have the guidance of God in these perplexities,

Very cordially Yours Charles Wood.

At this crisis the reunification of the Board seems to me of far more importance than the site of the Graduate School or even the existence of the School.

ALS (WP, DLC).

From Henry Burchard Fine *et al.*, with Enclosure

Dear Mr. President: Princeton, N. J. Jan. 11, 1910.

In transmitting to you this Supplementary Memorandum regarding the Graduate School we feel that we can safely authorize you to say that the views therein expressed are those held by the great majority of our colleagues on the University Faculty. So confident are we of this fact that we should welcome a test vote, if the opinion we express as to the opinion of the majority of the Faculty seems to any to be at all doubtful.

We remain, with great respect,

Very sincerely yours, H. B. Fine
Edward Capps
E. G. Conklin
W. M. Daniels

E N C L O S U R E

From Edward Capps *et al.*

Dear Sir: Princeton, January 10, 1910.

In view of the division of opinion in the Faculty Committee on the Graduate School which developed in the discussion of the question of the site of the proposed building, the undersigned members of that Committee feel it their duty to supplement the majority report then presented to you[1] by a fuller statement of their convictions as to the fundamental considerations involved. We feel impelled to this action because the divergence of opinion between the majority and the minority of our Committee proved to be radical, and because if we continue as members of this Committee we may be placed in the embarrassing position of being obliged to cooperate with the minority in carrying out plans to which we, the majority, cannot subscribe.

The presence of a body of serious-minded and well-equipped graduate students, working along with and under the immediate supervision of a well-chosen staff of instructors primarily interested in graduate study and research is the one essential condition of a true graduate school. The University should, in our opinion, subordinate to this end, so far as may be consistent with the legal obligations which have been assumed, any and all schemes of community life of graduate students. In short, we hold that all residential considerations should be duly subordinated to the one end of a graduate school, viz. the work of study and research. Furthermore, we question the wisdom of laying emphasis upon the supervision and direction of the life of graduate students. The conditions of life and residence of the normal graduate student should be as free and untrammeled as those of other professional students. Nor do we believe in the advisability of the segregation of graduate students from the general student body, nor in the separation of a certain part of this body of graduate students from their fellows.

A strong faculty and proper equipment are the legitimate and effective attractions for desirable graduate students. We believe that the best graduate students are likely to be repelled rather than attracted by any scheme which lays emphasis upon considerations other than those of scholarship. It has not been to the advantage of this University that the scheme of a residential college has been so largely identified with its graduate school, to the exclusion of more fundamental considerations.

Dependent as we are, in the main, upon the good will of our

colleagues in other universities for our graduate students, we must deserve and win their approval of our graduate school. It is therefore indispensable that our graduate school be distinguished as a place of learning. Such a school can be secured only by the abandonment of our present emphasis upon non-essentials.

An unusual opportunity for building up a strong graduate school is now presented to Princeton by reason of the widespread interest in and approval of our programme of undergraduate study; because of the general belief that we have entered upon a definite plan for enlarging and strengthening the work of instruction in the graduate school; and because of the recent additions to our material equipment in the shape of the new scientific laboratories.

We cannot have a great graduate school without a great graduate faculty; and we cannot have a great graduate faculty unless the conditions here are of such a character as to attract strong men. And we cannot attract strong men by adherence to dilettante ideals.[2] Respectfully submitted, EDWARD CAPPS

E. G. CONKLIN

W. M. DANIELS

H. B. FINE

TL (WWP, UA, NjP).

1 That is, the report of Oct. 19, 1909, printed as an Enclosure with A. F. West to WW, Oct. 19, 1909.

2 In Merwick, they had a model of the kind of graduate establishment that they were sure West meant to reproduce on a larger scale. "'Merwick,' 1905-1913, and its ambience," according to one historian of the Princeton Graduate School, "were elitist." Willard Thorp (ed.), "When Merwick was the University's 'Graduate House,' 1905-1913," *Princeton History*, No. 1, 1971, p. 55.

A contemporary account of life at Merwick by a resident, Leonard Chester Jones, offers ample evidence of the accuracy of this description. Jones, Princeton 1907, A.M., 1909, Ph.D., University of Geneva, 1916, lived at Merwick from 1908 to 1910. The original manuscript of his account, "The History of Merwick," written in 1914-15, is in the Princeton University Archives, and much of it is printed in Thorp, cited above.

From Jones's account, it is clear that Merwick was a luxurious gentlemen's club. After a late breakfast, many of the residents "would dawdle over newspaper, cigarette and coffee." (All quotations are from the manuscript unless otherwise noted.) Then followed classes and work on theses. Luncheon at one o'clock was usually preceded by conversation, reading, and games. Residents devoted most of the afternoon to sports, including tennis on the Merwick court. "At all seasons we walked a great deal—to Cherry Valley, Lawrenceville, the Junction, Rocky Hill, Kingston, or around Carnegie Lake." Dinner was the splendid occasion of the day. All around the table wore academic gowns—to the amazement and scandal of many undergraduates and faculty members—and the master said grace in Latin. The food was so sumptuous (according to another resident) that it was reported about town that the students dined on peacocks' tongues and similar delicacies. In fact, favorites were Virginia ham and beaten biscuits. After dinner came bridge, chess, conversation, and, occasionally, dances, followed by work. Sunday was a leisurely day with a late breakfast, a prolonged dinner in the middle of the day, conversation, and a formal tea. The Wednesday night dinners were the most elaborate occasions of the week. Students bearing large candles escorted Dean West to Merwick from his home across Bayard Lane. There was usually a guest who spoke after dinner, and all diners wore evening clothes under their gowns. A Canadian student "was so awed by the elegance of Merwick and the excellent manners of its inhabitants that he disappeared for ten days after his arrival (Thorp, p. 70). "To me," Jones concluded, "the years on Bayard Lane were invaluable. My fund of facts was, perhaps, not startlingly increased: I doubt if I showed much 'progress,' yet those two years revolutionized my scale of values and outlook on the world, so much so that everything before them seems to belong to another and a dimmer life."

From Richard Spencer Childs

Dear Dr. Wilson: New York Jan. 11th, 1910.

I am glad to be able to say that you are mistaken in your intimation regarding Gov. Hughes. We have not only converted him, but have done it thoroughly. His reference to the Short Ballot in his message[1] was put in in response to our request. He will not be at the banquet, but I think is genuinely sorry that he cannot be there. He is anxious that the Short Ballot shall not be used as a back fire to Direct Primaries, and we must be careful not to let it be used that way.

Speaker Wadsworth of the State Assembly[2] will be at our dinner. He is very much interested, and is very popular at Albany. Between his influence and that of the Governor and Herbert Parsons,[3] who has recently come out in our favor, together with several of the leading men in the legislature, I actually think that we may be able to get a series of appropriate constitutional amendments introduced in the legislature this year with hope of passage.[4]

Regarding the plans for the dinner, I shall write you more definitely after our Executive Board has had a meeting, which will be tomorrow.

We would appreciate it if you will plan to let us have copy of at least part of your speech in advance, in order that we can send it out on our clipping sheets and secure the maximum publicity.

We expect that in your remarks you will cover the Short Ballot doctrine completely, and also outline the plan and scope of the Organization. There will be other speakers, of course, but the plans are not yet complete.

Yours very truly, Richard S. Childs Secretary.

TLS (WP, DLC).

1 Enc.: printed news release dated January 6, 1910, featuring Hughes's endorsement of the short ballot and a "private call" by Wilson for the dinner meeting on January 21, 1910, which read as follows: "It is plain that the way of reform lies in the direction of simplification. If the voter is to know what he is about, the number of persons he is to be called upon to vote for must be reduced to a minimum. When it is so reduced, both nomination and election will become direct, simple and intelligible. I believe that the Short Ballot is the key to the whole question of the restoration of government by the people." In his Annual Message to the New York legislature of January 5, 1910, Governor Hughes did

indeed indicate his support of the principle of the short ballot, coupling it with his belief in the need for increased concentration of executive responsibility in the state government. "I am in favor," he said, "of as few elective offices as may be consistent with proper accountability to the people, and a short ballot." "But," he continued, "while this is a desirable aim, it does not justify closing our eyes to the situation as it exists and losing sight of improvements which are more closely within our reach." He went on to list the large number of elective state offices and suggested that administration would be greatly improved if many of these positions became part of a cabinet of administrative heads appointed by the governor. He concluded: "But it is apparent that such a change would require revision of our constitutional scheme. Some progress might be made by the reduction of elective officers in municipalities and in the case of certain minor statutory offices. It is idle, however, to expect under the present Constitution to achieve what is really a short ballot, and those who limit themselves to this effort neglect, in my judgment, present opportunities so far as this State is concerned." His only specific recommendation was for a *simplified* ballot in which each candidate's name would appear only once, in columns grouped under the names of the offices. See State of New York, *Public Papers of Charles E. Hughes, Governor,* 1910 (Albany, N. Y., 1910), pp. 28-31.

2 James Wolcott Wadsworth, Jr., Speaker of the New York Assembly, 1906-10.

3 United States Representative from the Thirteenth District of New York, 1905-11, and an important figure in the Republican party in New York City and New York State.

4 Constitutional amendments designed to have certain state-wide officers such as the Secretary of State, Treasurer, and Attorney General appointed by the Governor rather than elected by the people, and hence to shorten the ballot, were introduced in the New York legislature in 1910 and in each following year up to the next constitutional convention in 1915, but none ever passed the legislature.

ADDENDA

From Albert Jeremiah Beveridge

My Dear President Wilson: [Washington] June 12, 1902.

I have learned with sincerest pleasure of the great honor that has come to you in your elevation to the Presidency of Princeton University. I have read your various articles with keen interest and sincere admiration; and since I met you at the New England dinner and heard you speak there[1] my regard for you has had a personal coloring and atmosphere. It makes one feel good to know that a man of your comprehensive and far seeing views on questions of our national policy is to be in charge of one of the world's great educational institutions.

I know you will have a distinguished career of increasing success.

With kindest regards and best wishes, I am,

Sincerely, [Albert J. Beveridge]

CCL (A. J. Beveridge Papers, DLC).

[1] Wilson's address to the New England Society in the City of New York is printed at Dec. 22, 1900, Vol. 12.

Two Letters to Albert Jeremiah Beveridge

My dear Mr. Beveridge: Princeton, N. J. June 17th, 1902.

It was certainly very thoughtful and generous of you to write me your kind letter of the 12th, and I appreciate it most sincerely. I remember our meeting at the banquet of the New England Society with a great deal of pleasure. I remember also what satisfaction it gave me to find myself in sympathy upon public questions with a man like yourself,[1] who stands in the midst of affairs. Pray accept my warmest thanks and my most sincere assurances of appreciation.

Sincerely yours, Woodrow Wilson

TLS (A. J. Beveridge Papers, DLC).

[1] Beveridge spoke with Wilson and others at the dinner of the New England Society of the City of New York on December 22, 1900. The Indiana Senator's speech was typical of the many pro-imperialist and nationalistic addresses that he was giving at this time.

Remarking that the Pacific was an American ocean, that the proposed isthmian canal would be American, and that the Gulf of Mexico was in effect an American lake, he exclaimed: "The future of the world is in our hands. This is not enthusiasm; it is geography." Turning to the government of the new American empire, he said that the Constitution gave Congress full power to govern territory and other property belonging to the United States. However, it was only partially true to say that the Constitution followed the flag. The Constitution had grown with the nation; it was made for the American people, not they for it. And the people of dependent territories had to be governed by laws most suited to their needs. The important point was that American institutions followed the flag—"the simplest first, later the more complex, and finally, when the way is prepared, our noblest institution, the American Constitution, follows the flag. Free schools, equal laws, impartial justice, social order, and at last, when these have done their work and our wards are ready to understand and rightly use it, our Constitution, which is our method of government, follows the flag."

Moreover, Beveridge continued, any canal which joined the "American Pacific" to the "American Gulf" had to be owned and operated exclusively by the United States. "Geography and interest, not altruism, are the basis of fundamental national rights."

However, in governing and developing its empire, the United States had to act in the constructive spirit and stern honesty of Puritanism: "Develop, build, cultivate, create. No robbing, no looting, no piracies in the name of commerce! . . . Let no man fear because the Constitution gives the American people a free hand to do this giant's work. Let no man fear because our treaties and our foreign relations shall be so arranged that the American people shall have a clean future in which to do this work. The motto of Americanism henceforth must be: A clean future and a free hand. . . . America is to-day the young man of the Nations, eager for his work, and with that work waiting to be done. We will not tie his hands. We will not bind his future. Mr. President, I propose this sentiment: 'America, the young man of the Nations, the proudest development of the Puritan spirit. Give him a clean future and a free hand, and he will make of this new epoch the beginning of mankind's golden age.'" *Ninety-Fifth Anniversary Celebration of the New England Society in the City of New York* (New York, n. d.), pp. 50-54.

There is little wonder that Wilson liked Beveridge's speech, which followed his own. He said essentially the same things as Beveridge, if in somewhat less chauvinistic words.

My dear Mr. Beveridge, Princeton, 11 Nov., 1903

I am sincerely obliged to you for your very kind note[1] about my history.[2] I wrote it, so to say, with my whole blood and with full pulses, and it is matter of the deepest gratification to me that it should seem to you to be worthily done. Your note was an act of thoughtful kindness.

Sincerely Yours, Woodrow Wilson

ALS (A. J. Beveridge Papers, DLC).

[1] It is missing.

[2] That is, his *History of the American People*.

INDEX

NOTE ON THE INDEX

THE alphabetically arranged analytical table of contents at the front of the volume eliminates duplication, in both contents and index, of references to certain documents, such as letters. Letters are listed in the contents alphabetically by name, and chronologically within each name by page. The subject matter of all letters is, of course, indexed. The Editorial Notes and Wilson's writings are listed in the contents chronologically by page. In addition, the subject matter of both categories is indexed. The index covers all references to books and articles mentioned in text or notes. Footnotes are indexed. Page references to footnotes which place a comma between the page number and "n" cite both text and footnote, thus: "624,n3." On the other hand, absence of the comma indicates reference to the footnote only, thus: "55n2"—the page number denoting where the footnote appears. The letter "n" without a following digit signifies an unnumbered descriptive-location note.

An asterisk before an index reference designates identification or other particular information. Re-identification and repetitive annotation have been minimized to encourage use of these starred references. Where the identification appears in an earlier volume, it is indicated thus: "1:*212,n3." Therefore a page reference standing without a preceding volume number is invariably a reference to the present volume. The index supplies the fullest known forms of names, and, for the Wilson and Axson families, relationships as far down as cousins. Persons referred to in the text by nicknames or shortened forms of names can be identified by reference to entries for these forms of the names.

A sampling of the opinions and comments of Wilson and Ellen Axson Wilson covers their more personal views, while broad, general headings in the main body of the index cover impersonal subjects. Occasionally opinions expressed by a correspondent are indexed where these appear to supplement or to reflect views expressed by Wilson or by Ellen Axson Wilson in documents which are missing.

INDEX